D1393870

Property of

S. Patrick

ADVERTISING WORKS 12

Proving the effectiveness of marketing communications

ADVERTISING WORKS 12

Proving the effectiveness of marketing communications

Cases from the IPA Effectiveness Awards 2002

Edited and introduced by

Marco Rimini
Convenor of Judges

**World Advertising
Research Center**

First published 2003 by the World Advertising Research Center
Farm Road, Henley-on-Thames, Oxfordshire RG9 1EJ, United Kingdom
Telephone: 01491 411000
Fax: 01491 418600
E-mail: enquiries@warc.com

A CIP catalogue record for this book is available from the British Library

ISBN 1 84116 126 8

Typeset by Marie Doherty
Printed and bound in Great Britain
by Biddles Ltd, Guildford and King's Lynn

Dedicated to Dr Simon Broadbent 1928–2002.
Scientist and scholar.

Contents

SECTION 3: BRONZE WINNERS (SUMMARIES)

CONTENTS

IPA Effectiveness Awards 2002

DEMONSTRABLE ADDED VALUE

The IPA Effectiveness Awards exist to reward best practice in the development and assessment of commercially effective marketing communications. The Awards do this by promoting a way in which IPA practitioners can share best practice in order to build up a body of evidence to convince senior clients and the financial community of the added value that agencies bring.

It is important for any business to prove the financial worth of what it does. This is particularly true of our industry, which is part art and part science, part intuition and part process, part predictable and part impossible to forecast.

There have now been successive academic studies, learned books and commercial evidence concerning the value of a company's intangible brand assets. Similarly well-documented is the vital role that agencies and their marketing clients play in creating, building and maintaining these assets. Despite this there is a frustration within the IPA agency community that the worth of their strategic and creative product is still undervalued by members of the broader business community – CEOs and CFOs in particular.

This is why the IPA Effectiveness Awards are so vital to the agency sector and to the marketing function. The cases written for the IPA Effectiveness Awards are the only regular, extensive, accurate and public examples of best practice in the measurement of the effectiveness of communication available today.

A DECLARATION OF INTENT

There are now 765 case histories in the IPA dataBANK covering all product sectors and categories from automobiles to utilities. However, the full significance of these cases has never lain just in their factual content, or in what they teach us, valuable though this is. Similarly the lure of winning prizes has not been the only motivation of authors in writing them.

The IPA Effectiveness Awards are also important for what they symbolise, for they are a very public declaration of intent. A declaration that, irrespective of discipline, IPA agencies accept responsibility for measuring the part that their work plays in the achievement of their client's business objectives.

Although the measurement of this contribution is a responsibility they share with their clients, it is one IPA agencies should chiefly bear the burden of. They should also be proud to share with others in the industry, both in the UK and around the world, what they have learned in taking on this burden.

Intense competition leads to innovation, and this most closely-fought of awards schemes has generated more than its fair share of insights into how advertising and marketing communications contribute to business success and profitability.

It has also built an increasingly prevalent 'effectiveness culture' within IPA agencies. This means the setting of realistic objectives for brand communications in partnership with a client and then putting in place the requisite measures of effectiveness at the outset, so it becomes a continuous working process, rather than an episodic activity to try to win an award every couple of years.

A BRIEF HISTORY

The IPA agency of the 1980s was mainly concerned with the strategic and developmental process of creating advertising campaigns, and within that television commercials had primacy. Therefore the IPA Advertising Effectiveness Awards (as they were known then) tended to concentrate on proving their particular worth in competition with other 'below the line' alternatives.

Within this mainly advertising-centric context over the years, the Awards have nevertheless reflected the issues of their times. The changes that were made to the structure, format and judging of successive competitions were always intended to ensure that the agencies measured effectiveness in terms of what their clients' practical concerns were.

Thus the gradual evolution of the competition can be traced as its focus shifts over the first decade. Can we measure the effects of advertising at all? What do we know about effectiveness in fast moving consumer goods? How can we prove advertising works for financial services, for cars, or for retailers? What about privatisations, or Government, or charity advertising?

Then into the 1990s with more sophisticated concerns. How do we measure the longer and broader effects of advertising on brands? Can we determine the influence of communications on brands in terms of impact on a company's share price? What are the measurable 'manifold effects' of advertising such as the impact on employees or other key stakeholders?

By addressing each of these issues in turn, the papers written for the Awards, and the knowledge gained from them, have raised the level of understanding about the commercial impact of advertising as opposed to other key elements of the marketing mix.

EVOLUTION CONTINUES

In the meantime the nature of the member agencies of the IPA has continued to evolve with the changing communications landscape.

The separation of the creative and media functions into discrete agency sectors is now almost universal (although there are some signs of a reversal of the process in the newer agency start-ups) and some 22% of IPA agencies are now specialist media planning and buying companies.

The compartmentalisation of the sector continues apace and IPA agencies can now be found which have specialisms in ambient, digital, direct, sms (mobile marketing), sponsorship and web media. Even advertising agencies aren't calling themselves advertising agencies anymore, they are now communication companies, idea factories, brand agencies, or media investment managers which cover all the different channels through which a client's brand can be brought to market.

This has led to a rethinking of the purposes and content of the Awards.

A NEW DECLARATION OF INTENT

Following an analysis of the results of the Awards of 2000, and having conducted a thorough review of the prevailing concerns of clients, it was decided that a new declaration of intent should be made for the 2002 competition.

In a sense the new challenge the IPA membership gave itself was as daunting as the original aim in 1980, which was to prove whether advertising worked at all. Having risen successfully to this challenge with increasingly sophisticated but (with some notable exceptions) largely advertising-orientated cases, could agency authors in 2002 not only isolate the effect of the brand's advertising (TV, print, cinema, radio, posters) but also that of other communication channels used (DM, PR, web, sponsorship)?

Could our agencies now achieve the Holy Grail of effectiveness and measure the inter-relationship of these different media, demonstrating their combined brand-building effect and their impact on profitability?

Could a new era of case histories teach us about the optimal media mix in a variety of brand scenarios, and perhaps at the same time apply some of the energy and enthusiasm previously concentrated on advertising to some of the other less well documented media channels?

So the new ambition for 2002 was to start to collect quality cases on all channels to describe better their effectiveness in combination and to demonstrate their uniqueness. We want to get closer to the answers that clients ask today about effectiveness – how do I effectively divide up the entire marcomms budget? What evidence is there to show what channels work best in combination?

BUILD IT AND THEY WILL COME

In order to reorient the focus of the competition and encourage authors to rise to this new challenge, a number of apparently minor changes were made to the format. These are all detailed in the Guide to Entrants in the Effectiveness Awards section on the IPA website at *www.ipa.co.uk*, and when considered individually, they might seem innocuous, but when taken together they add up to the most fundamental re-staging of the Awards since their inception.

The most important of these changes was that the basis of the competition was no longer to be 'advertising-centric' in any way, but overtly 'media neutral'. It was to be opened up to any and all member agencies in the IPA, and specifically to media, direct marketing, integrated and other specialists who might previously have thought that the Awards were 'not for them'.

To reinforce this repositioning the specialist judging panel included senior figures from the direct marketing, sales promotion and media sectors. The 'how to win' seminars were designed to give particular assistance to IPA Effectiveness Awards debutantes from across the industry.

In a similar vein the client judging panel comprised very senior figures, many of whose brands have multi-media campaigns. Our Chairman, Ian MacLaurin, has had prior involvement with Tesco and is now working with Vodafone and the England & Wales Cricket Board. This has given him personal experience across the communications spectrum from dotcom to sms.

WHO ROSE TO THE CHALLENGE?

'Waiting for the response from agencies was an anxious time', stated the 1982 Convenor of Judges in *Advertising Works 2*. So it was this time, but happily our agencies have responded with a healthy increase in entries, 61 compared to the 2000 total of 52. A statistically significant shift, which has halted a gentle decline and turned the graph upwards.

1990	1992	1994	1996	1998	2000	2002
87	80	73	70	54	52	61

The nature of agencies entering saw a welcome resurgence in support from the leading IPA members, with eight out of the top ten submitting cases. We were also pleased to receive entries, which had previously done well in the IPA AREA and Scottish Effectiveness Awards.

In all 33 different agencies entered; of the papers four were joint entries and many were produced with the collaboration of several other companies. In particular we were delighted to get solo entries from media agencies and that two of these companies ended up as winners in the first year of the new competition.

Perhaps our only disappointment was in not receiving winning cases from direct marketing agencies and rectifying this must be a key aim for 2004, especially given the claims made for the accountability of DM.

LESSONS LEARNED

Every paper shortlisted contains lessons of relevance to the marketing communications business, but it is perhaps helpful to highlight those cases that have taken strides in the direction of the broader effectiveness agenda and our renewed declaration of intent.

First Barnardo's. The case showed how the idea of 'Giving Children Back Their Future' worked through several channels, and proved to redirect and re-energise the whole organisation. The execution of this big idea for all channels, internal and external, was demonstrably effective. The authors explain and detail how these channels were selected, what their role was, and how well each delivered within the overall campaign.

Halifax and Police Recruitment both demonstrated how each individual element of their communications programmes worked. These are therefore important examples of the difficult science of structuring a clear framework of objectives to allow for the thorough and reliable measurement of results.

The two Volkswagen cases deserve reading for their admirably clear approach to proving how each channel was planned and how each worked. These cases also start to look at the important area of combining different media to arrive at channel strategies. These two papers have a clarity of structure and a refreshing honesty of approach, which, I'm sure, will prove to be important building blocks for future entries.

Individual channels received special attention. Marmite models the PR effect and its combination with advertising. Hovis, the packaging effect, and Domino's Pizza talks us through how effective TV sponsorship and interactive TV can be. Stella and Tesco both have important comments to make on the relationship between advertising and sales promotion. Kellogg's show us how to use the web to best effect with children.

Alongside these broader papers were the deeper papers, which reflected best practice in the discipline of developing effective advertising through more traditional channels. Great advertising campaigns for Sainsbury's, Skoda, Walkers Crisps, the international case of Olivio/Bertolli, all proved that in broadening the Awards we haven't lost any of their depth.

CONCLUSION

Amongst many things, the IPA Awards are a declaration of intent. The intent is to prove to CEOs and CFOs that the commercial value of marketing communication created by agencies for their companies and brands in a multi-channel environment can be measured to their satisfaction, and that of their shareholders.

Those that wrote a paper, those that were shortlisted and the authors of the 23 published here, should be thanked by everyone in the industry for making that declaration loud and clear.

The Judges

Stewart Gilliland
Chief Executive
Interbrew UK & Ireland

Martin Glenn
President
Walkers Snack Foods

Andrew Harrison
Director of Marketing, Rowntree
Nestlé UK

Sharon Lang
Director of Brand Marketing
AOL UK

Ian Milligan
former Sales & Marketing Director
Camelot Group

Charlotte Oades
Marketing Director GB & Ireland
Coca-Cola GB

Raoul Pinnell
Vice President Global Brands &
Communications
Shell International Oil Products

Simon Tuckey
former Managing Director
Anchor Foods (New Zealand Milk UK)

David Walsh
Advertising Director Worldwide
Financial Times

Acknowledgements

The IPA Value of Advertising Committee

Stephen Woodford	(Chairman) WCRS
Joanna Bamford	Lowe
Les Binet	BMP DDB
Tim Broadbent	Bates UK
Michael Finn	DFGW
Trista Grant	BBJ Media Services
Laurence Green	Fallon
Chris Herd	Bates UK
Alison Hoad	CDD
Sue Little	McCann-Erickson Manchester
Katrina Michel	Cheetham Bell JWT
Sven Olsen	Banks Hoggins O'Shea FCB
Mark Palmer	OMD UK
Marco Rimini	J Walter Thompson
Malcolm White	Partners BDDH
Dylan Williams	Bartle Bogle Hegarty

Many people worked hard to make the Awards a success, especially the following: Stephen Woodford, Chairman of the Value of Advertising Committee; Marco Rimini, Convenor of Judges; Alison Hoad, Deputy Convenor of Judges; and Mark Palmer and Trista Grant, who also sit on the IPA Media Policy Group.

At the IPA, the core team were Jill Bentley, Tessa Gooding, Emma Kane, Clare Laverty, Angela Lucey-Harmer, Hamish Pringle and Justin Van de Velde.

Sponsors

The success of the IPA Effectiveness Awards 2002 owes a great debt to our sponsors. The IPA would like to thank the following companies whose support made the presentation possible, especially the *Financial Times*, our overall sponsor, whose long-term commitment to the competition has been so important to the industry.

OVERALL SPONSOR

FINANCIAL TIMES

INDIVIDUAL AWARD SPONSORS

World Advertising Research Center

   adforum.com

SUPPORTED BY

Marketing

Prizes

AGENCY OF THE YEAR (BILLINGS ABOVE £100M)

BMP DDB

AGENCY OF THE YEAR (BILLINGS BELOW £100M)
Bartle Bogle Hegarty

GRAND PRIX
Bartle Bogle Hegarty for Barnardo's

JOHN BARTLE AWARD FOR BEST NEW AGENCY
Fallon for Skoda Auto

BEST NEW CLIENT
Bartle Bogle Hegarty for Barnardo's

BEST LAUNCH
AV Browne for Hastings Hotels

BEST INSIGHT AND INNOVATION
M&C Saatchi for The Home Office (Police Recruitment)

BEST CHANGE OF DIRECTION
Fallon for Skoda Auto

BEST CONSISTENCY
BMP DDB for Volkswagen UK

BEST INTERACTIVE
BLM Media for Domino's Pizza Group Ltd

BEST MEDIA THINKING
BLM Media for Domino's Pizza Group Ltd

BEST INTEGRATION
Delaney Lund Knox Warren for HBOS plc (Halifax)

BEST INTERNATIONAL
Bartle Bogle Hegarty for Unilever Best Foods (Olivio/Bertolli)

CHARLES CHANNON AWARD
Not awarded this year

IPA EFFECTIVENESS AWARDS 2002

GOLD AWARDS

Bartle Bogle Hegarty for Barnardo's

Delaney Lund Knox Warren for HBOS plc (Halifax)

Fallon for Skoda Auto

SILVER AWARDS

McCann-Erickson Belfast for Dept of the Environment NI (Anti-drink driving)

PHD Media for BT Cellnet/O$_2$

Walsh Trott Chick Smith for Britannia Building Society

BMP DDB for Anheuser-Busch (Budweiser)

BLM Media for Domino's Pizza Group Ltd

Abbott Mead Vickers.BBDO for The Economist

AV Browne for Hastings Hotels

BMP DDB for British Bakeries (Hovis)

Leo Burnett for Kellogg's (Kellogg's Real Fruit Winders)

BMP DDB for Unilever Best Foods (Marmite)

BMP DDB and OMD UK for The Dairy Council (Milk)

Bates UK for Ocean Spray Inc.

Bartle Bogle Hegarty for Unilever Best Foods (Olivio/Bertolli)

M&C Saatchi for The Home Office (Police Recruitment)

Abbott Mead Vickers.BBDO for Sainsbury's Supermarkets Ltd

Lowe for Tesco

BMP DDB for Volkswagen UK (brand)

BMP DDB for Volkswagen UK (Volkswagen Passat)

Banks Hoggins O'Shea FCB for Waitrose

Abbott Mead Vickers.BBDO for Walkers Snack Foods (Walkers Crisps)

BRONZE AWARDS

Burkitt DDB for Nestlé Purina Pet Care (Bakers Complete)

Bates UK for Pfizer Consumer Healthcare (Benadryl)

Abbott Mead Vickers.BBDO for BT Retail

Cheetham Bell JWT for ACDOCO (Dr Beckmann Rescue Oven Cleaner)

Bartle Bogle Hegarty for Lever Fabergé (Lynx)

Cheetham Bell JWT for Manchester Evening News

Saatchi & Saatchi for Manor Bakeries (Mr Kipling)

Publicis for Post Office

J Walter Thompson and OMD UK for Coty UK Ltd (Rimmel)

Prager Proximity/Proximity London for Sainsbury's Supermarkets Ltd

McCann-Erickson for Dept of the Environment NI ('Damage' Seatbelts)

Lowe for Interbrew UK (Stella Artois)

J Walter Thompson for Tommy's: The Baby Charity

Section 1

Gold Winners

1

Barnardo's

'Giving Barnardo's back its future'

Principal authors: Dan Goldstein, Bartle Bogle Hegarty,
and Mary Daniels, Barnardo's

EDITOR'S SUMMARY

This case documents how in just two and a half years Barnardo's transformed its image among a generation of brand rejectors. A powerful advertising campaign spearheaded the re-launch, renewing the charity's relevance today along with the perceived deservedness of its work. To capitalise on the resurgence of interest that the advertising had created, a new communications channel was employed: Face-to-face. The net result is a younger more valuable base of donors guaranteeing millions of pounds of donations income well into the future.

INTRODUCTION

This is the story of how babies injecting heroin and adults committing suicide changed the face of Britain's oldest children's charity forever. Of how integrated communications turned a generation of brand rejecters into brand supporters and influenced diverse audiences from MPs to students. How one of the most ambitious recruitment programmes ever conducted by a UK charity has ensured millions of pounds in donations for years to come. This is the story of how Barnardo's divorced itself from its orphanage past and embraced the future.

THE BRAND PROBLEM

The importance of donations

A crisis in donations is probably the worst set of circumstances in which a charity such as Barnardo's could find itself. Donations mean so much to a charity. They are a measure of its popularity, of public support for its work, and as such a source of pride. Donations are also of strategic importance:

- Donations income spells independence. An increase in state funding experienced over the '90s meant that Barnardo's was becoming far too reliant on the public sector. This had compromised the charity's ability to lobby and campaign among MPs, a major area of the charity's work.[1]
- Money from donations gives Barnardo's the opportunity to work in areas too politically sensitive to be funded by the state, e.g. the charity's work with young asylum seekers.
- The state pays only for existing services and doesn't joint invest in new projects; without money from donations there is no new money to invest in new projects.[2] Donations are the only source of income that makes the charity grow.

Donor age profile

The reason Barnardo's donations income was under threat lay in the profile of the charity's donorbase (Figure 1). The people donating (Figure 2) to Barnardo's were from an older age group; over half were over 65.[3] This age profile is peculiar to Barnardo's, not to the charity market as a whole.

---

1. Local authorities and voluntary organisations like Barnardo's have always had a close relationship, where the local authority by contract or grant funds the charity's work in the community as an efficient means to outsource. Recently this relationship has become formalised as policy; in 1993 following The Community Care Act there was a transfer of responsibility and funding from central government to local authorities. As a part of this policy shift at least 85% of the additional money provided to local authorities had to be spent in the independent sector. Service provider charities such as Barnardo's receive a total of £1.4bn or 3% of total local authority expenditure a year (source: Local Government Financial Statistics, No. 9, Department of the Environment/DETR/HM Treasury).
2. Projects is the term given to the services Barnardo's provides to its 'service users', these being the children that the charity works with. These range from bricks-and-mortar services such as schools and drop-in centres to intangibles such as legal advice and counselling.
3. Active donorbase is defined by the people that have donated during the past two years.

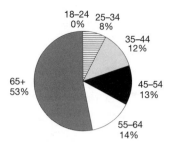

Figure 1: *Age profile of Barnardo's active donorbase, 1999*
Base: 425,122 donated to Barnardo's past 2 years Sep 97–99
Source: Claritas

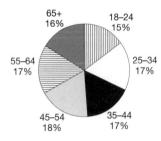

Figure 2: *UK adults donating to charity in the year 1999*
Base: 4142
Source: Family Expenditure Survey 1999

The vast majority of Barnardo's donorbase was recruited via the charity's direct mail programme. These people were affectionately referred to as 'Dorothy Donor'.[4] Dorothy presented the charity with a series of problems:

- Dorothy wasn't going to be around forever and there were few recruits coming in to replace her (it was estimated that 5% of Barnardo's donorbase was dying each year).
- Dorothy was giving one-off cash gifts when prompted to do so by direct mailers. This made it expensive for Barnardo's to maintain this type of donor relationship.
- To cut the costs of the relationship Barnardo's had tried to change Dorothy's donating habits (Figure 3) from prompted giving to a 'committed' donation via a standing order. This had proved very difficult and by 1999 only 3% of Barnardo's donorbase were giving via this method.[5]
- Dorothy was also a less valuable donor, giving less money in the way of donations than younger age groups.

---

4. As we will be describing several different profiles of donor we will use the term 'Dorothy Donor' in reference to direct mail donors. In reality there is an approximate 60/40 female/male split (source: Claritas).
5. There were only 11,397 committed donors in September 1999 and 425,122 cash donors (source: Barnardo's).

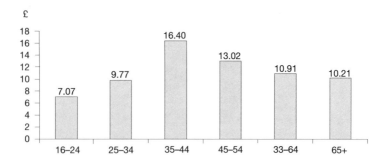

Figure 3: *UK average value of monthly donations by age, 1999*
Base: 4142
Source: Family Expenditure Survey 1999

It was clear that Barnardo's needed not only new donors but a *new profile of donor*:

- younger
- committed in their method of payment
- longer term
- higher value.

The 'lost generation'

In the past Barnardo's was a children's charity famous for its orphanages, and attracted financial supporters on that basis. However, in 1966 Barnardo's began closing its orphanages.[6] Over the next 35 years the charity was relatively quiet and there was little communication with the public about its new areas of work. This lack of dialogue had had a profound effect on how the charity was seen, particularly among younger age groups. For these people, 88% spontaneously associated Barnardo's with homes, orphanages and institutions.[7] It was these people that Barnardo's was looking to recruit and yet the charity's function appeared irrelevant to them in today's society:

'I see Barnardo's as outmoded; it hasn't moved with the times – we associate it with the nineteenth century.'

Female, 35–45

---

6. Barnardo's has undergone a number of significant changes since its first 'home for boys'. Established in 1870 by Dr Thomas Barnardo, the home was a response to the devastating effects of a cholera epidemic in the East End of London that left many children orphaned and homeless. Perhaps the most significant change in the charity's work took place in 1966: The Children and Young Persons Act of 1964 for the first time placed a duty on local authorities to reduce the need to take children into care by giving advice, support and even financial aid to families experiencing difficulties. As a result the number of children Barnardo's received was decreasing along with their length of stay in the homes. Following a comprehensive review the charity set a new policy in place to 'concentrate an increasing proportion of its resources on meeting new and hitherto unmet needs' – a policy that stands to this day. A commitment was made to cut down on residential services and to develop new work with disabled children and those with emotional and behavioural problems. To reflect this, the charity changed its name in 1966 from Dr Barnardo's Homes to Dr Barnardo's. The last home was closed in 1980 and in 1988 the charity changed its name again to Barnardo's.

7. Source: Quadrangle Tracking, October 1999, *'What area of work do you associate with Barnardo's?'*

'I think for all of us, we have a mindset that says Barnardo's equals homes that are no longer needed. I personally wouldn't give money to keep children in institutions.'

Male, 35–45

'I remember at school putting pennies into their collection box which was in the shape of a little children's home, but what they're actually doing today I haven't a clue. If they don't have any homes now, where is Barnardo's?'

Female, 35–45

Source: Plus Four Market Research Limited, March 1999
Creative development research for recruitment direct mail

Barnardo's orphanage past was a barrier for younger people. For them the charity was outmoded, old-fashioned and irrelevant. This lack of modernity was in contrast to how other major children's charities were perceived (see Figure 4).

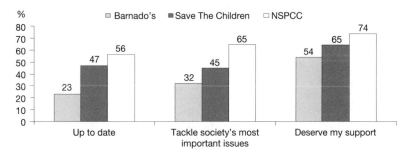

Figure 4: *'Which statement do you believe applies to the following charities?'*
Base: 292
Source: Quadrangle Tracking Study–Oct 99 (pre relaunch)

Not being relevant to younger generations meant that Barnardo's was perceived to be less deserving (Figure 5).[8] The years of 'silence' had meant that the charity's supporters had grown old with the brand. Termed the 'lost generation', Barnardo's had been aware of these people's views for some time. In the past however there had never been such a pressing need to change their perceptions of the charity. When Barnardo's approached Bartle Bogle Hegarty (BBH) in 1998, it was this generation of brand rejecters that the agency was tasked with recruiting into the brand.

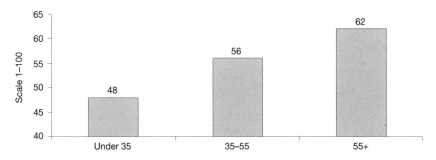

Figure 5: *Barnardo's perceived deservedness by age*
Base: 292
Source: Quadrangle Tracking Study–Oct 99 (pre relaunch)

8. Deservedness is measured using Manders Unbounded scale.

THE BRAND CHALLENGE

A new brand vision

The brand challenge was a considerable one – *to replace Barnardo's orphanage past with a new vision.*

The new vision for the brand had to represent the diverse work that the charity did today. *'What was the role that this 130-year-old organisation performed?' 'What did it do?' 'What was its purpose?'* The process employed by BBH in the development of the new vision involved:

- Interviewing the heads of each major department within Barnardo's.
- Interviewing children that had benefited from Barnardo's work.
- Visiting the projects themselves and interviewing the social workers.
- Exploring Barnardo's rich history.

BBH identified a common and powerful theme. It was based on the unique way in which Barnardo's approached childcare – one that differed from other children's charities, notably the NSPCC.[9] Where other charities intervene in the immediate circumstances, affecting the well-being of the child, Barnardo's works to ensure the child's long-term 'emotional health'. Through this process Barnardo's changes the future for children. The power of this thought lies in its 'truth' as an observation on how we develop as human beings and how our experiences shape all of our lives.

The brand vision was by no means a cosmetic exercise. This thought became the absolute basis of how Barnardo's sees its role today:

> 'Barnardo's purpose is to help the most vulnerable children and young people transform their lives and fulfil their potential.'

> Source: Barnardo's Corporate Plan 2000/05

For communicating the new purpose BBH needed to distil the vision further and expressed it as: *Giving children back their future.*

Internal communication

The next task was to communicate Barnardo's new purpose to all 12,500 people who work for the charity. BBH, together with the marketing and communications department, ran 'Brand Roadshows' that travelled the country and visited each of the 16 regional offices. Within each office the new vision was presented to the heads of each department who in turn ran their own workshops for their own staff. By autumn 1999 all the people working for Barnardo's understood that their efforts, their passion and commitment was in the pursuit of a single definable cause: children's futures.

---

9. The NSPCC is an approved child protection body, legally empowered to remove children from 'situations of distress or danger'. In reality their function is largely complete at this point and in a number of cases hands the child over to Barnardo's who would then work with the child's long-term needs in the way of repatriation to the home, psychological distress, working alongside other family members, etc.

Giving Children Back Their Future became Barnardo's purpose. It began to shape the way in which the diverse functions within the charity operated as well as the way they lobbied the charity's set of opinion formers:

- *Lobbying and influencing.* MPs were subject to literature and reports using children's futures as the context for their policy recommendations.
- *Public relations.* Journalists were now courted on points of view and issues affecting the future welfare of children in the UK.
- *Corporate volunteering.* Barnardo's relies upon volunteers for much of their fundraising and retail effort. The charity began motivating them with 'future branded' literature.
- *Corporate relations.* Barnardo's now approached big consumer-facing companies with a brand partnership proposition not just as a 'good cause'.
- *The projects.* When pitching for funding Barnardo's made sure that councillors were aware that the issue at stake wasn't money but 'children's futures'.

For the first time in decades there was a definable 'cause' by which Barnardo's could rally these audiences. These groups have a disproportionate impact on Barnardo's ability to fulfil its new vision.

THE COMMUNICATIONS PLAN

The communications activity had a single objective: to recruit younger people into the brand to ensure future donations income. To this end, a broad target of 35–55-year-olds was selected. This age group not only gave more money in donations but they had more reason to care about children's futures, being likely to have young children of their own. *The task was to turn this lost generation of brand rejecters into active brand supporters.*

The communications model

The relaunch date was set for 21 October 1999. All marketing and communications activity changed its content and branding to *Giving Children Back Their Future*. To recruit the lost generation the relaunch consisted of three core activities:

1. Advertising was to reposition the brand as modern and deserving to the 35–55-year-olds. As well as this central objective, it needed to impact opinion formers.
2. Face-to-face recruitment: a new channel to bring in new donors.
3. Direct mail would see some of its budget cut in order to fund the Face-to-face activity. However its function would remain constant: the continued recruitment and maintenance of Dorothy Donor.

[See Figure 6 for complete integrated communications activity.]

'What we developed was an holistic communications plan. Advertising was to aggressively punch through the old-fashioned views that people had of Barnardo's. The direct mail was to keep the cash rolling in so to speak, and the Face-to-face was our key to unlocking future donations income.'

Andrew Nebel, Marketing and Communications Director, Barnardo's

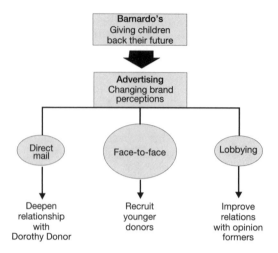

Figure 6: *Communications model*

Advertising

The advertising that BBH developed dramatised the 'future thought' in all its power.[10] Children were shown acting out their future lives as a result of their disadvantaged childhood: a 4-year-old robs a bank, a 6-year-old solicits as a prostitute, an infant injects heroin. The copy described the troubled circumstances of their childhood, explaining how their lives took such a destructive path. A second campaign showed images of dead adults. The copy described the childhood event that led to their death: sexual abuse from a relative, exclusion from school, being beaten by a parent. Without Barnardo's help they died as children, their fates sealed from the moment their rights were abused. In both campaigns each 'life story' was designed around an area of Barnardo's work.

The advertising was in many ways designed to shock because it had to. To overwrite 130 years of history the communication needed to shake people from an entrenched view that Barnardo's ran orphanages and was therefore redundant today. We needed to present a cutting-edge, modern organisation at the forefront of childcare. There was no doubt in our minds that shock was important strategically and morally. During the process of developing the advertising the creatives were provided with case histories and visited some of the projects themselves. All the individuals in the advertising were based on real individuals and the ones used were not the most 'shocking' (see Figures 7–18).

---

10. Barnardo's advertising has won a total of 23 creative awards including: Gold Lion at Cannes International Advertising Awards, 2 Campaign Press Silver, has appeared in the D&AD annual with both campaigns and numerous photographic awards.

Figure 7:
Heroin Baby

Figure 8: *Alcoholic*

Figure 9: *Prostitute*

Figure 10: *Homeless*

Figure 11: *Prison*

Figure 12: *Robber*

Figure 13: *Suicide*

Figure 14:
Dead Prostitute

Figure 15: *Drowned*

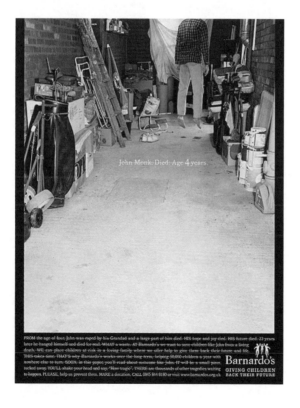

Figure 16: *Hanging*

Figure 17: *Jumper*

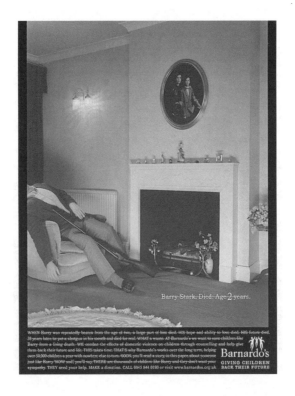

Figure 18: *Shotgun*

First campaign: 'Prostitute'

'Neglected as a child, it was always possible that Kim would be an easy victim for pimps.

'With Barnardo's help an unhappy childhood need not mean an empty future.

'We no longer run orphanages but continue to help thousands of children and their families at home, school and in the local community.

'Please help us by making a donation. Call 0840 844 01 80.'

Second campaign: 'Hanging'

'From the age of four, John was raped by his Granddad and a large part of him died. His hope and joy died. His future died. Twenty-two years later he hanged himself and died for real. What a waste. At Barnardo's we want to save children like John from a living death. We can place children at risk in a loving family where we offer them help to give them back their future and life. This takes time. That's why Barnardo's works over the long term, helping 50,000 children a year with nowhere else to turn. Soon, in this paper, you'll read about someone like John. It will be a small piece tucked away. You'll shake your head and say: "How tragic".'

Figure 19

Divorcing oneself from such an historic past was a brave step; a great number of people had dedicated their lives to the charity and the thought of change was traumatic. In a speech given to the ruling council at Barnardo's, the Chief Executive, Roger Singleton, captured the organisation's feelings at the time, but laid out in the simplest terms the importance of the relaunch: *We are fiercely proud of our past, but what concerns us most is our future.'* The change was set to go forward. The public was about to be educated as to Barnardo's function and the realities of childhood disadvantage in today's society.[11]

---

11. What helped convince people inside Barnardo's to go ahead with such a powerful advertising campaign came from the good doctor himself. Dr Barnardo had never been afraid of controversy and had made use of the then new technology of photography. He had used images of dirty and malnourished children dressed in rags to actively court discomfort among Victorian patrons from whom he sought financial support (see Figure 19).

Media

The media choice for the advertising was the broadsheet press, the role of which fulfilled several strategic functions:[12]

- A good coverage of our 35–55-year-old target audience.
- A readership who were more likely to be responsive to the advertising's 'challenging' content.
- A medium read by 'social influencers': not just potential donors, but audiences key to Barnardo's lobbying and corporate relationships.
- The advertising itself was of a serious subject matter – one that was felt to be in line with a broadsheet's editorial tone.
- The size of the layout presented an ideal format to give the advertising even greater levels of power and impact.
- The immediacy of a newspaper environment helped position Barnardo's as relevant in today's world.[13]

Face-to-face

The new purpose of *Giving Children Back Their Future* was to make people understand what it was that Barnardo's did today. If people feel that Barnardo's is working towards a deserving cause they are more likely to see the charity as deserving of their money. It was clear that direct mail was not the communications channel to finish this recruitment process. A new channel needed to be employed – one that was better set to recruit a younger age group in the volumes required.

A new channel for just such an ambitious recruitment programme had recently been introduced into the UK called Face-to-face recruitment. Face-to-face is conducted by a specialised recruitment agency.[14] The recruiters wore Barnardo's branded apparel, with *Giving Children Back Their Future* prominent to act as the prompt for passers-by, aided by the recruiters stock-in-trade question *'Could you spare a moment for Barnardo's?'* Face-to-face was an ideal choice for the recruitment of 'high-quality' younger donors:

- Face-to-face recruits only committed donors – people paying a monthly fee by standing order.
- Like any other communications channel, Face-to-face could be targeted. To reach Barnardo's 35–55-year-old brand target, shopping precincts in urban centres were chosen. These are places of high footfall where this age group spend their leisure time, go to and from work or are out shopping.

---

12. The majority of the press insertions appeared in broadsheet newspapers. The *Daily Mail* and Sunday colour supplements were used to extend the coverage of the campaign as a way of maximising OTS. Overall, the coverage of the 35–55 ABC1 target achieved since October 1999 is 84% at 19 OTS. This has been achieved despite the low levels of spend, ensuring that the campaign's 377 press insertions to date have had the greatest degree of impact and at the best price. *'Performance against the market was excellent. Not only were the negotiated costs below our pool averages but Barnardo's was one of our top performing customers in terms of position quality.'* Source: Billets, Independent Media Auditor.
13. The second round of creative work used the serious nature of advertising's broadsheet environment to lend immediacy and 'news value' to its message.
14. The recruitment agency does not get paid per recruit instead agreeing a fee against the expected number of successful conversions made. This fee is renegotiated by both parties at predetermined intervals throughout the process. In other words there is no commission; the only incentive the recruitment agency has for 'upping its sales pitch' is to reduce the costs of person-hours.

- Face-to-face is a two-way conversation with people. This was important given the re-education process involved in overwriting Barnardo's orphanage past.
- Face-to-face communicated modernity. The image of charity boxes and tin-shakers associated with old-style charity collection was replaced with an army of branded communication points (see Figure 20).

Figure 20

Direct mail

The content of the direct communications to Dorothy Donor changed in line with the new brand vision: from mailers to telemarketing scripts. Their content was inspired by the idea that 'In your hands lies a child's future' (see Figures 21–25):[15]

Figure 21: *Recruitment Mailer: EHS Brann*

---

15. There are three key activities employed in this programme:
    - Recruitment Mailers are targeted at people that fit the Dorothy Donor profile.
    - After making her gift Dorothy is subject to successive mailers asking her for more donations. These 'Warm Mailers' are the source of most of Barnardo's direct mail income.
    - Approximately six weeks after Dorothy has responded with her first cash gift, Barnardo's telemarketing agency call her by phone. This is to thank her and ask if she would like to become a committed donor.

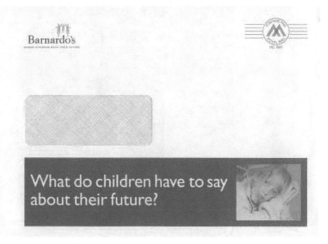

Figure 22: *Poverty: Direct Mail – EHS Brann*

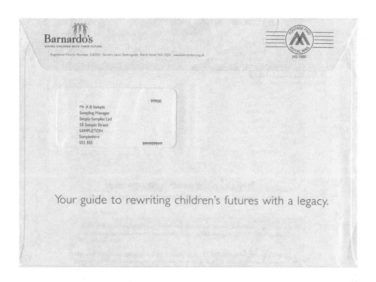

Figure 23: *Legacy Envelope: Direct Mail – EHS Brann*

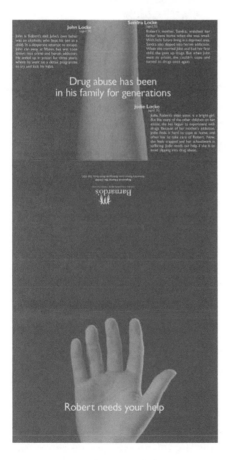

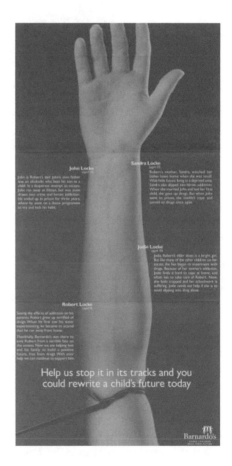

Figure 24: *Drug Mailer: Direct Mail – EHS Brann*

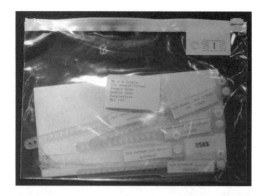

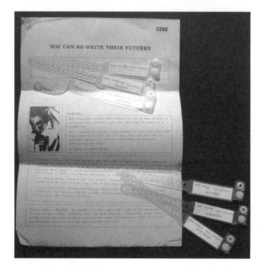

Figure 25: *Direct Mail: Babytags – BBH*

'The new brand vision for Barnardo's has allowed us much more leverage in how we can engage people using direct mail. The resultant creative has been far more powerful and far more effective than anything we have used before.'

Julian Horberry, Barnardo's Account Director, EHSBrann, London

'We run centres where we work with children and their families, helping them to rebuild their lives, free from the tyranny of drugs. By providing advice and support to parents we can help rewrite children's futures and save young lives.'

Barnardo's Telemarketing Script

HOW THE RELAUNCH IMPACTED ON THE BUSINESS

Total income

Twenty-nine months have passed since 21 October 1999. Since this date Barnardo's total income has increased by £46.6 million on the 29-month period before the relaunch (see Figure 26).

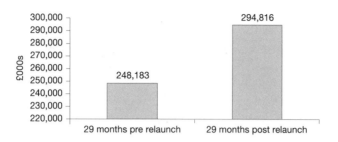

Figure 26: *Barnardo's total income £000s, 29-month period pre and post relaunch compared*
Source: Barnardo's

The fastest-growing source of income was from the 'direct marketing' programme: this represents all the money generated from the direct mail and Face-to-face activity (see Figure 27).

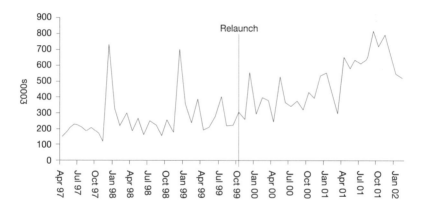

Figure 27: *Direct marketing monthly income £000s*
Source: Barnardo's

As a whole, direct marketing increased its contribution by 86% over the same time period prior to relaunch (see Figure 28).

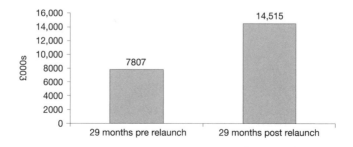

Figure 28: *Barnardo's total direct marketing income £000s, 29-month period pre and post launch compared*
Source: Barnardo's

Face-to-face performance

The recruitment activity began in London during October 1999, tying in with the advertising launch. Its success during the first six months led Barnardo's to roll-out the programme across the UK and Ireland. To date (February 2002) Barnardo's has both recruited and retained 107,205 people via this method and the programme continues with no sign of exhaustion.[16] As the base of recruits grows so too does the income from this source, totalling over £4 million to date (see Figure 29).

Figure 29: *£000s monthly income from Face-to-face recruits*
Source: PFP

The combined communications strategy in recruiting the lost generation of younger donors had been highly effective. The majority (58%) of the new recruits were the previously brand-rejecting 35–55-year-old age group (see Figure 30).

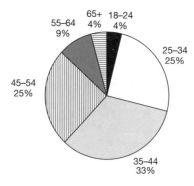

Figure 30: *Age profile of Face-to-face recruits, February 2002*
Base: 107,205
Source: PFP

---

16. The total number of people recruited over the 29-month period was in fact 110,995 but a small number have since cancelled their standing order. So successful has Barnardo's been with the Face-to-face activity that the charity has become synonymous with this recruitment method.

The addition of over 100,000 Face-to-face recruits shifted the entire age profile of Barnardo's active donorbase (see Figure 31).

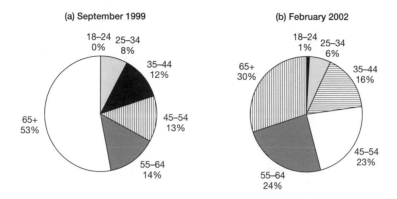

Figure 31: *Age profile of Barnardo's active donorbase*
Base: (a) £425,122 donated to Barnardo's past 2 years (Sep 97–Sep 99)
     (b) £469,837 donated to Barnardo's past 2 years (Feb 00–Feb 02)
Source: Claritas

The communications activity had also increased the quality of donors. In September 1999 (the month prior to relaunch) only 3% of Barnardo's donorbase were using committed methods of payment. *By February 2002 29% of donors were committed* (see Figure 32).

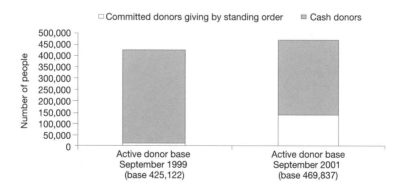

Figure 32: *Barnardo's active donorbase by method of donation, pre and post relaunch compared*
Source: Barnardo's

Direct mail performance

Even recruitment and retention of Dorothy Donor has improved since the brand relaunch. More people responded to recruitment mailers – an increase of some 400% (see Figure 33).

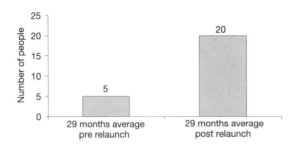

Figure 33: *Recruitment mailers: people responding per 1000 mailers*
Source: Barnardo's

Post relaunch the number of standing order accounts opened from each phone contact more than doubled (see Figure 34).

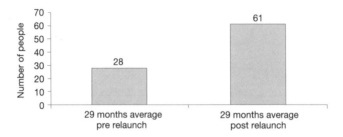

Figure 34: *Telemarketing: number of people contacted that opened a standing order account*
Source: Barnardo's

There has been a sharp increase in the number of committed donors recruited and developed through direct mail (see Figure 35).

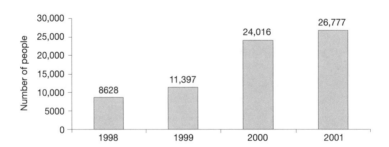

Figure 35: *Number of committed donors recruited through direct mail*
Source: Barnardo's

The success of this in migrating people up the value chain to a high-value committed gift means that despite fewer mailers being sent out overall, total income has increased by 27% on the 29-month period before brand relaunc (see Figure 36).

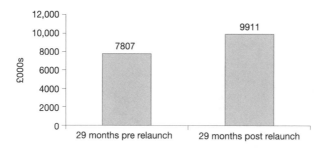

Figure 36: *Direct mail total income £000s*
Source: Barnardo's

Advertising performance

It was advertising's role to drive the change in the way that people defined Barnardo's. Of all communications it was the advertising that had attracted the most awareness (see Figure 37).[17]

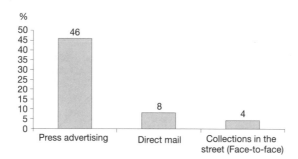

Figure 37: '*Where did you see Barnardo's communication?*'
Base: 403 people aware of Barnardo's communication (March 00)
Source: Quadrangle Tracking Study

For Face-to-face to successfully recruit people in such high volumes the advertising needed to start changing their opinions from the outset. The power of the advertising's content ensured that it did. The following charts are taken from a tracking survey conducted in March 2000, five months from the start of the campaign and after just 147 press insertions.

Barnardo's experienced the greatest leap in awareness of all UK charities (see Figure 38). It was now seen to be more modern, in line with other children's charities (see Figure 39).

---

17. Although the advertising was not designed to be a direct response medium it did have a telephone number to call for more information along with Barnardo's website address. Since the first campaign over 5000 calls have been made to this number. The website had a growth in traffic to an average in 2001 of 2050 individual visits a week – an increase of 300% prior to the advertising.

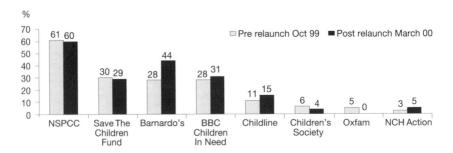

Figure 38: *'If I ask you to think of the names of charities, which ones come to mind?': spontaneous awareness of any charity*
Base: 292 (Oct 99) 403 (March 00)
Source: Quadrangle Tracking Study

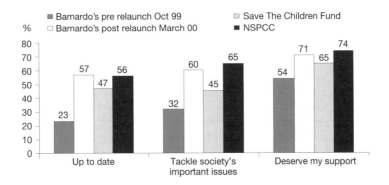

Figure 39: *'Which statement do you believe applies to the following children's charities?'*
Base: 292 (Oct 99) 403 (March 00)
Source: Quadrangle Tracking Study

Their associated areas of work were now much more modern issues and commensurate with the issues used in the advertising (see Figure 40).

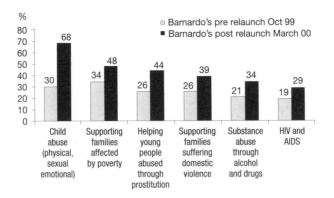

Figure 40: *'Which of the following areas of work do you associate with Barnardo's?'*
Base: 292 (Oct 99) 403 (March 00)
Source: Quadrangle Tracking Study

Immediately people's spontaneous association of Barnardo's with orphanages began to decline – a trend that continued throughout the life of the campaign (see Figure 41).

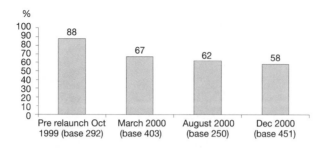

Figure 41: *'What type of work do you associate with Barnardo's?': % of all respondents saying 'home for children or orphanages'*
Source: Quadrangle Tracking Study

The net result of these perception shifts meant that people now saw Barnardo's as more deserving. The bigger moves were among the younger audiences (see Figure 42).

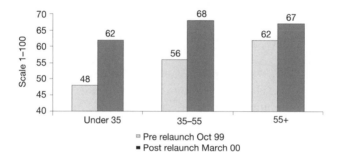

Figure 42: *Barnardo's perceived deservedness by age, pre and post relaunch compared*
Base: 292 (Oct 99) 403 (March 00)
Source: Quadrangle Tracking Study

It was the advertising that drove this deservedness (see Figure 43).

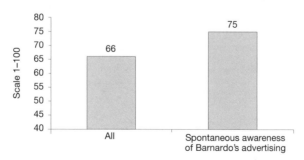

Figure 43: *Barnardo's perceived deservedness post relaunch*
Base 403 (March 00)
Source: Quadrangle Tracking Study

As the perception of the charity's deservedness increased so too did people's propensity to donate, the most dramatic change being among the 35–55-year-old age group (see Figure 44).

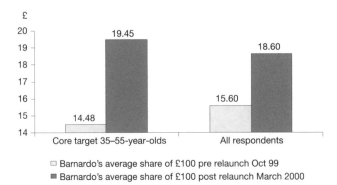

Figure 44: *£100 as shared by respondents between charities, pre and post relaunch compared*
Base: 292 (Oct 99) 403 (March 00)
Source: Quadrangle Tracking Study

TOTAL COMMUNICATIONS EFFECT

As well as repositioning Barnardo's in the minds of potential donors, the relaunch also needed to create a change in how the opinion leader audiences perceived the charity. The total communications effect can be demonstrated throughout the major areas of Barnardo's the organisation.

Public relations

The advertising was the major communications channel to influence journalists, among which the campaign had a high awareness, second only to the big-spending NSPCC (see Figure 45).

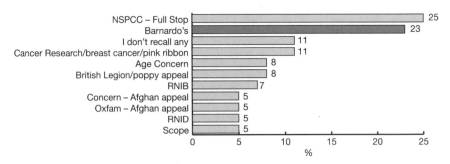

Figure 45: *'Do you recall any specific media campaigns carried out by charities, voluntary organisations or pressure groups over the last six months?'*
Base: 61 journalists (local, regional and national: across media)
Source: Charity Media Monitor, NFP Synergy/Future Foundation (Jan 02)

Not only were they aware of the advertising but they were impressed by the charity's relaunch (see Figure 46).

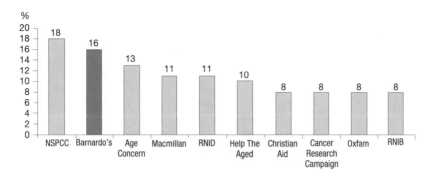

Figure 46: *'In your work as a journalist, which charities have directly impressed you in the last six months?'*
Base: 61 journalists (local, regional and national: across media)
Source: Charity Media Monitor, NFP Synergy/Future Foundation (Jan 02)

The campaign's provocative and shocking content made Barnardo's a subject of a national debate, which took place in newspapers, magazines and on TV. The Committee of Advertising Practice (CAP) urged media owners not to run the controversial Heroin Baby execution.[18] This was contrary to public opinion: there were only ever 28 complaints made to the Advertising Standards Authority (ASA). Fifty-seven per cent of people agreed that the advertising was *'shocking but effective'*.[19] Even Barnardo's head office received over 300 phone calls of support.

Paul Betts (father of Leah who died of an ecstasy overdose in 1995) said:

'Anything that brings attention to drug abuse and opens the debate is to be welcomed ... Even if this advert creates a stink, I don't care. It keeps people thinking.'

The advertising became a subject of political discussion:

'Barnardo's is a very reputable charity that does a lot of good. I hope this advert does help them to attract greater public support. It sounds shocking, but sometimes people need to be shocked to be made aware of how appalling both child abuse and drug abuse can be.'

David Liddington, Conservative Home Office Affairs Spokesperson

Even academics were turned to for comment:

'The statement that Barnardo's is making is quite accurate. People are likely to pay attention to something they see rather than something they hear. I think Barnardo's motives have been pure and it is based on research which is available.'

Professor Portwood, leading drugs psychologist quoted in the *Daily Mail*, April 2000

In response BBH ran the Bonny Baby execution to further fuel the debate (see Figure 47).

---

18. Only the *Daily Telegraph* adhered to the ban.
19. Source: Quadrangle Tracking Study March 2000. Base: 403.

Figure 47: *Bonny Baby*

In response to the public outcry CAP withdrew their 'ban' and made a public apology:

> 'We made a misjudgement in our view of how the ASA would consider your ad and for this I can only apologise.'

Andrew Brown, CAP Chairman

The value of the PR surrounding the Heroin Baby execution is alone worth £630,000.[20] The nature of this coverage is far from simply a mention in editorial and in many cases is equivalent to free advertising space (see Figure 48). Advertising did not only 'wake' the public to the shocking nature of childhood disadvantage in this country, it also created brand reappraisal among the journalists themselves.

> 'The turnaround of Barnardo's from old news to headline news is remarkable. From an institution that we would never have turned to for comment Barnardo's has become a continued source of breaking stories.'

Katie Weitz, Features Editor, *The Sunday People*

This in turn has led to more articles being written about the charity, aiding its ability to inform the public of its work. The number of articles about Barnardo's has risen 40% on the 12 months prior to the advertising. Barnardo's was also being written about in greater depth: the average number of column inches in articles where Barnardo's appeared increased from five to seven. Together these two factors amount to an extra half-mile of editorial coverage per year (see Figure 49).

---

20. Source: Aylings and Associates.

Figure 48: *PR*

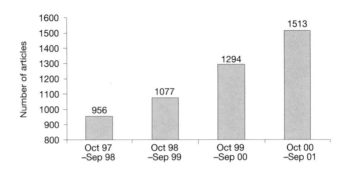

Figure 49: *Number of national newspaper articles referencing Barnardo's*
Source: MMS

Lobbying and influencing

The powerful advertising had created a high awareness and impact among MPs (see Figure 50):

'Barnardo's advertisements are very powerful. They communicate the effects of disadvantage on children and make policy makers think about what we need to do to help overcome this.'

The Right Honorable Julie Morgan, MP, Labour Member for Cardiff North

'The advertisements made clear to me what Barnardo's work is today: showing a credible, modern organisation and a powerful voice for children.'

The Right Honorable Lembit Öpik, MP, Liberal Democrat Member for Montgomeryshire

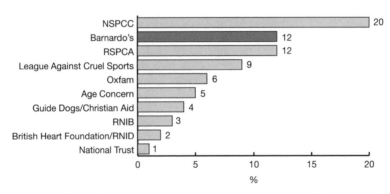

Figure 50: *'Do you recall any media coverage or advertising carried out by charities in the last six months?'*
Base: 113 MPs
Source: Charity Parliamentary Monitor, NFP Synergy/Future Foundation (July 01)

An important part of Barnardo's work is the lobbying of MPs on issues of policy affecting the welfare of children in the UK. The brand vision *Giving Children Back Their Future* has provided a simple definable cause, which has been incorporated into all policy recommendations and literature, targeted at MPs:

'The advertising is part of putting forward our case to politicians across the board. One could say that the advertising is part of our delivery of the argument; it has contributed and added to our ability to impress.'

Nigel Bennett, Director of Lobbying and Influence, Barnardo's

Barnardo's profile was further enhanced among MPs by the appointment of the Prime Minister's wife Cherie Booth as the charity's president in the autumn of 2001. Since her appointment she has become an outspoken supporter of the advertising:

'I have always been a strong supporter of Barnardo's work with children, and in recent years I have also come to support its powerful advertising campaigns. Its thought-provoking advertising alerts the public to the urgent issues affecting today's children and shows Barnardo's for what it is – a modern, forward-thinking organisation that no longer runs orphanages ... I am proud to be a member of such a modern organisation that not only helps thousands of UK children every year but also communicates relevant messages to the public through its advertising campaigns.'

Cherie Booth

Corporate relations

The brand relaunch has changed Barnardo's approach to potential corporate partners:

'The change in Barnardo's brand identity means we have to support the modernity of that image. We have woken up to the fact that if we wish to hit at that level [of corporate sponsorship] we need to follow through with our relationships; recognising that we are not just a good cause but also a beneficial business partner.'

Mark Smith, Head of Corporate Sponsorship, Barnardo's

Partnering with a modern Barnardo's is now seen as beneficial to how other brands are perceived by their own consumers, namely the 35–55-year-old age group. As a result Barnardo's has been partnered with bigger brands, committing more money than ever before.

'As the deservedness of Barnardo's increases so too do the benefits of our partnership. The impressive re-branding of Barnardo's has led us to review our work with the charity; which can be evidenced by an increase in financial commitment as well as plans to lift the profile of the relationship Barclays has with Barnardo's.'

Simon Gulliford, Marketing Director, Barclays

Argos named Barnardo's their charity of the year for 2002 and a 'major high street retailer' named Barnardo's their charity of the year for 2003.[21] The value of these partnerships alone is estimated to be worth between £3–5m for Barnardo's.

As well as being courted by big corporate partners, Barnardo's has received more income from small businesses than ever before, the total value of which since relaunch amounts to £2,029,000 (October 99 to February 02).[22]

Volunteering

In the past Barnardo's volunteers consisted mainly of older 'Dorothy Donor' types or BHGs (Barnardo's Helper Groups). BHGs raised money through the running of independent fund-raising events. Since the relaunch, Barnardo's has been able to

---

21. This retailer cannot be named at the time of going to press.
22. Barnardo's is beginning to set in motion the dual funding of services with corporate sponsors, pioneering the way in which charities might receive income from external partners in the future: "... this could happen in response to some organisations now wishing to associate their name with the Barnardo's brand. For instance we run catering schools to teach young care leavers a trade in Harrogate and Bristol. One can imagine Marriott or McDonalds wishing to lift their 'community profile' by joint funding these projects with us. It's that sort of idea, to get close to corporate partners that as a direction we are definitely considering for the future.' *Chris Hanvey, Barnardo's Director of Operations.*

recruit much younger volunteers in sectors of the community where it has had no record of recruiting fund-raisers before. These volunteers are not just donating their money but are actively engaged with Barnardo's, dedicating their time and effort to raising money on the charity's behalf. One such example is the student sector, where Barnardo's is now the principal charity operating:

> 'Barnardo's is cool. To raise money for them is more interesting than Oxfam or another *****
> "save the whale" campaign.'
>
> Dan Ferguson, Student President and Rag Week Organiser, Norwich University

> 'We could never have broken into the student market without being seen as modern and relevant today. Before the advertising we were seen as old and about orphanages. We're certain that the campaign has helped us to recruit more young people generally and it has certainly helped us in fund-raising where we are getting two or three thousand pounds a day rather than just a thousand.'
>
> David Booker, Head of Corporate Volunteering, Barnardo's

We cannot place a definite figure on the money raised every year by the student body of volunteers, but it is estimated to be around £50k. Active volunteers within the student market have benefits beyond monies raised: as higher earners in later life they represent a valuable source of future income as well as holding the potential to become society's future influencers – leaders of industry, journalists, politicians, etc.[23]

Local authorities

The advertising has been warmly received by the social workers in the projects themselves.

> 'The women who use our services felt the re-branding really got the message across that Barnardo's work has changed over the years and that now we work with very complex and difficult family problems.'
>
> Project Leader, Domestic Violence[24]

> 'The adverts are making people think about what is happening to children and young people which puts them at tremendous risk and makes them old before their time. Girls and young women involved in prostitution have to access us to just be kids again – and hopefully then they have a chance of a better adult future.'
>
> Project Leader, Barnardo's project for girls and young women abused through prostitution

It is the social workers that negotiate with the local authorities for state funding. Anecdotal evidence suggests that the total communications effect has helped enhance these relationships.

> 'The re-branding of Barnardo's has ensured that the organisation has raised its profile as a market leader amongst those national charities tackling social issues that for many others remain taboo. As a Local Authority it is important we have confidence in potential delivery agents in order to get the best service possible for those young people trying to survive in a hostile world. Barnardo's has enabled us to do that in Bradford.'
>
> Joyce Thacker, Head of Youth Service, Bradford Metropolitan District Council

---

23. There are no historical records of the number of volunteers by which to compare current recruits, but as evidence of their increasing number Barnardo's is now investing in a database to keep track of this growing resource.
24. Most social workers are unwilling to have their name and position revealed. This is due to the very real threat to them posed by individuals associated with the people that they work with.

DISCOUNTING OTHER FACTORS

Targeting change

Direct mail hadn't changed its targeting over the relaunch period:

- The recruitment mailers were to the same Dorothy Donor profile.
- The lists were purchased from the same company – Claritas.
- The warm mailers were sent to Barnardo's own donorbase.

Given it was communications' aim to recruit a different profile of donor through Face-to-face we can discount a targeting change for this activity.

Seasonal effects

It is true that there has been one more Christmas in the 29 months since Barnardo's relaunch. However, the increased number of committed donors has ironed out direct mail's seasonal income peaks (see Figure 51).

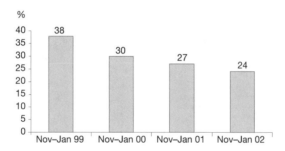

Figure 51: *Percentage of annual direct mail income from Nov–Jan quarter*
Source: Barnardo's

The Face-to-face recruits as a group are wholly-committed donors paying by monthly standing order. Thus with this group of donors there can be no seasonal fluctuations in income. In fact most cancellations of standing orders from Face-to-face recruits occur over the Christmas period as people tend to review their personal finances at the year's end.

Donation behaviour

It is true to say that there has been an increase in the number of donors in the UK since 1999. However the 1.3% increase in donor participation is considerably less than the 10.5% increase in Barnardo's active donorbase over this period. The increase in participation rates is equal to an additional 606,905 people donating. Considering Face-to-face recruited 110,995 in total, Barnardo's is responsible for nearly 1 in 5 of these new UK donors.[25]

---

25. There are 46,685,000 adults in the UK (over the age of 18). 1.3% of 46,685,000 = 606,905/110,995 = 5.46.

One also notes that there is a marked decline in the number of 35–55-year-olds donating to charity from 1999 to 2001. Yet it was this age group that represented the majority of Face-to-face recruits (58%) even though there were 250,000 fewer donating to charity (see Figure 52).[26]

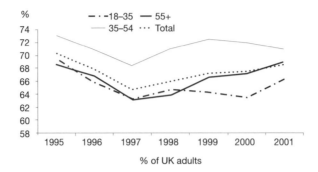

Figure 52: *Percentage donating to charity by age and year*
Base: 3912
Source: Family Expenditure Survey 2001

There was an 8.8% increase in the average value of UK donations to charities between 1999 and 2001. The 86% rise in total direct marketing income far exceeds this national increase (see Figure 53).

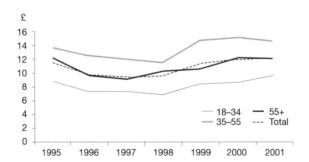

Figure 53: *UK adult monthly donations expenditure by age and year*
Base: 3912
Source: Family Expenditure Survey 2001

The charity market

It is difficult to determine the level of fundraising activity that took place over Barnardo's post relaunch period. What is significant is the NSPCC's activity over this timeframe. During 1999 the NSPCC began its 'big spending' Full Stop Campaign that continued to significantly outspend Barnardo's advertising activity

---

26. There are 16,121,000 35–55-year-olds in the UK. Source: Office of National Statistics. There was a 1.6% drop in the number of 35–55-year-olds donating to charity between 1999 and 2001. 1.6% of 16,121,000 = 257,936.

over the duration of the relaunch. Barnardo's success isn't simply a function of increased share of voice (see Figure 54).

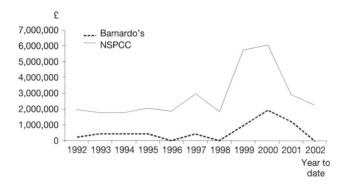

Figure 54: *Media spend: Barnardo's and the NSPCC*
Source: MMS

PAYBACK: COMMUNICATIONS' CONTRIBUTION

The advertising had driven the brand relaunch which set in motion an entirely new future for Barnardo's. Thus far *Giving Children Back Their Future* has been lived out across a range of departments and impacted upon their work. It is therefore very difficult to place an absolute figure on the 'income generated' as a result of the integrated communications activity.

To be ultra-conservative in our payback calculations we will use only the income generated by the Face-to-face recruits. Face-to-face donors have already contributed over £4m to Barnardo's since October 1999. Over time people do drop out of this committed donorbase. The fewer people in the donorbase, the less money is received. It is the number of people one expects to have at any future point that determines future income. By looking at cancellation behaviour over time we can calculate how many people we expect to retain and thus the future value of these recruits.[27]

To further build its relationship with the Face-to-face donors, Barnardo's has put into place an additional direct mail and telemarketing programme. This aims to:

- Keep people donating for as long as possible.
- Recommit those who fall out of the brand.
- Increase the value of individual donations.

We will discount all of these activities to calculate the payback, using only the natural fall-out rate of donors and the amount pledged at the time of their recruitment (see Figure 55). The 'life-time' value of these people over four years including the income Barnardo's has already received is £15,681,961.

---

27. The way Barnardo's calculates life-time value is based on the monthly attrition rates out of the donorbase. This is calculated by using the 29 months of data collected since the recruitment began.

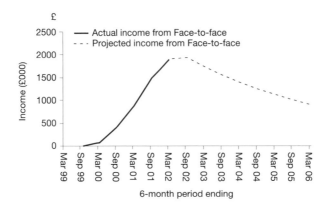

Figure 55: *Face-to-face biannual income, actual and projected*
Source: Barnardo's

In April 2000 the government launched a new initiative called Gift Aid. Gift Aid is a tax-aided relief on all charitable donations where the government gives an additional 28p in the pound. All the figures represented thus far have excluded Gift Aid. If we were to include the 71% of Face-to-face recruits opting for Gift Aid, the four-year 'life-time' value would amount to £18,979,535. It is this figure we will use in calculating the communications payback.

Barnardo's total expenditure since October 1999 on the advertising (including agency and production fees) and the cost of the Face-to-face activity = £8,766,779.[28] This means the return on the advertising and Face-to-face investment is £10,212,756. Or this can be expressed as a return of £2.16 on every £1 invested.

CONCLUSION

This paper has demonstrated how an integrated communications campaign has turned around Barnardo's fortunes. For Barnardo's the relaunch has been a resounding success, and some of the measures of that success have been outlined in this paper, namely:

- Greater public support.
- Recruitment of younger donors.
- A complete change in Barnardo's donor profile.
- Recruitment of more valuable donor relationships.
- Increase in income from direct mail.
- Recruitment of younger volunteers.
- Rise in corporate sponsorship.
- Enhanced relationships with local authorities.
- Improved perceptions among journalists.
- Enhancement of lobbying power among MPs.

---

28. The total cost of Face-to-face and the advertising is not broken down in respect of client confidentiality.

Traditional businesses express their profits in pounds and pence, thus any return on a communication's investment is expressed using a financial measure. Barnardo's doesn't count its profits in pounds and pence: its profits are counted in children and their futures. We will express Barnardo's return on investment by calculating the future benefits to children and society for its continued work.

We will base our calculation of 'Barnardo's Profits' using the *Counting The Costs of Child Poverty*[29] document as inspired by the advertising and presented to MPs. We will use the examples of Duane and Dean, the highest and lowest ratio of investment to societal saves (see Tables 1 and 2).

TABLE 1

Costs to date	Dean	If only...
	Age 0–5 Lack of 'normal' childhood experiences and attention from mother	Health visitor £924; parental support/ education £383; drop-in attendance at a family centre £11,475
Continuing exclusion in a pupil referral unit £13,000	**Age 9** Irregular access to education	Educational support from age 9: £6000
Barnardo's Community Family Centre group drama work £766; theft and other offences £19,500	**Age 13** Introduced to family centre; lack of stable adolescence; offending begins	
Failure to invest has cost £33,266		**Total for all suggested investments** £18,782
Early investment would have cost		£12,782

TABLE 2

Costs to date	Duane	If only ...
Social services £632.30; Barnardo's Family Centre assessment £10,000	**Age 0–5** Health costs to Hannah and her children; loss of normal childhood experience	Support for Hannah while pregnant £1,000; parental support/education £383; drop-in attendance at a family centre £11,475
Local authority care £424,944	**Age 8** Taken into care of social services	
Arson to cars and shops £56,706; arrest, sentencing and incarceration £29,000; intensive treatment programme, Barnardo's Project £1621	**Age 14** Loss of education; offending begins	
Failure to invest has cost £522,903		**Total for all suggested investments** £12,858
Early investment would have cost		£12,858

29. A document presented to MPs demonstrating that investment in disadvantaged children today would save society money in the future.

Barnardo's spends 72p in the pound on the child, 28p going towards administrative costs. Thus we will use 72% of the advertising and Face-to-face payback: 72% of £10,212,756 = £7,353,184.

Using the total suggested investment:

- We could help 391 Deans, saving society a future cost of £13 million.
- We could help 572 Duanes, saving society a future cost of £299 million.

In 2001, Barnardo's changed the future of over 100,000 children, young people and their families. Integrated communications has ensured that Barnardo's, the oldest children's charity, will help many more children well into the future.

2

Halifax

Taking on the high street banks by communicating like a high street retailer

Principal author: Richard Warren, Delaney Lund Knox Warren

EDITOR'S SUMMARY

This case describes how an integrated communications idea – 'Staff as Stars' – transformed Halifax from a 'former building society' to an aggressive competitor to the big four clearing banks in the space of just 12 months. Taking its inspiration from retailers, not from banks, this case shows how the idea galvanised a 35,000-person organisation, and cut through the most crowded sector in advertising, to produce a 150% increase in sales and 43% increase in profit per current account customer.

'A star is born – you can bank on it.
Howard Brown, the Halifax bank worker who appears in their new TV campaign, is brilliant.
He'd be a hit in a programme, never mind in the adverts.
And, unlike a lot of singers on the telly, he wouldn't need a little Xtra help.'

The Sun, 6 January 2001

INTRODUCTION

This case will demonstrate the value of taking communications learning and techniques from one sector, retailing, and applying them to another sector, banking. It will illustrate the power of an integrated communications idea to provide a galvanising and cohesive focus for a 35,000-person organisation.

It will show how this idea cut through the most crowded sector in advertising to produce a 150% increase in sales and a 43% increase in profit per current account customer. It will demonstrate that this idea created a momentum that did not just preserve Halifax's independence, but provided the platform for a powerful merger with Bank of Scotland. Finally, it will show that all this was achieved in a remarkably short period of time – just 12 months. Unlike previous 'effectiveness' cases, Halifax did not have the luxury of assessing communications effect over a period of years. As is increasingly the case in a shareholder environment, commercial effects had to be instant. Halifax's communications idea had to work from day one. It did.

FROM NO. 1 BUILDING SOCIETY TO NO. 6 BANK

Until 1997 Halifax had been Britain's biggest building society, and market leader in the traditional building society areas of mortgages and savings.

Following demutualisation in 1997, Halifax plc became Britain's sixth biggest bank, rated and analysed as a 'bank' by shareholders, the city and journalists; and competing with other banks – HSBC, RBS (including NatWest), Lloyds TSB, Barclays and Abbey National – in consumer banking, particularly current accounts.[1]

Little progress in consumer banking

For its first three years as a bank (1997–2000), Halifax, while holding share in its core areas of mortgages and savings, failed to make any headway in consumer banking. In fact, in current accounts Halifax went backwards (see Figure 1).

The share price languished below the banking sector (see Figure 2).

This lack of progress led to considerable pressure to merge with one of the bigger banks.

'The likelihood of more bids and mergers in the banking sector sent several leading financial services companies higher on Thursday. Halifax, the largest mortgage lender in the UK, was most prominent.'

Financial Times, 22 August 2000

---

1. Consumer banking consists of current account, credit cards and personal loans. Of these current account is by far the largest product area.

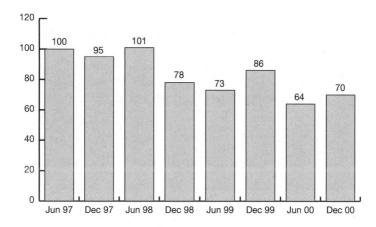

Figure 1: *Halifax share of all new current accounts (indexed data),*[2] *1997–2000*
Source: NOP Financial Research Survey (FRS), Dec 2000

Figure 2: *Halifax and banks sector rebased: June 1997 to December 2000*
Source: Halifax

The launch of the 'Extraordinary Growth' strategy in 2000

Lord Stevenson and James Crosby, the new Chairman and Chief Executive respectively (both appointed in 1999) refused to accept that a take-over was the only way forward. As Lord Stevenson wrote in the Chairman's Statement in the 1999 Annual Report, published in 2000: 'We believe that consolidation is guilty until proven innocent.'

2. All market data are provided by NOP Financial Research Survey (FRS). Due to the fact that this is a syndicated study shared by all the main financial institutions it is not possible to reveal actual market shares of either Halifax or the competition. We have therefore indexed these figures.

And as James Crosby wrote in the Chief Executive's Statement: '...it's the future that matters and that's about nothing less than achieving a transformation in this business and its prospects.'

The 'Extraordinary Growth' strategy was born – a commitment to steal market share aggressively from the big four clearing banks.[3] It was a courageous strategy, and one that *had* to work immediately to avoid a takeover.[4]

The importance of the current account to the 'Extraordinary Growth' strategy

The focus of the strategy had to be the current account. This was for three reasons:

1. It has the highest penetration of any of the banking products. (Of all current account customers, 55% have a credit card and only 18% have a personal loan – the other banking products. Source: NOP/FRS, Feb 02.)
2. It is the 'anchor' banking product. (Salary, direct debits and standing orders are all mandated to the current account making it the most used product.)
3. It acts as a gateway to the other products. (Sixty-eight per cent of current account customers of the main four banks who have a credit card and 35% of customers who have a personal loan have it with the same institution as they have their current account. Source: NOP/FRS, Feb 02.)

Quite simply, 'Extraordinary Growth' in banking had to come from 'Extraordinary Growth' in current accounts.

An aggressive target was set for 2001: to double Halifax's current account sales (see Table 1).

TABLE 1: CURRENT ACCOUNT TARGET 2001 VS. AVERAGE

Average annual acquisition 1997–2000	Target 2001
200,000	400,000

Source: Halifax

Current account recruitment – the difficulty of the task for Halifax

Current account recruitment breaks down into three equal segments (source: NOP/FRS):

1. 'First' accounts (starting at university/first job, etc.); these accounts involve various incentives/inducements that reduce profitability.
2. 'Additional' accounts that are run alongside an existing account; these accounts rarely have the salary/direct debits mandated and therefore are unprofitable.
3. 'Switchers' where the main current account is transferred from one bank to another.

---

3. Whilst Abbey National was at the time the fifth biggest bank, it was suffering from many of the same problems as Halifax. The two were often bracketed together as the 'mortgage banks'. Halifax's business strategy was only viable if it started competing with the biggest banks – Abbey National could not be the competition.
4. In the summer of 2001, the Competition Commission ruled against the hostile bid by Lloyds TSB for Abbey National on the grounds of anti-competitive market share in key banking sectors. This was a defining ruling but it did not come until nearly a year after Halifax had launched the 'Extraordinary Growth' strategy. Halifax's aggressive quest for organic growth was launched in a climate of pressure on the banking sector to consolidate. Halifax had no knowledge that it might be subject to the same regulatory protection subsequently afforded Abbey National.

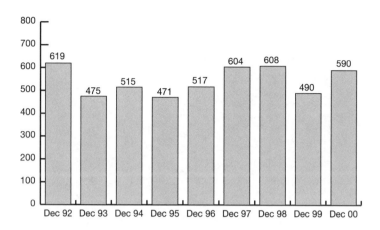

Figure 3: *Size of current account switching market (000s) – 1992–2000*
Source: NOP/FRS, December 2000

'Switchers' were not only the most profitable, but also most directly met the business strategy of stealing share from the clearing banks.

As Figure 3 shows, the current account 'switching' market had, however, remained small and flat for at least eight years (the earliest point for which we have data). Consumers believed 'all banks are the same' and were deterred from moving because of the hassle of switching over standing orders and direct debits.

Worse, Halifax's share of the 'switching' market had declined markedly since demutualisation (see Figure 4).

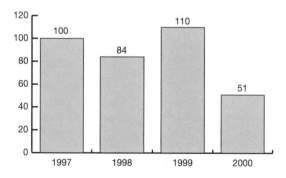

Figure 4: *Halifax share of the current account switching market (indexed data) – 1997–2000*
Source: NOP/FRS, December 2000

The strategy of focusing solely on 'switchers' meant that the doubling of sales (an additional 200,000 accounts) was going to have to come either from taking 40% of the existing switching market, or by growing the market by a third.

This task had never been attempted by any of the main clearing banks. For Halifax it would be even more difficult. As Figure 5 shows, Halifax was the last bank on people's current account consideration list.

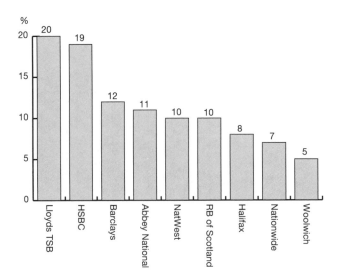

Figure 5: *Current account shortlisting – December 2000*
Source: Hall & Partners' tracking study

For Halifax to achieve its business strategy, the least likely brand was going to have to jump-start a market that had been static for over eight years.

The new Halifax current account

With so much inertia in the current account market, Halifax realised that it could not just do something incremental. It had to behave like a new entrant and give people a radical reason to switch. The new Halifax current account was developed paying significantly more interest than the high street clearing banks (see Table 2).

TABLE 2: INTEREST PAID ON CREDIT BALANCES (%)	
Halifax	4.0
Barclays	0.1
HSBC	0.1
Lloyds TSB	0.1
NatWest	0.1

It would be launched in January 2001.

Supporting products

Halifax also decided to focus on credit cards, the next most important banking product, and mortgages, its key area of business strength. The business propositions for each were as follows:

Credit cards

For credit cards 3.9% APR for the first five months on balance transfers and purchases; 17.9% APR standard rate.

Mortgages

Mortgage review: Every year Halifax will invite you into a branch to make sure your mortgage suits your circumstances.

The business strategy was in place. What was now needed was a new marketing strategy.

Following an agency pitch, Delaney Lund Knox Warren (DLKW) was appointed in September 2000.

THE NEED FOR A COMPLETELY DIFFERENT KIND OF MARKETING STRATEGY

There were two options to achieve 'Extraordinary Growth': market these products like a bank or market them in a completely different way. Bank marketing was not geared to getting rapid share growth; it was designed to consolidate inertia. It had not worked for Halifax so far. Something different had to be done.

One of the trends we had observed in the mortgage market was the huge rise in remortgaging – consumers being prepared to switch products to save money (see Figure 6).

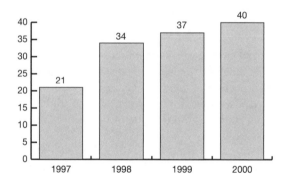

Figure 6: % of all mortgages that are remortgages
Base: All remortgagers with same and remortgagers with different
Source: NOP/FRS, June 2000

It was happening in credit cards too. As Tables 3 and 4 show, in both these markets consumers were 'shopping around' on the basis of 'price'. Loyalty to a 'provider' was far less important.

TABLE 3: TOP FIVE REASONS FOR SELECTING
AN ADDITIONAL BRAND OF CREDIT CARD

	%
Low introductory rate	44
Low standard rate	19
No annual fee	18
Existing relationship	9
Cashback scheme	8

Base: All new additional brand credit card holders
Source: NOP/FRS, December 2000

TABLE 4: TOP FIVE REASONS FOR SELECTING A MORTGAGE

	%
Interest rate on the mortgage	29
Recommended to me	26
Hold other products there	17
Discounts on the interest rate	10
They would lend the amount required	11

Base: All new mortgages
Source: NOP/FRS, June 2000

The credit card and mortgage markets were becoming 'retail markets'. With a current account that paid 40 times better interest, surely we could turn the current account market into a retail market too, and encourage the kind of switching we would need to achieve our business targets.

With this objective in mind, we decided to position Halifax, not as a bank, but as 'Britain's leading modern financial services retailer'. This meant it had to communicate like a retailer.

Communicating like a retailer, not like a bank

There are two components to communicating like a retailer. (In considering the merits of communication in the retail sector, we focused particularly on Tesco, Asda and Sainsbury's):

1. A determination to focus on 'substance' in all communications. Banks traditionally divide their advertising between a brand message on TV and a product message in press. Retailers, however, focus on 'substance' in all of their communications (deals, price comparisons, new products or services). In all of its communications Halifax would focus on the most motivating 'substance' in financial services – 'value'.
2. A realisation that a strong communications idea is often the fastest way to motivate staff. Given that 80% of Halifax sales come from the branch network and 55% of staff, known within Halifax as 'colleagues', are customer facing, highly motivated colleagues were a prerequisite of business success. Our communications idea could be critical in achieving this.

The new Halifax brand proposition

One part of the new Halifax brand proposition was clear – a focus on 'value'. But this on its own was not enough – it would be too easy for competitors to emulate. We also needed to define a brand equity that would be motivating to consumers and colleagues alike, and differentiated from the competition.

We undertook qualitative research among colleagues and consumers. What emerged from colleagues was great pride in the building society heritage, and consistently across all the interviews, a pride in being 'people not bankers'.

'It's important to be the same person at work as you are outside it.'

'The more yourself you are the better the job you do for your customers.'

DLKW Qualitative – Halifax colleagues

This 'human' approach was consistent too with consumers' existing perception of Halifax.

'Halifax people are people like us.'

DLKW Qualitative

And it was reinforced by Halifax's historical advertising equity – the well-recalled and liked 'House' campaign (which ran from 1991–1997) and the X made of people.

This led us to believe that focusing on Halifax as a 'human' organisation was a powerful platform. It was true and motivating to consumers and colleagues alike.

Halifax's brand proposition became simply a combination of *'value'* and *'human'* (Figure 7). Or as we branded it: *Extra value. Extra friendly.*

Not only was this proposition motivating but it was also differentiated from the more corporate, image-based competition.

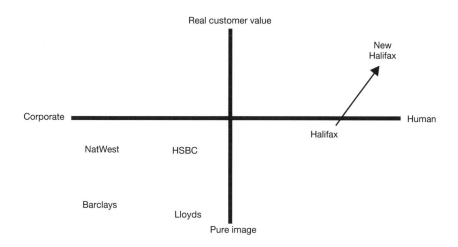

Figure 7: *Brand mapping – Halifax vs. competition*

A further communications opportunity that Halifax could exploit

We recognised that there was a further march we could steal on the clearing banks. All of the banks, including Halifax, were suffering from two basic communications problems: firstly their campaigns were failing to cut through, despite high spend (Figure 8), and secondly they were poorly branded (Figure 9).

In 2000 Barclays was running its 'Big' campaign; Lloyds TSB was running its 'How can we help you live you life' campaign; HSBC was running its 'Animals' campaign and NatWest had just ended its animation campaign. During 2000 NatWest spent £24m on TV, Barclays £13.2m, Lloyds TSB £11.6m, Halifax £8.9m and HSBC £7.4m.

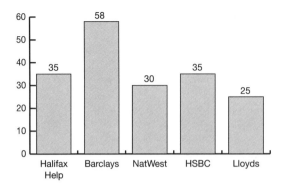

Figure 8: *Highest % prompted recognition of advertising stills during 2000*
Source: Taylor Nelson Sofres

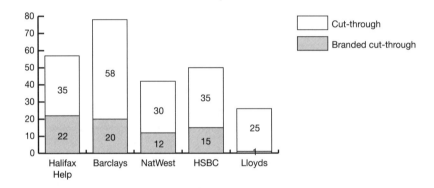

Figure 9: *Highest % branding during 2000*
Source: Taylor Nelson Sofres

Conventional wisdom was that these figures were to be expected, that banking is a low-interest category with high levels of competitive clutter where you cannot expect the levels of cut-through and branding that you can with high-interest areas such as packaged goods and retail. (According to MMS, £807m was spent in the financial services category in 1999, making it Britain's biggest spending category.)

Communicating like a retailer would, we believed, enable Halifax to get much higher levels of cut-through and branding – levels that would be essential to achieving 'Extraordinary Growth'.

The brief for communications

The brief for communications was as follows:

Target
- All adult customers of the clearing banks.
- Halifax colleagues.

Brand proposition
'Extra Value. Extra Friendly'.

Support
Extra value products – primary: current account; secondary: credit cards and mortgages.

Requirement
- Advertising that is branded and cuts through immediately.
- Advertising that merges brand and product.

THE COMMUNICATIONS IDEA

We knew from the outset that it would take more than an advertising idea to transform a 35,000-person organisation. We needed a communications idea that had the potential to permeate and inform everything Halifax did, both internally and externally.

In order to get branded cut-through we had to avoid the reverence and restraint of most bank advertising. We wanted communications that were populist and competitive in equal measure. Communications that would get talked about.

The creative solution was to use real Halifax staff. The big difference was that they would be singing in their own pop video. The communications idea, which we called 'Staff as Stars', precisely reflected the importance that the 35,000 colleagues had in achieving the business strategy.

We also introduced a new end-line, 'Always giving you extra' to reflect the Halifax's commitment to offering value.

Launching the communications idea – internally

To maximise the effect of the communications idea internally, it had to start working from the moment it was launched.

The campaign was launched internally on 18 October by Jonathan Ross appearing on Halifax TV (a weekly internet broadcast to all 35,000 employees; see Figure 10). It was a request for colleagues to come forward and star.

A total of 1169 people applied and were auditioned in eight regional castings, and 20 appeared in a national final in London.

Figure 10: *Jonathan Ross launches 'Search for a Star' on Halifax TV*

Launching the communications idea – externally

TV

The first ad, 'Howard', starring Howard Brown from the Sheldon branch and promoting the current account, broke on Boxing Day 2000 (see Figure 11).

To the tune of Tom Jones' 'Sex Bomb'. Maybe I'm a banker who's completely obsessed, got a little something that's bound to impress, this current account pays a higher amount of extraordinary interest.

Now you probably think it's all too tough to change, those debits and credits to be rearranged, just give me the signal and without any fuss, you can leave the whole thing to us.

Extra extra I know you want more, I'll give you something extra when you walk through my door.

Extra extra, though I cannot deny, terms and conditions apply.
VO: It's easy to change to the account paying the most extraordinary rate on the high street.
Halifax. Always giving you extra.

Figure 11: *'Howard' – Current Account 60-second*

Twenty-second cut-downs of the ad were used later in the year to promote other rational benefits (online banking and the switching service).

'Yvonne', starring Yvonne McBride from the Belfast branch, promoting the credit card, broke on 20th February (see Figure 12).

To the tune of Ricky Martin's 'Livin' La Vida Loca'. They think I'm slightly crazy but I'm just a banking babe. You're starvin' for a bargain, this card's gonna help you pay.

It might look simple plastic but it's worth its weight in gold, and don't it feel fantastic when there's more of this to hold, so if I may be so bold.

We've just caused a splash, we're living to give you extra, this card's extra flash, Livin' to give you extra. We've gone oh so low, you're gonna really rate us, it's the way to go, subject to age and status.

VO: The new Halifax Credit Card has a great rate. Apply now and for the first five months you'll get an extra low 3.9% APR.

Figure 12: 'Yvonne' – Credit Card 60-minute

And 'Matt', starring Matt Thornfield, from Halifax, Trinity Road, promoting mortgages, broke on 8th April (see Figure 13).

To the tune of the BaHa Men 'Who Let The Dogs Out'. You know I'm the man who understands mortgage, (yippee-aye-ay) so if you're about to check out a loan (maybe today), you might have a flat, a house or a cottage (it's gonna pay).

The question to ask when you finance your home...is...Who gives you extra? (Who? Who? Who?). So once every year I will send you a letter...(mortgage review).

Your life may have changed and we're eager to see... (what's happened to you), there may be a rate that could be much better (it's possibly new), I'll change it for you, just leave it to me...so.

Who gives you extra... (Who? Who? Who?) Who gives you extra? (Who? Who? Who?).
VO: A Halifax mortgage starts good value and, with our mortgage review, it stays good value.

Figure 13: 'Matt' – mortgages 60-second

National press

We used national press just as a retailer would, aggressively comparing our prices to those of the other banks (see Figure 14).

Figure 14: *Current account press advertising*

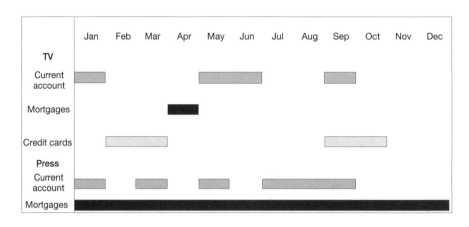

Figure 15: *TV and press plan – 2001*
Source: BBJ

Media plan

The media plan in Figure 15 above shows the TV and press laydown for the year. National press was used as a retail medium for mortgages and current accounts.

Other communications

The communications idea was also used in-store, in direct marketing and online. And even tactically (Figure 16).

So what happened?

Figure 16: *Current account tactical ad – Budget 2000*

Results

In evaluating the effectiveness of the Halifax communications idea we will seek to establish that:

- The advertising worked harder than any other bank advertising ever.[5]
- The communications idea motivated colleagues.
- The communications idea led directly to a significant uplift in sales and profitability.

THE ADVERTISING WORKED HARDER THAN ANY OTHER BANK ADVERTISING EVER

It cut through immediately and was well branded. It stood out and was liked. It communicated clearly. It changed the target's mind about the Halifax brand. But most importantly, by doing all of the above, it changed behaviour.

It cut through immediately

The Howard commercial achieved massive cut-through instantly. All three commercials enjoyed far higher recognition than any of the big four banks and by October 86% of the sample recognised the advertising (see Figure 17).[6]

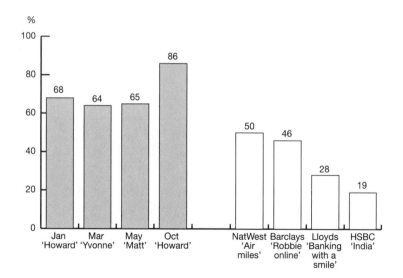

Figure 17: *Cut-through: 2001 vs. highest figures for other banks*
Base: All respondents (a representative sample of customers of the high street banks and Halifax)
Source: Hall & Partners[7]

5. In addition to the TV activity, and current account press Halifax did continue to run press for mortgages, savings, personal loans and insurance. Because these programmes are constant year-on-year, and designed to elicit direct response, we have not considered them here. It was TV that drove the changes in brand and sales.
6. Levels of cut-through in 2002 have now reached over 90%.
7. In December 2000 Halifax changed their tracking study from Taylor Nelson Sofres to Hall & Partners.

In order to eliminate the effect of media spend we have taken the best figures achieved by the competitors during 2001. During 2001 Halifax spent £14.1m, NatWest £13.7m, Lloyds TSB £11.0m, Barclays £1.9m (behind a campaign on which they had spent £13.1m in 2000) on TV and HSBC £2.4m on cinema (source: MMS).

These high levels of cut-through were corroborated by *Marketing* magazine's Adwatch survey[8] where Howard went straight in at number one with 71% recall – the first time a bank had ever gone straight in at number one.[9]

It was well branded

The cut-through was branded cut-through. Howard achieved 69% correct branding in its first burst, and 76% in October. Yvonne and Matt achieved 75% and 83% respectively.[10] All of these levels were far higher than the best level achieved all year by the clearing banks (see Figure 18).

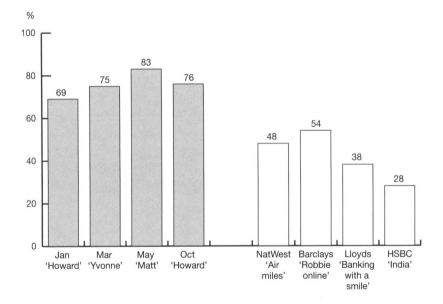

Figure 18: *Branding: 2001 vs. highest figures for other banks*
Base: All respondents
Source: Hall & Partners

It stood out and appealed more than any other bank campaign

The campaign stood out far more than any other bank campaign, *immediately* (see Figure 19).

And it was more liked (see Figure 20).

---

8. Adwatch data are collected every week in the form of a weekly NOP telephone omnibus survey of more than 500 adults. The results are published each week in *Marketing*.
9. Both Yvonne and Matt also went straight in at number one, and this year Howard 'Angel', the new current account commercial launched in January 2002, also went sttraight in at number one and remained there for four weeks running.
10. The branding levels in 2002 are now over 90%.

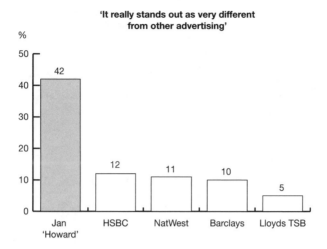

Figure 19: *Advertising stand-out vs. other banks*
Base: All ad recognisers
Source: Hall & Partners

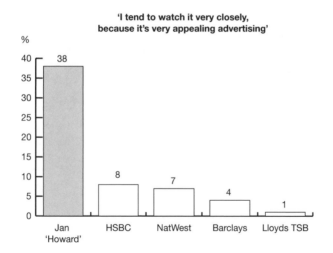

Figure 20: *Advertising appeal vs. other banks*
Base: All ad recognisers
Source: Hall & Partners

It stood out and appealed as much as the best fmcg campaigns

The campaign's stand-out and appeal were matched only by universally popular fmcg campaigns, confirming our belief that being a bank was no impediment to producing populist, well-loved advertising (see Figures 21 and 22).

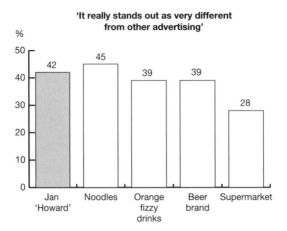

Figure 21: *Advertising stand-out vs. other fmcg brands*[11]
Base: All ad recognisers
Source: Hall & Partners

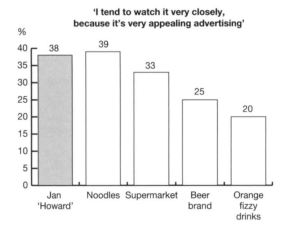

Figure 22: *Advertising appeal vs. other fmcg brands*[11]
Base: All ad recognisers
Source: Hall & Partners

It differentiated Halifax from the clearing banks

The advertising led to immediate changes in the perception of the Halifax brand.

We have looked at non-customers here. Not only were they our primary external target audience, but they provide a purer read on the effect of advertising since advertising is their primary source of brand perception.

By comparing non-customers of each of the banks we can see from Figures 23, 24 and 25 that in terms of the three key brand measures (being ahead of the others in providing the sort of things people want, valuing customers and service reputation), the 'Staff as Stars' campaign achieved an immediate and significant

11. These are the highest scores achieved by any fmcg brand tracked by Hall & Partners.

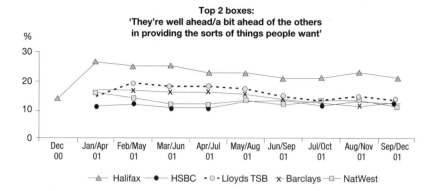

Figure 23: *Non-customer perceptions of banks*
Base: Non-customers of each bank
Source: Hall & Partners

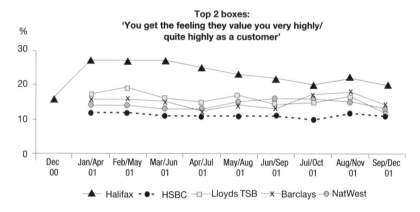

Figure 24: *Non-customer perceptions of banks*
Base: Non-customers of each bank
Source: Hall & Partners

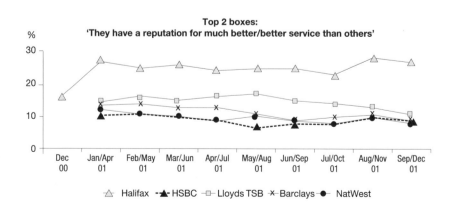

Figure 25: *Non-customer perceptions of banks*
Base: Non-customers of each bank
Source: Hall & Partners

uplift from December 2000 (pre)[12] to January 2001 (post). This differentiation from the clearing banks was sustained throughout the year.

It communicated clearly

As Figures 26, 27 and 28 show, each of the commercials was successful in communicating both a brand and a product message.

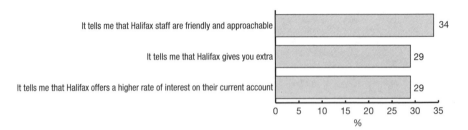

Figure 26: *Prompted communication of 'Howard'*
Base: All ad recognisers
Source: Hall & Partners

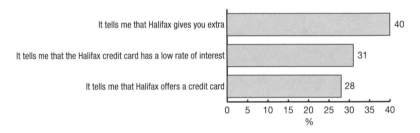

Figure 27: *Prompted communication of 'Yvonne'*
Base: All ad recognisers
Source: Hall & Partners

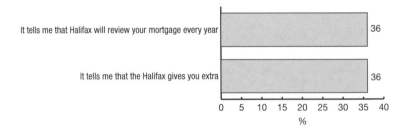

Figure 28: *Prompted communication of 'Matt'*
Base: All ad recognisers
Source: Hall & Partners

12. For the pre-stage only brand perceptions of Halifax were tracked as a benchmark.

Most importantly, it prompted people to shortlist the products

a) Current account

Halifax immediately jumped from seventh position to first position on the shortlisting chart the moment 'Howard' broke. It remained the most shortlisted current account throughout 2001 (Figure 29).

Dec	Jan	Feb	May	June	Sept	Oct	Dec
7th	1st	1st	1st	2nd	1st	1st	1st

Howard

Figure 29: *Shortlisting of current account*[13]
Base: All respondents
Source: Hall & Partners

b) Credit cards

'Yvonne' led to a growth in shortlisting throughout the year (Figure 30).

Dec	Mar	April	July	Oct	Nov
7th	5th	5th	5th	5th	4th

Yvonne

Figure 30: *Shortlisting of credit cards*[13]
Base: All respondents
Source: Hall & Partners

c) Mortgages

'Matt' extended Halifax's gap as most shortlisted brand (Figure 31).

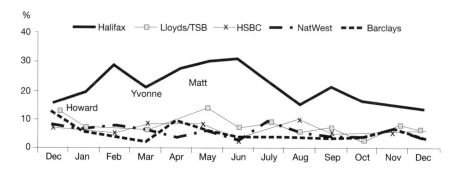

Figure 31: *Shortlisting of mortgages*[13]
Base: All respondents
Source: Hall & Partners

---

13. While mortgages are tracked every month, the other products are rotated to correspond to the timing of the TV advertising.

The advertising had done everything we had asked of it, and more. We will now look at how it was received internally.

THE COMMUNICATIONS IDEA MOTIVATED COLLEAGUES

First we will demonstrate that the advertising was very positively received by colleagues, and second, that the communications idea was so powerful and flexible internally, that it was adopted and embraced in all internal communications.

Hugely popular among colleagues

Extensive qualitative research was undertaken before the campaign was launched. The response was positive.

'It shows Halifax doesn't take itself too seriously.'

'It will be really good for Halifax but there's no way I'm doing it!'

Carne Martin Qualitative Research – September 2000

We have subsequently undertaken internal quantitative research which demonstrates that the colleagues believe that the campaign is having a very positive effect (Table 5).

TABLE 5: INTERNAL EMAIL SURVEY

	% agree	% neither agree nor disagree	% disagree
The campaign represents colleagues in a positive way	76	10	14
The campaign has given Halifax real momentum	84	6	10
The campaign has made Halifax a real competitor to the other high street banks	78	18	4

Base: 150 branch colleagues

The final measure of the popularity of the campaign among colleagues was that the number applying to star in the campaign went up from 1169 in 2001 to 1851 in 2002.

The communications idea has been widely adopted and embraced internally

One of most compelling demonstrations of the appeal of the communications idea is the breadth of uses to which it has been put internally. This is an idea that has been used organically by the organisation in a multitude of ways.

As Halifax role models, the stars are the perfect vehicle for recruitment advertising (see Figure 32).

Figure 32: *Halifax recruitment advertising*

Public appearances in the network

Product literature

Figure 33: *Use of stars in the network and for product literature*

The stars feature throughout the year in the internal magazine, *Retail Fax*; they are the focus for all internal PR – branch openings, special appearances, competition winners, etc.; and they are used on all product literature (see Figure 33).

They are the stars of every sales conference. In fact, just as with retailers, commercials are now timed to be launched at the key sales conferences each year (see Figure 34).

They have even been used on the front cover of the Annual Report (see Figure 35).

Figure 34: *The stars appearing at the sales conference January 2002*

Figure 35: *Cover of Halifax plc Annual Report 2000*

THE COMMUNICATIONS IDEA RESULTED IN AN UPLIFT
IN SALES AND PROFITABILITY

We will now show the impact of the idea on sales and profitability, and discount the effect of the products.

Current account sales

Halifax captured a near sixfold increase in share of the current account switching market in 2001 vs. 2000 (see Figure 36).

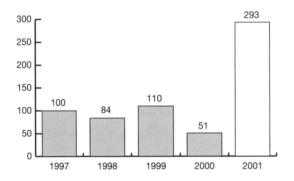

Figure 36: *Halifax share of the current account switching market (indexed data) – 1997–2001*
Source: NOP/FRS, December 2001

Halifax also grew the switching market as a whole for the first time in nine years (see Figure 37).

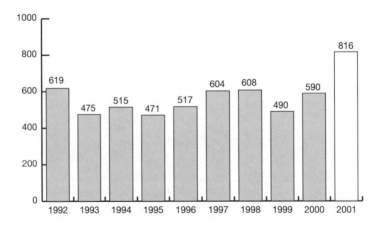

Figure 37: *Size of current account switching market (000s) – 1992–2001*
Source: NOP/FRS, December 2001

As a result, Halifax achieved a 150% uplift in sales, 25% above target (Table 6).

TABLE 6: CURRENT ACCOUNT SALES 2001 VS. TARGET

Average acquisition 1997–2000	Target 2001	Actual 2001
200,000	400,000	504,772

Source: Halifax

Current account profitability

We will now compare the profit generated by the campaign in 2001 with the profit generated by the campaign in 2000 (Table 7).

TABLE 7: PROFITS GENERATED BY THE CAMPAIGN IN 2001 VS. 2000

	2000	2001
Total communications spend	£1.16m	£6.91m
New current accounts	198,467	504,774
Accounts attributable to marketing	42,467	348,774[14]
Cost per current account	£27.32	£19.81

While the spend increased, the cost per current account came down by 28% due to the huge uplift in sales.

Regrettably, for reasons of commercial confidentiality, we are unable to share the NPV[15] of a current account either for 2000 or 2001. Using indexed figures we can show that profit per account increased by 43% in 2001 (Table 8).

TABLE 8: PROFIT PER CURRENT ACCOUNT 2001 VS. 2000

	2000	2001
Profit per current account	100	143

The increase in profit per customer is attributable to the reduced cost of acquisition and the higher NPV of customers recruited by the new current account.

Discounting the effect of the product

The most common objection that could be levelled against the effectiveness of the Halifax campaign is that the current account was so good that any campaign would have been successful.

Notwithstanding the fact that we have just proved that the communications idea *did* achieve an extraordinary growth in profitable sales in current accounts, and the fact that we have established that the idea provided a cohesive and motivating focus for the organisation, we will now demonstrate that its effectiveness *transcends the potency of individual product*s.

---

14. Halifax operates on an internal assumption that 156,000 current accounts is the natural level of acquisition attributable to the branch network without any marketing.
15. The NPV includes profit over the lifetime of a current account and expected cross-sales.

Ideally, we would have a region where we had not advertised current accounts to look at the uplift without advertising, but commercial requirements meant we needed to be a national advertiser.[16]

What we can do though is show that:

- A reduction in the current account interest rate had no effect on current account shortlisting.
- The advertised products (current accounts, mortgages and savings) performed far better than the non-advertised products (savings, personal loans).

The effect of the campaign versus interest rates

The key proposition on the current account was the 4% interest rate. As base rates were reduced throughout the year, Halifax had to cut the interest rate on the current account, first to 3% and then to 2%. As Figure 38 shows, neither of these cuts had any effect on the shortlisting of the current account. (We have used shortlisting data rather than sales data to eliminate the seasonality of current account sales.)

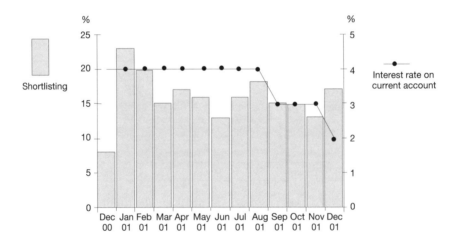

Figure 38: *Change in shortlisting vs. interest rates*
Base: All respondents
Source: Hall & Partners/Halifax

The effect of the campaign on credit card and mortgages

If we compare the two other advertised products (credit cards and mortgages) with the non-advertised products (personal loans and savings) we can see that there was

---

16. This paper has used exclusively descriptive data to prove the communications effect. The change in tracking study methodology and the low frequency of sales points since the start of the campaign (FRS sales data are only available every six months) have rendered the construction of a complex model premature. While we would look to do this in the medium term, this paper shows that in a modern commercial environment there isn't often time to wait for such a model to be constructed. This methodology we have used here, we believe, is equally valid and, for Halifax, more actionable.

significant growth in share of the former, and actually a decline in market share of the latter (Table 9).

TABLE 9: MARKET SHARE – NEW ACCOUNTS (INDEXED DATA)
– 2001 VS. 2000

	2000	2001
Other advertised products		
Credit card	100	315
Mortgages	100	116
Non-advertised products		
Personal loans	100	88
Savings	100	85

Source: NOP/FRS, December 2001

Not only was there an enormous leap in share of new credit cards, but even more impressively, Halifax's biggest business area, mortgages, grew significantly.

The only factors, other than the communications idea, that could have led to this increase in market share for the advertised products are first, a change in relative competitiveness of the products and second, an uplift in media spend.

In order to isolate these factors we will now compare one advertised product (mortgages) with a non-advertised product (savings). We have taken these products as they are Halifax's two largest and most stable product areas, and therefore the fairest comparison.

Comparing relative competitiveness of financial products year-on-year is virtually impossible – there is no such thing as an 'average basket price'. What we can say about mortgages and savings, though, is that they are both linked directly to the base rate. As brand leader in both mortgages and savings, Halifax cannot change the relative competitiveness of these products without having an enormous effect on profitability. For both 2000 and 2001 these products both enjoyed a consistent relationship to the base rate. Therefore we feel confident in stating that their relative competitiveness remained the same year-on-year.

Looking at media spend we can see that while mortgage spend went down year-on-year, savings spend actually went up. In terms of pure media spend we would have expected mortgage market share to go down, and savings to go up – the reverse of what actually happened (Table 10).

TABLE 10: MEDIA SPEND FOR MORTGAGES AND SAVINGS
– 2001 VS. 2000

	2000: £m	2001: £m
Mortgages	9.76	5.73[17]
Savings	0.45	2.17

Source: MMS

In 2001 mortgages had neither a higher media spend nor a more competitive product range than in 2000. The gains in market share can only be ascribed to the communications.

---

17. Not only was the total media spend on mortgages lower for 2001 than for 2000 but TV spend was also lower (2000: £5.1m: 2001: £2.4m). There was no change in allocation of resources that could have affected market share.

OTHER EFFECTS OF THE COMMUNICATIONS IDEA

Greater media efficiency

Because the campaign is so effective at generating branded cut-through, by modelling the Hall & Partners data against weekly TVR, we have been able to cut our weekly ABC1 TVR from 120 in 2001 to 98 in 2002. In a market that is year-round, this means we have been able to increase the number of weeks we advertise from 20 in 2001 to 24 in 2002 on the same advertising budget. Equally, we could have kept the number of weeks constant and reduced the budget by 10% – a saving of £1.4m (source: BBJ).

Effective in direct marketing

In 2001 we did a two-cell mailing for credit cards, both featuring the same proposition (3.9% APR for five months), one pack using 'Yvonne', one not. As Table 11 shows, 'Yvonne' resulted in a reduction in acquisition cost of £47 per card.

TABLE 11: RESULTS OF DIRECT MARKETING – YVONNE VS. NON-YVONNE

	Yvonne	Control (same proposition, without Yvonne)
Mailed volume	780,000	400,000
Total cost	£241,800	£124,000
Opened credit cards	2216	797
Cost per card	£109	£156

Source: Halifax

Effective in online media

Click-through rates after the introduction of 'Staff as Stars' are far higher than before for the same product propositions.

TABLE 12: CLICK-THROUGH RATES (%)
PRE 'STAFF AS STARS' VS. 'STAFF AS STARS'

	Pre 'Staff as Stars'	'Staff as Stars'
Share dealing	0.18	5.27
Mortgages	0.61	3.82
Websaver	0.33	0.97

Source: Zenith Media

Effective in PR

As Table 13 shows, 'Staff as Stars' created more PR than any other campaign in Britain during 2001, *without* the use of a PR agency.

Because Halifax does not employ a consumer PR agency we cannot calculate the equivalent cost of the amount of coverage the campaign received. What we can calculate is the cost of not employing a PR agency. Typically, a PR agency would expect to be on a retainer of £20,000 a month (source: Halifax). A communications

TABLE 13: ADS THAT MAKE NEWS –
NUMBER OF NATIONAL PRESS ARTICLES
– JAN–JUNE 2001

1. Halifax	17
2. Pepsi – Britney Spears	15
3. Coke – Christina Aguilera	15
4. Opium – Sophie Dahl	14

Source: Propeller Marketing Communications

idea that generated its own PR therefore saved Halifax a further £240,000 during 2001.

An effective internal communications programme

The communications idea has articulated and disseminated the brand proposition internally far better than any number of brand workshops that might typically be used for this purpose. Industry estimates of the cost of these programmes range from £7 to £35 per full-time employee (source: Halifax). In a 35,000-person organisation this works out to a saving of between £240,000 and £1.23m.

Effective use of agency resource

A 'single communications idea that fits all' has saved significant internal and external resource. Unlike other banks, Halifax does not require different concepts and different photography for branch window displays, product literature, sales conferences and presentations. A rough internal estimate places this saving at about £500,000.

Two banks, one idea

In September 2001 Halifax and Bank of Scotland merged to become HBOS. In January 2002 Bank of Scotland launched its own 'Staff as Stars' campaign, starring Angela Anderson from the Glasgow branch. Not only does using the same communications idea reap significant economies of scale (two brands managed by one marketing team and one agency, two commercials from one shoot), the fact that both Halifax and Bank of Scotland now have the same, albeit their own, campaigns has had a very positive effect on the merger. Both brands are able to use and benefit equally from the communications idea.

Every other bank has changed its campaign

Since 'Staff as Stars' broke, every one of the big four banks has changed its advertising agency, leading to a disruption in its marketing activity. As the Marketing Director of Lloyds TSB put it:

'It is Halifax, though, that has most shaken up the financial services market with its upbeat, headline-grabbing fmcg approach.'

CONCLUSION

Halifax did not have time to act like a bank. By refusing to accept that becoming a bank meant that you had to advertise like a bank, Halifax has, in the space of just 12 months, become an aggressive competitor to the clearing banks. 'Staff as Stars' has been the most popular, talked about, and effective campaign in British financial services marketing during 2001. Taking its inspiration from retailers not banks, the campaign has proved that financial services advertising can cut through, be well branded, stand out, be very appealing, communicate clearly, differentiate a brand and generate profitable sales in a very short space of time.

Halifax, far from being taken over, has now merged with Bank of Scotland and is stronger than ever. Two brands now share the same vision and the same communications idea, providing competition to the clearing banks north and south of the border.

The most exhilarating effect of the communications idea has been the internal effect. Galvanising large organisations in a very short space of time is extremely hard. We have demonstrated here the power that a strong, integrated communications idea can have in achieving this.

As Lord Stevenson wrote in the Chairman's Statement in the Annual Report the following year:

'... nothing emphasises the importance of the contribution made by our front line colleagues better than the television advert featuring Howard Brown from our Sheldon branch. In a way that corporate language cannot convey, Howard epitomises the enthusiasm our people have for what they are doing. Growth and enhanced shareholder value cannot become a reality until people like Howard, Halifax people, make it happen.'

3

Skoda

'It's a Skoda. Honest': the profitable return on brave communication

Principal authors: Laurence Green and Felicity Morgan, Fallon
Collaborating authors: David Hall and Karina Wilsher

EDITOR'S SUMMARY

'Skoda jokes' were so entrenched in British culture that, despite the brand's acquisition by VW in 1991, radical product improvements had continued to fall on deaf ears.

The repositioning that accompanied the launch of the Fabia in March 2000 challenged that prejudice head-on and reduced marque rejection from 60% to 42%. UK sales have since grown by 64%, dramatically outstripping other markets with the same model mix; £15m of marketing spend is estimated to have returned £37m of profits.

This paper relates the turnaround of a brand so maligned that until recently the very notion of an IPA submission on its behalf would have had a marketing audience bracing themselves for the inevitable punchline.

INTRODUCTION

Despite the car industry's stranglehold on the nation's airwaves (£863m was spent on automotive advertising in 2001, second only to retail expenditure), there are remarkably few established effectiveness cases. The category's purchase cycle is typically made scapegoat: the fact that cars are bought infrequently and after much consideration means that car advertising expenditure is unlikely ever to pay back over the short term.[1] In Skoda's case, however, we believe that we can already demonstrate a short-term return on advertising investment. (A return on investment achieved despite the brand's history and a category share of voice of less than 2%.)

For all the smart integration of marketing efforts on the brand's behalf (DM, PR and design efforts were swiftly aligned behind a new strategic approach), our story is in some ways an old-fashioned case of 'only advertising can do this', as the brand's very public problem demanded broadcast – as opposed to private – communication.

The pub version of the Skoda brand turnaround is this: ridiculed brand and ailing business stumbles on decent car and radical advertising and the VW Group's ugly duckling is reborn as a swan.

The truth, inevitably, is more complex than this. This paper scrutinises four key periods:

1. A brief history of Skoda's UK performance until 1997, a period of creeping growth within the limits of the budget sector and against a small base of loyalists.
2. The (failed) launch of the Octavia[2] in 1998.
3. The launch of the Fabia[3] (and brand relaunch) in March 2000 onwards demonstrating the broad effects of brand marketing and intermediate evidence of advertising effectiveness.
4. A specific focus on the 2001 relaunch of the Octavia, a model whose sales curve we noticed had behaved contrarily, and an analysis which allows us to strip out new product effect.

PRE 1997

British consumers know nothing of Skoda's genuinely splendid engineering heritage, having first become acquainted with the brand during the dog days of

---

1. The IPA itself was once moved to describe the business of demonstrating advertising effect in the car category as 'fiendishly difficult' – a turn of phrase which papers have since invariably played back. Including this one.
2. The Octavia competes in the upper-medium sector against the likes of the Vauxhall Vectra, Nissan Primera and Renault Laguna.
3. The Fabia supermini competes against the likes of the Ford Fiesta, Renault Clio and Vauxhall Corsa.

communist rule in Czechoslavakia and Skoda's unhealthy monopoly on car production. The Skoda joke, a uniquely British phenomenon, the unfortunate outcome.

As the jokes peaked in the late 1980s, change was afoot. Czechoslovakia's Velvet Revolution prompted courtship from Volkswagen and a partnership which soon bore fruit in the form of the Felicia, a car impressive enough to win seven consecutive *What Car?* 'Budget Car Of The Year' Awards.[4]

Though ridiculed as a brand, Skoda's UK sales grew through the mid-1990s (see Figure 1), and extraordinary levels of loyalty were achieved (see Figure 2).

No one could argue that the Skoda brand was ill-defined or its franchise particularly open to competitive incursion. But nor could it be argued that Skoda was making genuine inroads against the broader consumer base; rejection figures for the brand remained stubbornly fixed at around 60% over the period.[5]

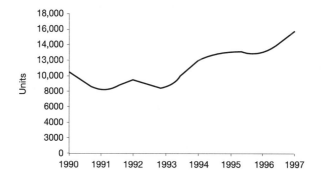

Figure 1: *Skoda UK volume sales 1990–1997*
Source: JATO/SMMT

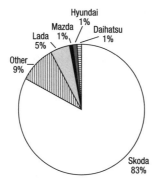

Figure 2: *1997 Skoda source of sales*
Source: JATO/SMMT

---

4. Volkswagen took a stake in Skoda in 1991 and became sole owners 10 years later.
5. Source: Quadrangle tracking. To put this into perspective, Fiat (a brand also plagued historically by product prejudice) was well clear of Skoda, with only 1/3 of prospects rejecting the marque.

And as the brand's future product reality became more obvious, it was apparent that Skoda's image deficiencies would soon become a critical commercial limitation. Higher-quality, more expensively priced cars would be rolling off the production line (as VW moved to a shared platform production strategy): Skodas that would have to compete for different consumers and against a new competitive set.

Skoda's brand rehabilitation in the UK was not just a matter of pride then, but a commercial imperative.

THE LAUNCH OF THE OCTAVIA, 1998

The first unarguable demonstration of the product transformation led by Volkswagen emerged with the launch of the Octavia in 1998. Launch reviews were invariably flattering:

'The Octavia is far and away the best car Skoda has ever made.'

What Car?

The Octavia's £10m launch advertising budget remains Skoda's largest ever. Skoda braced itself for success.

The launch was a failure:

- Only 2569 Octavias were sold in 1998 (that's an advertising cost per car in the region of £4000). By the year end, Octavia accounted for only 12% of Skoda sales, so that the Felicia remained overwhelmingly the Skoda car most often seen on the road.
- Skoda's brand image was unaffected, with no significant image improvements recorded over the launch period.

The failure, in retrospect, was one of strategy. The Octavia's marketing had been model-specific and product-centric, targeted at the small band of brand considerers; in short, Skoda was behaving like a brand without a problem rather than facing the truth and addressing the stigma.

2000–2001: FABIA LAUNCH (BRAND RELAUNCH) ONWARDS

Strategic foundations

When Fallon was awarded the advertising account in 1999, it was clear a new approach would be needed if Skoda's next launch – of the Fabia supermini – wasn't also to fall on deaf ears. Although the Fabia was once again rumoured to be a 'great product' it was clear that product alone wouldn't be enough to drive people to reappraise the Skoda brand; and indeed that we had to win reappraisal of the Skoda brand for any product to achieve its potential.

While, again, positive motoring press coverage was to accompany the Fabia's launch, we understood the role for marketing to be to complement product endorsement by directly attacking the prejudice against the Skoda brand.[6]

---

6. And prejudice there remained: the three 'Skoda joke' websites on the internet were still doing good business.

Despite the Fabia winning the *What Car?* 'Car of the Year' Award at launch the popular press gave us a truer representation of the car's likely reception:

> 'I see the Fabia has been named "Car of the Year" but I don't think I'm ready to drive one yet. I still think that it's less embarrassing to be seen getting out of the back of a sheep than getting out of the back of a Skoda.'

> *The Mirror*, 26 February 2000

We concluded that the stigma attached to Skoda had become a shared cultural phenomenon, and that to target only those who might consider buying one was to ignore the vast mass of their friends, neighbours, colleagues and even children who were likely to ridicule that decision (as well as leaving that broader base of prospects unmined).[7]

To summarise our two key strategic building blocks:

1. A new role for advertising: use the Fabia to confront the biggest barrier to buying a Skoda – the irrational prejudice against the brand.
2. A new target audience: create a *general* shift in attitudes so that potential buyers feel confident they can choose Skoda without being laughed at.

As a result, our media plan was contrary, eschewing the narrowcast and the new in favour of an old-fashioned broadcast plan: *Coronation Street*, posters and all.

PR played a critical role at launch; since press coverage was part of the problem, it had to be part of the solution. PR was charged with convincing opinion-formers that Skoda had changed (with car and campaign as evidence) and more generally to create an impression of success for the advertising to work against.

The creative idea: repositioning the consumer

Our objectives and strategy were well understood, but the consumer of course sees neither. The creative response to our brief – summarised in the line 'It's a Skoda. Honest' turned our ambitions into tangible reality. Skoda would make advertising featuring people who still thought their cars were poor. But by gently ridiculing these people, the consumer would conclude that he/she 'wasn't one of them'.

Launch executions featured an enthusiastic but buffoonish diplomat on a factory tour; a know-it-all motorshow supervisor; and a faintly moronic car park attendant. Each thrown by the evidence of Skoda's transformation sitting right before their eyes.

The creative work didn't so much reposition the brand as reposition *the consumer's attitude to the brand*. This was later to be summarised as follows:

> 'The brand's existing memorability – a poisoned chalice if ever there was one – is made into a plus. How stupid the mistaken fools in the ad are, thinks the viewer, who ten seconds ago wasn't aware of what the new Fabia looked like either. The commercials tell us something and make us feel superior about knowing it with the speed of light. How clever is that?'

> *Creative Review*, February 2000

---

7. In moments of doubt, we reminded ourselves of a peculiarly poignant remark from our client during briefing: 'We've had children crying in our showrooms'.

In creative development research, respondents responded as hoped and the campaign's strategic basis was validated:

> 'It's a bit tongue in cheek. They're obviously well aware of their reputation and this comes across as proud of what they've got.'

> 'Skoda used to be the joke. Now the joke is the joke.'

> 'This research strongly indicates that it will be important to acknowledge consumers' prejudices – to accept them. To start the conversation with agreement – finding common ground with the customer. Ignoring these perceptions risks leaving them festering.'

Shaw Research and Planning, November 1999

Setting objectives

Faced with a new objective and audience, we established a tracking study based on that used by Volkswagen and spanning prospects across the relevant sectors.

Though the study would gather the usual advertising diagnostics, these were of marginal interest. The objectives we had set could only really be measured by changes in Skoda's brand imagery and ultimately in marque consideration (which, remember, had been static for a decade). In the car market, as in most mature markets, imagery and consideration figures are remarkably obdurate and often follow rather than lead behavioural change.[8] Our first burst success criteria duly became simply whether or not we could achieve the following:

- Statistically significant improvements in brand imagery.
- A statistically significant decrease in marque rejection.

Campaign results

The Fabia launch/Skoda relaunch campaign broke in March 2000 and key TV spend since has comprised the following (see Figures 3 and 4):

Our first evidence of in-market effectiveness came from an unlikely source, the campaign being voted top of *Campaign*'s 'People's Jury'.[9] Some plaudit for such a much maligned brand, but no use to us if the campaign was failing to win minds as well as hearts.

Factory   Motorshow   Vandal

Figure 3: *Fabia executions (launched March 2000)*

---

8. The 1992 VW Golf IPA submission concludes: 'The propensity to consider or "desirability" of a marque seems to move slowly, if at all.'
9. 'The People's Jury' comprised a telephone omnibus survey conducted against a sample of 1000 adults by Taylor Nelson Sofres on the weekend of 14–16 April.

Transporter   Forensic

Figure 4: *Octavia executions (launched January 2001)*

Given our ambition to *publicly* reshape the brand's reputation a truer measure of effectiveness was the apparent sea-change in attitudes towards the brand in the national press which coincided with our advertising and PR efforts. Best exemplified by *The Mirror*'s sudden about-turn:

> 'History's biggest comeback since Bobby Ewing stepped out of the shower, new Skoda is hip and sexy – yes, sexy.'

Mirror Magazine, 28 March 2000

Our first tracking results confirmed that consumers had not just noticed the advertising, but responded favourably:

> 'Rather cheeky, very effective.'

> 'A true reflection on how people relate to Skoda.'

Millward Brown Verbatims, April 2000

More importantly, after only one burst of advertising, key image measures had responded rapidly (Table 1).

TABLE 1

	Pre (%)	Post (%)	Change (%)
Skodas are better than they used to be	54	79	+25
Skoda make cars you can't take seriously	47	32	−15
I'd be proud to have one on my drive	20	33	+13

Source: Millward Brown, July 2000

There was also dramatic impact on consideration. Having proved impervious to product innovation and previous marketing efforts, the number of prospects who would not consider Skoda dropped from 60% to 42%, a rejection figure now lower than the equivalent figures for Fiat and Citroën for the first time ever.

Since that first burst these results have been remarkably consistent and the top box measure of 'active consideration' has grown from 18% to a peak of 28% (source: Millward Brown, April 2001).[10] Even those left rejecting the brand are

---

10. At the peak of ad awareness, consideration of Skoda among the ad-aware was over twice that of the non-ad-aware; consideration had never previously correlated so strongly to ad-awareness.

now far less entrenched in their rejection. Fabias, for example, are now more commonly rejected on the basis of unfamiliarity than brand reputation (Table 2).

TABLE 2: REASONS FOR REJECTING FABIA

	March 2000 (%)	March 2001 (%)
Bad reputation	24	15
Negative image	21	10
Don't know what they're like	21	28

Source: Millward Brown

The Fabia relaunch was the start of an amazing two-year period for Skoda. The advertising and PR campaigns spearheaded a dramatically re-thought marketing programme that included innovative media thinking, new 'brand-led' direct marketing, POS and website.

All catalysed and were catalysed by the change in direction. DM, for example, adopted the advertising objective, strategy and tone and coordinated targeting, timing and creative. (For example, a Skoda badge was mailed to 100,000 prospects with the invitation to 'live with it for a while'.) DM response increased by between 50 and 100% and 2050 sales directly generated at an average cost per sale of £279 (source: AIS).

PR efforts against opinion-formers, meanwhile, continued to pay back across the period.

> 'I knew my Skoda was trendy, but not that trendy. I'd parked it on Shepherd's Bush Road to find both badges missing. To lose both looks like a style phenomenon ... the green arrow silhouetted against a white background has become the twenty-first-century equivalent of the VW badge.'
>
> Toby Young, *GQ*

Collectively, these efforts have had a striking business impact. The rest of this paper is devoted to demonstrating the scale of that impact and attempting to provide further proof that these effects can at least in part be attributed to marketing activity.

Topline business results

Since the Fabia launch, volume growth has easily outstripped the market, winning record share for the brand (Table 3).

TABLE 3

	Skoda volume growth (%)	Market growth (%)	Skoda market share[11]
1999	5	−2	1.0
2000	35	1	1.3
2001	23	11	1.5

Source: JATO/SMMT

---

11. Skoda's value share has grown even more precipitously, but there is no acknowledged industry standard for computing and presenting this figure.

We have already reflected on the direction and degree of response to our marketing efforts. Now we discount other factors which might have driven Skoda's business.

Eliminating other variables

Price

The years 2000 and 2001 witnessed sharp price deflation in the car market following the Byers' Report.[12] Skoda bucked the trend, the average price paid for a Skoda now 60% higher than in 1997. Skodas had always been priced competitively and the deterioration in the brand's relative price position over the campaign period means that we can rule out price as the source of sales success.

Distribution

Though Skoda continually seeks to upgrade the retail experience, there were no step changes in either numbers, share or quality of distribution over the period which might explain the dramatic sales uplift. (We would expect price and distribution variables anyway to work hardest against live brand considerers, while it is our contention – supported by data – that marketing has served to broaden the total base of considerers of the brand.)

Fleet marketing

Given the British car market's unique reliance on fleet sales, we must also eliminate this variable. Skoda's fleet business has always represented a small fraction of total sales (c. 18% compared to Vauxhall's 65%). More tellingly, retail sales have grown three times faster than fleet sales over the period in question. Fleet, in short, has not been the brand's engine of growth.

Product

This can be less easily dismissed as a factor in its own right, and we would not seek to diminish the importance of the Fabia itself in the transformation of Skoda's fortunes.

But at its most basic, marketing publicises products. At the very least then, marketing activity has catalysed awareness of the Fabia and therefore its effect on parent brand perceptions (Table 4).

TABLE 4

	Ad-aware (%)	Non-ad-aware (%)
Have seen the Fabia on the road, in a showroom or anywhere else	64	36

Source: Millward Brown, July 2000

Without marketing efforts, the Fabia might have been written about in the motoring press and would of course have been 'on display' in Skoda's dealerships. As we know, though, Skoda had enjoyed favourable motoring press for years,

---

12. The Alliance and Leicester Car Price Index reported a 10% price decline in 2000 and a 6% decline in 2001.

without any step-change sales effect, and dealerships tend only to be visited by active considerers. We would contend therefore that the mere presence of impressive new product (unamplified by marketing) simply would not have generated the sales step-change and broadening of franchise we have seen.

The following observations also put the product effect in context:

- The launch of the Octavia in 1998 (arguably even more of a step-change car) had not created a step-change in Skoda's fortunes.
- The effect of great product alone might most plausibly have been to win high levels of repeat purchase from existing Skoda loyalists. But what has happened – mimicking our tracking data – is that the brand's source of business over the last two years has broadened considerably (see Figure 5). It seems unlikely that product alone could have prompted this effect so quickly.

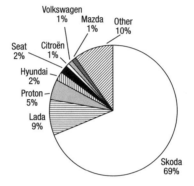

Figure 5: *2001 Skoda source of sales*
Source: JATO/SMMT

- Perhaps most emphatically, despite a common product mix and launch timetable across Europe, Skoda UK sales dramatically outstripped those of Skoda's other major markets over the period (see Figure 6).

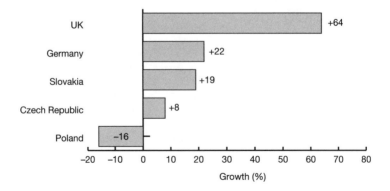

Figure 6: *Skoda sales change 1999–2001*
Source: Ex-factory sales

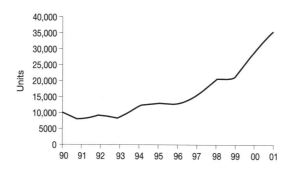

Figure 7: *Skoda UK volume sales 1990–2001*
Source: JATO/SMMT

Summary and payback

In years 2000 and 2001, then, Skoda's business accelerated from its trend line and the market trend line (see Figure 7).

Comparing actual sales to projected sales, we see an incremental revenue uplift of £185 million and profit uplift of £18.5 million, an uplift that already pays back on a total marketing spend of £15.4 million over the period.[13] Factoring-in predicted repeat sales and profit from those incremental customers, this profit uplift amounts over the longer run to £37 million.[14]

To summarise, we have a dramatic sales uplift which we can logically ascribe only to either the peculiar product power of the Fabia, the Skoda brand's repositioning in communications, or both. We have seen how we must be sceptical of the former (given Skoda's previous experience of breakthrough product, and international comparisons); how the brand's franchise has broadened as predicted; and how the marketing relaunch coincides with a dramatic decrease in rejection, which we would then expect to turn into sales over time.

In a last attempt to account for product effect, we turned to modelling.

Though it's increasingly rare for an IPA submission to be unsubstantiated by an econometric model, early attempts at modelling Skoda's business over the period proved fraught with difficulty.[15] We found correlations between spend, awareness, consideration and sales, discovered that the previously loose correlation between media spend and awareness had intensified during the last two years of activity, and that media spend and sales only *started* to correlate in 2000 – but none to a persuasive standard of proof.[16]

Our search for proof that marketing lay at the heart of Skoda's recent success continued. Attracted by an atypical sales curve, we began to stare harder at the

---

13. Setting trend sales at 5% (Skoda's 1999 growth, and the car market's average growth over 2000/2001; multiplying the resulting 18,517 incremental sales by the average selling price of £10,000 and applying an average car industry margin of 10%).
14. Car marques boast generally high loyalty rates so the principle of 'lifetime value' is well established. We computed long-term profit uplift by applying a recurring likelihood to repeat purchase of 50% (the market average; Skoda's loyalty figure is currently much higher). We have not attempted to factor in the profit made for dealers or from ongoing maintenance, repair and parts.
15. Essentially we had too few data points, too much seasonality, and too many models to manage.
16. Source: Tortilla 71 Econometric Modelling.

effect of advertising on sales of the Octavia (in market since 1998, marginally facelifted in 2001).[17] By removing 'new product effect', this, we hoped, might be the effectiveness case within the effectiveness case.

2001: OCTAVIA REVISITED

As demonstrated in previous papers, new car models have predictable sales and share curves, new models winning sales exponentially at launch, then tapering off as they lose competitiveness to other, newer launches (source: VW Golf IPA paper).

The Octavia's sales curve defies car category precedent, peaking three years after launch, at precisely the point where it should have lost its competitive advantage (see Figure 8) (source: VW Golf IPA paper).

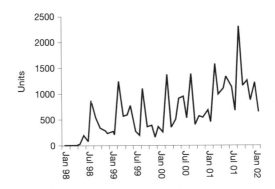

Figure 8: *Octavia monthly sales 1998–2001*
Source: JATO

Our hypothesis at the time of campaign planning had been this: that the Octavia had been burdened by the Skoda name at launch (a burden unrelieved by model-specific marketing efforts) and might therefore be highly responsive to advertising now the 'brand burden' had been lifted (as well as itself contributing to the ongoing assault on the brand's previous imagery).

Although we deployed a dramatically smaller ad budget against the Octavia at relaunch than it had benefited from at launch, the effects had been dramatic:

- First six months' sales at relaunch 79% up on launch equivalent.
- A 1.77% share of sector achieved, versus 0.76% at launch.

We decided to focus our modelling efforts on quantifying the impact of media spend and product changes on sales of the Octavia.

By isolating four key periods in the Octavia's recent life (see Figure 9) we were able to model three factors (those three factors jointly responsible for the observed sales curve):

---

17. This facelift was truly cosmetic, remodelled headlamps and grille the most obvious changes.

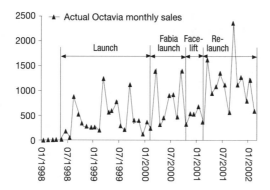

Figure 9: *Key periods within Octavia sales curve*
Source: JATO

1. The effect of the Fabia launch (i.e. Skoda relaunch) on Octavia sales.
2. The effect of the Octavia facelift on Octavia sales.
3. The effect of Octavia's marketing relaunch on sales.

Because of the difficulties of modelling monthly sales in such a seasonal market, our analysis was based on moving annual totals. We ran various scenarios:

- The first, that there had been no Fabia launch (Skoda relaunch) and that Octavia had continued to grow at 5% p.a.[18]
- The second, that Octavia sales had continued to grow at the rate set during the Fabia launch (a rate of 24%).
- Lastly, that Octavia sales during 2001 had continued to grow at the overall rate set in 2000 of 28%: i.e. no uplift due to 2001 marketing activity (see Figure 10).

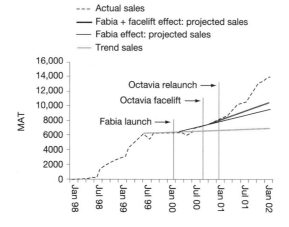

Figure 10: *Octavia sales projections*
Source: JATO

18. An optimistic projection: its sector declined continuously though 1999, 2000 and 2001.

By comparing the various projected sales figures, we established the relative effects of each force on Octavia sales (Table 5):

TABLE 5

Projected sales excluding Fabia launch/Octavia facelift/ Octavia relaunch	22,911		
		Fabia contribution	3864
Projected sales excluding Octavia facelift relaunch	26,775		
		Facelift contribution	1344
Projected sales excluding Octavia relaunch	28,119	Relaunch contribution	3691
Actual sales	31,810		

The results made intuitive sense: that the facelift had been a relatively weak force on Octavia sales, but that the Fabia launch (Skoda relaunch) and Octavia marketing relaunch had been strong effects.

The 'Fabia contribution', as we have already seen, is at least partially due to marketing. The 'Octavia relaunch' contribution (now that we have isolated the product contribution) is pure marketing effect and results in incremental short-term revenues of £41 million, incremental long-term revenues of £81 million and incremental long-term profit of £8.1 million.[19] This effect against an Octavia-specific re-launch budget in 2001 of £5.2 million. So without taking into account the value of considerers who have not yet purchased, the Octavia's halo effect on overall brand consideration, dealer profits or profits from parts and maintenance, the Octavia marketing spend still pays back handsomely.

CONCLUSIONS

Enough analysis. We will leave the last word to the people at the sales frontline – the dealers, typically cynical and critical of advertising efforts made on their behalf by central marketing. In 2001, Britain's dealers rated Skoda 'best make' in terms of 'product advertising by manufacturers' (source: Dealer Satisfaction Survey 2001).

ACKNOWLEDGEMENTS

This Skoda case is best summarised as an advertising-led brand repositioning.

Though Fallon are the paper's primary authors (encouraged by the Skoda client team), acknowledgement is due to Mediacom, Archibald Ingall Stretton, Sputnik and Duffy, co-authors all of the brand's marketing turnaround.

And for their respective roles in evaluating the campaign to date, we acknowledge also the contributions of Millward Brown, Shaw Research and Planning, and Tortilla 71.

---

19. Setting Octavia average price at £11,000 and again setting margin at 10% and repeat purchase at a recurring 50%.

Section 2

Silver Winners

4

Anti-drink driving
'Shame' campaign

Principal authors: David Lyle, Julie Anne Bailie, Pamela Baird and
Dawn Reid, McCann-Erickson Belfast
Collaborating authors: Robert Lyle, John Brolly and Sinead Holland

EDITOR'S SUMMARY

This paper demonstrates how 'Shame', the anti-drink driving campaign, contributed to 97% awareness, with 75% being 'very influenced' by it; a 68% improvement in zero alcohol safe driving perceptions; a 35% decline in the acceptability of driving after *one* drink among the target audience; and an improvement in the perception that drink-driving is 'extremely shameful', which increased to 97%. The target audience were responsible for 13.5% fewer deaths in 2001 compared to 2000.

THE CONTEXT

Northern Ireland has the highest levels of road traffic fatalities and injuries in the UK as shown in Figure 1.

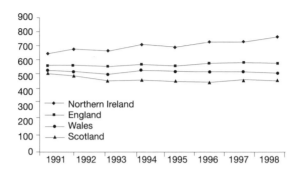

Figure 1: *How does Northern Ireland compare? Road traffic injury accident casualty and death rates per 100,000 population: UK regions, 1991–1998*
Source: Northern Ireland Annual Abstract of Statistics 1999

The problem costs the economy of Northern Ireland around £450 million a year, as shown in Table 1.

TABLE 1: ECONOMIC COST OF ROAD CASUALTIES

	Number	Cost per casualty (£)	Total (£m)
Deaths	141	1,089,130	154
Serious injuries	1509	122,380	185
Slight injuries	11,799	9440	111
Total			450

Source: DETR, DOE

THE PROBLEM

The Department of the Environment (DOE) has identified driver-alcohol as a major cause of road deaths in Northern Ireland. Driver-alcohol is the second biggest killer on the roads after excessive speed, contributing to 15% of road deaths in the five years 1995–1999 (see Figure 2).

CAMPAIGN OBJECTIVES

1. To position drink-driving as *socially* and *personally shameful.*
2. To influence attitude improvements among target male drivers:
   - Decreasing the acceptability of driving after consuming alcohol.
   - Increasing the number of safe drivers who believe they cannot consume *any* alcohol without affecting their driving.
3. To save lives.

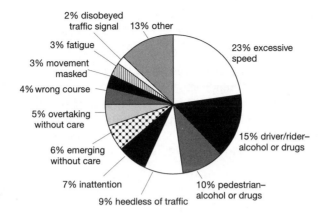

Figure 2: *What causes road deaths? Road deaths by principal factor 1995–1999*
Source: Police Service Northern Ireland

The target audience

Extensive five-year analysis of road casualty statistics identified male car drivers as being responsible for 94% of alcohol-related fatalities between 1995 and 1999.

Thirty-nine per cent of drivers responsible for alcohol-related fatal crashes between 1995 and 1999 were 17–24-year-old males and 36% were 25–34-year-old males. The primary target audience of the campaign is 17–24-year-old male drivers who are over-represented by 600% when indexed against the driving population (Figure 3).

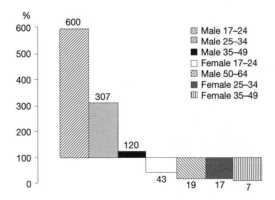

Figure 3: *Over and under-representation of car drivers responsible for alcohol-related* fatal *crashes by age/gender (1995–1999) (indexed against drivers by age/gender)*
Source: Police Service Northern Ireland/DOE data

UNDERSTANDING THE MINDSET

Male car drivers were responsible for 94% of alcohol-related 'killed' and 'seriously injured' collisions from 1995–1999.

An independent research company conducted a programme of qualitative strategy development research in February 2000. The objectives of the research were:

- To understand why certain males persist in driving after drinking and what the most powerful deterrents might be.
- To inform the creative strategy for a new anti-drink driving campaign with deeper insights into the most powerful psychological and creative triggers.
- To study the motivations of males who admit to driving after two pints or more than two units of alcohol, isolating those who live in areas with a lower police presence.

Ten groups were conducted in rural areas with male drivers who drink alcohol and aged 17–24, 25–34 and 35–49. The following components of an ideal anti-drink driving advertisement were identified by the research.

- Realistic/needs accident scene (post and pre)
- Child(ren) – maimed?
- Focus on conscience of driver
- Momentary lapse of concentration
- Depict as responsible/confident 25–30-year-old.

Source: Ulster Marketing Surveys,
Qualitative Focus Groups, March 2000

Consumer insight

A key insight into the 17–24-year-old 'young male chancers' who formed the epicentre of the drink-drive target audience was that, overconfident, in love with life and believing they would live forever, they were driven by a good time.

In the main, they were responsible in their pursuit of fun – not planning to drink and drive but, on occasions, doing so when faced with the choice of ending the fun or not. They post-rationalised their behaviour on the basis that it was neither pre-meditated nor excessive (unlike drunk drivers who set out to drink and drive in excess) and that any risk was outweighed by their confidence in their ability to handle a couple of drinks on one-off occasions.

The actual moment of decision was blurred by the heady elation induced by a moderate amount of alcohol – fuelling their confidence and desire to continue the fun further. As a result, the advertising communication needed to *remove any such room for negotiation and rationalisation.*

The imperative was to confront them with another choice – did they want to risk the good times turning into the very worst of times, in a split second, by succumbing, in the heat of the moment, to alcohol when driving?

The advertising also needed to dramatise how personal shame would be heaped on them – they would no longer be able to use the already stigmatised *drunk* drivers to justify their less deviant behaviour. A key trigger was the death of a child – a much greater motivation to modify behaviour and counteract the 'invincibility syndrome' than the suggestion that they could kill themselves.

A highly cynical audience, quick to dismiss any form of didactic communication, insisted that the advertising *had* to engage them in the narrative with a high degree of self-identification, to maximise the impact of the cognitive dissonance, leaving them *with no choice* but that of total abstinence when driving if the good times are to continue.

CAMPAIGN CREATIVE STRATEGY AND RATIONALE

Every unit of alcohol has an impairing effect on driving so the creative strategy was singular and clear, communicating 'Driving on even *one* drink can turn the good times into the worst of times.'

The strategy was to move drink-driving from a position of social stigma to one of personal shame. To take the target audience's core desire for 'a good time' and to dramatise how driving even on one drink can turn 'the best of times into the worst of times'. Therefore the outcome is shown to be dissonant or in conflict with their core desire, psychologically encouraging the target audience to change the dissonant attitude or behaviour.

The core thought is *shame* – designed to work in tandem with the established 'brand' of *never ever drink and drive*.

Shame as a concept and emotion spans every aspect of drink-driving. The end sequence line 'Never ever drink and drive – could you live with the shame?' is delivered over the tragedy on-screen as a challenging, probing question – not a didactic preachy tone of voice, which research indicated would alienate the target audience.

'*Could you live with the shame?*' evokes not just the shame of killing a child with all its haunting, life-destroying traumatic consequences, but also the sequence of shame which is implicitly consequential to drinking and driving – arrest, imprisonment, loss of job, loss of licence, loss of dignity, and personal humiliation.

Personal relevance is a vital component of the creative strategy. This is designed to be everyone's story – and everyone's nightmare. '*Shall I tell you about my life?*', the opening lines from 'Man of the World' by Fleetwood Mac, musically drives home personal relevance, with ironic potency.

The creative involves us in both the world of the victim and in the world of the perpetrator, before showing how these two worlds collide instantly because of the impairing effect of alcohol on driving.

THE CAMPAIGN

Shame opens on a cute, captivating little boy playing innocently in his front garden. He kicks a football and scores into his little football net and runs round like a professional punching the air. The ad then dissolves to an ordinary decent bloke (ODB) in a suit, (23 years old, attractive, carefree) as he throws his sports bag into his car. We then mix to ODB at football training with his mates as he scores a goal and replicates exactly the triumphant action of the little boy. The ad then cuts to ODB having a pint of beer after training. We then see him driving home, totally relaxed. He loses concentration, his car clips the kerb, which results in the car rolling over dramatically before crashing down over a hedge into a garden and falling on the little boy, who is crushed to death. We end on the tragic scene and ODB standing shocked, stunned and *shamed* amid the tragedy. Voice-over and end titles reveal:

NEVER EVER DRINK AND DRIVE – Could YOU live with the shame?

The media strategy

The media objectives were to intercept potential drink-drivers at the two key seasonal periods – pre-Christmas and summer – and to reach this group, and also the general public, at the point of danger before they went out or when they were out.

The key media was television, which enabled the DOE to reach 90% of 15–34-year-old adults in Northern Ireland. Television is the only medium which can quickly reach 90%+ of the target audience. Plus it possesses the inherent qualities of sound, vision, drama, narrative and emotional impact.

Over the five-week launch (November 2000–January 2001) 814 TVRs were bought in Northern Ireland, which were divided 50/50 between the two buying audiences – all adults and 16–34-year-old males. These particular audiences were bought to communicate to both the main target group (17–24-year-old males) and other influencers in their lives (all adults). The airtime was upweighted Sunday through to Thursday to intervene in the planning processes of those young people organising their weekends.

The television campaign was pre-publicised in the main regional titles in entertainment sections or in solus positions, to achieve appointment-to-view coverage of the launch (Figure 4).

Figure 4: *Launch press ad*

Post-launch, 227 TVRs were bought in March 2001 over the heavy drinking period of St Patrick's Day weekend, 583 TVRs for the summer 2001 campaign (July/August) and 552 for the Christmas 2001 campaign (November–December). A proportion of the television budget was also set aside for buying into high-profile football matches, the Grand Prix and The Brits.

Figure 5: *Bus rear ad*   Figure 6: *Washroom ad (also used in* Big Buzz *magazine)*

In Northern Ireland television was supported by province-wide cinema; bus rears (Figure 5) gave a weekly coverage of 88% of 16–24-year-old adults and A3 format washroom advertising (Figure 6) in over 108 pubs and clubs gave an extra 1.1 million impacts.

Post-launch, 310 bus rears were utilised province-wide during the summer and Christmas 2001 campaigns – to provide the communication *constantly* when drivers were thinking about barbecues or Christmas parties. Some 144 cinema screens were also used each week, for four weeks for the summer campaign and five weeks for the Christmas campaign, carefully targeting films directly aimed at 17–34-year-olds. These media channels were also supported by a solus front-page advertisement in the *Belfast Telegraph* (Figure 7) and also an advertisement in the *Big Buzz* magazine (Figure 6).

Car park barriers were also used for ads at all main entrances and exits at Odyssey, Northern Ireland's largest entertainment venue (Figure 8).

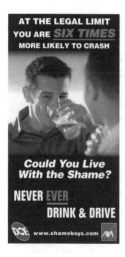

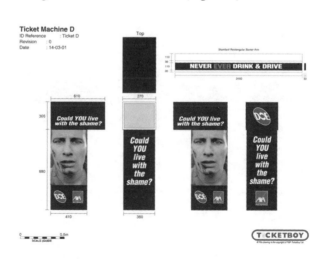

Figure 7: Belfast Telegraph, *solus front-page ad*

Figure 8: *Car park ad*

Figure 9: *Full colour ad placed in local titles*

As part of a more localised approach to the drink-driving problem, full colour advertisements were placed in 19 local titles in the run-up to Christmas 2001 (Figure 9).

Weekend radio promotions gave away free rugby match tickets to Celtic League matches sponsored by the Department of the Environment. Admobiles (Figure 10) were strategically placed at the matches and anti-drink drive tannoy messages were announced before and after the match and also at half time, to reach spectators leaving the beer tents.

Posters were placed around the stadium; there was an advertisement in the programme, pitch side banners and exit signage (Figures 11 and 12).

Figure 10: *Admobile strategically placed at Celtic League matches*

Figure 11: *Exit signage at Celtic League matches*   Figure 12: *Exit signage at Celtic League matches*

These are all part of an intervention strategy designed to interrupt target audiences at their most vulnerable point of danger.

The 'Shame Boys' penalty box

The launch of the Belfast Giants, Ireland's first Super League Ice Hockey team at the Odyssey Arena, where alcohol is served throughout games, provided an innovative opportunity to bring the message to life. Starting with the Giants' first home game on 2 December 2000, sponsorship of the 'Shame Boys' penalty box (Figure 13) provided an average of 11.5 anti-drink-drive messages per game. These messages were conveyed to the sell-out crowds, and clearly linked the idea of the shame associated with drink-driving accidents with the players being sent off to the 'sin-bin' for fouls or fighting.

Figure 13: *The 'Shame Boys' penalty box*

EVIDENCE OF EFFECTIVENESS

Massive campaign awareness

The 'Shame' TV campaign scored the highest rate of spontaneous recall of any advertising campaign in Northern Ireland in January 2002 (Figure 14).

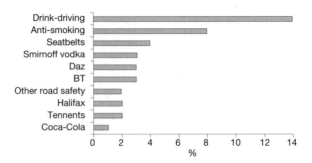

Figure 14: *Top ten spontaneously recalled advertisements in Northern Ireland 21–28 January 2002*
Base: All respondents 1116
Source: Independent survey by Ulster Marketing Surveys

By January 2001, awareness of the campaign was at 94% and by January 2002, 14 months after the launch, the campaign had achieved awareness levels of 97% (an increase of 3%) among all drivers who drink any alcohol.

In the same period awareness among the target audience of 17–24-year-old male drivers had reached 94% (an increase of 1%).

Washroom advertising in Greater Belfast was recalled by 92% of the target audience in March 2001.

PR effectiveness

The campaign generated free PR coverage valued at just over £½m in the first year, receiving extensive coverage in all the main media across Ireland – TV, press, radio and websites. The launch of the campaign achieved the lead story in the main TV news bulletins, BBC Newsline and UTV Live. All PR was advertising-led and driven by the television campaign.

ATTITUDE CHANGE SINCE LAUNCH

In January 2002 52% of 17–24-year-old male drivers who drink alcohol agreed they could not drink *any* alcohol without their driving being affected (a 68% improvement on baseline) (see Figure 15).

Prior to the launch of the campaign, 29% of drivers who ever drink any alcohol felt they could drink *more than one* unit of alcohol without affecting their driving. By January 2002, 13% of *all* drivers, who ever drink alcohol, felt they could drink *more than one* unit of alcohol without affecting their driving. This equates to a 55% improvement on baseline attitudes (see Figure 16).

Decrease in the acceptability of driving after one and two drinks

Among 17–24-year-old male drivers there was a 35% decline in the acceptability of driving after *one* drink (Figure 17a). Among 17–24-year-old male drivers there was a 40% decline in the acceptability of driving after *two* drinks (Figure 17b).

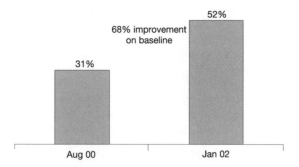

Figure 15: *Units of alcohol you can personally drink without affecting your driving – none at all 17–24 male drivers*
Base: All drivers who ever drink alcohol, August 2000: 484/January 2001: 433/January 2002: 443
Source: Ulster Marketing Surveys

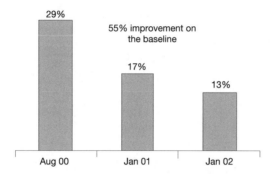

Figure 16: *Units of alcohol you can personally drink without affecting your driving – more than one*
Base: All drivers who ever drink alcohol, August 2000: 484/January 2001: 433/January 2002: 443
Source: Ulster Marketing Surveys

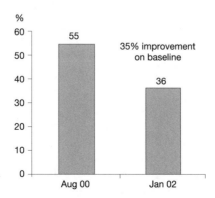

Figure 17a: *Acceptability of driving after having one drink – 17–24 male drinkers, very/fairly acceptable*
Base: All drivers who ever drink alcohol, August 2000: 484/January 2001: 433/January 2002: 443
Source: Ulster Marketing Survey

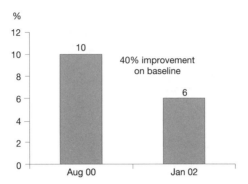

Figure 17b: *Acceptability of driving after having two drinks – 17–24 male drivers, very/fairly acceptable*
Base: All drivers who ever drink alcohol, August 2000: 484/January 2001: 433/January 2002: 443
Source: Ulster Marketing Survey

Improving the social climate

Prior to the launch of 'Shame', drink-driving was considered to be *extremely* shameful by 91% of an all-adult sample representative of the adult population in Northern Ireland, when compared to other shameful behaviour such as sexual abuse, drug dealing and shop lifting. In the 14 months following the launch, the perception of the shamefulness of drink-driving had increased, with 97% of adults believing it to be 'extremely shameful'.

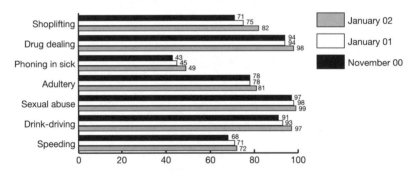

Figure 18: *Extremely shameful, nine or ten on ten-point scale*
Base: All respondents, November 2000: 1114/January 2001: 1116/January 2002: 1123
Source: Ulster Marketing Surveys

Impact on drivers who drink any alcohol

When asked to what extent the campaign made them think about the dangers of driving after one or more drinks, a huge 87% of drivers who ever drink alcohol felt the campaign made them think 'a lot' about the dangers. A further 8% claimed it made them think 'a little' about the dangers. The campaign has impacted a little or a lot on 95% of drivers who ever drink alcohol by making them *think* about the dangers of driving after one or more units of alcohol.

Behaviour change – saving lives

The following results are based on provisional figures for 2001.

Fewer deaths on the roads
In 2001 there was a 13% reduction in *all* road deaths, compared to 2000 (171 in 2000). Specifically, 17–24-year-old male drivers were responsible for 13.5% fewer deaths in 2001 (37 in 2000).

Fewer deaths due to driver alcohol
There were 44% fewer fatalities due to driver/rider alcohol/drugs in 2001, down from 43 in 2000 to 24 in 2001. The economic value of this reduction is £20.691 million sterling.

Crucially, 17–24-year-old male drivers were responsible for 40% fewer alcohol-related fatalities in 2001, down from 10 in 2000 to 6 in 2001.

In the longer term, analysis of five-year fatality and serious injury figures will provide more robust evidence.

CAMPAIGN INFLUENCE

The role of advertising in driving these attitude and behaviour improvements is revealed in the post-campaign research. A large sample influence survey, conducted after the launch, in December 2000, revealed that 75% of respondents are 'very influenced' by 'Shame'. This outscores the influence of the police by 59 percentage points; outscores the influence of TV advertising by 65 percentage points; and outscores politicians, celebrities, journalists and technical experts by 60 percentage points and more. 'Shame' outscores the influence of scientists and victims by more than 50 percentage points and outscores doctors by 44 percentage points. 'Shame' outscores radio, poster and press articles about road safety by more than

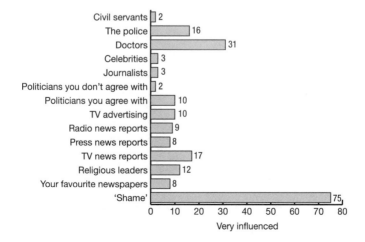

Figure 19: *Level of influence of 'Shame' ad campaign*
Base: December 2000, all respondents 1128
Source: Ulster Marketing Surveys

30 percentage points, and outscores TV reports about road safety by 23 percentage points.

This survey clearly isolates the power of the 'Shame' advertising as opposed to all other methods of communication and influence. The efficacy is in the advertising (see Figure 19).

RESEARCH EVIDENCE

All Attitude Tracking evidence, unless otherwise stated, was independently conducted by Ulster Marketing Surveys Group, now trading as Millward Brown Ulster.

5

Britannia

Keeping Britannia great: a small share of voice needs a big idea

Principal authors: Polly Evelegh and Alan Read, Walsh Trott Chick Smith
Collaborating author: Alan Long

EDITOR'S SUMMARY

It's what you do with what you've got that matters. With just 0.32% advertising share of voice, Britannia Building Society met ambitious marketing objectives, following the launch of a new campaign. Saliency increased from 17% to 29%; consideration leapt from just 4% to 20%, while mortgage advances increased 68% year-on-year, versus market growth of 17.8%. How? The campaign adopted a big idea that was used on every 'piece' of communications. Effective share of voice increased because each piece of communication reinforced the other.

INTRODUCTION

Vast sums of money are spent promoting financial services, a sector which is fragmented, complex and confusing. It is a challenge to make a mark with a large budget; to do so with a small one is a Herculean undertaking.

Our paper concerns Britannia Building Society. Its advertising budget for 2000 was £2,710,000. This had to cut through a total financial category spend of £879,550,000. By developing a campaign with a 'big idea', which was extended through every form of consumer communications, we aim to prove that 0.32% share of voice *can* make a difference.

The 'share of voice' theme may seem to lack imagination. However, it is an ongoing issue for advertisers and agencies, especially during recessional times, with pressure to cut budgets. It warrants further debate.

Please note that we have masked data due to confidentiality.

BACKGROUND

Britannia Building Society set up home in 1856.[1] It was one of a number of organisations established during the industrial revolution by local people to help them buy land and build houses. They existed for the mutual benefit of its members.

Today's building societies continue to be 'mutual'. A building society is not a company, nor is it listed on the stock market, so there are no shareholders requiring dividends. Surplus is returned to the organisation to benefit members, '*often through interest rates which can be higher for savers and lower for borrowers, and through better services*'.[2]

Rather than simply dropping rates, Britannia delivers value through the 'Members' Loyalty Bonus Scheme'. Members of three or more years' standing receive bonus payments.[3]

> 'Britannia's pricing, though broadly competitive, has tended not to be used as the main way to demonstrate mutual status.'
>
> Source: Agency Briefing Document 2000

Demutualisations and the rise of carpetbagging

Regulatory changes led to many building societies rescinding mutuality to become banks. Abbey National was the first to convert, floating on the stock exchange in 1989. Over the next decade, other building societies which demutualised included Cheltenham & Gloucester, National & Provincial, Alliance & Leicester, Woolwich, Halifax, Northern Rock, Bristol & West, Birmingham Midshires and Bradford & Bingley. Members generally received 'windfalls' in the new company.[4]

---

1. Originally the Leek & Moorland Permanent Benefit Building Society but the name was changed to Britannia Building Society in 1975. Source: Britannia website.
2. Source: Building Society Association website.
3. Members of three or more years' standing receive points for a combination of product holding, size of holding and tenure with the society. At year end, a value per point is announced and the annual value paid out to each qualifying member.
4. Source: Building Society Association.

Carpetbagging[5] began in the early 1990s, following the windfalls received by Abbey National's members. People opened accounts in remaining building societies with the intention of receiving a windfall, as cash or shares, should they convert. Carpetbaggers have also used their membership rights to force societies to convert by putting forward resolutions at annual general meetings (AGMs).[6]

Despite attempts to make Britannia convert, it has not. It is committed to mutuality as a way of benefiting its members. But the threat of 'pro-conversion' forces knocks constantly at the door.

THE THREAT TO BRITANNIA

By 1999, Britannia was the No. 2 building society behind Nationwide;[7] impressive for a society with a regional bias rather than national representation. However, Britannia was profoundly concerned about its future.[8]

Market concerns

Tumbling base rates cutting profits

To remain profitable, so benefiting members, Britannia needed to increase mortgage sales dramatically.

Increasing competition

This needed to be done in an increasingly competitive market. Strong competition came from new entrants using traditional and new channels, and consolidation among existing players, offering fantastic rates. The likes of Virgin had entered the market, and Egg had been offering exceptionally good rates that 'overshadowed the rates offered by the mutuals'.

Independent financial advisers (IFAs)

Fifty per cent of mortgages are sold through IFAs. Only 10% of Britannia's business comes through this channel,[9] because Britannia does not pay procurement fees.[10] Britannia had to compete without the benefit of IFA introductions.

---

5. The term *carpetbagger* comes from the American Civil War, when people from the north packed all their belongings into carpetbags and headed south to lay claim to land which wasn't theirs.
6. Source: Building Society Association website.
7. This is No. 2 within building societies, not No. 2 within the total category of mortgage providers which includes banks.
8. Source: Britannia's Marketing Director, Alan Long.
9. Source: Britannia.
10. When an independent financial adviser 'introduces' a borrower to a mortgage provider, it is normal practice for the IFA to charge the mortgage provider a fee.

Britannia's status within the market

Regional sales profile

Britannia's Heartland region springs from Staffordshire.[11] However, even in the Heartland, the likes of Halifax and Nationwide were bigger, better known and had bigger advertising budgets (Table 1).

TABLE 1: COMPETITIVE BRAND AWARENESS AND ANNUAL SPEND
IN THE HEARTLAND (PRIOR TO ACTIVITY)

	Spontaneous brand awareness (%)	Total brand awareness (%)	Total UK advertising spends in 1999 (£m)
Halifax	66	92	14.92
Nationwide	28	89	4.45
Britannia	15	87	1.89

Wave: August 2000, pre-campaign wave (only available pre benchmark)
Source: MMS and Hall & Partners tracking study.[12]

In addition, Britannia was weak in the south. Britannia needed to improve value share in this region to take advantage of the active housing market and higher value mortgages being demanded.

Britannia's customer profile

The customer base was older than the market average.[13] Many were near paying off mortgages; others had small, inactive savings accounts. Britannia needed to acquire new members and to rebalance its customer base. This included attracting first-time buyers with a lifetime's worth of financing ahead of them.

Increasingly old-fashioned image

High-profile mergers and acquisitions, demutualisations and trendy internet banks were revolutionising finances. As a regional, branch-reliant, mutual organisation, Britannia was looking dusty.

'I associate Britannia with years and years ago, one your granny's with. They've never moved on.'

'Research tells us that the society is currently not a well known player. It is seen as a trusted and long-standing brand by those who know it. However, it is perhaps not seen as *contemporary* enough to be a long term or credible player.'

Source: Britannia Agency Briefing Document, 2000

The need to differentiate

To get on to consideration lists Britannia had to differentiate. Otherwise it would be ignored in favour of organisations that had been advertised a lot or were just offering cheap rates, or recommendations from IFAs, friends or family.

---

11. Heartland is defined as South Cheshire, North Staffordshire and East Anglia.
12. Tracking study: Periodic waves/in-home interviews. Base: men and women aged 25 to 50, either moving from rented accommodation to own flat/house, moving from current flat/house or changing their current mortgage. Approximately 300 respondents per wave.
13. Source: Agency Briefing Document, 2000.

Britannia had a theoretically differentiating brand positioning, based on 'Home Building', and this needed to be communicated.[14]

Britannia's mutual status
In 1999 Britannia fought off an aggressively high-profile 'conversion' attempt, making it extremely aware of its vulnerability. The company needed to strengthen its mutual future, much of which depended on communicating the benefits of mutuality and on business success.[15]

NEW MARKETING PLAN INTRODUCED IN 2000

A new marketing plan was introduced with the following objectives:

Marketing objectives

1. Create differentiation via 'Home Building'.

2. Modernise image.

3. Increase brand saliency;[16] measured by results in the Heartland.

4. Increase consideration. At least 10% in the Heartland should put Britannia in their top five consideration list for mortgages.

5. Acquire new customers and rebalance the membership profile. Specifically, attract a core target, identified as good prospects for long-term growth.[17] Within this, first-time buyers were important.

Business objectives

6. Increase value share of gross advances,[18] focusing on:
   • the Heartland
   • South of England
   • while improving value share in all other regions.

7. Strengthen Britannia's mutual status.

---

14. Home Building was developed with Added Value. The idea of anchoring Britannia in the home, rather than just finances, was historically relevant to a mutual building society whose roots lay with helping people set up home. Home Building is about going further than just selling mortgages. It means the society can help with all sorts of financing that go into making a home, with services from helping with house moving, house/home insurance, even home maintenance.

15. It is hard to explain the depth of the mutual philosophy in this day and age. It is only through talking to members of staff at Britannia that it becomes clear that the egalitarian philosophy runs deep through everything Britannia does and stands for.

16. Measured in terms of Hall & Partners' definition: a combination of difference and relevance.

17. For confidentiality reasons we cannot go into detail about the core target, except to say that it included first-time buyers.

18. There are several different stages to getting a mortgage. The first stage is when a person applies for a mortgage. The person is 'credit-checked' and, if creditworthy, they are given an 'approval' to borrow the money. Later, when the purchase of the property is 'completed' the mortgage provider 'advances' the money to the borrower. Gross advances measure all of the 'advanced' money being lent. This can be measured in terms of actual value, or volume of gross advances. Or it can be measured in terms of value share of the market; either of the advances made only by building societies (Building Society Category) or of advances made by all mortgage lenders, including banks (Total Mortgage Category).

THE NEED FOR COMMUNICATIONS

In 2000, Britannia appointed Walsh Trott Chick Smith (WTCS) to develop an advertising campaign that would *help* meet objectives. An advertising campaign had run in 1997 based on sharing. While effective, it was felt that the new financial context, the hard-hitting objectives and the new but as yet theoretical brand positioning about the home, required new communications. WTCS was to work hand in hand with MGOMD.[19] Later, WTCS recommended that Joshua should execute below-the-line activity.

THE COMMUNICATIONS CHALLENGE: UNDERSTANDING THE PROBLEM LEADS TO AN EFFECTIVE SOLUTION

The biggest problem was the small advertising budget, equating to a tiny share of voice (SOV). In 1999, Britannia's annual advertising SOV within the Total Financial Category (all financial products) was just 0.27%. It is important to consider the SOV within the Total Financial Category because of the sheer weight of financial messages, above which Britannia needed to be heard. Assuming similar category spends in 2000, Britannia's SOV would remain low. SOV did remain low at 0.32%. While adspend increased to £4.22m in 2001, share of voice was just 0.50%.

Annual SOV within the Mortgage Category (advertising of *just* mortgages) was no more encouraging (Table 2).

TABLE 2: ADVERTISING SPEND AND SHARE OF VOICE 1999 TO 2001

	1999	2000	2001
Total Financial Category (£m)	693.99	879.55	845.53
Mortgage Category (£m)	54.68	85.13	60.65
Britannia adspend (£m)	1.89	2.71	4.22
Britannia SOV of Total Financial Category (%)	0.27	0.32	0.50
Britannia SOV of Mortgage Category (%)	3.46	3.18	6.96

Source: MMS/MGOMD

In these circumstances, communications had to have impact and stand out. Otherwise Britannia would be wasting its money. Instead of a 'pure' advertising campaign, WTCS recommended a through-the-line campaign. A consistent message and look should be presented everywhere a customer came into contact with Britannia. Impact is increased because each 'piece' of communications would reinforce another, causing a multiplier effect. This could be achieved at minimum additional cost to the annual direct marketing and point-of-sale budgets, beyond restyling. An integrated campaign needed a transferable 'big idea'. 'Home Building' should be central to the idea.

---

19. Manning Gottlieb OMD (formerly MGM) had been Britannia's media agency since 1997.

'Home Building' was great in theory but how could it be brought to life, avoiding conventional, undifferentiated, images of domesticity? Qualitative research among the target *and* staff informed the creative idea:[20]

- A home was not a building made of bricks and mortar.
- Products themselves made sense of 'Home Building'. Products needed to be featured in every 'piece' of communication. The conventional approach of using TV to communicate only a conceptual brand message should be avoided.
- It should be clear that Britannia was there to forge a long-term relationship beyond just selling mortgages.

Regarding modernising Britannia, WTCS observed that 'old-fashioned' building society values such as 'caring' and 'helpful' never went out of date. Furthermore, as these values supported 'mutuality', it was about presenting caring and helpful values in a modern, original way. Stereotypical depictions of modernity should be avoided.

Presenting caring and helpful values would make Britannia seem approachable, so side-stepping IFAs.

To help generate enquiries, direct response advertising was recommended. Specific direct response objectives were introduced for 2001: to generate 17,000 responses.

CREATIVE SOLUTION: ANIMAL HOMES

By using animals' homes, the creative idea was true to the meaning of homes: a place that isn't about bricks and mortar.

The animated white-on-black style was inspired by chalk on school blackboards. This gave the idea a caring, helpful and approachable feel in a differentiated way. The style was also easily transferable.

Products were communicated in every execution, from TV advertising right through to in-store materials.

The line, 'In a word, your home for life', summed up Britannia's long-term approach to helping make homes.

FURTHER RESEARCH CONFIRMED THE APPROACH

Further qualitative research conducted among the target and staff confirmed the direction.[21] A Millward Brown Link Test gave the final thumbs up.

---

20. Qualitative research conducted by WTCS among target audience and staff members. The latter involved moderating 'groups' in branches.
21. Source: WTCS qualitative research 2000.

MEDIA STRATEGY

Brand-building and regional requirements led to the use of TV advertising. TV advertising broke in September 2000 with a heavyweight in the Heartland,[22] using ITV, C4, C5 and satellite. The rest of the country received a lower exposure through C4, C5 and satellite. In February 2001, heavierweight activity rolled out to the South,[23] while continuing use of national C4, C5 and satellite. Two further TV bursts occurred in the Heartland and the South later in 2001, again with C4, C5 and satellite running nationally. Two longer length commercials aired alongside a shorter 10-second call-to-action commercial.

Press ran continuously from September 2000 and focused on brand-cum-product promotion. For 2001, MGOMD devised a two-level strategy with product information 'strip' ads alongside small 'rate led' press ads and a call to action. A high number of small '10 × 2' ads allowed cost-effective responses.

Media planning required translating Britannia's target segments and regional needs through TGI and Acorn to arrive at precision media choice (see Figure 1).

	2000				2001									
	Sept	Oct	Nov	Dec	Jan	Feb	Mar	Apr	May	Jun	Jul	Aug	Sept	Oct
Total £	1.42	0.58	0.01	0.01	0.01	0.86	0.49	0.18	0.11	0.74	0.56	0.05	0.43	0.73
TV	1.19	0.47	0	0	0	0.75	0.36	0	0	0.59	0.44	0	0.31	0.64
Region	Heartland + C4, C5 and satellite					Heartland and South + C4, C5 and satellite				Heartland and South + C4, C5 and satellite			Heartland and South + C4, C5 and satellite	
Press	0.21	0.10	0.01	0.01	0.01	0.11	0.13	0.18	0.11	0.14	0.12	0.05	0.12	0.08

Figure 1: *Summary main media plan: spend, region, medium*
Source: MMS (rounded to two decimal points)
Heartland: Central, Granada, Anglia South
South: Meridian, HTV

Tactical

Small tactical poster and radio campaigns ran in the Heartland before the springtime AGMs.

The campaign broke (see Figures 2 to 8).

---

22. Heartland TV regions: Central, Granada and Anglia South.
23. South TV regions: mainly Meridian but including HTV.

MVO: When you get a flexible
mortgage with us

you get a discount upfront

And you'll get two more discounts at
set dates

which could help you pay off your
mortgage quicker.

And if something unexpected happens,

we'll even let you take a payment
holiday

Britannia

In a word, your home for life

Figure 2: *Britannia 30-second TV – Spider/Flexible Mortgage*

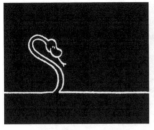  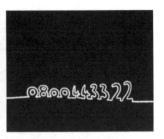

MVO: If you'd like Britannia to tell you more   call free on   0800 44 33 22

Figure 3: *Britannia 10-second response TV – Snake*

Figure 4: *Britannia launch press*

Figure 5: *Britannia press – strip ads*

Figure 6: *Britannia press – small space*

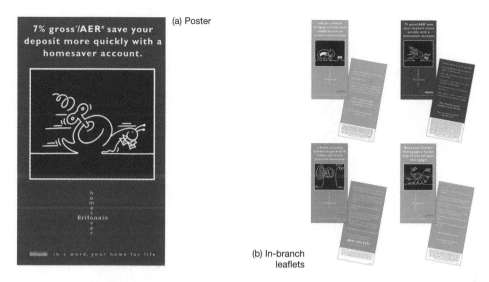

(a) Poster

(b) In-branch
leaflets

Figure 7: *Britannia in-branch materials*

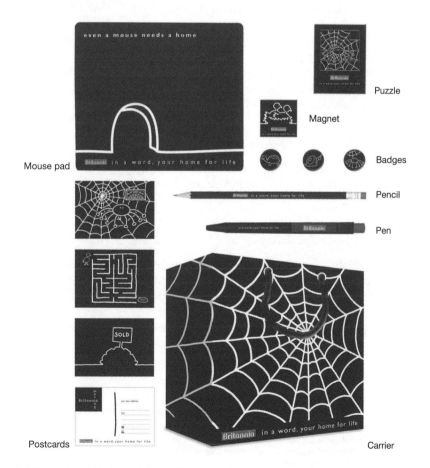

Figure 8: *Britannia brand identity pack (for staff)*

WHAT HAPPENED?[24]

Within one year there were remarkable improvements across all objectives:

- Britannia became more differentiated; 50% agreed with 'stands out as different from other financial providers'.
- Perceptions of Britannia as 'caring', 'helpful' and 'approachable' improved.
- 'Home Building' took hold.
- Saliency and consideration built dramatically.
- New customers, especially first-time buyers, flowed through Britannia's doors.
- Mortgage advances went through the roof with a 68% increase in value of gross advances compared to the previous year. This was in the context of a growth in the Total Mortgage Category (all providers) of 17.8% and of only 7.2% in the Building Society Category (only building society providers).
- By early 2002 'mutuality' was on firmer ground.

PROVING THE CONTRIBUTION OF THE CAMPAIGN

Communications were intended to affect every level of the marketing plan and to do so in a causal way. By generating impact and differentiation, by improving image, and so improving saliency and consideration, communications could attract customers, leading to better performance and the strengthening of mutuality. Communications affected every level.

Britannia differentiated

That the campaign successfully differentiated Britannia from other financial providers is evident from the 'difference' score; a huge increase by the end of the first year of the campaign, from just 29% to 50% (Figure 9).[25]

Image improved as intended and Home Building started to build

Significant image shifts were recorded in the post-waves of tracking across key prompted image dimensions. Approachability was measured in terms of 'Someone whose advice I respect' and 'Easy to do business with'. The notion of 'home' began to seed.

The timing of shifts and the absence of other factors to explain them is evidence of an effect driven by the campaign (Figure 10).

---

24. In the main, analysis of 'what happened' goes up to a year from the start of the campaign, depending on available data. Of course 11th September 2001 was also taken into consideration.
25. All tracking results are represented within the Heartland only. Since tracking began only in the Heartland we have used it as a consistent measure of performance over time. Tracking was introduced outside the Heartland in 2001.

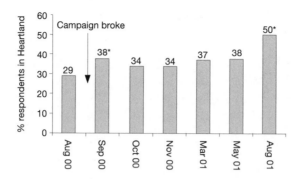

Figure 9: *Difference*
Base: All respondents in the Heartland
Definition: % agree with 'they really stand out as different'
*Statistically significant shift (at 95% level) from previous period
Source: Hall & Partners tracking study

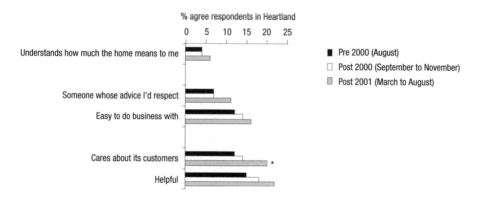

Figure 10: *Positive shifts in Britannia's image*
Base: All respondents in the Heartland
Definition: Pre 2000: single wave prior to the start of the new campaign (August). Post 2000: average post-launch 2000 waves (September to November). Post 2001: average post-launch 2001 waves (March to August)
*Statistically significant shift (at 95% level) from previous period
Source: Hall & Partners tracking study

*Brand saliency and consideration positively shot up
when the campaign started in September 2000*

Salience responded immediately to the start of the campaign. The levels recorded since then have been consistently higher than before the campaign (Figure 11).

Mortgage consideration reinforces the pattern for salience. Consideration leapt from 4% to 20%, exceeding the target by 100%, and remained above pre-campaign levels (Figure 12).

Before the campaign, one person in 25 would put Britannia on their shortlist of five mortgage providers. After the first month of the campaign one in five would do so.

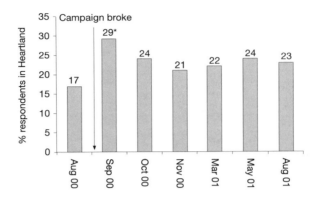

Figure 11: *Salience*
Base: All respondents in the Heartland
Definition: % agreeing with either of the statements, 'Really stands out as different from other financial providers and has a got a lot going for it right now' or 'It stands out as different from other financial providers with something going for it right now'
*Statistically significant (at 95% level) change on previous period
Source: Hall & Partners tracking study

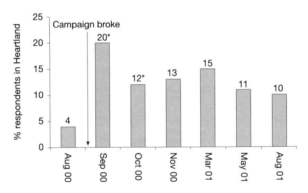

Figure 12: *Consideration*
Base: All respondents in the Heartland
Definition: % who put Britannia in their top five shortlist for mortgages
*Statistically significant (at 95% level) change on previous period
Source: Hall & Partners tracking study

Strong customer acquisition and rebalancing

Given the longevity of the mortgage relationship and the years of trading, the annual growth in the customer base was pleasing, at 0.7% in 2000 to 2001.

Segmentation of new customers demonstrates a growth rate four times faster among the key customer groups than among all others. This is testimony to focused targeting (Figure 13).

Comparing customer types among mortgage applicants in two six-month periods immediately before and after the campaign began shows that the uplift was almost solely attributable to new customers and first-time buyers (Figure 14). Coinciding with the campaign, we hypothesise that it successfully expanded and rebalanced Britannia's customer base.

Figure 13: *Growth in customer segments, 2000 to 2001*
Data: Customer segment numbers
Region: National
Time periods: January to December 2000 compared with January to December 2001
Source: Britannia

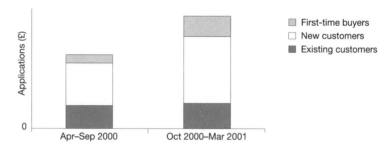

Figure 14: *Britannia customer profile: value of mortgage applications*
Data: Mortgage applications value six months before/after start of campaign
Region: National
Source: Britannia

Massive uplift of gross advances in line with the campaign

Evidence of the campaign's contribution lies in timing of uplifts in value share of gross advances. Moving annual total (removing seasonal effects) value share grew dramatically following the campaign (Figures 15 and 16).

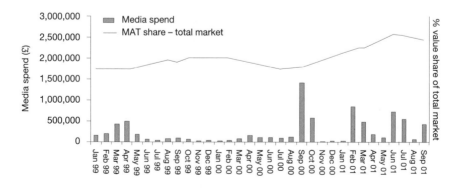

Figure 15: *Britannia value share of total market gross advances and media expenditure*
Region: National
Source: Britannia, CACI National Mortgage Database, MMS

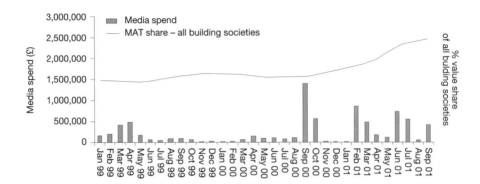

Figure 16: *Britannia's share of all building society gross advances and media expenditure*
Region: National
Source: Britannia/BSA/MMS

Monthly analysis provides further evidence of the relationship between the campaign and the increase in Britannia's value share, particularly when a time lag in the mortgage negotiation period is considered (approximately two months between application and advance) (Figures 17 and 18).

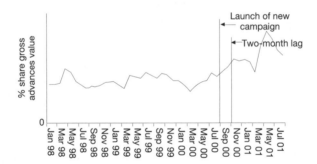

Figure 17: *Monthly Britannia share of gross advances within the building society market*
Region: National
Source: Britannia/BSA

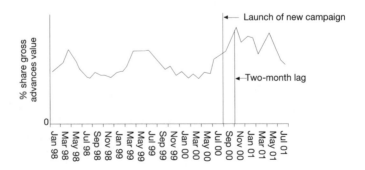

Figure 18: *Monthly Britannia share of gross advances within the total market*
Region: National
Source: Britannia, CACI National Mortgage Database

That value share increased in both the Building Society Category and the Total Mortgage Category refutes that Britannia was simply mopping up business as a result of demutualisation of other building societies.

Regional weights

The step change in value share was greater in the Heartland and South where there was heavierweight advertising and so greater depth to the campaign (Figure 19).

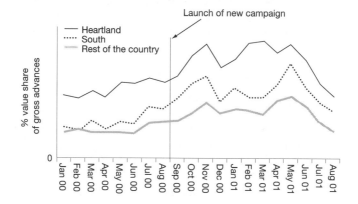

Figure 19: *Britannia value share of gross advances – total UK mortgage market by region*
CACI regions: Heartland = Midlands + North West + Anglia; South = South East + Wales; rest of country = all others
Note: CACI is based on standard regions so some approximation is involved when replicating TV regions
Source: Britannia Gross Advances, CACI National Mortgage Market Database

Examining share rather than absolute value of advances removed seasonal effect and market trend. To illustrate Britannia's relative rate of growth, Figure 20 shows an index of gross advances against all building societies. Britannia grew faster in line with the timing of the campaign.

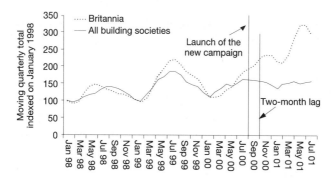

Figure 20: *Moving quarterly value of gross advances in building society category*
Region: National
Source: Britannia, BSA

Did the campaign help strengthen the mutual status?

An *unprecedented* five-to-one vote in favour of continuing mutuality, at the 2002 AGM, proves strengthened mutuality.

Britannia stated that the campaign contributed to the pro-mutuality vote by making members more 'involved' with the society.

We go further to prove the campaign's effect on strengthening mutuality.

Before 2002's AGM a tactical campaign ran in the Heartland, reminding members to vote at the AGM. Posters and radio referred to Britannia's recent business successes with the overall campaign line, 'Vote to Keep Britannia Great'. This message was possible only with improved performance in 2000 and 2001, which we have shown relates to the campaign as a whole. So ultimately the total campaign helped performance, which helped secure Britannia's future mutuality.

Summary

Various factors prove the campaign effect on all of Britannia's objectives. The majority involve the timing of the campaign from the massive leaps in saliency and consideration, through to advanced growth. Shifts in image perception, which can have come only from the campaign, support our assertion.

PROVING THE CONTRIBUTION MADE BY ADVERTISING

We have demonstrated a campaign effect. We will now prove advertising's contribution via:

1. Qualitative evidence that the advertising worked as intended.
2. Quantitative evidence that the advertising had high impact and differentiation.
3. Comparing perceptions, saliency and consideration between advertising recognisers and non-recognisers.
4. Regional comparisons.
5. Reviewing 'traffic' to Britannia against advertising activity.

Qualitative evidence that the advertising worked as intended

Qualitative research proved advertising had impact, modernised Britannia, presented a caring, helpful image and communicated the brand positioning:

'Distinctive and eye-catching.'

'It looks like its trying to be contemporary and probably succeeding.'

'Can help you with everything to do with buying and maintaining a house.'

'They are a friend there to help you with all your needs and advice to make that dream home come true.'

'That line, Home for Life, makes you think they won't just take your money and run. They are with you for a long time and have your interests at heart.'

'It was a subtle indication of the services offered, and nothing like those dreadful singing employee ads, used by a competitor.'

Sources: Qualitative research conducted as part of Millward Brown Link Test in 2000 and further post-campaign qualitative research 2002

Quantitative evidence of impact

Advertising was perceived as very different. Figure 21 shows how different the advertising was against a competitor's financial advertising.

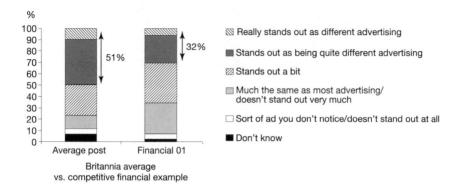

Figure 21: *Britannia (on the left) vs. competitive financial advertising (on the right)*
Base: Campaign Recognisers in the Heartland
Source: Hall & Partners tracking study

Advertising positively affected perceived 'difference', image, saliency and consideration

Advertising recognisers were more likely to perceive Britannia as different, caring, helpful and approachable (where approachability is measured in terms of: 'easy to do business with' and 'someone whose advice I respect') (Figures 22, 23, 24, 25 and 26).[26]

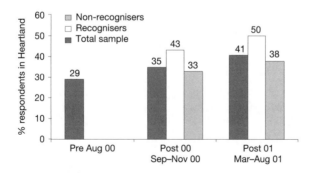

Figure 22: *Britannia: difference*
Base: All respondents in the Heartland – all waves combined for September to November 2000 and February/March to August 2001
Note: Recognisers significantly higher (at 95% level) than non-recognisers in post 2000
Source: Hall & Partners tracking study

---

26. Of course, this runs up against the Rosser Reeves theory whereby campaign recognition could be a result of being a member of Britannia rather than the other way round. However, given that there were minimal Britannia members included in the tracking study this is unlikely.

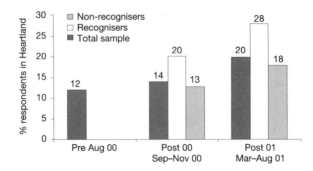

Figure 23: *They care about their customers*
Base: All respondents in the Heartland
Note: Recognisers significantly higher (at 95% level) than non-recognisers for both post waves
Source: Hall & Partners tracking study

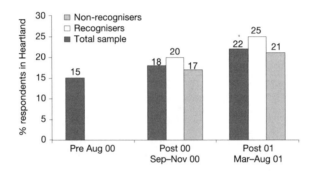

Figure 24: *Helpful*
Base: All respondents in the Heartland
Source: Hall & Partners tracking study

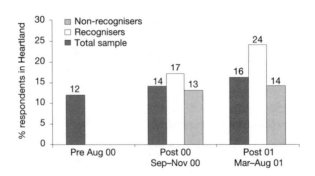

Figure 25: *Easy to do business with*
Base: All respondents in the Heartland
Note: Recognisers significantly higher (at 95% level) than non-recognisers post 2001 wave
Source: Hall & Partners tracking study

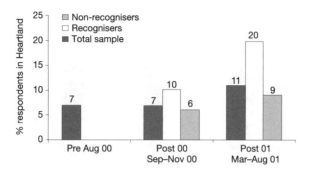

Figure 26: *Someone whose advice I'd respect*
Base: All respondents in the Heartland
Note: Recognisers significantly higher (at 95% level) than non-recognisers post 2001 wave
Source: Hall & Partners tracking study

Advertising recognition promoted agreement with 'Britannia understands how much my home means to me' (Figure 27). The delay is not surprising as 'brand meanings' take time to develop.

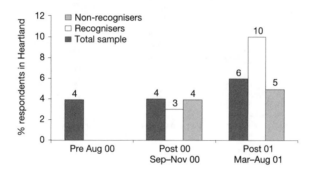

Figure 27: *Understands how much my home means to me*
Region: Heartland
Base: All respondents
Source: Hall & Partners tracking study

Advertising recognition correlates with stronger brand saliency and mortgage consideration (Figures 28 and 29).

While mortgage consideration fell during the second post wave, it remained considerably higher than before the advertising broke.

We have attempted to compare growth in brand salience and mortgage consideration against the competition. Halifax was a major spender in this period and by matching our tracking periods as closely as possible to their burst in early 2001, we have calculated relative performance.

With significantly greater share of voice, Halifax's brand saliency increased by only slightly more than Britannia. Expressing this as a ratio shows that Halifax was

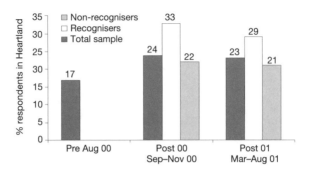

Figure 28: *Britannia: salience*
Base: All respondents in the Heartland
Note: Recognisers significantly higher (at 95% level) than non-recognisers both post waves
Source: Hall & Partners tracking study

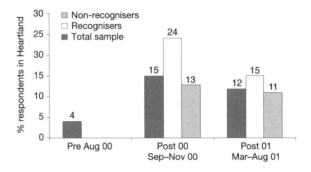

Figure 29: *Mortgage consideration (top five)*
Base: All respondents in the Heartland
Note: Recognisers significantly higher (at 95% level) than non-recognisers in post 2000 wave
Source: Hall & Partners tracking study

less than half as efficient at converting share of voice to saliency (Tables 3 and 4). In terms of mortgage consideration, there was a decline in Halifax over this period.

TABLE 3: THE RATIO OF BRAND SALIENCY TO SHARE OF VOICE WITHIN THE MORTGAGE CATEGORY

	% SOV	Uplift	Ratio	Index
Britannia	15.1 (September 2000)	+12% (August to September 2000)	0.79	100
Halifax	42.8 (January to April 2001)	+14% (November 2000 to May 2001)	0.33	42

Base: All respondents in the Heartland
Source: Hall & Partners tracking study and MMS data

TABLE 4: THE RATIO OF CONSIDERATION TO SHARE OF VOICE WITHIN THE MORTGAGE CATEGORY

	% SOV	Uplift	Ratio	Index
Britannia	15.1 (September 2000)	+16% (August to September 2000)	1.06	100
Halifax	42.8 (January to April 2001)	−4% (November 2000 to May 2001)	−0.09	−84

Base: All respondents in Heartland
Definition: % who put the organisation in their top five list for mortgages
Source: Hall & Partners tracking study and MMS data

Regional comparisons

We cannot make a true comparison of performance in advertised regions versus non-advertised regions because advertising also ran nationally on Channel 5, Channel 4 and Satellite TV. However, we can compare Britannia's advertising effect in different regions by looking at share of voice.

The point of our paper is to look at the success of Britannia's campaign relative to a noisy market with huge spending competitors. Examining 'internal' performance does not refute the overall argument.

Regionally, a higher share of voice correlates with stronger growth, in terms of growth in value and volume share of gross advances (Figures 30 and 31).[27] This proves that advertising contributed positively to growth.

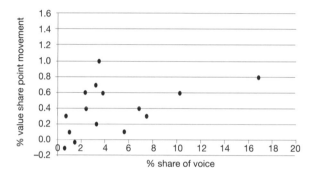

Figure 30: *Regional share of voice and value share point movements*
Note: It was necessary to relate share of voice by TV region to share by standard region. Share of voice in a particular region will be higher than total SOV
Source: Britannia, CACI, MMS

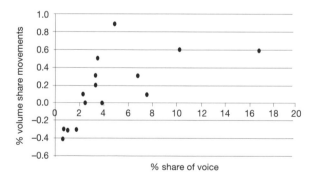

Figure 31: *Regional share of voice and volume movements*
Note: It was necessary to relate share of voice by TV region to share by standard region
Source: Britannia, CACI, MMS

---

27. Percentage share point movements show the change in Britannia's share of total market gross advances in the three months following an advertised period compared with the three months immediately before it. Therefore each point represents a period of advertising in a given area, which explains why there are more 'points' than regions. Some small negative share movements occur if the region experienced particularly strong growth in a previous burst. Figures 30 and 31 plot regional share movements (on the y axis) against Britannia's share of voice (on the x axis). They show a positive correlation from which we conclude that a higher share of voice results in a higher share movement.

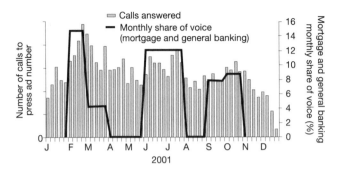

Figure 32: *Mortgage direct calls answered and monthly share of voice (advertised regions)*
Source: Britannia

Advertising drives traffic to Britannia

Advertising activity correlates with calls made to Britannia. Figure 32 shows calls against SOV in advertised regions.

Direct response advertising was particularly effective at driving enquires. All media were effective at doing so (Table 5).

TABLE 5: RESPONSE SUMMARY 2001

Medium	% share of spend	% share of responses	Index responses over spend
TV	67	61	91
Interactive TV	3	5	166
National press	27	26	96
Magazines	1	2	200
Yellow Pages	2	6	300

Target responses: 17,000; actual responses: 22,784; Actual vs. original target: 134%
Source: Britannia, MGOMD

Increased traffic to the website correlates with advertising activity (Figure 33).

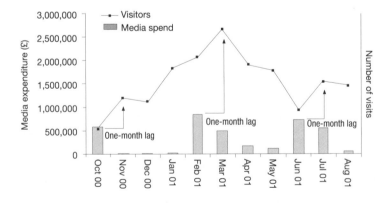

Figure 33: *Britannia website visitors and media expenditure*
Data: Visits to Britannia website (data available from October 2000)
Source: Britannia, MMS

Summary

There is no doubt that advertising had a significant impact on Britannia meeting its marketing objectives. Every indicator at our disposal proves this.

ASSESSING THE CONTRIBUTION MADE BY OTHER COMMUNICATIONS IN THE MIX

Integrating the campaign created a multiplier effect. The synergistic scope of the campaign meant what little advertising money there was would be magnified in other paid-for communications. Spend didn't increase on direct marketing or point of sale (Table 6), except for restyling. Yet effectiveness of these 'tools' improved.

TABLE 6: DIRECT MARKETING SPEND
(POS SPENDS UNAVAILABLE AT TIME OF WRITING)

Year	Spend (£000)
1997	642
1998	564
1999	418
2000	559
2001	571

Source: Britannia

Direct marketing

Britannia stated, '*If the whole campaign has been successful it is likely, but not proven, that direct marketing would have benefited.*' We have proven the campaign successful. Unfortunately data do not exist to compare the overall percentage response rates before and after the campaign.

Another source indicates that the campaign improved response levels. Thirty per cent response levels regarding direct mail prior to the 2002 AGM was very high. Britannia has partially attributed this to the fact that the overall campaign raised members' involvement with the society.

In-store materials and the customer

Qualitative research confirmed that in-store materials worked to extend the advertising campaign to the high street. On showing advertising in research groups, we heard:

'I remember now. Yes, I've seen that in the branch.'

'I've seen their posters in the window. *It's all over the place actually.*'

Source: WTCS creative development qualitative research, 2002

The fact is that Britannia was not all 'over the place', but it felt as though it was to this respondent. By taking the idea through the line, the campaign had a much bigger impact but at no extra cost.

Staff effects

Staff response was fantastic. From feeling that the branches were old-fashioned and untidy, the new campaign instilled a renewed sense of professionalism, modernity and pride. Furthermore, the campaign helped launch the new brand positioning to staff, ultimately making it easier to explain and sell to customers.

ELIMINATING OTHER FACTORS

We have proved that the campaign was effective at meeting Britannia's objectives. Here, we eliminate other factors that could have been responsible for both the ultimate business performance and strengthening of mutuality.

1. *The strengthening of mutuality*: The five-to-one pro-mutuality vote cannot have been driven by anything else except improvements in involvement with the brand, and performance of the society, which have been affected by the campaign as a whole.
2. *AGM activity*: Tactical campaigns in the Heartland in springtime, encouraging members to vote could not have affected the dramatic uplift in gross advances immediately following the launch of the campaign in September 2000.
3. *Performance was not driven by market growth*: Growth has been measured in terms of value share, removing the effect of market growth. Britannia grew faster than the market.
4. *Performance was not driven by carpetbaggers*: Carpetbaggers are more likely to open savings accounts, not take out mortgages.
5. *Performance was not driven by an increase in outlets*: There was no increase in branches during 2000, so this cannot account for the uplift post September 2000.[28]
6. *Performance was not attributable to a decrease in competitive outlets*. There were no decreases.
7. *Britannia website*: Traffic to the site 'was minimal' until the campaign began.
8. *Online advertising*: There was no online advertising for mortgages until 2002.

WHAT ABOUT RATES AND PRODUCTS?

Low rates are a great consumer motivator in this market – enormous savings can be made over the lifetime of a mortgage. But, quite obviously, unless consumers are made aware of a competitive rate or product they can hardly include it in their decision-making.

Without direct communication a mortgage provider is at the mercy of IFAs, friends, family and the financial pages. The Animal Homes campaign promoted Britannia's products. We can demonstrate that Britannia's rates and products were not solely responsible for the uplifts:

- Advertising recognisers were more likely to consider Britannia than were non-recognisers.

---

28. In 2001 a branch share scheme started with Yorkshire branches. This was after the uplifts in late 2000. The 'shared' branches did not enable opening of new accounts, only to pay in and take out money.

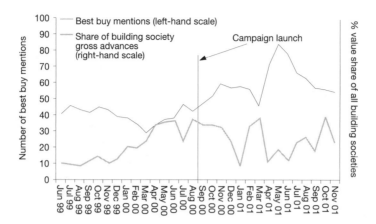

Figure 34: *Britannia best buy mentions vs. share*
Source: Britannia, BSA

- Correlation between share of voice and growth means uplifts were not due solely to rates or products.
- Mortgage providers appear in newspapers' best buy tables if they have a product that is deemed worthy. Britannia features regularly in best buy tables.

Best buys *do* affect growth, but it is unlikely that best buy tables were solely responsible for the huge uplift from September 2000. Figure 34 shows the total number of mentions in which Britannia appeared in a best buy table each month against Britannia's share of all building society gross advances.

Best buy appearances increased during the course of 2000. Share corresponded. By 2001, appearances in best buy tables fell back. Despite this, share continued its upward trend. Thus advertising augmented best buy appearances.

- We have looked at Britannia's *relative* competitiveness by comparing the standard variable rate against two key competitors. Figure 35 shows Britannia offering a comparable rate at the beginning of the campaign. In a period of falling base rates there is no evidence to suggest that Britannia was gaining a competitive advantage by reducing its rate faster than the competition.

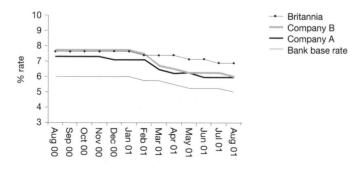

Figure 35: *Interest rates: standard variable rate for Britannia and two key competitors*
Source: Britannia

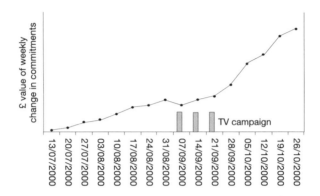

Figure 36: *Launch of the Flexible Mortgage*
Source: Britannia

- There is one product that needs special consideration. Britannia launched its Flexible Mortgage shortly before the campaign. Take-up was strong. But when the campaign broke, growth accelerated. This product was communicated in TV advertising at the time of launch. Figure 36 compares growth rates before and after the product was advertised.

ECONOMETRIC MODELLING

To understand further the relationship between products and interest rates we used econometrics. Factors contributing to Britannia's share were statistically calculated using econometric modelling. From an extensive list of potential influences we identified those which had an effect on share:

- External factors (e.g. economic indicators, consumer confidence, competitive advertising expenditure, seasonality).
- Britannia's headline rates (the APR quoted on advertising) vs. key competitors.
- The launch of new products and distribution channels.

Finally the contribution of advertising was calculated as:

- TV spend decayed by 60% per month.
- Press spend as a share of total mortgage press spend decayed by 40% per month.

The resulting model successfully explained 87% of historical variance in share with an especially good fit in the later periods. This was judged to be a significant achievement in our understanding of the impact of advertising in the total mix. Figure 37 (with scales removed for confidentiality reasons) clearly demonstrates that advertising contributed to value share alongside rates and products, proving that communications did contribute to Britannia meeting its objectives.

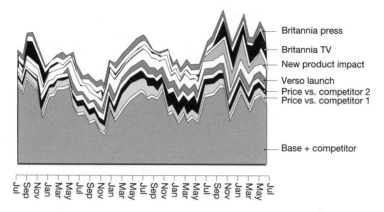

Figure 37: *Britannia market share decomposition by econometric model*
Source: Britannia, CACI Mortgage Market database, MGOMD

THE FINANCIAL CONTRIBUTION OF ADVERTISING

The model allowed us to assess the financial contribution of advertising to share and therefore to the incremental gross advances yielded by advertising.

Commercial sensitivity prevents us from including further detailed evidence here. However, even using reported spends (generally well above the actual cost to client) it was calculated that £1 spent on advertising resulted in £114 of additional gross mortgage advances. The net product value over the lifetime of these mortgages alone (and ignoring any halo effect on other Britannia products) represents a 'considerable' return on investment for Britannia. Therefore, advertising paid for itself several times over.

CONCLUSIONS

This paper demonstrates how a tiny share of voice can be used to maximum effect in a category traditionally associated with huge spending campaigns.

The core of the approach was to understand Britannia's objectives and to design a communications solution wedded to meeting those objectives.

Clearly, impact within a cluttered market is essential, or else Britannia would be wasting its money. A campaign which is adaptable to every point of contact with the consumer results in a multiplier effect on advertising spend alone. The whole can be much greater than the sum of its parts. Embedded within the idea were all the elements required to meet Britannia's objectives from the essential 'Home Building' brand meaning through to 'mutual' values presented in a modern way.

We have proved that the approach worked at every step, in a causal fashion, leading the target through to taking out a mortgage with Britannia and strengthening Britannia's mutual future.

Britannia was delighted with the results of the campaign.

6

BT Cellnet

How broadcast sponsorship of Big Brother 2 became a business partnership and consumer brand experience

Principal authors: Adele Gritten and Tony Regan, PHD Media
Collaborating authors: Laurence Munday, Simon George and Jonathan Fowles

EDITOR'S SUMMARY

BT Cellnet's £4m sponsorship of *Big Brother 2* communicated key brand messages and made the brand more familiar and relevant to the key 16–24-year-old audience. But it was a business partnership that went beyond broadcast sponsorship – and the brand's involvement made a TV show into a 24/7 experience that consumers could participate in via their mobile phones. This generated incremental revenue for BT Cellnet of £880,000, as well as over £10m media value from TV, and incalculable PR value from BT Cellnet-branded editorial.

INTRODUCTION

BT Cellnet's sponsorship of *Big Brother 2* was conceived and developed as a business partnership, not simply a broadcast sponsorship. As well as featuring in sponsorship idents around the programme broadcasts and website, BT Cellnet provided the mobile telecomms infrastructure that brought an extra dimension to the second series by making it into a 24/7 fully mobile interactive experience.

As a result, the activity became an exercise in brand participation, not just communication – with the benefit that key brand messages were communicated about text services and new internet applications. BT Cellnet's involvement in the programme became well-known among consumers, particularly the 16–34-year-old audience that was key to the brand. They saw the sponsorship as relevant, appropriate, well-executed and enjoyable.

Consumer interaction with the programme via BT Cellnet mobile applications resulted in incremental revenue of £880,000, in addition to calculations of a media value in excess of £10m – all for a total investment of around £4m.

We believe this case study provides important learning and ample encouragement for brand owners seeking to develop new ways to engage with consumers and overcome the limitations of a changed media landscape where traditional spot advertising may not have the power it once did.

It was an achievement that was a collective effort, as is increasingly typical in a more complex marketing communications environment. PHD Media (PHD) itself is responsible for BT Cellnet's media strategy and planning, and Drum PHD, the UK's largest broadcast sponsorship specialist, worked with Channel 4 and with Endemol UK, creators of Big Brother, to put this partnership together. Many other agencies were involved in marketing activity built around the sponsorship – as well as many parts of BT Cellnet itself.

Sponsorship of *Big Brother 2* has been the foundation of a longer-term and broader relationship between BT Cellnet and Channel 4, the first example of which will be collaborating on *Big Brother 3* in 2002, this time featuring O_2, BT Cellnet's new brand name.

BT CELLNET AND THE MOBILE PHONE MARKET

Tougher competition

The mobile phone network market had been experiencing strong growth through the 1990s. In consumer perception, the mobile phone had changed from a businessman's aspirational accessory in the late '80s to become, ten years later, a practical and everyday item owned by two-thirds of the population – male and female, young and old. Innovations such as 'pay as you go' had boosted penetration, particularly among younger audiences. By 2001 growth opportunities were less likely to come from penetration increases – most people who were going to get a mobile already had one (see Table 1).

The mobile phone industry was now turning its attention to stimulating growth by increasing 'average revenue per user' (ARPU). This meant attracting

TABLE 1: MARKET GROWTH SLOWING

	1990	1991	1992	1993	1994	1995	1996	1997	1998	1999	2000	2001
Connections (000)	1140	1225	1397	2002	3060	5410	6810	8264	13,001	23,938	40,066	49,000
% year-on-year	–	+7.5	+14.0	+43.3	+52.8	+76.8	+25.9	+21.4	+57.3	+84.1	+67.4	+22.3

Source: Mintel

subscriptions to added value services such as internet-based applications and text services. While SMS (texting) had begun to take off in popularity, consumers had been disappointed about some technological advances (e.g. WAP-based services), and they were in a mood to judge for themselves the potential benefits of new services.

In a rapidly maturing market, the other focus for growth had to be market share gains. Brand switching had always been inhibited by two key factors – the prevalence of service contracts that locked people in, and the lack of number 'portability' which meant that people changing to a different network provider would usually have to face the inconvenience of losing their existing phone number. New regulations in October 2001 saw the four major network providers agreeing to allow consumers to switch networks and still keep their existing number. The market share battle was set to begin.

The challenge for BT Cellnet

In 2001, BT Cellnet was finding these market conditions challenging, and faced tough competition from market leader Vodafone and fastest-growing competitor Orange. In the third quarter (Q3) of 2001, the company relinquished second place in the market, after becoming the first UK network to report a reduction in subscribers in the three months to June 2001, as is shown in Figure 1 (*Marketing*, 19 July 2001).

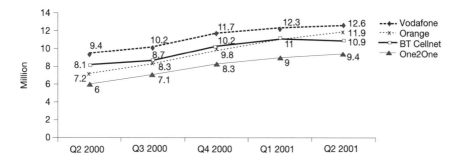

Figure 1: *Subscriber numbers Q2 2000–Q2 2001*
Source: *Marketing*, 19 July 2001

BT Cellnet's brand was, in contrast to its competitors, relatively weak among the young consumers who would offer the best growth opportunities. Overall market penetration among the youngest segment of 15–24-year-olds was at 80%, and the broader 15–34-year-old audience was the one most likely to be motivated by the text-based services, internet applications and technology advances that could drive ARPU. However, BT Cellnet's particular strengths were among the over-64s and among ABs.

Furthermore, the brand was under increasing pressure given heavy advertising investment from competitors. One2One, in particular, had been advertising heavily in efforts to attract younger consumers, and had achieved the strongest share of all the networks among the key 15–24-year-old segment (Table 2).

TABLE 2: BIG INCREASES IN COMPETITOR ADSPEND REDUCED
BT CELLNET'S SHARE OF VOICE (£000)

	1996	1997	1998	1999	2000
Vodafone	16,697	11,016	19,901	25,775	46,416
One2One	13,834	24,215	38,835	46,662	33,638
Orange	18,806	18,660	27,478	26,154	26,016
BT Cellnet	12,666	16,895	25,980	29,412	15,881
Virgin	–	–	–	4,088	15,475
Others	3,210	940	2,368	9,544	11,456

Source: MMS/Mintel

Together the four main networks accounted for almost £150m of advertising spend in 2000, with a further £110m being spent in the same year primarily by handset manufacturers and retailers. Achieving standout for BT Cellnet, and communicating key brand advantages, was set to be a challenging task.

The focus for BT Cellnet in 2001

BT Cellnet's brand objectives for 2001 were summarised by their Consumer Director Cath Keers as: 'To position BT Cellnet as the undisputed leader in the provision of content/information to your mobile phone, whilst driving incremental revenue through our value added services.'

This led to specific communications objectives, which were to:

- Gain reappraisal of the BT Cellnet brand among key 16–34-year-olds – a high value audience.
- Showcase relevant products and services (aiming to help reduce churn and encourage switching).
- Drive revenue and growth – increase usage and interaction with BT Cellnet and Genie[1] WAP services.
- Increase registrations to Genie.

In developing the media strategy, PHD conducted an analysis of BT Cellnet's tracking study data. Key brand measures showed there was little to distinguish any of the major brands.

More disturbingly, PHD's analysis showed that the significant TV advertising spends in the market were largely failing to communicate key information to

---

1. Genie was originally the BT Cellnet brand for mobile internet services, promoted heavily in 2000, and later sold off as a separate network. However, this continued to be the brand under which internet-based services were packaged for BT Cellnet subscribers.

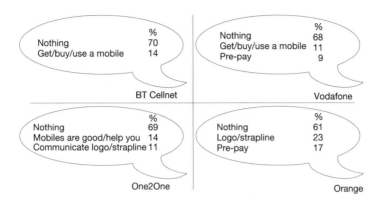

Figure 2: *Spontaneous ad recall of main network providers*
Base: All respondents who have seen TV advertising for each network, weeks 1–3, 2001

consumers. All the brands were suffering from this, according to the data (Figure 2).

PHD's conclusion was that advertising and conventional media strategies across the whole market were not doing enough for brand differentiation – for any brands. They recommended broadcast sponsorship for communicating more effectively, particularly to the younger audience that was a key weakness for the brand.

However, while broadcast sponsorship of a relevant 'young' programme was certainly in consideration to support the 'reappraisal' task, it would not typically be expected to deliver on the other objectives above. But it was becoming a more sophisticated tool. Broadcasters were recognising the importance of offering advertisers more than just 'name awareness', and specialists such as Drum PHD were extending the discipline.

A strengthening advantage of sponsorship was the opportunity to create ways for consumers to 'participate' in brands, not simply be exposed to the brand name. This would be an important advantage for a mobile phone network, where users had to switch networks *before* they could sample the alternative brand experience.

BT Cellnet had begun to exploit sponsorship as a means to make the brand more relevant to younger people – as headline sponsor of the Ministry of Sound's first tour of UK universities in 2000, extending the association to the Ministry's magazine, website and CD-compilations.

PHD's recommendation was for BT Cellnet to become the broadcast sponsor of *Big Brother 2*. This would offer much more than the communications benefits traditionally associated with broadcast sponsorship. Drum PHD investigated the opportunity, and set to work developing the eventual complex partnership.

It was immediately clear that the opportunity lay beyond communications alone. PHD put the case to the BT Cellnet board, to gain buy-in from parts of the business beyond the marketing function, and to the teams responsible for product development, sales, and network infrastructure.

THE *BIG BROTHER* 2 OPPORTUNITY

The social phenomenon of Big Brother – the first series

TV's role as a social lubricant is widely acknowledged, but Britain had been quite unprepared for what hit Channel 4's screens in July 2000. Overnight, *Big Brother 1* became part of the nation's cultural life. Within weeks the press were enthusing about what a landmark in TV history the show had become:

'Every so often a TV show comes along which grips the nation and becomes part of our lives.'

Leader, *The Mirror*, 19 August 2000

'It has pulled off a trick thought possible only in television's golden past – creating a shared collective experience.'

Jonathan Freedland, *Guardian*, 9 August 2000

Indeed, McClaren PR valued the press coverage in 2000 at over £13m at advertising equivalent prices. Stories about Big Brother featured in the national media every day of its 65-day long run, and on August 18, the day after Nick's eviction, Big Brother was on the front page of *every* national newspaper. But the impact of the show went beyond its ability to dominate the popular press and boost newspaper circulations. The Big Brother website became the biggest in Europe with Nasty Nick's eviction scoring 7.5m internet impressions in one day. As *The Sun*'s leader announced on 19 August 2000:

'[Nick's eviction] was maybe also the day the Internet came of age in Britain.'

The use of the internet had been a huge innovation in the concept of the original series – offering viewers an additional point of access to the 'house' outside the times of the edited broadcast footage, via the Big Brother website. The success of combining broadcast TV with internet-based accessibility had a huge impact on the show's creators (Endemol UK) and Channel 4. Work began immediately into how they could build more technological innovation into the second series, and involve viewers *even more* in the programme.

They realised that by incorporating mobile technology, the Big Brother experience could become truly multi-platform, accessible beyond home and the workplace. It could take interactivity much further than phone-voting and interactive TV (provided by E4, Channel 4's digital TV channel).

Mobile technology was at an interesting stage of development – SMS was becoming more widely adopted, but other applications were not yet mainstream. Research from *uboot.com* suggests that under-25s showed little loyalty to the use of SMS service in the months leading to June 2001 (*Loyalty*, 1 June 2001, p. 8). A recent survey from Marterna however, suggests text messaging is only now coming of age (*Computeractive*, 21 March 2002, p. 7). Incorporating a range of mobile technologies into the programme would help viewers see that the game had certainly moved on. For Channel 4 it would extend their revenue streams even further. By the time *Big Brother 2* went on air, Andy Anson, Channel 4's Head of iTV, had this to say:

'This year we will get revenues from iTV voting, pre-paid SMS cards with BT Cellnet, e-commerce and sponsorship. We have made sure we have turned over every commercial stone.'

Big Brother 2 – *a golden opportunity for BT Cellnet?*

Big Brother 1 had been such a major television success that the second series would inevitably attract interest from advertisers targeting the 16–34-year-old audience and looking to advertise around the programme, or become broadcast sponsors.

The challenge for any sponsor was to be perceived as doing more than simply jumping on the bandwagon of the show's success. The 16–34-year-old viewers would reject any brand they considered to be an inappropriate sponsor, or one that simply 'borrowed' youth credibility from the programme.

It was clear that BT Cellnet could indeed contribute the expertise that would increase people's enjoyment of the show and their ability to get involved in it, both on-screen and off-screen. The brand would be a credible sponsor, and participation could be expected to help towards achieving the full range of communications objectives.

BUILDING THE PARTNERSHIP

It became evident that it was in all parties' interests to invest time and effort in extending the partnership as far as possible. This would ensure maximum impact on the show, and provide more opportunities for BT Cellnet to showcase its services to a relevant audience. It would also enable BT Cellnet to communicate its involvement to a wider audience, and benefit still further from the association. The outcome was a multi-media campaign, including mobile telecommunications, TV, interactive TV, press, direct mail, online (internet and microsite), point of sale (POS), product and PR (Figure 3).

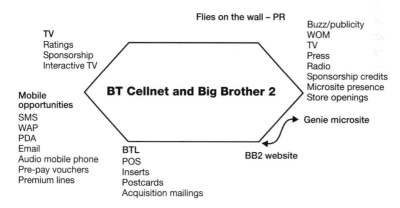

Figure 3: *Multi-platform, multi-media campagin*

Ultimately, viewers were able to receive instant updates on the show through digital and interactive TV, email, audio mobile phone, SMS, WAP or PDA. BT Cellnet brought technology for mobile applications and wireless internet.

Accessing Big Brother gossip via mobile phones

For viewers, the key benefit of incorporating mobile technology into the show was that they would get instant updates. BT Cellnet created the infrastructure to make

24/7 access to Big Brother gossip available to users of *all* the mobile networks. Consumers could interact with Big Brother in a variety of ways, courtesy of BT Cellnet:

- By registering for a free basic Big Brother text alert service, and then receiving text alerts and interactive quizzes throughout the series.
- By subscribing to premium services, giving access to exclusive Big Brother text alerts, ringtones and icons. Consumers had to buy vouchers available on the high street (cost £4.99) or purchase them online by visiting *www.buzzchannel4.com*.
- By accessing the first 'live-feed' audio service, allowing them to listen in to events in the house direct from contestants' microphones. This service was available via a premium rate number.

Existing subscribers of BT Cellnet had additional *exclusive* Big Brother services, including shortcode 1220 for the live-feed audio line.

All these services were promoted at the end of programmes, online, through retail POS in 15,000 outlets, and through mailings to existing and potential customers. In addition, a dedicated information line provided callers with all they needed to know about Big Brother services.

These applications placed the brand at the front of people's minds even when they were not watching the show. All offerings were enhanced by competitions and promotions with exclusive prizes, including tickets to 'eviction nights', visits to the house and house memorabilia.

Viewer participation through Genie (BT's wireless portal)

It was important for BT Cellnet to use *Big Brother 2* to improve consumers' unfavourable perceptions of WAP, which had got off to a stumbling start in 2000. *Big Brother 2* was, as *Marketing* magazine observed on 29 November 2001, an opportunity to showcase Genie by delivering content that was easy to use and entertaining, to introduce the mobile internet to many who had not tried it, and to stimulate repeat visits.

A *Big Brother 2* microsite exclusive to BT Cellnet included latest news from the house updated several times a day, gossip, a daily hour-by-hour log of developments, and an online game, *Big Brother 2* Lifestylers. Navigation was kept simple to provide a positive experience for inexperienced users of WAP technology.

COMMUNICATING BT CELLNET'S ASSOCIATION WITH THE PROGRAMME

The primary platform for communicating BT Cellnet's involvement in the programme was the sponsorship credits featured around the broadcast on Channel 4 and E4. These 'break bumpers' needed to work hard for the brand, which led to a challenging creative brief:

- Drive awareness of BT Cellnet's role as sponsor
- Enhance brand perceptions
- Deliver product messages

- Entertain
- Be relevant to the programme
- Be extendable through the line.

Transmissions on Channel 4 and E4 would be going out several times a day, seven days a week. Viewers would be seeing the broadcast many more times than they would see a 'normal' programme in the same time frame. As a result, the creative idea needed to be:

- *Flexible* – to allow it to incorporate references to the way the programme narrative was developing.
- *Affordable* – to allow multiple executions that would be needed to keep the sponsorship fresh.

Working with Channel 4 Creative Services, Drum PHD conceived BT Cellnet's very own 'Fly on the Wall' correspondents, Horse and Fruit (Figure 4). At the heart of house action and appearing at the start of each Big Brother episode, they commented on events in the show. The fly on the wall theme was linked to the BT Cellnet brand and the gossipy nature of the programme using the strapline: 'It's the Buzz'.

Figure 4: *Horse and Fruit enjoying the show*

Horse and Fruit were also created in cartoon format for use in print and online. They had a daily column on the *Big Brother 2* microsite where they engaged in humorous banter about the day's proceedings.

EVALUATING THE ACTIVITY

Exceptional performance

To gain maximum value from the investment of time, effort and money, BT Cellnet needed *Big Brother 2* to be a ratings success.

It was. Eight million viewers tuned in to see Brian win *Big Brother 2* on Friday 27 July 2001 (according to PHD, BARB, DDS and SPC). The series, which ran from 28 May to 27 July, was the highest rating programme on Channel 4 for 16–34-year-old adults in 2001, attracting between four and five million viewers per episode.

In audience share terms, *Big Brother 2* far outshone the first series, gaining an average 21% audience share on Channel 4. Compared to the first series, it made the strongest progress among the core 16–34-year-old audience, where share was +8% compared with 2000. In fact, share of viewing was up among all demographics, except those aged 55+ (Figure 5).

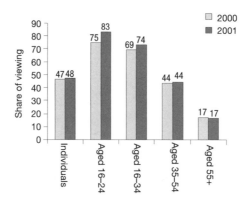

Figure 5: *Big Brother vs. Big Brother 2 – share of viewing for final episode*
Source: BARB/SPC All homes

Moreover, the programme boosted viewing to E4 significantly (peaking at 25% audience share),[2] and boasted enormous success for its interactive elements. Digital E4 coverage was rolled out live on E4 18 hours a day. At its peak E4 was delivering higher audiences than Sky One.

Against Cellnet's core target of 16–34-year-olds, Channel 4 and E4 activity achieved 4363 TVRs, 83.3% cover at a staggering 52.4 OTS overall (Table 3). Compared against a typical burst of TV activity, this was a massive achievement, and made the brand very conspicuous for the 16–34 audience (PHD).

TABLE 3: £4M BT CELLNET SPONSORSHIP VS. CONVENTIONAL TV
BURST FOR 16–34-YEAR-OLDS

	Conventional TV airtime burst	BT Cellnet Big Brother sponsorship
Ratings (TVRs)	800	4363
1+ coverage	85%	83.3%
Frequency (OTS)	9	52.4

Source: BARB/PHD analysis

2. *Big Brother 2*, Thursday 26 July 2001 on E4 (time 2432–2458) gained 25.5% audience share.

PHD calculated that the broadcast sponsorship credits alone delivered BT Cellnet value in excess of £10m at realistic media buying rates, with online and interactive activity taking the sponsorship to greater heights.

Impact on perceptions

Perceptions shifted, making the brand more relevant to the 16–34-year-old audience.

The sponsorship was an extremely effective communications tool. Quantitative research was undertaken by IPSOS RSL in order to understand the impact of the brand communication on awareness, image and consideration among BT Cellnet users and non-users.[3] The results were extremely positive.

BT Cellnet strongly associated with *Big Brother 2*

In fieldwork conducted during the first two weeks of the series, 40% of 16–34-year-old mobile users were aware that BT Cellnet was the sponsor. This rose to 66% by the series end, beating the figure for Nescafé's long-running association with *Friends*.[4]

Spontaneous awareness was strong too. Respondents were asked, without prompt, 'Which brand or company do you think sponsors Big Brother on Channel 4?' A total of 31% of the target knew which company was the Big Brother series sponsor. This was higher among BT Cellnet's key targets – 16–24-year-olds (36%), lower social grades, and readers of mid-market and popular newspapers.

BT Cellnet seen as an appropriate sponsor

Viewers believed BT Cellnet to be an appropriate sponsor and enjoyed the idents. A total of 51% of 16–24-year-old viewers, and 48% of 25–34-year-old viewers, considered the sponsorship very/quite appropriate. By the end of the series, perceptions of appropriateness increased as viewers experienced the role that BT Cellnet had played (Figures 6 and 7).

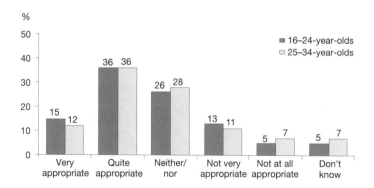

Figure 6: *BT Cellnet perceived as appropriate sponsor*
Base: All respondents (wave 1 and wave 2)

---

3. Two waves were conducted on a 350 sample of 16–34-year-old mobile phone owners, interviewed via multimedia omnibus.
4. Wave 1 (early wave) fieldwork ran from 1–10 June 2001, wave 2 (late wave) ran from 27 July–5 August 2001. Precise data on sponsorships by other companies are confidential.

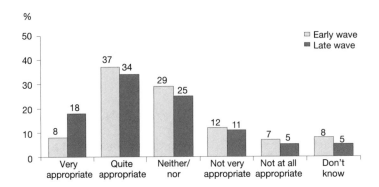

Figure 7: *Perceptions of BT Cellnet as appropriate sponsor of Big Brother grew*
Base: All respondents

Consumers (71%) enjoyed the creative executions, again 16–24-year-olds in particular – and the number of consumers who enjoyed them also increased by the end of the series. Consumers strongly rejected the idea that 'sponsorship spoils my enjoyment of the programme' with only 14% prepared to agree with this statement. This is a remarkable achievement given the massive amount of repeat exposure, and it endorses the decision to make 95 separate idents to keep the sponsorship relevant to events in the programme, and avoid 'wearout' (Figures 8, 9 and 10).

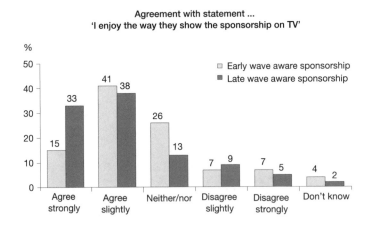

Figure 8: *Increased enjoyment of creative execution*
Base: Respondents aware of sponsorship

Key messages conveyed about text messaging via BT Cellnet

Text messaging (at 51%) and text message alerts (at 36%) dominated recall of products communicated by sponsorship (Figures 11 and 12).

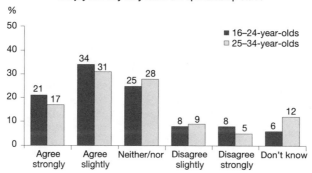

Figure 9: *Sponsorship enjoyment higher among 16–24-year-olds*
Base: All respondents, waves 1 and 2

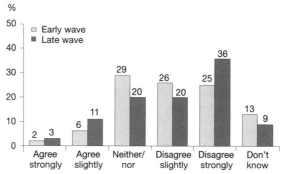

Figure 10: *Sponsorship enjoyment*
Base: All respondents

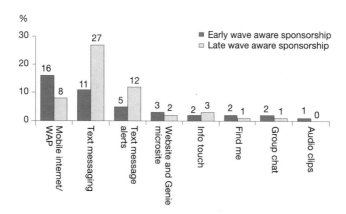

Figure 11: *Spontaneous awareness of products as part of sponsorship*
Base: Respondents aware of sponsorship

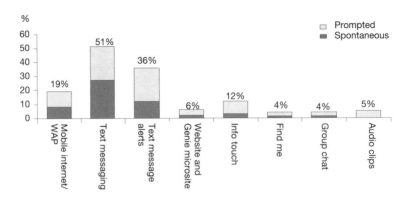

Figure 12: *Total awareness of products and services as part of sponsorship*
Base: All respondents aware of the sponsorship (wave 2)

Brand perceptions strengthened among Big Brother viewers

Brand perceptions strengthened significantly among *Big Brother 2* viewers, versus non-viewers, in all key image statements including 'Straightforward', 'Passionate', 'Approachable', 'Fun', 'Open', 'Clear' and 'Trusted' (Figure 13).

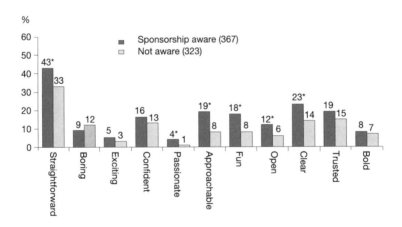

Figure 13: *Significant image improvements*
Base: All respondents (wave 1 and wave 2)
*denotes significant difference at 95% confidence level

To quote Mike Jackson from Ipsos RSL: 'It is difficult to shift brand image and perceptions in nine weeks! However, the sponsorship has worked hard in a short, intensive period of time.'

Sponsorship credits had a life beyond the programme

As an ideal PR vehicle and a regular part of *Big Brother 2* stories, Horse and Fruit attracted extensive interest from columnists and radio presenters alike. They gained much press coverage about a potential release (cover version) of Curtis Mayfield's 'Superfly', alongside speculation about having their own late night chat show. They also took part in store openings and promotional tours.

The *Daily Record* reported on 21 July 2001 that they would have been on TV 5000 times – 'not bad for eight weeks work!'

PR alone generated 108 million OTS across press and radio, and the online viral marketing campaign generated 230,000 hits in just five weeks.

Branded BT Cellnet interactions

BT Cellnet facilitated huge numbers of mobile-based interactions with Big Brother. Beyond the communications effect of exposure to sponsorship credits, it was clear that huge numbers of consumers got involved with Big Brother via branded BT Cellnet interactions. For example:

- Over five million Big Brother gossip text alerts were sent out via BT Cellnet.
- A total of 172,000 people signed up for the basic text alerts service.
- There were 150,000 calls to the audio line for real-time live feeds from the house.
- In all, 26,000 vouchers were sold at £4.99 through high street retail outlets for access to the premium Big Brother services, plus an additional 34,000 calls were made to the voucher registration line, and 3600 were made to the voucher download line.
- Altogether, 227,000 people called the Big Brother information line.

In addition to the 'brand experience' effect, the scale of this activity generated £880,000 in additional revenue to BT Cellnet.

Extensive sampling of mobile internet via Genie wireless portal

The *Big Brother 2* WAP microsite, available through the mobile internet platform Genie, recorded more than 21 million WAP page impressions, equivalent to 286,000 per day. This was achieved for an investment in the production and hosting of the website of just £50,000.

Because the microsite was constantly being fed with new information from the programme as it evolved, the *Big Brother 2* WAP service was able to reach and maintain a position as the third most popular site in Europe.

The microsite proved a unique opportunity for consumers to sample the benefits of WAP, since they were so motivated to find the information they wanted about the show. Because BT Cellnet was able to monitor site usage closely, the exercise provided instantaneous and valuable learning about how to change and improve the user experience.

Top five position among European websites for BT Cellnet sponsored site

With animated versions of the Horse and Fruit characters from the TV sponsorship icons featuring on the website, this was another platform for BT Cellnet's association with the programme.

The main Channel 4 Big Brother site received over 159 million page impressions, making it one of the top five European sites. Moreover, 10% of that traffic (16 million page impressions) visited the BT Cellnet microsite linked to the main site. Other calculations show that the BT Cellnet microsite had over 446,000 unique visitors.

Jupiter MMXI reported that the website recorded 7.4 million page impressions per day on days when a key contestant was expelled, matching the online impact of Nasty Nick's eviction in the 2000 series.

CONCLUSION AND SUMMARY

Sponsorship of 2001's most talked-about media event, and Channel 4's highest-rating programme of the year, helped BT Cellnet achieve significant exposure and relevance to the important 16–34 audience.

This success was achieved in only 32 days from conception to execution, and involved energetic teamwork across many companies – BT Cellnet, Genie, Endemol UK, Channel 4, Drum PHD and PHD. It brought focus to the collective effort inside BT Cellnet, bringing together teams from marketing, product development and technical infrastructure.

For an outlay of around £4m, it brought incremental revenue to the company of £880,000, and delivered media value (through TV alone) of £10m (PHD), with additional *incalculable* value from the scale of positive PR exposure through press and radio.

Besides the above, the activity achieved a number of key objectives that were important to the company in a maturing market where the key battles were now market share and ARPU (average revenue per user), and where traditional communications strategies were struggling to convey brand differentiation, or provide brand experiences. These objectives were:

- Brand association with the hottest and hippest media property of 2001.
- Brand awareness, image and empathy uplifts.
- Driving consumers to try out new mobile and WAP technologies – through exclusive interactive media content.
- Facilitated text and WAP services with over 100,000 subscribers (BT Cellnet figure).
- The setting up of four premium-line services and the development of the first ever 'live feed' audio service.
- Increased connections to BT Cellnet.

While the broadcast output was undoubtedly the driving force for the scale and momentum of *Big Brother 2*, it was BT Cellnet's involvement in providing a technical infrastructure and developing purpose-made applications, that enabled *Big Brother 2* to become a 24/7 mobile interactive experience.

BIG BROTHER 3

Big Brother returned in 2002, and this time with BT Cellnet rebranded as O_2. All the partners were again aware of the need to keep innovating with the programme. For O_2, key requirements were to boost awareness of the rebranded company, as well as to showcase a variety of new products and services.

The investment made by BT Cellnet – in infrastructure and in the relationship with Channel 4 and Endemol – reaped rewards in *Big Brother 3*, and will continue to do so.

7

Budweiser

Frogs, Lizards, Whassup?
Market share that's what

Principal authors: Emmet O'Hanlon and Andrew Deykin, BMP DDB
Collaborating authors: Les Binet and Sarah Carter

EDITOR'S SUMMARY

Budweiser's market share had slipped into decline in mid-1998 as 18–34-year-old drinkers ('adult lads') began to lose their connection with the brand. Subsequent research led the authors to conclude that the current advertising campaign had run its course. Adult lads were no longer engaged by classic American provenance and imagery – ads where tough men battle with adversity and ultimately triumph were not going to cut it anymore. Our target market expected something different, especially from one of the UK's leading beer brands. This case demonstrates how Anheuser-Busch, owner of Budweiser, and DDB worked together to ensure that the subsequent advertising which was produced – 'Frogs', 'Frogs & Lizards' and 'Whassup' – was the lynchpin of the brand's recovery. Three years on, Budweiser's fortunes have been rejuvenated. The brand consistently appeals to its target audience, and most importantly market share decline has been arrested, turned around and is rising steadily once again.

INTRODUCTION

Anheuser-Busch, the company behind Budweiser, is known throughout the world for its dynamic workforce and innovative approach to sales and marketing. This paper tells the story of how Anheuser-Busch, and its advertising partner DDB, identified a market share decline in the UK but took swift, decisive action to turn it into a steep growth curve. During the course of this paper, we will show how advertising commissioned and bought by Anheuser-Busch spearheaded this return to growth.

Budweiser had slipped into decline in mid-1998. While it can be very difficult to turn a brand's fortunes around, we succeeded. This paper will show how we started rejuvenating Budweiser by improving, first, brand awareness, then image and, finally, market share. We will show that outstanding advertising was the lynchpin of our recovery programme. But we will also demonstrate how advertising's effects were heightened by applying some important lessons which we learnt along the way.

Lesson 1:
Outstanding advertising is a base requirement for success in the lager category. Budweiser has now become synonymous with providing this.

Lesson 2:
Outstanding advertising alone can't turn a troubled brand around. It must have the appropriate amount of media spend behind it. In Budweiser's case, getting our spend levels right helped ensure that our advertising wasn't just talked about, it became famous.

Lesson 3:
Advertising which takes off and becomes a cultural phenomenon in its own right is difficult to create, but if it can be achieved, this will multiply effectiveness several times over. In Budweiser's case, it put our brand name on the lips of the target market for months on end.

Lesson 4:
Most importantly, if you can make these three engines of growth work together in tandem, then you can really start to turn a brand's fortunes around.

BACKGROUND

Budweiser was launched in the UK in 1984 as a bottled lager (Premium packaged lager or 'PPL'). As an American brand, it enjoyed kudos and style. Budweiser was cool. People liked being seen with it. So growth was steady (see Figure 1).

It was so popular that by 1998 it was the number 1 PPL brand in the UK (see Figure 2).

But then something started to go wrong. In mid-1998 overall market share started to fall for the first time ever (see Figure 3).

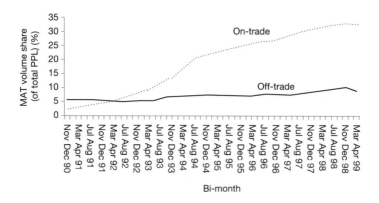

Figure 1: *Budweiser PPL volume share*
Note: MAT = moving annual total
Source: Nielsen

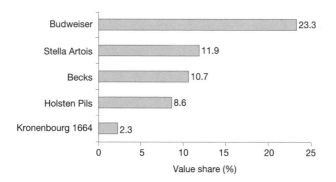

Figure 2: *Value share of leading PPL brands 1998 – on- and off-trade combined*

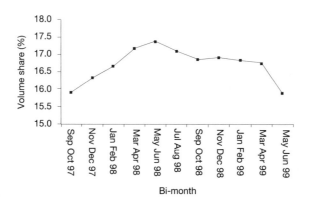

Figure 3: *Budweiser PPL volume share*
On- and off-trade 6-month moving average
Source: Nielsen

UNDERSTANDING WHAT WAS GOING WRONG

Managing a lager brand is interesting because it operates in two sectors: the on-trade and the off-trade.[1] Each is different from the other in terms of consumer profile, pricing structures and competitive environment. We decided that without ignoring the off-trade, we needed to focus on the on-trade. This was for two reasons: volume of sales and because it is where brands are 'adopted'.

Sales
The on-trade is over twice the size of the off-trade in value and volume terms (Figure 4). So it's where the biggest opportunity lies.

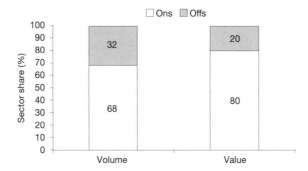

Figure 4: *Sector share of total lager 1998*
Source: Nielsen

In part, the size of the on-trade market is a reflection of the fact that pubs are where the heaviest lager consumers congregate (Figure 5). As you might expect, these people tend to be 18–34-year-old men ('adult lads').

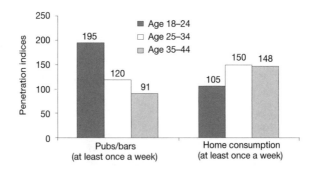

Figure 5: *Lager penetration indices relative to all adults*
Base: All adults
Source: TGI

---

1. The 'on' trade is where people buy alcohol to drink *on* the premises (bars, clubs, pubs, etc.). The 'off' trade is where people buy alcohol to drink *off* the premises (supermarkets, off-licences, etc.).

Where brands are adopted

The on-trade is where people try out and adopt brands. If you want to recruit new drinkers then a strong on-trade presence is paramount. Critically, the habits acquired in the pub are taken into the off-licence. To succeed in both sectors, you must be successful in the on-trade.

> 'Going to pubs and clubs is a badge of adulthood that every young man yearns for, so it is unsurprising that the 'on'-trade and everything to do with it has more cachet than the 'off'-trade ever could.'

> 'If there's no special offers on [in the off-licence], I'd buy whatever I drink in the pub.'

> Male, aged 24, Manchester

> 'Drinking preferences tend to be defined in the 'on'- trade because men are surrounded by different brands and products, which they discuss and experiment with as part of the evening.'

> Source: Q Research 2000

How would we regain market share?

If Budweiser were to regain market share, success in the on-trade would be crucial. Once it had firmly re-established itself here, then off-trade sales should follow. But there were two big challenges facing Budweiser in pubs and clubs: salience and image.

Salience

Over 90% of the Budweiser sold in the on-trade is in bottles. But there's a huge range of bottled drinks to choose from nowadays. To further complicate things, the bottles tend to be hidden away in fridges behind the bar so they're not as obvious as draught taps. That's why brand salience is crucial. But Budweiser's spontaneous brand awareness had been declining (Figure 6).

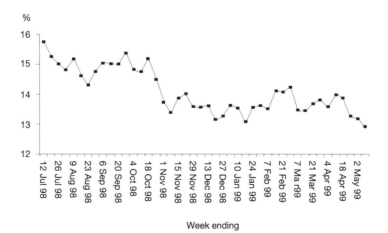

Week ending

Figure 6: *Budweiser spontaneous awareness – first mention*
Base: 18–34-year-old men
Source: Millward Brown rolling 16-week data

Image

Image counts for more in the on-trade than the off-trade. What you drink at home is private. What you drink in a pub is a matter for all to comment upon. This is particularly the case for PPLs over draught lager because of the label on the bottle. Millward Brown image measures had fallen slightly. These don't tend to move much in any market, so even a small drop made us realise Budweiser was losing its 'cool' credentials (Figure 7).

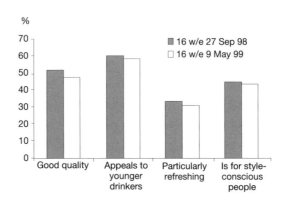

Figure 7: *Budweiser brand image*
Base: 18–34-year-old men
Source: Millward Brown rolling 16-week data

Qualitative research told us we shouldn't merely be concerned, but actively worried:

'Verging on the boring.'

'It doesn't have an edge.'

'I wouldn't want to stay very long at that [Budweiser] party.'

'It's an '80s thing, but lacks retro cool.'

Source: BMP/Fathom Brand Healthcheck 1998/1999

Why were we going out of fashion?

There were two main issues with our communication approach: we weren't connecting with adult lads, and we weren't spending enough.

Connecting with adult lads

American imagery had become much more familiar to adult lads over the years. They no longer automatically bought into classical US provenance in the way that they used to:

'America can be cool but it can also be pretty cheesy.'

Source: BMP qualitative research 1998

Our brand advertising of the time featured working class American Bud drinkers. They would get into sticky situations but invariably triumph over adversity. The campaign worked brilliantly at launch. But in our increasingly post-modernist society, where irony and self-deprecation are all the rage, its time seemed to have passed.

Figure 8

'Currently some problems with the "American mythology"; overfamiliar [cf cynicism about Irish mythology] can become just a convention ...We suggest that overt American "hero" drinkers fail to speak relevantly to the target market.'

Source: RDS Brand Healthcheck 1998

Spend
Our share of voice (SOV)[2] had fallen from its earlier levels.

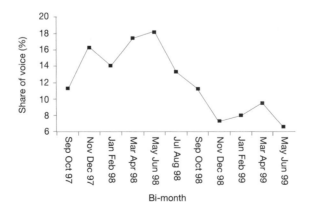

Figure 9: *Budweiser share of voice*
Source: MMS 6-month rolling data

---

2. SOV is defined as share of total lager adspend. It is not possible to define share of PPL adspend, since much of the advertising in this category works at the total brand level, supporting both packaged and draft products.

OBJECTIVES

Armed with this understanding of what was going on, Anheuser-Busch set new objectives. It seemed unrealistic that we would be able to turn things around immediately, so these were long-term.

Business objectives

1. To maintain value market share in 1999 and move to value share growth in 2000. The focus was on value because Budweiser commands a price premium, which it was intent on maintaining.
2. To concentrate on the on-trade because success here would lead to subsequent success in the off-trade (on-trade is also the biggest sector).

Marketing objectives

Halt the drift of 'adult lads' from the brand, especially 18–24-year-olds. These people are the heart of the on-trade. They also represent the future of the brand. If we can win them over when they reach adulthood then they'll stick with us as they age.

Advertising objectives

We had two requirements if we were to reconnect with adult lads:

1. To make Budweiser famous. As we've explained, salience is critical for a PPL in pubs and clubs. We had to put Budweiser on the tip of every adult lad's tongue.
2. Make the brand desired. Famous wouldn't be enough. The image had to strike a chord.

So what did we do?

We knew what we needed – a different take on our US provenance. Something more offbeat, edgy and surprising. We researched a selection of ads which we had already generated in the USA for the American market, alongside some scripts written in the UK.

The US routes had an edge. Adult lads somehow sensed that they were written by Americans and that made them seem more original and authentic. But even better, we had found the campaign that we were looking for – a truly different type of US provenance. Also, it was ready to go; we could use it immediately.

So in October 1998, we began what was to be a three-phase recovery plan.

- Phase 1, 'Frogs', October '98–April '99: outstanding advertising
- Phase 2, 'Frogs & Lizards', July '99–July '00: outstanding advertising, increased media spend
- Phase 3, 'Whassup', September '00–June '01: outstanding advertising, *significantly* increased media spend, cultural phenomenon

As we moved into the second and third phases, we started learning and applying the lessons mentioned earlier. Great advertising can't work to full potential unless it has the correct amount of media spend behind it, and that the right amount of spend becomes a relative fortune if you have advertising that creates a cultural phenomenon.

Phase 1 'Frogs'

This campaign featured three frogs in a swamp. Each one croaks one syllable of the word 'Bud – Weis – Er' as if in a relay. Although the brand is central to the advertising, the product isn't even featured – a radical departure from our existing campaign.

Rather than showing the full campaign, we adapted the two best ones and put all of our spend behind them to really seed the concept in.

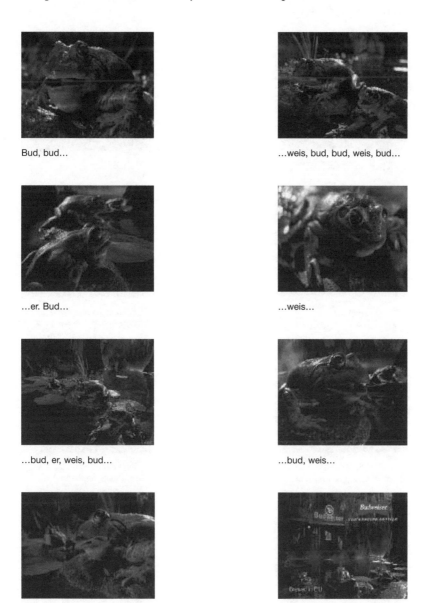

Bud, bud...

...weis, bud, bud, weis, bud...

...er. Bud...

...weis...

...bud, er, weis, bud...

...bud, weis...

er....

Bud, weis, er. Bud, weis, er
(repeat)

Figure 10

Phase 2 'Frogs & Lizards'

Our campaign was subsequently given a new twist by Goodby Silverstein & Partners, another Budweiser roster agency. This time the frogs were being observed by a pair of wisecracking lizards. Louis (bad lizard) would slag the frogs off. Meanwhile, Frankie (good lizard) attempted to calm him down. Subsequent executions brought twists and turns to the plot and the campaign began to unfurl like a mini soap opera. It had lads falling around with laughter in the USA and British lads did exactly the same when we researched it here.

Bud, bud, weis, bud, bud...

...weis, bud...

...er, bud, weis...

– Oh if only I could swim. I would swim over there; then I would go up and say...

...hi my name is Louis, how are you? Then I would grab their heads...

... and hold them under the water like this and this, ha, ha, ha!

Louis, you are one sick lizard.

Figure 11

BMP analysis of the previous 'Frogs' campaign concluded that, although it had been very well received, more spend was needed to really begin turning the brand's fortunes around. So this time budgets were increased. Again, we cherry-picked six of the best ads from the campaign, made some amendments and put them on air.

Furthermore, an award-winning media approach was conceived in conjunction with OMD, UK.[3] Additional airtime was bought at strategic moments in the saga, such as the lizards' plot to assassinate the frogs. This helped constantly rekindle interest in the campaign.

Other activity

We wanted the campaign to be as ubiquitous as possible. The theme of fighting frogs and lizards lent itself to a variety of media so we spread our resources.

Radio

A radio campaign was used – for the first time in Budweiser's history – to reach our target more effectively and to remind people of the storyline.

Online

A computer game was developed, allowing people to interact with the characters (Figure 12).

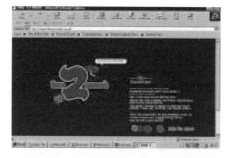

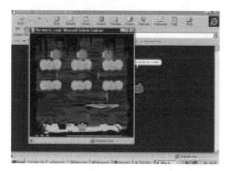

Figure 12

---

3. Winner Mediaweek Integrated Campaign of the Year, 2000 award

Tactile media

Again, 'guerrilla' media were used to keep the campaign fresh and signpost major moments in the saga.

Figure 13

Phase 3 'Whassup'

So things were looking good, but then in September 2000 we played our ace. The initial ad set it all off. We ran a campaign that launched a phrase, that became the catchphrase of the nation, echoing, quite literally around the land. It features a bunch of black guys hanging out in their apartment. They lounge around and yell 'Whassup' at each other over and over again (see Figure 14).

Anheuser-Busch knew that 'Whassup' would be a winner when they bought it. But nobody could have foreseen that it would turn into a cult phenomenon. Almost as soon as it was aired, everybody was shouting 'Whassup' at each other. The catchphrase entered the vernacular, was constantly discussed in the media and the actors from the ads became stars. It was certainly a different campaign to 'Frogs & Lizards', but once again it was a new and offbeat side of American provenance.

We researched it in the UK where, once again, it went down a storm with adult lads. It made them do more than just talk about the ads. It made them all start shouting 'Whassup'. Knowing that we needed to launch with a bang, Anheuser-Busch upped media budgets once again.

Media

The initial ad was intended to set the whole campaign up and launch the phenomenon, so we wanted to get it out to as wide an audience as possible. Anheuser-Busch had rolled the campaign out in the midst of high-profile programming in the USA and wanted to take a similar approach here. So we booked airtime in the 'grand finale' of 'Big Brother'.

Internet

A 'Whassup' website game was set up which encouraged people to download ads and screensavers (see Figure 15).

– Hello?
– Yo, whassup?

– Nothin'. Watchin' the game. Havin'
a Bud.
– True. True.

– Yo, who's that?
– Yo, yo, pick up the phone.
– Whassupp

– Yo, Dookie
– Aaaaahhhhh
– Whassuuupp

– Aaaaaahhhhh

– Whassuuup

– So, whassuuup B?
– Watchin' the game, havin', a Bud.

Figure 14: *Budweiser – Whassup*

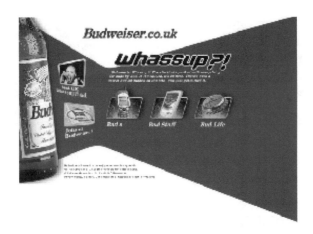

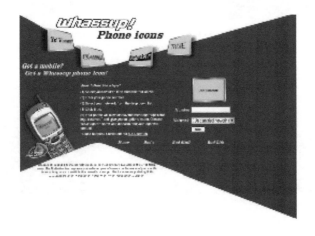

Figure 15

Sponsorship

Budweiser also branded certain concerts and music festivals with elements of the campaign, i.e. 'Whassup'/'True' music.

Miscellaneous

Several other activities were organised which helped keep the brand and catchphrase top of mind. One promotion involved the actors from the ads being flown over to the UK for an extensive publicity tour. Another involved a competition in bars where punters were filmed for amateur 'Whassup' ads (the winning versions being shown on TV and the internet).

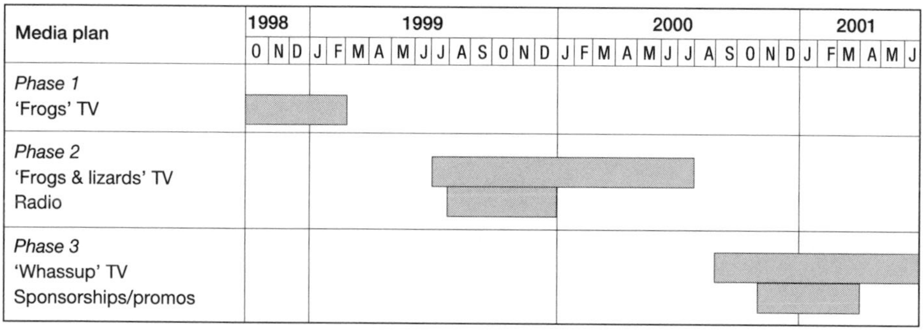
Media plan
1998
1999
2000
2001
O N D J F M A M J J A S O N D J F M A M J J A S O N D J F M A M J
Phase 1
'Frogs' TV
Phase 2
'Frogs & lizards' TV
Radio
Phase 3
'Whassup' TV
Sponsorships/promos

Figure 16: *The overall rollout plan*

Media spend was increased progressively as the different campaigns were rolled out.

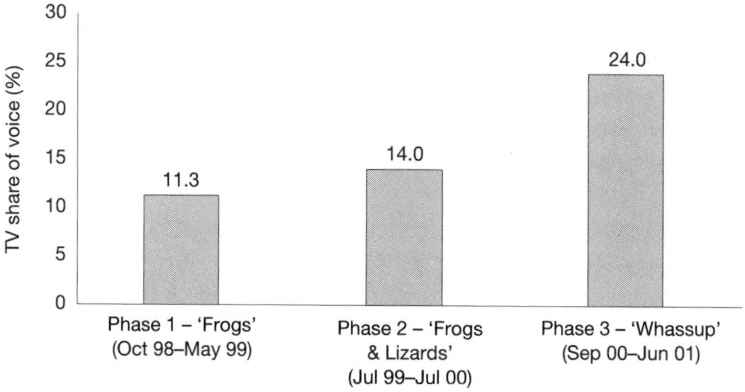
TV share of voice (%)
30
25
20
15
10
5
0
11.3
14.0
24.0
Phase 1 – 'Frogs' (Oct 98–May 99)
Phase 2 – 'Frogs & Lizards' (Jul 99–Jul 00)
Phase 3 – 'Whassup' (Sep 00–Jun 01)

Figure 17: *Budweiser campaign periods and share of voice*
Source: MMS

WHASSAPPENED?

Anheuser-Busch successfully achieved its objectives

After a period of decline, not only did we achieve our objective of maintaining share, the brand actually returned to share growth. As predicted, gains were first achieved in the on-trade. This growth was sustained as media weight was increased, right through 'Frogs & Lizards' and 'Whassup' (see Figure 18).

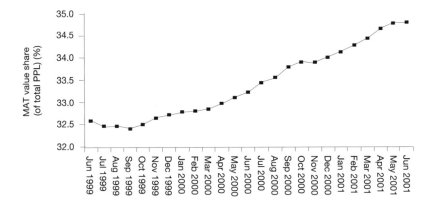

Figure 18: *Budweiser PPL value share, on-trade*
Source: Nielsen

Then, as predicted, once we had turned the on-trade around, the off-trade followed. Budweiser had returned to growth.

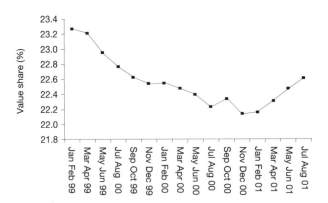

Figure 19: *Budweiser PPL value share: on- and off-sales*
Source: Nielsen

We will now demonstrate that it was advertising that achieved this remarkable transformation in the brand's fortunes, and show how it did so.

Evidence that the advertising worked ... and how

The new ads made a big impact

To say that the advertising was noticed would be a massive understatement. As soon as the new 'Frogs' ads were aired in Phase 1, advertising awareness started to rise. 'Frogs & Lizards' and 'Whassup' ratcheted levels up even higher.

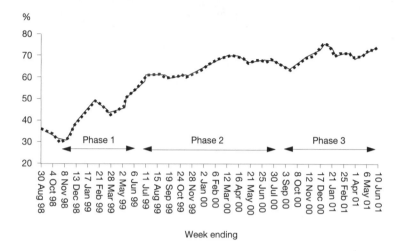

Figure 20: *Budweiser TV advertising awareness*
Base: 18–34-year-old men
Source: Millward Brown, rolling 16-week data

These increases are even more impressive when compared to our competitors. By the end of the campaign, twice as many people had noticed our ads as Stella's.

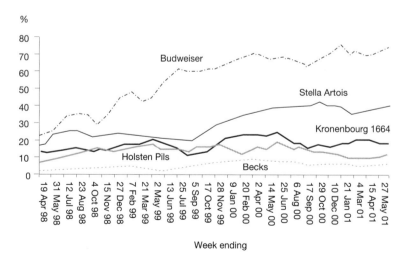

Figure 21: *TV advertising awareness*
Base: 18–34-year-old men
Source: Millward Brown, rolling 16-week data

These awareness gains were clearly driven by the new advertising (Figure 22).

169

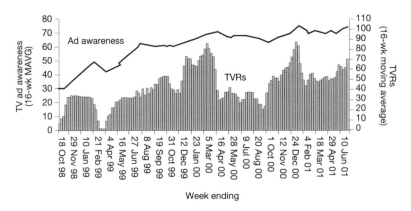

Figure 22: *TV ad awareness vs. TVRs*
Source: Millward Brown, BARB

There is a clear and immediate correlation[4] between ad awareness and TVRs.

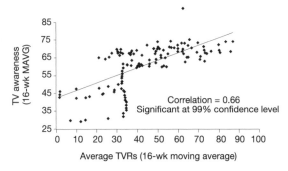

Figure 23: *TV ad awareness vs. TVR October 98 to June 01 (Phase 1 to Phase 3)*
Source: Millward Brown, BARB

Furthermore, the biggest gains in ad awareness were among our target audience of young men.

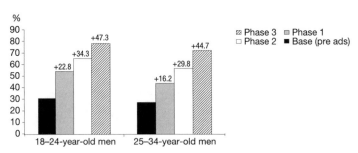

Figure 24: *Budweiser TV ad awareness*
Source: Millward Brown

4. The level of statistical significance tells us how likely it is that there is a link between these two variables. So here we can say that there is a 99% probability that TVRs are one of the drivers of ad awareness. The square of the correlation is then a measure of how much of the variation is explained by this link. So a 66% correlation means that 44% of the variation in awareness is due to ratings.

People loved the new ads

Qualitative research consistently showed that 18–34-year-old men loved the new ads. Of 'Frogs' they said:

'It's brilliant, a load of frogs selling the beer, only Budweiser could do that.'

'That's so different from normal; Budweiser always takes itself so seriously and this is really taking the piss out of itself.'

2CV qualitative research 1998

Of 'Frogs & Lizards' they said:

'Those ads are talking my language now.'

'Doesn't take itself too seriously, [it's much] less stuffy now.'

'No one has done this before.'

'They've moved from being like a Gillette ad with the big hero whose face you'd love to rub in the mud into this foreign planet where the frogs love the beer, but the... iguana wants to get them. I never could have thought it up, but it's brilliant.'

Fathom/BMP 1999

And by the time 'Whassup' broke, Budweiser had established a new reputation for making cracking ads:

'That's brilliant, Budweiser just does it again and again.'

'They always do advertising that's totally in tune with your sense of humour.'

'I'd put their ads on a level with Lynx or Levis, it's the best of the best.'

'Listen, listen, I have to tell you that I've never seen an ad that's made me piss myself more than that Whassup.'

BMP/Firefish 2000/2001

It was also clear, from early on, that our new take on American-ness struck a chord with young British lads:

'I've just realised it's the clean cut Hollywood I hate, but this is cool Hollywood.'

'You'd just love to be one of those blokes, being naturally cool instead of acting it like we have to because we only come from Leeds and not LA (widespread laughter).'

Fathom/BMP 1999/2000

The ads increased brand awareness

To recap from earlier, brand salience is particularly important for bottled lagers as they're usually hidden away behind the bar in fridges. But Budweiser's brand salience didn't improve immediately. Advertising awareness improved as soon as we aired the new ads, but *brand* awareness didn't improve until we increased media spend, in phase 2 (see Figure 25).

Once we increased our share of voice, however, spontaneous awareness climbed, reaching its peak at the height of the 'Whassup' campaign. At this point, Budweiser had better salience than any other lager brand, despite lacking a major draught presence (see Table 1).

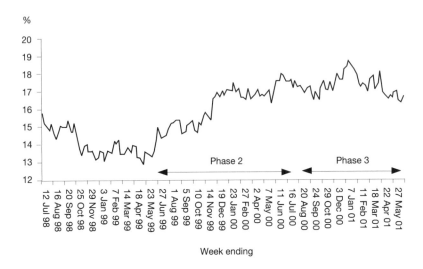

Figure 25: *Budweiser spontaneous awareness, first mention*
Base: 18–34-year-old men
Source: Millward Brown, rolling six-week data

TABLE 1: BRAND AWARENESS

Brand	Spontaneous brand awareness (%)
Budweiser	17.6
Stella Artois	15.8
Becks	8.1
Kronenbourg 1664	2.7
Holsten Pils	1.5

Source: Millward Brown, Oct 2000

We can demonstrate that the new advertising was driving these gains. Firstly, there is a significant correlation between brand awareness and share of voice (see Figure 26):

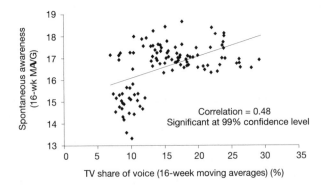

Figure 26: *Spontaneous brand awareness vs. TV share of voice*
Base: 18–34-year-old men
Source: Millward Brown, BARB

Secondly, the awareness shifts were greatest among our core target market of 18–24-year-old adult lads.

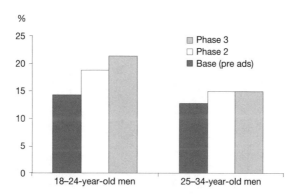

Figure: 27: *Budweiser spontaneous awareness, first mention*
Source: Millward Brown

The ads got people talking about Budweiser
One way that we achieved this increase in salience was by getting people talking about the ads, and hence about the brand.

This phenomenon started with 'Frogs'.

> 'Me brother used to do that with his mates. They'd be watching telly and someone would go "Bud" and then someone else would go "Weis" and "Er". You'd all laugh.'

BMP qualitative research 1998

'Frogs & Lizards' kept the momentum up. The campaign was valuable social currency for lads. On the assassination of the frogs:

> 'You knew for ages that someone was going to get killed but the build-up to it was just as good.'

> 'The lizards were different, they never had a chorus [sic] like Whassup, but you'd always end up talking about them, because there'd be a new angle to the story and it was always good for a laugh.'

BMP qualitative research 1998

But it wasn't until 'Whassup' that we really hit pay-dirt. This wasn't just a talked-about campaign – it was a massive cultural phenomenon. The catchphrase took off like wildfire:

> 'You walk outside the pub any Friday or Saturday night and all you hear is people screaming "Whassup" up and down the street.'

> 'Everybody's doing it on the telly, Thierry Henri did a big "Whassup" to the crowd when he scored that goal against Man Utd at Highbury last week. The crowd went mad.'

> 'I know about four different people who have it on their answering machine.'

BMP/Firefish 2000

The media were quick to latch on to it. 'Whassup' was imitated on the *Big Breakfast* and discussed on the news among others.

Media mania was further heightened by the actors from the ads coming to the UK for a publicity tour. The number of press mentions jumped while our campaigns were on air (especially 'Whassup').

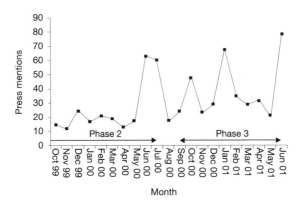

Figure 28: *Budweiser press mentions*
Source: Reuters

And the bootleggers got busy. You can really tell that something has taken off by the number of people who jump on the bandwagon. A walk down Carnaby Street revealed a host of 'unofficial' items: 'Whassup' mobile phone covers, T-shirts, rucksacks, hats, cups, pens... you name it.

Not only that, but the catchphrase actually got its own dictionary listing – true proof that it had become a cultural phenomenon:

> **Whassup** *interj.* American slang word meaning 'hello', from
> 'What's up?' used especially as a greeting to someone you
> know well.

> Source: *Longman Dictionary of Contemporary English*, 2001

Fans of the phenomenon even began making their own ads and circulating them on the internet. At the last count, over 69 different versions were available on www.adcritic.com and www.trevc.net. They've got everything covered. Bill Gates, Grannies, Northern lads ... There's even one of some very British guys going 'Hellew' to each other.

People's awareness of Budweiser 'Whassup' activity on the internet correlated well with TVRs (see Figure 29).

The Budweiser 'Whassup' website was inundated with hits once the campaign was on air (see Figure 30).

Brand image improved

As brand salience improved, so did brand image. As we mentioned earlier, quantitative image measures are notoriously difficult to shift, especially for well-established brands. Yet Budweiser's key image measures did increase once we had started to improve salience in phase two. The improvements continued throughout phase three (see Figure 31).

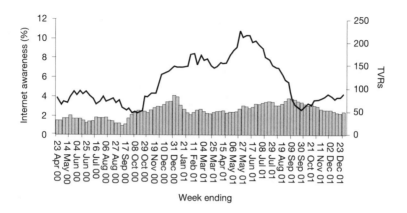

Figure 29: *Internet awareness vs. TVRs*
Base: 18–34-year-old men
Source: Millward Brown, 16-week rolling data

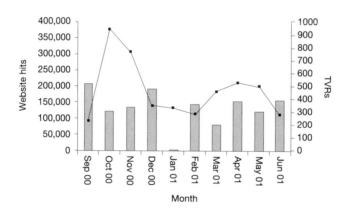

Figure 30: *Website hits vs. TVRs*
Source: Circle

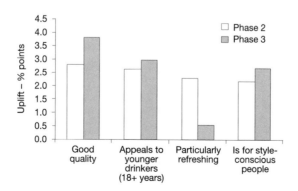

Figure 31: *Budweiser brand image – uplifts while ads on air*
Base 18–34-year-old men
Source: Millward Brown

So we got uplift in image dimensions, but it also appears that there was a 'halo' effect because product measures lifted as well ('particularly refreshing' and 'good quality'), even though we didn't talk about them in our ads. Once we had got people to like our ads and our brand again, they started to think positively about it in every sense.

Market share started to improve in the on-trade

We've shown how the new ads boosted ad awareness in Phase 1, and how they increased awareness and image in Phase 2, with additional media spend. We'll now show how advertising reversed the decline in market share.

As expected, the first signs of recovery appeared in the on-trade. Once again, although there were some encouraging signs in Phase 1, it wasn't until share of voice increased in Phase 2 that a clear growth trend emerged in both volume and value terms. This growth was sustained right through Phase 3 when 'Whassup' was on air.

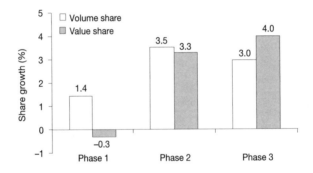

Figure 32: *Budweiser share growth: on-trade*
Source: Nielsen

It's interesting to note that these increases in market share lagged behind those in brand awareness that we observed earlier. Salience appeared to be driving market share, not vice versa.

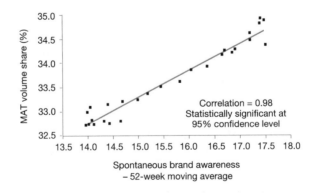

Figure 33: *Budweiser volume share vs. spontaneous brand awareness, on-trade: April 1999 to June 2001*
Source: Nielsen, Millward Brown

Once again, we can show that advertising was responsible. Market share followed share of voice, with a slight lag (Figure 34).

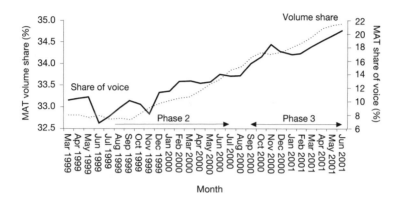

Figure 34: *Budweiser PPL volume share vs. share of voice, on-trade*
Source: Nielsen, MMS

Once the lag is accounted for there is a clear correlation between the two (Figure 35):

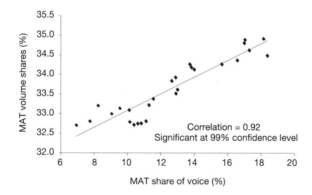

Figure 35: *Budweiser PPL volume share vs. share of voice, on-trade: April 1999 to June 2001*

Sales in the off-trade followed the on-trade
As expected, the off-trade took a little longer to respond. It wasn't until Phase 3 that market share clearly started to rise, in both volume and value terms (see Figure 36).

With everything in place, the brand's fortunes turned around
By the time 'Whassup' broke in Phase 3, everything was in place. We had great ads, decent share of voice and the buzz of a cultural phenomenon. As a result, Budweiser's overall market share stopped falling and began to rise once again (see Figure 37).

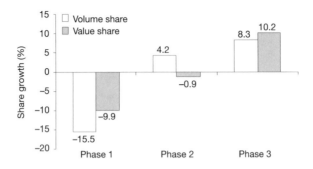

Figure 36: *Budweiser share growth, off-trade*
Source: Nielsen

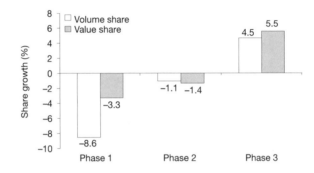

Figure 37: *Budweiser share growth total (on- and off-trade)*
Source: Nielsen

Not only that, Budweiser's sales actually began to increase, something we hadn't anticipated.

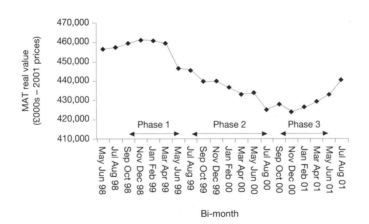

Figure 38: *PPL Budweiser real value sales on- and off-trade*
Source: Nielsen

This success was clearly linked to the new advertising. We've shown how the new ads, together with an increase in share of voice, increased brand salience and how that led to share gains in the on-trade, and how share gains in the off-trade followed in turn. As a result, there is a clear correlation between overall market share and share of voice (Figure 39).

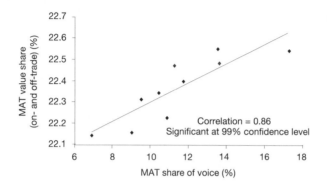

Figure 39: *Budweiser value share vs. share of voice, November/December 1999 to May/June 2001*
Source: Nielsen, MMS

Note that overall market share lags behind share of voice by 18 months. This reflects the fact that on-trade market share lags slightly behind increases in brand salience, and off-trade market share lags further behind on-trade market share (Figure 40).

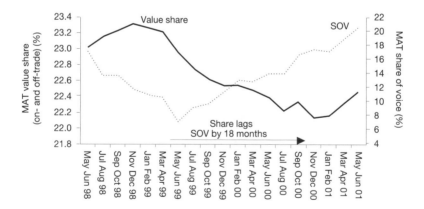

Figure 40: *Budweiser value share vs. share of voice*
Source: Nielsen, MMS

MEASURING THE EFFECTS OF THE ADS

The direct contribution of the advertising was estimated using two econometric models – one on-trade and one off-trade.

The econometrics show that the advertising was the main factor behind Budweiser's growth in the on-trade. Without any advertising support, share would have barely grown since the beginning of 1999.

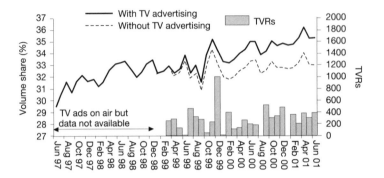

Figure 41: *Budweiser: estimated effect of TV advertising on-trade volume share*
Source: Econometric model

We've demonstrated that share in the off-trade took longer to turn around. The econometric model for this sector shows that without the advertising, Budweiser's share would actually have suffered a significant decline (Figure 42).

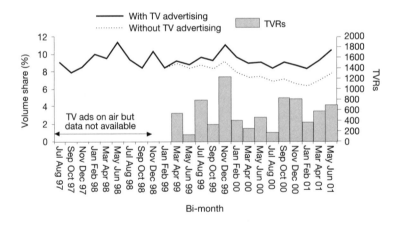

Figure 42: *Budweiser: estimated effect on TV advertising on-trade volume share*
Source: Econometric model

So the advertising worked as expected

The advertising worked exactly as intended. Advertising awareness increased with each new campaign, until we reached the point where our ads were getting scores twice as high as our nearest rival, Stella Artois. The ads got people talking about them and about Budweiser. Brand awareness improved, and so did brand image. As a result market share started to rise, first in the on-trade, and then in the off-trade. At each stage we've shown that the improvements in Budweiser's fortunes correlate with advertising. Finally, we've measured the size of the effect using econometric modelling. We will now demonstrate that no other factor can explain the brand's new-found success.

Discounting other factors

The state of the market

None of the improvements in Budweiser's fortunes can be attributed to the state of the PPL market – we have seen market share gains in both on- and off-trade sectors.

Brand distribution

Although Budweiser already has very high distribution, there was a small increase in on-trade brand distribution over the period. But rate of sale also rose and at a faster rate than that of distribution.

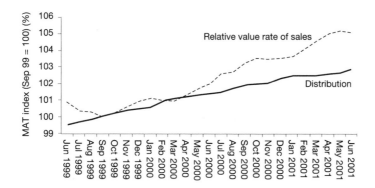

Figure 43: *Budweiser 330 ml bottle distribution and relative value rate of sale, on-trade*
Source: Nielsen

Furthermore, we have measured the effects of this distribution change using the on-trade econometric model. They are small relative to the advertising effect.

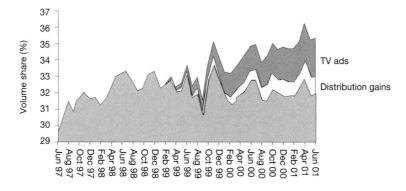

Figure 44: *Estimated effect of TV ads and brand distribution gains, Budweiser on-trade volume share*
Source: Econometric model

In the off-trade, brand distribution has remained static (Figure 45):

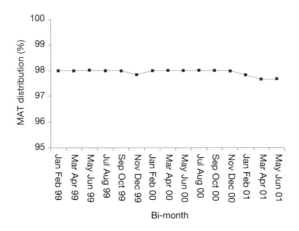

Figure 45: *Budweiser distribution, off-trade*
Source: Nielsen

Product range

Two new variants were launched while the campaigns were on air – a 500 ml can and a 946 ml bottle. These launches couldn't be responsible for a significant proportion of Budweiser's growth over the period because:

- since launch, they have accounted for only 2% of Budweiser's value share
- they have been available only in the off-trade, which has enjoyed lower growth than the on-trade.

We've also accounted for the effects of changes in the product range in the off-trade using econometrics. This confirms that the contribution of new launches has been small relative to that of the advertising.

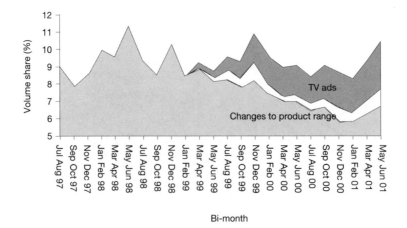

Figure 46: *Estimated effect of TV ads and product range changes, Budweiser off-trade volume share*

Price

Budweiser's relative price has changed little over the two years since 'Frogs & Lizards' was first shown. In fact, relative price has hardly moved in both the on- and off-trades. Price, therefore, cannot have helped increase share while the ads were on air.

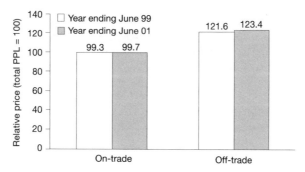

Figure 47: *Budweiser relative price*
Source: Nielsen

Promotions

Unlike many of its competitors, Budweiser does not have an active policy of continuous price promotions, although a small number are undertaken from time to time. This activity has not changed over the period of this paper.

The advertising paid for itself and more

Between January 1999 and June 2001,[5] Anheuser-Busch spent £25m on Budweiser's TV advertising.

The models tell us that this increased sales by the equivalent of 67 million bottles and increased value by £80m. But this is just the effect of the ads when they were on air. The econometrics also tells us that the ads have other long-term effects. The £25m that Anheuser-Busch spent over the two-an-a-half-year period will continue to generate a further 72 million bottles and £77m of extra revenue over the next six years. So, in total, *our spend of £25m will generate extra sales worth £157m.*

TABLE 2: ADDITIONAL BUDWEISER VOLUME AND VALUE DUE TO ADVERTISING

	While ads on air (Jan 99 to Jun 01)	Subsequent effect	Total effect on *retail* sales
Volume (330 ml equivalents)			
On-trade	17.5m	12.7m	30.2m
Off-trade	49.3m	59.2m	108.5m
Total	66.9m	71.9m	138.8m
Value			
On-trade	£36.9m	£27.2m	£64.1m
Off-trade	£43.0m	£50.2m	£93.2m
Total	£80.0m	£77.4m	£157.4m

Source: Econometric models

---

5. Although the 'Frogs' activity started in October 1998, data limitations mean that the econometric models are estimated from January 1999.

Anheuser-Busch has a strict company policy of not disclosing any figures relating to profitability. However, they are prepared to confirm that the advertising has been a strong financial success.

Efficiency

We have shown that the ads were effective – they achieved and exceeded their goals. But were they efficient? One measure of efficiency is Millward Brown's AI score.

The ads achieved the highest Millward Brown AI scores ever recorded by Budweiser or *any* other brand in the category.

TABLE 3: AI SCORES, PPL CATEGORY

Budweiser (1997 maximum)	5
Budweiser (1998 maximum pre 'Frogs')	7
Budweiser ('Frogs')	18
Budweiser ('Frogs & Lizards')	20
Budweiser ('Whassup')	20
Stella Artois ('Heroes Return')	14
Kronenbourg ('Femme Fatale')	4
Holsten Pils ('Crisps')	2
Becks ('Naturally')	2

Source: Millward Brown

So why didn't we do more?

After six months, it was inevitable that the novelty would wear off.

'I knew it was time to drop it ['Whassup' catchphrase] as soon as my dad started saying it.'

BMP qualitative research 2001

So it was time to bow out gracefully. In any case we already had a world-class successor to 'Whassup' standing by.

Although the scope of this paper is UK only, we have undertaken some quantitative analysis[6] of Budweiser's image in markets where 'Whassup' ran versus those where it did not. We cannot prove that the campaign alone is responsible for brand health in those markets. But it is interesting to note that Budweiser's health has seen positive shifts wherever 'Whassup' ran.

People state that they are more likely to buy Bud in advertised markets (see Figure 48).

There is also an uplift in the number of people claiming to have a better opinion of the brand (see Figure 49).

---

6. Proprietary quantitative survey administered on a global basis by DDB.

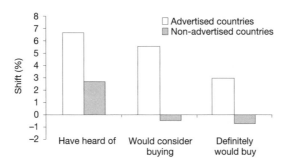

Figure 48: *Shifts in purchase intention*
Source: DDB International Quantitative Study

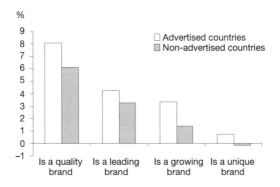

Figure 49: *Shifts in perceived image*
Source: DDB International Quantitative Study

SUMMARY AND CONCLUSIONS

Anheuser-Busch and DDB returned Budweiser to share growth via a winning triple formula of outstanding advertising which bravely re-expressed Budweiser's American provenance in a highly appealing way for 18–34-year-old men.

The effects of this advertising were maximised by giving subsequent campaigns the correct levels of media spend for them to achieve their real potential.

Finally, the brand's fortunes were turned around by a mixture of the above two elements, but with the added impetus of a cultural phenomenon which helped to make Budweiser the buzzword of a nation. All testament to an innovative, pioneering approach to marketing from Anheuser-Busch.

8

Dairy Council

*From bland to brand: how the Dairy Council
showed it was made of 'The White Stuff'*

Principal authors: Andrew Perkins, Myriam Vander Elst and Sara Donoghugh,
BMP DDB, and Helen Croxson, OMD UK
Collaborating authors: Les Binet and Sarah Carter

EDITOR'S SUMMARY

'The White Stuff' campaign of 2000–2001 dramatically improved the fortunes
of milk. A strong insight into the image of milk and its consumers led to a
powerful creative idea and a media strategy that used an unprecedented range of
communication channels, from TV and radio, to packs, milk trucks and even
farmers' fields. This made the campaign four times more efficient than had
been predicted, to give farmers and dairies a £20.8m return on their £8.2m
investment.

This is a paper about turning a bland commodity into a desirable brand. It shows how even the most overlooked, taken-for-granted product, in long-term decline, can reinvent itself and reverse its fortunes.

When BMP DDB and OMD UK won the Dairy Council account, milk was a product going downhill fast. It had a poor image, it was a victim of changing demographic and social trends, and it was being squeezed out by increasingly competitive and sophisticated soft drinks marketing.

And then came 'The White Stuff', a combination of insightful strategy and systematic use of every possible communication channel.

In 18 months milk underwent a metamorphosis. The sales decline was reversed, branded bottles sold at a 133% price premium and ultimately farmers and dairies saw a return of almost double their investment.

'I can imagine a man on the moon but I can't imagine them selling milk in cans from the machine in school.'

'It'd be like trying to sell tap water at a premium.'

Source: Transparent Research June 1999

THE CHALLENGE: REVIVING A MARKET IN STRUCTURAL DECLINE

Hard times: milk was threatened on all sides

Consumption was in long-term decline

When BMP DDB and OMD UK won the Dairy Council account in March 2000, milk was in a sea of troubles. The total consumption of milk had been in almost continuous year-on-year decline since the mid-1970s (Figure 1).

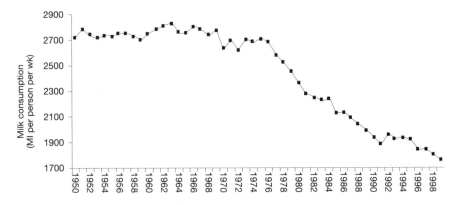

Figure 1: *The relentless decline of milk consumption*
Source: National Food Survey

Eating and drinking habits were undermining consumption

The times were conspiring against milk, with changing demographics and a decline in home cooking, sit-down breakfast and tea consumption. Changing purchasing behaviour had made the situation even worse. People who have milk delivered to

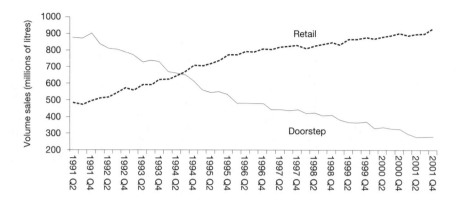

Figure 2: *Cannibalisation of doorstep by retail sales*
Source: MMD

their doorstep tend to consume more, but doorstep sales were losing out badly to retail.

The combined effect was a rapid and apparently unstoppable decline in total sales (Figure 2).

Milk's image was dire

The Dairy Council's ad campaigns have traditionally focused on milk as a drink rather than as an ingredient, since it is the only usage they can act upon independently of other food manufacturers.

But here the situation looked even worse. Research showed that people's relationship with the drink had soured. It was so familiar that it went almost unnoticed, and lacked any sort of strong personality. In other words, it was a commodity. Any personality it did have was fairly abysmal – bland, boring, babyish.

Competition was tough, and marketing minimal

Consumers were bombarded on all sides by superbly marketed soft drinks, splendidly packaged and backed by heavy advertising spend. Increasingly brand-conscious and independent children were being wooed by the likes of Sunny Delight, while an ever-expanding range of waters, fruit juices and smoothies were being targeted at adults (Figure 3).

Meanwhile, poor old milk was suffering; supermarkets stocked it in rickety wet crates; packaging was distinctly unappealing; and advertising spend had fallen dramatically as the 1990s had gone on.

The Dairy Council fights back

A new marketing campaign

In 1999, dairy farmers and the dairy trade agreed to fund a new generic marketing campaign for milk. The Dairy Council was appointed to implement and monitor the communication strategy, and we were appointed to tackle the creative and media solutions.

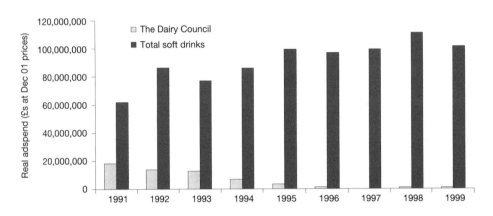

Figure 3: *The David and Goliath battle for share of voice: NDC and competitors' adspend*
Source: MEAL, MMS

An ambitious business objective
The objective of the campaign was to slow the decline in sales.

By 1999 the Dairy Council had been using an econometric model, built by MMD,[1] for 12 years, which allowed it to project milk sales to calculate optimum marketing budgets. MMD predicted that a £7m campaign would slow the decline in sales by 35m litres after 12 months and 63m litres after 18 months. This was our target (Figure 4).

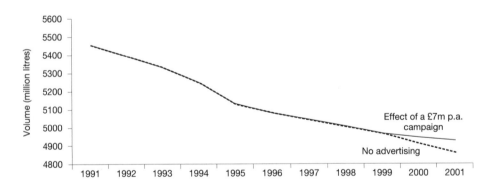

Figure 4: *Predicted effects of advertising on milk sales: household liquid milk consumption 1991–2001*
Source: MMD

Three key client mandates
We had a well-thought-through brief from the Dairy Council. The Council had commissioned extensive research prior to appointing agencies and had a clear idea of what the communication needed to do.

---

1.   MMD is a business consultancy that specialises in econometric and financial modelling.

- *Promote milk as a drink.*   Although drinking 'neat' makes up only 8% of all milk consumption, this is the only area where communication could have any kind of control independent of cereal, tea or coffee advertisers.

- *Target parents.*   Many previous milk campaigns had targeted children (e.g. 'Accrington Stanley' and 'Cool for Cats'), who drink by far the greatest volume of milk. But those were different times. Now the feeling at the Dairy Council was:

  > 'Competing head on with soft drinks and targeting children is not an option ... This is primarily because the budget available is only a fraction of what is spent by individual soft drinks manufacturers. A further weakness in such a strategy is the fact that the Dairy Council has no control over milk packaging and distribution.'

  Instead, the campaign needed to encourage *parents* to drink milk, 'thereby endorsing it through their actions'.

- *Reach children via their parents.*   While the campaign needed to be accessible to children, its long-term success would come through creating 'virtuous circles' of milk drinking: kids would keep up the milk-drinking habit because their parents did, and would then grow up to be milk-drinking parents themselves (Figure 5).

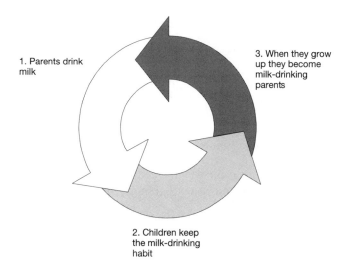

1. Parents drink milk

2. Children keep the milk-drinking habit

3. When they grow up they become milk-drinking parents

Figure 5: *Creating a virtuous milk-drinking circle*
Note: Children with milk-drinking parents are 25% more likely to drink themselves
Source: The Dairy Council pitch brief, Omnibus

The communications strategy: from bland to brand

So we had an extremely tough task.

Our strategy would be to turn milk from a bland commodity into a credible brand, through heroism and 'surround sound'.

Parents were too narrow a target

The Dairy Council's brief to us then was to target parents. However, there simply weren't enough milk-drinking parents out there to achieve our sales volumes. Research had already shown that encouraging *non-drinkers* to drink milk was definitely out. Non-drinkers of milk tend to be unswervingly non-drinking; once you drop the habit, you drop it for good.

To hit our targets, we would have to increase frequency among current parent drinkers, but also cast our net far wider, and appeal to *all* milk drinkers, including children and non-parents.

The communications would have to have extremely broad appeal and reach.

Making milk heroic, modern, public and ubiquitous

We knew that milk had seriously lost its bottle with consumers. Now our strategy had to centre on finding that nugget which would help us reinvent its image.

Milk had a very peculiar image. When you asked consumers about it, they tended to reel off the facts they were taught in school: it's healthy, full of calcium and vitamins, makes you fit and strong. So milk drinkers are pretty fantastic people then?

Well, not quite.

When respondents in groups were asked what milk drinkers were like, this was the sort of thing we heard:

'A quiet child, she would be intelligent, but wouldn't have too much to say. She wouldn't wear shoes through the house.'

'Boring rucksack-types who go walking in the Dales.'

'White skinned, skinny with big teeth. He'd be a loner, not popular or funny, he'd be picked on. I wouldn't want to sit by him.'

'Not a party animal, she should be at a WI meeting.'

Source: Transparent research

Milk drinkers were dull, dull, dull. They were old-fashioned and they were anonymous.

And because most milk is drunk at home and straight from the fridge, it also has a private, slightly tawdry feel to it. As one respondent said:

'You're standing in the kitchen with your kids in your underpants – it's hardly fashionable.'

Source: Transparent research

Scary stuff. Milk was the shabby, unnoticed granny in the soft drink family. We needed to make milk modern, visible and high profile.

And no milk drinker wanted to be told that milk was healthy. They all *knew* that already. But this goodness wasn't being translated into any emotional feel-good. How unfair can you get? People who drank the lowest kind of yucky, sugary toxin were constantly made to feel great about it through swanky lifestyle ads. But the noble, underground race of milk drinkers never felt any kind of emotional reward for treating their bodies like temples.

This wasn't about health. It was bigger than that. This was about pride, about doing something fine and noble, about having emotional strength, guts and gumption.

Milk drinkers aren't hill walkers.

They're heroes.

Now all we needed to do was overturn years of seeing milk as a bland, over-looked commodity, and make it a public, ubiquitous, modern brand that said 'hero'.

Tricky.

TABLE 1: THE FOUR IMAGE-SHIFTS MILK NEEDED

Dull and boring	→	Heroic
Old-fashioned	→	Modern
Private	→	Public
Anonymous	→	Ubiquitous

The task demanded a multi-channel approach

We had set ourselves an immense task. We were effectively trying to turn tap water into wine. Media and creative would have to work extremely hard to do this.

We had to say that milk was heroic, in a contemporary way that would make it live again. But we were fighting years of ingrained prejudice, and the muscle of the big soft drinks brands dwarfed our budget. We needed to get clever, exploiting all possible channels, and get everyone to work on our behalf: farmers, dairies, the news media, schools, retailers. Only by creating a 'surround sound' campaign would we be able to get the job done.

Most importantly, media and creative work were integrated from the beginning to tackle the specific problems we faced.

The total makeover of milk

We systematically tackled the four image-shifts – heroic, modern, public and ubiquitous.

From dull and boring to heroic

- *TV and radio led the campaign.* We chose TV and radio as our lead channels. Using broadcast media would reinforce stature. The ads showed milk-fortified characters performing acts of everyday heroism. They had gumption and they had backbone. And each of the ads was signed off with a classic piece of British pluck: the theme tune to *The Great Escape*. Best of all, we had a bold, modern image of a glass of milk, ironically referencing Guinness, and a ballsy, challenging endline.

- *The icon let us go into outdoor.* We had a great icon, which we knew would have massive impact when translated into 48-sheet posters, building our stature.

Figure 6

SFX: We hear screams of terror...

Eubank: Do thumthink Pwinth Nath!

Naseem: ...But I hate them!
Eubank: Not more than me. I hate them more than you.
I do.

Eubank: Be careful. Don't hurth ith legths!
Naseem: Throw it out the winda!

Eubank: Yeth, well done, well done.

V/O: The White Stuff. Are you made of it?

Figure 7: *Boxers*

Assistant: Bestie!
George: I'd like a football shirt, please.

Assistant: Right. You talking home or away. First strip, second strip, European Champions strip, this season, last season, next season?

George: No. Just your basic red shirt. No logos. No name on the back. No holographic sponsors message. No funny squiggly bit. No Designer label. No limited edition Designer label.

Assistant: Here George. You been drinking?

George: Yeah! What of it?

V/O: The White Stuff. Are you made of it?

Figure 8: *Bestie*

Rolf: Little bit here. He he. And a bit there. He He.

Kid: Oh Dad!
Rolf: Ah, poor little mites. If they don't get some tucker soon, they'll be too weak to make it through the day.

Rolf: Allow me. I'll just wet my whistle first.

SFX: Didgeridoo and wobble board.

Kids: YEAH!

V/O: The White Stuff. Are you made of it?

Figure 9: *Rolf*

Boy: 'Grandma Thora?'

Thora: 'Yes, love?'

Boy: 'There's a spiritual being with a black cloak and a scythe outside.'

Thora: 'Oh well, let's have some milk.'

Boy: 'OK.' (glug glug)

(Ding-dong)

Being: 'I am the reaper.'

Thora: 'Look, I don't need pegs, encyclopaedias or double-glazing.'

Being: 'I am here to claim...'

Thora: 'I don't need me knives sharpened, me drive tarmacked or my religious views changed.'

Being: 'But you...'

Thora: 'In fact I don't need anything – now hop it.'

V/O: The White Stuff. Are you made of it?

Figure 10: *Thora (radio)*

- *PR amplified the heroic theme.*   The heroic theme was interpreted in the most creative ways to get great PR results. For example, the intrepid Dairy Council Marketing Manager Andrew Ovens got very excited about the campaign. So much so that he entered the 'Bird Man of Bognor' competition, flying a replica Spitfire named 'The White Stuff'. Although he only managed a measly 4.25 metres before plunging into the icy waves, he did get coverage in national newspapers.

  He's fine now, in case you were worried.

From old-fashioned to modern

- *The ads had a cool, modern style.*   The ads took place in a cool, animated world that made milk feel contemporary. In this 'White Stuff World' celebrities live side by side with ordinary folk – a world where George Best pops into the local sports shop, and Rolf Harris is your next-door neighbour. The advertising had broad appeal, speaking to parents, but without being 'mumsy' and alienating non-parents or children. The work appealed to the adult in the parent, rather than the parent in the adult.

- *'The White Stuff' appeared in 'zeitgeist programmes'.*   We set the advertising in an adult and contemporary environment, avoiding all children's airtime. In addition we supplied specially made 'White Stuff' props in programmes that are central to the zeitgeist, such as *Eastenders* and *Big Brother*. By setting 'The White Stuff' firmly in contemporary culture, we helped milk find its place in modern life.

- *Going online reinforced milk's modernity.*   We totally revamped the Dairy Council's website to represent 'The White Stuff' world (Figure 11). This featured the ads themselves, pocket biographies of the stars, and a 'Great Escape' ringtone and 'White Stuff' visual to download on to your mobile phone.

Figure 11

From private to public

- *The ads brought milk drinking out of the closet.* We had to break that tawdry, private image of milk drinking and bring it out of the closet. So the ads featured acts of brazenly open swigging.

    The most public media – TV and outdoor – were used.

    Parents were the epicentre of the campaign, but media made sure we reached families when they were together, in order to make milk more communal and help reinforce the 'virtuous circle' of milk drinking. We advertised in top jointly viewed programmes, school holidays, videos of family audience films that were also heroic (e.g. *Chicken Run* and *The World Is Not Enough*) (Figure 12).

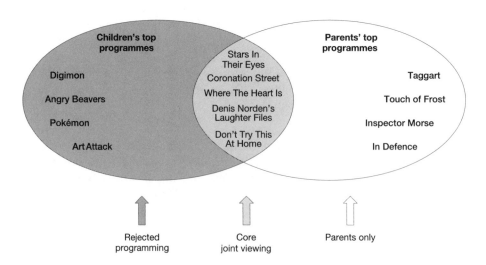

Figure 12: *Reaching families watching TV together*
Source: BARB, June–July 2000

- *Branded bottles made milk a public drink.* In its original brief, the Dairy Council had said it had no control over packaging. With the success of our campaign however, independent dairies took up 'The White Stuff' on their bottles. Over the course of the campaign, Wiseman Dairies branded over 300 million packs of milk with The White Stuff.

  Then in the summer of 2001 the fully branded 'White Stuff' bottle hit the shelves.

Figure 13

- *Point of sale drew attention to milk.* BMP and OMD travelled around the country to present 'The White Stuff' to the main supermarket chains, persuading them to support the campaign. As a result, point-of-sale material ran in Sainsbury's and Safeway stores, and Sainsbury's ran free of charge a six-sheet poster campaign worth an estimated £80,000.

Figure 14

Figure 15

- *Roadshows took milk outside.* The Dairy Council set up a White Stuff Sampling Experience, which visited 20 shows throughout 2000 and 2001. At the St Helen's show in July 2000, the stand proved so popular that it had to be roped off to protect staff from the scrum that formed, and 5000 bottles were given away in less than four hours.

  In the summer of 2000 as a whole, 135,000 White Stuff branded bottles were distributed.

- *Milk bars took milk back to school.* The farmer-owned co-operative First Milk launched the first White Stuff branded milk bar, at Sandbach School in Cheshire. First Milk's Deputy Chairman, Roger Evans, said:

  'The potential for milk in schools is enormous. The White Stuff graphics and packaging are striking and perceived as cool. First Milk's school bars present an up-to-date image to enable milk to compete on an equal footing in schools with the soft drink brands.'

  Thanks to White Stuff branding, including branded 250 ml bottles, the milk bars sold 8944 more pints in 2001 than in 2000 (a 55% increase). Martin Mills, Milk Bars Manager, said:

  'The White Stuff livery and the generic campaign encouraged the dairies, in particular the Co-op, to make use of the milk bar (and the Roadshow vehicles) more than ever before when milk marque and the farmers had the sole interest in the milk bar.'

- *PR kept milk in the news.* By using celebrities, we knew we could get good PR and raise the profile of milk. We were ironically fortunate to begin with, as George Best was hospitalised when 'Bestie' ran. But we couldn't rely solely on lucky breaks. As the campaign developed, PR agencies Keizo and Red Rooster were able to plant stories about future celebrity ads in order to gain extra publicity.

  While Jerry Hall was appearing naked in *The Graduate* in the West End, we had a caricature mocked up, and spread the story that she was to be the latest

'White Stuff' star. And while it may have been bad news for pop music, planting a story about a forthcoming 'Hear'Say' ad got the campaign great publicity in *The Sun*.

From anonymous to ubiquitous

Milk was the invisible drink. We had to spread 'The White Stuff' wherever you went, creating 'surround sound' to the extent of creating new channels.

- *Media strategy splashed 'The White Stuff' everywhere.* Our media strategy made maximum use of the budget. Radio gave us high-value frequency, at times when our audience wouldn't be watching TV. By complementing TV, we could follow our target throughout the day. Meanwhile, a poster campaign helped us establish the endline and reach people outside the home.

- *Media strategy made the campaign last longer.* The media planned a burst-and-then-drip approach with the television ads modelled to obtain optimum continued awareness. The burst phase was multimedia and created a 'surround sound' effect. In the drip phase we continued advertising at breakfast when media are good value. We could therefore allow for multiple creative executions, letting us build a 'White Stuff World'.

- *We reached people at their 'milk moments'.* Research had shown us when milk was drunk during the day. We focused the media activity at these times to nudge people when they were most likely to drink, focusing on point of consumption rather than point of purchase. The drip phase centred on breakfast, when consumption is highest. Luckily most of these times correlated with the times when most people jointly viewed television (e.g. teatime with the children).

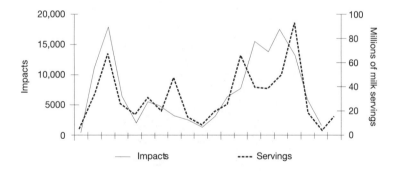

Figure 16: *Bought airtime reflected 'milk moments'*

- *Creating new communication channels to take the campaign further.* After meeting with various farmers' groups and rallying them around the campaign we produced a 'How to post your own 48 sheet' guide. Barns and fields all over the country proudly displayed posters of the White Stuff. In total, 1300 were erected by farmers (Figure 17).

Figure 17

– Throughout 2001, milk tankers all over the country were plastered with the logo (Figure 18). In total 1400 liveries were run, and at the time of writing most trucks still bear the icon.

Figure 18

– Merchandising: In the 18 months of the campaign, the Dairy Council distributed 5000 postcards, 10,000 stickers, over 5500 T-shirts, 30,000 bumper stickers, 30,000 car stickers and 200 Stetson hats (Figure 19).

Figure 19

We had systematically tackled the four problems: fighting to make milk heroic, modern, public and ubiquitous.

And in the process, with the new bottle, the POS and website, the big TV and prompting radio, we had achieved something greater.

Milk had started behaving like a brand.

	2000							2001											
	J	J	A	S	O	N	D	J	F	M	A	M	J	J	A	S	O	N	D
TV burst (all channels)	▇			▇								▇							▇
TV drip (breakfast emphasis)		▇			▇				▇					▇		▇			
TV prop supply (mini-posters, branded bottles)										▇	▇	▇	▇	▇	▇				
Radio	▇		▇					▇						▇					
Outdoor (48 sheet roadside)	▇		▇																
Outdoor (48 sheet in farmers' fields, etc.)				▇	▇	▇	▇	▇	▇	▇									
Video					▇						▇	▇	▇						
Roadshows (White Stuff merchandise = hats, T-shirts, stickers and postcards)	▇	▇	▇									▇	▇	▇					
Tanker livery								▇	▇	▇	▇	▇	▇	▇	▇	▇	▇	▇	▇
POS (Sainsbury, Safeways, Wiseman's Express, Dairy Crest, etc.)		▇														▇	▇	▇	
Car/bumper stickers	▇	▇	▇	▇	▇	▇	▇	▇	▇	▇	▇	▇	▇	▇	▇	▇	▇	▇	▇
PR	▇	▇	▇	▇	▇	▇	▇	▇	▇	▇	▇	▇	▇	▇	▇	▇	▇	▇	▇
Website (inc. downloadable ringtones)	▇	▇	▇	▇	▇	▇	▇	▇	▇	▇	▇	▇	▇	▇	▇	▇	▇	▇	▇
School milk bars												▇	▇	▇	▇	▇	▇	▇	▇

Figure 20: *The Dairy Council's channel exploitation*

MADE OF IT: ACHIEVEMENTS

In what has been a tough couple of years for the farmers, 'The White Stuff' has been a tremendous success. In 18 months we have seen:

- A massive turnaround in consumption and value sales.
- A sustained price rise.
- Increased revenues for farmers and dairies.
- Outstanding returns on investment.

In the following section we will see how this fully integrated campaign met and then outstripped the targets set. We will look first at the business and marketing results, and then prove that it was the Dairy Council's campaign that was responsible for this dramatic reversal of the fortunes of milk drinking.

Finally, we will attempt to calculate the financial returns that the campaign delivered.

The reversal of fortunes

It worked – business results

'The White Stuff' set off a dramatic turnaround in the levels of milk consumption. Within two years we have reversed a decline that had been going on for 25 years. Indeed, this is the first time milk has enjoyed two consecutive years of growth in consumption since 1963 (Figure 21).

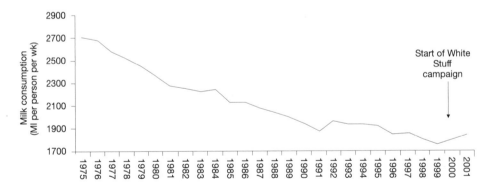

Figure 21: *Two consecutive years of growth in consumption*
Source: National Food Survey, Expenditure and Food Survey

This is all the more remarkable given that the retail price of milk has risen. After a long price war by retailers, the average price of milk since 2001 has increased by over 6% on the doorstep and by over 11% in the shops (Figure 22). Consumption has risen, with shop prices at their highest levels since 1996.[2]

---

2. Source: Milk Monitor 2002.

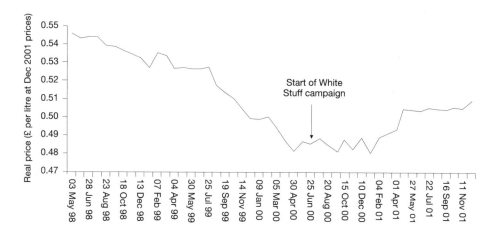

Figure 22: *Milk no longer a casualty of the price war*
Total milk real price
Source: Taylor Nelson Sofres

The effect of the price rise and the growth in consumption has been a substantial turnaround in the value sales of milk. Since the start of the campaign, the decline in value sales rapidly slowed, until by the summer of 2001 we were seeing continued and accelerating growth (Figure 23). It is hard to exaggerate what a revolution in the recent history of milk this represents.

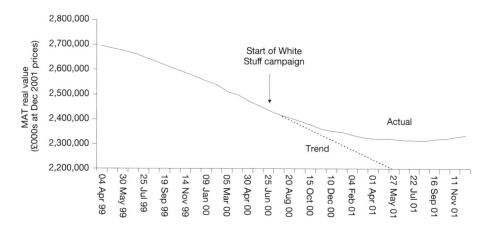

Figure 23: *Slowing down the decline in sales*
Note: MAT = moving annual total
Source: Taylor Nelson Sofres

This wasn't just increased revenue for the supermarkets and dairies however. The farmers themselves have benefited, as the farmgate price of milk (the price at which farmers sell on milk to dairies) also rose (Figure 24).

The combined effect is dramatic – a sustained growth in milk producers' revenue (Figure 25).

So, the campaign has worked to turn around the business fortunes of milk.

205

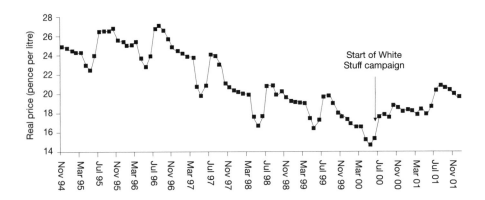

Figure 24: *A turnaround in the downward spiral of farmgate prices*
Source: Milk prices surveys DEFRA, SEERAD, DARD (NI)

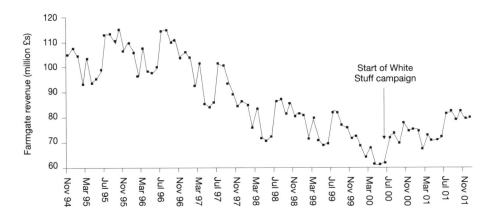

Figure 25: *The income of milk producers increased*
Source: Milk Monitor, Milk prices surveys DEFRA, SEERAD, DARD (NI)

How it worked – marketing results

We had planned the campaign to be loud and proud, stressing the heroism of milk drinkers and squeezing every last drop of sound from the channels we used.

And this is precisely what we saw.

The Dairy Council had set us the target of achieving the equivalent of a Millward Brown awareness index of 5. This translated into an awareness score of 35% in the Martin Hamblin tracking study. In fact, the campaign regularly achieved awareness scores far exceeding the target. Awareness peaked among adults in January to February 2001 at 46% (Figure 26).

- *'The White Stuff' on everyone's lips.* This was a campaign that punched well above its weight. Scores for campaign recognition were extremely high, far outstripping what one might expect from the level of adspend. Recognition of the phrase 'The White Stuff. Are you made of it?' peaked at a massive 91% in September/October 2001. The fact that nine out of ten people recognised the

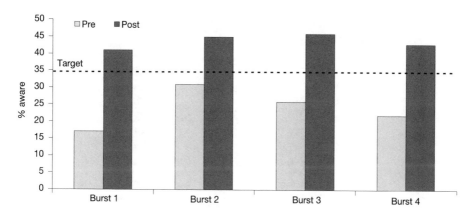

Figure 26: *The campaign exceeded advertising awareness targets at every burst*
Base: All adults
Source: Martin Hamblin

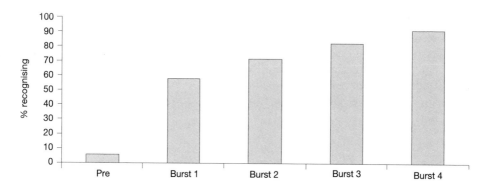

Figure 27: *Recognition of 'The White Stuff. Are you made of it?' peaked at 91%*
Source: Martin Hamblin

phrase is strong testament to the combined success of media and creative (Figure 27).

> 'It's the Phrase 'The White Stuff' that sticks more than anything else.'
>
> Source: Mark Lifton Research, March 2000

In addition to the tracking study, there is good evidence that 'The White Stuff. Are you made of it?' has taken on a life of its own, and has become part of the vernacular.

> 'My son says that all the time. "Get some more of the White Stuff in, mum."'
>
> Source: Forrest Associates research

After years of newspapers referring to milk as 'bottle' in headlines, we have started to see 'White Stuff' become the set phrase.

In other words, 'The White Stuff' was public.

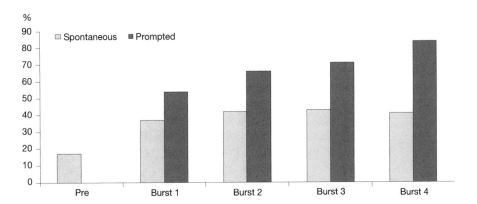

Figure 28: *TV advertising reached record levels of awareness*
Source: Martin Hamblin

- *Breadth of media was key.* There is strong evidence that the high scores achieved were only made possible thanks to the breadth of media used. As expected, television accounted for a large proportion of attributed campaign awareness and recognition (Figure 28).

  As can be seen, each burst of TV advertising saw a substantial growth in recognition. One execution alone, 'Rolf', was recognised by over three-quarters of adults in September 2001.

  And posters, despite low spend, also tracked very well with recognition at 61% (Figure 29).

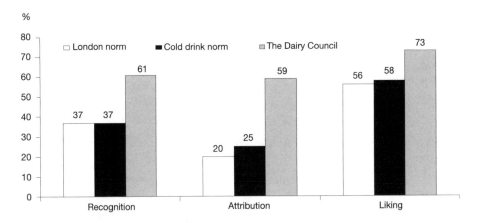

Figure 29: *Poster tracking broke category norms*
Source: IPSOS RSL/Maiden Outdoor

'Excellent recognition levels (61%) especially for an infrequent user of the medium. Outstripped both the London and cold beverage norms ... Excellent attribution levels achieved (59%) against both the London (20%) and cold beverage (25%) norms (high brand awareness due to strong branding).'

Source: Ipsos RSL/Maiden Outdoor

Radio recognition peaked at 29% among adults who listen to commercial radio. On average, radio added an extra 3% to total advertising recognition in each period.

Although not tracked, we know from qualitative research that the other channels of the campaign were being noticed. In March 2001, we were meeting respondents who enthused about having seen 'The White Stuff' on the sides of milk lorries, on packs, and also in farmers' fields.[3]

There is evidence that the more media people were exposed to, the more positively they viewed milk (Figure 30).

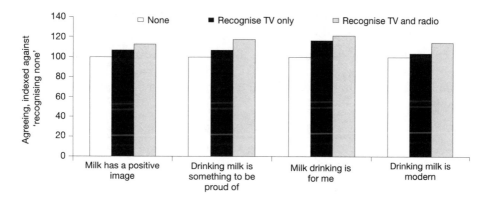

Figure 30: *Image scores higher among those recognising TV and radio*
Base: All adults
Source: Martin Hamblin

- *The campaign was greatly enjoyed.* But we wanted more than noise. We wanted to endear people to milk through a loveable, charming campaign. This is exactly what we achieved. We know from the tracking study that the ads were extremely well liked (Table 2).

TABLE 2: ATTITUDES TO ADS

% agreeing	Average for all four TV executions
I like the ad	85
Different from other ads	83
Appealed to my sense of humour	81
Easy to follow	89

Source: Martin Hamblin

And this sentiment has been backed up fully by qualitative research.

'They were really enjoyable for a change.'

'It would make you think have you seen the next one?'

'They've got characters that appeal to the kids but the humour is more adult.'

Sources: Mark Lifton research and BMP research

3. Source: Forrest Associates research.

It wasn't just the TV ads that did it for people. The 'Thora' radio execution has also proved a firm favourite.

> 'I actually thought that was really good, because you'd think they'd never have the balls to do something like that with Thora.'
>
> Source: Transparent research

But best of all was the end frame. Anything that is recognised by over 90% of the population must have something going for it. Qualitative research confirmed that it *'works very well to endear people to milk. The line was extremely popular in groups'*.[4]

Our brief had been to come up with big, populist advertising. 'The White Stuff' certainly provided that.

- *The campaign communicated well.* But it wasn't just about being loud and loved. The campaign needed to make people feel proud about being a milk drinker. Tracking showed that the TV ads strongly communicated our message (Table 3).

TABLE 3: RECEPTION OF MESSAGE

% agreeing	Average for all four TV executions
Showed milk in a positive light	79
Made milk drinker look like a hero	55
Would encourage people to drink more	63
Made milk look modern	68

Source: Martin Hamblin

Qualitative research confirmed that the ads managed to convey both the heroism of milk drinkers and encourage people to think of milk as a drink for today.

> 'He doesn't solve the problem because he is Rolf Harris. He solves it because he is a milk drinker, an everyday hero.'
>
> 'Milk is said to make her strong. Not physically but in the sense of having the willpower to do the right thing. She is an everyday hero.'
>
> Source: Forrest Associates research

> 'It says she's plucked up her courage after drinking milk.'
>
> 'Milk makes you brave.'
>
> 'It's cool to drink milk.'

Again, the endline proved extremely successful, conveying the intended message perfectly.

> 'It's saying get more in.'
>
> 'Are you getting enough?'
>
> 'Calling it The White Stuff means it's not plain and ordinary anymore.'
>
> 'The line is fighting talk, it symbolises a perceived new vigour and self-confidence surrounding milk.'
>
> Source: Forrest Associates Research

---

4. Source: Forrest Associates research.

- *The image of milk improved.* So 'The White Stuff' was reaching and being remembered by people. It was a campaign that was greatly enjoyed, and it was communicating as intended.

  But it was also vital that the campaign improved the image of milk (Figure 31).

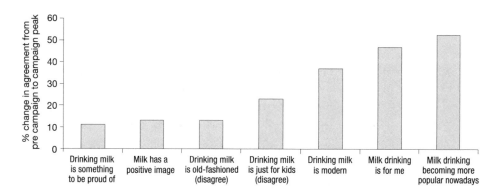

Figure 31: *Improvements in milk's image*
Base: Parents
Source: Martin Hamblin

- *From bland to brand*: But this was about more than simply improving the image of milk. Something more revolutionary was going on.

  As shown earlier, the feeling at the Dairy Council had been that milk simply could not compete with branded soft drinks. It was too bland, too old, too much of a commodity. But there was something about that in-your-face line, and that tongue-in-cheek 'Guinness negative' image of a cool, white glass of milk that insidiously got to people.

  While we knew that the phrase was tracking extraordinarily well, it wasn't until The Dairy Council commissioned qualitative research that we really began to see what the campaign had done.

  It had turned a commodity into a brand.

  > 'Many lines work because they evoke well-established advertising properties. They are the endlines that call a piece of audiovisual communication to mind. *The White Stuff is bigger than this. It transcends the status of endline. It is a brand idea. "The White Stuff" is not just a nickname; it is a brand identity* ... By making milk more of a brand it allows it to compete with other brands for share of throat. It raises it from commodity status to brand status.'

  Source: Forrest Associates research

- *Commanding a price premium.* Once milk started looking like a brand, it could start behaving like one. The best example of this took place in schools. One of milk's great problems was its lack of presence in schools. Before the campaign the Dairy Council had said that targeting children was 'not an option'.

  Before 'The White Stuff' was born, we were hearing comments like this:

  > 'I can imagine a man on the moon but I can't imagine them selling milk in cans from the machine in school.'

Enter the school milk bar.

> 'This is out chill cabinet where we keep all the bottled drinks, cartons of drink and our sandwiches, and as you can see we're just adding extra milk, The White Stuff. The White Stuff – it's a repackaged bottle of milk in a small plastic container, says 'The White Stuff' on it, which the kids seem to love. It's selling very, very well. When we were asked to promote it I was very, very sceptical and I said they'll never buy it but it's selling excellent ... The White stuff's selling at 35 pence ... *we used to sell it in small glasses at 15, 20 pence a glass – the kids wouldn't entertain it but since it's been repackaged in the bottles at 35 pence, they don't question the price.*'

> Christine O'Hagan, Kitchen Manager, Walbottle Campus School, Newcastle
> Source: BBC Radio 4, *You and Yours*, 19 October 2001

Once it really started behaving like a brand, milk could command a massive 133% price premium, and still hugely increase sales.

The Bursar of Sandbach School said:

> 'It is a fabulous resource. We were selling six milk drinks a day before we had this bar. Now it's 200 drinks a day.'

> Source: *Yorkshire Post, Farmer's Guardian,* the Dairy Council

It was official. Milk was a brand.

Proving the campaign's effectiveness

There is substantial evidence that it can only have been 'The White Stuff' that caused the reversal in the fortunes of milk.

Timing

The improvement in the hard measures began at the same time as the campaign broke. Looking at year-on-year growth, we can see that the turnaround in consumption levels took place in the same year as the launch of the campaign (Figure 32).

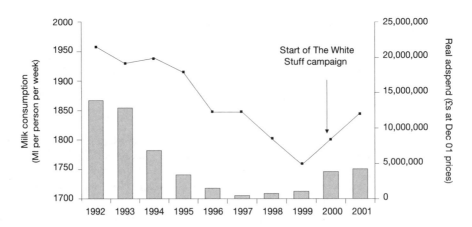

Figure 32: *Consumption rises at the start of the campaign*
Source: MEAL, MMS, National Food Survey, Expenditure and Food Survey

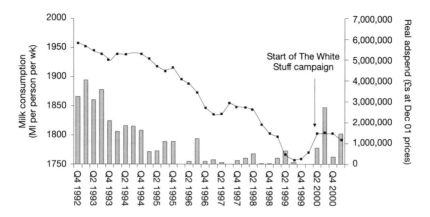

Figure 33: *The campaign had an instant impact on consumption*
Source: MEAL, MMS, National Food Survey

When we investigate more closely, we can in fact time the significant growth in consumption to the exact quarter in which 'The White Stuff' was born (Figure 33).

Perhaps the clearest demonstration of this effect is in the turnaround of value sales. Here the change occurs at the exact month in which the campaign broke (Figure 34).

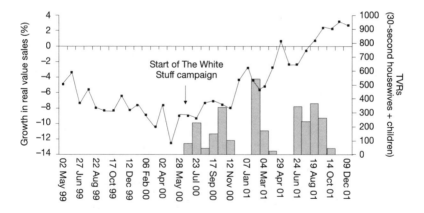

Figure 34: *The instant effect of the campaign on value sales*
Year-on-year change in 4 w.e. value total milk sales
Source: Taylor Nelson Sofres, BARB

But there is more evidence than simply the timing of the sales turnaround.

Behavioural proof

We expected the campaign to have a greater impact on retail sales because our target audience buys its milk mostly from supermarket chains. Retail sales also tend to respond more quickly to changes in consumption habits than doorstep sales. In fact, this is exactly what we saw (Figure 35).

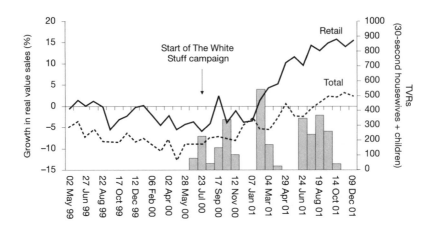

Figure 35: *The turnaround benefited retail sales greatly*
Year-on-year change in 4 w.e. value total and retail milk sales
Source: Taylor Nelson Sofres, BARB

In addition, media were bought at times when people might be prompted to grab a glass of milk. This would often mean they would have to pop into their local corner shop or garage. We therefore predicted that we would see a particularly strong uplift in impulse above all other sales channels. Again, we were proved correct in our predictions (Figure 36).

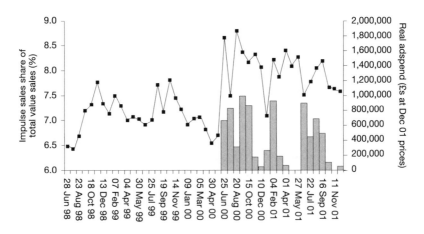

Figure 36: *The contribution of impulse sales grew immediately*
Source: MMS, Taylor Nelson Sofres

Note here also that the timing of the rapid increase in impulse sales corresponds, to the month, with the start of the campaign.

The plan was always to increase frequency rather than penetration of milk drinking, and this is exactly what we saw happen (Figure 37). Since day one, the growth in consumption has been driven by the rise in frequency.

This growth in frequency has come at a time when frequency of total drinking has fallen slightly – a clear indication of the turnaround in milk's fortunes over the period of the campaign (Figure 38).

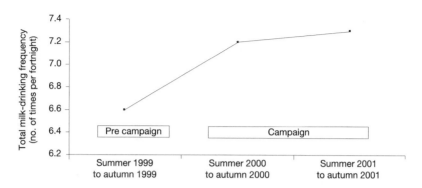

Figure 37: *In line with the strategy, frequency of milk drinking grew*
Source: TNS Family Food Panel, children and adults

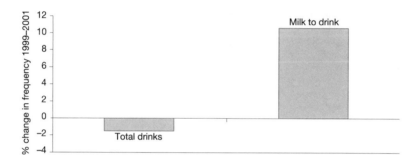

Figure 38: *Between 1999 and 2001, milk frequency grows strongly while frequency of total drinks falls*
Source: TNS Family Food Panel

Again, in line with our strategy, the growth in frequency has not been restricted to one age-range, but has in fact been true for all ages (Figure 39). This is strong testament to 'The White Stuff' having been the big, populist campaign that we intended.

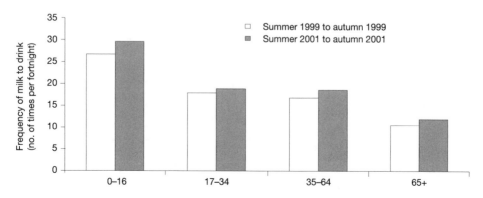

Figure 39: *Increase in frequency of milk drinking across all ages*
Source: TNS Family Food Panel

Awareness and attitudes

Satisfyingly, awareness seems to be particularly high in households where there are three or more people present, suggesting that we were successful among our core target of parents (Figure 40).

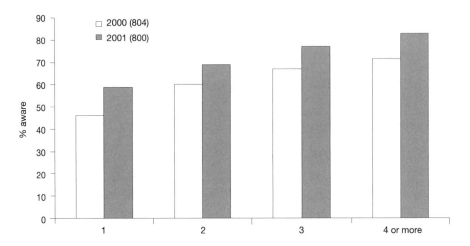

Figure 40: *Highest awareness scores in households with three or more people*

Attitude and image statements correlate with TVRs and awareness, which clearly demonstrates that advertising is responsible for changing attitudes (Figures 41 to 44).

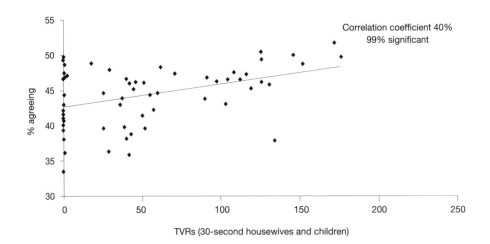

Figure 41: *Making milk a more popular drink*
Base: Parents
Source: Martin Hamblin, BARB

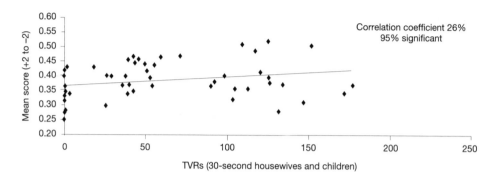

Figure 42: *'Milk is something to be proud of'*
Base: Parents
Source: Martin Hamblin, BARB

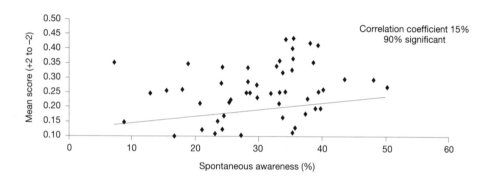

Figure 43: *'Milk drinking is for me'*
Base: Parents
Source: Martin Hamblin, BARB

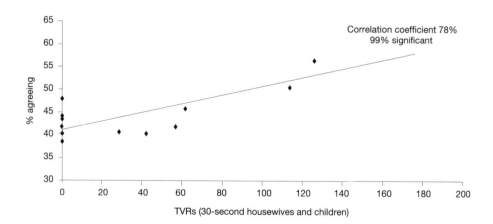

Figure 44: *'Milk has an up-to-date image'*
Base: Parents
Source: Martin Hamblin, BARB

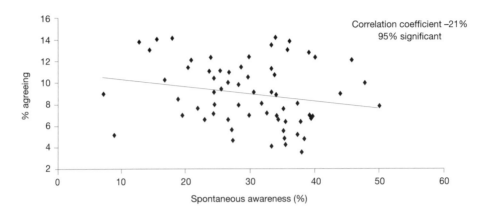

Figure 45: *'Drinking milk is just for kids'*
Base: Parents
Source: Martin Hamblin, BARB

Awareness of the campaign has a corrective effect on the negative attitude towards milk (Figure 45).

Having looked at other factors that may have affected the growth of milk, we have been unable to find anything significant; demographics have not changed quickly enough to have any effect, and there has been no change in distribution or pack size. Other factors, such as the economy, competitor activity and health scares, will have only worked against us.

To recap, we have shown that the fully integrated 'The White Stuff' campaign was responsible for the turnaround in the fortunes of milk between June 2000 and December 2001. We will now go on to show the payback of the campaign, and demonstrate how efficient our integrated strategy has been.

Payback time

Econometric modelling
The original target was for the campaign to generate additional sales of 35m litres after 12 months and 63m litres after 18 months.

In fact, 'The White Stuff' has far outstripped these targets. Econometric modelling shows that the actual additional sales generated were 121m litres after 12 months and 266m litres after 18 months (Figure 46). In other words, it has generated well over three times the sales predicted originally.

This means that the campaign has given fantastic return on investment for both farmers and dairies.

Dairies will have had a £9.9m return on a £4.1m investment by December 2002 alone (Figure 47).

By the same date, farmers will have received a £10.9m return on their £4.1m investment (Figure 48).

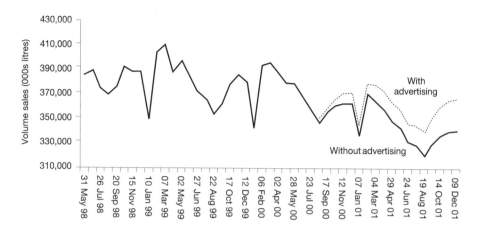

Figure 46: *Milk sales would have been lower without advertising*
Source: BMP econometric model

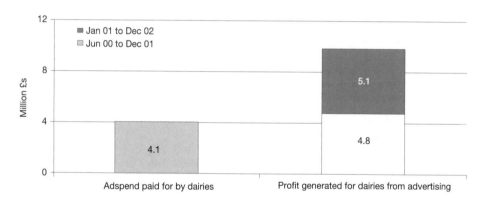

Figure 47: *Dairies will more than double their investment by December 2002*
Source: BMP econometric model, *Dairy Industry News*

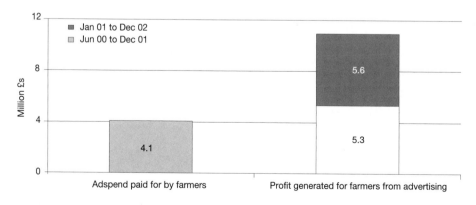

Figure 48: *Farmers will more than double their investment by December 2002*
Source: BMP econometric model, DEFRA

Price increase

Obviously, due to the commercially sensitive nature of the information, we are unable to provide direct evidence from retailers on the influence of our campaign on the price rise. However, the Dairy Council said:

> 'The White Stuff played an important part in creating an environment in which supermarkets were prepared to increase the retail price of milk.'

Efficiency

- *Media buying efficiency.* We bought TV, radio, video and outdoor extremely efficiently.

  - Video delivered extra exposure at 60% discount off TV
  - Radio added cover and frequency cheaply
  - TV 'drip' airtime was bought into more cost-effective channels (GMTV, satellite).

    > 'The Dairy Council pricing is very sharp – cheaper than the pool in every way.'
    >
    > Source: TV Media Audits buying review 2001

  - Posters we printed and stored for free in advance, enabling us to play the short-term market to maximise return.

    > 'The flexibility shown by the Dairy Council permitted an extraordinary 60% discount to the pool to be negotiated. This did not reduce the quality of the campaign.'
    >
    > Source: Outdoor Media Audits buying review 2001

- *Efficiency of the new channels.* Making full use of free media gave the campaign massive extra muscle (Table 4).

TABLE 4: FREE MEDIA

	Worth (£)
Prop supply (media ratecard value)	516,000
Sainsbury's own posters	80,000
Farmers' 48 sheets	1,500,000[5]
Tankers	3,500,000[6]
PR value estimate	750,000
Total	6,346,000

- *Sales efficiency.* We have shown throughout this section how 'The White Stuff' has punched well above its weight in so many ways. The big Dairy Council campaigns of the past have also increased consumption, but it is only 'The White Stuff' that has achieved two consecutive years of growth (Figure 49).

This is unprecedented in recent milk history.

---

5. Source: Outdoor Connection/OMD estimate based on 75% take-up of materials requested and two months' run.
6. Source: Outdoor Connection/OMD estimate based on eight months' run. Since many tankers are still running the ads, the figure of £3.5m may well be much higher.

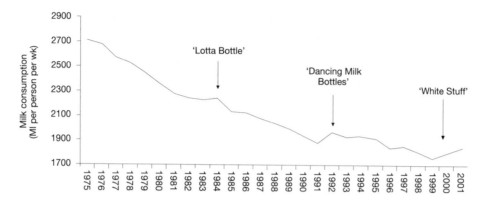

Figure 49: 'The White Stuff' tops advertising efficiency
Source: National Food Survey, Expenditure and Food Survey

The MMD model used to set our sales targets was based on the efficiency of previous campaigns. The fact that we exceeded those targets suggests that the new campaign was far more efficient.

We are confident that it is thanks to our successful utilisation of more channels than ever before that we can see something like this (Figure 50).

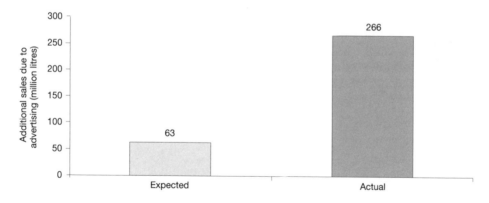

Figure 50: 'The White Stuff' was four times more efficient than we expected
Volume uplift from advertising: generic milk campaign vs. White Stuff
Source: BMP econometric model, MMD econometric model

A land flowing with milk and honey

We were going to call this paper 'Against All Odds', but then we thought it sounded a bit cheesy.

The sentiment is right though. We have demonstrated how a strong enough insight into the consumer's heart, and integrated communication across *all* channels (even creating some new ones), can give even the most bland-seeming commodity all the emotional values of a brand.

And, of course, once you start looking like a brand, you can start behaving like one. This means creating pride in your consumers, justifying a price rise, and ultimately increasing returns.

Milk, after all those years in the wilderness, had suddenly got a wiggle in its walk. It had earned the right to show off.

Now what was that about selling tap water at a premium?

9

Domino's Pizza
Building a high street brand through a change in media strategy

Principal author: Charlie Makin, BLM Media
Collaborating authors: Chris Moore, Steve Booth and Graham Hawkey Smith

EDITOR'S SUMMARY

This case study highlights how Domino's became brand leaders in the pizza delivery market on a significantly smaller spend than its main competitor. More so, how brand leadership and the efficacy of communication helped drive a highly successful AIM listing and how a subsequent shift in brand-responsive advertising has demonstrably driven sales.

There are few examples where a change in media strategy has altered the fortunes of a business over a sustained period.

This paper highlights how Domino's became brand leader in the pizza delivery market on a significantly smaller spend than its main competitor, how brand leadership and the efficacy of communication helped drive a highly successful AIM listing and how a subsequent shift to brand-responsive advertising has demonstrably driven sales.

> 'Domino's total sales in the UK and the ROI for 2001 grew 29.4% to £98 million ... every time Domino's ran national terrestrial TV advertisements in the UK and Ireland, our sales increased. In turn, every time our sales increased, the size of our national TV advertising fund increased with it. This means we are in an excellent position whereby each TV campaign we run helps to support the next.'
>
> Stephen Hemsley, CEO Domino's, *Financial Times*, 9 January 2002

The Domino's story is a collective effort from a small but highly dynamic team determined to build a brand; a marketing team, a media agency, a committed media owner and franchisee operators who improved service levels to deliver the communication promise.

Our approach to this paper is to demonstrate the collaborative essence of the team; it has therefore been prepared as a series of interviews with key players to demonstrate how a highly successful strategy emerged as it was played out.

However, there are certain landmarks in the story:

- In 1998, Domino's sponsored *The Simpsons* on Sky One.
- In 1999, Domino's was the first advertiser on Sky's Open shopping channel and delivered Europe's first digital TV order.
- In 1999, Domino's floated on AIM.
- In 2000, Domino's was the first advertiser to run transactional interactive TV campaigns on Sky.
- In 2001, Domino's ran national terrestrial campaign focusing on the HeatWave technology.

THE STRATEGY

Chris Moore – Sales and Marketing Director, Domino's Pizza

Chris, can you briefly describe the delivery pizza market in the UK?
Broadly we compete against any form of convenience food; this ranges from kebabs to hamburgers. Within pizza delivery itself, the industry is divided 50:50, half being independent stores and the other half branded companies: Pizza Hut, Perfect Pizza (Papa John's) and ourselves.

What prompted Domino's to consider an integrated communication strategy?
Domino's had a poor brand image. We had an old logo that had been designed in 1960. On top of that we had a reliance on delivery by moped. The only part of the image we could control was the leafleting. But it provides no barrier to entry. Pizza delivery has always been seen as the daggy end of the convenience food market. What we needed to do was to extract ourselves from that and put Domino's in a

position where we could offer a premium service, a premium product and get the premium price that comes with that.

Evidence: Domino's produces 120 million leaflets a year. Some households in London receive 15 leaflets a week from pizza delivery companies.

Is is true that building a brand was especially important given your business is predominantly franchisee owned?

Fifteen per cent of our stores are corporately owned and 85% are franchisee owned and to attract new franchisees into the system you have to show great returns. This means attracting customers and getting repeat purchase.

Evidence: Mintel shows only 27% ordered a take-away or home-delivery pizza in the past three months; increased penetration is clearly an opportunity.

Evidence: independent research commissioned in January 2002 demonstrates that by far the top reason for a franchisee to join the Domino's system is the brand.

In 1998 you sponsored The Simpsons *on Sky One. Was that the first attempt in trying to build a brand?*

That really was the first shift.

Using TGI's 'Specially Choose to Watch' analysis BLM identified *The Simpsons* as the ideal programme for our target audience.

There were three further factors that were crucial to the selection of *The Simpsons*. First, it's the right time of day (6 p.m. to 7 p.m.) to prompt purchase. Second, it's a great fit, and the attitude and personality of the show differentiate the brand (Figure 1).

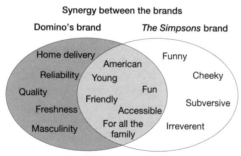

Figure 1: *Brand imagery*
Source: SPA Quantitative Research

The final consideration was audience delivery. *The Simpsons* offered a large audience with remarkably little wastage for the task of reaching pizza eaters (67.6% of those who 'specially choose to watch' *The Simpsons* 'like to eat take-away foods'; 44.3% of Pizza Hut customers 'specially choose to watch' *The Simpsons*).

In 1998 *The Simpsons* was the highest rating programme on Sky One. In 2002 it still is.

Can you talk about how you generate budgets?
We have a national advertising fund (NAF) based on a levy we charge franchisees (4% of net sales). If those figures increase dramatically, as they have in the past 15 months, we plough more money back into TV advertising; it's a virtuous circle.

In 1999 Domino's floated on AIM. How important has marketing been in driving shareholder value?
It has been vital because shareholders and potential investors know what Domino's stands for.

You've recently started, perhaps, a more conventional advertising strategy on terrestrial television. Can you talk how that has driven your business?
Over the first three years *The Simpsons* sponsorship created a competitive positioning for Domino's based on personality rather than product differentiation or innovation. In January 2001 Domino's stores used a major technological innovation called HeatWave that guaranteed your pizza was delivered 'oven hot' to your door.

Our competitors didn't have the technology. Therefore we had the opportunity to attract two sets of new customers while adding to the service already provided to our existing customers.

Qualitative research identified two new target audiences:

1. Customers of competitor stores (specifically Pizza Hut).
2. Lapsed/occasional pizza eaters who have (through experience) low expectations of home-delivered pizza.

> 'You don't expect them to be hot – you know they never are – they're warm.'
> Source: SPA Research, September 2000

We wanted to reach these audiences quickly, efficiently and at the right time of day to prompt purchase. Pizza Hut's heavy use of TV effectively defined the media battleground for the launch of HeatWave. However, on the limited budgets available we had to deliver a highly targeted TV campaign.

Of the top 50 TV programmes selected by these target audiences as 'specially choose to watch':

- 18 are on satellite channels (all between 5 p.m. and 10.30 p.m.)
- 18 are on Channel 4 (15 between 5 p.m. and 10.30 p.m.)
- Six are on Channel 5 (all between 5 p.m. and 10.30 p.m.)
- Nine are on ITV (only four between 5 p.m. and 10.30 p.m.)

The TV strategy for the launch of HeatWave therefore used satellite and Channel 4 exclusively with a programme-specific buying strategy.

Can you instantly attribute sales to a specific advertising campaign?
Yes. The classic example is right at the beginning of 2001 when we ran terrestrial TV advertising for the first time for HeatWave. We were convinced we could afford only three weeks of advertising, and those three weeks were going to be a one-time hit in January, but then events really took over and we saw the virtuous circle begin to work its magic. We had a huge increase in sales in January as a result of the TV

advertising and quite astonishingly that gap between 2001 and 2000 remained constant, so by April we had already generated enough funds to go back on TV. We ended 2001 with a total of five TV bursts.

Evidence: sales for the first seven weeks of 2001 were up 30.5%.

And you attract more franchisees ...
I think the story on franchisees is twofold.

We have seen an increase in the number of enquiries, a 40% increase in 2001. We have also seen a huge increase in the quality of the candidates.

So your communication strategy has implications for the entire business?
Absolutely.

Another intangible benefit of *The Simpsons* sponsorship is that like all fast-food companies we are competing in a fairly small labour pool. To handle increasing business we need drivers, pizza makers and order takers all the time on a regular basis. Now it's cooler to work for Domino's and that makes a big difference when you are trying to hire people.

Steve Booth – Chief Executive, BLM Group

What was the initial thinking behind sponsorship? Why did it fit the brief better than advertising?
Advertising would not have given us any long-term advantage, we would have spent the budget in two to three weeks and that would have been that. Sponsorship allowed Domino's to own a property and also allowed us to be on air every day of the year.

How important was BSkyB as a media partner?
Sky was fantastically supportive when we struck the original deal. It was a massive leap of faith for Domino's. Sky was as equally confident as we were that it was a good fit and, as such, gave us the opportunity to test for three months.

Sky was also crucial in helping us push back the barriers with the ITC of what was achievable in terms of sponsorship credits.

The Simpsons offers us a great franchise with Sky viewers which we have been able to exploit with lots of other platforms, such as 'Great Nights In'. Unlike many media owners, Sky will look at different commercial relationships, such as Meal Deals which have gone right through to our leafleting where you package up a pizza and a pay-per-view movie with Sky Box Office.

Chris Moore – Sales and Marketing Director, Domino's Pizza

Chris, you committed the majority of your national advertising budget to broadcast sponsorship in 1998. Did you consider it a risk?
Absolutely. First because it was a fairly new area in the media market. Second, with sponsorship there were some pretty draconian laws around at that time about what you couldn't say in the credits; for example, we couldn't show the product, we couldn't talk about the product overtly, we could only make a reference to the programme and show the logo.

I think the one thing that swung the decision for us was that we were going to get our brand on national TV every single day of the week at dinnertime, plus we were going to be associated with a hip programme. Literally, within six months, we went from being known for mopeds to the guys that sponsor *The Simpsons*.

So you saw immediate results?
Immediate results in terms of perception and in terms of sales. We had something in the stores that was known as 'The Simpsons Rush'. Which was amazing if you think the actual sponsorship didn't show a product, didn't get people's appetite going and simply talked about Domino's – a fresh slice of family life delivered in 30 minutes.
    Evidence: see Figure 2.

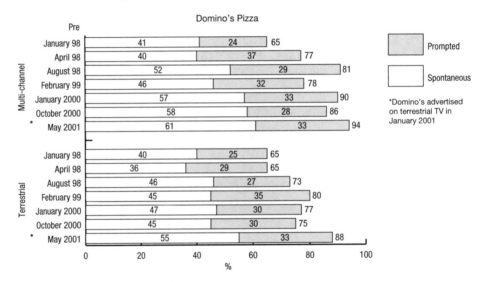

Figure 2: *Brand awareness*
Base: All respondents (WI pre *n* = 337, WII *n* = 318, WIII *n* = 321, WIV *n* = 335, WV *n* = 350, WVI *n* = 338, WVII *n* = 348

So it worked way beyond any expectations of either you or the franchisees?
Hugely. Our awareness before *The Simpsons* started was 65%. Within one year that had moved to 81%.

Which is extraordinary considering you were on only one channel in a small proportion of homes that were multi-channel at that stage.
Exactly, but I think that serves to really underline the success of the programme which resulted in lots of appointment viewing. People who don't have Sky will go to their mate's house to watch *The Simpsons*.

I suppose in many respects the relationship with BSkyB has been critical to how your business has developed?
I think the whole relationship with Sky has been critical, starting with *The Simpsons* and with Open and Sky Active, and from that we have had many other opportunities. The list is endless.

Mark Wood – Commercial Director, BSkyB

Do you think BSkyB has added value for Domino's beyond the normal remit of a media owner?
One of the problems of getting advertisers and media owners to work together is to find advertisers for whom those new developments are relevant. Just because you can do something doesn't mean you should. Domino's was the first to get real value from all the extensions that we have done.

What Domino's managed to do was to use the new technology of interactive television and internet ordering to take an existing relationship with a programme into new media and generate substantial returns through transactional channels.

Do you search out specific innovations and ideas for them?
Yes, unquestionably. If you were to look at the advertisers that were first to use interactive television with Sky, it's no coincidence that it's our long-term sponsors.

Stephen Hemsley – Chief Executive, Domino's Pizza

You were recently quoted in the Financial Times *as saying that Domino's investment in television is a major driver of sales. Can you describe the underlying business strategy that helps deliver this?*
The underlying business strategy is to deliver what you promise. The message communicated via TV last year was home delivery, superior quality and hot pizza.

To make sure we got a payback on that we had to go back to the stores and to make sure we could deliver on that promise. One of the focuses at store level was what we called PSI – product, service and image.

Our credibility would have been blown if we had gone out with extensive TV advertising and the experience that the customer enjoyed did not meet or exceed what we promised.

Domino's moved from being a poor number two to being the dominant brand in the market in a relatively short period of time. What factors helped achieve this?
Brand awareness. The last four years the awareness of who we are and what we do has grown out of all proportion. *The Simpsons* sponsorship certainly helped with our flotation. Also product quality has been critical and what we call 'kerb appeal'.

As Chief Executive you have a lot of stakeholders to satisfy. How important is the communication strategy in terms of servicing them?
It's vital. The particularly difficult dynamic is with the franchisee; our ability to deliver our promise to the customer is not a direct one. It's a vicarious route and the communication strategy helps us manage it.

John Shedden – Domino's franchisee, south-west London

As a franchisee, how important was it for Domino's to build a brand identity through television?
I think it's critical; it's something we had been anxious to do for quite some time.

Were you worried when the idea of sponsoring The Simpsons *was suggested? Did you think it was a risk?*
Yes. I'm 55 years old. At the beginning I was sceptical of who watched *The Simpsons* and Sky One, but over the years I have become firmly convinced it's been nothing but a good thing. I didn't realise the power of the programme. I'll tell you how deep that one goes. We have a shop in Springfield Road,[1] Horsham, and you can't believe the amount of time I get the mickey taken out of me.

When you first started running advertising at the beginning of 2001, did you see any effect?
You don't need a chart to see the weekends when we are on the TV. Just being in the stores, it's immediately apparent, it's that noticeable. Ten or 15 per cent of the lift we saw last year came as a direct result of being on TV. I have no doubt it made a really dramatic impact.

Chris Moore – Sales and Marketing Director, Domino's Pizza

You have moved from what has been a highly successful niche marketing strategy to mainstream broadcast media. Did you have a grand vision or has the strategy evolved?
It's really evolved: if we do more sales, we do more advertising. We believed HeatWave was very relevant to the customer, so we decided to leverage it, nationally, through conventional advertising. Tracking research tells us awareness is not an issue; what we need to do is highlight innovations and offers and we now have a proven range of channels that almost guarantee the return we will generate.

Chris, the channel market strategy you have developed is highly sophisticated. It now embraces the internet and interactive television, as well as driving sales through more conventional channels. Could you describe how you arrived at the strategy and how effective it has been?
The synergy between watching TV and ordering a pizza means it makes a lot of sense for us to be within the interactive TV environment. Also the numbers were mushrooming. When we first started with Sky Active there were 1.8 million households and there are now 5.9 million households. It also happens to be exclusive to us. Our competitors have chosen not to follow us, probably because of an ever-increasing cost to entry.
    Evidence: See Table 1.

TABLE 1: VIEWING HABITS OF TAKE-HOME PIZZA CONSUMERS

Media	Index vs. adults
Receive satellite/cable	131
Channel 4	111
ITV	103
BBC 2	103
BBC 1	101

Base: Take-away food – type used, all pizzas combined
Source: TGI

1. *The Simpsons* live in Springfield.

The other motivation was that by going into things such as interactive TV and the internet it rang all the right bells with our target audience. Our core target audience is largely 18- to 24-year-olds, and the internet, interactive TV and new technology is their environment.

Our first port of call was to get the deal with Sky Active, and then within six months we had established an e-commerce platform with every single major interactive TV platform as well as having the on-line presence. What that has given us is an exclusive position; no other competitor has gone into this type of environment to this extent.

One reads of horror stories of e-commerce strategies failing. How have you managed to develop one that is successful?
We have not sought to ramp up the costs of putting our e-commerce infrastructure into place. We have had very lean budgets right from day one with minimal numbers of people involved and we've created a very tight network of people to make it happen. We have a system that is profitable.

We can show each product, change the prices and offer up our menu in a far more dynamic way and ultimately, it's a lot more exciting and a lot more relevant to our target audience.

Also cannibalisation was limited, but was our great fear. Only 25% of Sky Active sales were pure cannibalisation; the rest were first-time customers through interactive TV.

Is the market driven purely by innovation or do you feel that Domino's has built brand positioning that gives a competitive edge?
Obviously HeatWave was our biggest win, but it's also down to the type of company we portray ourselves as. We launched a Domino's branded popcorn with Sky Box Office and we may not sell hundreds of thousands of them, but it shows we are an off-beat company that takes its lead from *The Simpsons*.

So it's focused on in-home entertainment?
Yes, rather than a pizza being delivered as a meal replacement we want to fit within their particular lifestyle. So hence deals with Sky Box Office, for example. The other benefit of the presence on Sky with the interactive ordering ability is that we can get our message in front of millions of customers at short notice. In the England and Germany game last year, we had a reminder on Sky Digital to 3.9 million homes which said don't forget to order your pizza for the match; nothing else, no special deal. It's easy; we can do those kinds of things immediately because we are there. We had a record night that night.

THE RESULTS AND PROOF OF EFFECTIVENESS

Jon Priest – Managing Director, SPA Ltd (research agency)

How does the sponsorship of The Simpsons *work at a consumer level?*
It does work. The evidence from research is that awareness of Domino's as a home-delivery company has gone up to be the market leader in the time of the

sponsorship. What makes it special? It's the consistency and duration of the sponsorship, which is key. Domino's is becoming in the consumer's mind *The Simpsons* brand. We all know what *The Simpsons* stands for and Domino's borrows that brand equity. You only achieve that by prolonged involvement, and consumers start to decode it at a subconscious level. It's a naturally good fitting sponsor.

What about as the communication strategy has moved on into more mainstream and interactive TV? How do you see that working?
The communication still has synergy with the original communication approach; the sponsorship lays the foundations for this.

Domino's had to use the sponsorship to create critical mass for mainstream spot advertising. They all have a lot more credence because awareness has been built.

Chris Moore – Sales and Marketing Director, Domino's Pizza

Can you demonstrate that your investment in interactive TV is working?
Total e-commerce sales in 2001 were nearly £4 million, 64% year on year. The first quarter of 2002 is already 40% up on last year. This is a channel that is attracting new users every day and is paying back in spades. We are now testing and refining the customer acquisition on an ongoing basis to drive revenues. For example, we are now at the stage where we are targeting lapsed customers of both Sky Active and Domino's with on- and off-line direct marketing to maximise sales potential.

Graham Hawkey Smith – Strategic Planning Director, BLM Media

Can you prove this strategy has worked?
In the period 1998 to 2002 there is an inextricable link between communication investment and incremental sales.

1. *The Simpsons* sponsorship. An investment of £2.4m generated incremental sales in excess of £12.7m.
2. TV advertising. An investment of £0.9m in TV advertising generated incremental sales of £17.2m in 2001.
3. Competition. Although outspent 8:1 by Pizza Hut, Domino's has grown market share in a growing market.
4. Number of stores. The growth in store numbers has increased the efficiency of advertising investment. The brand stimulated demand from franchisees.
5. Individual store sales. Average weekly sales for individual stores have increased in line with advertising investment (Table 2).

TABLE 2: SHARE OF VOICE VS. MARKET SHARE

	Pizza Hut (£m)	Domino's (£m)	Domino's share of voice (%)	Domino's market share (%)
1998	5.804	0.805	12	17.2
1999	6.724	0.810	11	17.9
2000	7.284	1.100	13	20.0
2001	2.484	1.712	19	23.0

The way Domino's raises advertising funds (the weekly levy on franchisees) is key to driving the virtuous circle of commercial return from advertising investment. We have developed a model that enables us to value the financial contribution made by each phase of advertising investment since 1998. The model uses a like-for-like store basis to measure the return-on-investment for both sponsorship and TV advertising. Pre-1998 sales data form the base (Figure 3).

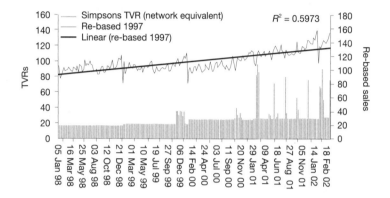

Figure 3: *Ad investment phase model*

Between 1998 and 2002, the correlation between media weight and sales (*R*-squared value) is 0.2651 (Figure 4).

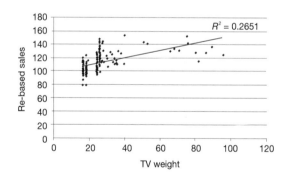

Figure 4: *Correlation between sales and weight of advertising 1998 to 2001*

Between 1998 and 2000 (*Simpsons* sponsorship only) the *R*-squared value decreases to 0.1447 (Figure 5).

This demonstrates the step change in advertising effectiveness that the evolution of media strategy delivered from January 2001.

The return on investment is expressed as both a ratio (incremental sales: advertising investment) and as an absolute cash value. Table 3 shows the initial growth of return on investment. Two key factors contributed to the increased

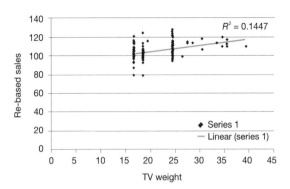

Figure 5: *Correlation between sales and weight of advertising 1998 to 2000*

efficiency of the sponsorship vehicle; *The Simpsons* sponsorship was being exposed to a growing cable and satellite universe, while more areas of the country had access to new stores.

TABLE 3: INITIAL GROWTH OF RETURN ON INVESTMENT

	Incremental sales (£m)	Domino's spend (£m)	Ratio
1998	2.04	0.805	2.5:1
1999	3.85	0.810	4.75:1
2000	6.88	1.100	6.25:1
2001	24.08	1.712	14:1

In 2001 there was a significant improvement in advertising return on investment. The HeatWave advertising reached a wider audience more quickly and efficiently than the sponsorship had previously.

Although we cannot prove the same causal link between advertising and share price performance, given the method of generating budgets and efficacy of the advertising, there is a strong likelihood that the turnaround in Domino's share price from a low in December 2000 coincides with the investment in terrestrial TV advertising (Figure 6).

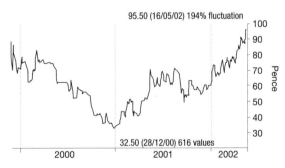

Figure 6: *Domino's share price 2000 to 2002*

The share price reached a high of 104p (double the opening price of 50p) on 17 May 2002.

10

The Economist

The importance of selling a brand, not next week's issue

Principal authors: Clare Phillips and Annabelle Watson,
Abbott Mead Vickers.BBDO
Collaborating authors: Tony Regan, Paul Gummer and Nick Crisp

·EDITOR'S SUMMARY

Unlike most media brands, *The Economist* decided, in 1988, to invest in brand advertising rather than in a tactical, content-led approach. It was a decision that paid dividends. Over the past 14 years, the award-winning 'White out of Red' campaign has helped *The Economist* to enjoy a circulation increase of 64%, against a market decline of 20%; subscriptions to the title have almost doubled; and an advertising rate card growth seven times greater than its competitors.

> The average IPA paper has an eight-word title, featuring a pun about the product, which is the maximum the exhausted entrant can manage after three months hard slog. This, however, is a paper about *The Economist*.

INTRODUCTION

A revolution has taken place in the media. Since 1985 there have been over 1500 magazine launches, over 300 new TV channels, more than 200 new radio stations and the number of websites has increased from zero to millions.[1] This dramatic fragmentation has left media owners needing to fight even harder for consumers' time and money. This paper shows how a media brand established in 1843 can compete successfully in today's increasingly competitive media market.

MANAGEMENT SUMMARY

When establishing a brand identity, a key question media businesses face is whether their communications should be brand- or content-led. Should they be judged by what they stand for or what they contain? Media brands often choose to make their communications content-led because of the pressure of short-term targets and the need for an immediate return on investment.

The Economist was ahead of its time when, in 1988, it decided to invest in the brand rather than week-by-week content. The award-winning 'White out of Red' advertising campaign established a positioning in people's minds, but more than that, a role for the brand in their lives.

As a result of its brand-building advertising, *The Economist* has enjoyed circulation and ad revenue success that outstrips its competitors; competitors who adopted content-led advertising hoping to achieve these very goals. Building the brand has also led to broader business benefits such as a huge increase in customer loyalty and scope for additional revenue streams through brand extension and expansion. All this has been achieved on a modest annual advertising budget of *c.* £1 million.

The Economist won an IPA award in 1992 by proving the substantial advertising payback over the first four years of the campaign. This paper looks at the long-term effects of advertising and provides new learning by showing how:

- A long-term brand-building campaign can be more effective for a media brand than the short-term tactical activity which dominates the newspaper market.
- Keeping a powerful creative idea consistent over 14 years has enabled continued success on a modest advertising budget.
- A consistent campaign has retained its impact because the thinking has been kept fresh and the advertising has moved with the times.

---

1. Source: PHD.

THE ADVERTISING AND MEDIA STRATEGY

The advertising problem

In 1988, Abbott Mead Vickers.BBDO and *The Economist* recognised the need for a new advertising campaign. People's choice of media was expanding (Figure 1).

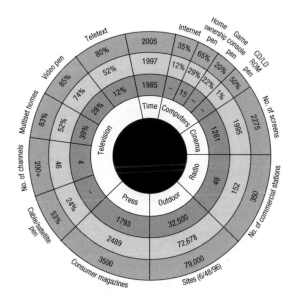

Figure 1: *Media explosion 1985 to 2005*
Source: PHD

However, people's time to consume this expanding media remained unchanged.

'We are unlikely to spend much more of our leisure time or money on the media in 2003 than we did in 1986.'

Source: The Henley Centre, *Your Money Your Time* 1998

As a result, *The Economist*, with its traditional positioning as a weekly newspaper, was competing for share in a highly aggressive marketplace. A publication with a worthy and rather intellectual image could easily be driven out of readers' repertoires, as was the case for the weekly *Business Magazine*, forced to close in the recessionary early 1990s.

The advertising objective and strategy

The objective was to encourage more people to read *The Economist* by positioning it as an essential weekly read and a brand with which they wanted to be associated.

The campaign's target audience was ambitious, busy business people. The campaign needed to both consolidate the customer base and acquire new readers.

Qualitative research conducted by AMV.BBDO provided the key that unlocked the new strategy.

When people spoke about the publication, even if they found it hard-going, they almost all revered it. They did so because of what it said about them.

> 'You don't want to be seen on the tube reading the *Mail* but you'd be rather pleased if you were spotted with a copy of *The Economist* under your arm.'
>
> Source: AMV.BBDO Qualitative Research 1988

We found that there was a link between *The Economist* and success. An emotional link that would prove to be extraordinarily powerful.

> 'There's always something in there which you can use to drop into conversations which makes you seem really clever. I wouldn't admit it but it's great for impressing people.'
>
> Source: AMV.BBDO Qualitative Research 1988

Rather than advertising content as most of our competitors did, we decided to dramatise the emotional benefit of reading *The Economist*. The creative strategy was to play on the cachet of reading *The Economist* – if you were a reader, you were part of an exclusive club of successful people. The price of admission was the price of the magazine. The creative guidelines insisted that the tone of the advertising reflect the personality of the successful club – clever, urbane – with an undercurrent of wit to move the brand away from its somewhat stuffy image.

"I never read The Economist."
Management trainee. Aged 42.

Figure 2

A poster should contain no more than eight words, which is the maximum the average reader can take in at a single glance. This, however, is a poster for Economist readers.

Figure 3

The media strategy

It is now impossible to imagine a time when any medium other than outdoor might have been considered for this campaign. Yet other media had competing claims, and it is important to take note of *what might* have happened, as well as what *did*.

It would have been cost-effective to have targeted business people more accurately and with minimal 'wastage' by identifying media that specifically reach that audience. Three such options were:

* business sections of national newspapers
* highly targeted radio stations
* *News at Ten*, which was regarded as the pre-eminent showcase for reaching opinion-formers, business people and politicians.

So why posters?

The use of posters supported the creative insight of suggesting that readers are an exclusive 'club' of successful people. If exclusivity is defined as much by those who are *not* members of the club as by those who are, then using a broadcast medium was vital to bringing the creative strategy to life.

This loyalty to posters also created a point of difference in its competitive set – no other newspaper or magazine has made significant use of the medium, allowing *The Economist* to 'own' the news category in outdoor (Figures 4 and 5).

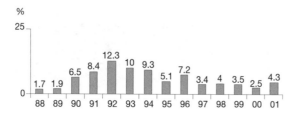

Figure 4: The Economist *overall advertising SOV within market of quality newspapers*
Source: PHD: share of total ATL media spend

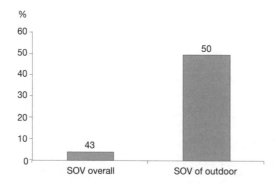

Figure 5: The Economist *SOV of outdoor within quality newspaper market vs. overall SOV in 2001*
Source: PHD

A further benefit of using posters was the creative opportunity built on the characteristics of poster exposure:

- Major sites bought on a two-week basis alongside commuter routes into city centres meant that each poster would be seen repeatedly by consumers on their daily journey to work. It gave them time to decipher the double meanings and wordplay that became an integral part of the campaign.
- Posters also allow for several executions within each campaign, which create a more rounded expression of the brand.

Finally, the medium formed a vital part of the message and the two mutually reinforced the brand communication.

This rotating poster, which was deliberately prevented from 'spinning', ran in 1997 when accusations of political spin were rife (Figure 6).

Figure 6

This 1999 'Eclipse' design on 96' Advan routed past Stonehenge down to prime viewing areas in Cornwall. From left to right the poster reads: 'Total', 'Three Quarters', 'Partial', 'The Economist' (Figure 7).

Figure 7

Poster sites at airports and train stations exploited the environment to witty effect.

'Nothing to declare' in green, '*Economist* readers' in red at Heathrow:

Figure 8

This ad ran at Waterloo Station during major rail disruption in autumn 2000:

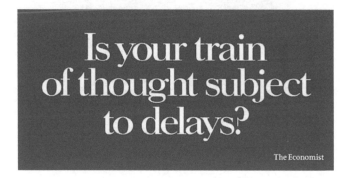

Figure 9

Consistency has been key to the success

Not only have the media and advertising strategies remained consistent over time, but the campaign creative has been consistent through the line.

Everything from direct mail and point-of-sale material, to corporate gifts such as eye masks and matchboxes, have a consistent look and tone.

Figure 10: *Eye masks on Virgin Atlantic*

Counter
intelligence.
Air trouble

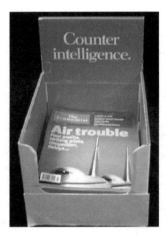

Figure 11: *Point-of-sale material*

Illuminating

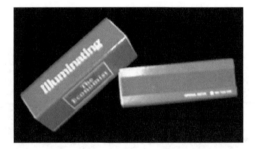

Figure 12: *Matchboxes*

The campaign has been constantly refreshed

The creative strategy and the look and feel of the campaign have remained consistent because the thinking behind them is updated continually. The brand proposition has evolved over the past 14 years to reflect the changing business, social and economic climates.

In the late 1980s, the advertising focused on business success and the conspicuous consumption of the Thatcher era with the proposition: '*The Economist* gives you the edge in business.'

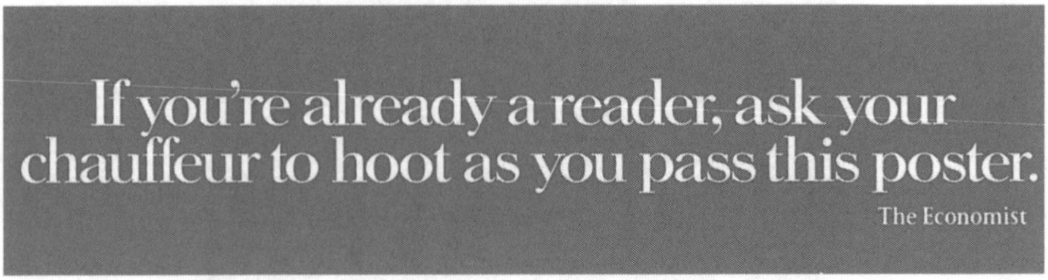
If you're already a reader, ask your chauffeur to hoot as you pass this poster.
The Economist

Figure 13

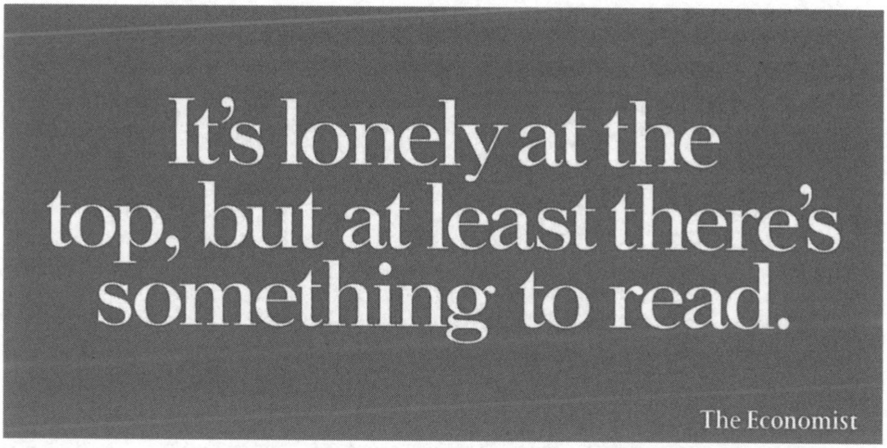

It's lonely at the top, but at least there's something to read.

The Economist

Figure 14

Hot air blowers belong in the washroom, not the boardroom.

The Economist

Figure 15

The early 1990s saw John Major's struggle against recession. Success was all about hanging on to your job. The proposition changed to 'Don't get caught out' in order to tap into that uncertainty.

If your assistant reads The Economist, don't play too much golf.

Figure 16

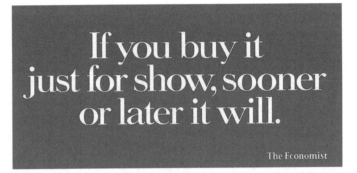

Figure 17

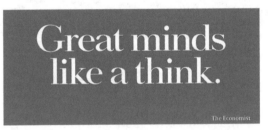

Figure 18

At the end of the 1990s with 'Cool Britannia' and the quest for a more inclusive society, the proposition was changed once more to reflect the shift towards more inwardly focused 'personal' success.

Figure 19

Figure 20

Figure 21

The fact that the campaign continues to win creative awards year after year is testament to the continuous 'fresh thinking' (Table 1).

TABLE 1: THERE HAVE BEEN 66 CREATIVE AWARDS FOR *THE ECONOMIST* 'WHITE OUT OF RED' CAMPAIGN 1988–2001

Year	Award
1988	Campaign poster: 2 × Silver
1989	Campaign press: 1 × Silver
	Campaign poster: 2 × Gold and 2 × Silver
1990	Campaign press: 1 × Silver
	Campaign poster: 1 × Silver
	Creative circle: 2 × Bronze
1991	Campaign poster: 1 × Gold and 2 × Silver
	One show (New York): 1 × Silver and 1 × Bronze
1992	Campaign press: 1 × Silver
	Campaign poster: 1 × Silver
	D&AD: 2 × Silver
	EPICA: 1 × Winner
1993	National Newspaper Campaign Awards: 1 × Winner
	Campaign press: 2 × Best of Category
	Campaign poster: 2 × Silver
1994	Creative circle: 1 × Bronze
	National Newspaper Campaign Advertising Awards: 2 × Winner
	One show: 1 × Gold and 1 × Silver
	Campaign press: 1 × Gold and 2 × Silver
	Campaign poster: 1 × Silver and 1 × Special Commendation
1995	National Newspapers Campaign Awards: 1 × Winner
	One show (New York): 1 × Bronze
	Campaign poster: Silver
1996	One show (New York): 1 × Bronze
1997	Campaign press: 1 × Bronze
	Campaign poster: Best Use of Bus Advertising and Best Media or Entertainment
1998	Cannes: 1 × Gold, 1 × Silver and 1 × Bronze
1999	Creative circle: 1 × Silver and 1 × Bronze
	One show: 1 × Gold
	Cannes: 2 × Bronze
	Campaign poster: 1 × Silver and 1 × Commendation
2000	Campaign poster: Silver
2001	Campaign press: 2 × Silver
	D&AD: 1 × Silver
	Clios: 1 × Silver and 1 × Bronze
	Cannes: 1 × Silver
	Campaign poster: 2 × Gold and 2 × Silver
	London International Advertising: 3 × Winner

Media has also helped to refresh the campaign

Large format posters have formed the heart of the media schedule since the launch; however, additional media opportunities have been exploited which helps keep the campaign salient (Figures 22–25).

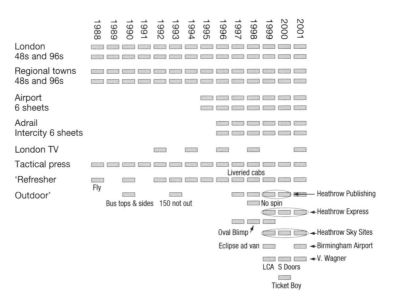

Figure 22: *Media laydown*

Figure 23: *Bus tops: 'Hello to all out readers in high office.' Bus sides: 'Get on'*

Figure 24: *London liveried cabs: 'Tips included', 'The Knowledge', 'Avoid the Pedestrian', 'Know almost as much as the Driver'*

Figure 25: 'Overview' and 'No Hot Air' on a blimp tethered adjacent to the Oval Cricket Ground for the Fifth Summer Test Match, 1997 to 1999

How the advertising works
We have developed a model which:

- summarises the advertising strategy
- outlines the way in which the advertising works (Figure 26).

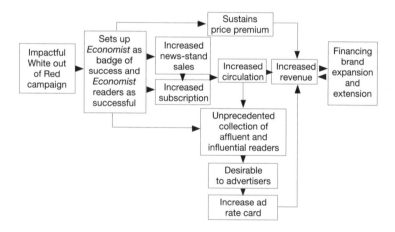

Figure 26: The effectiveness of the advertising
Source: AMV.BBDO

The consistency and continuity of *The Economist* brand campaign has paid dividends.

Increased circulation
During the campaign, *The Economist* increased its circulation by 64% (from 86,000 in 1988 to 141,000 in 2001). This is against a backdrop of decline in newspapers and magazines of 20% over the past 15 years.[2] Most of

---

2.   Source: AA, *Decline in Newspaper and Magazine Circulation 1985–2000.*

The Economist's 'competitors' – the quality dailies and news magazines – have suffered declines in circulation over the period: 40% decrease for *The Independent*; 10% decline for the *Financial Times (UK)*; 27% decrease for *The Guardian*; static circulation for *Management Today*. Indeed the only competitor to increase its circulation significantly during this period was *The Times* (62% increase), but this was accompanied by deep price-cutting (Figures 27 and 28).

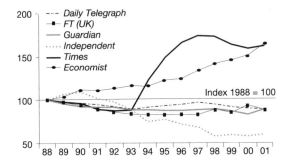

Figure 27: *Newspaper circulation figures indexed against 1988*
NB: All circulation figures include bulk sales
Source: AA and ABC

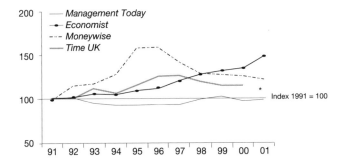

Figure 28: *News magazine circulation figures indexed against 1991*
*2001 data not available
NB: All circulation figures include bulk sales; complete data 1988 to 1990 not available
Source: ABC

Increased loyalty

In the case of *The Economist*, increasing customer loyalty means increasing the subscriber base. Over the 14-year campaign, the number of subscribers in the UK has increased, from 37,000 in 1988 to 72,000 in 2001 – an increase of 95%. As a proportion of total circulation, this is an increase from below 50% in 1988 to 64% in 2001 (Figure 29).[3]

---

3. Source: *The Economist* – proportion of subscribers excluding bulks from circulation.

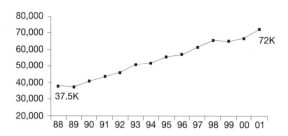

Figure 29: *Increase in subscriptions to* The Economist *between 1988 and 2001*
Source: ABC

Strengthened readership profile

The Economist's ad revenues are dependent not only on circulation but also on the profile of its readership. So it was not enough just to increase readership. *The Economist* had to attract more of the right kind of readers. Since 1988 the magazine has increased the proportion of ABs by almost 10% (Figure 30).

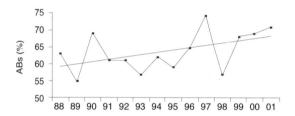

Figure 30: *Proportion of ABs in readership of* The Economist
Source: NRS

Increased advertising revenues

Between 1988 and 2001 *The Economist* increased the cost of a single page advertisement at a faster rate than the competition. For confidentiality reasons, actual rates cannot be disclosed, but looking at the indices for mono and colour page increases versus the market average (Figure 31), the uplifts for *The Economist* are considerable.

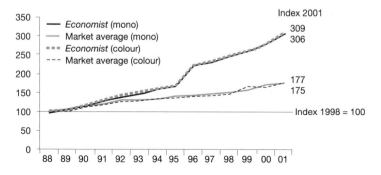

Figure 31: *Rate card for* The Economist *versus average for quality dailies indexed against 1988*
Source: BRADNET

Further evidence of *The Economist*'s success is the fact that it doesn't discount off the rate card. This is in a market of increasingly greater discounting. Over the past 15 years, the average rate card discount for quality dailies has increased from 14% to almost 40% (Figure 32). It is worthy of note that, since 1988, there have been two media recessions, yet *The Economist* has never deviated from this policy.

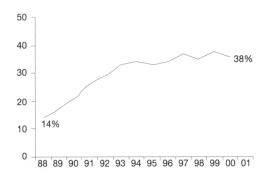

Figure 32: *Average discount from rate card for the quality dailies since 1988*
Source: AA

Indeed if we apply the average discount to the average rate card for quality dailies, we can see that *The Economist*'s performance versus the competition is even stronger (Figure 33).

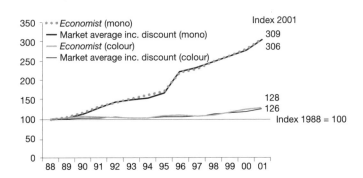

Figure 33: *Rate card for* The Economist *versus average for quality dailies indexed against 1988*
Source: BRADNET

How do we know it was the advertising that fuelled The Economist's *success?*

We have five key pieces of evidence:

1. The direct effect of advertising on circulation and loyalty using econometric modelling.
2. How this increase, along with advertising's strengthening of the readership profile, has led to a substantial ad rate card increase.

3. How the creative and media strategy has enabled *The Economist* to achieve extremely high levels of advertising and brand awareness despite a decreasing share of voice.
4. How the advertising has built the quality credentials of the brand.
5. Finally, we will account for the contribution of other factors.

First, a note on the data

The Economist has a relatively small research budget. This, coupled with monitoring a brand over such a long time period, has inevitably created difficulties. The most obvious gap in the data is a lack of brand measures, as these were never captured on the advertising tracking used during the 1990s. However, a more comprehensive tracking study was put in place in 2001 to rectify these issues.[4] This is why in some cases we are able to look only at brand measures relative to the competition and not over time as well.

Circulation

Econometric modelling shows a direct effect of advertising on circulation. Because news-stand sales and subscriptions behave differently, we developed a model for each.

These models cover only the past five years (1997 to 2001) as there are not enough data available to cover the entire campaign period. Had we been able to model the 14-year effect of advertising, we would have seen a larger impact on circulation.

The models reveal that every £1000 spent on advertising generates 60 news-stand sales and 6.4 subscriptions. Each year we spend approximately £1 million on the brand campaign, so that figure generates 60,000 news-stand sales and 6400 subscriptions. This equates to 2.4% of news-stand sales and 5.7% of subscriptions.

Since *The Economist* has a very high base level of sales (*c.* 80%), effectively only 20% of sales are 'influenceable'.[5] So when expressed as a proportion of influenceable sales, we can see that the advertising contribution is key to driving circulation growth: 12% of variable news-stand sales and 29% of variable subscriptions (Figures 34–36).

Loyalty

The advertising doesn't just generate new customers, it generates *loyal* customers. As the model illustrates, the campaign has twice the effect on subscriptions as it does on news-stand sales. It encourages people to form a relationship with *The Economist,* literally 'buying into' the brand by going straight to subscription. This is remarkable given no response mechanism or call to action is used in the brand advertising.

In addition, the model shows that the advertising has made a significant contribution to the base level sales of 80% over time. Advertising has increased

---

4. Hall & Partners.
5. Base level sales are the modelled estimate of sales without marketing activity, stripping out the impacts of *Economist*-controllable activity (such as cover design or distribution).

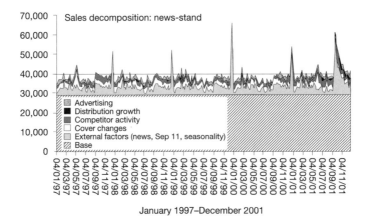

Figure 34: *News-stand sales decomposition for* The Economist *showing very high base level sales*
Source: ROI

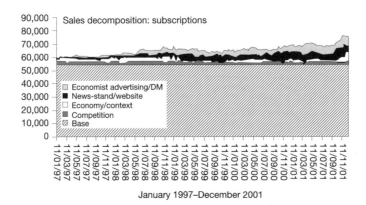

Figure 35: *Subscriptions decomposition for* The Economist *showing very high base level sales*
Source: ROI

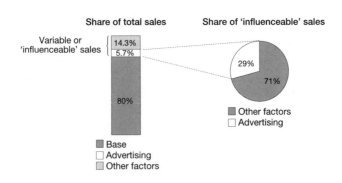

Figure 36: *Advertising's impact on variable subscription sales*
Source: ROI

base level sales by an estimated 1% for news-stands and 1.4% for subscriptions every year.[6]

Increasing the premium for ad space

Advertising revenue is dependent upon circulation and readership profile. We have already shown that advertising contributes to circulation uplift but it has also helped attract more upmarket readers. The advertising campaign positioned the brand as a badge of success with which successful, affluent people want to be associated. However, the advertising has not only affected *The Economist* readers but it has also had a direct influence upon advertisers and media buyers. They want *The Economist* on their schedule because they believe it is a unique medium for reaching such a concentration of affluent and influential people. This demand is borne out by the fact that the increase in the ad rate card exceeds expectation, given circulation increases of 64% and AB readership increases of almost 10%.

> 'A key challenge for our advertising sales team is to positively differentiate *The Economist* as an advertising medium. The advertising campaign has consistently reinforced *The Economist* brand as being distinct from and superior to other media brands.'

> David Hanger, Publisher, *The Economist*

Raising awareness

One of the first tasks of advertising is to get the brand noticed in order to successfully communicate its message. The data show that the campaign has achieved high levels of cut-through and raised ad and brand awareness despite the modest budget.

Ad awareness

Advertising awareness built rapidly in the early years of the campaign and has continued at its high levels ever since, despite a decreasing share of voice (Figures 37 and 38).

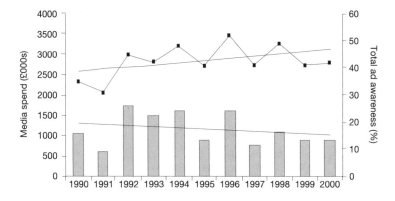

Figure 37: *Ad awareness and adspend for* The Economist *1990 to 2000*
Source: BMRB and PHD

---

6.   Derived from a separate piece of analysis breaking down the five-year time span into sections and remodelling.

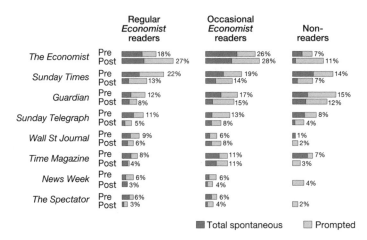

Figure 38: *Ad awareness for* The Economist *and competitors 2001*
Source: Hall & Partners 2001 Tracking

Examining it today, *The Economist's* ad awareness still outstrips the competition who have spent on average three-and-a-half times more on advertising.[7]

This pattern is mirrored when we look at brand awareness.

Brand awareness
Relative to the competition, *The Economist* has extremely high spontaneous brand awareness (Figure 39).

	Regular Economist readers	Occasional Economist readers	Non-readers
The Economist	95%	73%	18%
The Times	55%	60%	25%
Financial Times	52%	37%	16%
Guardian	48%	52%	45%
Daily Telegraph	44%	60%	36%
Sunday Times	41%	50%	33%
Observer	36%	34%	26%
Independent	33%	32%	22%
Sunday Telegraph	31%	30%	11%
Time Magazine	28%	30%	10%

Figure 39: *Spontaneous brand awareness for* The Economist *and competitors 2001*
Source: Hall & Partners 2001 Tracking: Pre wave

There is strong evidence to suggest that the advertising is responsible for this. There are uplifts in brand awareness, particularly among our key target of occasional readers, following the autumn 2001 poster burst (Figure 40).[8]

---

7. Source: PHD. Comparing total ATL media spend 1988 to 2001 for *The Economist* with the market of quality newspapers.
8. September 11 happened during the fieldwork period. However, this would have affected brand awareness for all newspapers and magazines.

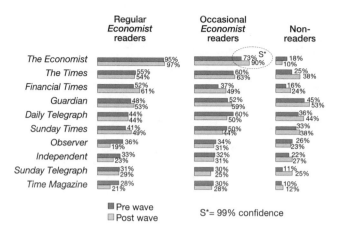
Figure 40: *Spontaneous brand awareness pre and post autumn 2001 poster burst*
Source: Hall & Partners 2001 Tracking

The magnifier effect of a consistent creative and media approach

A testament to the campaign's consistency is its magnified effect on the advertising.

Econometric modelling shows that consistent advertising has led to a weekly adstock carry-over rate of 98% (Figure 41). This is incredible given that the norm for outdoor is 70 to 90%, and it is, to quote our econometrician,[9] '*far higher than any other advertising that's used the outdoor medium*'.

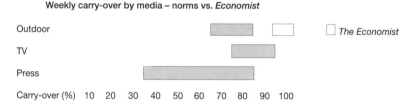

Figure 41: The Economist's *outdoor advertising carry-over rate vs. the norm*

With a media strategy of biannual two-week bursts, the remembering rate of one burst of advertising has never declined fully before the next burst begins, such that the effect of the advertising is building constantly without ever increasing adspend (Figure 42).

Increasing quality perceptions

The advertising has also increased quality perceptions. Tracking shows that 'intelligence', 'cleverness', 'well informed' and 'witty' are the key communication take-outs from the advertising (Figure 43).

---

9. Sally Dickerson, Managing Director, ROI.

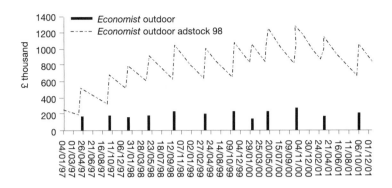

Figure 42: The Economist's *outdoor adstock is 98%*
Source: ROI

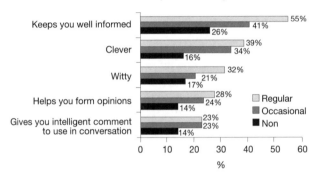

Figure 43: *The key communication take-outs from the advertising*
Source: Hall & Partners 2001 Tracking

These advertising messages have remained consistent during the campaign and over time have translated into brand image, as shown in the brand studies conducted among subscribers periodically through the 1990s (Table 2).

TABLE 2: *THE ECONOMIST* BRAND IMAGE MEASURES 1990 TO 1998

Subscriber survey		1990	1994	1998
	Base	1561	1523	1121
Valuable international perspective	Agree strongly (%)	54	65	85
Provides a global interpretation of world affairs	Agree strongly (%)	48	62	n/a
More authoritative	Agree strongly (%)	n/a	41	63
Essential weekly reading	Agree strongly (%)	n/a	50	58

Source: Ipsos/RSL brand study

All this has contributed to *The Economist*'s strong reputation today. Relative to a key 'quality' competitor such as the *FT Weekend*,[10] readers see *The Economist* as

---

10. *FT Weekend* and *Time Magazine* are the competitors against which we track quality perceptions and regular *FT Weekend* readers were the only base size big enough for this comparison to be made.

more prestigious, authoritative and intelligent. Interestingly, this is even true among a base of regular *FT Weekend* readers (Figures 44–46).

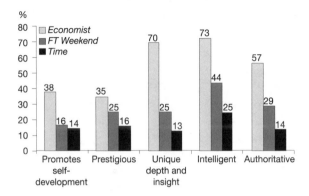

Figure 44: *Quality image ratings – regular* Economist *readers*
Source: Hall & Partners 2001 Tracking

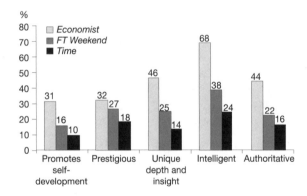

Figure 45: *Quality image ratings – occasional* Economist *readers*
Source: Hall & Partners 2001 Tracking

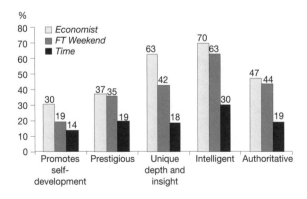

Figure 46: *Quality image ratings – regular* FT Weekend *readers*
Source: Hall & Partners 2001 Tracking

We have shown that the advertising has improved the image of the brand but it also increases desire for the brand. The 2001 tracking shows a significant uplift in propensity to buy *The Economist* among the key target of occasional readers following the autumn burst of advertising (Figure 47).

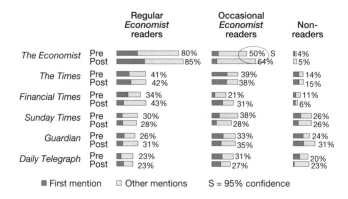

Figure 47: *Brand consideration pre and post autumn 2001 advertising*
Source: Hall & Partners 2001 Tracking

What else could explain *The Economist*'s success?

The advertising does not act in isolation. Other parts of the marketing mix – PR, promotions and DM in particular – all played an important part in the success story. However, these and the other possible influential factors (listed below) remained relatively unchanged, or, if anything, worked against *The Economist*. Furthermore, they are all accounted for in the modelling:

- *Distribution*: Overall, levels have not changed. A recent rise in supermarkets and convenience stores has been balanced out by a decline in CTNs.
- *Cover price*: This has increased steadily over the past 14 years from £1.40 to £2.80 and is now at a real premium versus competitors (Figure 48).
- *Covers*: Econometric modelling shows a minor impact of covers on news-stand sales; however, the quality and variety of the covers has not changed throughout the campaign period.

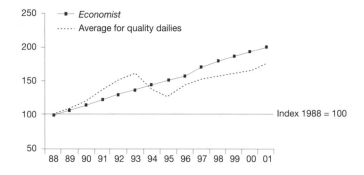

Figure 48: The Economist's *cover price vs. average for quality dailies against 1988 prices*
Source: AA

- *Editorially*, *The Economist* has remained relatively unchanged. A new technology supplement was added recently, but this appears only quarterly.[11] In May 2001, *The Economist* added colour throughout and a new layout; however, this has occurred too recently to be responsible for the 14-year success story.
- Finally, *competitor activity* has increased significantly over the advertising period, doubling from £13.7 million in 1988 to £27 million in 2001.[12]

Payback to the business

Econometric modelling shows a revenue return on investment of 1:1.8. Over the 14-year campaign, this equates to a minimum return in revenue to *The Economist* of £25.2 million on an ad spend of £14 million.[13] Due to confidentiality reasons, the profit return is not disclosed, but it is considerable.

However, the advertising has paid back in more ways than this.

Securing future revenue by increasing customer loyalty

By driving subscriptions the advertising has secured *The Economist*'s future revenue streams. On average, 54% of subscribers resubscribe in the first instance, 66% of those resubscribe a second time and 80% of those renew their subscription for a third time or more.[14] This means that the average life of a subscriber is 3.3 years.[15] When we account for this, the revenue return on investment becomes 1:5 which equates to a payback in revenue to *The Economist* of £70 million, for an investment of £14 million.

Creating an ad rate card premium

The Economist has generated significant extra ad revenue because its rate card has increased faster than the competition and it has a no discounting policy. The advertising is not wholly responsible for this success but it has played a significant part. In the interests of confidentiality, actual revenues cannot be disclosed. However, using *The Economist* average annual advertising pagination for the UK edition,[16] and the proportion of mono pages versus colour,[17] we estimate that in 2001 alone, extra advertising revenues of £19.5 million were accrued. Over the life of the campaign, assuming the same average pagination and mono/colour split, this becomes £130 million.[18]

Opening up new revenue streams through brand extension

The advertising has helped to strengthen *The Economist* brand and consequently has enabled it to extend into other areas such as Economist conferences, rights and syndication, pocket books, 'The World In' series and *The Economist* shop on Regent Street.

---

11. *Technology Quarterly*.
12. Source: PHD. Total ATL spend for quality newspapers.
13. 'Minimum' because based on modelling from the last five years of data (1997–2001). Had data been available from 1988 we would have seen a greater contribution of advertising to sales and thus a higher overall return.
14. Source: *The Economist*.
15. Source: ROI econometric modelling.
16. Source: *The Economist* – average of pagination data 1998–2001; fractional sizes have been excluded.
17. Source: *The Economist* – average of colour/mono page data 1998–2001.
18. According to MMS Medialog, the annual number of full ad pages for *The Economist* has not changed significantly between 1991 and 2001 (data pre 1991 not available).

'The strength of *The Economist* brand allows us to be active in commercial areas where many of our competitors cannot play; or at least, it allows us to adopt a premium pricing policy and achieve higher margins than most.'

Des McSweeney, Director of Economist Enterprises

Furthermore, in recent years, *The Economist* has launched a very successful website, *Economist.com*, which is based on a business model that is funded partly by subscription, not just advertising revenues alone. Since mid-1997, UK traffic has grown from 120,000-page views a month to 1.2 million and registered users in the UK from 10,000 to 120,000. Advertising has played an important part in this success because of its role in building *The Economist* brand.

'We run a subscription model to complement the print product and it is a testament to the brand that users are prepared to pay, even for individual articles.'

Paul Rossi, Publisher of *Economist.com*

Opening up new revenue streams through brand expansion
The 'White out of Red' campaign has been adapted for a European audience and is proven to be driving sales in Europe.

Figure 49: *Ran in Paris – 'Fill up every Friday'*

There is an estimated potential *Economist* audience of 1.7 million in continental Europe and current circulation is 170,000, so there is huge future growth potential (Figure 50).

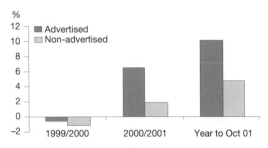

Figure 50: *Circulation change for* The Economist *in continental Europe in advertised and non-advertised countries*
Source: The Economist & PHD

The Economist's long-term brand advertising has paid back more than a content-led approach

The return on advertising investment to *The Economist* is considerable and part of the reason is the decision in 1988 to invest in the brand, not week-by-week content.

We can prove this because *The Economist* uses tactical press alongside the brand campaign to promote next week's survey editions and we monitored both in the econometric modelling (Figures 51 and 52).

Figure 51: Technology Quarterly, *September 2001*

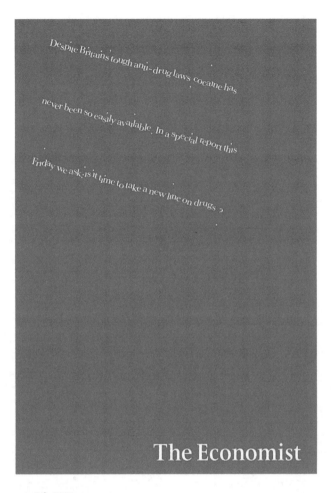

Figure 52: *Drugs survey, July 2001*

The modelling results show that this tactical press actually generates less news-stand sales than brand advertising on a per £1000 basis, despite the tactical press containing a call to action (Table 3). This is because its effects are concentrated in the week of advertising and quickly die out. This tactical press has an adstock carry-over rate of 70% per week versus 98% per week for the brand advertising. This means it is more disposable and easily forgotten and thus ultimately doesn't work as hard as the brand advertising. That said, 70% adstock is still above average for press advertising (Figures 53 and 54).

TABLE 3: IMPACT OF £1000 SPEND ON NEWS-STAND AND SUBSCRIPTIONS
FOR BRAND ADVERTISING (OUTDOOR) VERSUS TACTICAL PRESS

	Economist outdoor spend	*Economist* press spend
News-stand	60	53
Subscriptions	4.5	0
Subscriptions via news-stand sales	1.9	1.7

Source: ROI

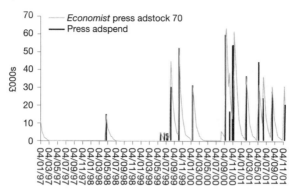

Figure 53: The Economist's *tactical press has an adstock of 70%*
Source: ROI

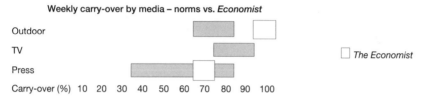

Figure 54: The Economist's *press adstock is above average compared with the norm*
Source: ROI

Furthermore, we can see that the tactical activity does little to improve customer loyalty, as it has no direct effect on driving subscriptions. Subscribers are hugely valuable to *The Economist* because they provide guaranteed revenue. The brand advertising encourages people to invest in the brand long term, the tactical only asks them to buy *The Economist* that week.

This isn't to say that all tactical advertising should be abandoned; there is a clear role for it in boosting short-term sales.[19] However, *The Economist*'s case demonstrates that if content-based advertising is the mainstay of a communications plan, as it is for many media brands, then the business can suffer in the longer term.

CONCLUSION

This paper shows that *The Economist* made a wise decision in 1988 to invest in brand advertising. It made an even wiser decision to continue doing so for the next 14 years, since it has resulted in an iconic brand and a stronger business.

Figure 55: *'Smarties'*

19. The issue containing the Drugs Survey, advertised in the UK (Figure 52), was the eighth biggest selling issue of 2001.

11

Hastings Hotels

Welcome to Northern Ireland: how advertising attracted golfing tourists back to the province after an absence of thirty years

Principal authors: Mike Fleming and Sam McIlveen, AV Browne Advertising, and Julie Maguire, Hastings Hotels

EDITOR'S SUMMARY

This case demonstrates how a radical marketing strategy, coupled with intelligent media solutions, contributed a significant short-term profit and a valuable database for future direct marketing activity. Hastings Hotels tapped into a niche opportunity of golf coverage of the Senior British Open on Sky Sports to attract cash-rich golfers to their Slieve Donard Hotel. As a result of the advertising over £45,500 gross income was generated within one month, while annual golf room bookings increased by more than 300% to over 1500. And all for a spend of just £12,000.

INTRODUCTION

This case history sets out to demonstrate how low-budget tactical advertising can exploit a topical situation for both short- and long-term benefit. It will show how:

- A 'local', 'regional' advertiser can gain national and international exposure within a niche market.
- Effective advertising can be delivered by targeting the moment rather than the audience
- A powerful, cogent advertising strategy overcame a long-held fear of travelling to Northern Ireland.

Most important of all, it will prove that a substantial return on a small budget is possible.

BACKGROUND

The Hastings Hotels Group is Northern Ireland's premier hotel chain.

However, with the cessation of 'the troubles' and the subsequent business regeneration, a number of global network hotels have sprung up over the past ten years, mostly in response to predicted, rather than actual, traveller demand. Holiday Inn, Jury's and Hilton are just three brands which have taken room rates in the province to a value/budget level. The number of hotel rooms in Northern Ireland has leaped from 3110 in 1991 to 4890 last year – a 58% increase according to Northern Ireland Tourist Board (NITB) figures. This has resulted in the slow, but steady, erosion of Hastings' traditional revenue stream (see Figure 1).

As Hastings was unlikely to be able, or even want, to compete in this cut-price room rate war, it was evident that they had to re-evaluate their marketing strategy to explore and exploit fully the opportunities afforded through carefully targeted niche marketing. They had to compete effectively with global rivals on a local level and find ways to maximise their limited budget.

Yet, in comparison to its nearest neighbours, Northern Ireland has a long way to go to fulfil its tourism potential. While headline figures indicate growth, this is

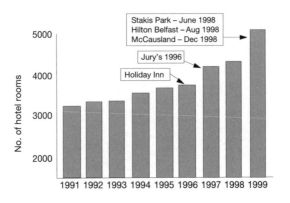

Figure 1: *Brand share of hotel bedrooms in Northern Ireland*

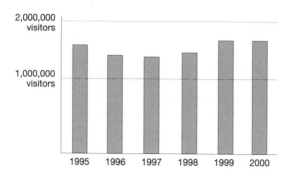

Figure 2: *Tourist visitors to Northern Ireland*
Source: Northern Ireland Tourist Board

from a very low base. Visitor numbers recently exceeded 1.5 million, but Northern Ireland still lags significantly behind Britain and the Republic of Ireland. Tourism currently makes up 2% of the North's GDP, compared to 7% in the Republic and 5% in Scotland.

At approximately 300,000, the number of pure holiday visitors has yet to show a significant increase. The number of these holiday visitors still comprises less than 1 in 5 of the total number of visitors.

Public disorder associated with 'ongoing' disputes continues to deter visitors while global media coverage of the continued unrest does untold damage to tourism prospects (see Figure 2).

This scenario is starkly confirmed by Jennifer Miller's 'Tourism' report in *Technology Ireland's* Business Industry Review:

'The tourist industry in Northern Ireland has fared poorly in comparison to Great Britain and the Republic of Ireland due largely to terrorism. Visitor numbers dropped from 1,080,000 in 1967 to 321,000 in 1976. The amount of international visitors has only recently begun to rise to the numbers that were achieved before the "Troubles".'

Historically, the Hastings Hotels Group has attracted infrequent bookings from people interested in playing golf through their hotels' close proximity to some of the province's top golf courses. Building on this and the desire to play named links courses, an exclusive tailored golf package was created.

MARKETING OBJECTIVES

Objectives were:

- To market Hastings Hotels as the perfect golfing holiday partner in Northern Ireland, and encourage golfers to visit more than one hotel and stay for longer.
- To extend the Hastings Hotels product portfolio to include the Royal Tour (see subsection entitled 'The new product') and integrate this new product into the Group marketing activity.
- To exploit the opportunity provided by inclusive golfing break packages through the Hastings Hotels Royal Tour and build on the growing popularity of golf as a leisure activity (25 million players in North America).

- To deliver a coordinated communications plan employing advertising, PR, online activity and direct sales to maximise level of enquiries from golfers from Great Britain, Republic of Ireland and beyond.
- To maximise conversion of enquiries into sales to generate additional income for the Group.
- Actively to promote Northern Ireland in general as a golfing destination and secure additional funding from appropriate organisations.

THE CAMPAIGN

Objectives

The campaign brief was to generate sufficient levels of enquiry to achieve 120 room nights from the launch of the campaign in order to fund ongoing marketing activity.

Playing to our strengths – golf in Northern Ireland

Long overlooked as a golfing destination because of the ongoing political conflict, Northern Ireland can boast a rich heritage in this sport. Royal Portrush Golf Club on Antrim's north coast is the only course outside Scotland and England to have hosted the British Open (1952). Further south in the province, Royal County Down Golf Club has been the scene of British Amateur Championships, Senior British Opens and PGA events. Indeed, since the launch of the definitive *Golf World* biennial survey of the Top 100 courses in the British Isles, Royal County Down has rarely been outside the top five and was ranked fourth in the world by America's *Golf Digest* magazine in 2001. Add to this over 80 other high-quality private members' clubs within 90 minutes drive of each other and you have a golfer's perfect holiday location.

TABLE 1: *GOLF WORLD* TOP 10
BRITISH ISLES COURSES

1. Royal Birkdale
2. Muirfield
3. Turnberry (Ailsa)
4. Royal Country Down
5. Carnoustie
6. Ballybunion (old)
7. St Andrews (old)
8. Royal Portrush (Dunluce)
9. Ganton
10. Sunnydale (old)

Source: *Golf World*, November 1998

Target audience

The target audience was identified as active golfers in mainland GB and Republic of Ireland with a propensity to take a golfing holiday every year.

Problems to overcome

There were three main 'problems'.

Budget

Given the limited budget for the campaign, our initial recommendation was to look at either a press campaign using a combination of specialist golf titles, in-flight magazines and daily/Sunday press classified travel sections, or a direct mail campaign using lists from the Northern Ireland Tourist Board.

While both were safe options, the Agency felt that neither was strong enough to launch the campaign to highlight the quality of golf courses available in the province. To overcome people's natural reluctance to visit Northern Ireland we had to show the target audience the high quality of the golf courses.

'The troubles'

'Regrettably, public disorder associated with the "parades dispute" has again deterred tourists from coming here in what should be the peak business season. Global media coverage of continued unrest during July does untold damage to the realisation of future tourism prospects.'

Roy Bailie, Chairman, Northern Ireland Tourist Board, 2000

To overcome the chill factor for tourists we knew that we needed to produce a very compelling argument for golfers to visit Northern Ireland. We needed to identify a media platform that would provide the endorsement necessary to make this campaign a success.

Adverse media coverage

As you can see from the NITB quote above, July is a flashpoint month in the Northern Ireland calendar and, as such, attracts huge media coverage. The unpredictability and volatility of the situation demanded that we put 'clear blue water' between our campaign and any adverse coverage. Media selection, as you will see, played a crucial role in overcoming this problem.

The solution

In 2000, the Senior British Open moved venue from Royal Portrush to Royal County Down. It was a welcome change for the players who compete every year and was welcomed even more by Hastings Hotels as their luxurious Slieve Donard Hotel is situated no more than 150 yards from the course! It would mean a full house for them during the four days of competition and also gave them a perfect opportunity to market their hotel group on an international stage.

The new product

Recognising the opportunity created by world-class golf combined with top-class accommodation and believing that this was a credible extension of Hastings Hotels, we created a new product: tailored golfing packages. We named it 'The Royal Tour' as the package consisted of golf at Royal Portrush, Royal County Down and Royal Belfast, along with top-quality hotel accommodation.

By creating an exclusive three-destination tour Hastings Hotels would be able to extend the golfers' stay and encourage them to visit more than one of the Group's hotels. In addition, the positioning of the Royal Tour allowed for a price premium to enhance revenue.

Media strategy

We knew from TV Span (a research product commissioned and used by ITV) that an attentive viewing environment is crucial. We also knew that advertisements seen in extended viewing sessions are more effective at driving up sales. The same research also highlights the importance of frequent exposure to the advertising message. So what better time to advertise for Hastings Hotels' golfing breaks than in the coverage of the Senior British Open? This presented avid and affluent golfers with the world-class golfing opportunity awaiting them at The Royal County Down/Slieve Donard Hotel.

The editorial content in which the advertisement appeared was the key driver in media selection. Rather than targeting the audience (i.e. active golfers in GB and Republic of Ireland), the campaign targeted the coverage of the British Seniors on Sky Television. By focusing on the tournament at Royal County Down we were able to reach golfers who were already being exposed to the magnificent vistas of the Mourne Mountains, the Irish Sea, the stunning beaches along the County Down coastline and the golf course itself. Thus the viewing environment was already promoting Northern Ireland as a top golfing and holiday destination. The Slieve Donard Hotel itself also featured heavily in coverage of the tournament.

While the airtime was concentrated into a four-day period there was the reassurance that the viewing profile of Sky was 'spot on' and this allowed us to maximise geographical coverage, and by being very specific in the programming selection, we were able to minimise wastage (see Figure 3).

This media strategy also avoided the possibility of adverse media coverage 'colouring' potential visitors' decision to come to Northern Ireland. Sky Sports carries no news and is therefore an inert platform.

Players such as Gary Player, Hubert Green, Tommy Horton and Christie O'Connor Jnr add credibility to the package as well: that is, 'if they are playing there it must be good'. The advertising strategy was to use the coverage of the

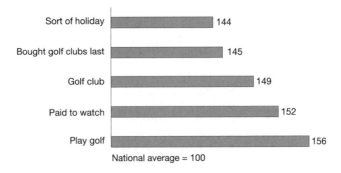

Figure 3: *Profile of Sky viewer versus national average*
Source: TGI 1999, ©BMRB International

Figure 4: *Scenes from the Sky coverage of the British Seniors (reproduced with permission of BSkyB)*

tournament to sell golfing in Northern Ireland and for the Hastings Slieve Donard commercial to provide a point of reference (see Figure 4).

The creative concept

The ad concept focused on the close proximity of the Slieve Donard Hotel to Royal County Down golf club and delivered four key messages:

1. The hotel is very close to the golf course hosting the Senior British Open.
2. The hotel is a luxurious accommodation.
3. Booking a stay at the hotel is simple.

Figure 5

4. Although Hastings Hotels have a high-class, quality brand image, they also have the ability to laugh, joke and be 'human', 'warm' and 'friendly' – essential attributes in any hotel.

The ads delivered a strongly branded message and provided viewers with a telephone number and web address to contact Hastings Hotels for further information (see Figure 5).

The media plan

The media plan was: 17 transmissions to be broadcast during live and recorded highlights on Sky Sports One and Two, between Thursday 27 July to Sunday 30 July 2000.

Short-term results and long-term impact

We measured the success of the campaign in three different areas to show its effects, both short term and to be built on over the next five years. Those areas were:

1. Instant 'direct response' bookings via telephone and email
2. Enquiries for more information for database building
3. Long-term Tourist Board funding and relationship building.

Instant enquiries during the tournament coverage and campaign (only four days remember!) reached 187. Of these, 39 were converted into bookings, resulting in 91 paying guests for an average stay of three nights (273 room nights), generating a gross income of £45,500. Net revenue is difficult to evaluate but taking the average internal room tariff, hotel spend and green fee as £103.25 per paying guest per night, it is estimated that the campaign resulted in a profit of £17,312.75 for

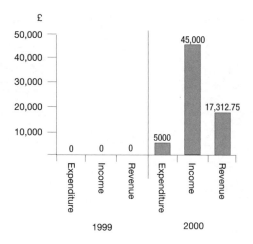

Figure 6: *Golf package – specific advertising activity and results*
Source: Hastings Hotels

Hastings Hotels. All from a media expenditure of just £5000 and production budget of only £7000 (see Figure 6).

THE RESULTS

The short-term effect of the television advertising had a threefold payback on the initial investment, as Figure 7 demonstrates.

Following the television campaign at the end of July, a tactical press campaign ran in specialist golfing publications including *Golf World* and *Irish Golf Review*. This campaign built on the endorsement of the Seniors Tour, employing the headline: 'Play where they played, stay where they stayed'.

In addition, golf tours were promoted on Hastings Hotels' website and through a combination of web advertising, PR and direct marketing. The revenue generated by the initial campaign created the impetus to fund new activity that has been extended to include direct mail, a readers' competition (part of a four-page editorial feature on Royal County Down in the June issue of *Golf World*) and increased coverage in the golfing press. The press treatments (Figure 7) included 'Play where they played, stay where they stayed', highlighting that Northern Ireland had hosted the British Senior Open. A second treatment was developed based on the *Golf World* Top 100 survey, in which two of the top ten courses in the British Isles are in Northern Ireland. Both the creative treatments and the media placement, which was in editorial featuring Northern Irish golf courses, were planned to maximise third-party endorsement.

The rate of conversion from enquiry to booking has slowed from that experienced in the initial campaign. This may be attributed to a number of factors including foot and mouth, September 11th and an increase in tension in Northern Ireland caused by the Holy Cross protests and sectarian violence in North Belfast.

Hastings Hotels also repeated the Sky Television campaign during the coverage of the British Seniors tournament in July 2001. For the second burst of activity

Figure 7
Reproduced with permission of *Golf World*

expenditure was increased to £10,000. This campaign generated slightly fewer enquiries, at 280, and a lower level of conversion to bookings was achieved at 47. The 47 bookings resulted in 102 paying guests staying for an average of just under three nights (295 room nights). These room nights generated a gross income of £49,165. Applying the same formula to estimate net revenue, it can be calculated that the second burst of television activity resulted in a revenue of £18,706.25 from the £10,000 media expenditure.

Added value

Additional benefits for Hastings Hotels were recognition of innovative approach by Sir Reg Empey and coverage by local journalist Barbara McCann. As Minister for Department of Enterprise, Trade and Industry, Sir Reg Empey is directly responsible for tourism.

> 'Of course the decision by Hastings Hotels to air its first television advertisement on Sky Television during the coverage of the Seniors was indeed a very clever marketing move. The advert promoting golfing holidays at the Slieve Donard Hotel made Hastings the only Northern Ireland company to advertise during the Senior British Open championship.'

Extract from *Belfast Telegraph*, 3 August 2000

The database built up over the last year will now be used as part of our ongoing below-the-line campaign and has a value exceeding £11,750 (the cost of buying such a niche list from a broker). Both the Northern Ireland Tourist Board and Kingdoms of Down (the organisations responsible for promoting tourism to Northern Ireland and the region of County Down) provided funding for the campaign.

Long-term impact

Historically, the Hastings Hotel Group has attracted bookings from people interested in playing golf. Prior to the launch of the Royal Tour in July 2000 the

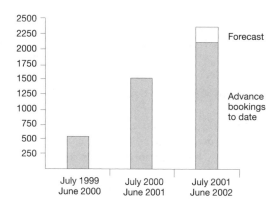

Figure 8: *Year-on-year golfing room night comparison*
Source: Hastings Hotels

number of golf bookings averaged 472 room nights per year, peaking at 517 between July 1999 and June 2000.

Since the launch of the Royal Tour the number of golfing room nights has risen almost threefold to 1533 room nights for 2001. For July 2001 to June 2002 they had over 2000 confirmed golf room nights at the time of writing, while the number of enquiries generated by the communications plan was over 1100. Their forecast for 2002 was 2350 room nights (see Figure 8).

The rate of growth far exceeds any natural market growth in visitor numbers, which actually dropped last year by 2%.

The control

The control for this campaign is easily evaluated as the previous year the Senior British Open took place at Royal Portrush Golf Club and received almost identical levels of coverage on Sky.

Hastings Hotels have two hotels in this region (The Ballygally Castle and Everglades) and did not market them at all during the event. In total, no bookings can be attributed to the coverage.

Isolating the advertising effect

Television led all marketing activity for this campaign.

Although we understand that all Effectiveness Award submissions must eliminate other factors which may have influenced campaign success, in this case we actively encouraged other factors to help build the strength of our message. The coverage on Sky became a 16-hour ad for our client. The event had a thrilling climax, within which our spots appeared, helping to elevate the Hastings Hotels brand.

Any tactical campaign with such a small spend must rely on piggybacking other coverage and events (third-party endorsement) to maximise the budget. Our campaign for Hastings Hotels is the perfect example of this in action.

What we can isolate is any special offers enticing golfers to stay; new refurbishments at the Slieve Donard; plane or ferry travel discounts; changes in the peace process or particularly brilliant summer weather. None of these took place.

SUMMARY AND CONCLUSIONS

The threefold sales returns on our four-day TV campaign were excellent. The reason for this can be attributed to the advertising coupled with the Sky coverage. But *only* the advertising can have driven the calls and email enquiries direct to Hastings.

In the longer term we now have a client who had never before advertised on television, took a risk by targeting one four-day golf tournament and now has faith in the process. The Hastings Group has successfully launched and funded ongoing marketing of a new product.

They also have a robust and growing database which they are using.

Despite the difficulties in attracting visitors to Northern Ireland, reflected by a 2% downturn in numbers last year, the results of the campaign indicate that we were able to achieve significant growth.

The number of golfing nights has risen from 517 three years ago to a projected figure of 2350 for 2002. Although this increase cannot *all* be attributed directly to marketing activity, a significant number can be linked to the advertising.

Hastings Hotels have a new product which is making them money and one which, when advertised in an intelligent, creative manner, is a powerful enough reason to make people overcome their fears about travelling to and around Northern Ireland.

12

Hovis

Repackaging goodness

Principal authors: Vicki Holgate and Andrew Deykin, BMP DDB

EDITOR'S SUMMARY

This case demonstrates how the relaunch of Hovis resulted in massively increased profits. The relaunch included radical new advertising and packaging based on the core brand value of 'everyday goodness'. They drove demand to such an extent that Hovis was able to increase volume at the same time as increasing price – totally counterintuitive. Hovis was the fastest-growing non-alcoholic grocery brand over the past year (+26%). Both the advertising and packaging more than paid for themselves.

INTRODUCTION

This case study is important for three reasons:

1. Instinctively we tend to view volume increases as an indicator of business success. This case study shows, however, that this may not always be such a good measure. We demonstrate how communication tackled the problem of declining brand equity, thereby supporting an increase in price which made brand growth much more profitable.
2. For the first time in an IPA paper, this case study evaluates the role and effect of packaging as a communication channel in its own right, over and above the effects of advertising.
3. Finally, we also demonstrate how brand activity can increase the value of the total market.

BACKGROUND

Back in the spring of 2001, British Bakeries was about to celebrate Hovis's 115th birthday.[1] On the surface, things were looking good. Hovis's sales were rising. This was made all the more impressive by the fact that the market as a whole was in decline (4% p.a.[2]). Hovis's market share had almost doubled in the last two years (Figure 1).

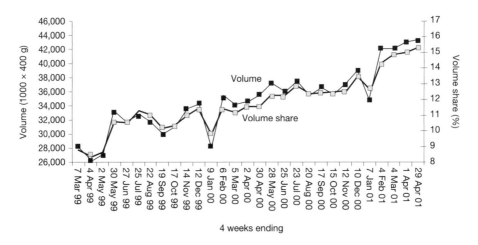

Figure 1: *Hovis volume and volume share*
Source: TNS

False success

However, under the surface, all was not well. British Bakeries was selling more and more bread, but it was making less and less money out of it. Since May 1999, profits had been in decline, despite the increase in volume (Figure 2).

---

1. British Bakeries owns the Hovis brand.
2. Source: TNS.

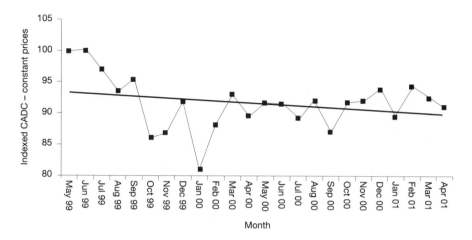

Figure 2: *Total Hovis: contribution after distribution costs*
Source: British Bakeries

Everyday low profits

To understand what was going wrong, we needed to understand why sales were rising. During the period in question, Hovis had been forced to accept Everyday Low Pricing (EDLP) by most of the major retailers. While this marked an end to price promotions in the stores that ran it, it meant that the average price that people were paying for Hovis fell by 10% in real terms. Hovis's price was forced down particularly aggressively, so the relative price of Hovis compared to its competitors also fell (Figure 3).

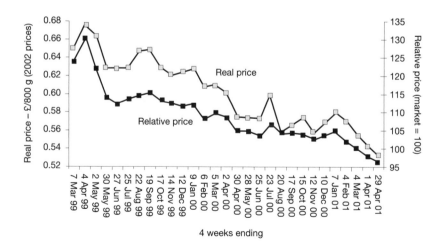

Figure 3: *Hovis real and relative price*
Source: TNS

As the relative price of Hovis fell, so its market share grew. As Figure 4 shows, the way share grew almost exactly mirrors the way price fell.

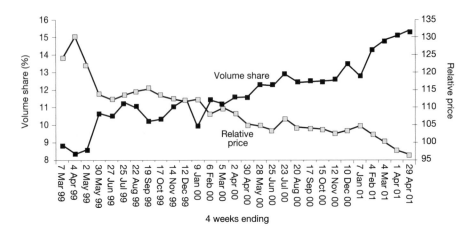

Figure 4: *Hovis volume share vs. relative price*
Source: TNS

Plotting these data in the form of a classic 'demand curve' demonstrates just how strong the correlation between market share and relative price actually was (Figure 5). In fact, regression analysis shows that 93% of the variation in Hovis's market share over this period may be explained purely in terms of price movements. To put it simply, pretty much the only reason people were buying more Hovis was because it was getting cheaper.

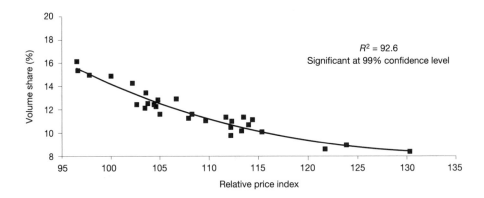

Figure 5: *Hovis demand curve before relaunch (March 1999 to May 1999)*
Source: TNS

In order to achieve the low prices of EDLP, British Bakeries had been forced to cut their margins. Unfortunately, margins had been cut to such an extent that profit actually went down, despite the increase in volume.

Increasing sales volume is often regarded as a sign of success, but it is important to remember that it is really only a means to an end. Sales value is a slightly better indicator, but profit is the only real measure of success.

The retailers acknowledged bread had been devalued

It wasn't just Hovis that had been devalued. The retailers had been using bread as a loss leader to prove their overall good value for money. This resulted in extraordinary situations like the 7p own label economy loaf in early 1999[3] and, later that year, EDLP. Retailers had been forced to cut their margins too, in order to achieve EDLP. This was a shared pain. Therefore, the retailers were also beginning to realise that they needed to start increasing profits from the bread aisle. They looked to manufacturers to lead a recovery.

HOVIS'S BUSINESS OBJECTIVE

This couldn't have been clearer.

> **Hovis's Business Objective**
> To increase Hovis's profits significantly by the end of 2001.

In doing this, British Bakeries wanted to build value back into the bread category to try to reverse the devaluation that had occurred during the 1990s.

Business strategy

The aim was to increase volume and price *together* by increasing the underlying demand for the brand. As an economist would put it, we needed to shift the demand curve (Figure 6).

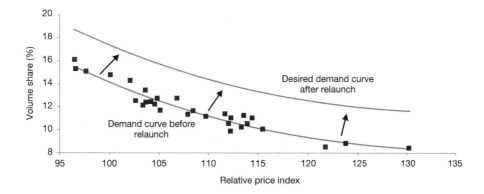

Figure 6: *Shifting the Hovis demand curve*
Source: TNS

A shift of this magnitude would allow Hovis to come off EDLP and put up its price (thereby improving margins) while increasing volume *at the same time*.

---

3. To put this in context, a normal white sliced loaf of Hovis typically costs around 57p these days.

UNFORTUNATELY HOVIS'S BRAND EQUITY WAS DECLINING

To shift the demand curve you need a strong healthy brand. It is hard to increase the underlying demand for a brand when its value in consumers' minds is declining. And that was the problem with Hovis – declining brand equity.

By 'brand equity' we mean brand strength, not a brand valuation. Unfortunately, there is no direct measure for this kind of brand equity. In this particular case, British Bakeries was alerted to the decline in Hovis's brand equity via a number of different measures: price elasticity, brand awareness and brand image.

Price elasticity was high and increasing

High price elasticity is a classic symptom of a weak brand and any price elasticity over 1 is considered high for a food brand. Therefore, not only was Hovis alarmingly price sensitive (with an initial price sensitivity of 1.75), but the brand's price elasticity had also increased significantly over the past couple of years to 2.5 (Figure 7).[4]

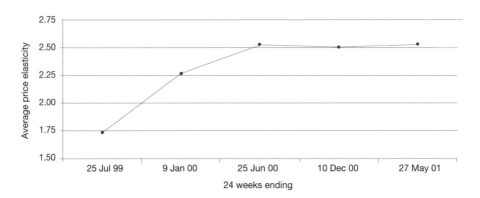

Figure 7: *Hovis price elasticity (estimated using demand curve)*
Source: TNS

Effectively the value of the brand had been eroded in the eyes of the general public by the constant price cuts imposed by the retailers. This meant that simply putting up the price would have resulted in volume dropping like a stone.

Spontaneous brand awareness was in decline

Spontaneous brand awareness of Hovis was in long-term decline. Conversely, spontaneous awareness of Kingsmill (Hovis's closest competitor) was on the rise, to the point that it had even overtaken Hovis for a brief spell in 2000 (Figure 8).

---

4. In July 1999, if Hovis had increased its price by 1%, it would have lost 1.75% of sales. By spring 2001, if Hovis had increased its price by 1%, the brand would have lost a massive 2.5% of sales.

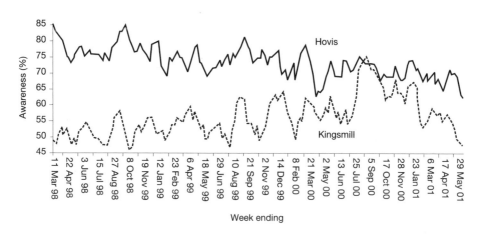

Figure 8: *Spontaneous brand awareness*
Source: NFO

Brand image was out of date

Hovis was seen as old-fashioned and was becoming increasingly distant from bread buyers.

Quantitative research showed that Hovis (and Hovis brown in particular) was seen as significantly more old-fashioned than Kingsmill (Table 1).

TABLE 1: PERCEPTIONS OF BRANDS (%)

	Hovis white	Hovis brown	Kingsmill
Old-fashioned	18	38	3
Contemporary/up to date	15	14	23

Source: RSGB U&A, 1998

Qualitative research had revealed that people were distancing themselves from the Hovis brand. Previously, when asked to describe a 'Hovis room', people had talked about being in a warm, cosy kitchen with a traditional oven and a baker removing freshly baked loaves. By 2001, people were still describing the same kitchen, but now they were standing outside the kitchen looking in through the window, unable to find the door to get in. British Bakeries took the hint and realised that the Hovis brand was becoming more remote.

More people were seeing Kingsmill as the dynamic bread brand that was going places (Table 2).

TABLE 2: PERCEPTIONS OF BRANDS (%)

	Hovis	Kingsmill
One of the leading brands and getting better all the time	38	45

Source: NFO Tracking Study, April–June 2001

What was responsible for this dilution of brand equity?

Hovis was in the 'wrong' market

White bread has always dominated the market. Brown bread made some inroads during the 'no pain, no gain' diet-conscious 1980s, but began to fall away again

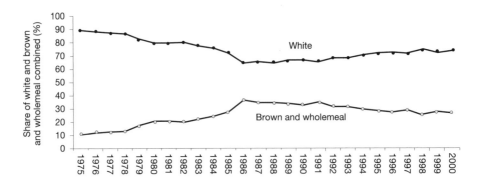

Figure 9: *Consumption by bread type*
Source: National Food Survey

from the 1990s onwards (Figure 9). Once again, the white bread market was the place to be.

Unfortunately Hovis's strength has always been in brown bread, where it dominates the market. Back in 2000, Hovis's share in white was approximately half the size of its share in brown. Hovis remained firmly behind Kingsmill in the more dynamic white bread market (Figure 10).

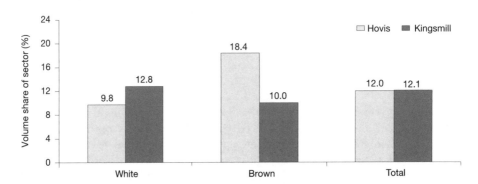

Figure 10: *Volume share (2000)*
Source: TNS

Even though the two brands were actually neck and neck in the race to be No. 1 in the total bread market, Kingsmill had the advantage. Public perception is important and Kingsmill had a massive perceived advantage in the more modern and popular white bread market. Perceptions of Hovis were resolutely tied to brown bread (Table 3).

TABLE 3: PERCEPTIONS OF BRANDS (%)

	Good at white (%)	Good at brown (%)
Hovis	13	38
Kingsmill	32	13

Source: NFO Tracking Study, Positioning Shares, August–October 2000

Hovis was going to have to dramatically improve its performance in white bread, both in terms of perception and reality, if it was going to increase its standing in consumers' minds and significantly grow volume.

Advertising investment had fallen
Another contributor to Hovis's declining brand equity was that Hovis simply had not had enough advertising support in recent years, either in real (Figure 11) or relative terms (Figure 12).

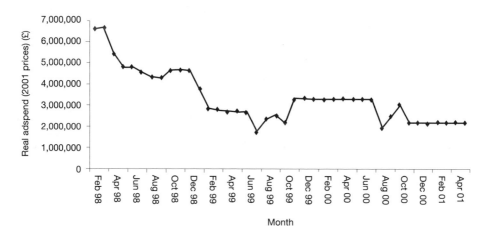

Figure 11: *Hovis adspend*
Source: MMS

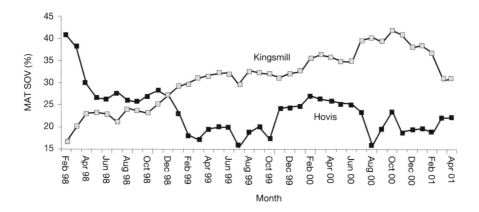

Figure 12: *MAT share of voice*
Source: MMS

The effect that falling investment had on brand awareness can be clearly seen in Figure 13.

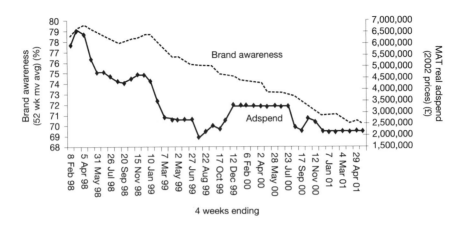

Figure 13: *Hovis spontaneous brand awareness vs. adspend*
Source: NFO, MMS

Advertising funds had had to be redirected to fund the EDLP activity, and Hovis had fallen victim to the vicious circle of EDLP (Figure 14). (NB: This vicious circle effectively also applied to those retailers that were still running big promotions.)

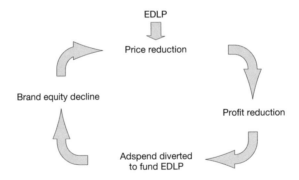

Figure 14: *Vicious circle of EDLP*

BREAKING OUT OF THE VICIOUS CIRCLE

In order to improve the underlying demand for the Hovis brand and break out of this vicious circle, Paula Moss (Brands Director for British Bakeries) decided that nothing short of a total relaunch would suffice. Hovis would be relaunched on 11 June 2001 with a £4.2 million advertising investment. This was double the spend of the previous year and was anticipated to give Hovis at least an equal share of voice with Kingsmill. The relaunch would coincide with the planned price rises.

The relaunch communication would drive demand by increasing brand equity. The planned price rises could be implemented without fear of volume loss due to this underlying increase in demand. The resulting increase in volume *and* value would meet the business objective of increasing profits substantially.

BUILDING BRAND EQUITY THROUGH COMMUNICATIONS

Holistic communications

The philosophy behind the relaunch communication plan was that it should include every opportunity people had to interact with the Hovis brand. It would therefore comprise:

- radical new packaging
- new advertising
- updated website
- significant PR.

Being consistent with 115 years of history

The communications were going to have to build Hovis's brand equity. But more than that, if they were to increase the underlying demand for the brand, they were going to have to build brand equity in a way that was motivating. As we discussed earlier, it was going to have to be particularly appropriate to the white bread market.

As brand guardians, we looked for something from Hovis's heritage that could be made relevant and valuable for today's bread buyers. This way the message would build on the past, making the most of the 115 years of history and, as a result, be more believable. We were looking for some 'consistency'.

'Goodness' provides the consistency

Although most people eat white sliced bread at some point, the core of the market is families. They are getting through up to a loaf of bread a day! The mother in the family is the key bread buyer.

Looking at all the qualities of the Hovis brand, one stood out as both differentiating and also very motivating for mums – goodness.

'Goodness' has always been at the heart of the Hovis brand (Table 4). From its very inception, back in 1886, Richard 'Stoney' Smith found a way to retain the wheatgerm (the goodness) in the flour, thereby producing a loaf that was more nutritious.

TABLE 4: PERCEPTIONS OF BRANDS (%)

% agreeing with statement:	
Hovis is good for you	66
Kingsmill is good for you	36

Source: Millward Brown, pre relaunch

'We are programmed that Hovis is good for you'.

Source: BMP Qualitative, mums with children aged 2 to 10

Nowadays, goodness is of massive importance to mums faced with the prospect of junk food and nutritional compromises at every turn.

'Kids want junk, and we want them to eat healthily.'

Source: BMP Qualitative, mums with children aged 2 to 10

Consistency alone was not enough

Unfortunately, the link between Hovis and brown bread was so strong that it threatened to jeopardise any attempt at communication about white bread, however full of goodness it was.

The biggest handicap that Hovis had was actually the very element of the brand that it was probably most famous for – The Boy on the Bike ad (Figure 15).

Figure 15: *The Boy on the Bike*

Talk to bread buyers for more than 30 seconds about Hovis and they will probably mention that ad (or, worse, start singing the music). And it had not been on TV for 15 years! They couldn't remember any of the intervening ads. The association between 'The Boy on the Bike' ad and the Hovis brand was incredibly strong. Unfortunately, the ad stood for brown bread and old-fashioned values – the very opposite of what Hovis was now trying to be. Worse still, any reference to that ad (even a hint of sepia or a few bars of Dvořák's *New World* Symphony) took people straight back to brown bread and they didn't listen to another word you had to say to them.

We realised that whatever we did in communication terms, it was going to have to be very noticeable and very different to get people to think again about Hovis. We were going to have to 'disrupt' their thoughts.

The watchwords of every element of the communication mix, therefore, became 'consistency and disruption' – '*consistency*' through goodness and '*disruption*' through tone and style.

THE COMMUNICATIONS CAMPAIGN

The advertising

The creative brief put 'goodness' in a context that was relevant to today's hassled mums (Table 5).

TABLE 5: CREATIVE BRIEF

What do we want people to believe?
If I buy Hovis for my family, then, whatever else might happen, at least I know
I've given them a damn good start.

Proposition
Hovis is one good thing you can do for your family everyday.

Target audience
Hassled mums who want to do the best for their family. Anything they can rely
on for a spot of 'goodness' is appreciated.

Tone of voice
Honest, of the people.

We just had to make sure that the ads looked totally different from anything
that had gone before for Hovis. And they did.

The advertising was developed by John Webster at BMP and features a cartoon
family who suffer all the problems and battles of real families – squabbling kids,
rude words and so on. They are Harry Hovis, his family (sister Hannah, mum
Hilary and dad Hugh) and his friend Alfie. From the first frame, the viewer is hit
by the bright primary colours of the cartoon – not a hint of sepia in sight
(Figure 16).

Figure 16: *The Hovis family*

The endline for the campaign is 'Get something good inside' – a realistic and
modern way to talk about 'goodness'. This line is featured throughout all the
communication and has even been incorporated into the Hovis logo (Figure 17).

Figure 17: *The new logo*

The launch ad for the campaign was 'Dustbin' (Figure 18). This was quickly
followed by two more – 'Conversation' (Figure 19) and 'Tuesdays' (Figure 20).

Harry: I'm a kid. My job?

Eating junk.

I'm supposed to eat what you call good food
... like Hovis and stuff grown in earth

OK I'll go for the Hovis – but earth!

A caterpillar could have poohed on it!

You think we have no discretion?

VO: White Hovis. Get something good inside.

Figure 18: 'Dustbin'

Harry: Pooh
Alfie: Bra

Harry: Bogies
Alfie: Er …

FVO: When the witty conversation starts to
drag …

FVO: give them a break with peanut butter
and banana in fresh White Hovis

Harry: Mmm

Alfie: Mmm
FVO: Things'll soon start to pick up again

Alfie: Belly button
Harry: Pants

MVO: White Hovis. Get something good
inside

Figure 19: *'Conversation'*

Hannah: Tuesdays are excellent

Hovis chicken salad rolls – excellent to the max

Trouble is …

Deirdre Sims always wants a swap with one of her dry cheese sandwiches – gross …

'cept I have to be nice cos she helps me with my maths homework. Miss Penny's thirty …

and how are you supposed to concentrate when she's got that thing on her neck – gross

Anyway, I'm going to be a TV weather girl except I'm not very good at talking

VO: Hovis Rolls. Get something good inside.

Figure 20: 'Tuesdays'

The media schedule

The advertising was bought against the core white bread market – housewives with children (Figure 21).

Month	June	July	August	September	October	November	December	January	February	March	April
ITV/C4/C5/Sat											
HWS with kids TVRs											
Total 1753		748		512			291			202	

Figure 21: *Media schedule*

The packaging

It was very important to the success of the campaign that when people got to the shelf in the bread aisle they were not presented with 'the same old Hovis'. It was decided that the packaging should change as radically as every other element of the communication mix. This is a very unusual decision. Usually, pack design is changed in almost unnoticeable steps. But this was *'revolution, not evolution'*.

The packaging designs were developed by Williams Murray Hamm. The 'goodness' message is communicated by photographs of good, honest, everyday food. The disruption comes because the packs are quite literally covered in baked beans, tomatoes, cucumbers, eggs and cheese on toast (Figure 22). They are quite unlike anything ever seen before on the bread fixture and stand out a mile.

Old packs　　　　**New packs**

Figure 22

The website

Hovis already had a website in 'traditional' livery. Along with every other channel of communication, the site was redesigned to fit in with the new Hovis style. Tribal DDB Interactive was responsible for the transformation. The site became 'Harry's site' and contained information on the new packs, the Hovis family and the new advertising (Figure 23). The primary purpose of the site was to provide information for journalists, but it also served as an entertaining destination for anyone interested in finding out more about the new campaign.

Figure 23: *The website*

The PR

The PR coverage, generated by Borkowski, was excellent. Newspapers ranging from the *Sun* to the *Telegraph* ran stories commenting on the change in Hovis.

The PR also helped introduce people to the new pack designs through fly posters featuring baked beans and the Hovis logo. And it continued with British Bakeries' Commercial Team doing a photocall, dressed to the nines in baked bean suits (Figure 24). Second from the left is British Bakeries' Managing Director, the aptly named Peter Baker.

Figure 24

Price rises

Hovis came off EDLP as planned and the price was increased dramatically over the first six months of the campaign. For example, the average price of a Hovis Great White loaf rose from 49p to 57p.

Relative price did not increase as much as real price because other brands were able to follow suit. However, Hovis was able to keep ahead of the pack (Figure 25). The very fact that other brands were able to follow suit is an indicator that Hovis was beginning to help put value back into the whole market.

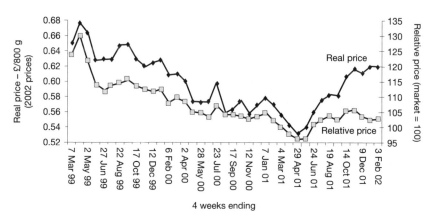

Figure 25: *Hovis real and relative price*
Source: TNS

HOVIS ACHIEVED ITS BUSINESS OBJECTIVES

As we have discussed, prior to the relaunch, Hovis's volume was already rising, due to its falling price. However, one would have expected to see volume begin to fall as soon as the price rises were implemented (in the absence of any other supporting activity). Using predictions based on the demand curve that we saw earlier, we can see that the drop in share would have been quite significant (Figure 26).

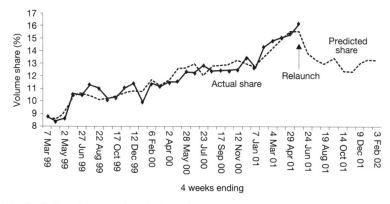

Figure 26: *Predicted effect of price rise from the demand curve*
Source: TNS, BMP

However, quite the opposite happened. Volume continued to rise (Figure 27).

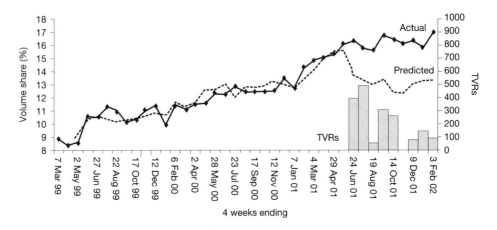

Figure 27: *What actually happened*
Source: TNS, BARB, BMP

As a result of the increase in price, revenue growth was much more healthy (Table 6).

TABLE 6: COMPARISON OF REAL REVENUE GROWTH
WITH VOLUME GROWTH

	Volume (%)	Real value (%)
Pre relaunch:	+17.9	+7.0
52 w/e 4 February 2001		
Post relaunch:	+21.7	**+22.6**
52 w/e 3 February 2002		

Source: TNS, National Statistics

The combination of increases in volume at the same time as increases in price meant that the business objective of increasing profits significantly by the end of 2001 was soundly achieved (Figure 28).

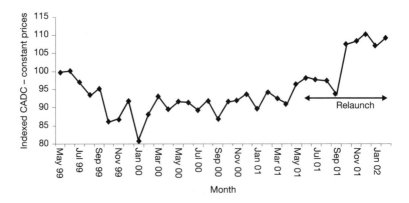

Figure 28: *Total Hovis: contribution after distribution costs*
Source: British Bakeries

Hovis increased its share of white bread dramatically, becoming No. 1 in white bread, and therefore No. 1 in every area of the bread market (Tables 7 and 8).

TABLE 7: BEFORE: SHARE RANKING AMONG
BRANDED BREAD – 4 WEEKS ENDING
4 FEBRUARY 2001

	Total	White	Brown
Volume share	2	2	1
Value share	2	2	1

Source: TNS

TABLE 8: AFTER: SHARE RANKING AMONG
BRANDED BREAD – 4 WEEKS ENDING
3 FEBRUARY 2002

	Total	White	Brown
Volume share	1	1	1
Value share	1	1	1

Source: TNS

STRENGTHENED BRAND EQUITY INCREASED DEMAND

If we look again at the demand curve shown earlier, we can see that the underlying demand for Hovis altered radically after the relaunch in June (Figure 29).

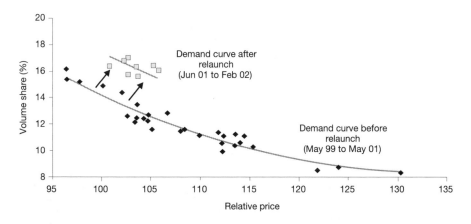

Figure 29: *Hovis demand curve before and after relaunch*
Source: TNS

We are now going to show that the underlying demand for Hovis increased due to improvements in people's perceptions of the Hovis brand (i.e. the strengthening of Hovis's brand equity). This increase in demand more than outweighed the negative effects of the price increase, allowing volumes to continue to rise, but at a higher price.

Brand awareness shot up

Spontaneous brand awareness did a sudden turnaround after the relaunch (Figure 30).[5]

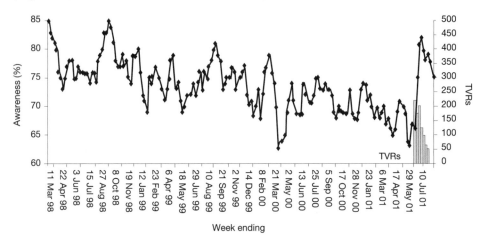

Figure 30: *Hovis spontaneous brand awareness*
Source: NFO, BARB

Improvements to brand image

Hovis's brand image improved on all the key dimensions communicated by the advertising and the packaging. The improvements across these measures were even more pronounced for our communication target of families.

These results are particularly impressive because brand image statements are usually slow to move and the campaign had been running for under six months when we measured it. Hovis already scored very highly on 'good for you', so the fact that this increased even further was a major achievement (Figure 31).

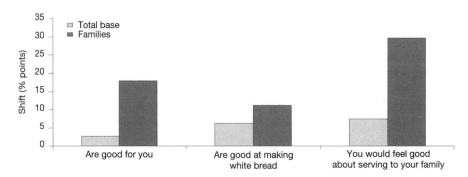

Figure 31: *Image shifts, total base vs. families*
Source: Millward Brown

---

5. Just before the relaunch, British Bakeries made the decision to change tracking companies from NFO to Millward Brown. Millward Brown began collecting data just before the relaunch. The NFO study was continued for a month into the relaunch. The data you will see are therefore drawn from a combination of these two sources. In particular, where the historical picture is of importance, NFO has been used, even though it covers only the first month of the relaunch.

Hovis retook its rightful place in people's minds as not only the leading brand of bread, but one that was improving all the time (Figures 32 and 33). Again, there were much greater increases among our core target of families.

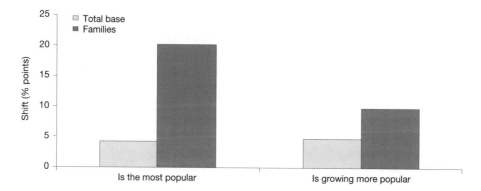

Figure 32: *Hovis popularity, total base vs. families*
Source: Millward Brown

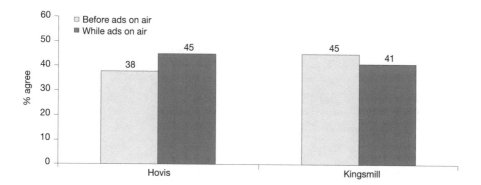

Figure 33: *'One of the leading brands and getting better all the time'*
Source: NFO

Demand for Hovis grew

After the relaunch, people claimed to be much more likely to buy Hovis, particularly Hovis white.[6] And, just as we saw with all the brand equity measures, this was even more strongly the case for our core target of families (Figure 34).

---

6. Consideration is defined as anyone who, when asked to describe their attitude towards the purchase of Hovis, said yes to any of the following: 'It's the only brand I would ever consider buying', 'It's one of my preferred brands', 'It's not one of my preferred brands, but from what I've heard about it, I'd like to try it'.

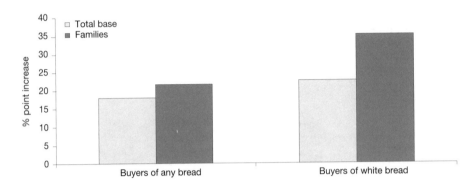

Figure 34: *Hovis consideration increases while ads on air*
Source: Millward Brown

An analysis of actual sales reveals that, although sales increased impressively overall, increases were similarly even stronger among our core target of families (Figure 35).

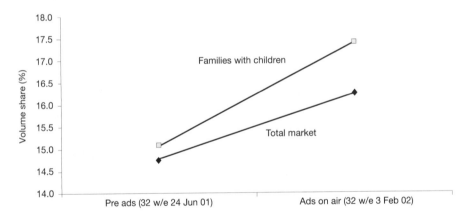

Figure 35: *Hovis volume share*
Source: TNS

COMMUNICATION MIX STRENGTHENED THE BRAND EQUITY

There is strong evidence that the relaunch communication (including all elements of the mix from packs to ads) was responsible for the strengthening of Hovis's brand equity.

First, to be viewed as a brand that is getting better all the time, it is necessary to be seen to be doing things. And the relaunch certainly created quite a stir (Figure 36).

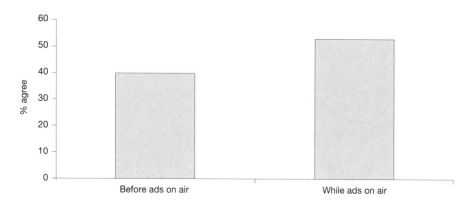

Figure 36: *Hovis: 'Heard a lot about recently'*
Base: All adults
Source: Millward Brown

People saw the campaign

We can demonstrate a significant increase in awareness of all elements in the communications mix.

Advertising awareness increased impressively (Figure 37).

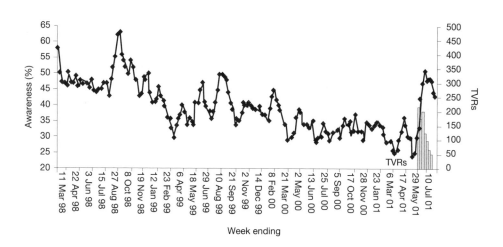

Figure 37: *Hovis spontaneous advertising awareness*
Source: NFO, BARB

Awareness of the packaging also grew steadily and most people are now aware of at least one of the new designs (Figure 38).

Our best measure of awareness of the website is to compare the number of visits before and after the relaunch, which shows an impressive increase (Table 9).

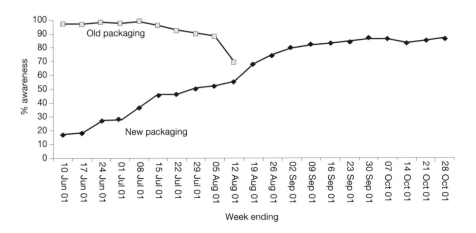

Figure 38: *Hovis packaging awareness*
Source: Millward Brown 4-week rolling data

TABLE 9: VISITS TO WEBSITE

	Before relaunch	After relaunch (to March 2002)
Average visits per month to *www.hovis.co.uk*	700	4300

Source: Tribal DDB Interactive

For the PR campaign, we have to look at the absolute number of opportunities that people had to see it (not ideal, but due to the nature of PR it is very difficult to measure awareness in the same way one does with ads). The PR campaign was independently audited by Cutting Edge, which estimated that the coverage would have cost £1.5 million to buy and that it amounted to 55 million individual opportunities to see (Figure 39).

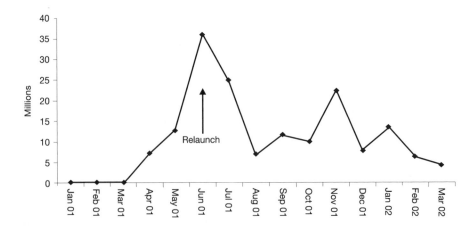

Figure 39: *Circulation for all media*
Source: Romeike Media Intelligence Ltd

People liked the advertising

People loved the ads and genuinely felt they could relate to the characters and situations (Figure 40). Again, mums have been even more positive.

'I think it's brilliant.'

'Very funny.'

'Very true to life as well.'

'We've all got one in the family.'

'That's my daughter!'

'Boys are like that ... girls are too!'

Source: BMP Qualitative, mums with children aged 2 to 10

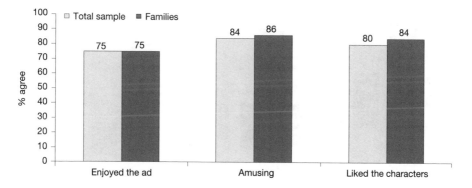

Figure 40: *Responses to 'Dustbin' execution*
Source: Millward Brown

People also liked the packaging...after the initial shock

People are, relatively speaking, used to seeing radical change in advertising, but they are not used to seeing it in packaging. And with something as fantastically different and 'disruptive' as the new Hovis pack designs, you could expect to get a polarised response. Over 3000 people wrote into Hovis after the relaunch to comment on the packaging. Initially the response was more negative than positive.

email

```
Dear Sirs,

Congratulations for creating such a visually revolting
design ... Perhaps the money would have been better spent on
redundancy payments within the marketing department, thereby
offering long-term benefits to the company.
```

As you would also expect with such a major change, initially people had difficulty finding their usual loaf. There was a particular problem with identifying the correct slice thickness (although this was rectified after a couple of weeks with a slight tweak to the packaging). But this is the kind of pain you have to accept with such a momentous change.

email

... At the weekend, we picked up two of our usual baked bean
square-cut medium-sliced loaves, but when we went to use the
second one, we found it to be the extra-thick sliced … Sorry
if this sounds petty, but I bet we aren't the first to have
made the same mistake.

With such a strong response to the packaging change initially, it would have
been very easy for British Bakeries to panic. But they held their nerve and this
bravery certainly paid off. The balance shifted quickly to a more positive response
(Figure 41).

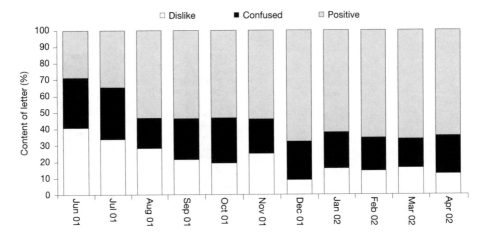

Figure 41: *Letters of response to new packaging*
Source: British Bakeries

> Letter
>
> Dear Sir or Madam,
>
> I *love* the new bread wrappers! They are cheerful
> and colourful and should have come out ages ago.
> Instead of bread being put away in the breadbin,
> I'm happy to leave it out as the wrapper is so
> funky and up to date. I do like Hovis bread
> anyhow, but I bought it even more so because of
> the wrappers! It's a great idea, don't stop. Great
> way to start the day, colourful wrappers Hovis way.

People understood and believed the communication

We have evidence that both the advertising and packaging clearly communicated
the core messages that helped to build brand equity.

The advertising was clearly communicating the key messages, with improvements over previous Hovis advertising. The increases were again greater for our core communications target of families (Figure 42).

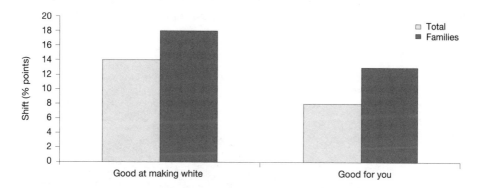

Figure 42: *Shifts in prompted communication of Hovis advertising*
Base: Seen advertising
Source: Millward Brown

What was the advertising saying about Hovis?:

'Try to get something good inside your child amongst all the other food that they eat.'
'Good for your children. Something wholesome amongst the junk.'
'Hovis white bread is healthy and nutritious.'
'Hovis bread is healthy food – even white sliced is good for you.'

Source: BMP Qualitative, mums with children aged 2 to 10

When recounting the ad, people demonstrated how clearly the goodness message was integrated within the advertising.

When asked 'Tell me everything you can remember about the ad,' people said:

'A little boy in a cartoon figure saying there are certain good things he should eat such as Hovis and things grown in the earth. Tries the bread but won't eat anything grown in the earth, as a caterpillar might have pooed in it.'

'It was a cartoon with two kids saying kids eat anything. Then one of them emptied a dustbin full of rubbish into his mouth. Then he opens some Hovis bread and says give them something good and he eats it.'

Source: Millward Brown Tracking

Quantitative testing on the packaging showed that it was also working strongly to communicate goodness in a modern way (Table 10).

TABLE 10: PACKAGING COMMUNICATION

% agreeing with the following statements about the packaging:	
Contains bread that's good for you	77
Modern and up to date	81

Source: TNS Consumer, May 2001

The packaging and advertising turned decline into profit

Using British Bakeries' econometric model we are able to separate the effects of the advertising and, for the first time in an IPA paper, packaging on sales.

Both communication channels had a considerable effect on sales and made the difference between a disastrous decline and massive profit (Figure 43).

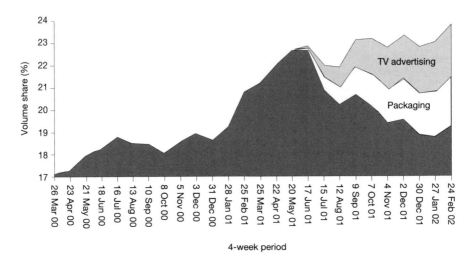

Figure 43: *Hovis: estimated effect of TV advertising and new packaging (volume share)*
Source: Econometric model

Price elasticity has begun to decrease

Using the econometric model, we are also able to estimate the effect of the activity on price elasticity (Figure 44). It is early days, but this reduction in price elasticity indicates a strengthening of the Hovis brand and has helped cushion Hovis sales from the negative effects of the price increases.

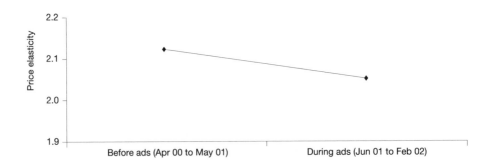

Figure 44: *Hovis price elasticity (estimated using econometric model)*
Source: Econometric model

ELIMINATING OTHER VARIABLES

So far we have demonstrated that the relaunch communications (in particular the advertising and the packaging) have driven sales and profits. But could anything else have been responsible?

We have already discussed the increase in price which was such a crucial part of the relaunch strategy and which, on its own, would have resulted in a decrease in sales. The variables that we have not yet examined are distribution and new product launches.

Distribution

Hovis had almost total distribution before the relaunch. This level of distribution has remained constant throughout the relaunch (Figure 45). Distribution can therefore be eliminated as a possible cause of Hovis's success.

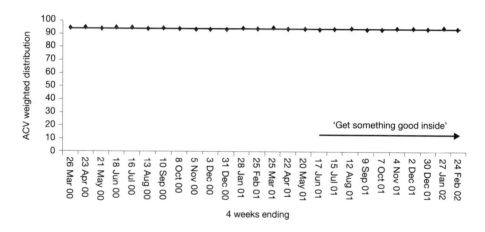

Figure 45: *Hovis distribution*
Source: IRI

New product launches

There were two product launches around this time.

Square Cut Wholemeal was launched on the day of the relaunch. Its contribution to sales has been tiny – less than 1% of volume.

Best of Both, a white loaf with all the goodness of brown, was launched one month later. Although more important, it cannot explain all of Hovis's success because:

- it still only constituted 5% of sales
- it was launched *after* demand improved
- Hovis did just as well in stores that didn't stock it.

The contribution of both of these new variants has been accounted for in the econometric model.

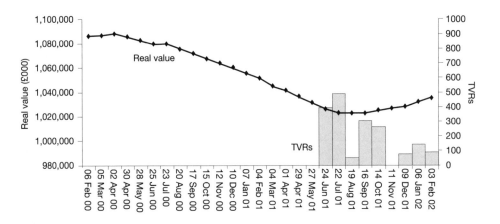
We can therefore discount all the above factors as the contributors to Hovis's success. This leaves the price rises, supported by the communication, as the sole drivers of increased profit.

EFFECT ON TOTAL BREAD MARKET

As was mentioned in the background section of this paper, British Bakeries shouldered some of the responsibility to help drive value back into the bakery market. By justifying an increase in Hovis prices, the Hovis brand also helped justify a price increase for other brands in the market. Figure 46 shows that there has been an unusual and satisfying increase in the value of the bakery market, the start of which coincided exactly with the relaunch of Hovis.

Figure 46: *Total bread market real value (MAT)*

THE RELAUNCH HAS BEEN EXTREMELY PROFITABLE

Both Hovis volume *and* value grew massively. Hovis is now No. 1 in all areas of the market. Its value growth is so impressive that TNS has calculated that it has been the fastest-growing non-alcoholic grocery brand over the past year. These things are pleasing, but, from a business perspective, what is ultimately important is profit. The relaunch, in its entirety, has transformed the profitability of Hovis. Profits increased by over 32%.[7]

Using British Bakeries' econometric model, we are able to show that the advertising pays for itself more than one-and-a-half times over. Every £1 spent on advertising generates £1.67 of extra profit. This equates to a return on investment of 67%.

---

7. Source: British Bakeries.

The financial value of the Hovis brand has also increased dramatically. Before the relaunch, British Bakeries had the Hovis brand valued independently by Interbrand. The Hovis brand value has recently been re-estimated internally by British Bakeries, which found that the brand has increased in value by over 31% compared with its value before the relaunch.

SUMMARY AND CONCLUSIONS

This paper has three important lessons for us:

1. It demonstrates how profit is the only real measure of business success, and that looking at volume alone can conceal the true picture. When volume and value are increased at the same time, then amazing turnarounds in profit are possible.
2. It is an excellent example (and a first for an IPA paper) of how packaging, in addition to advertising, can be an important communication channel. The holistic nature of the relaunch, where every element conformed to the same 'Consistency and Disruption' Strategy, was a bold and brave move for British Bakeries. But it is one that has paid off. We have demonstrated how communications can quite literally add value to a brand.
3. Finally, we have shown how the activity of one brand can increase the value of the whole market. Hovis led the way and the rest of the market was able to follow (albeit at a distance).

13

Kellogg's Real Fruit Winders

Unwinding the effects of
an integrated campaign

Principal authors: Janey Bullivant and Gurdeep Puri, Leo Burnett
Collaborating author: Lachlan Badenoch

EDITOR'S SUMMARY

The Kellogg's Real Fruit Winders entry shows how an integrated multimedia campaign of PR, ambient, web and TV was used to create a very different brand experience that went far beyond simple enjoyment of the product and gave kids the means to interact with the brand on a number of levels on their own terms.

The paper also describes how an integrated approach can further enhance a brand's value, in this case pushing sales up to £21.5m in the first year.

INTRODUCTION

This paper tells the story of the launch of Real Fruit Winders, a new fruit snack from Kellogg's. It shows how an integrated multimedia campaign of PR, ambient media, web and TV was used to create a very different brand experience – one that went far beyond simple enjoyment of the product and gave kids the means to interact with Real Fruit Winders on a number of different levels on their own terms.

It is our contention that this innovative communications approach has been a major factor in Real Fruit Winders' success. By giving kids the building blocks of the brand rather than a script to follow, we enhanced its overall value. After one year in the market, Real Fruit Winders is worth £21.5m, more than either Rice Krispies Squares or Cereal and Milk bars at the same stage of launch (source: Kellogg's ex factory sales, IRI Retail Audit). It has also outsold established favourites, Nestlé's Smarties and Rowntree's Fruit Pastilles (source: 24 weeks w/e 9th September 2001 total multiple value sales, IRI Retail Audit).

Communications worked by getting Real Fruit Winders onto kids' radars, by inviting them to participate, by creating the desired sense of 'cool' and driving trial, at a level far higher than expected.

The campaign also helped the Kellogg's brand to enter the world of kids in a way it had never done before, moving from home out into the tougher environment of the playground.

Finally, the success of Real Fruit Winders has proved the ability of Kellogg's to diversify into new markets outside of cereal for the first time, paving the way to deliver shareholder value in the longer term.

This case will reflect the mission of the 2002 awards to demonstrate the effectiveness of integrated communications. The launch campaign was a collaboration between Leo Burnett, Leonardo, Cake, Mindshare and M Digital.

BACKGROUND

Kellogg's ventures beyond cereal

Kellogg's has been making cereals for over 100 years. By the 1990s, the search was on to find new growth opportunities beyond the breakfast table. The cereal market was mature, the UK population profile was changing as were people's breakfast habits (source: Mintel Breakfast Cereals Report, February 2002). In 1997, Kellogg's launched its first snack brand – Nutri-Grain.[1] This was a relatively safe brand stretch for Kellogg's. Both the product and the missed breakfast proposition were close to Kellogg's heartland. Three other cereal bar launches followed: Rice Krispies Squares, Cereal and Milk bars and Special K bar.

With these successes behind it, Kellogg's felt confident enough to take the brand beyond cereal and beyond any breakfast association for the first time.

There appeared to be an opportunity with kids. Kids' purchasing power was on the increase and kids' need for snacks seemed set to grow as meal occasions

---

1. See *Advertising Works 11* for the Nutri-Grain launch case (World Advertising Research Center, 2000).

fragmented (source: Mintel: Snacking Report 2000). Kellogg's had built a successful adult snack business while, with kids, it had done little more than give them their favourite cereals in another form. For Kellogg's the kid snack opportunity lay in leveraging its strength as a 'kid enjoyed/mum endorsed' brand which would provide a point of difference in the market. The search was on for a product that fitted this brief.

Kellogg's struck upon a market that was dynamic in the States but non-existent in the UK – fruit roll-ups worth $400m. The 'fruit' sector would allow Kellogg's to exploit its nutritional heritage in a new area.

Kellogg's developers set about producing their own version of a fruit roll-up. Real Fruit Winders were in essence long, soft strips of tasty fruit snack, made from over 60% real fruit. Initial food scores were excellent (source: Concept Food Test 1999).

THE CHALLENGE

The challenge was to successfully launch Real Fruit Winders as the first non-cereal product from Kellogg's, creating a platform for future growth in fruit snacks. This was diversification of a different order. As early qualitative research confirmed, 'Real Fruit Winders represent a significant departure from the tried and tested for Kellogg's' (source: Conway Smith Rose Research 2000). This was a new proposition in a new sector. Established brands spent millions competing for kids' attention. In 2000, £88m was spent advertising toys and games, £34m on crisps and savoury snacks and £28m on sugar confectionery alone (source: MMS approximate annual spends 2000). The audience was elusive too. Kids could be notoriously fickle, quick to adopt and quick to drop.

In business terms, Kellogg's was aiming higher too: for a value of £25m by the end of year two, against £15.9m for Cereal and Milk bars (source: Kellogg's targets, IRI Retail Audit).

Communications would have to work very hard to get the brand on kids' radar and earn their approval.

CAMPAIGN DEVELOPMENT

The magnitude of the task meant we had to work and think differently. Right from the start, we worked as a multidisciplinary team. The search was on for groundbreaking ideas not 30-second launch ads. We needed something that would fire the imagination of kids in an intensely crowded marketplace. We went to toy fairs, we studied the success of Pokémon, we scoured the Japanese snacks market for inspiration. Our key strategic breakthrough was to redefine the business we're in – entertainment not just taste satisfaction.

Target kids

We would only target kids in communications. We would position Real Fruit Winders as a genuinely cool snack that every ten-year-old in the playground wanted. To do this, we would have to give kids ownership of the brand and not let mum in on the act. We felt confident that the packaging descriptor of 60% real fruit, the name '*Real* Fruit Winders' and the Kellogg's brand would reassure her 'behind the scenes'. This reassurance was important as Kellogg's expected mums to generate most of the volume via multipack purchasing. But in communications terms, it gave us free rein to talk to kids in their own language and adopt a new tone of voice for Kellogg's advertising. (Other Kellogg's kids' brands had never been as single-minded, with the result that advertising had a much safer, 'mumsier' tone of voice.)

Target insight

Our key insight came from beyond the snack market. In their struggle to make sense of the world and to assert themselves, kids have a deep desire for control. One of the things in their universe that satisfies this desire is interactivity. It was the common theme of the things kids were most into: Gameboy, CD-Roms, the internet, email, SMS messaging. Interactivity put them in charge, allowed them to make the decisions and express themselves freely.

By contrast, there was little true interactivity in the snack market. It was often just an add-on such as a website with some games rather than the glue which held the brand together.

Our big idea

This gave us our big idea – to take on some of these interactive properties and position Real Fruit Winders as an edible toy. We knew from early research that the product had real play value (source: Leo Burnett Qualitative Research, December 1999). The product was long, soft, squidgy and stretchy. Kids could eat the whole roll as one or tear strips off. In our own play sessions, we had also discovered that the food was soft enough to be imprinted upon, suggesting exciting new possibilities for interaction. It was now a case of exploiting this through the entire brand experience.

The creative brief

The creative brief for the launch campaign read as follows:

- *Role for advertising.*   Put Real Fruit Winders into the hands and minds of kids.
- *Target audience.*   10–12-year-old kids (broader audience 6–12 years).
- *Proposition.*   Interactive fruity fun that goes on and on.
- *Tone of voice*
  - Street smart
  - Groundbreaker.

Our brief was for an integrated and inescapable campaign that explored where kids were hanging out and what they were doing.

The creative solution

The creative idea was that Real Fruit Winders were an anarchic form of fruit – one that kids could eat, play with and use to communicate with each other. We created a world that this fruit would inhabit and that kids could interact with. This was the world of the Chewchat gang, a team of mutant fruit whose mischievous pranks centred round 'winding up' terrified fruit and squishing them into Real Fruit Winders. We created three characters – Strawberry Sorbabe, Orange Blabber and Blackcurrant Booster.

The invention of a 'language' gave our idea its edge. The Chewchat gang would converse in Chewchat, an iconic symbol language, initially composed of 22 symbols. Chewchat would also be used to spread the word about the brand virally and to take kids' involvement with it to another level.

The Chewchat symbols were iconic enough to have a base level of recognition and meaning yet still open enough for kids to interpret and use in their own way.

Collectable stampers connected the language back to the food. These would allow kids to stamp their favourite messages into the food and chat with their mates in a new and exciting way.

Media strategy

Our intention was to engage kids by building the brand from the ground up. This would be accomplished in three phases: initial underground communication, a kid discovery phase and a broadcast phase.

Real Fruit Winders was launched in mid-January 2001.

Phase one: underground – pre-launch
The aim of phase one was to seed the Chewchat language among opinion leaders. A PR programme was created to direct them to *www.chewchat.com*. This included distributing chewchat.com stickers at concerts, in magazines and in cinemas. Chewchat clothing was created for key kids' celebrities and a giant Chewchat symbol appeared at Victoria station. On the website, kids could use the 'Chatterbox' to download symbols and email them to friends.

This activity was all unbranded.

Phase two: kids' discovery – launch
The objective of phase two was to put kids 'in the know' about Chewchat, the gang and the product. Again, activity focused on reaching playground leaders who could be relied upon to spread the word, ensuring a trickledown effect on awareness and sales. A total of 300,000 branded chewchat.com stickers were inserted into kids' magazines. Terrified fruit and members of the Chewchat gang began to appear on the website.

Three high-profile kids' sites were chosen to drive awareness of the brand online. Instead of simply using banner advertising, new microsites were created on *www.capitalfm.com*, *www.citv.co.uk* and *www.diggit.co.uk* to build kids' relationships with the characters. For example, *Capitalfm.com* featured 'Sorbabe's Pop Club' where kids could access celeb gossip, music news, competitions and a Strawberry Sorbabe music game.

Phase three: mass awareness and trial

Phase three aimed to get the Real Fruit Winders message across to a broader audience of kids and mums and build critical mass for the brand. TV broke at the beginning of June, with two ads. Prior to this, a series of fruit 'wind up' stunts occurred around the country. These included blocking roads with giant strawberries and blackcurrant rain showering a stately home. On April Fool's Day, it was revealed that this was a hoax from Kellogg's in the *News of the World*.

www.chewchat.com was continually updated until August 2001, with features such as games, new Chewchat symbols and updateable screen savers. These chatpads let kids receive online comic strips and Chewchat messages while retrieving emails or viewing other sites.

Figure 1: *Chewchat sticker sheets*

Figure 2: www.chewchat.com *home page*

Figure 3: www.capitalfm.co.uk

It's the longest, stretchiest, fruity snack around, around, around.

New orange Fruit Winders from Kellogg's.

In three fruity flavours. New Kellogg's Real Fruit Winders... Unwind the fruity fun forever.

Figure 4: *TV advertising*

It's the longest, stretchiest, fruity snack around, around, around.

New strawberry Fruit Winders from Kellogg's.

In three fruity flavours...

New Kellogg's Real Fruit Winders... Unwind the fruity fun forever.

Figure 4: *TV advertising (continued)*

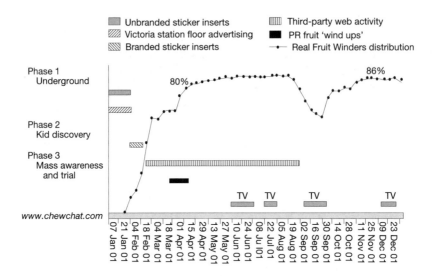

Figure 5: *Media plan 2001 and Real Fruit Winders distribution*
Note: This is the average of all variants' distribution in multiples. Distribution dipped in September as the orange variant was out of stock
Source: Mindshare

WHAT HAPPENED?

The launch of Real Fruit Winders has been a resounding success. By the end of December 2001, it achieved the following:

- Real Fruit Winders has a market value of £21.5m RSP (retail selling price). (This is based on Kellogg's ex-factory volume and IRI average price.) This compares favourably with a figure of £14.4m for Cereal and Milk bars in its first year. It is already close to its second year objective of £25m.

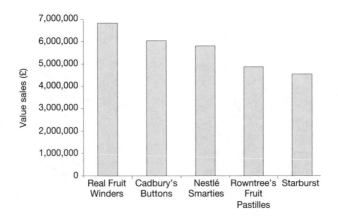

Figure 6: *Value sales total multiples 24 w/e 9 September 01*
Source: IRI Retail Audit

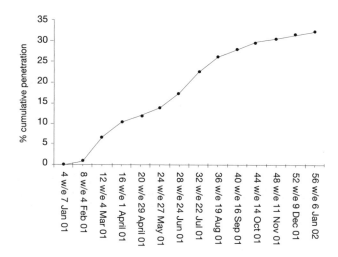

Figure 7: *Real Fruit Winders cumulative penetration in households with kids*
Source: TNS Superpanel

- It has outsold several key kids' brands in grocery (Figure 6). (Please note that Kellogg's purchases limited confectionery data from IRI on an ad hoc basis. This does not allow us to provide a comprehensive brand ranking. We have only looked at sales in multiples as Real Fruit Winders did not reach more than 13% Impulse distribution.)
- It has achieved penetration of 32% in households with children. This is almost double the launch target of 17% (Figure 7).
- It has attained strong repeat rates – 51% first repeat and 65% second repeat among households with children, against targets of 46% and 65%.
- It has built Kellogg's equity outside of cereal for the first time and created a platform for future growth in fruit snacks.

THE COMMUNICATIONS EFFECT

In the following sections, we will prove that the campaign has been instrumental in achieving these results. We will consider the evidence in a number of ways:

1. We will confirm that the campaign worked as intended.
2. We will analyse each phase in turn and illustrate its effects.
3. We will use econometric modelling to measure the contribution of communications.
4. We will show that additional factors cannot fully explain the sales growth.

THE CAMPAIGN WORKED AS INTENDED

We shall demonstrate that the campaign got the brand noticed, involved kids, created the desired brand image and got mums to buy it by the boxful.

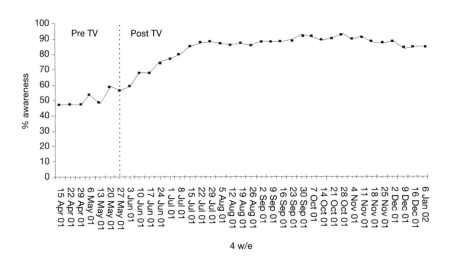

Figure 8: *Real Fruit Winders 4-weekly rolling prompted awareness among 6–15-year-olds*
Source: Millward Brown

It got the brand noticed

Real Fruit Winders achieved a remarkable 59% prompted awareness among kids with only PR and web activity. This rose to 77% after the first TV burst and peaked at 93% in October (Figure 8).

Later on, we shall show a strong correlation between brand awareness and TV ad awareness.

These scores are further validated by an Omnibus study which records high levels of spontaneous awareness among 7–12-year-olds, suggesting that the brand had attained real salience (Table 1).

TABLE 1: BRAND AWARENESS AMONG TARGET

	August 2001
Spontaneous brand awareness	77%
Prompted brand awareness	83%

Source: Carrick James Market Research

It involved kids

It was our desire to involve kids by opening the brand to participation. In communications terms, the Chewchat language and *www.chewchat.com* were the tools kids could use to interact with the brand. The best quantitative indicators of success are the number of visitor sessions and the measure of time spent on *www.chewchat.com*.

Table 2 shows the number of visitor sessions on *www.chewchat.com* since January 2001 with figures for *www.cocopops.co.uk* as a point of reference. These

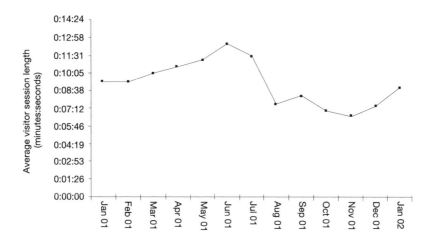

Figure 9: *Average visitor session length on* www.chewchat.com
Source: WebTrends

figures are a conservative estimate of total visitor sessions due to the limitations of the tracking methodology.[2]

TABLE 2: VISITOR SESSIONS 12 MONTHS SINCE LAUNCH

www.chewchat.com	www.cocopops.co.uk
416,820	306,257

Source: Webtrends

Between January and July 2001, when PR and online advertising were live, kids spent an average of 10 minutes 37 seconds on the site per session (Figure 9). This compares favourably with industry norms for 2000: 2–16-year-olds browsed entertainment sites for an average of 40 minutes per month (source: MMXI Europe, October 2000).

Qualitatively too, the evidence suggests that we created an interactive brand experience. The post-launch review, conducted via CKC Research KidsLink sessions in schools, concluded:

'One of the reasons that we believe Real Fruit Winders have been so successful is that they appeal to kids on multiple levels.'

Source: CKC Research, November 2001

In terms of the usage of Chewchat, we are hampered by lack of data. At a qualitative level we have clear indication that it infiltrated kids' conversations and was seen as part of their world. In respondents' words:

---

2. WebTrends tracks visitor sessions through the IP address of the visitor. If the Internet Service Provider filters data through an intermediate proxy server as in the case of AOL, individual IP addresses will not be picked up, thus the total number of visitor sessions will be underestimated. WebTrends also counts several requests to the same IP address within 30 minutes as a single visitor session.

'I have used the site and sent messages – a heart to my best friend to make up and say sorry after a fight.'

'It is more secret than text messaging – my mum wouldn't know what was going on.'

Source: CKC Research, November 2001

We also know that celebrities appeared on *Live & Kicking*, *SMTV*, *GMTV* and MTV wearing Chewchat T-shirts between February and June 2001. This led to phone calls to Kellogg's customer services with people asking where they could buy the clothing. While anecdotal, this story is evidence that Chewchat was something kids wanted to be in on and that they had made the connection with Real Fruit Winders and Kellogg's.

It gave Real Fruit Winders the desired image

The campaign also gave Real Fruit Winders a slight edginess which was new for a Kellogg's brand. The Chewchat gang contributed to this.

'All three are considered 'cool' and are liked by both girls and boys.'

'What is interesting is that the characters are perceived as mean, a bit wicked, but they are still liked.'

Source: CKC Research, November 2001

Overall, the brand was seen as 'cool'. This was the verdict of an Omnibus Study[3] and qualitative research where kids scored Real Fruit Winders 5 out of 5 on a 'cool-o-meter' scale (source: CKC Research, February 2002). Kids based their judgement on a number of cool criteria, including:

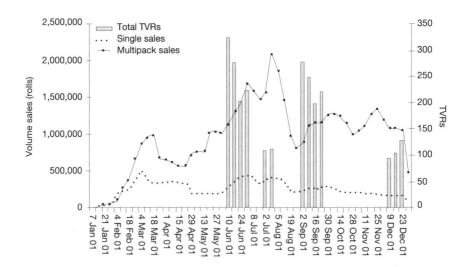

Figure 10: *Multipack and single sales versus TVRs*
Source: IRI Retail Audit, Mindshare

---

3. A total of 46% of kids agree Real Fruit Winders are cool; 42% agree Real Fruit Winders are OK; but only 8% believe Real Fruit Winders are not at all cool. Source: Carrick James Market Research.

- Everybody eats it, talks about it, wants it; all my friends like it.
- It makes you look more popular and older.
- You can do something with it.

In contrast, sweet snacks as a whole were not deemed cool. In the words of an 11-year-old respondent, 'sweets aren't cool, they are just sweets' (source: CKC Research, November 2002). With Real Fruit Winders, kids got more than just great taste. This was a brand with real play value that they wanted to be seen with in the playground.

It got mums to buy it

Finally, the campaign worked by getting mums to stock up. Figure 10 shows the huge rise in multipack sales once the brand was on TV.

THE EFFECTS OF EACH PHASE

It may be helpful to refer back to the media plan (Figure 5) at this stage.

Phase one

In January 2001 a total of 25,583 visitor sessions to *www.chewchat.com* was recorded. It is our contention that PR drove curious kids to the website as there was no other above-the-line activity at this time and product availability was very limited.[4]

We can even pinpoint the effect of the first magazine release (Figure 11). *Top of the Pops* magazine hit the shelves on 3 January 2001, leading to a 325% rise in

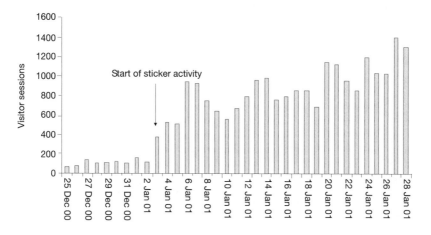

Figure 11: *Daily* www.chewchat.com *visitor sessions for January 2001*
Source: WebTrends, Mindshare

---

4. The unbranded PR activity was scheduled to take place before launch. Due to differing launch windows by retailer, the product was actually launched mid-January. However it only reached 14% £ distribution w/e 28 January. It had 1% and 5% distribution the previous weeks. In Impulse it attained less than 2% £ distribution by the end of January.

visitor sessions that day. Visitor sessions continued on an upward trend through January.

Phase two

The aim of phase two was for kids to discover the secret world of Real Fruit Winders through contact with the brand online. During this phase, we see a continuing rise in web usage, as expected. We also note a magnified effect on trial and awareness, as the early web adopters spread the word to other kids in the playground.

Figure 12 shows the increase in visitor sessions to *www.chewchat.com* and the correlation with PR and online advertising.

Third-party sites provided an effective introduction to the brand, generating the following clickthroughs:

TABLE 3: CLICKTHROUGHS FROM THIRD-PARTY SITES

	Clickthroughs (by number of visitors)
www.capitalfm.com	22,650
www.diggit.co.uk	177,578
www.citv.co.uk	244,383

Source: Doubleclick

These figures are a measure of clickthroughs to both *www.chewchat.com* and to the Chewchat microsites created within *capitalfm.co.uk*, *diggit.co.uk* and *citv.co.uk*. Average click rates varied from site to site, with a monthly average of 0.45% for *capitalfm.co.uk*, 6% for *diggit.co.uk* and 10.28% for *citv.co.uk*. This compares to an industry norm of 0.33%. We know that we were successful in getting kids to interact with the brand once they logged on, as we have shown

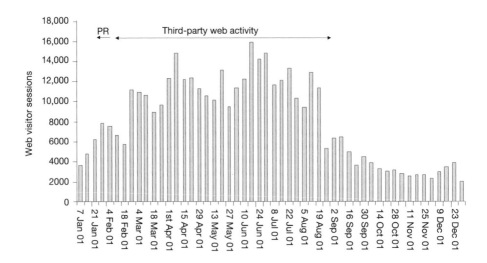

Figure 12: *Weekly* www.chewchat.com *visitor sessions and third-party web activity*
Source: WebTrends, MindShare

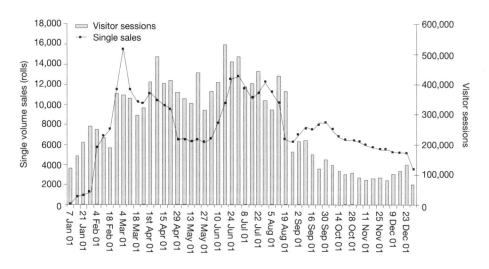

Figure 13: *Real Fruit Winders single volume sales and* www.chewchat.com *visitor sessions*
Source: IRI Retail Audit, WebTrends

already in the measure of average session length (Figure 9). From February, we see an increase in trial, measured as the uplift in singles sales, corresponding with web usage (Figure 13).

Penetration grew to 13.8% households with kids by the end of May,[5] or one million actual households. The brand was bought by far more households than logged onto the web at this stage (199,150 visitor sessions), suggesting that PR and web did indeed have a viral effect.

Prompted brand awareness reached 59% prior to TV,[6] providing further evidence that this phase worked as intended.

Phase three

TV broke in June. At exactly the same time, we see a step change in the brand's awareness, volume and penetration. This is absolutely in line with the strategy of reaching a broader audience.

Figure 14 demonstrates that TV awareness was a key driver of brand awareness.

Not only did the TV create awareness, it was very efficient at doing so. It achieved an Awareness Index score of 30, versus the norm of 11 for kids' ads (source: Millward Brown).[7] This is essentially a measure of the increase in ad awareness resulting from 100 TVRs delivered to the target group.

In Figure 15, we can see a strong correlation between sales of Real Fruit Winders and the ads being on air.

---

5. This figure is likely to be a conservative estimate of trial as it only reflects in home penetration.
6. We cannot show the awareness build as we only have continuous data from April 2001.
7. The Link Test AI was only 6, suggesting the ads way outperformed expectation.

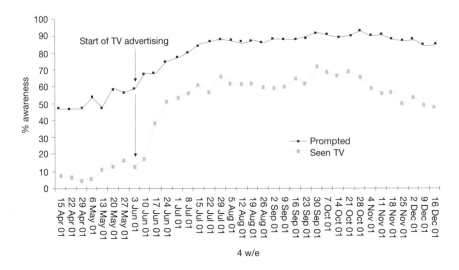

Figure 14: *Real Fruit Winders 4-weekly rolling TV awareness and 4-weekly prompted brand awareness*
Source: Millward Brown

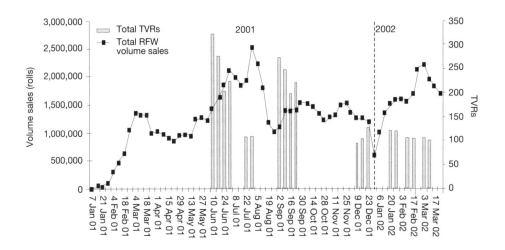

Figure 15: *Real Fruit Winders volume sales and TVRs*
Source: IRI Retail Audit, Mindshare

In Figure 16, we show sales by variant versus TVRs. We have included this chart to explain why the sales uplift from the September burst of TV was lower than for the first two bursts. The orange variant was out of stock during this period and while strawberry and blackcurrant showed strong sales, this situation clearly inhibited overall brand performance.

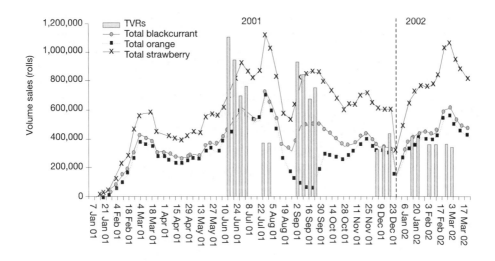

Figure 16: *Real Fruit Winders 4-weekly volume sales by variant (rolls) and TVRs*
Source: IRI Retail Audit, Mindshare

In December 2001, sales of Real Fruit Winders actually dipped. We have included the most recent sales data (Figures 15 and 16) to establish this was not an ongoing trend but a Christmas effect.[8] Kellogg's advertised at this time to insulate the new brand as far as possible from this effect.

Gains in household penetration also correlate with the ads being on air (Figure 17).

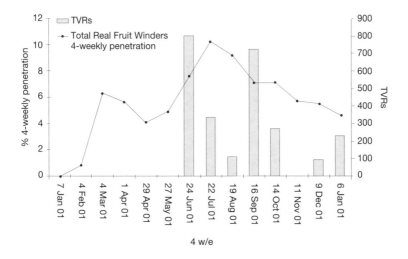

Figure 17: *Real Fruit Winders 4-weekly penetration in households with kids and GRPs*
Source: TNS Superpanel, Mindshare

---

8. Retailers reduce the space given to individual countlines to make way for Christmas packs.

Phase three also included a PR element with fruit 'wind up' stunts generating national and regional press coverage. We have limited ability to judge the effectiveness of this activity as we have no awareness data for mums. We can say that PR generated 58 articles on Real Fruit Winders and 21 articles on the fruit 'wind ups' (source: Millward Brown Precis, Cake). These appeared in newspapers including *News of the World*, *Daily Express*, the *Guardian*, the *Independent*, *Funday Times* and on Channel 5 news. A total of 98% coverage was positive or factual and 92% coverage carried at least one key message.[9]

ECONOMETRIC MODELLING

Modelling techniques were employed to disentangle the effects of the media and marketing variables involved. This was not an easy task given the complexity of the communications and the relatively limited period from launch. Nevertheless, a model was produced which performs acceptably against a range of standard statistical diagnostics. This gives us an indication of the advertising contribution.

The key drivers of Real Fruit Winders' volume sales were found to be the average price of each pack size, its distribution, its TV adstock, the combined effect of PR and visitor sessions and the combined effect of TVRs and visitor sessions.

Other variables were initially included but were found to be statistically insignificant. Figure 18 shows the actual volume sales versus the model fit.

The contribution of TV for 2001 is calculated to be 11.3 million roll sales (Figure 19). The additional combined effect of kids seeing the ads and logging on to *www.chewchat.com* is estimated to be 2.2m roll sales.

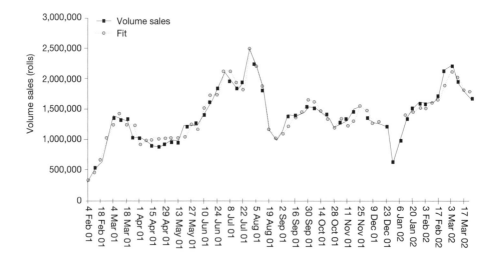

Figure 18: *Actual Real Fruit Winders' volume sales vs. fit*
Source: Econometric model

---

9. Cake's intended messages were 'branded Real Fruit Winders from Kellogg's, 50% real fruit, character mentions, snack not a sweet, fun snack for kids, fruity fun'.

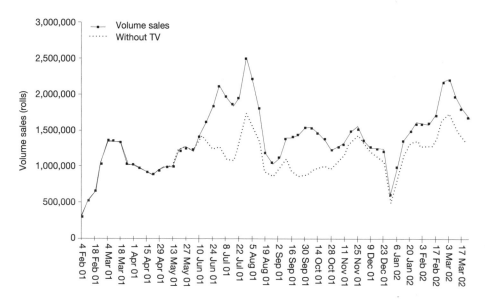

Figure 19: *Estimated effect of TV advertising*
Source: Econometric model

The combined effect of PR and visitor sessions from February to April is 400,000 roll sales. This calculates only the sales that came directly from kids seeing PR and logging onto the website. It does not reflect any viral effect, whereby early web adopters bought the product and spread the word to other kids in the playground. In this sense, the econometric model underestimates the true contribution of PR and web to Real Fruit Winder sales.

We have also been unable to estimate the contribution of third-party online advertising to sales as we could not find an acceptable way to include it in the model.

Based purely on the model, we calculate the total contribution of communications to be 22% Real Fruit Winders sales.

ADDITIONAL FACTORS

Promotions?

The major retailers promoted Real Fruit Winders on average twice in 2001. Promotions were either price discounts or multibuys. They have been taken into account in the model through the inclusion of average price variables.

Category growth?

Real Fruit Winders has created its own sector. It competes within the overall snacking market but replaces a broad range of snacks – sweets, chocolate, biscuits, crisps, fruit (source: Carrick James Omnibus Study, April 2002). This makes it hard to explain sales as the result of a particular category's growth. Even if we do look at an apparently close competitive category such as fruit confectionery, we see it cannot account for Real Fruit Winders' success as it is in decline (source: Mintel Sugar Confectionery Report, 2001).[10]

BROADER EFFECTS OF THE CAMPAIGN

What about mum?

Our strategic decision to talk only to kids has paid off in creating a desirable kids brand. But what about mum? As the main expected purchasers of Real Fruit Winders, mums' perception of the brand was also crucial.

We have evidence that the 'real fruit' message got through.

> 'Most of the mums were aware of the fruit content of Winders and considered them a healthier alternative to the other sweets their children like.'
>
> Source: CKC Research, November 2001

In the latest Omnibus study, 61% of mums claimed to be using Real Fruit Winders 'as a treat that's better than sweets' (source: Carrick James Omnibus Study, April 2002).

We have created a snack brand with appeal to both kids and mums. Kids were our main advocates, but mums became willing accomplices once they knew about the fruit content and the Kellogg's branding. This is a powerful position to hold in the snack market.

Effect on the Kellogg's brand

Stronger equity with kids

The strong status of Real Fruit Winders among kids has also increased the salience of the parent brand.

For the first time, kids are happy to eat a Kellogg's product in the playground in front of their mates (source: CKC Research, 2001; DUCKFoOT Research, 2001). While enjoyed for their taste, other Kellogg's brands did not cut it as social snacks. A major segmentation study for Kellogg's in 2000 concluded that its existing products satisfied two need states: 'solid fill' and 'mumsy health' (source: icon brand navigation, 2000, the findings of which cover cereals and cereal bars). Kids ate these products because they were filling and nutritious and because 'mum likes you to have them' rather than for peer approval.

Real Fruit Winders in contrast are 'cool' and have direct appeal to kids.

They have added a new dimension to the Kellogg's brand, adding 'a mischievous facet to its personality' (source: Conway Smith Rose Research, 2000).

Equity outside cereal

At the outset of this paper, we described Kellogg's brave decision to build equity in a new market. Was this a risk worth taking?

---

10. Fruit confectionery declined from £477m in 1998 to £414m in 2000.

In a word, yes. The success of Real Fruit Winders has created a platform for further expansion in fruit snacks. In particular, Kellogg's has identified potential for 'line extensions featuring terrified fruit in other guises' (source: CKC Research, 2002), underlining the contribution of communications to the uniqueness of the brand.

Future new product development will provide an important engine of growth for Kellogg's, helping to deliver shareholder value over the longer term.

From the trade perspective, the success of Real Fruit Winders has secured Kellogg's reputation as an outstanding innovator. It has opened new channels, the most notable of which is Woolworth's.

PAYBACK

Through econometric modelling, we have shown that the campaign accounted for 22% total Real Fruit Winder sales. We believe the actual contribution to be higher than this, as the model does not include the effect of online advertising or the viral impact of PR.

Even without these other media effects, we can show that the campaign has paid for itself and generated incremental revenue. TV advertising, the combined effect of TV and web and the combined effect of PR and web account for 13.9m roll sales, equivalent to £3.1m value sales. As our data source has only reported 65% total sales,[11] the actual revenue generated by the campaign is £4.8m. The total cost of the campaign was £3.3m, including media and production (source: Kellogg's data, Mindshare).

Not only has the campaign paid back in the short term, it has helped establish a brand that we expect to be profitable for many years to come.

CONCLUSION

The purpose of this paper has been to prove the contribution of advertising to the launch of Real Fruit Winders. The numbers are conclusive: 22% sales came directly from advertising. We have demonstrated that while TV remains the key volume generator, an integrated approach can further enhance the value of a brand and build a more involved relationship with the target audience. We concur with the argument of John Grant in *The New Marketing Manifesto*:

'It is a paradox of New Marketing economics that the less you do and the more they participate, the more you are worth.'

We also conclude:

- A relevant and engaging website can increase the effectiveness of TV advertising.
- Although we cannot measure the viral effects of the campaign, we have a strong indication that they exist. Real Fruit Winders was bought by a million

---

11. This is based on the difference between Kellogg's ex-factory sales and IRI volume sales.

households with kids pre-TV – five times more than the number of web visitor sessions. It also achieved awareness of 59% among kids. At this early stage of launch, it seems unlikely that distribution alone could account for these results. Part of the explanation must surely lie in the trickledown effect of early adopters surfing the web and 'infecting' other kids in the playground.

- By talking only to kids, we have created the first Kellogg's brand with true kid cachet. At the same time, we have retained the approval of mum – a win–win situation all round.

14

Marmite
'Please don't spread it thinly'

Principal authors: Laurence Parkes and Les Binet, BMP DDB
Collaborating author: Emma Wright

EDITOR'S SUMMARY

This case documents how, despite being in a declining market, Marmite managed to grow at an average of 5% p.a. between 1995 and 2001. This was achieved with little more than an extremely effective advertising campaign and associated PR. This activity was instrumental in repositioning Marmite's brand image and reintroducing lapsed users. Econometrics showed how the £12.4m spent on advertising increased sales by £53.5m and that without the advertising and PR the sales would have fallen by 26%.

INTRODUCTION

Nowadays, communication needs to work harder to break through the increasing advertising noise. It is commonly believed that getting a foothold in the public's attention requires a presence across a greater number of communication channels.

This paper, however, will show how quite the opposite can be true.

We show how a brave and focused new strategy, concentrating firepower (both creatively and in media terms), elevated an already strong brand to new heights.

The two linchpins of the strategy were:

1. Just one media channel (TV advertising) was used to give Marmite a radical new adult-oriented direction.
2. A second communication channel (PR) was used to amplify the fame-generating potential of the provocative advertising campaign. And for the first time in an IPA paper, we believe we quantify the additional sales contribution of this PR.

Concentrating, not fragmenting, marketing communication – doing fewer things but doing them well – has transformed Marmite's fortunes and made it into a national icon.

BACKGROUND

Marmite has a heritage as strong as its taste. It has been popular as a healthy foodstuff since this useless leftover of the brewing industry was first made edible and sold to the British public 100 years ago. Full of B vitamins, Marmite was getting publicity in the *Lancet* as early as 1903. The brand established itself as a healthy spread for children through promotion in traditional 'village hall' clinics. However, in the 1970s, these clinics were replaced with welfare centres where retail sales were forbidden. To compensate for this, the owners of Marmite began to use consumer marketing more heavily.[1]

THE PROBLEM

At first the heavier investment in consumer marketing appeared to work; sales growth had been strong during the 1980s. But by the early 1990s growth had slowed (Figure 1).

Several factors contributed to this slowdown:

- *Marmite's reliance on bread consumption.* Ninety-six per cent of Marmite is eaten as a spread on bread. The first half of the 1990s saw UK bread consumption moving into a decline.
- *Marmite's reliance on breakfast.* More than 55% of all Marmite eating occasions are breakfasts. Breakfast has been a declining meal occasion since 1990.
- *The decline in the number of children in the population:* In line with Marmite's heritage, under-four-year-olds are an important group for driving sales. This age group began to decline in 1993 and this decline was projected to continue.

---

1. As shown in an earlier IPA paper 'How "The Growing UP Spread" just carried on growing' (1998).

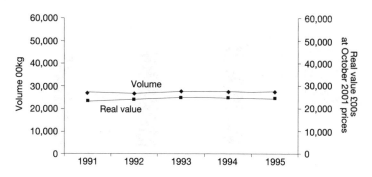

Figure 1: *Annual sales of Marmite*
Source: Nielsen

MARKETING OBJECTIVES AND STRATEGY

An impossible task...

This paper picks up the story in 1996. Following an expensive restructuring programme and a period of aggressive acquisition, CPC (then owner of Marmite) was keen to squeeze more profit out of its brands to pay off debts. This meant, despite recently stalled sales and no increase in marketing budget, that Marmite's sales target was set at an ambitious 5% growth per annum.

... Made even harder

This target appeared even more ambitious when we assessed the strength of the brand. Levels of 'brand goodwill'[2] had declined over recent years (Figure 2).

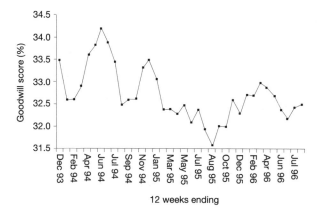

Figure 2: *Marmite brand goodwill*
Base: All adults.
Source: TABS

---

2.   'Brand goodwill' was measured on a 10-point scale of appeal ('for me' to 'not for me').

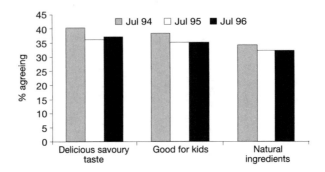

Figure 3: *Marmite brand image scores*
Base: All adults.
Source: TABS

And when looking at more specific brand measures, we saw that important brand image attributes had been eroded (Figure 3).

The brand malaise was obvious from qualitative research showing consumers' emotional detachment from the brand:

'Marmite is taken for granted by its users (it is in the store cupboard but not top of mind) and its rational values dominate its emotional values in consumers' image of the brand.'

Source: The Leading Edge Consultancy

An explanation for this reduction in important attributes and overall appeal was that Marmite was becoming less top of mind. This was shown by perceptions of the amount of publicity Marmite was getting (Figure 4).[3]

This decrease in presence was, in part, because Marmite's advertising wasn't working hard enough to cut through. Falling advertising awareness (Figure 5), despite an increase in advertising activity, showed this.

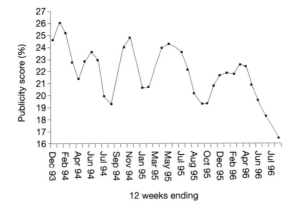

Figure 4: *Marmite publicity score*
Base: All adults
Source: TABS

3. Publicity score was measured on a 10-point scale ('recently had lots of publicity' to 'had no publicity at all').

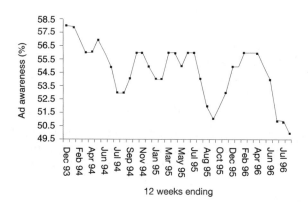

Figure 5: *Marmite advertising awareness*
Base: All adults
Source: TABS

So what was wrong with the advertising?

Marmite's marketing was complicated by the 'Marmite life cycle' (Figure 6). Marmite's unique taste means that people usually acquire a liking for it when young. Britons first acquired their taste for Marmite when it was recommended by the village hall clinics. Nowadays, the habit is passed from generation to generation when parents, who have acquired the taste as children, feed it to their children as a healthy spread.

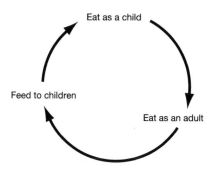

Figure 6: *The Marmite life cycle*

Within this life cycle, there are two junctures when Marmite usage can lapse:

1. When older children get greater autonomy over food, they often reject Marmite in favour of sweeter spreads. Often, they will not return to it until they themselves are parents.
2. Once their kids have grown up, older people often lapse out of the brand, having less reason to eat it.

This leaves five potential options for boosting sales:

1. Get Marmite parents to feed it more often to their children.
2. Increase trial among children.
3. Increase trial among adults.
4. Get adult users to eat more.
5. Get lapsed adult users back into the brand.

The previous five years' marketing activity had attempted to chase a variety of these objectives simultaneously. The multiple marketing objectives were reflected in confused advertising messages. It was this that caused the reduced advertising cut-through (Figure 7). The adult objectives (using a taste message) were given equal priority to the traditional family-focused objectives (using a health message). As a result, the activity was spread too thinly and none of the messages got through.[4]

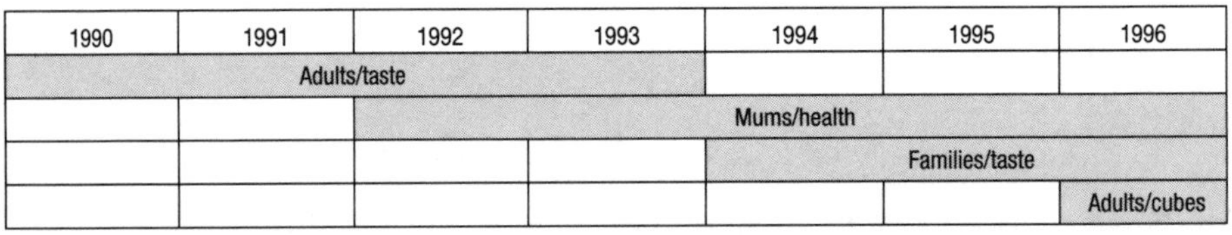

1990	1991	1992	1993	1994	1995	1996
Adults/taste						
		Mums/health				
				Families/taste		
						Adults/cubes

Figure 7: *Marmite TV advertising activity (1990 to 1996)*

There were also attempts, using advertising, to increase penetration in the North. Marmite was much stronger in the South (82% of Marmite households were southern), as a result of historical NHS support in that region. Returns on investment for this northern activity were not good and it distracted money away from Marmite's heartland.

As a result, the advertising activity was spread thinly over different target audiences, messages and regions. This inevitably led to a weak brand image:

'The weakness and imbalance in the brand image appears to be a direct result of the brand's advertising over the last five years. This has severely eroded the brand–consumer relationship to the point at which consumers lack a strong emotional attachment to Marmite.'

Source: The Leading Edge Consultancy

A more focused marketing strategy

We acknowledged that, in order to achieve the ambitious sales target, we had to be brutally focused in our thinking. We advised that marketing should concentrate ruthlessly on just one of the possible objectives. After evaluating each option, we decided that adult lapsed users should be targeted. This was a large group of people who had already acquired a taste for Marmite.

We believed that focusing on lapsed users would get the required volume growth. Calculations showed that if just one in ten lapsed users became a light user we would achieve our sales target (Table 1).

---

4. This was made worse when, in 1996, Marmite stock cubes were being supported.

TABLE 1: CALCULATION OF ADDITIONAL VOLUME
BY FOCUSING ON LAPSED USERS

Lapsed users = 25% of population
10% of lapsed users = 1,166,667
Eating 3 portions of Marmite (12 g) per month = 144 g p.a. per person
Total additional volume = 168 kgs p.a. = 5% growth

We knew this was a brave strategy. But we were confident that we could attract enough lapsed users, while the existing user group would carry on eating Marmite.

In summary

Attempts to cover all bases had proved to be the root of Marmite's weakness in 1996. Having decided that we must be strictly single-minded, a very specific marketing strategy was set. We aimed to get lapsed adult users back into the brand.

COMMUNICATIONS OBJECTIVES

With a weakened brand as a result of diffuse marketing activities, the need to have tightly focused communications was clear. Concentration on influencing lapsed adult users should give the brand a new and reinvigorated direction. Therefore, it was agreed that the role for communications would be:

1. Raise Marmite's profile with lapsed adult users.
2. Give Marmite a revitalised image.

It was also hoped that it would play another, indirect role. It was possible that the communications would have a knock-on effect, re-engaging current adult users with the brand.

DEVELOPING THE COMMUNICATIONS STRATEGY

A focus on TV advertising and PR

We needed to focus on fewer marketing activities and do them better. We wanted to raise the profile of the brand. We needed to make it famous. The obvious choices of activity were advertising and PR.

- Advertising would be key to getting lapsed users to reappraise Marmite's image.
- It would also allow the general public to overhear and raise Marmite's profile with them.
- PR would amplify advertising effects for both of the above.

In order to make the most of the modest budget and focus as much as possible, we chose to concentrate almost all the communications budget in advertising. The small but significant amount that was being spent on PR would continue. This would be used to make the advertising itself a talking point among the general population. This was much more concentrated than previous Marmite budgets and that of a typical UK firm (Figures 8 and 9).

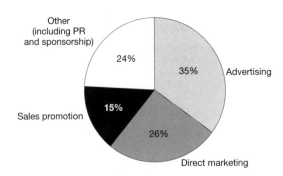

Figure 8: *How the average UK firm allocates its budget*
Source: IPA Bellwether Report 2000–2001

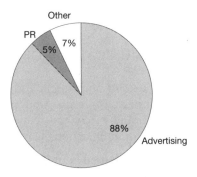

Figure 9: *How we allocated our budget 1997 to 2001*
Source: Unilever Bestfoods

To focus further we felt that we had to concentrate on just one advertising medium to get cut-through. It was felt that television would be ideal for re-engaging people with the brand and making it famous.

A tightly defined target audience

We chose TV advertising partly for its mass broadcast potential. But to make our advertising effective we still needed a clear idea of who our core target audience were. We knew we wanted to recruit lapsed users but could we be even more specific?

The two junctures at which people lapse out of the brand are indicated in the penetration levels in adult life-stages (Figure 10). Penetration is low due to lapsing at the pre-family stage, escalates when people have their own children and then slowly drops off again when people lapse back out as their children grow older.

The post-children lapsed group (including people from maturing, established and post-family life-stages) is by far the biggest of the two, but the pre-family group is much more **valuable** to influence because:

1. They have longer to live and consume Marmite.
2. They would have Marmite in the house when they establish their own families.

So we would focus on this group.

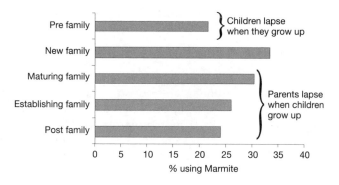

Figure 10: *Marmite penetration by life-stage*
Source: Omnibus 1995

Understanding pre-family lapsed users

In seeking to make what we communicate more relevant to our target audience, we discovered that:

- It was Marmite's strong heritage as a healthy baby spread that caused lapsing among this group:

  'Young adults lack sufficiently strong reason to stay with the brand, which for them is predominantly about childhood, motherhood and family. There is a need to break though this emotional "baggage" in order to bring lapsed users back into the brand.'

  Source: RDS Research, May 1996

- The primary reason young adult users gave for eating Marmite was the taste.
- Food advertising targeted to this marketing cynical group had developed in recent years. Brands such as Tango, Pepperami and Pot Noodle were beginning to act more like beer brands. To be noticed by its target audience, Marmite's advertising had to compete in this new world.

The creative brief

Summary of BMP creative brief (February 1996)
- *Opportunity for advertising.* Get people to reappraise 'good Old Marmite', to make it famous again, by showing that it is relevant, accessible and 'out and about'.

- *Target audience.* Infrequent and recently lapsed users of Marmite, especially younger men and women, who are setting up home and establishing their own eating/snacking habits. They like the taste, but take Marmite very much for granted and tend to forget about it. They value Marmite highly but think of it as something they were given as kids and it feels a bit authoritarian and distant.

- *Personality.* A popular hero for our time. An old friend who has a new lease of life.

- *Tone of voice.* Vital, fresh, irreverent but still steadfastly familiar and unpretentious.

- *Proposition.* Get Marmite out of the cupboard and into your life.

The creative brief was a good summary of our strategic thinking. However, to be honest, it was the creatives who came up with the consumer insight at the heart of the new campaign. That particular flash of inspiration was the result of a fortunate dynamic that existed within the creative team: one of them loved Marmite and the other loathed it. They felt that this element of the brand would be the perfect way to communicate Marmite's unique taste. Research showed that their reactions were not unusual:

'It's so true. Everyone knows someone who hates it.'

'You know that if someone is eating it they must love it 'cos there's no middle ground with Marmite.'

Source: 2CV research, April 1999; RDS research, March 1997

The creative team wrote two launch executions for the Hate/Mate campaign: one showing people loathing Marmite and the other showing people obsessively loving it (Figures 11 and 12).

[Low Rider music throughout]

Singer: I hate Marmite

Singer: I hate Marmite

[Low Rider music]

Figure 11: *'I Hate'*

[Low Rider music throughout]

Singer: My mate Marmite

Singer: My mate Marmite

[Low Rider music]

Figure 12: 'My Mate'

The strength of the Hate/Mate idea

The creative idea was particularly strong for two reasons:

1. It was ground-breaking in its honesty. This appealed to our marketing-cynical target audience and would also generate publicity.
2. It would allow both users and non-users to get involved with the campaign – a useful quality in bringing this campaign into public consciousness.

Creative development research backed up our belief that this campaign would get Marmite talked about again.

'The campaign is a jolt, bringing the brand back into lapsed users' minds:

- It puts the target audience back in touch with the brand.
- It brings the brand into the public domain (sparks off debate, gets people talking about it, challenges you to declare where you stand).'

'It's going to make people sit up and talk about it.'

'Everyone would want the T-shirts.'

'They could set up a spoof Marmite help line.'

Source: RDS research, May 1996

THE MEDIA STRATEGY

So far this paper has shown how we focused on just one target audience, aiming to communicate one message. We were also more focused in our media strategy.

1. As mentioned, we concentrated on TV (Figure 13).

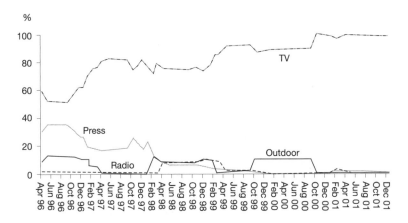

Figure 13: *Total adspend for each media (%) (MAT)*

2. Marmite's strength in the South meant that by focusing activity there we would be talking to many more lapsed users (Figure 14). So we increased the proportion of spend in the South and decreased it in the North (Figure 15).

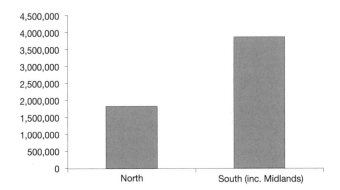

Figure 14: *Number of lapsed users*
Source: Omnibus 1995, Homescan 1995

3. A 1994 econometric model showed the most efficient time of year to advertise was in the winter (Figure 16). So this is when bursts of activity were bought (Figure 17).
4. The ads were concentrated in a different (more adult, later evening) context, helping people to reappraise Marmite as a more adult-orientated brand (Figure 18).

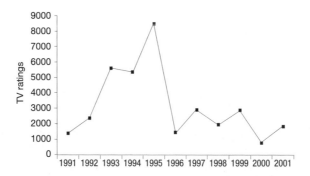

Figure 15: *Level of Marmite advertising in the North*
Source: BARB

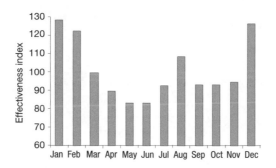

Figure 16: *Marmite TV advertising effectiveness by time of year*
Source: 1994 Econometric model

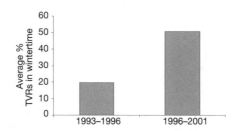

Figure 17: *Percentage of TVRs in winter time*
Source: MMS

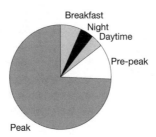

Figure 18: *TVRs by day part 1996 to 2001*
Source: MMS

CAMPAIGN DEVELOPMENT

More focus as the campaign evolved

The second burst of activity after the launch executions (Figure 19) brought the two elements of love and hate together in one ad for media efficiency purposes.

Madam, can I interest you in trying some Marmite today?

Thank you

Urgh!

Not you again
One more?

[Low rider music begins]

SFX: Shrieks

Nooooooo....

Super: You either love it or you hate it.

Figure 19: *'Promotion'*

The third burst of activity (Figure 20) focused on what appeared (in research) to be one of the strengths of the creative idea; depicting how Marmite affects relationships between people. It was at this point that the campaign became truly famous.

Sorry about the mess...

Would you like to sit...coffee?
Great

Mmm...

Urgh...

Yuck...

[Low Rider music begins]

YOU EITHER **LOVE** IT
OR **HATE** IT

Figure 20: 'Apartment'

The fourth burst of activity (Figures 21 and 22) closely followed the same structure.

Urgh...

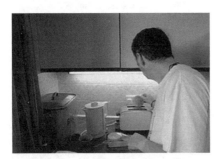

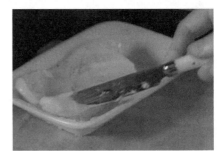

Mmm...

Blah!

[Low Rider music begins]

Figure 21: *'Milk'*

SFX: Stomach growling

Yuck!

[Low Rider music begins]

Figure 22 *'Tramp'*

BUSINESS RESULTS

The new campaign has been a tremendous success. After five years of stagnation, sales saw an immediate increase and have been increasing ever since (Figure 23).

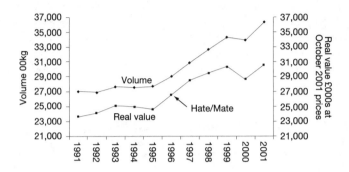

Figure 23: *Annual sales of total Marmite paste*
Source: Nielsen

As a result of this we have achieved the marketing objective of achieving 5% growth per annum (Table 2).

TABLE 2: GROWTH RATE IN SALES

	Volume sales (%)
1995–1996	5
1996–1997	6
1997–1998	6
1998–1999	5
1999–2000	–1
2000–2001	7
Average annual growth rate 1996–2001	5

PROOF OF THE EFFECT OF ADVERTISING AND PR

So how can we tell that the advertising and PR were responsible for the brand's success?

We will now show that we created:

1. Famous advertising.
2. Advertising that, with PR, generated publicity.
3. Advertising and publicity that revitalised the brand.
4. Advertising and publicity that affected consumer behaviour.
5. Advertising and publicity that had a direct effect on sales.
6. Advertising and publicity that had other beneficial effects.

After that we will eliminate any other possible factors that would influence sales.

Finally, we will quantify exactly how much the advertising and PR contributed to sales, using an econometric model.

FAMOUS ADVERTISING

People began to notice Marmite's advertising

With the launch of the new, more focused campaign, ad awareness suddenly increased (Figure 24).

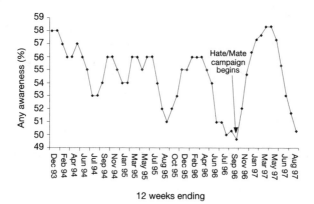

Figure 24: *Marmite advertising awareness*
Base: All adults
Source: TABS

This increase in ad awareness was sustained and has grown during the campaign, reaching a peak with 'Apartment'/'Burst 3' (Figure 25).

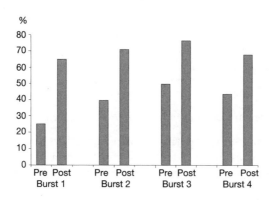

Figure 25: *Ad awareness*
Source: Research International

The ads were loved

The appeal of the advertising was strong from the launch and, since then, has grown even higher (Figure 26).

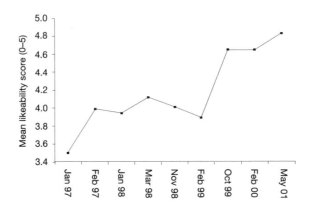

Figure 26: *Likeability of ads*
Source: Research International

When 'Apartment' was pre-tested, the research agency found it was one of the best ads it had ever researched (Figure 27).

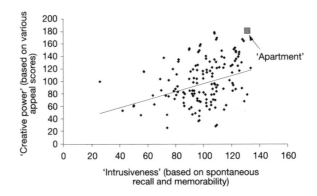

Figure 27: *'Apartment' was one of the best ads ever tested*
Source: Research International database of 300 ads

The campaign communicated the desired message

Communication of the polarising nature of Marmite's unique taste has strengthened over the campaign, despite starting from a high base. As hoped, this has boosted the belief that Marmite has a delicious taste (Figure 28).

The ads became famous

The campaign has worked as planned. The ads became famous and people started talking about the brand:

'It's one of those ads where the kids shout you into the room…"quick mum it's on."'

'You're likely to talk about it, like – "did you see … ?"'

Source: RDS research, March 1997; Navigator research, September 1997

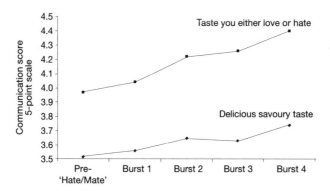

Figure 28: *Ad communication*
Source: Research International

The advertising became more front-of-mind for our tightly defined target audience but the campaign is also a topic of conversation for the general population (users and non-users alike) (Figure 29).

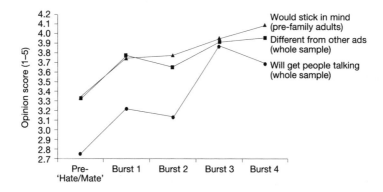

Figure 29: *Opinion of ads*
Source: Research International

ADVERTISING THAT, WITH PR, GENERATED PUBLICITY

The advertising generated publicity for Marmite

As planned, the campaign got the media talking about Marmite. An indication of this is the number of newspaper articles that mentioned the brand. Press mentions[5] more than quadrupled during the course of the campaign (Figure 30).

---

5. Note that, because we only have data on a selection of press titles, this chart significantly underestimates the total amount of publicity Marmite was getting. The effect was actually even bigger than this.

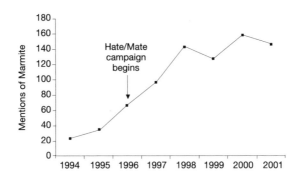

Figure 30: *Mention of Marmite in national newspapers*
Source: Reuters, Lexis

And, although we do not have hard data on other media, it is clear that they were picking up on Marmite as well:

'Marmite is everybody's favourite. It's a brave campaign, very funny ... hats off to Marmite for going out on a limb and saying "you either love our product or you don't."'

Chris Evans Breakfast show, Virgin Radio, October 1999

'I could do with some toast and Marmite right now. Me and Erica love Marmite, Posh doesn't of course ... You either love it or hate it – it's polarising, everyone's got an opinion.'

Jono, Heart FM

'But that's the way it is with *The Sound of Music*. It's like Marmite. Something you either love or hate.'

Woman's Own, December 1999

'We are the Marmite of radio, no doubt.'

Chris Evans, Virgin Radio

'But *Imagine* (by John Lennon) is a record that's as built into the British psyche as Marmite – and, like Marmite, it's a love-it or hate-it thing.'

Heat, January 2000

So why did the media suddenly start paying so much attention to Marmite? As mentioned, the paid-for PR support for the brand had not increased during this period. And there was little real 'news' for the PR agency to use – no new product launches or any other major events that are likely to have caught the attention of the media.

But the PR agency had new ammunition – the press were interested in the new advertising. Prior to the Hate/Mate campaign, none of the press articles mentioning Marmite had referred to its ads. Now an increasing proportion of news articles were doing so (Figure 31).

In fact, press coverage related to advertising grew almost five times faster than other press coverage. Further evidence that advertising was driving media coverage comes from comparing annual press coverage with advertising ratings. There is a clear correlation between the two, as Figure 32 shows.

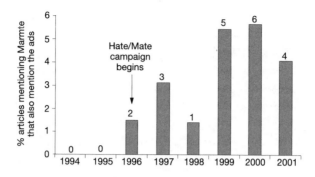

Figure 31: *More newspaper articles about Marmite mentioned the ads*
Source: Reuters, Lexis

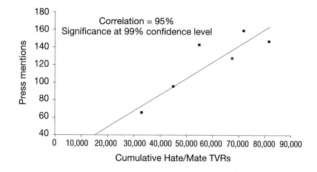

Figure 32: *Press mentions correlate strongly with advertising TVRs*
Source: Reuters, Lexis

The final proof comes from the regional data. Coverage in English newspapers increased substantially during the course of the campaign (Table 3). But in Scotland,[6] where there was very little advertising support, there was no such increase.

TABLE 3: MENTIONS OF MARMITE IN REGIONAL NEWSPAPERS

	Mentions 1997–1998	Mentions 2000–2001	% change
English papers	13	23	+77
Scottish papers	29	29	0

Source: Reuters, Lexis

6. Note that the base level of mentions is higher in Scotland because our sources audit more Scottish than English titles.

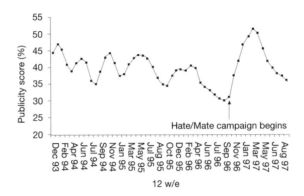

Figure 33: *Marmite publicity score*
Base: Adults
Source: TABS

People noticed the publicity

As a result of the new advertising and its PR amplification, people felt that Marmite was getting more publicity than ever, with no increase in the communication budget (Figure 33).

We therefore conclude that:

- The PR campaign helped generate more publicity for the brand.
- The advertising was essential in generating much of this extra publicity.

Much has been said about the talk-value of advertising over the years, but we believe this is the first time that the effect has been quantified in this way.

It is very difficult to separate the individual effects of advertising from the associated publicity. They were intimately linked. However, their seamless integration (the fact that publicity could not have occurred without the advertising) makes it acceptable to look at their combined effect on the brand in most areas.

However, by inputting levels of national and regional press publicity into our econometric model, we have been able to isolate the effect publicity had on sales (separate to the advertising) – another evaluation 'first'.[7]

ADVERTISING AND PUBLICITY THAT REVITALISED THE BRAND

The brand becomes strong again

Advertising, and PR amplification, combined to get Marmite back into the public's consciousness. This began with the first burst of activity in the campaign (Figure 34).

It has continued ever since (Figure 35).

---

7. The PR account for Marmite has changed hands several times over the course of the campaign; from Manning, Selvage and Lee to Hill and Knowlton to Freud Communications.

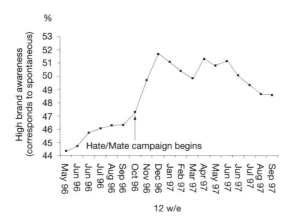

Figure 34: *The new campaign immediately boosted brand awareness*
Source: TABS (adults)

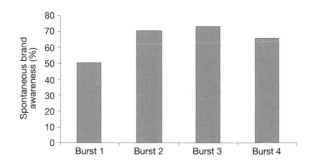

Figure 35: *Brand awareness continued to build as the campaign progressed*
Source: Research International

While top-of-mind awareness increased, so did those important brand attributes that we had seen falling before the campaign (Figure 36).

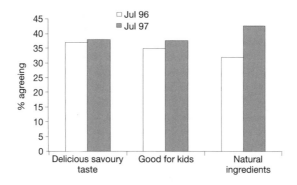

Figure 36: *Marmite brand image scores*
Base: All adults
Source: TABS

Far from making the brand more modern to the detriment of more traditional attributes, we have seen all aspects of the brand strengthen (Figure 37).

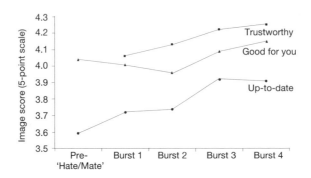

Figure 37: *Brand image and personality*
Source: Research International. 'Trustworthy' added to questionnaire at Burst 1

In line with the increases in brand awareness and image, the appeal of the brand increased (Figure 38).

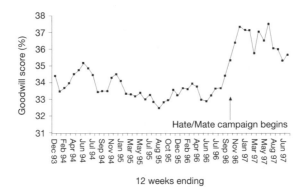

Figure 38: *Marmite brand goodwill*
Base: Adults
Source: TABS

Marmite becomes a national icon

Over the course of the campaign, Marmite became a national icon (Figure 39).

It has been the subject of discussion with people as far-ranging as Chris Moyles on Radio 1 and John Waite on Radio 4's *You and Yours*. Marmite had clearly 'made it' when MP Tony Banks tabled a parliamentary motion to debate Marmite's role as a national icon in the House of Commons:

'We take intense satisfaction from the essential Britishness of the product and its lack of appeal for the majority of the world's population. And we look forward to another century of the wonderful savoury being spread over soldiers and crumpets.'

Signed by Paul Flynn, Stephen Pound and Tony Banks

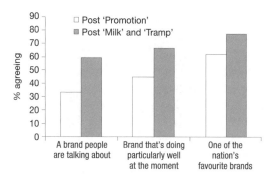

Figure 39: *Marmite becomes a national icon*
Source: Research International

ADVERTISING AND PUBLICITY THAT AFFECTED
CONSUMER BEHAVIOUR

We have shown that over the advertised period, the ads were noticed, loved, communicated the desired message and generated publicity for the brand. We have also shown that, at the same time, the brand grabbed the nation's attention and rose in the nation's esteem. But what effect did the advertising appear to have on consumer behaviour?

Lapsed users became users

Research showed that the advertising worked in the way we expected:

> 'Watching it for the first time it did make me think, cor, I haven't had Marmite for ages and I started eating it again because I had had some in the cupboard for ages.'

Source: RDS research, March 1997

'Increased talkability has led to:

- reminder of how good Marmite tastes
- reinvigoration in terms of personality/perceived popularity
- loyalty disposition augmented still further across user groups.'

Source: Research International, March 2000

During the campaign we have seen a reduced lapsing rate, especially with our target audience (Figure 40).[8]

As expected, the reduction in lapsed users has occurred only in the more heavily advertised South (Figure 41).

Because we have succeeded in reducing the number of lapsed users, penetration levels have increased over the course of the campaign, especially among the target group (Figure 42).

---

8. Over 60% of pre-family adults are aged 16 to 24.

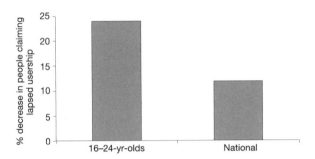

Figure 40: *Decrease in lapsed usership during Hate/Mate campaign*
Source: Audience Selection/TNS Phonebus 2002 vs. 1995

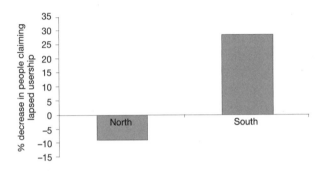

Figure 41: *Change in lapsed usership during Hate/Mate campaign*
Source: Audience Selection/TNS Phonebus 2002 vs. 1995

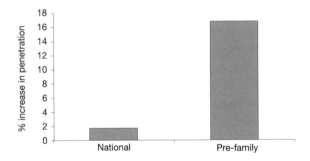

Figure 42: *Increase in Marmite penetration during Hate/Mate campaign*
Source: Nielsen Homescan, 2001 vs. 1995

Penetration increased in the more heavily advertised South and fell in the North (Figure 43).

Marmite users used more

As we hoped, when we were setting our communications objectives, the advertising and publicity appear to have had another, indirect effect. Giving Marmite a higher

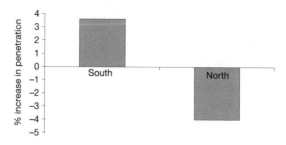

Figure 43: *Increases in Marmite penetration during Hate/Mate campaign*
Source: Nielsen Homescan, 2001 vs.1995

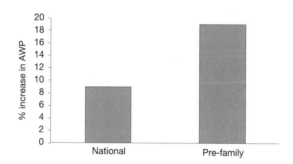

Figure 44: *Increases in average weight of purchase during campaign*
Source: Nielsen Homescan, 2001 vs. 1995

profile appeared to make current users use the brand more. The weight of purchase increased over the campaign, especially among the target group (Figure 44).

In total, between 1995 and 2001, sales to pre-family households increased by 51%. We have just shown how the advertising and publicity worked in exactly the way it was supposed to.

Now we will prove beyond doubt that it was the advertising and publicity that led to the sales increase.

ADVERTISING AND PUBLICITY THAT HAD A DIRECT EFFECT ON SALES

The rate of sale increased dramatically after the campaign launch, in line with the increased penetration (Figure 45).

The average jar size sold increased from the same point, in line with the usage increase (Figure 46).

As a result of these two factors, the total sales increased. And this increase coincided exactly with the launch of the new campaign (Figure 47).

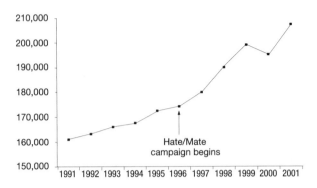

Figure 45: *Rate of sale in jars*
Source: Nielsen

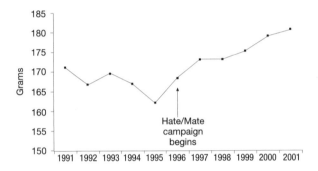

Figure 46: *Average size of jar sold*
Source: Nielsen

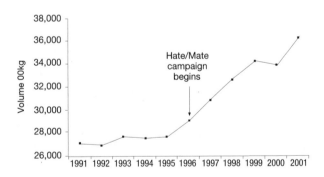

Figure 47: *Marmite sales vs. advertising*
Source: Nielsen, MMS

The relationship between the weight of advertising and sales growth is clearly shown when looking at each year of the campaign (Figure 48).

This relationship can also be seen when looking at different regions. Owing to our strategy of concentrating activity in the South, there were significant differences in levels of support in the North and South. It should come as no surprise by now to see that sales growth was much stronger in the South (Figure 49).

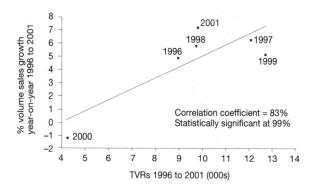

Figure 48: *Sales growth vs. TVRs*
Source: Nielsen, BARB

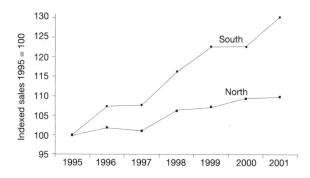

Figure 49: *North vs. South: indexed volume sales*
Source: Nielsen

The weight of evidence becomes overwhelming when observing the strong correlation between levels of support and sales growth, by Nielsen sales region (Figure 50).

Finally, our econometric model proves conclusively that the advertising and publicity had a positive effect on the sales. We will return to this in detail later on.

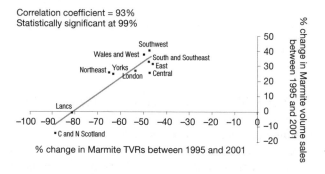

Figure 50: *Regional Marmite volume sales vs. TVRs*
Source: Nielsen, BARB

ADVERTISING AND PUBLICITY THAT HAD
OTHER BENEFICIAL EFFECTS

As well as basic sales, there were other ways in which the advertising had a positive effect on the brand.

Brand partnerships have been more successful

Since the start of the Hate/Mate campaign, brand partnerships have been very successful. In 2000, Sainsbury's 'Love It' Marmite sandwich won the Sandwich Association Sandwich of the Year. This year, Marmite-flavoured Walkers crisps look like becoming a permanent fixture after a trial promotion period.

Marmite improves Unilever Bestfoods' standing in the City

The business press gave Marmite undue attention (considering its tiny global turnover) during the coverage of the 2001 Unilever Bestfoods merger (Figure 51). The business press has never been a target for Marmite's PR agency. The fact that this strong brand was part of the merger was undoubtedly considered important by the financial world.

Recent coverage shows Marmite has become one of Unilever Bestfoods' flagship brands in the eyes of the business press.

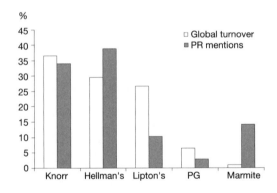

Figure 51: *Comparison of global turnover vs. amount of PR during Unilever/Bestfoods merger**
Source: Reuters, Unilever Bestfoods website
*Looking at the five brands most mentioned.

PROOF OF THE EFFECT OF ADVERTISING AND PUBLICITY – SUMMARY

We have shown how famous advertising, and the publicity it helped generate, has got Marmite back into the public's consciousness.

We have also demonstrated that, as planned, the number of lapsed users within the tightly focused target audience and the more general public has declined and penetration and usage have increased.

In addition we have shown how regional sales prove that the advertising and publicity have had a direct effect on sales. The evidence clearly shows that the advertising and publicity and the brand's fortunes are linked.

ELIMINATING OTHER FACTORS

No other factor can explain the change in the brand's fortunes, as a whole, and its particularly strong growth in the South.

Distribution was not a factor

Marmite's growth cannot be explained by distribution gains, as Table 4 shows. Distribution actually fell a little at the brand level, and the only significant gain at the size level was for the small 57 g jar. As the table shows, its contribution to growth was minor. The main sales increases came from the big 250 g and 500 g jars, and neither of these made significant distribution gains.

TABLE 4: DISTRIBUTION GAINS

	Percentage increase in distribution	Contribution to brand growth (%)
8 g	−100	−1
57 g	+38	+8
125 g	−2	+4
250 g	−2	+63
500 g	+3	+28
600 g	−100	−2
Total brand	−2	100

Source: Nielsen (year to December 2001 vs. year to September 1996)

Furthermore, distribution gains occurred equally in the North and the South so it couldn't have caused the greater level of sales growth in the South.

There was no NPD

NPD could not explain the sales growth since no new products were launched. In fact, three products were withdrawn during the campaign: Marmite cubes, an 8 g jar and a 600 g jar.

Growth was not driven by price

There have been no significant changes in price over the campaign. The effect of price on sales of Marmite has been accounted for using econometrics. The minor changes in price turn out to have contributed very little to the long-term growth of the brand.

Prices do not vary by region so they can't explain the faster growth in the South.

Demographics

Growth in the general population cannot explain Marmite's success since this was mainly accounted for by an increase in volume sales per head (Figure 52).

Nor could it have been caused by a growth in the child population, which has declined since 1992 (Figure 53). This decline was as great in the South as it was in the North so cannot have caused the regional variation in sales.

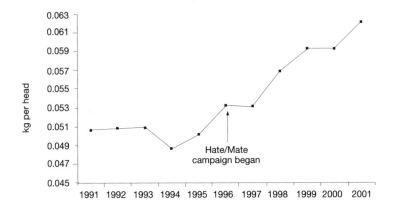

Figure 52: *Volume sales per head of the population*

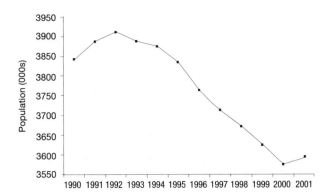

Figure 53: *Population of children aged 0 to 4 years*

Economic factors

As the economy grows, it seems unlikely that people will spend their extra cash on a non-luxury item such as Marmite. And even if they did, economic growth patterns were similar in the North and the South during this period, as the unemployment data show (Figure 54). So the economy cannot explain the regional differences in sales growth.

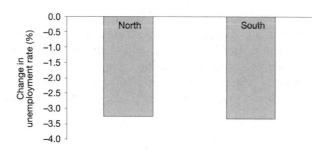

Figure 54: *Fall in the unemployment rate: North vs. South*
Source: ONS

Market context

As established in the Problem section, Marmite sales rely heavily on consumption of bread, since it is the main 'host food'. But the rate of bread consumption couldn't have contributed to Marmite's sales growth. It fell over the advertised period (Figure 55) and did so in both the North and the South.

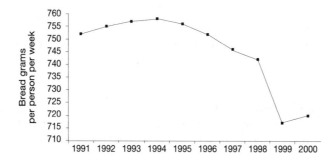

Figure 55: *Bread consumption was falling*
Source: National Food Survey

There was also no growth in the general spreads market to explain Marmite's growth (Figure 56).

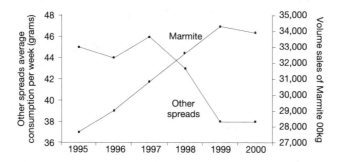

Figure 56: *Other spreads vs. Marmite*
Source: NFS, Nielsen

Competition

Marmite's gains weren't due to lack of competition. Marmite's immediate competitors are Vegemite and Own Label, and if anything they were making life slightly tougher. Their combined distribution increased by 3% over the course of the campaign (source: Nielsen MATs). These competitors weren't supported with advertising or other marketing activity during our campaign, but then they never had been.

Advertising spend

With no growth in total ad spend the sales growth could not have been the result of any increase during the campaign.

PR spend

There was no increase in PR spend during the campaign so this could not explain the sales growth.

Promotions

The few small-scale promotions there were had all been on-pack, and therefore national. They cannot explain the phenomenal sales growth in the South.

Sampling

The one big sampling drive (in October 98) was solely in Scotland. There was some small-scale national sampling activity. Neither of these can explain the sales growth in the South. Sampling has been accounted for in the econometric model.

Eliminating other factors – summary

We have shown that there were no factors that can explain the extent of Marmite's growth over the advertised period, nor the speed of growth in the South.

QUANTIFYING THE CONTRIBUTION OF ADVERTISING AND PUBLICITY

We have shown that advertising and the publicity that it generated were the main factors driving Marmite's growth. Using econometrics, we have measured their effect on sales (Figure 57).

The model tells us that advertising was indeed the main engine of growth. In fact, annual sales would have actually *fallen* by 26% without advertising. Publicity also boosted sales, although the effect is smaller.

The model tells us that the advertising was highly effective. Bestfoods spent £12.4m on ads during the first five years of the campaign, and this directly increased sales value as measured by Nielsen by £47.0m (Figure 58).

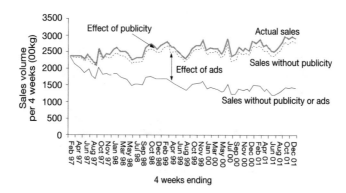

Figure 57: *The effect of ads and publicity on sales volume*
Source: Econometric model

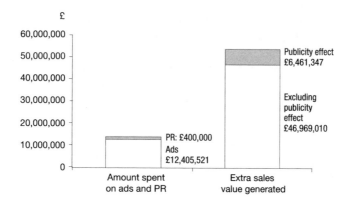

Figure 58: *The effect of advertising and publicity on sales value 1997 to 2001*
Source: Econometrics, Nielsen

Furthermore, the indirect effect of advertising, via the publicity it generated, increased sales by a further £6.5m. Without revealing confidential information, we can state that these effects make advertising a very attractive option for Marmite.

Note that publicity significantly increases the effectiveness of advertising. In fact, by amplifying the effect of advertising, publicity increases effectiveness by 14%. We believe this is the first time that this effect has been quantified.

EFFICIENCY

We have shown that the advertising was effective, in that it achieved the stated objective of 5% sales growth per annum. Now we will show that it did so efficiently.

1. One measure of efficiency is the Awareness Index. This compares awareness gener-ated to TV ratings used. As Figure 59 shows, the Hate/Mate campaign was almost four times more efficient than the average food ad at generating awareness.

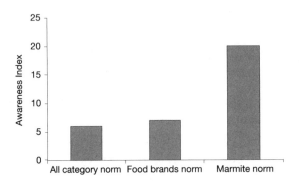

Figure 59: *Awareness Index norms*
Source: Research International

2. The new campaign was also highly efficient at generating sales – much more so than previous campaigns, as Table 5 indicates.

TABLE 5: THE SUCCESS OF THE NEW CAMPAIGNS

Campaign	Dates	Total TVRs	Real increase in annual sales (£m 2001 prices)	Sales gained per 100 TVRs
'Soldiers'	1987–1991	3011	£2.3m	£78k
'Early Words'/'Celebration'	1991–1993	2405	£1.0m	£60k
'Low Rider'	1994–1996	3333	–£49k	–£1k
'Hate/Mate'	1996–2001	4281	£4.3m	£100k

Sources: Nielsen, MMS

CONCLUSION

Five years of stagnating sales and a weakening brand were the results of multiple objectives and diffuse communications. In 1996, the lesson was learnt and we focused with a vengeance. The exceptional use of just two communications channels working hand in hand, a tightly defined target audience and an extremely focused media strategy, all helped make the campaign not only effective but highly efficient.

Although it is tempting to spread your money across many different channels, concentrating it can be far more efficient. One of the ways this works is through the power of a strong, creative idea, strong enough to create fame for your brand. Making a big splash on TV can, with the help of some PR spend, generate publicity that can make your budget go even further.

AFTERWORD

To mark Marmite's Centenary, the elements of the Hate/Mate campaign that have made it successful continue; this time using Zippy from Rainbow to create impactful advertising that generates publicity (Figure 60).

Hello, it's breakfast time and I'm really hungry

SFX: Zip!

[Low Rider music begins]

Figure 60: 'Zippy'

So at 100, Marmite continues to gain strength. In the week this paper was submitted, it was published that Marmite was chosen (by 20- to 30-year-old Brits) as one of the top five brands that would ideally represent Britain in the future:

1. Virgin
2. Cadbury
3. Dyson
4. Marmite
5. The Body Shop

> Source: Corporate Edge (based on quantitative and qualitative research with 20- to 30-year-olds). Published in *Marketing Week* (9 May 2002)

Not bad for the 'useless leftover of the brewing industry'!

15

Ocean Spray

The longer-term effects of advertising over promotions

Principal author: Martin Smith, Bates UK
Collaborating author: Matthew Critchley

EDITOR'S SUMMARY

This case examines advertising's role in the overall marketing mix and in particular in relation to how price promotions changed the course of Ocean Spray's fortunes. With 0% year-on-year growth and household penetration in a steady decline, Ocean Spray's combined use of above-the-line and sales promotion strategies resulted in household penetration increasing by 1.8 million households and total payback from advertising amounting to £2.6 million combined with £2.2 million from promotions.

INTRODUCTION

This paper examines advertising's role in the overall marketing mix and, in particular, in relation to price promotions. It gives a real-life test of marketing theory, versus actual marketing practice.

We will show how price promotions effectively delivered short-term sales increases for Ocean Spray, while advertising generated longer-term revenue growth and therefore profitability. Both mechanics are a necessary part of any marketing director's arsenal. However, the means by which they work and the effects they have differ.

For Ocean Spray, price promotions gave consumers a value-incentive to purchase. Advertising's effect was to create a stronger bond with the Ocean Spray brand, through communicating a reason to drink cranberry juice drinks that led to greater repeat purchase at full prices (Figure 1).

Figure 1: *Scene from the advertising*

MARKETING PRINCIPLES

In uncertain times, one of the first things to be cut is a company's marketing budget. Or, to be more specific, its advertising budget. Lower-cost and other more direct methods of generating improvements to the bottom-line in the short term often take precedence over longer-term investment (Richards, 2002). It has been argued that currently advertising expenditure is counter-intuitively low, in relation to GDP growth and overall patterns of household consumption (Lind, 2002) (Figure 2). Where growth in these two indicators weakens, advertising expenditure suffers still further (Figure 3).

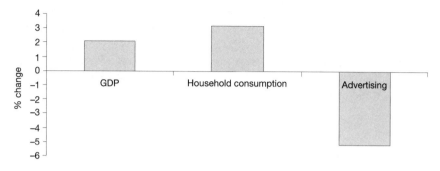

Figure 2: *Change % 2001 vs. 2000 (constant prices)*
Source: National Statistics, AA/WARC, *Quarterly Survey of Advertising Expenditure*

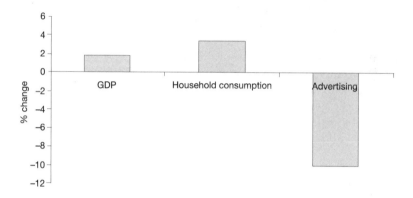

Figure 3: *Change % Q4 2001 vs. 2000 (constant prices)*
Source: National Statistics, AA/WARC, *Quarterly Survey of Advertising Expenditure*

Increasing price promotions, despite limited long-term profitability

'The double jeopardy of sales promotions' (Jones, 1990), warns *against* the profit-stripping effects of promoting by cutting prices.

Promotions have two effects. They incentivise deal-seeking consumers who have no other interest in the brand and therefore do not buy it on full price, or encourage existing buyers to 'stock up', effectively bringing forward existing sales that the brand would have benefited from, irrespective of the promotion (Ehrenberg & Hammond, 2001).

In the soft drinks category, where products have a limited larder life, qualitative insight has suggested that promotions encourage a brand's existing consumers to drink more for a shorter period, rather than increase stocks for a later date.

The longer-term effects of advertising

Advertising, on the other hand, is typically associated with increased penetration and longer-term revenue growth (Ambach, 2001). On average it has been demonstrated that a customer who buys a brand following a burst of advertising is

2.5 times more likely to buy it again over the course of a year than a customer who buys the same brand when on promotion. This would suggest that an immediate sales uplift of 5% is actually worth 12% over the course of a year (Roberts, 2001). Taking this a stage further, the true long-term value of advertising lies in the 'multiplier effect' of penetration increase, repeat purchase and advertising's role in justifying a brand's premium price (Broadbent, 2001).

MARKETING STRATEGY

Ocean Spray: the market situation

Ocean Spray is the world's largest grower of cranberries and producer of cranberry-related products, accounting for over 70% of total cranberry production. It is wholly owned by a collective of North American cranberry and grapefruit growers. Its portfolio in the UK is primarily driven by cranberry juice drinks, of which the key line is Cranberry Classic, an ambient cranberry juice drink.

Globally, cranberry is in over-supply. Following the early '90s surge in cranberry popularity, buoyant trading conditions and years of good harvests, the cranberry crop far outstripped demand.

In the UK, as elsewhere, the need to generate short-term volume sales was considerable. In order to meet volume targets, a programme of grocery sales promotions and above-the-line advertising was undertaken.

A commodity category

Thanks to the dominance of own label in the juice and juice drinks category (64% overall category volume), consumers have been educated *out* of the kinds of automatic brand beliefs and quality assumptions that operate in most market categories. They are uniformly presented with private label juices that are 15% to 20% cheaper than their branded counterparts and believed to be of acceptable quality. The consumer perception that 'fruit juice is just fruit juice' is all-pervasive and the few brands in the market have to work unusually hard to justify their premium price.

A stagnant market

As Figure 4 shows, the ambient juice drinks category is not growing. Year-on-year volume growth in May 2001, immediately before Ocean Spray advertising went on air, was 0%, with household penetration in steady decline (Figure 5). The only relevant sector in growth has been chilled juices, in which Ocean Spray is not present, and on which neither the advertising, nor this paper, focuses.

The business requirement

With 75% share, Ocean Spray had traditionally owned the cranberry juice drinks category. However, against a burgeoning own-label threat, Ocean Spray had to protect both its volumes and its margins from considerable own-label share growth.

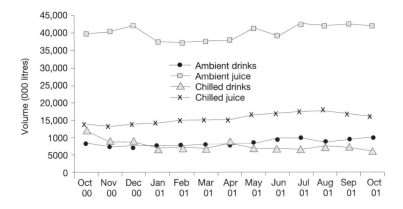

Figure 4: *Juice and juice drinks market volume*
Source: AC Nielsen

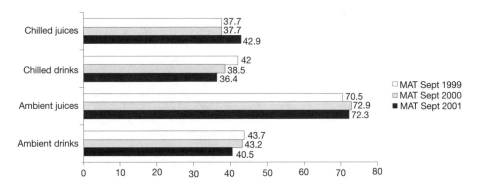

Figure 5: *Household penetration %*
Source: AC Nielsen

Ocean Spray's awareness as a cranberry brand was more than 80%. It had no *branded* competitors in the UK market, although the own-label cranberry offering was becoming increasingly powerful. The task at hand was to grow the cranberry category by bringing in new users (primarily from other juices), in a way that strengthened the Ocean Spray franchise, against the threat of own label.

Advertising strategy

Health is cranberry's strongest motivator, but drinkers' belief in its health properties far surpasses the reality. Over the last ten years or so, news had spread of doctors' recommending cranberry as a cure for cystitis and a rumour about its 'special properties' had gathered momentum.

The natural overclaim of the cranberry mystique (and consumers' belief in it) offered a huge opportunity for growth, but one that advertising had to handle with care. Mystique thrives on a lack of evidence, so to communicate the one-sided *truth* about cranberry health benefits would destroy the rumour of its multifaceted properties.

ABC1 women account for over 80% of cranberry volume consumption, with hard-core drinkers displaying an almost evangelical zeal about what they saw as *their* drink, and Ocean Spray as *their brand*. The job for advertising was to bring new users to the brand, by stimulating the curiosity among a new wave of women.

The advertising dramatised the proposition of 'the modern-day elixir' with something that mythical power transcends, namely science. A total of three 20-second ads were made, dramatising ridiculous mock-scientific experiments that attempted, in vain, to establish what is special about cranberries. They reached no sensible conclusion, except that 'there's definitely something in it'.

Above-the-line media strategy

Total media spend was £923,000, generating 420 network ratings on a two-weekly 'pulsed' basis, from 1 June to 25 July 2001. Reach among ABC1 housewives was 78% (1+ cover), at an average OTS of 5.4. Nationally, C4, C5 and satellite were used to provide a national backdrop, with key ITV regions selected where there was a high index for Ocean Spray drinkers (see Figure 6).

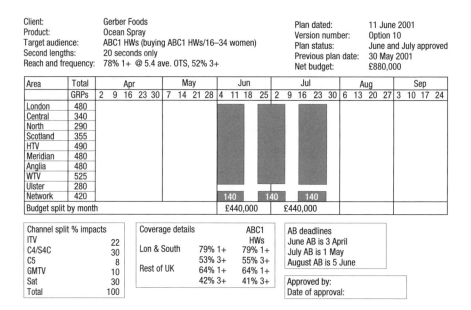

Figure 6: *Above-the-line media plan*

Promotions strategy

A combination of 'buy one, get one free' (BOGOF) and 'three for two' multi-buy offers ran across all grocery retailers before, during and after the advertised period. Promotions were staggered across retailers, with the typical duration of 2–3 weeks. Above-the-line advertising was never on air without the presence of price promotions in at least three major retailer chains. Total expenditure on promotions

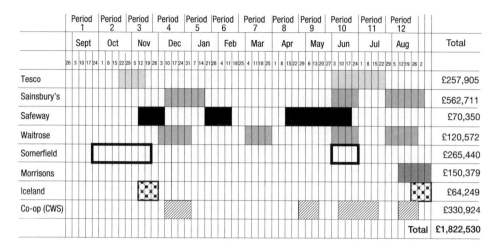

Figure 7: *Promotions plan*

was £1.81 million over the course of 2001. During the advertised period, spend on price promotions was £1.17 million (see Figure 7).

MARKETING EFFECTIVENESS

A significant sales increase over the campaign period

Despite flat category growth, Ocean Spray volume sales grew by 28% over the June–July campaign period. Brand share increased from 41% to 45%. Compared to June–July 2000, Ocean Spray volume sales increased by 42%.

PRINCIPLES IN PRACTICE – ISOLATING THE SALES EFFECTS OF ADVERTISING AND PROMOTIONS

At no point was advertising on air *without* some form of price promotions being in place. Econometric analysis has suggested that advertising worked in tandem with sales promotions to maximise Ocean Spray sales. It is the objective of this paper to establish how advertising worked harder to increase business profitability.

The contribution of multi-buy promotions

Since multi-buy promotions ran *before* the advertising, it was possible for the econometric model to isolate the specific contribution of multi-buys to sales, independent of advertising. Furthermore, promotions ran for a full year. It is possible, therefore, to gauge the effect of a year's worth of promotions.

Cranberry Classic multi-buys generated an elasticity of 0.031, with chilled multi-buys generating an elasticity of 0.009. This means Ocean Spray's total promotional spend (£1.87 million) generated 2.16m litre sales, at an average price of £1.02 per litre. Therefore, £1.87m on promotions generated £2.20m in revenue, meaning that each £1 spent on promotions generated £1.18 in revenue.

The contribution of advertising plus promotions

The econometric model gauged the effect of a year's worth of advertising, using a carry-over formula, based on adstock. Ocean Spray's carry-over effect was 80%, based on four years of advertising.

The short-term increase in Ocean Spray sales per single TVR was found to be 1312 litres. Therefore, assuming that each month's sales effect will be 80% of the preceding month, each TVR will, over one year, generate 6109 litres in additional sales.

Ocean Spray's 2001 TV expenditure of £923,000 translates into 449 TVRs, making the total year's sales generated through advertising 449 × 6109 = 2,742,941 litres. The average retail price of one litre of Ocean Spray Cranberry Classic is £1.02, making the total year's advertising plus promotions payback 2,742,941 × 1.02 = £2,797,800. This means that, over the course of 2001, each £1 spent on TV advertising with promotions generated 2,797,800 ÷ 923,000 = £3.03 revenue.

Isolating the contribution of advertising from sales promotions

We have seen that multi-buy promotions generated a return of £1.18 per £1 expenditure and advertising plus promotions generated a return of £3.03 per £1 expenditure. Therefore, we can assume that advertising alone would have generated a return of 3.03 − 1.18, i.e. £1.85.

The 'decomposition' of Ocean Spray sales, by marketing activity is illustrated in Figure 8.

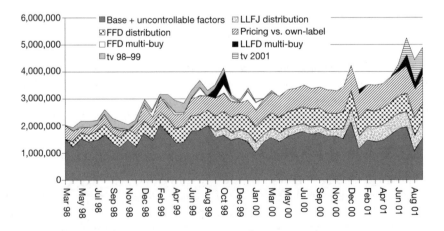

Figure 8: *Sales decomposition, Ocean Spray brand sales UK*
FFD = fresh fruit drinks
LLFJ = long-life fruit juice
LLFD = long-life fruit drink

Put another way, econometric analysis seemed to suggest that advertising was 57% more effective in generating revenue than price promotions. Half the expenditure generated more than twice the revenue payback. However, this analysis fails to take into account two further, crucial factors, namely premium price and repeat purchase. It has been hypothesised that advertising works harder than price promotions to bring in new users, who continue to purchase the brand. In addition to this, they buy the brand at its full price. Calculations of long-term payback must take these factors into account.

Isolating longer-term advertising plus promotions effects

AC Nielsen's Homescan panel monitors the weekly purchase of household items by 10,000 respondents, who scan the bar codes from items bought into a computer. It is therefore possible, with near absolute accuracy, to compare individual respondent purchase of a given brand on promotion, versus at full price. Nielsen analysis has isolated two groups of consumer:

- Trialists who went on to buy Ocean Spray again (trialists who repeated).
- Trialists who did not buy Ocean Spray again (trialists who did not repeat).

Trialists who repeated versus trialists who did not

Nielsen data show that, between the end of April and the beginning of September 2001, Ocean Spray's household penetration increased by 1.8 million households. Nielsen were also able to demonstrate the relative contributions of new visitors and new converts, to this overall figure: 607,000 households were trialists who repeated; 1,200,000 households were trialists who did not repeat (Figure 9).

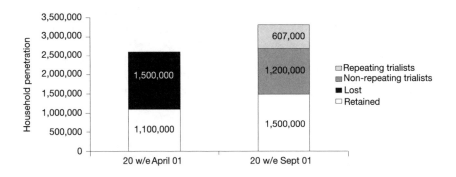

Figure 9: *Ocean Spray penetration shifts*
Source: AC Nielsen

Promotions drove short-term sales increases, advertising brought in trialists who became repeat buyers

Of the trialists who repeated, only 42% had bought Ocean Spray on price promotion. Taken another way, this means that the majority of trialists who

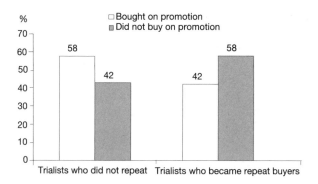

Figure 10: *New buyers, source of purchase*
Source: AC Nielsen

repeated (58%) were brought into the brand by factors *other than* price promotion (Figure 10).

Penetration increase, versus repeat purchase generation

We can see that promotions were hugely effective in driving sales increases through increased penetration: 996,000 additional trialists were brought into the brand. However, this must be seen as a short-term increase, since these buyers did not then go on to repurchase Ocean Spray after the promotional period (Figure 11).

Advertising worked less well than promotions in driving short-term trial, bringing in an additional 504,000 trialists who did not repeat. However, the contribution of advertising was to encourage a greater number of trialists who repeated. The 352,060 people who bought Ocean Spray *when not on promotion* then went on to buy the brand again subsequently.

The number of trialists who repeated, who were brought into Ocean Spray by advertising, is 38% higher than the 'repeating trialists' who originally bought on promotion. This forms the basis of advertising's greater long-term payback.

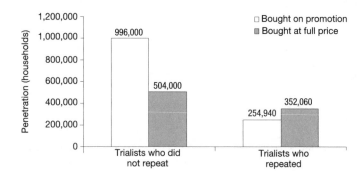

Figure 11: *Penetration increases over campaign*
Source: AC Nielsen

Advertising brings in a more profitable group of consumers

Trialists who repeat would appear to offer by far the most profitable source of revenue for Ocean Spray. Not only do they appear to be more loyal to the brand, but they bought it at its full premium price.

Price promotions had been effective in driving short-term sales but, perhaps as a measure of people's price sensitivity, they had brought in consumers with a weaker motivation towards Ocean Spray. Advertising, on the other hand, had created a stronger bond for consumers with the brand and created more repeat purchase.

A reason to drink is more motivating than a reason to buy

Tracking research suggests that this lay in communicating the functional health benefits of Ocean Spray (Figure 12). Those who recalled the advertising were significantly more likely to attribute health benefits to Ocean Spray than those who had not. Even non-drinkers who recalled the advertising believed Ocean Spray to be healthier than those who did not.

In essence, while promotions had given consumers a short-term reason to purchase, advertising gave people a tangible, long-term reason to drink and continue drinking Ocean Spray.

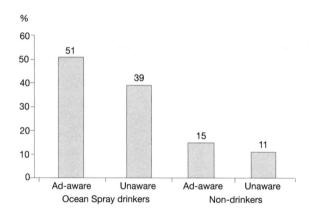

Figure 12: *Believing Ocean Spray to be a great-tasting, healthy drink (summary)*
Source: Hall & Partners Tracking

EVALUATING THE CONTRIBUTION OF NON-ADVERTISING FACTORS

In order to establish advertising's contribution to sales, it was necessary to take into account the effect of factors *other* than advertising. Ocean Spray commissioned an econometric model, some six months after the advertising and promotional period, to investigate this. The model proved very robust, accounting for 96% of all historical Ocean Spray sales variation.

It is worth noting that this model focused on sales of Ocean Spray's key line, 'Cranberry Classic'. This accounts for over 80% of total Ocean Spray drinks volume and represents to consumers the recognisable face of a brand with comparatively low awareness, versus other juices. With this in mind, the advertising also focused on Cranberry Classic.

Pricing

Perhaps not surprisingly, the econometric model highlighted price as having the strongest effect on sales, with an elasticity of –1.15. According to this analysis, a 10% decrease in the price of Cranberry Classic would, assuming the prices of all other brands remained constant, generate an increase in sales of 11.5%.

However, pricing decreases were not unique to Ocean Spray. Owing to increased commoditisation of the juice and juice drinks sector, burgeoning retailer power and EDLP, downward price pressure on fruit juice was considerable, and prices across all brands and private label had been falling for some time.

Figure 13 shows that Ocean Spray was no exception to its competitors in lowering the price of its key classic line. Given the almost uniform downward pricing trend across the sector as a whole, there was no automatic competitive advantage gained by the similarly gradual decrease in Ocean Spray's prices.

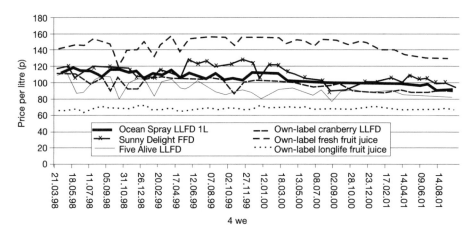

Figure 13: *Other brands show downwards price trend Price per litre p*
Source: AC Nielsen

Distribution

Historically, Ocean Spray had benefited from two main distribution increases, and econometric analysis cited these as the second two strongest factors. Figure 14 shows Ocean Spray's distribution changes over time.

Historically, distribution increases have had a profound effect on Ocean Spray sales. A 10% increase in the distribution of Ocean Spray ambient pure fruit juice would have generated an increase in sales of 0.34%. A 10% increase in Ocean Spray chilled juice distribution would have generated a 2.6% sales increase.

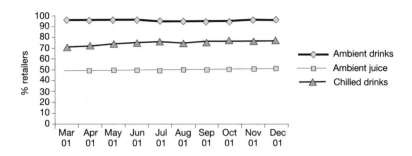

Figure 14: *Ocean Spray grocery distribution*
Source AC Nielsen

Crucially, however, Ocean Spray distribution has not changed throughout and since the period in question. Cranberry Classic has been in around 96% of grocery multiples since November 1999. Therefore, distribution gains did not affect Ocean Spray sales during or after the advertised period.

Weather

Intuitively, weather is a key influence upon drinking behaviour and variations in both rainfall and sunshine had been observed in 2001, versus the preceding year. However, econometric analysis found that the only significant effect of weather on sales was a negative one, i.e. that of rainfall. According to the model, a 10% increase in rainfall would decrease Ocean Spray sales by 0.4%.

The campaign period in 2001 saw on average only 0.5% less rainfall (see Figure 15) than the same period in 2000. There was no discernible difference in rainfall and therefore no effect of rainfall on Ocean Spray sales.

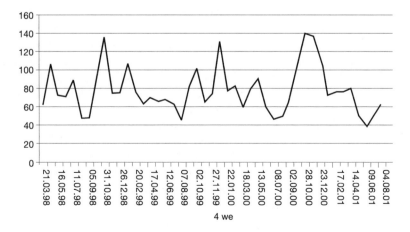

Figure 15: *UK rainfall (mm)*
Source: UK Met Office

Consumer confidence

Historically, consumer confidence was found to have an interesting effect on Ocean Spray sales. Negative confidence has actually *increased* sales – perhaps through consumers staying at home, or seeking the reassurance of known brands. However, over the advertised period, consumer confidence was significantly more positive than during the preceding two months, *and* versus the same period the preceding year (Figure 16). Therefore, consumer confidence could not have accounted for the increases in Ocean Spray sales over the period concerned.

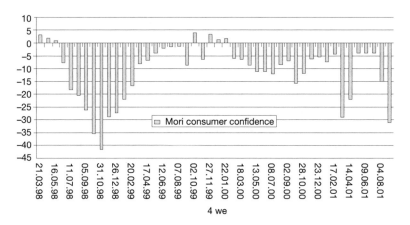

Figure 16: *Consumer confidence – net %*
Source: Mori

CALCULATING TOTAL PAYBACK

As previously noted, overall payback from any kind of marketing expenditure must be seen in terms of a 'multiplier effect' – that is, the combination of short-term sales uplift, repeat buying and premium price.

We have established that 58% of trialists who repeated are brought to Ocean Spray by advertising and 42% by promotions. We know that 42% of trialists who do not repeat are attracted by advertising and 58% by promotions. This means that advertising brought in (607,000 × 58%) = 352,060 trialists who repeated and (1,200,000 × 42%) = 504,000 trialists who did not repeat. Sales promotions brought in (607,000 × 42%) = 254,940 trialists who repeated, and (1,200,000 × 58%) = 696,000 trialists who did not repeat.

Nielsen analysis has also shown that the average household purchase of Ocean Spray Cranberry Classic during one year (AWOP) is 5.8 litres. It is therefore possible to calculate the total payback of advertising, versus sales promotions. Average unit price for Ocean Spray cranberry Classic, over the last year is £1.02. Total payback calculations are based on these figures, and are summarised in Figure 17. Therefore, the total payback

- from advertising was £2,596,867
- from promotions was £2,218,145.

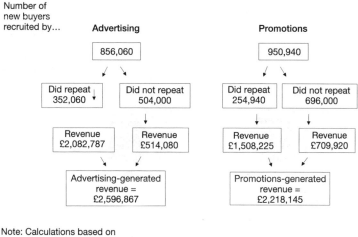

Figure 17: *Payback calculations summary*

Advertising was more efficient at generating payback

Comparing total payback with expenditure, we see that advertising was 48% more efficient in generating revenue per £1 expenditure, than sales promotions (Table 1).

TABLE 1

	Advertising	Sales promotion
Cost of	£923,000	£1,170,000
Return from	£2,596,867	£2,218,145
Payback per £1	£2.81	£1.90

Naturally, it is not possible to disclose individual clients' profit margins. However, if we were to assume the client made a profit margin typical of most fmcg categories (i.e. not just juice and juice drinks), the advertising would have been profitable.

Summary

In a time where immediate justification for marketing spend is increasingly imperative, it is important to bear in mind that the different means at a marketer's disposal drive sales in very different ways. Growth always costs money, either by reducing profit margins (sales promotions) or by increasing marketing costs (advertising spend).

We have demonstrated that, whilst price promotions were more effective than advertising in driving short-term sales volume, advertising's long-term revenue payback is significantly greater. Price promotions work harder to provoke immediate, discounted sales, that may not be repeated, whereas advertising works harder to create a bond between consumer and brand, that leads to higher levels of repeat purchase, at premium prices (Figure 18).

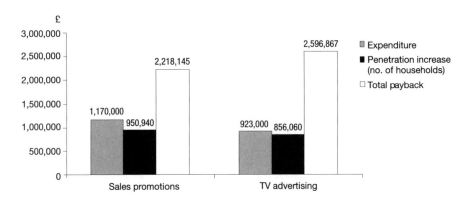

Figure 18: *2001 Expenditure vs. payback summary*

REFERENCES

Ambach, G. (2001) Measuring marketing's long-term effect, European Advertising Effectiveness Symposium, Copenhagen, June.

Broadbent, T. (2001) How advertising pays back, *Admap*, November.

Ehrenberg, A. & Hammond, L. (2001) The case against price-related promotions, *Admap*, June.

Jones, J.P (1990) The double jeopardy of sales promotions, *Harvard Business Review*, September–October.

Lind, H. (2002) The case of the missing ads, *Admap*, May.

Richards, P. (2002) Rumble in the brand jungle, *Admap*, May.

Roberts, A. (2001) The medium-term sales effect of television advertising, European Advertising Effectiveness Symposium, Copenhagen, June.

16

Olivio/Bertolli

'Divided we dine, united we dream':
how the UK campaign for Olivio spread
crossed borders against all odds

Principal authors: Helen Firth, Patricia McDonald and
Mike Holmes, Bartle Bogle Hegarty

EDITOR'S SUMMARY

This case documents how the UK Olivio spread campaign was successfully rolled out for Bertolli spread in three other European markets, taking it from a €40 million to a €100 million brand in just four years. Advertising has been fundamental in building a brand image relevant above and beyond local food culture, by appealing at a deeper emotional level. Sales uplifts attributed to advertising average 65% and the production efficiencies of using a single campaign led to savings of £3 million.

INTRODUCTION

'There is not one kind of food for all men.'

David Henry Thoreau

Food is one of the most difficult categories to internationalise. Different eating habits make developing international food advertising challenging, if not impossible. One man's meat is another man's poison.

This paper demonstrates how Olivio spread and its Continental equivalent, Bertolli, has developed successful international advertising in this most parochial of categories. By expressing a higher-order benefit – an idea about the way people want to live, rather than the way they to want to eat – Olivio/Bertolli has created powerful emotional resonance across markets. The power of this brand has taken Olivio from a *c.* €40 million brand in 1997 to a *c.* €100 million brand in 2001, growing 150% in just four years.

We will demonstrate that advertising is primarily responsible for this growth and that we have created a campaign that not only works across countries, but – as predicted – works in exactly the same way in all markets.

We offer a solution to one of the most pressing business issues of the twenty-first century: how to sell the same brand in the same way to people who use it, buy it and understand it differently. Olivio/Bertolli's answer is to focus not on realities that divide, but fantasies that unite.

RECAPPING THE UK STORY

'The best international advertising campaign I know started off as the best single–market advertising campaign I know.'

John Hegarty

Olivio – the first spread to contain olive oil – was created in the UK by UnileverBestfoods with a view to possible roll-out in other markets. It grew strongly in the UK over several years, growing from a 0.6% share of the margarine and low fat spreads market in 1995, to over a 2% share at the close of 1997.

Olivio's success in the UK was driven by a campaign which built genuine emotional resonance for the brand, setting it apart from own label imitations which had dogged Olivio since launch and stolen share. This campaign generated a complete turnaround in Olivio's fortunes. Our 1998 IPA paper documents that:

- Targets were met ahead of schedule, achieving record 182% growth 1995–97.
- Share of olive oil spreads rose from 23.1% to 43.7% over the relaunch period.
- Own label users traded-up to Olivio.
- Price premium over own label increased from 37p in 1996 to 45p in 1997.
- Sales-driven distribution grew from 73% to 88%.

The 1998 paper used statistical modelling to demonstrate a strong correlation between Olivio advertising and sales, showing that:

- Advertising sold 13,088,000 more tubs.
- Sales were 148% higher than they would have been without advertising.

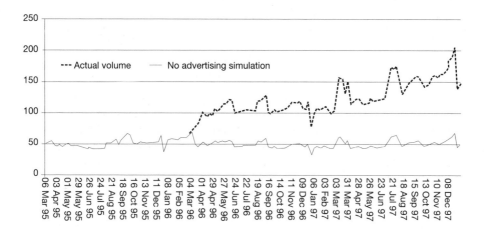

Figure 1: *UK volume actual and with no advertising simulation, indexed*

Figure 1 shows actual sales and simulates actual sales (indexed) with no advertising support to quantify the contribution of advertising.

Given the success in the UK, plus a changing business climate focusing on international synergies, it was decided to roll out the Olivio mix across Europe. UnileverBestfoods already had an olive oil presence under the Bertolli brand name and chose to introduce olive oil spreads as Bertolli, but retained the Olivio model in all other aspects of the mix, including communications.

This paper focuses on how we developed advertising for Olivio/Bertolli spread in four key markets – UK, Belgium, Germany and Holland.

BUSINESS RATIONALE, IRRATIONAL CONSUMER

The 1997 roll-out was driven by a requirement for international efficiencies and improved operating margins. This requirement has become more pressing over time. The outcome is the rationalisation of brands seen today – Unilever alone has undertaken to cull its brands from 1600 to 400, focusing on a smaller number of global 'Power Brands'.

> 'We dissipate our energy and resources on far too many brands ... Our aim is to build a core portfolio of no more than 400 leading brands, each one No. 1 or 2 in its market or segment ... There will be a number of power brands, which we aim to grow at between 6% and 8% a year.'
>
> Niall Fitzgerald, Unilever Chairman

As we will discuss, spread roll-out was highly successful and Olivio/Bertolli has been selected for further global development. From core products of olive oil and spread, it has a mandate to expand across categories and countries. This poses new challenges. From a business point of view, brand rationalisation is eminently sensible. From a consumer point of view, it can be seen as highly problematic.

Conventional wisdom states that food advertising does not work on a global level. Cultural sensitivities make it immensely difficult to find a globally relevant solution. While brands may strive to be global, food remains parochial.

'Food, more than any other, is the category most strongly influenced by local culture, climate and historical factors. People's diets and eating patterns evolved long before brands existed, as indeed did food 'retailers' (i.e. markets). So food habits still vary hugely around the world, and these patterns are not easy to break.'

Steve Thompson, Roper Starch International

Interbrand's ranking of the world's most valuable brands (excluding drinks) reveals just two packaged food brands in the top 50 versus nine IT brands, six financial brands and six automotive brands. Moreover, analysis of food advertising across the world shows that Heinz has aired 33 different executions across 19 countries, Knorr 95 executions across 32 countries and Lipton 35 executions across 28 countries.

Our paper offers an alternative approach – that one campaign can work in many countries, if rooted in relevant emotional associations. This learning provides a blueprint for today's task of extending across new countries and categories.

DIVIDED WE DINE: THE PROBLEM WITH GLOBAL FOOD BRANDS

'Some cultures are defined by their attitude to cheese.'

Benny and Joon director Jeremiah Chechik, MGM

We had a clear conceptual model for how the advertising worked in the UK, borne out by our statistical analysis. The campaign drove awareness and built engagement with the brand benefit. This drove trial, and the depth of our emotional connection would prompt trialists to talk about the brand, recruiting friends and family to Olivio. In this way, advertising drove a series of consistent steps upward in growth (Figure 2).

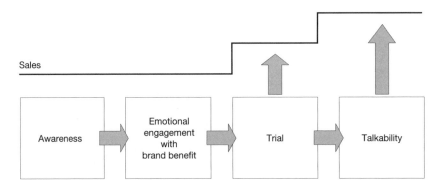

Figure 2: *Advertising model*

As seen above, building genuine emotional engagement was the single most important factor in driving success. However, at roll-out, we were initially unsure whether we could make the same emotional connection in other countries with very different attitudes to food.

BELGIUM

A nation divided by language, culture and cuisine.

> 'Southern Belgian cuisine is not unlike French, retaining the fondness for rich sauces and
> ingredients ... In Flanders the food is more akin to that of Holland, plainer and simpler on
> the whole.'
>
> *Rough Guide*

Chips feature heavily in the French-influenced side of Belgian cooking – mussels, chips and mayonnaise is the national dish.

Traditional Flemish cooking features 'Ghent Whaterzooi' (chicken stew) and rabbit with prunes in beer sauce. Meat features heavily, accounting for 20% of total food consumption.[1] This contributes to high per capita spend on food and high daily calorie intake.[2] Calorie intake is doubtless also driven by Belgium's famous chocolate and waffles.

Yellow fats divide the nation. Butter dominates the French region, margarine the Flemish. The butter and margarine market is fragmented, offering spreading *and* cooking margarines, 'melanges' (butter mixed with oil) and an array of cream cheeses. Butter is often bought direct from farms, leading to a profusion of tiny local 'brands'.

HOLLAND

Mashed potato is a staple, used in stamppot – mash with meat or vegetables, and hutspot – mash with vegetables and gravy. Traditional dishes such as herring and pancakes sit alongside imported cuisine such as Indonesian 'rijsttafel'. Meat and dairy produce are important to traditional cooking, with cheese a national speciality. The Dutch spend almost as much on cheese as meat,[3] earning the nickname 'cheeseheads'. Margarine is used extensively for cooking and shallow frying – liquid margarines enjoying new-found popularity.

GERMANY

Cuisine is dominated by meat – particularly sausages and salamis – potatoes, and pickled vegetables such as sauerkraut.

Regional specialities are important, such as brains from Niedersachsen and soft noodles from Schwabia. Beer is drunk with almost everything. Attitudes to food have changed since 10 million Germans were diagnosed as overweight in the 1970s – they now avidly consume salads, fruit and vegetables. 'Light' foods are not popular due to concerns over artificial content – Germans prefer to manage their health in natural ways. This preference for natural foods favours butter, while the margarine sector is less sophisticated and segmented than the UK. Curd cheese is a popular alternative to spreads.

---

1. Source: Euromonitor.
2. Source: Health and the European Consumer, 1997.
3. Source: Euromonitor.

UNITED WE DREAM: THE OLIVIO/BERTOLLI SOLUTION

Local differences meant that developing one meaningful advertising campaign across four markets appeared difficult, if not impossible. However, the key to successful international roll-out lay in the breakthrough thinking behind the UK strategy. This was rooted in extensive analysis among opinion formers which unearthed a new trend. In reaction to the punitive health regimes of the eighties, people were increasingly adopting a more holistic and natural attitude, which we termed 'positive health'. The Mediterranean was seen as the cradle of 'positive health', conjuring images of happy, relaxed individuals enjoying life. More importantly for Olivio, olive oil was seen as the epitome of this Mediterranean lifestyle.

The original Olivio launch ads ran a rational longevity message, but this generic built the category, not the brand. At relaunch, olive oil became a symbol of the whole Mediterranean approach to life. Rather than selling the generic of long life, Olivio created a whole brand world based on the Mediterranean idyll of enjoying a longer, fuller life (Figures 3 and 4).

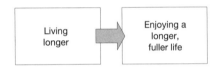

Campaign proposition
'Eating Olivio as part of an olive oil rich Mediterranean style diet can help you enjoy a longer life.'

Advertising idea
Elderly Mediterraneans living happy, stress-free lives.

Figure 3

Figure 4

There was substantial support behind the brand during the early years of relaunch.

Yellow fats constituted a highly prosaic category. By harnessing an idea about how people want to live, rather than how they want to eat, this campaign could transcend everyday attitudes to food and health to connect with consumers at a higher level.

'There seemed to be a willingness, even an eagerness, to suspend disbelief.'

Arnold Cragg, Cragg Ross Dawson Research

Examining other markets, we discovered that, although differences in specific eating habits were manifold, common trends emerged at this higher level. While attitudes to food remained diverse, attitudes to life were converging. Olivio's focus on higher-order benefits offered the key to extending the brand into other markets. Just as the Mediterranean dream could bypass everyday attitudes to food in the UK, it appeared to unite consumers across countries.

Extensive desk research into eating habits and attitudes across Europe revealed that consumers increasingly regarded health as the key to active enjoyment of life. There were more and more consumers aware of the need for a holistic approach, recognising the link between a healthy mind and healthy body, eschewing stress and punitive action in favour of balance.

The Institute of European Food Studies' report of 1996 revealed that the idea of balance was becoming increasingly important across Europe. When asked to define healthy eating, 'balance/variety' was mentioned by 48% of the sample within key countries, making it the highest scoring definition in these markets (Table 1). 'Balance/variety' was the most unifying statement, with the lowest standard deviation.

TABLE 1: PERCENTAGE OF RESPONDENTS MENTIONING
VARIOUS FACTORS AS CONTRIBUTORS TO HEALTHY EATING

	Less fat	More fruit and vegetables	Balance and variety	Fresh/ natural food
Belgium	56	n/a	73	52
Denmark	28	41	52	6
France	29	17	52	36
Germany	72	43	37	13
Netherlands	52	47	35	28
UK	65	63	44	9
Austria	24	40	46	27
Spain	31	49	44	32
Sweden	51	49	45	28
Average	44	44	48	29

Moreover, *Health and the European Consumer, 1996* stated that while actual levels of olive oil penetration and usage varied, there was a common association of olive oil with the Mediterranean lifestyle, and a shared belief in the pleasures and benefits of that lifestyle.

While people might wake up divided over what to spread on their toast, they dreamed the same dream about sunshine and olive groves, and a happy, healthy existence surrounded by friends and family. Food might be local, but the Olivio/ Bertolli vision seemed universal. The client teams in other European countries were also convinced that the appeal of positive Mediterranean health was a lifestyle shift that transcended local attitudes to food.

'You can't resist it – it's a dream you want to live.'

IMW Pan-European Research, December 2000

'In the north [of] Europe there is a fundamental trend towards well-being and quality of life: consumers are looking for naturalness and balance. The success of the Mediterranean lifestyle in Northern Europe is that it represents a passion for life, enjoyment and positive health.'

Unilever FBE Board, *A Proposal for Growth*

Our strategy's time had come beyond the UK, and the European markets were ripe for our message. Olivio/Bertolli had captured not just a health trend, but a macro-shift in the way consumers aspired to live.

'An invasion of armies can be resisted, but not an idea whose time has come.'

Victor Hugo

The Olivio/Bertolli model offers an unconventional way of thinking about global advertising, as it did not start out as an international campaign. There was an eye to long-term roll-out, but the immediate focus was to make it work in the UK. The secret of the campaign's success is that it thought big from the beginning; becoming brand leader in the UK required an emotional connection that would transcend the rational nuances of price and product differentiation. Success in the rest of the world required an emotional connection that would transcend local attitudes to food. The secret is not necessarily to think global, but to think big. Consumers do not know whether an ad is global – only whether it is great.

BIG IDEAS TRAVEL, BUT YOU HAVE TO HELP THEM GET THERE: MANAGING THE ADVERTISING ROLL-OUT

Although convinced that the same campaign would work across markets, we nevertheless needed to be aware of local sensitivities. When considering executional roll-out, we consulted creatives in local markets. This aided understanding of local relevance, building awareness of linguistic and cultural differences.

Belgium was the first new market to roll out communications. The spread was launched as Bertolli in 1997. As in the UK, Bertolli created the olive oil spreads sector, and the brand has been supported consistently ever since, beginning with 'Football' in 1997, followed by 'Tug' in 1998/99 (Figure 5).

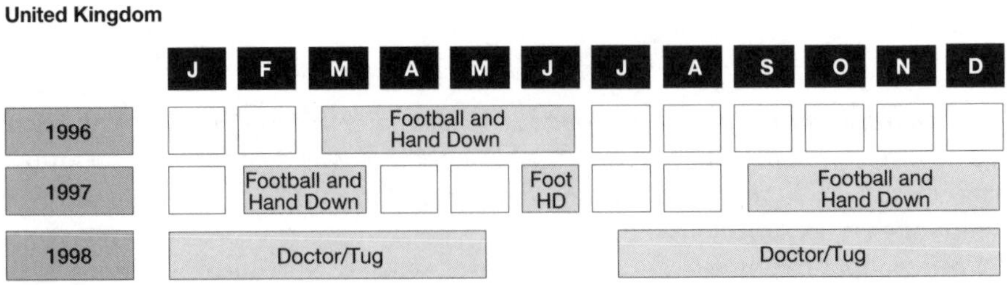

Figure 5: *Olivio communications, 1996–1998*

A consistent local voice-over artist was used across all executions, building warmth and familiarity towards the brand and becoming the 'voice' of Bertolli in

VO: All the goodness of olive oil on your bread.

Super: All the goodness of olive oil on your bread.

Figure 6: 'Tug' – Belgium

Belgium. While the Olivio world remained constant, we made subtle changes to voice-over and titling to accommodate local market dynamics. As the spreading margarine sector is less developed in Belgium, we needed to spell out the usage occasion and differentiate versus cooking products, with the endline 'All the goodness of olive oil on your bread' (Figure 6). Given Bertolli's olive oil presence, we emphasised Italian authenticity by referencing the brand's origins in 1865.

Belgium

	J	F	M	A	M	J	J	A	S	O	N	D
1997					Football							
1998	Tug							Tug				
1999	Tug		Tug									
2000		Hol/Ex B/Lilo		Hol/Ex B/Lilo			Hol/Ex B/Lilo					
2001		H/E B/L			H/E B/L							

Figure 7: *Bertolli communications, Belgium*

The media plan comprised substantial national investment, split more or less evenly across the Flemish-speaking north and French-speaking south. Bertolli spread was the most successful launch in the category for ten years, achieving 5000 tonnes in less than three years.

Mario "de hakker", 79 jaar

Paolo, spits, 82 jaar

BERTOLLI

BERTOLLI Olijfolie sinds 1865.

VO: Bertolli, all the goodness of olive oil on your bread.

Figure 8: *'Football' – Holland*

Success in Belgium accelerated roll-out plans in other countries. Holland launched Bertolli spread in 1998 without advertising. Sales were disappointing, leading to the client's observation:

> 'These test results are conclusive evidence that UK advertising is needed if we are to maximise the potential of Bertolli spread.'
>
> Garance Deelder, Marketing Manager for Health Spreads, Holland, 1998

In 2000, Holland began supporting the spread with the Olivio executions, namely 'Football' (see Figure 8) and 'Tug' (Figure 9). Media spend was low in year one, but encouraging results led to an increase in year two.

Holland

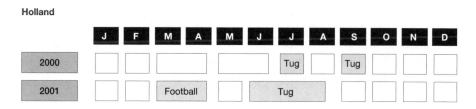

Figure 9: *Bertolli communications, Holland*

Germany relaunched its olive oil spread as Bertolli in June 2000, with 'Football', followed by 'Tug' in 2001 (Figure 10).

Germany

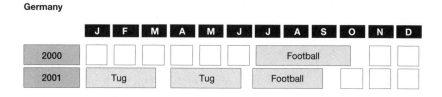

Figure 10: *Bertolli communications, Germany*

Holland and Germany also required creative tweaks to accommodate local tastes – while the Mediterranean fantasy was compelling, too strong an olive oil taste was not, and again, we needed to differentiate versus cooking products. In Germany, our endline was revised to *'The new spread with **mild** olive oil'*. In Holland we described *'Bertolli for your bread with **mild** olive oil'*. Again in each market a consistent voice-over artist with local appeal became the brand 'voice'.

REFINING THE STRATEGY

In the interim we refined our views about how the campaign was working in the UK. A 1998 review highlighted the opportunity to drive trial among consumers who found the Olivio world aspirational, but had not tried the product, particularly those at the younger end.

April 1999 also saw the launch of Benecol, a spread targeting Olivio's heartland with a promise to reduce cholesterol. We believed the role for Olivio was not to compete on a rational basis, but to deepen its emotional connection with consumers.

The campaign evolution sought to do two things:

- Draw in younger consumers by increasing relevance and 'youthfulness'.
- Create even greater emotional engagement with the Olivio world by heightening the emphasis on full *enjoyment* of life.

The creative idea was that eating Olivio meant joining 'Club 18–130'. Ads showed our familiar elderly Mediterranean characters on holiday, getting up to antics that were even cheekier than before. This played on the 'Club 18–30' pun and introduced a youthfulness and zest for life into the brand world.

Six executions were developed in 1999: two 30-second ads, 'Holiday' and 'Exposure'; two 10-second ads, 'Lilo' and 'Banana'; and two print executions for six-sheet posters and for women's magazines (Figures 11–15).

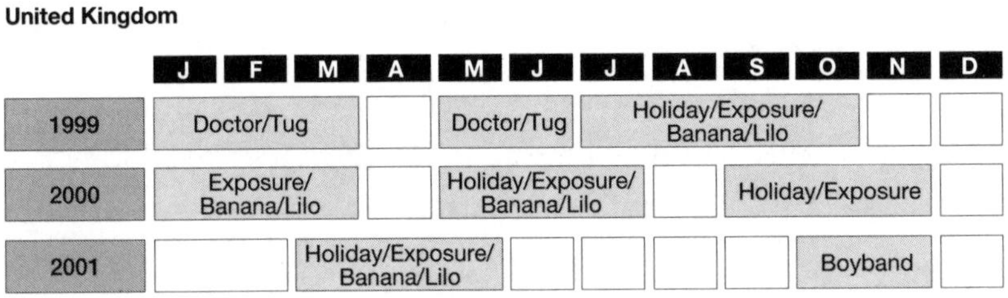

United Kingdom

	J	F	M	A	M	J	J	A	S	O	N	D
1999	Doctor/Tug				Doctor/Tug		Holiday/Exposure/Banana/Lilo					
2000	Exposure/Banana/Lilo			Holiday/Exposure/Banana/Lilo				Holiday/Exposure				
2001		Holiday/Exposure/Banana/Lilo							Boyband			

Figure 11: *Olivio communications, UK, 1999–2001*

'Club 18–130' successfully evolved our creative vehicle, deepening consumers' emotional relationship with the brand. It also drove a significant increase in volume gained from our younger target. Under-35s accounted for 10.3% of total volume in 1998, rising to 16.2% in 2001.[4] Penetration among this group in the UK rose by 5% year-on-year in the first year of 'Club 18–130'.

The brand grew at the fastest rate since launch, from 3.8% to 5.4% value share within three weeks. Belgium also rolled out this campaign, where value share rose to 12% and volume share to 9% at the peak advertising period.[5]

'Club 18–130' was followed in the UK by 'Boyband' in October 2001, continuing the youthful theme with the story of the homecoming of Italy's favourite 'boy' band (Figures 11, 16 and 17).

We now had a clear campaign evolution process. At launch, the brand would establish its proposition of enjoying a longer, fuller life, driving trial among the core target. Over time, it would evolve to embrace a broader view of Mediterranean zest for life, deepening the consumer relationship and drawing in a younger target.

---

4.   Source: TNS pre-2001, AC Nielsen post-2001.
5.   Source: AC Nielsen.

Figure 12: 'Exposure' – UK

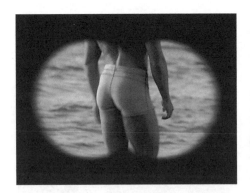

VO: Bertolli. The goodness of olive oil on your bread

Figure 13: *'Holiday' – Belgium*

Figure 14: *'Lilo'* – *UK*

Figure 15: 'Banana' – UK

Figure 16: 'Club 18–130' – UK print

VO: What is it that makes the women of Lucca act like teenagers? Is it Bertolli, first produced here in 1865, the olive oil at the heart of Olivio?

Or is it the homecoming of Italy's premier 'boyband'?

I mean – they've been around almost as long as Bertolli has!

Bertolli: the heart and soul of Olivio.

Figure 17: 'Boyband' – UK

BUSINESS EFFECTS

By the end of 2001 the brand had built critical mass in four markets, and was achieving significant results. The spread had achieved a total volume of *c.* 30,000 tonnes with combined sales worth *c.* €100 million, making it UnileverBestfoods' fastest growing food brand in Europe in 2001.[6]

As younger markets, Germany and Holland led the field, with an average 200% volume growth year-on-year since launch. The UK and Belgium have grown more slowly as they have matured, but nevertheless, volume grew 8.5% over a three-year period.[7]

As seen in Table 2, additional measures show positive growth over time – more rapidly in the newer markets of Germany and Holland. This growth has come from both penetration and average weight of purchase.[8]

TABLE 2: GROWTH IN KEY MEASURES (PRE/POST ADVERTISING)

	Penetration % (total households)		Average weight of purchase (per household)		Volume share % (total market)	
	Pre	Post	Pre	Post	Pre	Post
UK	3.8	19.8	2.5	2.75	2.0	4.2
Belgium	17.2	22.3	2.4	3.30	0.2	7.3
Germany	4.6	8.2	1.2	1.80	1.0	2.0
Holland	2.8	5.3	1.2	1.80	0.1	1.4

The UK experience had given us a clear model for how the advertising should work: building an emotional connection with the Mediterranean way of life to drive sales consistently upwards. The presence of similar beliefs about this lifestyle across countries had convinced us that we could build the same emotional connection in other markets. Our hypothesis was that, given similar levels of involvement with the brand, we could expect to see similar patterns of growth.

As Figures 18–21 demonstrate, there has indeed been consistent growth in all markets and, as predicted, growth has built in a remarkably similar way across the four, with a visible 'stepped' pattern across the board. This effect is more immediately evident in the launch years, but is still occurring in the more mature markets. The one consistent variable throughout has been the advertising. We will go on to demonstrate conclusively that the campaign is indeed the primary driver of this growth.[9]

---

6. Source: UnileverBestfoods data – approximate totals due to client confidentiality reasons.
7. Source: TNS/AC Nielsen.
8. 'Pre' and 'Post' refer to the figures reached before and after the advent of material advertising support in these countries. Actual dates vary based on time of roll-out. Source: TNS, AC Nielsen, IRI, GfK, UBKPIs.
9. Index base cannot be revealed for client confidentiality reasons.

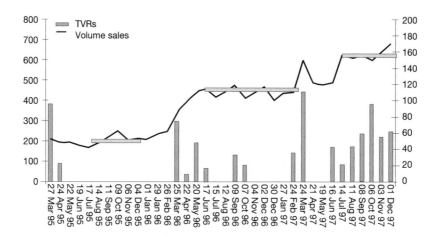

Figure 18: *UK volume versus TVRs 1995–1997, indexed*

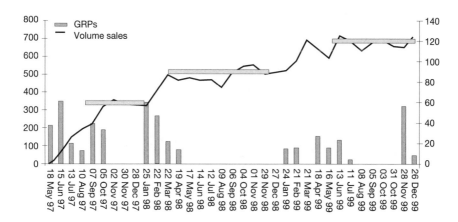

Figure 19: *Belgium volume versus GRPs 1997–1999, indexed*

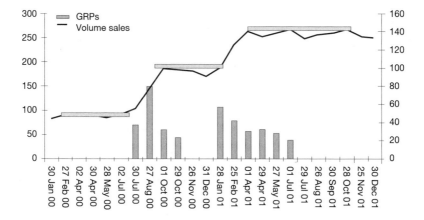

Figure 20: *Germany volume versus GRPs 2000–2001, indexed*

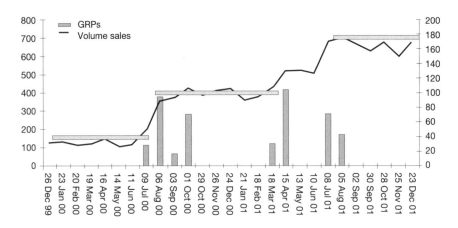

Figure 21: *Holland volume versus GRPs 2000–2001, indexed*

PROVING THE ADVERTISING EFFECT

Here we outline three proofs that advertising is the key driver of Olivio/Bertolli's performance:

1. Econometric modelling in all markets demonstrates the correlation between advertising activity and brand sales.
2. We use a combination of modelling and additional data sources to eliminate other factors that might have contributed to Olivio/Bertolli's growth.
3. A range of hard and soft measures prove that the advertising is working exactly as intended.

Econometrics

Statistical analysis was undertaken on UK, Belgium, Germany and Holland sales to test the hypothesis that, having created similar levels of emotional engagement in these markets, we should see advertising driving sales growth, in line with the UK picture in 1998.[10]

We took the general structure of the original Olivio model and applied it to the new data. Statistical diagnostics confirmed that there are remarkable parallels between the four sets of data and the nature of the advertising effect. Key findings regarding the advertising effect are:

- In all countries, after taking account of other important factors – pricing, distribution, promotions and direct marketing – advertising effects were a significant component of overall sales volume.
- The general effect of advertising was the same across all markets – sales display a series of 'steps' upward, coincident with advertising activity.

---

10. Data collection in Germany is by 13 periods per year. This causes periodic 'spikes' in the data when the period has five weeks rather than the standard four. To illustrate the 'true' pattern of sales growth, we have averaged out this effect, but elsewhere we have used data as recorded.

- These 'steps' upward are consistent with adstock with a 'zero decay' rate. In other words, when advertising comes off-air, there is usually a tailing-off of brand sales as advertising effect decays. Unusually, Olivio/Bertolli advertising displays no such decay, continuing to drive sales even when off-air. Figures 22 and 23 show volumes versus an adstock with zero decay.[11] The correlation is evident. Alternative adstock variables have been tested and the fit is significantly less impressive.[12]

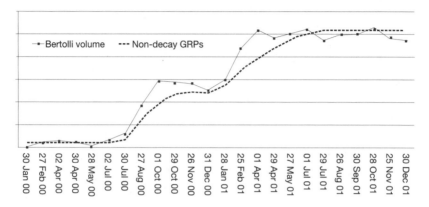

Figure 22: *Germany normalised data*

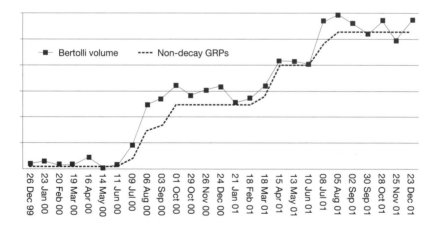

Figure 23: *Holland normalised data*

- This finding matches the result in the UK in 1998, when the 'zero decay' finding was proven but remained controversial, since there was then no clear hypothesis as to why this unique result occurred.
- Today, we not only have an hypothesis as to what drives this effect – an ongoing emotional connection to a higher-order benefit – we also have new data which support the hypothesis.

---

11. Data have been normalised in order to make sales comparable on one axis.
12. Once again, the pattern is most obvious in younger markets, but holds true in the UK and Belgium.

The corollary of these findings is that the strategy we developed in the UK and rolled out across other countries has worked exactly as intended.[13]

Figures 24–27 show model fits, indicating that the models adequately account for all major variations in sales.[14]

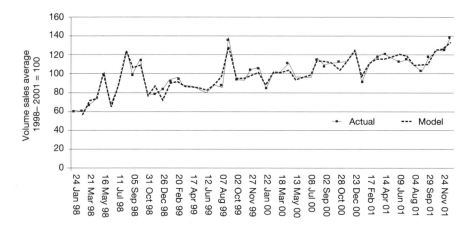

Figure 24: *UK volume: actual vs. model*

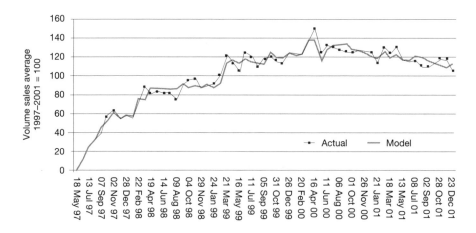

Figure 25: *Belgium volume: actual vs. model*

13. All four of the models are subsets of the original UK 1998 model, with the general structure working across all markets. However at a local level, the models have minor specification differences, due to different levels of market maturity and competitive activity.
14. R^2 is 93.5, 99.7, 98.7, 99.3 and estimated regression standard errors are 5.2%, 5.9%, 5.5% and 5.8% for UK, Belgium, Germany, and Holland, respectively.

412

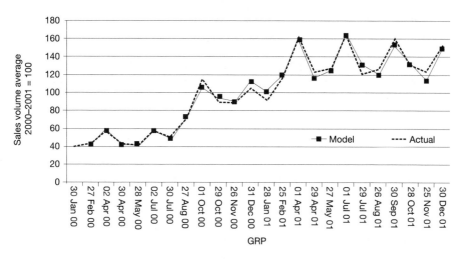

Figure 26: *Germany volume: actual vs. model*

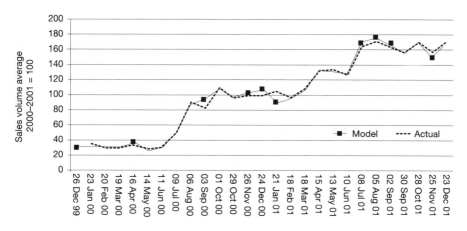

Figure 27: *Holland volume: actual vs. model*

Discounting other variables

Factors other than advertising could clearly have affected Olivio/Bertolli sales. We have examined these variables in detail and either quantified their impact or determined that they do not have a material effect. Therefore, the advertising effect is a true measure of the campaign and does not wrongly attribute other factors.

Pricing effects

Relative price

Olivio/Bertolli maintained a price premium above the total margarine market, and above other branded and own-label olive oil spreads. Price has been maintained in the UK, where Carapelli has declined 8.3% and own label 4.7%. In Germany, price has been maintained and is at a premium to own label. In Belgium and Holland, while the Bertolli price shows a slight decline, competitors show greater decline.

In Belgium, Belolive price has declined c. 25% more than Bertolli over the period, while in Holland, Mediterrane price has dropped twice as much as Bertolli. Market forces are clearly impacting price across the sector in Belgium and Holland, but despite slight declines, our relative positioning has been maintained. Where relative price becomes an issue, it has been quantified within the models and is not artificially augmenting advertising effect.

Promotions
Olivio/Bertolli does not generally follow a multi-buy promotional strategy (i.e. 'buy-one-get-one-free'). This means price promotions are captured in standard pricing data. Exceptions to this rule have been identified and quantified within the models. There have been no significant non-price promotions.

Sampling took place in Holland, where it drove penetration to an extent, but not to any degree that can be quantified within the model. In Germany, sampling was discontinued as inefficient. Additionally, panel data reveal that less than 5% of Bertolli sales are accounted for by promotions, versus for example 50–60% for Rama, a key competitor.[15]

Distribution effects
Distribution
Distribution has not changed significantly in the UK or Germany, rising from 59% to 66% in Germany for 2000–2001, and from 89% to 98% in the UK for 1998–2001. This effect is minor and has not been identified as significant. Belgium (16–90%) and Holland (23–92%) have seen material changes in distribution and the effect has been quantified in the models.

As a result of Bertolli brand strength in Holland, a competitor was de-listed from one store chain, Albert Heijn. The sales benefit to Bertolli could be wrongly attributed to advertising at this period. However, this only occurred within the last six months, and could not affect findings over a two-year period. We have calculated the contribution of this competitor's Albert Heijn sales to total volumes for the six months prior to de-listing. Even if Bertolli had acquired all these competitor sales within this chain – which is unlikely – it could not account for Bertolli's growth.

Shelf space
The introduction of new 500 g and 1 kg packs in some markets has increased the brand's facings in store – a factor which would not show as an increase in distribution, but would give increased presence and possibly boost sales. In the UK, all pack sizes were present before the period of this paper, so there can be no effect. In other markets, we have examined the introduction of new sizes as a proxy for increased shelf space; in markets where there is a material effect, this has been quantified and eliminated from advertising effect.

Competitive advertising
Competitive advertising could positively affect the sector as a whole, benefiting Olivio/Bertolli. There has been no significant spend behind any brand with a specific olive oil message, therefore it is unlikely that Olivio/Bertolli would benefit.

---

15. Source: GfK weekly PanelData Germany (all housewives).

However, increased spend behind new competitors in the total health spreads sector such as Flora/Becel Pro-Activ and Benecol means that Olivio/Bertolli has not had a disproportionately high share of voice.[16]

TABLE 3: SHARE OF VOICE

	UK		Belgium		Germany		Holland	
	Olivio	Flora Pro-Activ	Bertolli	Becel (Pro-Activ)	Bertolli	Becel (Pro-Activ)	Bertolli	Becel (Pro-Activ)
1998	19	n/a	18	15	n/a	n/a	n/a	n/a
1999	16	n/a	24	15	n/a	n/a	n/a	1
2000	16	14	21	22	7	2.1	8	24
2001	20	27	18	22	12	6.1	11	31

Health trends

Capitalising on an emerging health trend has benefited Olivio/Bertolli. One could argue this trend itself is the key sales driver, and that the brand would have shown natural growth without advertising, in line with 'positive health'. Separate health spreads data do not exist in all markets, but if we consider the UK and Germany (one mature, one growing market) we can see that in the UK, health spreads volume has declined by c. 8% for 1998–2001. In Germany, health spreads volume has grown just 9.3% year-on-year against 98.9% growth from Bertolli. Bertolli has grown ten times faster than the total health sector.[17]

Olive oil growth

Olive oil has grown steadily over the period of this paper and logic suggests this would affect olive oil spreads. However, Olivio/Bertolli's strong share performance indicates that it is not merely benefiting from sector growth, as would be the case if we were witnessing an olive oil effect. Olive oil users also have a greater propensity to use butter than margarine (indices are 112 and 96 respectively), so olive oil growth would not automatically translate into olive oil spreads growth.[18]

Other marketing activity

Other marketing activity has run at low levels across markets, including DM, press, posters and radio. We have been unable to identify a separate effect within the model for these other activities, with the exception of a burst of UK DM. Other marketing activities have been concomitant with TV advertising, with the result that they may be adjusting the TV effect slightly upwards. To avoid artificially inflating this effect, we have used advertising spend across all media when calculating payback.

Quantifying advertising effect

By comparing actual sales with modelled sales we would obtain without advertising support, we can quantify percentage of sales driven by advertising.[19]

16. Pro-Activ is not broken out from total Becel spend in these markets, but their step changes in share of voice can be attributed to the Pro-Activ spend.
17. Source: TNS/AC Nielsen/IRI.
18. Source: TGI 2002.
19. The effect of the advertising was quantified by simulating the model and setting the advertising input to zero; this shows what sales would have been with no advertising support, other factors being equal.

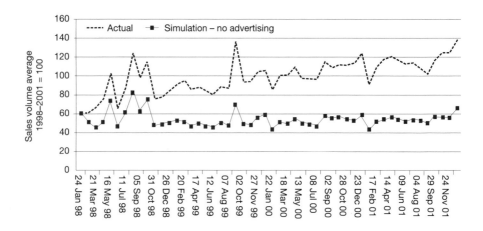

Figure 28: *UK: actual vs. no advertising simulation*

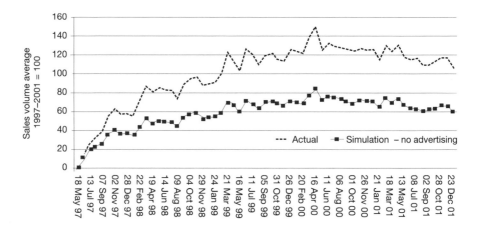

Figure 29: *Belgium: actual vs. no advertising simulation*

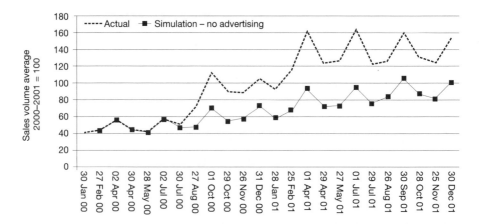

Figure 30: *Germany: volume: actual vs. no advertising simulation*

Figure 28 shows that sales in the UK were 83.6% higher than they would have been without advertising. In Belgium, sales are 72% higher than they would have been without advertising (Figure 29). In Germany sales are 47.5% higher than without advertising (Figure 30). Finally, in Holland sales are 58.7% higher than without advertising (Figure 31).

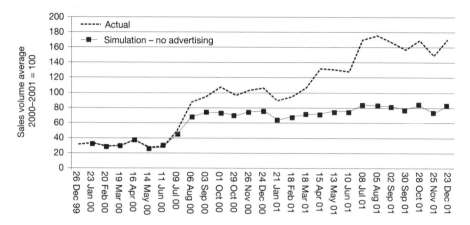

Figure 31: *Holland: volume: actual vs. no advertising simulation*

A control in Holland provides further evidence of the advertising effect. Bertolli was present in Albert Heijn before and after advertising. It launched in Albert Heijn in 1998, but TV advertising support did not begin in earnest until 2000. Sales in this chain grew rapidly once advertising was on air, doubling weekly volumes pre and post. This reflects the proportional increase seen in the national models. Distribution and pricing within the chain remained flat over the period concerned (see Figure 32).[20] The Albert Heijn control gives a true read of advertising effect, and further confirms effects quantified by the model.

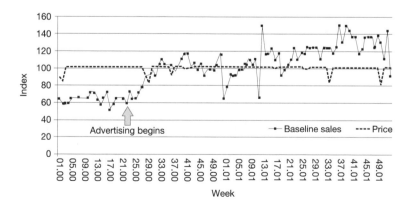

Figure 32: *Albert Heijn baseline sales vs. price (Holland)*

---

20. We acknowledge the caveat placed on baseline sales, but given flat pricing and distribution, we feel their use is legitimate in this case to eliminate promotional effect as far as possible.

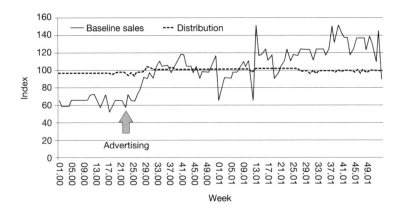

Figure 33: *Albert Heijn baseline sales vs. distribution (Holland)*

Additional support

We have revisited the strategic model for how the advertising should work developed in 1998, and shown that it holds good for all four markets. This offers further evidence that the advertising works as intended in all markets. We noted four key things that the advertising must achieve in order to drive sales success (see Figure 34). These have been met in all markets, as discussed below.[21]

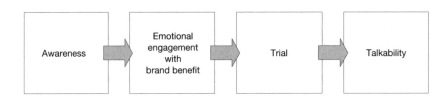

Figure 34: *Advertising model*

Raising awareness

UK unaided awareness has risen consistently since 1998. It stands at 23%, with aided awareness at 93% (see Figure 35).[22]

In Belgium, while no pre measures are available, unaided awareness is 30% and prompted awareness 92%.

Germany and Holland doubled unaided awareness in the six months between two dips in 2001, i.e. during the key period that advertising was on air.[23]

---

21. It is important to note that rolling data are available only for the UK. Where possible, we have used pre and post dips in the other markets. The scale of the effects is on a par with the UK and from similar performance overall we can infer that the pattern is similar also.
22. Source: Millward Brown tracking.
23. Source: Millward Brown Health Check, December 2001.

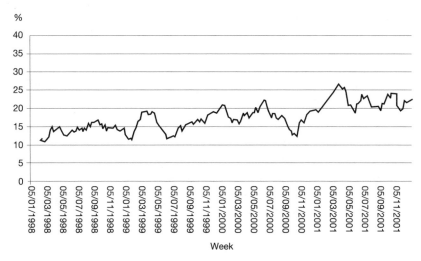

Figure 35: *Unaided awareness (UK)*

TABLE 4: AWARENESS (%) DURING PERIOD ADVERTISING WAS ON AIR

	Germany		Holland	
	March 2001	Sept 2001	March 2001	Sept 2001
Unaided awareness	11	20	7	14
Aided awareness	37	60	57	71

Qualitative research in Holland and Germany also reveals surprisingly high recall for a new campaign.

'[The campaign] is more well-known than one might expect ...an ad with uncommonly good impact' [Germany].

'It [the brand] is well known and being steered by high impact advertising' [Holland].

Bertolli Line Extension research, August 2000

Another measure of awareness is the advertising Awareness Index calculated by Millward Brown. It is particularly impressive for Olivio/Bertolli. In the UK, the brand has achieved an AI of 8 against a country average of 6. This is mirrored in the other markets, leading to the observation that:

'Olivio/Bertolli advertising is amongst the strongest within Unilever at the moment and is proving effective in all countries.'

Millward Brown Brand Health Check, December 2001

Communicating the brand benefit

The brand proposition of 'enjoying a longer, fuller life' is firmly established in all markets. 'Helps you enjoy a longer life' (Figure 36) in the UK stands at 30%.[24]

This measure shows 27% endorsement in Belgium, and impressive growth in Holland and Germany (Table 5), doubling between the two tracking dips undertaken in 2001.[25]

---

24. Source: Millward Brown tracking.
25. Source: Millward Brown Brand Health check, December 2001.

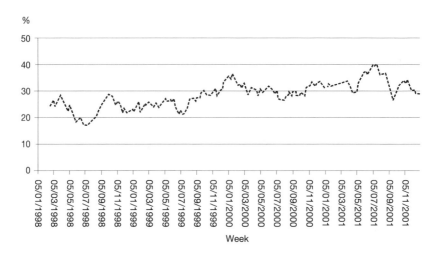

Figure 36: *Enjoy longer life (UK)*

TABLE 5: ENDORSEMENT (%) OF BRAND PROPOSITION

	Germany		Holland	
	March 2001	Sept 2001	March 2001	Sept 2001
Enjoy longer life	10	22	14	20
Enjoy life to the full	13	18	9	14

Further surveys confirm that the brand benefit is being clearly communicated. A 1998 survey in Belgium[26] shows 61% of spread users agreeing that the brand promotes longevity, with 68% agreeing that it offers 'enjoyment' (Table 6).

TABLE 6: AGREEMENT WITH BRAND
BENEFITS IN BELGIUM

	% users agreeing
High-quality brand	68
Authentic	68
Enjoyment	68
Longevity	61
Different from other brands	79
Open, spontaneous	61

Furthermore, we have extensive qualitative evidence to show that the brand promise is being communicated and appreciated across markets.

'Bertolli stands for Italian healthiness, growing old the "right" way.'

NPD Pan-European Concept Development research, December 2001

'In all markets, Bertolli is closely associated with zest for life – a positive, active appreciation of the good things in life.'

Sadek Wynberg Pan-European Research, January 2002

---

26. Source: IPSOS Quantitative Survey, Belgium 1998.

'The general message perception was that Bertolli stands for [a] healthy product which keeps you young, vital and active.'

Bertolli Marketing Mix Debrief Netherlands, April 2001

'Bertolli is seen as a sunny, warm, extrovert brand with abundant character.'

Censydiam Research, Belgium 1998

The evolution to 'Club 18–130' is also working as intended to maximise enjoyment across the UK and Belgium, building greater emotional proximity over time. This led to the Millward Brown comment:

'"Club 18–130" enjoyment scores are in the top 2% of all ads ever tested.'

Millward Brown PreView Debrief, UK, August 1999

Overall engagement with the brand deepened significantly over the life of this campaign (Tables 7 and 8).[27]

TABLE 7: ENGAGEMENT WITH THE BRAND (UK)

	UK (all 'Club 18–130')	
	Pre (%)	Post (%)
'Enjoy watching a lot'	55	79
'Made the brand more appealing'	39	67

TABLE 8: ENGAGEMENT WITH THE BRAND (BELGIUM)

	Belgium 'Exposure'		Belgium 'Banana'	
	18–44	45–64	18–44	45–64
'Enjoy watching a lot'	91	86	93	82
'Made the brand more appealing'	77	70	76	72

The power of the brand's emotional connection is best summarised as follows:

'I was astonished by the popularity of its advertising, and by the strength and clarity of the brand imagery. I can't immediately recall (in over twenty-five years of research on advertising) coming across another campaign that seemed to be performing so powerfully and exactly as intended.'

Arnold Cragg, Cragg Ross Dawson Research

In terms of more concrete measures, we can also show that the advertising performs as intended.

Driving trial

Penetration has increased in all four markets, showing ongoing increases in trial. 'Ever bought' as measured by Millward Brown continues to rise in the UK (now at 32%, see Figures 37 and 38), and is surpassed by Belgium, at 42%.

Germany and Holland show impressive increases in the six months between the two tracking dips in 2001 (see Table 9).[28]

---

27. Source: Millward Brown.
28. Source: Millward Brown Brand Health Check, December 2001.

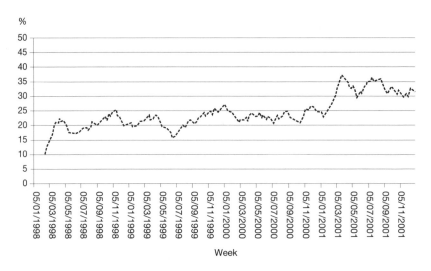

Figure 37: *Ever bought (UK)*

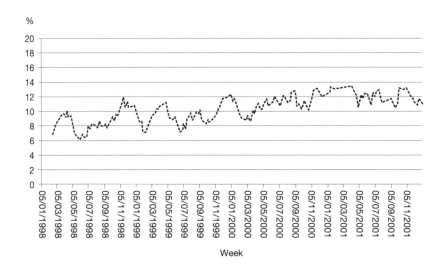

Figure 38: *Buy nowadays (UK)*

TABLE 9: PERCENTAGE OF SAMPLE BUYING BERTOLLI

	Germany		Holland	
	March 2001	Sept 2001	March 2001	Sept 2001
Ever bought	8	16	17	21
Buy nowadays	3	6	9	12

Client teams in our other markets firmly believe that the advertising had a significant effect in driving trial.

'The advertising seems to be highly effective in establishing the right brand values and communicating the proposition, driving consumer trial. TV advertising should therefore be absolutely central in the marketing mix of olive oil spreads.'

UnileverBestfoods FBE Board Presentation, February 2000

Getting the brand talked about

Part of our model for how the advertising would work was the expectation that the message would be interesting enough for people to discuss in the real world. This would extend the advertising effect by getting the brand talked about, even when off air. Our consumers would become brand advocates, recruiting friends and family. One hypothesis to explain the controversial 'zero decay' effect discussed earlier is this 'talkability' factor. This effect means that our ads are never out of mind. Further evidence of the brand's 'talkability' is the Millward Brown attribute 'Getting more popular' (Figure 39). This rises in the UK to 27% and in Belgium to 50%.

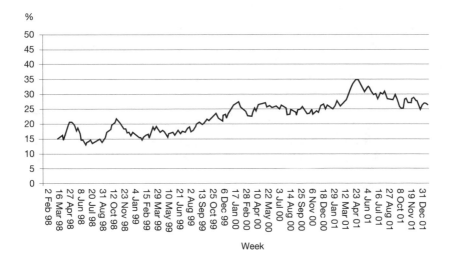

Figure 39: *'Getting more popular' (UK)*

Scores come through at equally strong levels across the other markets.[29]

TABLE 10: TALKABILITY (%)

	Germany		Holland	
	March 2001	Sept 2001	March 2001	Sept 2001
'Getting more popular'	17	21	30	42

We also found qualitative evidence of this 'talkability' effect.

'I started using Olivio after I had it at my mum's. She tried it because of the advertising, and I thought it would be a good idea because my little girl doesn't eat dairy.'

Van den Bergh Consumer Connection, UK, August 2000

29. Source: Millward Brown Brand Health Check, December 2001.

Omnibus findings also confirm the role of word-of-mouth in the UK. One third of respondents who had tried Olivio stated that they had tried it because friends or family recommended it.[30]

PAYBACK

This section focuses on the financial payback of the advertising. Figures 40–43 show the period at which this has been or will be achieved in each market. Using combined European figures, the advertising has already paid for itself across Europe and is now generating incremental sales benefits.

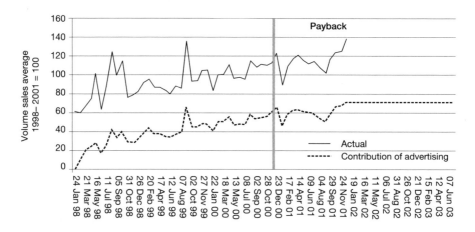

Figure 40: *UK volume: payback calculation*

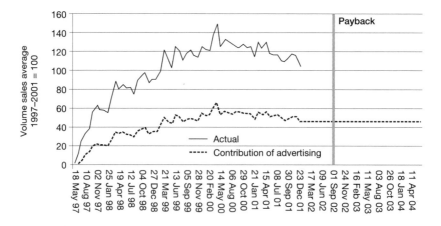

Figure 41: *Belgium volume: payback calculation*

---

30. Source: TNS Omnibus, May 2002.

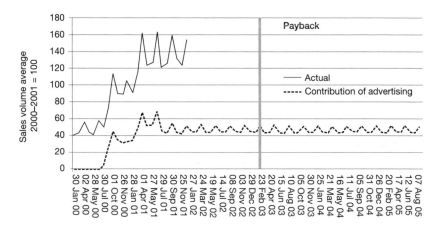

Figure 42: *Germany volume: payback calculation*

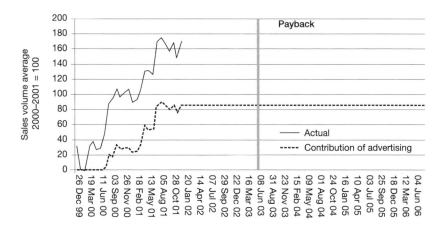

Figure 43: *Holland volume: payback calculation*

FURTHER EFFICIENCIES

The success of the Olivio/Bertolli advertising campaign has led to several efficiencies above and beyond spread sales growth. The international appeal of the campaign means that production of separate commercials to support Bertolli across markets was not required. We estimate that this has saved UnileverBestfoods in the region of £3 million. This saving does not take into account the considerable person-hours required to produce effective advertising, again estimated as a saving of 23%[31] in workload on the agency side alone.

---

31. We investigated the extent to which applying a consistent brand platform over a number of markets yields operating efficiencies compared to separate strategy executions for each market. Our experience of the client allowed us to make a direct comparison between single market agency workloads and global platform/ relationship workloads. This leads to our estimate of a 23% saving in agency workload compared to an equivalent relationship across four markets with work developed for each market to different marketing strategies.

SUMMARY

Despite notorious difficulties in creating food advertising that works across markets, Olivio/Bertolli has developed a successful international campaign. We have demonstrated conclusively that advertising was the primary driver of Olivio/Bertolli's growth and that it worked exactly as predicted. The campaign delivered success by building emotional engagement with the brand benefit of enjoying a longer, fuller life the Mediterranean way. The emotional richness of the brand world also prompted trialists to recommend it to friends and family, recruiting still more users. Sales growth driven by advertising in this way can be seen as a series of consistent upward 'steps'.

UK success led to roll-out in Belgium, Germany and Holland. Convinced that consumers would engage with the advertising as in the UK, we believed we should see a similar pattern in sales effects. This is exactly what we saw.

Our econometric modelling has demonstrated that:

- Advertising delivered significant sales uplifts across all markets.
- It has already more than paid for itself across Europe.
- It is now generating incremental profit.

The campaign has delivered additional production efficiencies of £3 million and an estimated saving in person-hours of 23%. Furthermore, the benefits of brand extension using a proven model for developing effective international advertising are inestimable.

CONCLUSION

We have quantified advertising's sales contribution over time and additional savings in terms of production efficiencies. What we cannot calculate today is the ongoing value of our learnings for international communications development. We have learned that:

- People in diverse countries can be united by emotional benefits that transcend local differences – realities divide, dreams and aspirations unite.
- Successful international advertising is not necessarily about thinking global, but about thinking big – big ideas unite people at a profound level.
- Emotional engagement is not limited by category – even a spread brand has permission to dream.
- Wrapping an emotional benefit in a distinctive brand world creates even greater international appeal, bypassing local tastes in casting, setting, etc., and allowing consumers to suspend disbelief.
- Emotional engagement is all very well, but a successful brand needs a clear model for how this engagement will translate into hard sales results.
- A successful international campaign can build momentum and cohesion behind a brand, giving it a sense of energy and consistency that bodes well for the future.

The 1998 paper finished by observing that the true test of that paper's learnings would be the number of future IPA papers written on the brand. If the same holds true of today's paper, there may be another one along in a minute …

'The Olivio/Bertolli advertising campaign is widely acknowledged within UnileverBestfoods as being an example of highly effective advertising. I myself do not doubt that it has played a major role in the commercial success of our brand. It provides an important case study for us in terms of learnings on issues of brand globalisation.'

Anthony Simon, President, Marketing Foods Division, Unilever plc

17

Police Recruitment

How thinking negatively ended the negative thinking

Principal author: Richard Storey, M&C Saatchi

EDITOR'S SUMMARY

This case examines how advertising that seemingly deters people from joining the Police Force had precisely the opposite effect. Respected figures' admissions that they could not do what police do elicited several positive effects. It boosted respect for the Force, after years of decline. It increased police morale and reduced public fear of crime. Most importantly it drove a 73% increase in recruits, dramatically reversing a seven-year decline in police numbers. This exceptional efficacy saved UK taxpayers more than £30 million.

COUNTER-INTUITION

This paper charts the transformational effects of two words – *I couldn't*.

Previous IPA Effectiveness papers demonstrate that advertising can effectively stimulate recruitment.[1] Beyond showing that police recruitment advertising works, this paper specifically examines *how* it works.

While most advertising encourages and persuades, this campaign set out to actively *discourage and dissuade*. This negative approach works counter-intuitively, producing positive effects that are especially powerful and widespread.

In particular, the campaign drives both specific action *and* widespread attitudinal change – a feat usually regarded as too ambitious for a single piece of advertising.

NEGATIVE THINKING

Deciding to join the Police means a life-changing commitment to unsociable hours, danger, personal insult, rules, responsibility and paperwork. Difficult at the best of times.

Compounding this, perceptions of the Police in 2000 were poor.

'There is no doubt that there were fundamental errors ... a combination of professional incompetence, institutional racism and a failure of leadership by senior officers.'

Sir William Macpherson's Report, Steven Lawrence Inquiry, 1999

'You come out of the pub drunk at the weekend and the policeman is the one that stops you and has a go and you think "what a tosser".'

Male, 23–30, Consumer InSight

'The Bobby on the Beat must be one of the least desirable jobs in England – alongside managing the England cricket team and running the Millennium Dome.'

Chairman, Constables Central Committee

Indeed, the Police's reputation had fallen steadily to a level where the public claimed they had more confidence in Coca-Cola, Asda and Chris Tarrant (Figure 1).

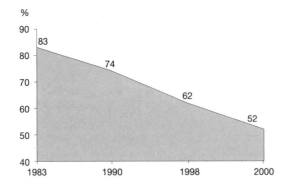

Figure 1: *Declining confidence in the Police*
Source: Henley Centre

---

1. Sources: RAF Officer Recruitment 1980, Nursing Recruitment 1986, Metropolitan Police Recruitment 1988, London Bus Driver Recruitment 1990, RAF Recruitment 1996, Army Recruitment 1996.

As a consequence of this malaise, applications to the Police were falling steadily and the strength of the service had dropped to a ten-year low.

The Home Office therefore instigated a national recruitment campaign to complement the Government's newly announced Crime Fighting Fund. This first ever *national* advertising for the Police was designed to complement the local forces' own recruitment campaigns.

M&C Saatchi was appointed with an objective of helping recruit 9000 police officers over three years.[2]

TURNAROUND

Advertising ran nationally from August 2000 using the theme *'I couldn't. Could you?'*

This resulted in a rapid uplift in police recruits, delivering a pronounced turnaround in the number of serving officers (Figures 2 and 3).

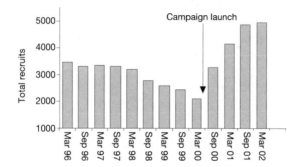

Figure 2: *Uplift in police recruits*
Six-monthly totals
Source: Home Office *Police Service Strength*

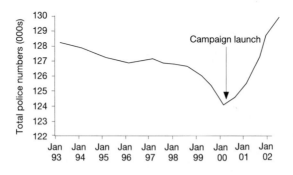

Figure 3: *Turnaround in police numbers*
Source: Home Office

---

2. The Crime Fighting Fund (CFF) provided £454 million '*to recruit and train 9000 extra officers over and above the number that forces had planned to recruit in the next three years to March 2003*'. Advertising was expected to be '*a significant factor*' in achieving this target. NB: All police are 'officers' irrespective of rank. The task was to recruit regular Police Constables.

The Home Secretary underlined the significance of this transformation:

'We have now decisively reversed the decline in Police numbers. The increase of 4578 Officers in under two years shows the success of our investment.'[3]

Source: No. 10 Press Release, 13 March 2002

A DIRECT LINK

For once it is easy to establish advertising's direct contribution to this turnaround. This is because the advertising response channels are unique.[4] Enquirers ringing or clicking on these channels must have been prompted directly by this advertising. Their details are captured and tracked separately from applicants via ongoing local channels.

We can therefore report that the campaign has generated 101,795 relevant enquiries. (This is the total number of telephone enquiries up to 12 May 2002. As will be shown below, many more enquiries were made via the web, but inconsistencies in the way the data are measured make it unreliable to provide a total unique visitor figure across the whole period.) This yielded 66,346 application requests[5] and 5998 officers recruited via the Crime Fighter Fund (CFF recruits to March 2002).

These recruits represent an incremental 52% over and above ongoing numbers (Figure 4).

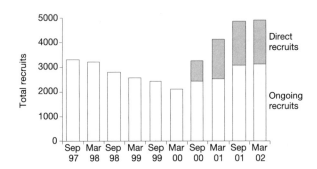

Figure 4: *Source of police recruits*
Six-monthly totals
Source: Home Office *Police Service Strength*

Having established the campaign's success, it is illuminating to look at exactly *how* this was achieved.

---

3. The increase in officers is lower than the number of recruits because of serving officers retiring or leaving the force.
4. 0845 6083000 and *www.policecouldyou.co.uk* are the unique national enquiry lines. The 'Could you?' advertising is the only realistic means whereby anyone could obtain these. Each of the local police forces uses a separate number and URL for applications in its own advertising and marketing.
5. Enquirers returned an 'Expressions of Interest' to receive their application form. This figure combines both telephone and internet enquiries.

HOW THIS HAPPENED

The campaign's counter-intuitive strategy was based on five key observations.

1. The task isn't *'more people to consider'*, but *'people to consider more'*.

   There's a massive disparity between the number of people prepared to consider a police career (25%) and the number who actually apply (0.07%). This disparity illustrates the extent to which people 'toy' with the idea of joining the Police.

   'Considerers' tend to have thought about a career with the Police only vaguely and without serious commitment. Typically, it's something they've mooted for a while, but done nothing about.

   Advertising needed to force them to consider the Police more actively and in more detail, ultimately making a decision one way or the other.

2. One in 4000.

   We needed to recruit less than one person in 4000,[6] which presented two profound dilemmas:

   - The advertising needed to target and motivate a highly specific minority.
   - Even then, however, it would effectively be 'wasted' on the remaining 99.9% seeing it, unless it served another purpose.

3. Quality is sacrosanct.

   The Home Office made it clear from the start that the requirement to boost numbers should in no way compromise quality of recruits. Standards would not be lowered to artificially 'make the numbers'.

   At the time, a typical, cynical view of the skills required was:

   > 'It doesn't take much to cruise around in a panda car, dishing out the odd speeding ticket.'
   >
   > Male, 25–35

   In marked contrast, our research with serving officers revealed the exceptional range of skills required: innate qualities such as mental toughness, objectivity, compassion, bravery, thoroughness, interpersonal skills and a drive to help others ahead of personal considerations.

   It was essential that advertising solicited a response from people of this mindset, rather than anyone motivated by superficial attractions – power, glamour, excitement, job security and so on.

4. Encouragement is too indiscriminating.

   The 'standard' recruitment strategy is to feature positive aspects of the job to encourage applicants; for example, spontaneous communication of Army recruitment advertising is 30% qualities needed to be a good soldier, 23% job

---

6. The task represented recruiting one out of every 4546 eligible adults. Sources: National Statistics, Home Office.

prospects, 20% positive role of the army, 19% exciting lifestyle (source: IPA Effectiveness paper).

Indeed, local police forces' advertising follows this encouragement route:

'Have you ever wanted a career where no two days are the same?'

'A life with variety. A career for life.'

Local force advertising

Research confirmed that these kinds of messages have broad appeal. Too broad in fact. They appeal disproportionately to less suitable candidates who are likely to withdraw or be rejected during the application process.

'That's what they should do. It's got helicopters, detective work, variety. That makes it more appealing to me.'

Male 21, rejected applicant

Advertising that 'over-sold' the job's attractions therefore risked diluting quality.

5. Low respect hinders willingness to apply.

While the decision to apply is deeply personal, potential applicants are swayed by family and peers' opinions. It is human nature to be influenced by the perceived status of your chosen career.

Low esteem for the Police was clearly affecting disposition to apply.

'Becoming a Police Officer was seen as something that would make you deeply unpopular.'

Source: BMRB, 2000

'Your mates'd think you've gone soft in the head.'

Male, 20–30, 2000

Indeed, perceived lack of respect for the Police ranks third among the major factors deterring applicants, above pay (Figure 5).

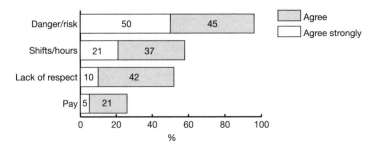

Figure 5: *Concerns about joining the Police*
Source: Consensus 2001

While advertising cannot alleviate these other concerns, it could have a role in combating low respect.

A DIFFERENT APPROACH

Combining these observations, it was clear that advertising needed a dramatically different strategy.

- It needed to issue a powerful challenge.
- It needed to actively *discourage* the vast majority of viewers, while inspiring a tiny minority of the most committed.
- Also, by driving widespread respect for the Police, advertising could encourage this minority to apply.

This is creatively expressed as:

> Make 999 out of every 1000 people
> realise they couldn't be a police officer,
> but respect like hell the one who could.

ADMITTING FAILURE

The resulting advertising was inspired by interviewing serving police officers. Each challenged us with profoundly difficult situations they had faced in the line of duty.

Reflecting on the qualities needed to handle scenarios such as these, the planner reported back:

'I, for one, couldn't do that.'

The advertising idea came directly from this comment. It features well-known, respected figures admitting they haven't got the qualities needed to be a police officer.

Each spokesperson contemplates a challenging police scenario, concluding that they themselves couldn't do it, raising the question '*Could you?*'

The featured scenarios are chosen to poignantly counterpoint each spokesperson's obvious strengths. For example, Lennox Lewis struggles to restrain himself from punching a wife-beater and Bob Geldof is unable to separate a child from its abusive parents.

THE POWER OF '*I COULDN'T*'

Research shows that the admission of defeat acts as a profound catalyst.

The challenge forces consideration which solicits two types of response. Most are put off, but nevertheless are filled with respect for the Police. Meanwhile, it triggers strong interest among a minority with a particular mindset, whose desire to apply is supported by the perceived respect. We illustrate this as shown in Figure 6.

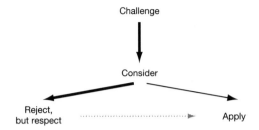

Figure 6

We will show how *'I couldn't'* drives these effects.

- By improving respect it helps boost morale, curtail resignations, reduce fear of crime and influence press reporting.
- Meanwhile the challenge encourages an exceptional rate, quality and speed of applications.

CREATING IMPACT

Most advertising seeks to attract attention by being enjoyable, colourful, pacy, noisy and easy to consume. And rightly so. Studies show enjoyability, liveliness and ease of viewing correlate strongly with impact.

> 'Enjoyability is a key component of the Awareness Index (AI), correlates with both message communication and persuasion and is a strong determinant of an ad's overall effectiveness.'

> 'The Link Test database shows that advertising rated highly on the active/passive scale tends to have higher branded impact.'

> Source: Millward Brown International

However, this is not to say that all advertising must be all these things to be effective. Far from it.

This campaign's negative approach is purposefully uncomfortable, mono-chrome, slow-paced, quiet and taxing. Research shows this makes it stand out from the media clutter and from other recruitment activity.

> 'The advertising is seen as highly distinctive within the break – still, slow paced, long periods of silence, sense of things left unsaid, stark, clinical, no music or special effects. In strong contrast with other fast, loud and quick-cutting ads.'

> 'There's not even a hint of glamour there. It's not like the "fast cars" approach.'

> Source: *The Nursery*

Furthermore, the thought-provoking approach stimulates engagement, making it particularly memorable (Figure 7).

> 'It forces you to concentrate on what the celebrity is saying and what it'd be like to be in that situation yourself.'

> *The Nursery*

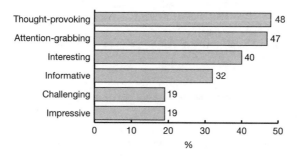

Figure 7: *Description of advertising*
Base: All aware of advertising
Source: Taylor Nelson Sofres

As a result, the advertising has lodged in the minds of an unprecedented 98% of the target.[7]

More importantly, its message has been steadily drilled into their consciousness (Figure 8).

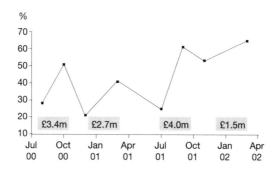

Figure 8: *Spontaneous replay of message*
Spontaneous recall of 'police do a difficult job', 'famous people saying they couldn't do it'
Source: Taylor Nelson Sofres

FORCING CONSIDERATION

The campaign doesn't simply generate passive message registration. The personal nature of others' fallibility forces people to consider themselves in relation to the scenarios and assess their own suitability.

> 'It's a very interesting approach that immediately made me ask myself what she is asking ... Oh my God, could I do it?'
>
> *The Nursery*

Unusually, people spontaneously credit advertising as the catalyst for their consideration of the Police.

---

7. Prompted TV recognition among the target of 18 to 34-year-olds. Source: Taylor Nelson Sofres tracking. We know of no higher score achieved by any campaign.

'It made my decision for me.
I suppose I'd had it at the back of my mind since I was about 12. I know people who've joined and I guess I'd always thought I might.
I thought about that old woman with the black eye and realised I didn't fancy that sort of thing. I guess I was really more interested in the glamorous side.'

Male, 26, non-applicant

'I thought seriously about it after seeing the advert. I hadn't really given it time to think before then.'

Asian female, 23, applicant

We can show that advertising influences active consideration by looking at people's curiosity about the job (Table 1). Whether or not they ultimately apply, those aware of the advertising are more likely to want further information.

TABLE 1: DESIRE TO FIND OUT MORE

	Among those spontaneously aware of advertising (%)	Among those *not* spontaneously aware of advertising (%)
Applicants	76	57
Non-applicants	61	33

Source: Consensus Follow Through Research

Web interactions also illustrate advertising driving consideration. Logs indicate that visitors directed to *www.policecouldyou.co.uk* by the advertising spend longer on the site, exploring it in more detail. Specifically, among the site's most visited areas are the simulation exercises, giving visitors an insight into the realities of the job, and the application pages (Table 2).

TABLE 2: APPLICATION PAGES

	policecouldyou.co.uk	Comparison sites*
Average pages viewed per visitor per visit	13.9	10.1
Average length of time spent on site (mins)	12.3	9.5

*Average of eight comparable Home Office sites on crime reduction, prisons, car crime, security on the web, drugs etc. As they are all information sites for particular 'interested' audiences these 'norms' are several times higher than the all-site average.

Sources: COI, Webtrends, eMC Saatchi

Significantly, research concludes that it is the admission of defeat that incites consideration. Scripts tested without '*I couldn't*' lack this impetus.

'Defeat is central. Seeing others admitting defeat acts as a spur to interrogate one's own abilities. Other routes communicate the same message but lack the motivational power.'

The Nursery

REJECTION DRIVES RESPECT

In line with the strategy, advertising creates a strong impression of the job's demands. In tracking, 'difficult' measures come through far stronger than 'positive' ones (Figure 9).

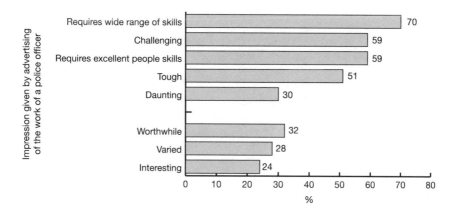

Figure 9: *Advertising shapes job perceptions*
Base: All aware of advertising
Source: Taylor Nelson Sofres

As a result, most people reject the Police, frequently blaming advertising as the cause.

'That's exactly why I didn't join.'

'They're asking for people who are superhuman.'

Non-responders

However, the act of considering and rejecting is not without value. Having ruled out the job personally, people appreciate the extent of what the Police do and view them with increased respect.

'You realise they're there to do something good, as opposed to just barging in and doing an arrest – more from a counselling side I suppose.'

'For somebody I respect as a brave person to say she couldn't do that job, the people who do must be braver than her.'

'It shows a more caring side, that they do other things and have a lot of emotional strength. Other things than just chasing after people and arresting villains.'

Rejecters, Consumer InSight

This fuels dramatic rises in respect and crucially *perceived* respect for the Police, previously in a 20-year decline.[8] The influence of advertising is particularly striking. The most recent data coincide with a negative PR period related to police reform. There was three times more negative than positive media coverage over this period (source: Echo). Nevertheless, the decline in respect among those aware of advertising is less marked (see Figures 10 and 11).

---

8. The perception of society's respect for the Police is a more relevant measure of the concern faced by potential applicants. Levels of perceived respect are markedly lower, but growing faster.

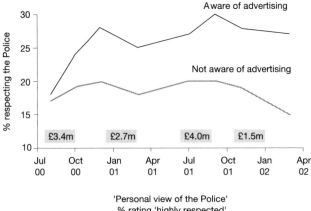

Figure 10: *Personal respect for the Police*
Base: 18–34-year-olds, split by aware/not aware of Police advertising
Source: Taylor Nelson Sofres

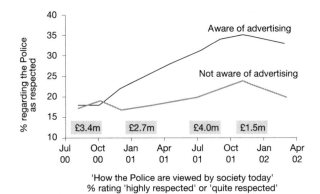

Figure 11: *Perceived respect for the Police*
Base: 18–34-year-olds, split by aware/not aware of Police advertising
Source: Taylor Nelson Sofres

This increased respect has in turn produced a number of useful knock-on effects which are outlined in the following subsections.

Morale

It is no secret that the service suffers motivation issues. A 1999 report indicated low morale in 84% of officers.[9]

Against this backdrop, serving officers praise the campaign for the public recognition it lends them.

---

9. Source: HM Inspectorate of Constabulary. Local force inspection. This was an isolated study, not repeated since.

There is strong anecdotal evidence of a positive campaign effect on pride in the job, perceived support and improved public regard, all powerful components of morale.

'There was universal support from Officers for the campaign. In particular, its ability to turn them into unsung heroes.'

Consumer InSight

'The perceived message to the public is "it's a difficult and necessary job that many people couldn't hack – it deserves your respect". For serving Officers, this flatters the job and the person.'

Cragg Ross Dawson

'When my wife sees that she understands exactly what I do. She realises why I come home late and stressed and sometimes don't even get home at all.'

Serving officer

By boosting admiration for the Police, the campaign has substantially improved perceptions of the appeal of the job (Figure 12).

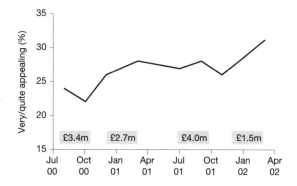

Figure 12: *Appeal of the job*
Source: Taylor Nelson Sofres

An indication of the value of this can be seen in 'wastage' from the service. The number of leavers has been gradually declining. However, as most are retirees, this is largely age related. Beneath this, resignations – a better indication of morale – were trending upwards.

Together with improved pay and conditions, the impact of advertising on morale has halted this trend (Figure 13).[10]

---

10. This does not only reflect the drop in the total number of leavers since the trend in resignations has levelled off as a proportion of all leavers as well as in absolute numbers. Pay levels did improve in 2001 at a level slightly above inflation and increases in previous years.

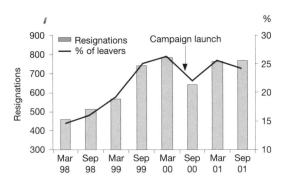

Figure 13: *Trend in resignations halted*
Six-monthly totals
Source: Home Office *Police Service Strength*

Fear of crime

The maxim 'perception *is* reality' is particularly apposite when it comes to crime figures.

While studies show UK crime steadily declining, public fear of crime is both substantially higher and has been increasing (Table 3).

TABLE 3

	% perceiving crime has risen over the last 2 years	Actual rise in crime over the last year (%)
UK adults	67	−12

Note: The British Crime Survey measures the public's claimed incidence of crime, which differs from police-reported crime figures. Nevertheless, both show the same downward trend in actual crime over the past five years.

Source: British Crime Survey, 2000

A number of factors fuel this disparity, including media reporting, amount of violent crime, fallibility of memory, and so on. By contrast, confidence in the Police and visibility of officers on the beat offers reassurance.[11]

By raising respect for the Police, advertising has boosted public confidence in the fight against crime (Figure 14). This goes some way to reversing the upward trend in fear of crime (Figure 15). The reduction is greater than could be explained purely by the increase in serving officers over the period. Furthermore, the rate of reduction in crime actually slowed over this period (−3% to −2%; source: British Crime Survey).

---

11. Source: 'Open All Hours – an inspection report on the role of police visibility and accessibility in public reassurance', Home Office.

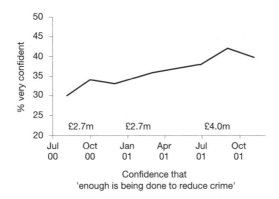

Figure 14: *Increased confidence in crime reduction*
Base: All adults
Source: Taylor Nelson Sofres

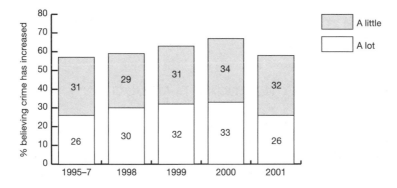

Figure 15: *Reduction in perceived crime*
Source: British Crime Survey

Media reporting

Police matters naturally attract large amounts of press coverage, much of it negative. Before the campaign this was in the ratio 20% positive to 53% negative.

We know the campaign has the same pattern of influence with national newspaper editors as the public at large.

> 'It's strong advertising. At a time when it's open season on criticising the Police, it's a timely reminder of all they have to deal with.'
>
> Andrew Neil[12]

> 'It proves one thing, I couldn't do that job.'
>
> Piers Morgan, Editor-in-Chief, Mirror Newspapers

It is therefore significant that, while negative stories still predominate, their proportion has declined significantly since the campaign (Figure 16).

---

12. Andrew Neil has been Editor of *The Economist* and *The Sunday Times*. At the time of this campaign he was Editor-in-Chief of the *Scotsman*, the *European* and *Sunday Business*.

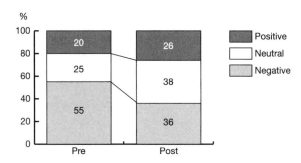

Figure 16: *Shift in media reporting*
Nature of national newspaper police stories 2001 versus 1999, analysis conducted December
Sources: Profound, Reuters, Echo

Furthermore, research suggests that the public's appetite for negative reporting has been suppressed.

'Sometimes the papers should leave off. With everything they do, the Police deserve a break.'

Male, 27, non-applicant

REJECTION PROMPTS APPLICATION

Having shown that rejection yields many indirect effects, we now illustrate its power at prompting direct response.

The idea of other people admitting defeat acts as a spur to a small but significant minority, many of whom openly credit the rejection idea with their desire to respond.

'Lennox Lewis, for all his fame, talent and money, couldn't do that job, whereas I reckon I could.'

Applicant

'Who could say for sure they could handle something like that? I was prepared to find out.'

Applicant, recent recruit

This explains the marked pattern of response corresponding to the advertising (Figures 17 and 18).

Despite only a tiny minority responding positively to the dissuasion strategy, the response in absolute numbers is significant. Comparison with previous IPA Effectiveness winners shows this is the most efficient published recruitment campaign (Table 4).

TABLE 4: RECRUITMENT CAMPAIGNS

	Cost per application (£)	Cost per recruit (£)
Police recruitment	151	583
Army recruitment	208	652
Metropolitan Police (1988)	156	819
Nursing recruitment	234	846
RAF recruitment	309	965
RAF officer recruitment	494	n/a
Navy recruitment	634	n/a

Note: Costs at 2001 prices
Sources: IPA data BANK, Broadsystems

SILVER

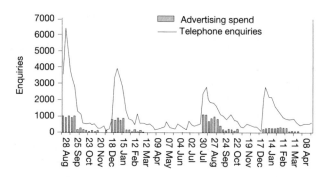

Figure 17: *Telephone response to advertising*
All recruitment enquiries on 0845 6083000
Source: Broadsystems

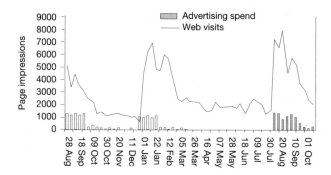

Figure 18: *Web response to advertising*
Impressions on *www.policecouldyou.co.uk* home page
Source: Home Office

The right kind of enquirers

The campaign is efficient not only in the number of enquiries generated, but also in the *nature* of enquirers.

The minority motivated by the challenge tend to have the right innate qualities.

'Those expressing interest were a close emotional fit with the Police.'

The Nursery

Thirty-seven per cent of enquirers phoning in response to the advertising request an application form, indicating the extent to which they have already self-selected. Prior to this campaign, the established enquiry-to-application ratio was 25%.

In addition, the desire to 'try before you buy' in private means that the website has played a vital role in engaging suitable applicants. People respond to the advertising by visiting the site for further consideration. The web received 93,315 such visitors in an advertised month, compared with 10,010 telephone enquiries.

We estimate that 19% of all site visitors complete a request for an application form online, indicating the further filtering that the site content produces.

We should note the web's power as a direct response channel. In line with common advertising practice, the phone number is far more prominent than the URL. However, the fact that customers need to consider, research and investigate before they commit means the web attracts nine times the response and accounts for 61% of applications (this compares favourably with 30% for Army recruitment).[13]

As well as being an efficient source of applications, the advertising is effective at driving final recruits. In total, the recruits-to-applications ratio is 1:5. The equivalent ratio prior to the campaign was 1:7. This further supports anecdotal feedback from recruiting officers on the high calibre of applicants.

As a result, the recruitment process is 13% more efficient, with less time spent processing unsuitable applicants.

Specific audiences

The campaign is also efficient at motivating particular subgroups. There are three demographics the Police are especially keen to attract: young, female and ethnic minorities.

However, there are sensitivities in overtly soliciting these groups. For example, some ethnic minorities regard being specifically targeted as a racist act in itself. Women likewise are sensitive to any suggestion that they are being recruited on a less than equal basis.

This campaign features spokespeople of the appropriate age/sex/ethnicity, who are suitable for reasons far more prominent than their demographic profile. This alleviates any suggestion of 'token' targeting, while ensuring the advertising registers disproportionately with the relevant groups (Table 5).

TABLE 5: RECALL BY SUBGROUP

	Total	18–34	Women	Black	Asian
Simon Weston	85	90	86	76	74
Patsy Palmer	68	83	76	59	50
Joan Bakewell	36	36	44	28	69
John Barnes	63	71	58	69	58
Lennox Lewis	73	85	69	90	78
Chris Bisson	49	54	52	63	69

Prompted TV execution by execution
Source: Taylor Nelson Sofres

This has attracted increased applications from women and ethnic minorities (Figures 19 and 20), and from young people (constituting 88% of all enquiries).

This has resulted in corresponding uplifts in recruits. Ethnic minority officer numbers are growing four times faster than the service in total and over twice the rate they were before the campaign. Likewise, female officer numbers are growing at twice the rate they were before advertising (Figures 21 and 22).

---

13. Source: COI/IPA Effectiveness Databank.

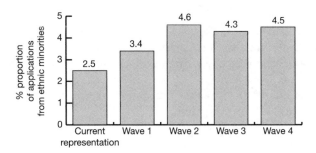

Figure 19: *Increased ethnic minority applications*
Source: Broadsystems

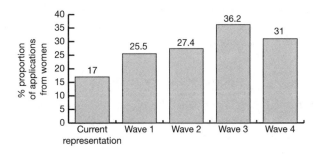

Figure 20: *Increased female application*
Source: Broadsystems

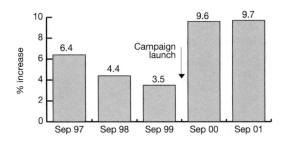

Figure 21: *Growth in ethnic minority officers*
Twelve-monthly totals
Source: Home Office *Police Service Strength*

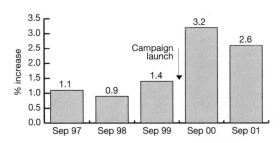

Figure 22: *Growth in female officers*
Twelve-monthly totals
Source: Home Office *Police Service Strength*

Speed of response

The 'purchase process' for the Police can take anything from days to several years. It is significant therefore that this campaign's effects begin almost immediately – within minutes of the advertising airing in the case of enquiries, within months for recruitment figures.

In part this is due to an increased urgency to recruit. However, it also reflects the galvanising effect of the campaign.

'I saw it and went for it. I'd been dithering for so long.'

Female applicant

Indeed, with applications currently being processed, the campaign has achieved its objective of helping recruit 9000 officers ahead of schedule. Such is the speed of response that the Home Secretary's new target for the campaign (130,000 officers by March 2004) has subsequently been brought forward by a year to spring 2003. Projections show that the campaign is on track to achieve this more testing target.

Boosting indirect response

Not all the uplift in recruits is explained by direct response to national advertising. Local force initiatives, from open days and career fairs through to local advertising, continue to successfully attract applicants.

While local forces are predisposed to champion the success of their own initiatives, 71% of them acknowledge that the national campaign has affected their recruitment, 70% commenting spontaneously on increased applications.[14]

Indeed, by discounting recruits attributable to the CFF, we can see that local activity has indeed been progressively more effective since the introduction of the national campaign (Figure 23).

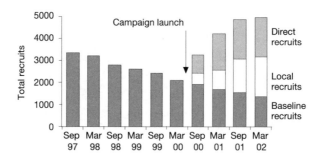

Figure 23: *Uplift in indirect recruits*
Six-monthly totals
Source: Home Office *Police Service Strength*

Indeed, the force's own activity, running in conjunction with '*Could you?*', is 72% more effective (on the assumption that baseline recruitment numbers would otherwise have continued their decline).

---

14. Source: PCRU research into local force selection and recruitment procedures.

Local activity is largely unchanged in nature across the period and only increased in volume by 21%, suggesting that the contribution of the national campaign to this boost in effectiveness is substantial. This is consistent with someone being intrigued by the '*Could you?*' advertising, then spotting and responding to local force advertising announcing vacancies.

Interestingly, the British Transport Police, whose recruitment processes are unrelated, has reported a similar uplift.

Sincere flattery

While not strictly an effectiveness measure, elements of this strategy have been adopted by other recruitment campaigns, notably:

'99.99% need not apply.'

Royal Marines recruitment endline

MULTIPLE EFFECTS

The effects of the advertising can therefore be summarised as in Figure 24.

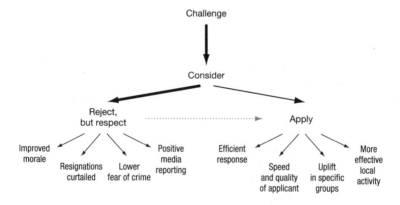

Figure 24: *Effects of advertising*

Good value

While profit is meaningless in the context of public service, we can assess the value for money the UK taxpayer receives from this approach.

The campaign has cost £15 million to date.[15] Across the lifespan of the CFF, advertising will represent just 6% of expenditure.

---

15. Source: COI. The total cost for 20 months' activity to date, including all production, media, professional fees, repeat fees and VAT, is £15.02 million.

To assess value for money, we examine alternative means of achieving the same result.

Cynics initially suggested '*they should stop wasting money on advertising and just pay the Police more*'. However, a modest increase of £2000 per head would have cost the taxpayer £428 million over this period alone, plus an ongoing £260 million per annum.

Alternatively, others suggest that officers themselves could stimulate enquiries by 'talking up' the job to the public. Conservatively, 1% of their time spent doing this would cost £124 million in lost Police resources.[16]

Conservatively, the costs of subcontracting the whole task to private sector recruitment consultants have been estimated at £43 million.[17]

The result could instead have been achieved by local activity. However, before '*Could you?*', local activity wasn't reversing the decline in numbers. Without the boost in effectiveness from the national campaign, approximately 2.3 times the budget would have been needed to achieve the same result – a cost of £62 million.

While it was never a viable option, the consequences of reducing application standards to boost recruitment are not without cost implications. A mere 10% decrease in recruits' efficiency 'costs' £52 million a year in police resources.[18]

On the basis of these calculations, the '*Could you?*' campaign has to date saved the UK taxpayer at least £30 million.

It is also reassuring to note that on a cost per response basis, the campaign represents at least 10% better value than other proven recruitment campaigns.

Added value

Response alone represents good value; however, the 'respect' factor contributes significant added value.

It is disingenuous to put a financial value on the improvements in respect, morale, resignations and press coverage. However, it is instructive to quantify the value of reduced fear of crime.

The advertising has contributed to a 13% reduction in perceived crime. To have achieved this via direct reduction in crime itself would have required £964 million, based on increasing the cost of running the force by 13% to achieve an equivalent reduction in crime. This is a modest assumption, since the returns on investment in crime reduction are not linear. Even if advertising were responsible for just 5% of the perceived reduction, its worth would be £48 million, more than three times its cost.

16. This is based on 1% of the £7.4 billion annual cost of financing the force, extended pro rata to 20 months (source: Police Funding).
17. This is based on a commission on salary. Given the difficulty in attracting the right candidates a rate in the region of 25% would be charged.
18. Ten per cent of 9000 officers represents 0.7% of Police resources, equivalent to £52 million.

CONCLUSION

Hopefully we have established that the counter-intuitive, negative approach produced this campaign's positive effects.

As a response-generating exercise alone, its efficiency represents 'best value' for the UK taxpayer.

The broader added value comes as a bonus. However, it alone is a significant multiple of the investment.

The wider lesson of this case is the benefit of establishing *exactly* how advertising is likely to work. The more rigorously defined and inventively articulated this is, the more powerful the advertising is likely to be.

18

Sainsbury's

A recipe for success

Principal authors: Bridget Angear and Rebecca Moody,
Abbott Mead Vickers.BBDO
Collaborating authors: Paul Baker and Beate Lettmann, OHAL,
and Nicola Rogers, Millward Brown

EDITOR'S SUMMARY

Since 2000, TV advertising has helped turn around Sainsbury's business fortunes, delivering £1.12 billion in incremental revenue and an ROI of £27.25 for every advertising pound spent. In reinvigorating the brand mission of 'Pioneering better-quality everyday food', it has given customers new food ideas that have encouraged them to shop, cook and eat differently. This has helped halt defection and enticed loyalists to spend more at Sainsbury's, ultimately helping to improve shareholder value – potentially to the tune of £1.76 billion.

INTRODUCTION

This paper demonstrates the contribution TV advertising has made to the turnaround in Sainsbury's business fortunes since 2000. It is an old-fashioned argument about the power of TV in effecting an attitudinal and behavioural change, resulting in sales uplift.

Econometric modelling shows that the Sainsbury's campaign featuring Jamie Oliver has delivered £1.12 billion of incremental revenue – making it 65% more effective in generating sales than any previous Sainsbury's advertising modelled – and delivered a substantial return on investment of £69,000 revenue per TVR, or £27.25 for every advertising pound spent.

It has done this by conveying a more modern expression of the Sainsbury's brand essence of 'pioneering better-quality everyday food', galvanising the entire business behind that single thought, and giving consumers new food ideas that have encouraged them to shop, cook and eat differently.

This encouragement has helped arrest defection and enticed loyalists to spend more of their grocery money with Sainsbury's, ultimately helping improve the value of the company to shareholders – potentially to the tune of £1.76 billion.

It has provided Sainsbury's with a recipe for success on which to build a brighter future.

A GLORIOUS HISTORY

J. Sainsbury's supermarkets were established 133 years ago in Drury Lane by the founder, John Sainsbury (see Figure 1).

Initially selling only the most basic provisions such as eggs, bacon and 'the best butter in the world', John aimed to set the highest product standards in London versus his early grocery competitors like Lipton. His initial sales pitch was 'Quality perfect, prices lower'.

Sainsbury's was a dominant player in the grocery market through to the 1990s. Between 1987 and 1992, sales saw double-digit increases, profit growth never fell below 20% and the company had a firm grasp on the No. 1 spot (sources: SSL Company Reports, Verdict).

Figure 1

THE FALL FROM GRACE

For many years, Tesco had been pursuing a policy of bullish acquisition, culminating in 1994 with the purchase of the Scottish chain William Low which gave them the critical mass needed to dominate the market.

Further clinchers included the instigation of new pioneering formats like Metro and Express, the opening of concessions such as pharmacies, and high levels of service innovation (most notably Clubcard), all under the profitable banner of 'Every Little Helps'.

Customers voted with their feet and Sainsbury's lost the No. 1 market share slot in 1995 (see Figure 2).

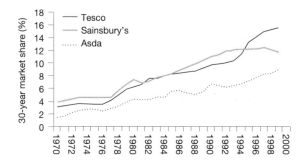

Figure 2: *1995 – Sainsbury's loses market leadership*
Source: IGD

Sainsbury's like-for-like sales[1] started to steadily decline and finally dropped into negative figures in the financial year 1999–2000 to –0.2% (see Figure 3).

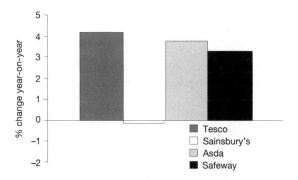

Figure 3: *Sainsbury's like-for-like sales decline 1999–2000*
Source: IGD Research, HSBC

---

1. Like-for-like sales = sales in stores that were open in the same period in the previous year.

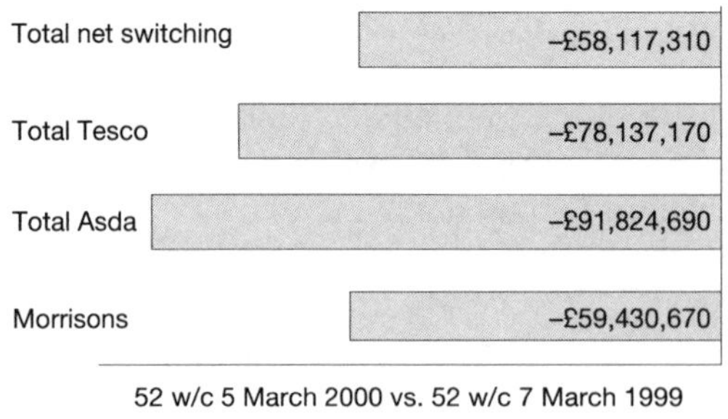

Total net switching	−£58,117,310
Total Tesco	−£78,137,170
Total Asda	−£91,824,690
Morrisons	−£59,430,670

52 w/c 5 March 2000 vs. 52 w/c 7 March 1999

Figure 4: *Sainsbury's switching 2000 vs. 1999 – heavy losses*
Source: TNS

In the same year, prior to the launch of the new advertising campaign, Sainsbury's was losing spend most notably to Tesco, Asda and Morrisons to the tune of £299 million (see Figure 4).

THE DAWNING OF A NEW AGE

In March 2000, Sir Peter Davis returned to Sainsbury's as chief executive after a fifteen-year absence. He was under no illusion regarding the enormity of the challenge:

'I don't think the problems were as severe as at Marks & Spencer, but they were quite severe. The decline in profitability was remorseless ... we were vulnerable to a takeover ... a raider could come in and look at £5 billion of property and say that is more than the market capitalisation of the whole company.'

Source: *The Sunday Times*, 5 August 2000

His strategy was simple: the company had to go back to its basics of quality fresh food. Sainsbury's had lost the mantle of being the UK's No. 1 supermarket, but it could be consumers' first choice for food. This meant embarking on a total business reinvigoration: store refurbishments,[2] streamlining the supply chain including overhauling stock control and ordering systems, and innovating once more within Sainsbury's own brand.

Sir Peter knew these changes would take time to come to fruition and wanted a more immediate signal to the outside world that Sainsbury's was changing. His marketing team, headed up by Sara Weller, was tasked with, among other things, developing a new TV campaign that could provide this signal and begin the much-needed process of brand reappraisal.

THE ROLE FOR ADVERTISING

The advertising had two key roles: to inspire people to want to shop at Sainsbury's again; and to galvanise the business behind a single thought.

---

2. The Reinvigorate store refurbishment plan started in January 2001, but rolled out in earnest in April 2001.

Inspiring people to shop at Sainsbury's again

While Sainsbury's had remained static for almost a decade, consumers had changed. They were spending more, specifically on eating out and food and drink, and many trends were pointing towards a heightened interest in food – whether it be experimentation with new ingredients, reassurance over sourcing, healthy eating, or a simple desire to be a better cook (source: Mintel British Lifestyles). The media were quick to embrace this interest via an increase in consumer food magazines, cookbooks and the rise of the '90s cult of the celebrity chef.[3]

Sainsbury's, with its heritage in food, had an opportunity to tap into these trends in order to reassert its relevance to consumers. Going back to its founding principles of pioneering better-quality everyday food would give the brand a strong point of difference given that the market leader (Tesco) increasingly owned service, while Asda and Morrisons owned price.

However, qualitative research had highlighted that tonally Sainsbury's had lost touch with consumers and was

'Too elitist, too upmarket and a little too arrogant.'

Source: Patrick Corr Qualitative Research 1998

Advertising therefore had to fuse the historical strengths of the brand with a more contemporary, down-to-earth personality (Table 1).

TABLE 1: A MORE CONTEMPORARY PERSONALITY

Elitist	$\longrightarrow$	Everyone
Arrogant	$\longrightarrow$	Approachable
Aspirational	$\longrightarrow$	Accessible
Patronising	$\longrightarrow$	Passionate
Fastidious	$\longrightarrow$	Fun-loving

Source: Patrick Corr Qualitative Research

The advertising would also need to create renewed salience for the brand. Throughout the early '90s, advertising for Sainsbury's had trickled along almost unnoticed while Tesco's 'Dotty' campaign went from strength to strength. Millward Brown modelled the Sainsbury's Awareness Index[4] to be 2–3 while Tesco was 7 on average.

Galvanising the business behind a single thought

Sainsbury's Supermarkets Limited (SSL) is a complex business comprising 480 stores, employing 140,000 staff and selling on average more than 56,000 different products in each store. The advertising would therefore need to act as a beacon that ensured everyone was working towards a single aim. It would also have to be flexible enough to carry a number of different innovations generated by such a multi-faceted business.[5]

---

3. In 2000, *Celebrity Ready Steady Cook* was drawing audiences of 7.4m mid-week, almost equal to that of *Casualty* on Saturday (Source: BARB).
4. Awareness Index = % increase in advertising awareness per 100 GRPs.
5. Innovations included new products, range extensions, value propositions, sub-brand launches.

THE ADVERTISING BRIEF

The advertising brief was a combination of two things (see Figure 5). The aim was to stop any more consumers leaving the brand, and to encourage existing shoppers to shop differently.

Figure 5: *The advertising brief*

THE ADVERTISING IDEA

The advertising idea needed to focus Sainsbury's brand strengths in quality food and innovation and then magnify their significance and relevance to customers. We wanted to use a chef as an advocate for Sainsbury's as he/she would demand high standards from the supermarket in which they shopped.

Inspiration arrived in the form of Jamie Oliver, a 24-year-old, moped-riding chef (see Figure 6) – a breath of fresh air in the fussy world of cooking and a living embodiment of the personality and values Sainsbury's was looking for. Jamie himself had a brand print that was an almost perfect fit with where Sainsbury's wished to be (see Figure 7). He's a man who lives and breathes passion for food and is genuine about his mission to get everyone to enjoy better-tasting food. And Sainsbury's gives him 11,000,000 shoppers a week to convert to the cause.

Figure 6

Brand vision	Brand benefits
Get stuck in!	I feel guided, not instructed
	I have the confidence to give it a bash
Brand mission	I love that feeling of accomplishment
Fresh ideas ...	
Better food ...	Brand promise
Fantastic times ...	To give people more than they expect
Happy days ...!	
	Brand position
Brand personality	Jamie Oliver takes the concept of cooking,
Accessible	food and fantastic times to a whole new
Passionate	level of accessibility
Inspiring	
Eclectic	By breathing passion and common sense
True	into everything he touches, he inspires
Fun	people, young and old, to keep things
Adventurous	simple and Get Stuck In!

Figure 7: *Jamie's brand print*
Source: Jamie Oliver Brand Consultancy

Qualitative research, conducted at the outset of the campaign, concluded:

'Response to the campaign has been very positive, and indicates that its development to date has been almost entirely well-founded ... Jamie Oliver contributes an accessible quality message and very considerable appeal. His most overt and immediate contribution is in terms of personality, and he works very well to raise brand perceptions. His use evokes a more down-to-earth, accessible brand image, but also one which is contemporary, youthful, dynamic, interesting, shaking off the past staidness of the brand and in itself making shoppers more disposed to Sainsbury's.'

Source: Sadek Wynberg Research, 2001

It was Jamie's 'realness' that helped set the Sainsbury's campaign apart from others in the category. As one observer put it:

'The reason why the Jamie Oliver ads work so well is because there is a genuine match between him and the brand values Sainsbury's is trying to project. If there wasn't, we wouldn't believe it was a real situation and it would come across as crass.'

Source: Nicola Medelsohn, Business Development Director BBH, quoted in *Retail Week*, June 2001

The combination of Sainsbury's, with its heritage in food, and Jamie with his passion, energy and 'do-able' recipes, had the potential to affect the nation's shopping, cooking and eating habits.

Since the campaign broke in June 2000, 41 executions have been made featuring Jamie and his family (see Figure 8), continually inspiring customers with new ideas to make everyday life taste better.

Figure 8: *Jamie and his family*

THE MEDIA STRATEGY

PHD's media strategy has been twofold. First, to use evidence from econometric modelling to optimise the laydown against driving short-term sales. Second, to ensure the quality of the airtime enhances the performance of the communication.

Econometric modelling

OHAL has been able to calculate the point of diminishing returns in the effectiveness of TV advertising in contributing to sales (see Figure 9).[6] From this a weekly ratings target has been derived. This information, combined with additional data about the best balance of coverage[7] and frequency,[8] has provided tight parameters for managing the airtime.

Figure 9: *Sales consequences of different budgets – TV*
Source: OHAL

'Quality' airtime

Despite these tight parameters, airtime quality has also been influenced. Billett & Company identified a link between advertising recall and position in break (Table 2).

TABLE 2: THE LINK BETWEEN ADVERTISING RECALL AND
POSITION IN BREAK

Airtime descriptor	Ad recall
1st, 2nd or last ad in break	28% higher recall
Centre break of programme vs. going-in break or end break	9% higher

Source: Billett & Company

Using this learning, airtime for Sainsbury's has subsequently improved relative to key competitors on 'position in break' and proportion of centre breaks (Table 3).

---

6. Actual numbers have been removed from this chart due to issues of confidentiality.
7. Coverage = the percentage of the target audience who have been exposed to the campaign.
8. Frequency = the average number of times they are exposed to the campaign.

TABLE 3: SAINSBURY'S IMPROVED POSITION IN BREAK (%)

	Pre-Jamie Jan–June 2002	Jamie June–Dec 2000	Jamie Jan–Dec 2001
1st/2nd/last in break			
Sainsbury's	63	64	73
Tesco	47	42	43
Asda	40	39	34
% in centre break			
Sainsbury's	64	68	75
Tesco	70	69	73
Asda	60	60	66

Source: Billett & Company

Performance in 2001 was particularly strong for advertising spots that appear first-in-break (see Figure 10).

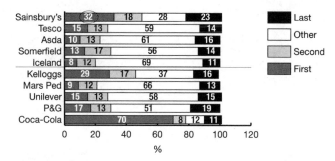

Figure 10: *Sainsbury's first-in-break more than competition*
Base: Housewives with children
Source: Billetts & Company

Another key assessment of airtime quality is the percentage of total TVRs that appear in 'Top 20' programmes. Figure 11 shows a definite improvement in the airtime quality since the onset of the campaign.

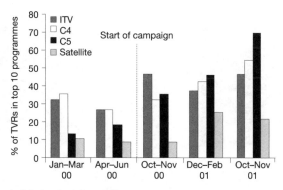

Figure 11: *Improvement in Sainsbury's airtime quality*
Source: PHD

EXAMPLES OF THE WORK

JO: Boys, do you fancy a ruby?
Right, your place, 20 minutes

JO: Garlic, lemongrass, coriander ... bit of coconut milk

JO: Right guys, how hot do you want it?

JO: I'm doing the garlic guys ... hope you're not seeing the girls tomorrow!

JO: right have you got the wok?

JO: Coconut milk ... happy days

JO: One spicy prawn curry
Mates: Nah, not up for it

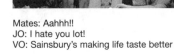

Mates: Aahhh!!
JO: I hate you lot!
VO: Sainsbury's making life taste better

Figure 12: *Lads' Night Out (40 seconds)*

Music: Elgar's *Pomp and Circumstance*

Music and fireworks sound effects

Series of explosions as the potatoes
bubble in the pan

Sound of crackers going off as Jamie
drops the sausages into the frying pan

Sounds of fireworks in time with the
chopping

MVO: Sainsbury's is committed to
bringing you great British food

MVO: Rediscover your British favourites
with Sainsbury's

MVO: Sainsbury's, making life taste better

Figure 13: *Fireworks (30 seconds)*

JO: Nice little bit of goose fat

JO: Bit of garlic

JO: Get the old zest in there, nice and Christmassy

JO: What else shall we have ... A nice bit of sage

JO: Let's chop up the old spuds

JO: Ah, the smell of that

JO: Nice and crispy

FVO: Roast potatoes with orange, sage and goose fat ...

FVO: ... at Sainsbury's

Figure 14: *Goose Fat (20 seconds)*

JO: Neh Dey Sown Ci Di Mu Yah
– Thai Go Choi, Eui Nan Choi, Szechuan
Choi?

FVO: Anyone can go oriental …

… with Sainsbury's new Oriental range,
the widest selection …

… of oriental delights in any supermarket

Mate: Buy Duck Haw Lian, Low Yow

JO: Pukkaa!

Figure 15: *Oriental (30 seconds)*

THE ADVERTISING EFFECT

Sales have shown the first green shoots of recovery

Sainsbury's like-for-like sales showed their first positive recovery in Q1 (April–June) 2000, lifting to a modest 2.1% by the end of the 2000–01 financial year. This growth has since increased with the company enjoying a '*magical Christmas*' (source: Sara Weller) in 2001 with customers returning from Tesco for the first time in several years and a rise of 6.8% in sales in the quarter ending March 2002 (source: IGD). Market share growth also started to stabilise in late 2000, turning positive in 2001 (source: IGD).

To quote Sir Peter Davis on the final quarter 2001–02 results:

'For the first time (in 5½ years) we are showing six months of market share gains.'

Source: *Wall Street Journal*, 15 April 2002

Retail analysts at Goldman Sachs have labelled this a '*creditable performance*' (source: *Wall Street Journal*, 15 April 2002).

While it would appear the supertanker has regained course, how much of this can we attribute to the TV campaign?

Econometric modelling indicates substantial TV advertising contribution

Sainsbury's have employed ongoing econometric modelling since the early 1990s through OHAL to help isolate advertising return. The latest modelling data from September 2001 estimated that the TV campaign has made a contribution of some £1.12 billion to sales since its introduction in June 2000, and a return on investment of £69,000 revenue per TVR[9] (see Figure 16). This makes it 65% more

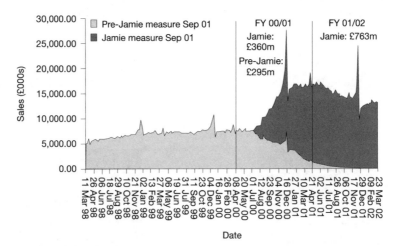

Figure 16: *Jamie TV advertising has contributed £1.12 billion revenue*
Source: OHAL

---

9. Based on the one complete year of the Jamie campaign (01/02), TV advertising has contributed £763m of revenue (six months measured, six months extrapolated). This suggests a better pro rata performance than the rival Tesco 'Dotty' campaign which delivered £552m p.a. over its first five years (source: OHAL, Tesco IPA Grand Prix 2000).

effective in generating sales than any previous Sainsbury's advertising modelled (source: OHAL).

How has advertising helped achieve sales success?

We now set out to demonstrate how advertising has helped boost Sainsbury's fortunes.

By making the brand more salient
A core objective of the new advertising was to make Sainsbury's front of mind again. To that end, claimed TV advertising awareness has risen significantly over the course of the campaign (see Figure 17). To quote Millward Brown in March 2002:

'... strong creative has increased TV ad awareness past Tesco ...'

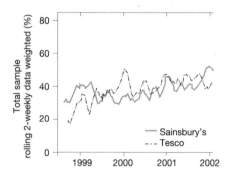

Figure 17: *Sainsbury's claimed TV ad awareness surpassing competitors*
Source: Millward Brown, March 2002

Low advertising efficiency had also been a serious issue. However, modelling of the Sainsbury's Awareness Index has shown steadily increasing returns over recent campaigns, culminating in an impressive AI of 12 for the Christmas executions of 2001 vs. the retail average of 6 (source: Millward Brown BIAT).

Sainsbury's now has a well-branded and competitive advertising property (see Figure 18), which has in turn proved itself enjoyable and involving over and above retail sector norms (see Figure 19).

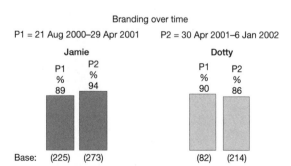

Figure 18: *A well-branded advertising property* vis-à-vis *competition*
Source: Millward Brown BIAT, March 2002

Enjoyment of 'Jamie Oliver' campaign

Jamie average	73
UK retail average	68

Figure 19: *Jamie enjoys higher than average 'enjoyment'*
Base: Total sample (661)
Source: Millward Brown BIAT, March 2002

By re-establishing the brand's role in people's lives

The campaign is deemed a close fit with the brand, reminding shoppers of the good things about the offer (see Figure 20).

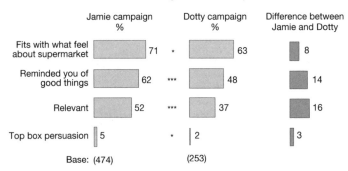

August 2000–January 2002

	Jamie campaign %		Dotty campaign %	Difference between Jamie and Dotty
Fits with what feel about supermarket	71	*	63	8
Reminded you of good things	62	***	48	14
Relevant	52	***	37	16
Top box persuasion	5	*	2	3
Base:	(474)		(253)	

Figure 20: *'Jamie' is felt to be a good fit with Sainsbury's*
* = 95% significant, ** = 99% significant, *** = 99.9% significant
Source: Millward Brown BIAT, March 2002

And a renewed understanding of its promise (see Figure 21).

Sainsbury's – diagnosis of presence vs. category

	1998		2001
Unaided awareness	36	*	43
Ever tried	18		24
Aware of promise[10]	21	*	27
Base:	(401)		(400)

Figure 21: *Jamie has improved Sainsbury's brand understanding*
* = 95% significant, ** = 99% significant, *** = 99.9% significant
Source: WPP BrandZ Study

---

10. Aware of promise is defined as having an opinion of the brand via endorsement on the image grid.

12/11/01–6/1/02	Sainsbury's	Asda	Tesco	Safeway
		Difference from expected		
High-quality fresh fruit and vegetables	3	+4	+1	+2
Have fresh ideas	7	+1	+1	0
High-quality own-label products	4	+7	+3	+4
Are food experts	6	+11	+12	+5
Wide range of luxury products	17	+12	+7	+5

Base: Total sample (661)

Figure 22: *Sainsbury's has reasserted quality image profile*
Base: Total sample (661)
Source: Millward Brown, BIAT, March 2002

This broader promise, over and above the communication of products and own-label ranges, is a rebirth in the understanding of Sainsbury's passion for 'good food for all'. This has in turn helped better distinguish Sainsbury's from competitors[11] (Figure 22).

Recent qualitative feedback corroborates that the campaign has provided a reinvigorating and fresh take on Sainsbury's:

'The idea that Jamie Oliver, who loves to cook, knows what he wants, is not prepared to compromise on quality, chooses to shop in Sainsbury's is a strong, credible endorsement of the brand.'

Source: Sadek Wynberg, March 2002

The campaign has also built greater affinity with Sainsbury's among shoppers (source: Brand Dynamics™) delivering both a performance which matched this promise (+7) and renewed market edge (+6) (Figure 23).[12]

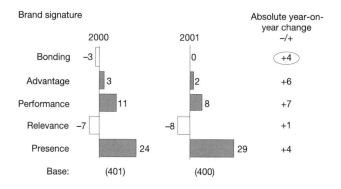

Figure 23: *Sainsbury's brand showing renewed market edge*
Source: WPP BrandZ Study

---

11. Millward Brown image profiles statistically remove the effect of brand size and generic statements in order to establish which characteristics brands are particularly associated with.
12. Sainsbury's Brand Signature™ (part of the Sainsbury's Brand Dynamics model) shows the ability of the brand to take consumers from brand knowledge to brand loyalty relative to competition. Bonded consumers who believe a brand has an edge in the marketplace account for the highest share of sales. The WPP BrandZ study includes 15,000 brands worldwide and is extensively validated against sales performance.

By affecting implied behavioural change in shopping, cooking and eating habits

Among the public at large, Jamie is strongly credited with encouraging people to try new and different things in the kitchen. For example when asked '*Which celebrity chefs, if any, have influenced your cooking?*', one in five UK adults answered Jamie Oliver, ranking him No. 1 choice (source: Nestlé Family Monitor/ Mori, December 2001).

The Jamie Oliver campaign, in its quest to make good food more accessible to all, has capitalised on that strength by rallying shoppers to branch out in their culinary experimentation (see Figure 24). Qualitative research endorses this, stating:

'Primary and secondary shoppers alike feel they are being inspired and helped to introduce new foods to their repertoire with Sainsbury's...'

'[Jamie's] particular approach to cooking is accessible and desirable for even the most hassled mum.'

Source: Sadek Wynberg, 2002

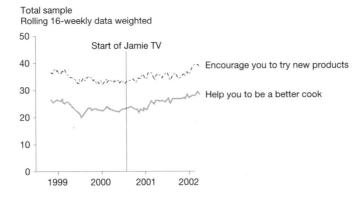

Figure 24: *Sainsbury's increasingly seen as source of food inspiration*
Source: Millward Brown BIAT, March 2002

The campaign has therefore not just served to better differentiate Sainsbury's from the price-fighting competition, based on its commitment and passion for food, but has also brought about claimed behavioural change:

'The ads make everything fun and make you want to try cooking.'

'They make you think you could have a go.'

Source: Sadek Wynberg, March 2002

By influencing actual changes in consumer behaviour patterns

Sainsbury's has enjoyed positive customer penetration gains of +7% since the start of the campaign (source: TNS). This has been largely attributed to an increase in spend from new store shoppers,[13] thanks to store openings and the refurbishment

---

13. New store shoppers = sales gained due to a shopper adding another retailer to their repertoire but still spending the same amount in the original retailer.

programme. It is plausible that the advertising has predisposed people to visit Sainsbury's stores. However, the main purpose of this paper is to show the major role advertising has played in helping to close the floodgates on the shopper exodus and secondly, enticing existing shoppers to spend more at Sainsbury's.

Negative switching (minus £58m to competitors in 99/00) has been eliminated and went into credit (+£751k) in the financial year 01/02 (see Figure 18) with losses to Tesco, Morrisons and Asda stemmed by £28m, £66m and £37m respectively over the same time period (Figure 25).

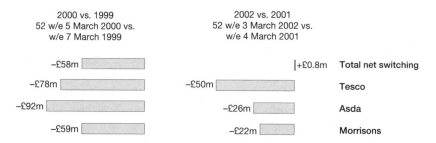

Figure 25: *Sainsbury's net switching eliminated in 2001*
Source: TNS

Crucially, the advertising has helped to give existing shoppers more reasons to spend more of their shopping budget with Sainsbury's. Sales gains from increased average weight of purchase[14] have risen almost tenfold from £46.5m in 99/00 to £447m in 01/02 (see Figure 26).

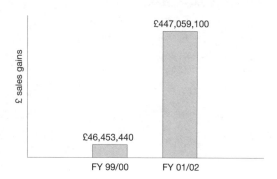

Figure 26: *Sainsbury's AWP increases almost tenfold*
Source: TNS, 52-week data

The advertising itself has had a direct influence on the products and lines sold (source: Sainsbury's):

• A total of 310,000 Jamie Oliver prawn and coriander curries were made in the six weeks following launch.

---

14. Increased average weight of purchase = a shopper who spends more in the retailer than they did in the previous period.

- Some 49,000 packs of Blue Parrot Café fish fingers sold in the first week of TVC airing.
- Sales of goose fat rose by 3000% to £201k in one week during Christmas 2001.
- Two million Jamie Easter lamb recipe cards collected in March 2002.
- Four-weekly sales of BGTY Balti Sauce increased by 1040%; BGTY lamb by 408%.
- Taste the Difference wild mushroom sauce sales have gone up 584%.

To this end, refocusing the brand on quality food has not just improved brand health, but has also driven short-term sales.

By galvanising the business behind a single thought

The campaign reignited Sainsbury's focus on food. Jamie is a consultant working behind the scenes with Sainsbury's innovations team to improve their offering. Their unique range of herbs is just one of the projects that has been worked on to date. Sainsbury's is now the only supermarket where it is possible to buy unusual herb varieties such as Golden Marjoram and Purple Sage, with culinary tips from Jamie on the back. He is often used on Sainsbury's business TV, broadcast to every store to talk to colleagues about these new projects (see Figure 27).

Figure 27: *Jamie Oliver and Mira Samani, New Product Development Manager, Fresh Herbs*

He also announces the opening of new and refurbished stores (see Figure 28), and is used in Sainsbury's recruitment advertising (see Figure 29).[15]

He is the PR face of Sainsbury's, and whenever Sainsbury's is in the press, Jamie's name is usually used in the headline.

---

15. Jamie may well have helped Sainsbury's leap 21 places in the Times Top 100 Graduate Employers Survey, from 63 to 42 (ahead of Tesco, which fell seven places to 52 from 45).

Figure 28: *New store openings*

Figure 29: *Recruitment advertising*

ELIMINATING OTHER VARIABLES

We are able to demonstrate the contribution of the new campaign, but what of other factors that could have affected this success?

Store refurbishments

Store refurbishments began in earnest in April 2001, nine months after the start of the new advertising. While only about one-third of the 480 stores have been refurbished to date, it is important to be able to eliminate the impact of these refurbishments.

Sales

The OHAL model is able to predict 97% of the variation in sales and thus isolate pure advertising effect. It is possible to look at the effects of the first nine months of the campaign on sales prior to any store refurbishments taking place. The model clearly showed an immediate sales effect with the campaign yielding an extra £47k of revenue per TVR for the first nine months (vs. £40k per TVR on average for the previous campaign, i.e. +17.5% more effective at generating sales) (see Figure 30).

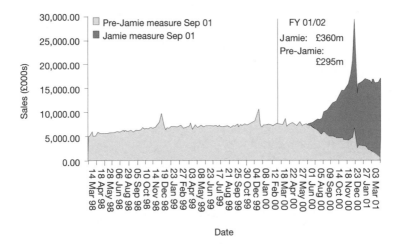

Figure 30: *Jamie sales contribution: the first nine months*
Source: OHAL

Brand image

Millward Brown BIAT also shows a shift in brand image during this period. Consumers were quick to accredit Sainsbury's with the intention to change (Table 4).

TABLE 4: SIGNS OF SHORT-TERM POSITIVE BRAND IMAGE SHIFTS

	May 2000	Dec 2000	+/–
Encourages you to try new products	34	44	+10*
Are food experts	39	46	+7*
Help you be a better cook	23	30	+7*
Have high-quality fresh fruit and vegetables	44	47	+3
Have a wide range of more luxury products	39	42	+3
Have high-quality own-label products	41	43	+2

Base: Total sample
* = 95% significant
Source: Millward Brown BIAT

Behavioural change

Negative switching (from –£58m to –£12m, 00/01) and average weight of purchase (£47m to £60m, 00/01) also began to show improvement in the first nine months (source: TNS).

Sub-brands

Sub-brands played a very important role in revitalising the Sainsbury's brand. Our contention was twofold. First, that the model strips out the contribution made by sub-brands. Second, the TV campaign has proved a very effective vehicle for driving these brands. For example, Be Good To Yourself saw volume sales up +183% in the first week of advertising in January 2001 and Blue Parrot Café +274% in March 2001 (source: Sainsbury's).

Media

Our contention here is that TV airtime has been largely governed by parameters set down by the OHAL model and this has consistently been the case since before the Jamie campaign, and throughout its duration. Sainsbury's SOV has risen marginally – 39% to 43% – and airtime quality improved in ways likely to enhance effectiveness. While we expect that these factors have helped the effectiveness of advertising, they cannot solely explain the sales effects and brand health improvements detailed in this paper.

Price

Throughout the period Sainsbury's price differential versus Tesco remained stable, so we are discounting price as having contributed to the sales uplift (see Figure 31).

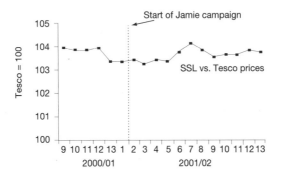

Figure 31: *Sainsbury's price differential: static vs. Tesco*
Source: SSL statistics

The Naked Chef

We acknowledge that this campaign leverages an existing TV property. However, we can be sure there is no direct sales effect of the BBC *Naked Chef* as the programme was not on air during the modelled time period.[16]

---

16. The TV campaign started in June 2001 and analysis ended 15 September 2001. The *Naked Chef* series II ended 31 May 2000 and series III did not resume until 16 October 2001 (source: BBC Information Service).

PAYBACK

OHAL has proven that Sainsbury's new TV advertising generated a total of £1.12 billion over its first 21 months.[17] Taking our full-year revenue figure of £763m, we calculate that, on a media spend of £28m (source: PHD), the campaign has provided a return on investment of £27.25 per £1 spent. Applying a marginal profit figure, which for the purpose of this paper we have set at 20%,[18] advertising has delivered £5.45 per £1 spent – equating to £153m per annum or £2.9m profit per week to the bottom line.

But what of its estimated contribution to shareholders' purses?

There are two ways of looking at increase in shareholder value. The first is to assume that the extra profit is at the rate reported in the accounts (for 2001 it was 3.7%) and the second is to assume that the marginal profit all filters down into the final accounts. Clearly neither is completely correct in that the first assumes that all group costs (e.g. head office) are increased pro rata, and the second assumes that there are no extra marginal costs (e.g. lorries) generated as a result of the extra turnover. However, Table 5 shows that the scale of shareholder return is so large that it is a question of personal judgement whether the Jamie TV is commercially successful.

TABLE 5: JAMIE'S ESTIMATED CONTRIBUTION TO SHAREHOLDER VALUE:
TWO POTENTIAL SCENARIOS

	1. Net profit 3.7%	2. Marginal profit 20%
Capitalisation of Sainsbury group	£7.61bn	£7.61bn
Declared operating profit	£663m	£663m
Earnings per share	19.2p	19.2p
Share price	£3.95	£3.95
Price/earnings ratio (P/E)	20.6	20.6
Loss in profit if Jamie did not take place	£28m	£153m
Profit loss as % of total	4.2%	23.1%
Assume no change in P/E ratio (20:6)		
Share price would be	£3.78	£3.04
Capitalisation would be	£7.29bn	£5.85bn
Loss in shareholder value	£320m	£1.76bn

Source: SSL Company Report 2001, OHAL, *The Guardian*

It is also feasible that in helping drive perceptions of an improved brand offering and brand affinity, the Jamie campaign has helped boost loyalty and gain more value from Sainsbury's customers, resulting in a less volatile cash flow and a subsequently healthier P/E ratio (see Figure 32).

In conclusion, the Sainsbury's TV campaign has delivered 'Good Food for All', leveraging the brand's heritage of expertise, knowledge and innovation via a more modern, accessible face – that of Jamie Oliver. We believe that Sainsbury's and Jamie working together has been, and will continue to be, a recipe for success and one that will help Sainsbury's consolidate its growth moving forward.

---

17. Interestingly, this £1.12 billion over 21 months is half the £2.06 billion achieved over five years by the Tesco 'Dotty' campaign (source: Tesco IPA Grand Prix IPA paper).
18. The majority of retailers operate at a marginal profit of between 15–25%. We have therefore taken the mid-point.

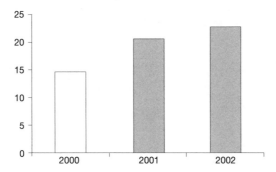

Figure 32: *Improved P/E ratios since Jamie started*
Source: SSL Company Reports, *The Guardian*

'The TV campaign has been an important galvanising event in our three-year sales-led recovery plan – it is an iconic signal of our passion for quality food made accessible to all, and its important impact on the pride of our colleagues and confidence of our customers cannot be underestimated.'

Source: Sir Peter Davies, May 2002

19

Tesco

Profitable carrots: how advertising price promotions had a positive, long-term effect on Tesco sales

Principal authors: Cathy Lewis, Lowe
Collaborating author: Joanna Bamford and Robert Black

EDITOR'S SUMMARY

This paper is not about the world of big brand advertising. It documents how a campaign of 10-second price promotion ads, with minimal media support, generated over £300m incremental revenue for Tesco. By exploring six different ways in which the campaign worked, the case sheds new light on how advertising price promotions can have a broader effect on sales than may typically be assumed.

TESCO AGAIN?

The Grand Prix winning IPA case for Tesco explained the role advertising played in transforming Tesco's brand image, helping it progress from a 'pile-it-high-sell-it-cheap' number two to become the dominant market leader.[1]

It would be a safe bet that the vast majority of award-winning IPA papers have also focused on advertising's valuable role in building successful brands.[2] These cases have been immensely instructive in helping to pin down something that is extremely difficult to measure.

It seems, however, that tactical advertising – at the so-called 'down and dirty' end of the spectrum – has fallen off the effectiveness radar. This may be because tactical advertising is usually intended to have an immediate sales effect – so what more do we need to do other than see whether or not there is one?

This paper aims to set the record straight. It's not about the big and powerful world of brand advertising. It's about how a dedicated campaign of ten-second price promotion ads, each with a media spend of just £250,000, generated over £300 million additional revenue for Tesco (source: Holmes and Cook). This was because advertising the promotions had a significant effect on sales over and above the promoted item and because these effects lasted for up to a year. We will outline the different consumer responses that help explain how this happened.

SUMMER 2000: IDENTIFYING A NEW REVENUE OPPORTUNITY

Beyond loyalty

Loyalty has become a key marketing mantra. Numerous papers and books (e.g. *The Loyalty Effect* by Reichheld) have been written on the subject. And the reason why this is so is clearly demonstrated in the supermarket sector, where the relationship between loyalty and market share is obvious.

A 'loyal' customer is defined by Superpanel as someone who spends 50% or more with that particular store.

TABLE 1: LOYALTY AND MARKET SHARE

	Tesco	Sainsbury	Asda	Safeway
% of store's customer base accounted for by loyal shoppers	32	29	28	21
Market share (%)	15.8	11.7	9.3	7.5

Source: Superpanel, 52 w/e July 2000 and IGD 2000

However, despite Tesco's success in securing loyal customers, there was still potential to generate more revenue from them. Moreover, 68% of Tesco's

---

1. IGD. Latest share figures give Tesco 16.5% of the market, ahead of Sainsbury's (11.5%), Asda (9.5%) and Safeway (7.5%).
2. Other examples might include: 'How do you create a most desired brand?' (Stella Artois); 'How advertising can steal brand leadership?' (Felix); 'How long term advertising investment can add real value to a brand within a tight budget?' (Solvite); 'How advertising can relaunch a brand in trouble?' (PG Tips), source: IPA Business Questions – Advertising Answers 2000.

consumers were spending at least half their weekly grocery budget elsewhere. This pool of 'secondary' shoppers was attractive for two reasons:

1. They represented a huge revenue opportunity: there were 4.2 million secondary shoppers[3] spending, on average, £26[4] per week.
2. Many of them were high-value shoppers. They were relatively upmarket and veered towards more expensive purchases – enjoying foreign food, keen to try new food products, and happy to buy ready meals.[5]

TABLE 2: THE DEMOGRAPHIC PROFILE OF
TESCO'S SECONDARY SHOPPERS INDEXED
VS. ALL ADULTS

AB	129	15–24	56
C1	113	25–34	121
C2	89	35–44	138
DE	73	45–54	123
		55+	75

Source: TGI, April 1999–March 2000

Finding the 'carrot'

What could entice these secondary shoppers to shop at Tesco more regularly? And could the same tool be used to encourage loyal shoppers to spend more?

By 2000, thanks to Tesco's efforts to improve their offer and advertising's role in using this to transform Tesco's image, the brand itself was no longer a barrier to entry. Tesco's secondary shoppers thought as highly of it as they did the other supermarkets where they shopped more often.

TABLE 3: TESCO SECONDARY SHOPPERS' OPINION OF TESCO
AND ITS COMPETITORS

	Tesco	Sainsbury's	Asda	Safeway
Excellent/very good overall reputation (%)	58	58	60	48
Excellent/very good overall store image (%)	57	53	60	45

Source: Taylor Nelson Sofres Image and Attitude Study 2000

So Tesco needed to find an additional hook to draw secondary shoppers to its stores. The answer came from trade-off analysis, which ranked the most important factors that determined where people chose to shop. It identified four priority improvements that would help make Tesco more attractive to secondary shoppers. It also identified four further, more emotional, factors that could tip the balance in its favour.

---

3. TGI, April 1999–March 2000; secondary shoppers are self-defined as those who shop at Tesco, but do not shop there most often.
4. Dunnhumby Clubcard data, average for 2000.
5. TGI, April 1999–March 2000, Tesco secondary shoppers, index vs. all adults: Enjoy eating foreign food: 124; Don't have time to prepare food: 106; Like to try new food products: 114.

TABLE 4: PRIORITY IMPROVEMENTS THAT COULD ATTRACT
TESCO SECONDARY SHOPPERS

Essential (rational) factors	Further (more emotional) factors
Availability of staff	Range of fresh food counters
Special offers	Range of food for eating healthily
Store layout	Friendliness of staff
Value for money	Range of organic products

Source: Taylor Nelson Sofres trade off analysis, May–June 2000[6]

Special offers looked like an easy win – provided they were done in a way which represented genuine *value for money* (rather than cheapness). The more emotional discriminators suggested that offers on quality products would be the way to achieve this. Special offers had the added advantage of being an attractive reward for loyal customers too. (Loyal shoppers didn't cite special offers as essential in determining store choice, but they did feature among the more emotional criteria that could make a difference.)

There were many special offer mechanics available to Tesco, but research showed that good old-fashioned price discounts would be most attractive:

'With money off you can still buy what you want and save money – not like those buy one get one free things. Or three for the price of two. They're a bit of a con. You have to buy more than you need. You just fill up your cupboards and forget you've bought it.'

Tesco/Lowe promotions research, summer 2000

The revenue potential of special offers

Health warnings about the dangers of price-promoting fmcg brands abound:

'The effects of price promotions appear to be transient. Once the promotion is over and the sales "blip" has subsided, it is as if it had not occurred (except for its cost).'

'This is explained by the additional finding that price promotions are mainly used just by past customers of the brand who therefore cannot be converted.'

Source: Andrew Ehrenberg and Kathy Hammond,
'The case against price-related promotions', *Admap*, June 2001

But there was a chance that price promotions for a *retail* brand could have a more noticeable, *positive* effect on revenue. There were six potential reasons why this might happen:

Attracting secondary shoppers
Here, it would counter the effect of loyal shoppers trading down on price. *'Perhaps I'll go to Tesco instead this week because of that special offer I saw.'*

Expanding the shopping list
Here it would be generating new revenue on top of someone's usual basket of goods. *'I don't usually bother with the wine aisle, but since it's on offer, I might as well take a look.'*

---

6. Taylor Nelson have a slightly different definition of secondary shoppers: they look at 'available shoppers' – which includes secondary and non-Tesco shoppers.

Attracting category enthusiasts

It would attract people who'd buy other things from the category at the same time as the promoted item. '*We like our meat and two veg for dinner, and I've noticed Tesco have got an offer on fresh legs of lamb. I might as well get some pork chops while I'm at it.*'

The whole basket benefit

'*I came in for the duty-free whisky, but now I'm here it makes sense to do the rest of my weekly shop.*'

Attracting high-value customers

Attracting people whose total basket would be particularly valuable. '*I don't usually shop in Tesco, but I thought the wine offer was really good. I was pushing my trolley around and came across their Finest range and loads of organic stuff too.*'

Longer-term disruption

The price promotion would disrupt spending patterns of loyal shoppers and secondary shoppers' store choice. '*I don't know why I used to buy wine somewhere else when I could have got it at Tesco at the same time as the rest of the shopping,*' and '*I hadn't been to Tesco for a while before they did that offer. It was better than I remembered and it's just as convenient as Safeway...*' This was the biggest potential prize. Tesco's superior ability to secure loyalty suggested it was not a forlorn hope.

The offers

To maximise all these revenue opportunities, it was important that the promotions were perceived to be high value. Given the trade-off analysis findings, Tesco couldn't afford for the promotions to look *cheap*. So it couldn't be 10p off white bread or 12 toilet rolls instead of 9. This paper covers the first eight advertised offers.

TABLE 5: THE OFFERS

Offer	Dates on offer
50% off whole fresh leg of lamb	11–17 September 2000
50% off whole fresh chicken	25 September–1 October 2000
20% off champagne	20–26 November 2000
VAT-free chart DVDs and videos	4–9 December 2000
Duty-free Glenfiddich whisky	6–11 December 2000
20% off Australian wine	20 April–1 May 2001
20% off French wine	9–22 May 2001
20% off American wine[7]	23 May–5 June 2001

---

7. The three wine promotions ran back to back, to form a 'Wine Festival'.

COMMUNICATING THE OFFERS

Clearly, special offers were not new to Tesco. But advertising had an important role in helping Tesco achieve their broad ambitions for these promotions. It needed to attract secondary shoppers (who didn't necessarily shop in Tesco enough to be aware of in-store announcements) *and* to help 'tune in' loyal shoppers to make them more likely to take notice of the offers.

Media strategy

There were two seemingly conflicting principles at the heart of the media strategy. Advertising needed to be intrusive to stir secondary shoppers. Yet it also needed to be disposable because the offers ran for only a short period of time *and* because we didn't want to displace 'Dotty' as Tesco's primary advertising property. ('Dotty' is the long-running campaign, featuring Prunella Scales as the mother of all shoppers, that has helped build Tesco's brand image around 'Every little helps'.)

We chose to run 10-second executions (which could easily accommodate the message but were more 'disposable' than longer time lengths).

Because the advertising needed to be disposable, we couldn't plan on the basis of ad awareness and neither could we risk using in-market testing to establish optimum efficiency. Instead, we worked with the 'rules' that have made Tesco's 'Dotty' campaigns so efficient, applying those that we knew helped drive home the main message, which we *did* want, and modifying those that drove high levels of awareness, which we *didn't* want. (Over the years, modelling, continuous tracking and structured testing of hypotheses has enabled us to establish a set of 'rules' that maximise the efficiency of each 'Dotty' campaign.)

Bending the 'rules' for the price promotion campaign
We decided to bend our 'Dotty rules' in the following ways for the price promotion campaign.

- Instead of six OTS (which maximised 'Dotty' awareness), we would achieve no more than three.[8]
- We would plan shorter period campaigns (since the offers were running only for one to two weeks, and to minimise the likelihood of displacing memories of 'Dotty').
- There was no requirement for regular activity. (Overall awareness of 'Dotty' is maintained by spending no longer than two weeks off air at any given time.)
- 'Dotty' campaigns are front-weighted to deliver maximum coverage quickly. The price promotion campaigns would be focused into the few days prior to the main store trading days. Generally, the campaigns ran across Monday to Friday, but were weighted towards the end of the week to deliver proximity of exposure to the heaviest (weekend) shopping periods.

---

8. Six OTS is the optimal frequency to deliver verifiable advertising awareness of 'Dotty' campaigns. However, in this case we were less interested in achieving verifiable ad awareness than we were in ensuring sales effects. According to TNS TV Span (whose single source data link TV viewing to shopping habits via Superpanel), those exposed to advertising three times in the three days prior to product purchase are 20% more likely to purchase than those not exposed at all. Comparatively, three exposures over 28 days deliver only a 5% increase in purchases.

- 'Dotty' spot placement 'rules' were applied, since these were key to getting the main message into consumers' minds efficiently. Communication is increased when ads are placed within programmes the target consumer has specifically chosen to watch. Buying centre or first/last position in break aids this effect.
- Since TV viewing is relatively old and downmarket, we aimed to maximise conversion to younger ABC1 housewives – particularly for the champagne and wine offers.

Maximising coverage against three OTS led to around £250,000 spend behind each execution.

Creative strategy

Our first question was whether we should follow the conventions of offer advertising. If nothing else, this gets the offer over loud and clear: the promoted product is centre stage, the discount is in huge typeface (plus obligatory starburst) and there's no getting away from the necessity to 'hurry' or 'act now....'. But what about the consequences for brand image and the loyalty that this engenders? We needed to find a way of bringing the offer to people's attention without damaging the brand.

An obvious solution would have been to use 'Dotty'. The campaign had many things going for it (familiarity, popularity and associations with quality among both loyal and secondary shoppers). But for all its upsides, there were good reasons to *not* use 'Dotty':

- 'Dotty' was *too* familiar. There was a risk that, in 10 seconds, the promotion itself might not shine through.
- 'Dotty' was about Tesco's broader 'Every little helps' philosophy, not short-lived one-offs.
- We were wary of overusing 'Dotty'. It would be better to find a new way to communicate price promotions than wear out Tesco's valuable brand vehicle.

The creative solution

The solution was to develop a separate campaign. It needed to borrow the more helpful aspects of the genre (clarity of the offer and urgency), hence the advertising proposition 'Don't miss out on this amazing offer at Tesco'. But at the same time, it needed to *enhance*, rather than feed off, the Tesco brand. So tonally, it had to sit comfortably with the humour of 'Dotty'. And it needed to suggest quality, rather than desperation.

The creative idea (yes, even though they were tactical ads, there was one) was to showcase offers so good that they were causing a stir among other products in store. Literally. The products on offer were brought to life – and their pleasure at being reduced was so infectious that it animated other products around it, which couldn't quite believe that such good products were on offer. Like 'Dotty', the ads used good clean fun. No starbursts and no one shouting at you to get down to Tesco.

The executions carried Tesco's red, white and blue livery and the familiar 'Every little helps' endline. To give a flavour of the campaign, three executions are described below.

Mumm 20% off champagne

In the run-up to Christmas, assorted bottles of champagne brands whimper 'Mum! Mum! Don't leave us!' as a discounted bottle of Mumm champagne is whisked away in a trolley of festive fare.

Figure 1: *Mumm champagne ad*

Lamb sources: 50% off whole leg of lamb

The half-price lamb execution features a wooden spatula standing on its shelf, telling another spatula the news that 'there's 50% off a whole leg of lamb this week'. The second spatula doesn't believe him and tells him he'd better check his *sources*. Overhearing, a lovely bottle of mint *sauce* pipes up: 'He's right you know. 50% off'.

Figure 2: *Lamb 'sources' ad*

Shrimp: 20% off Australian wine

As one Australian shrimp exclaims: 'Strewth, there's a great white!' the other shrimp panics 'where, where?' The first shrimp replies: 'Over there by the great red!' When the scene cuts to the wine bottles, the white turns slightly towards the shrimps.

Figure 3: *Australian wine 'shrimp' ads*

HOW DID PEOPLE RESPOND TO THE ADVERTISING?

Response to the advertising was extremely positive – particularly when compared with similar advertising from competitors.

Half-way through the campaign, in May 2001, Tesco's tracking study was changed from BJM to Taylor Nelson Sofres (TNS). We have shown both sets of data for completeness. In addition, we have compared responses to 'Talking products' with offer advertising from Asda that carried the familiar 'pocket pat' device.[9] (This sets a tough test, since Asda is synonymous with low prices.)

Recall

As we'd expected (and planned for), spontaneous recall of the advertising[10] was virtually nil. However, prompted recognition of the advertising was relatively strong. Encouragingly (and unusually), recognition was as high among secondary shoppers as it was among loyal shoppers. Most striking is that recognition for this new campaign was higher than that for Asda (Table 6).[11]

TABLE 6: PROMPTED RECOGNITION (%)[12]

	Asda offer ads	'Talking products'	
	All shoppers	All shoppers	Secondary Tesco shoppers
BJM	n/a	24	20
TNS	16	24	25

Base: Total sample

Branding
Branding was as strong as for Asda's 'pocket pat' executions (Table 7).

TABLE 7: CORRECT BRANDING (%)

	Asda offer ads	'Talking products'	
	All shoppers	All shoppers	Secondary Tesco shoppers
BJM	n/a	60	49
TNS	58	60	51

Base: All recognisers

Communication
'Talking products' was very clearly special offer, rather than brand advertising. It communicated more strongly than the Asda ads (despite the latter being part of a long-running price-based campaign).

---

9. The tracking looked at three of Asda's offer ads: two DVDs for £20 (20-second), low-price copies of Dido's 'No Angel' CD (10-second) and cut-price microwave ovens and pans (10-second). The figures shown are the average response across all three ads. Since the Asda ads ran from September–November 2001, analysis is available only from the Taylor Nelson tracking.
10. As measured by the question: 'Please describe in as much detail as possible the first television advertising for a super-market you have seen recently'. Inevitably, memories of 'Dotty' advertising outweighed those for 'talking products'.
11. Asda suffered from people remembering Asda advertising generally, but not being able to differentiate one execution from another.
12. All tracking data refer to the average response across all 'Talking product'/Asda offer ads.

TABLE 8: PROMPTED COMMUNICATION (%)

| | | Asda offer ads | 'Talking products' | |
		All shoppers	All shoppers	Secondary Tesco shoppers
Has good special offers	BJM	n/a	34	26
	TNS	8	32	38
Offers competitive prices	BJM	n/a	26	19
	TNS	16	27	18
Gives good value for money	BJM	n/a	30	24
	TNS	12	33	24

Base: All recognisers

Consumer response to the advertising communication
Importantly, the advertising helped the offers seem good value:

'They talk about the offers without making Tesco seem cheap.'

'They do offers as well ... but they're not cheap and nasty like Iceland ... Iceland's are for a pizza and chips mum who just feeds her kids junk food.'

Lowe Qualitative Research among Tesco secondary shoppers

How people liked the advertising
Unusually, for this kind of advertising, people liked it.

TABLE 9: LIKE/LIKE VERY MUCH (%)

| | Asda offer ads | 'Talking products' | |
	All shoppers	All shoppers	Secondary Tesco shoppers
BJM	n/a	49	36
TNS	12	52	44

Base: All recognisers

Brand image
The advertising did not work to the detriment of Tesco. In fact, it enhanced peoples' view of the brand. We have compared views of the brand among secondary shoppers who had seen the advertising against primary shoppers who hadn't. This is in an attempt to avoid concluding an advertising effect, when it might be simply that people who already have more positive views of the brand would be more aware of the advertising.

TABLE 10: BRAND IMAGE

	Secondary shoppers who had seen 'Talking products'	Primary shoppers who hadn't seen 'Talking products'
Cheaper prices on all/some of the products I regularly buy	76	76
Always/often have special offers on things I want to buy	77	77
Excellent/very good quality of products overall	61	61
Excellent/very good overall reputation	63	64
Excellent/very good overall store image	64	65

Base: Total sample
Source: TNS

So 'Talking products' appeared to be working harder than comparable offer ads, saying the *right things* to the *right people*, in an unusually engaging way. But did it make any difference to sales?

WHAT HAPPENED TO SALES?

Before we isolate advertising effects, we have outlined what happened to sales.

Increase in revenue from promoted products

Revenue from all the promoted products was significantly higher than in the same period the year before or the year after (Table 11). Either the promotion had encouraged loyal shoppers to take advantage of the promotion and/or it had attracted extra secondary shoppers to Tesco.

TABLE 11: YEAR ON INCREASE IN SALES REVENUE OF THE
PROMOTED ITEM DURING THE PROMOTIONAL PERIOD

50% off whole fresh leg of lamb	+105%
50% off whole fresh chicken	+42%
20% off champagne	+534% vs. three weeks pre;
	+238% vs. three weeks post
VAT-free chart DVDs and videos	n/a
Duty-free Glenfiddich	n/a
20% off Australian wine	+6%
20% off French wine	+20%
20% off American wine	+25%

Source: Tesco till rolls (see notes to Table 12)

Increase in revenue from category of promoted products

So sales of the promoted items increased. Less expected, sales of the promoted product's *category* also rose during the promotion vs. the same period the year before (see Table 12).

When we looked at the revenue comparisons it looked as if one (or both) of two things had happened:

Shopping lists had been expanded

People were shopping in a category they didn't usually frequent because of the promotion and were drawn into buying other category products at the same time. '*I don't normally buy wine from Tesco, but since I'm here because of the French wine promotion, I might as well try some of that New Zealand Chardonnay.*' This could be loyal shoppers visiting an unfamiliar aisle or secondary shoppers coming into Tesco because of the promotion.

Category enthusiasts were brought in by the promotion and switched some of their category purchases to Tesco

Secondary shoppers who *did* typically buy the category were taking advantage of the Tesco promotion and stocking up on the other products from the category at the same time. '*I was going to buy some lamb at Sainsbury's, but since I'm at Tesco to get it half price, I may as well get the pork chops I was going to buy too.*'

TABLE 12: YEAR ON INCREASE IN SALES REVENUE OF THE CATEGORY
DURING THE PROMOTIONAL PERIOD

Promotion	Category	Category uplift
50% off whole fresh leg of lamb	Total lamb	+44%
	Beef/lamb/pork joints	+31%
50% off whole fresh chicken	Total fresh chicken	+14%
20% off champagne	Champagne	n/a (offer was across whole category)
VAT-free chart DVDs and videos	–	n/a
Duty-free Glenfiddich	Malt whisky	+15%
	Total whisky	+2%
20% off Australian wine	Total wine	+8%
20% off French wine		
20% off American wine		

Source: Tesco till rolls (see notes on revenue comparisons below)

Notes:
a) Comparisons have been made with sales for the same week(s) in the following year (2001) for lamb, chicken and whisky and with the preceding year (2000) for wine. (This is because EPOS data are only available for these two years.)
b) Lamb, chicken and whisky, which were on promotion and advertised in 2000, were *not* on promotion in the comparative year, 2001. Champagne was on promotion *and* advertised in both 2000 and 2001. Wine, which was on promotion and advertised in 2001 was on promotion but *not* advertised in 2000. The year-on-year comparisons for wine can therefore be used to show an advertising effect. This is discussed in greater detail later in the paper.
c) The champagne uplift has been measured differently, since the promotion was advertised in both 2000 and 2001. In addition we need to take account of the natural sales build in the run-up to Christmas. The sales pattern pre/during/post is similar in both years. For these reasons, the comparisons shown are i) the average sales uplift in 2000/2001 vs. the average of the three weeks prior to the promotion; ii) the average sales uplift in 2000/2001 vs. the average of the three weeks post the promotion. We looked only at three weeks, to minimise the Christmas effect. It is clear, then, that the uplift during the promotional week was not simply due to sales growth in the run-up to Christmas.
d) Data for chart DVDs and videos are unavailable as Tesco do not collect chart sales as a separate category (instead their sales are included in their relevant film genre category).
e) We do not have sales of Glenfiddich whisky specifically. We show, above, total malt whisky and total whisky sales, which in some respects is a more interesting measure, since switching in this category (between and within malt and blended brands) is so high.
f) Wine data cover seven weeks (due to the promotions running back-to-back during the Wine Festival).

But what about the bigger prizes of *whole basket benefits* and *longer-term disruption*? Had the extra secondary shoppers attracted by the promotion bought more than just the promoted products? Had loyal shoppers who'd been 'introduced' to the category continued to buy from it after the promotion had ended? More valuable still, had secondary shoppers, brought into the category by the promotion, continued to do their whole shop at Tesco after the promotion had ended?

And how much had advertising the promotions contributed to their success?

Whole-basket and longer-term effects

Although it is very clear from raw sales data that sales in all categories have seen marked uplifts during the week(s) of the advertised promotions, it is difficult, at this level, to disentangle the wider (whole basket) and longer-term (post-promotional) effects. There are a number of reasons for this difficulty:

- Many of the promotions took place in 2000. The available EPOS data cover only 2000 and 2001. In many instances we have thus had to use 2001 as our control. Tesco sales have grown considerably between 2000 and 2001 for a number of reasons including a buoyant economy and their own marketing activity. Thus, the post-promotional period in 2000 is being compared against an overstated benchmark.
- Tesco have a busy ongoing promotional programme, at all times, in most categories, and it is impossible to factor out the impact of this with simplistic analysis. Hence, at sub-category level, we do not know whether we are comparing like with like over a longer period.
- The DVD/champagne/whisky promotions ran very close to Christmas. In the immediate post-promotional period sales are heavily affected by a massive seasonal uplift and then a decline. Because promotions ran in both years we do not know what the natural seasonal profile should be.
- Whisky and DVD promotions ran in the same week.

These problems are crucial. Increasing footfall and sales across all categories could have been a key benefit of advertising the promotions. Measuring advertising's contribution to the wider (whole-basket) and longer-term (post-promotional) effects thus requires a more comprehensive approach. Tesco uses 'dry grocery' sales as a proxy for footfall and has an econometric model which explains dry grocery movements in a panel of stores. This was used in the 2000 paper to evaluate the effects of the 'Dotty' campaign and has been used again to evaluate 'Talking products'.

The model is illuminating on two counts. First, it shows that by advertising the promotions, Tesco did indeed reap 'whole-basket' benefits, where people bought more than just the promoted item. Second, it suggests that longer-term disruption was achieved, since the effects of advertising the promotion last up to a year.

Whole-basket benefits
The model shows quite clearly that dry grocery, a category which did not feature in any of the promotions, has, all else remaining equal, benefited over the promotional period. The model shows a 1.46% uplift in revenue (on average) from the start of the campaign to November 2001.

Dry grocery consists of what can be described as staple products (tea, cereal, canned goods, pasta, etc.). Since dry grocery is a proxy for footfall, the model provides evidence that advertising brought more people into Tesco than would otherwise have been the case. It is unlikely that loyal shoppers would have increased their purchases of staple products as a result of a price promotion in a high-value category. So we can conclude that, as we hypothesised, secondary shoppers, brought into Tesco by advertising the promotion, must also have bought a further basket of goods at the same time.

Longer-term disruption
The model shows advertising effects that persist, at some level, for up to a year after advertising, though half of the total effect comes within 13 weeks of air-date.

It is unlikely that the promotions alone would have had such a lengthy effect. And it is unlikely that loyal shoppers would have significantly increased their longer-term expenditure on dry grocery staples. Again, since dry grocery is a proxy for football, the model suggests that the advertising did act as a 'carrot' that kicked off a chain of events. It brought more secondary shoppers (who wouldn't have seen the promotions in store) into Tesco to buy the promotion and this experience caused them to come back to shop at Tesco more regularly than they had before.

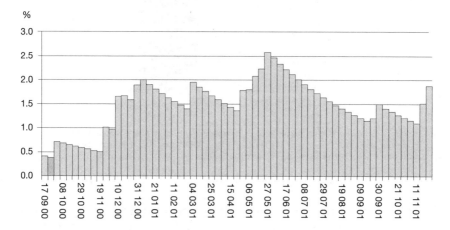

Figure 4: 'Talking products' campaign: effect on Tesco dry grocery sales
Note: 26/11/00 to 21/01/01 not included when model estimated. Effects have been projected on the basis of adstock growth over that period.

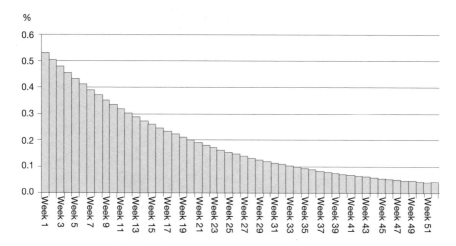

Figure 5: 'Talking products' campaign: effect of 100 TVRs
Note: TVRs occur in week 1. Effects continue up to and beyond week 52. This indicates the campaign is still generating some effect up to a year off air-time.

One way of assessing the scale of these uplifts is to look at what happened to the number of households shopping at Tesco pre, during and post the promotions period (see Figure 6). We can see that the overall number of households shopping at Tesco increased during the promotional period *and* was 3% higher after the promotions had ended than before. (This is reassuringly similar in scale to the uplift in dry grocery that the model shows.)

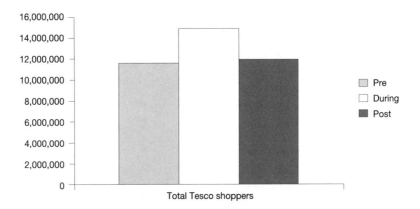

Figure 6: *Number of households shopping at Tesco pre, during and post the whole promotional period*
Source: Superpanel; pre is the 12-week period ending 20 August 2000; during is the 40-week period ending
27 May 2001; post is the 12-week period ending 19 August 2001

This was because there was a significant increase in the number of secondary shoppers during the promotional period. While this flattened out once the promotions were over, the number of loyal shoppers increased – suggesting that some previously secondary shoppers had been traded up by Tesco to become primary shoppers. While other factors will have contributed to this, the econometric findings show that advertising the promotions played a substantial part. (It's interesting, given that the model showed that half of the effect of the advertising comes within 13 weeks off air, that the number of secondary shoppers falls away to pre levels in the 12 weeks after the advertising.)

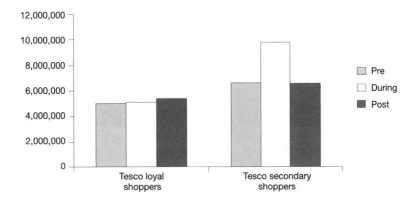

Figure 7: *Number of households shopping at Tesco by loyalty type pre, during and post the whole promotional period*[13]

---

13. We have not looked at other promotions individually: a) the Wine Festival is the only one where there is a year-on-year comparison of the same promotion with and without advertising; b) assessment of other offers is complicated by seasonality (whisky, champagne), lack of data (DVDs/videos and chicken) or one-off events (the start of the lamb promotion coincided with the fuel crisis).

IN SUMMARY

The model shows that advertising the promotions worked in four of the six ways we had hypothesised:

1. It attracted secondary shoppers into Tesco.
2. It expanded people's shopping lists.
3. It generated a broader, whole-basket benefit.
4. It brought about longer-term disruption.

Looking at the three promotions that made up the Wine Festival has allowed us to look at these four effects in further detail. It also suggests that the advertising also worked in the two other ways we hypothesised (attracting category enthusiasts and attracting high-value shoppers).

Further learning from the Wine Festival promotions

Further analysis has been conducted on the Wine Festival promotions only. We are able to look at what would have happened if the promotion had run *without* advertising by comparing the 20% off Australian, French and American Wine Festival promotions that were supported by TV advertising in 2001 with the same promotions that ran a year earlier without TV support.[14]

The findings support, and expand on, the effects we have already seen.[15]

---

14. In 2000 the Wine Festival was supported only by a small national press spend of £99k. The year-on-year comparisons are valid:
    - The offers ran at the same time of year (April/May/June).
    - The 20% off offer was the same.
    - The range of wines promoted was actually smaller in 2001.
    - In both years, £150k was spent on in-store promotion and the same material was used (hanging banners, car park banners, in-store posters, shelf-talkers, shelf dividers and floor stickers).
    - The average retail price of Tesco wine had not moved significantly (up 4% from £3.42 in 2000 to £3.56 in 2001, making the 20% off saving similar – 68p vs. 71p).
    - The number of consumers drinking wine had not grown: in both years 59% of adults bought wine for home consumption (source: TGI April 1999–March 2000, and April 2000–March 2001).
    - The number of consumers buying wine in Tesco had increased marginally (by 4%) year-on-year. Within that, the number of secondary shoppers buying wine in Tesco had decreased by 0.5%.
    - Spend on wine in Tesco in the six-week period prior to the Wine Festival was down 1% vs. 2000.
    - Consumers were not favouring Australian, French or American wines any more than they had a year ago. The percentage of Tesco's wine accounted for by Australian wine went from 19% to 20% in the six months to March 2000 vs. the six months to March 2001; French fell from 29% to 26% and American went from 10% to 11%.
    In both years, the promotions ran for two weeks each, back to back. Naturally, this affects response to each promotion. For example, the only 'clean' pre period is before the Australian promotion; the only 'clean' post period is after the American promotion. This makes analysis of the French promotion particularly difficult. As a result, even though three separate ads ran to support the discount on each type of wine, most of the analysis looks at the total Wine Festival period.
15. The source for this analysis is Tesco's Clubcard data through Dunnhumby. We chose to use Clubcard data since they give us a level of detail not available to us through other sources (such as Superpanel, where we run into difficulties with sample size). Around 80% of Tesco's transactions are made with a Clubcard. Inevitably these transactions are skewed towards loyal shoppers as Clubcards are held only by around a quarter of secondary shoppers. Nonetheless, Clubcard still captures the spending patterns of 1.3 million secondary shoppers (as well as 4.3 million loyal shoppers). So while it can give us a good idea of how secondary shoppers responded to the promotions, it underestimates their response.

Sales were higher

When it was advertised, a million and a half more bottles of promoted wine were sold during the Wine Festival and revenue nearly doubled. (The *uplift* in volume and revenue vs. the period before the Festival was over 300% greater in 2001 than in 2000.)

TABLE 13: WINE FESTIVAL VOLUME AND REVENUE

	2000	2001	Difference
Total Wine Festival volume (000s bottles)	2009	3516	+75%
Total Wine Festival revenue (£000)	8745	15,807	+81%

Note: These tables are different to those presented earlier because they are Clubcard sales, rather than Tesco till roll.

Advertising the promotions attracted significantly more secondary shoppers and expanded the shopping list of loyal shoppers

The uplifts in volume and revenue can partly be explained by the fact that significantly more people (54%) bought promoted wine in 2001 than in the previous year. Advertising brought the Wine Festival to the attention of more loyal shoppers than did the offer alone (in all likelihood, expanding their shopping list). But the biggest uplift vs. the non-advertised Wine Festival was among *secondary* shoppers.

TABLE 14: THE INCREASE IN THE NUMBER OF SHOPPERS BUYING
EACH TYPE OF PROMOTED WINE IN 2001 VS. 2000 (%)

	Loyal Tesco shoppers	Secondary Tesco shoppers
Australian	+44	+214
French	+64	+109
American	+18	+51

The advertising attracted high-value customers

One of the risks of advertising the promotions was that it might attract a disproportionate amount of low-spending bargain-hunters. In fact, across all three promotions, the majority of the people that advertising attracted were 'fine foods' buyers (Tesco's highest-value customer segment). 'Price-sensitive' shoppers, on the other hand, were the least likely to have been attracted by the advertising (according to Dunnhumby segmentation, based on Clubcard purchases).

TABLE 15: THE PROPORTION OF THE INCREASE IN THE TOTAL
NUMBER OF PEOPLE BUYING PROMOTED WINE ACCOUNTED
FOR BY EACH SHOPPER TYPE 2001 VS. 2000 (%)

Shopper segments (ranked in descending order of value to Tesco)	Australian	French	American
Finer foods	31	38	39
Healthy	14	17	16
Convenience	8	7	8
Mainstream	22	17	20
Traditional	16	14	12
Price-sensitive	8	8	5

This also is supported by the next finding.

The advertising appears to have attracted category enthusiasts

Spend per transaction went up

In both years, people who bought promoted wine spent *more* per transaction than in the six weeks prior to the promotion. This was not only because they bought more bottles, but also because they spent more per bottle. In 2001, when the promotion was advertised, the increase in spend-per-transaction vs. before the promotion was much more pronounced. This may have been due to people 'treating themselves' – taking advantage of the promotion to buy wine that's normally out of their price range. Or the promotion attracted people who were more 'into' wine. Either way, these people were of potentially greater value to Tesco because they were prepared both to spend more and buy significantly more.

TABLE 16: WINE FESTIVAL SPEND AND VOLUME PER TRANSACTION

	2000	2001
Amount spent per transaction		
In the six weeks before the promotion	£6.75	£6.95
During the promotion	£7.77	£9.04
	(+15%)	(+30%)
Number of bottles bought in each transaction		
In the six weeks before the promotion	1.7	1.6
During the promotion	1.8	2.0
	(+6%)	(+25%)
Amount spent on each bottle		
In the six weeks before the promotion	£3.97	£4.34
During the promotion	£4.34	£4.52
	(+9%)	(+4%)

Category sales went up

In 2000, when the Wine Festival was not TV advertised, wine category volume went down. In 2001, it went *up* (again, suggesting that category enthusiasts were brought in by advertising of the promotion).

TABLE 17: CATEGORY VOLUME

	2000	2001
Total wine category volume in six weeks *prior* to the Wine Festival (000 bottles)	15,457	16,405
Total wine category volume *during* the Wine Festival (000 bottles)	15,173	16,760
Difference	–2%	+2%

Longer-term disruption

Total wine sales went up by 10% *after* the promotion – whereas they returned to the same level in 2000. People the advertising had attracted to the promotion came back for more (see Table 18).

More significantly, compared to 2000, in 2001 44% more of the people brought into Tesco to buy Wine Festival promotions were still shopping at Tesco in the six weeks after the promotion ended. They had come in for wine, and ended up more loyal to Tesco.

TABLE 18: WINE CATEGORY REVENUE IN THE SIX WEEKS
AFTER THE WINE FESTIVAL VS. THE SIX WEEKS BEFORE

	2000	2001
Total spend on wine *pre* Wine Festival	£6.42m	£6.48m
Total spend on wine *post* Wine Festival	£6.42m	£7.12m
Pre–post change	–	+10%

Note: These tables are different to those presented earlier because they
are Clubcard sales, rather than Tesco till roll.

Summary

The analysis of advertising the Wine Festival promotions supports the econometric findings and sheds further light on how the advertising worked. We have, in total, six different ways in which this advertising generated incremental sales for Tesco. These are:

1. Attracting secondary shoppers
2. Expanding people's shopping list
3. Attracting category enthusiasts
4. Whole-basket benefits
5. Attracting high-value customers
6. Longer-term disruption of spending patterns and store choice.

We have shown already[16] that there were very few wine-specific differences year-on-year, and we can find no other macro factors that could explain the scale of the uplifts in the 2001 Wine Festival (see Table 19).

We have concluded, therefore, that the scale of the uplifts seen in the 2001 Wine Festival can be attributed to advertising.

BECAUSE OF ITS BROADER AND LONGER-TERM EFFECTS, THE ADVERTISING PAID BACK

The econometric model shows an average uplift of 1.46% in sales from the start of the campaign to November 2001, which equates to an increase in revenue in the panel of stores analysed of £13.7m. As the advertising works for a considerable number of weeks after air-time there will be future effects proportional to the rate of adstock decline. These total £5.2m, making a total of £18.9m extra revenue.

It is necessary to make assumptions about how sales in other categories and outside our panel of stores respond. During the promotions, the promoted categories saw much larger uplifts than 1.46%. However, the number of weeks with advertised promotions was relatively few within the timescale over which payback is calculated. Therefore, if we assume that, on average, all categories and stores experience an uplift of 1.46%, this produces a revenue increase of £349.4m. The cost of the campaign was £3.2m.[17] Tesco thus would have broken even (before the cost of investing in the promotions themselves) if their margin were 1%. It is in fact close to 6%.

Tesco's 'carrots' had been rather more profitable than might have been expected.

---

16. In footnote 14.
17. The model includes all executions with a total media and production spend of £3,234,550.

TABLE 19: POSSIBLE EXPLANATIONS FOR THE SCALE OF THE 2001 WINE FESTIVAL UPLIFT

Possible explanation	Change vs. 2000
More stores/ floor-space?	Tesco opened 33 more stores in 2001, expanding their floor-space by 6%.[18] This could have increased the number of transactions, but not spend-per-transaction (which grew by 30%). It is extremely unlikely, therefore, that increased floor-space generated the 81% revenue uplift.
More people shopping at Tesco?	Tesco penetration grew by 2.5% points.[19] Again, this slight increase cannot account for the 54% increase in the number of people buying promoted wine nor the 81% revenue uplift in wine during the 2001 festival.
Tesco's other advertising?	'Dotty' didn't advertise any of the promoted items (they didn't even feature in the background). Spend on 'Dotty' *fell* by 4% vs. 2000 and the balance of communication moved *away* from price.[20] Moreover, there was no significant change in the way consumers responded to 'Dotty'.[21]
Competitor advertising?	The competitive situation was, if anything, disadvantageous. Both Asda's and Sainsbury's share of voice increased vs. 2000.[22] In addition, Sainsbury's new Jamie Oliver campaign (which launched at the same time as Tesco's lamb promotion) improved the relative performance of their advertising.[23]
Increased price-consciousness (making savings more attractive)?	People didn't feel more price-conscious: no more people claimed to 'always look for the lowest prices when shopping' than in 2000.[24] In any case, spend per transaction went up in 2001, suggesting that it wasn't price-consciousness that drove people to the promotions.
Wealthier consumers?	Average income grew by 5.2% year-on-year,[25] in contrast to the increase in wine revenue of 81%. And Tesco's average basket price was slightly lower in 2001 than in 2000.[26]
The Millennium (making 2000 an odd year for comparison)?	The model suggests that dry grocery sales in 2000 were back to normal by the beginning of March,[27] making it very unlikely that the Millennium affected either year.

18. Tesco plc annual report and financial statements 2000 and 2001.
19. TGI; April 2000–March 2001 vs. April 1999–March 2000.
20. MMS: Tesco spent £18.9m on TV advertising in the year to June 2001 compared to £19.6m in the year to June 2000. In the year to June 2001, 'Dotty' communicated four price, five service and three quality messages. In the previous year, 'Dotty' communicated nine price, three Clubcard and three service messages.
21. BJM: Awareness grew only slightly (from 32 to 35%) and likeability remained stable at 80%.
22. BJM: Spontaneous awareness of Sainsbury's advertising grew from 5% to 24% between the start of the Jamie campaign in September 2000 and June 2001. Likeability of their advertising grew from 53% to 70%.
23. MMS, July 2000–June 2001 vs. previous 12 months.
24. TGI April 2000–March 2001 vs. April 1999–March 2000; 38% agreed in both years.
25. Government statistics.
26. Dunnhumby £25.52 in 2001 vs. £25.62 in 2000.
27. Holmes & Cook.

20

Volkswagen

'The road to purchase': the growth of Volkswagen UK, 1995 to 2001

Principal authors: Richard Butterworth, Matt Willifer and
Sara Donoghugh, BMP DDB
Collaborating authors: Tom Goodwin, Tribal DDB,
and David Parslow, Proximity London

EDITOR'S SUMMARY

This case shows how an integrated multi-channel communications approach based around car buyers' 'road to purchase' helped Volkswagen UK double its new car sales and value share over six years, as well as boosting sales of parts and used Volkswagens, without any erosion of the brand's 'cut above' status. The communications approach was highly efficient, and directly led to 151,000 extra sales and £1.99 billion extra revenue for Volkswagen UK.

In 1994 Volkswagen was a niche player in the UK car market. By the end of 2001 it had doubled its sales. This transformation was achieved efficiently. In addition, despite a massively increased on-road presence, it was achieved without any erosion of the brand's aspirational reputation.

This paper will show how marketing communications contributed to that transformation. In doing so, it builds on the five-star award-winning Volkswagen case study from 1998. That study showed the contribution made by one communications channel, national advertising, over two-and-a-half years between 1995 and 1997. This study goes far beyond that by examining how a battery of communications channels contributed to Volkswagen's growth over the past seven years. Our aim is to show how those marketing channels were used in a complementary and cost-efficient way, an approach which was grounded in a sound empirical knowledge of consumer behaviour rather than any grand theories about the dos and don'ts of multi-channel marketing.

MARKET CONTEXT

The UK car market

Every year about two million new cars are sold in the UK. Most of these sales are in the small, lower-medium and upper-medium-sized categories (Figure 1).

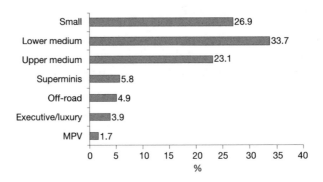

Figure 1: *The UK new car market by category*
Source: SMMT 2001

Until the late 1980s, the volume market was dominated by the 'domestic' manufacturers Ford, Vauxhall and Rover. Over the past 15 years, continental and Asian importers have grown at their expense. The premium car-makers such as Mercedes also increased their market share steadily (Figure 2).

Volkswagen UK

In 1994, when this paper begins, Volkswagen was a small player despite having competitively priced models in all the major volume market sectors.

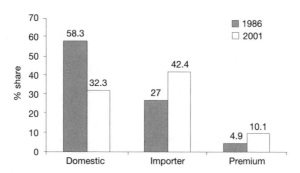

Figure 2: *UK car market 2001 vs. 1986*
Source: SMMT

TABLE 1: VOLKSWAGEN IN 1994

Unit sales	74,548 cars
Market share	3.9%
Rank	7th

Source: SMMT

Its sales mix and brand reputation were dominated by just one model: Golf (Figure 3).

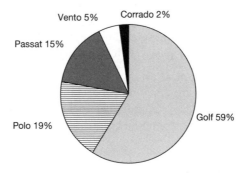

Figure 3: *Volkswagen sales in 1994 (by model)*
Source: SMMT

At this time, the French car-makers Renault and Peugeot were single-mindedly growing their UK share with heavyweight marketing budgets and aggressive tactical offers. This strategy – buying share with free insurance and 0% finance – had implications for Volkswagen: it too played the tactical game in order to retain its small share of an increasingly offer-driven market. This response eroded its profitability.

A CHANGE OF DIRECTION: NEW BUSINESS OBJECTIVES, NEW COMMUNICATIONS STRATEGY

It was against this background that Volkswagen in Germany decided to change its UK *business strategy*. It too wanted to grow market share: from 3.9% to 7% in five years. However, this ambitious growth objective came with two challenging caveats: it should be achieved profitably, and without erosion of Volkswagen's 'cut above' brand image.

The barriers to achieving this objective were threefold:

- Mass-market car buyers did not really see Volkswagen as a brand for them. The iconic GTi was a must-have for rich people in the 1980s – not a car for the likes of you and me.
- Golf was synonymous with Volkswagen. The Polo and Passat were neither as well known nor as highly regarded.
- Although prices had been realigned some years before, Volkswagen's upper-class image, and its association with a top-end variant meant that people wrongly believed its cars to be too expensive.

Volkswagen UK's resulting *marketing strategy* was based on using communications rather than incentives to solve these problems: communications which promoted brand values, and (in the short term) addressed the price misperceptions.

Communications strategy

Hitherto, the strategy had been relatively simple, commensurate with the brand's 'niche' market status:

- Overall communications spend was relatively low.
- Advertising talked only about Volkswagen, not the individual models.
- Direct mail was limited to promoting test-drives for new models.
- The Volkswagen Press Office liaised with motoring journalists and broadcasters.

Volkswagen and its communications agencies decided such an approach was no longer appropriate. In deciding how to progress, four areas were scrutinised: overall communications presence, optimum channel deployment, the messages that needed communicating, and the communications tone.

Increased presence

The overall communications budget was increased in line with Volkswagen's greater business ambitions. Direct-marketing and advertising budgets were substantially increased, PR was given greater resource, and the internet was introduced. These increases were funded partly by redirecting marketing budget from tactical offers.

Deployment by communications channel

The optimum role for each communications channel and the share of the marketing budget put behind it was determined by examining how people went about buying cars, and how different channels influenced this process.

Typically, people bought a new car once every three years. For most of the time between purchases these people were *'passive'*, and really not that interested in cars.[1] None the less, their opinions *were* being influenced, most commonly by word

---

1. At any given time, about 92% of Britain's six million new car buyers were in this passive phase. Source: Millward Brown.

of mouth, on-road presence, and direct experience of models they owned or had driven. One paid-for communications channel had a particularly strong influence during this time: intrusive mass media advertising.

Consequently, when people came to buy they had already drawn up a shortlist of three or four models. A more *active* stage then began, with people investigating in more detail those few shortlisted models: cost, equipment levels, performance in road tests and so on.

At this stage information-rich local dealer advertising and direct marketing exerted their greatest influence. PR, too, was vital. Prospective car buyers made much use of articles in motoring magazines or in the motoring pages of national newspapers. These media gave information-hungry prospective buyers the kind of information they were seeking at the time they most wanted it.

Between 1995 and 2001 internet penetration among new car buyers quickly rose to over 70%.[2] Although the internet appeared to have many potential strengths, we decided its most attractive quality was its ability to give active-phase car buyers comprehensive and convenient information, with easy reference to objective third-party websites (e.g. *What Car?*) (Figure 4).

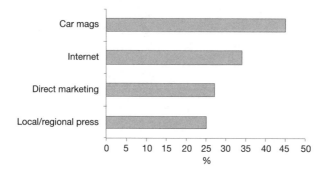

Figure 4: *Car mags, internet, DM and local press all used when buying a car*
Base: New car buyers
Question: 'What sources of information did you find useful when buying your last car?'
Source: NOP 2001

We devised our channel deployment strategy in response to these findings: use channels in a complementary way, where each plays to its strengths in terms of cost-efficient audience delivery and its ability to convey particular kinds of information, from broad emotive claims (at one end of the spectrum) to detailed descriptions of air-conditioned glove compartments (at the other).[3]

Channel deployment strategy

Passive phase
• *Role for communications*: Create demand for Volkswagen and its models among (i) those millions of new car buyers who weren't actively in the market

---

2. Source: NCBS.
3. To a greater or lesser extent, all the channels exerted some kind of influence on the people exposed to them at *both* stages in the new car-buying process: a TV ad could sway an active new car buyer's opinion about a car, and a well-written piece of direct marketing could shape a passive new car buyer's perceptions about a brand and its models.

for a new car; (ii) anyone who might influence their new car-buying decision;
(iii) second-hand car buyers.
• *Channels*: Mass media TV, cinema, press, poster and radio advertising.

Active phase
• *Role for communications*: Provide relevant information to those few hundred
  thousand people who were actively in the market to buy a new car.
• *Channels*: Local print and radio retailer advertising; direct marketing; PR;
  internet.

A range of messages
Having isolated the roles for different communications channels, we were in a
better position to determine what each should actually say.
   Passive stage. National advertising, in its primary role as a demand-generator,
was used to create a motivating identity for Volkswagen via the main models in its
range. With those models which required the most advertising support (Polo, Golf,
Passat), we picked messages that in the interests of efficiency did two things:
(1) promoted that model's merits to buyers within its own particular market sector;
(2) reinforced broader 'truths' about the Volkswagen brand to *all* car buyers. In
doing so, Passat ads (say) were not just to sell Passats, but also other Volkswagen
models.

TABLE 2: ADVERTISING CLAIMS SUPPORTED BOTH INDIVIDUAL MODELS
AND THE OVERALL VOLKSWAGEN MARQUE

Model	Model story upon which that model's advertising was based	Why that story was attractive within sector	What that story said about the Volkswagen brand
Polo	... feels sturdier than other small cars	You feel more protected and assured on the road	Safety, reliability and solidity
Golf	... is a refined design classic	You feel good about yourself and your car	Understated style and cars to be proud of
Passat	... is constructed with obsessive attention to detail	You feel you're driving a quality German car rather than a conveyer-belt rep's car	Engineering quality

Active stage. Recognising that local advertising, direct marketing, PR and the
internet were better suited to delivering more detailed information, we developed
messages which either supported the broad model claims in much more detail; or
which, more generally, told people about price and specification levels. This latter
category included short-term equipment-related offers (e.g. free air-conditioning for
summer).
   The direct marketing targeted people increasingly in the active stage of the car-
buying process. Inserts were placed in monthly motoring magazines, and direct
mail was sent to people who were looking for a car. Meanwhile, the website
provided both an informational main site and also a gateway to individual retailers'
micro-sites. This allowed customers to obtain details about the models in general,
how many were in stock, and when or where they could test-drive one.
   We resisted the temptation to simply reproduce and run broad brush-stroke
national advertising material in these active phase channels.

Tonal consistency

The Volkswagen brand tone of voice was well established. Intelligent, understated wit dated back to the 1960s American DDB work for Beetle, and a more premium edge had been added by the 1980s ads for Golf, most notably Casino (set in Monte Carlo) and Changes (featuring Paula Hamilton). To help retain the brand's 'cut above' status, we decided to keep this tone of voice – a brave decision given that a 'dumbing down' to cultivate broader mass market appeal seemed to be the more obvious consequence of Volkswagen's ambitious growth objectives.

Furthermore, we made sure this tone permeated our activity across *all* communications channels. In the interests of overall efficiency we judged it vital that Volkswagen spoke with one voice.[4]

MANY CHANNELS, MANY TASKS

The implementation of this new communications strategy was phased: overall presence was increased from September 1995 onwards, with channel-deployment plans being implemented in the following few months. More recently, online activity began in 1999.

Space limitations prevent us from outlining all the details of six years' worth of multi-channel, multi-campaign activity. However, Figures 5 and 6 give spend by channel, by model, and examples of the activity.

A key component of the above-the-line strategy involved making use of clever media buying to amplify the impact of particular creative ideas, thus making budgets work harder (Table 3).

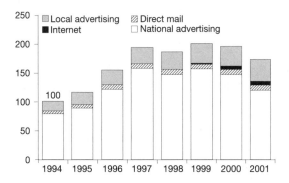

Figure 5: *How the communications budget was deployed (spend by channel by year)*
Sources: MMS, Proximity, Tribal DDB

---

4. Aiming for tonal consistency might sound like a bleedin' obvious thing to do. However, judged against the tonal diversity of activity for competitor car brands with many models to promote via many different channels to buyers within many market sectors, our decision went counter to the prevailing norm. In fact, for a car-maker with mass market ambitions and a communications approach to match, this decision was unprecedented.

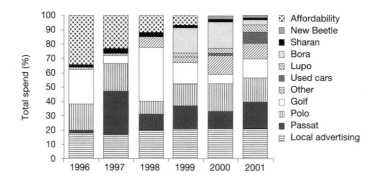

Figure 6: *Communications spend split by task*
Sources: MMS, Proximity, Tribal DDB

TABLE 3: MEDIA EXTENSION AND AMPLIFICATION OF CREATIVE IDEAS

Model/task	Creative idea	Media amplification
Beetle	*Fun on the outside, serious underneath*	Special-build poster using real 'fake fur' and pin-striped material
Bora	*Any excuse*	Saturation of motorway service stations with cars, 6-sheet posters, and posters in the Gents
Diesel	*You rarely need to fill your tank*	Ads on petrol-pump hand-nozzles
Golf	*Leave it alone*	'Would the person who..?' announcements on the ground PA at major football matches
Polo	*Protection*	Bubble-wrapped 6-sheet and 48-sheet posters

VOLKSWAGEN EXCEEDED ITS BUSINESS OBJECTIVES

The brand grew

Volkswagen's growth objectives were achieved. By 2001, Volkswagen's new car sales had more than doubled, and the 7% share target had been exceeded (Figures 7–9).

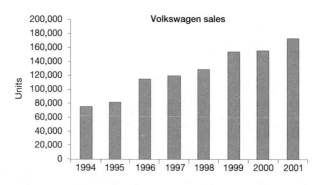

Figure 7: *Sales grew*
Source: SMMT

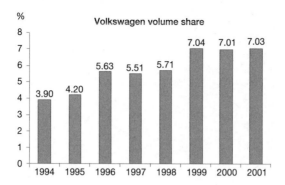

Figure 8: *Volume share grew*
Source: SMMT

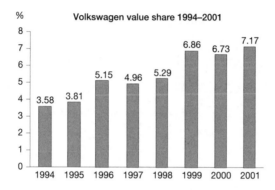

Figure 9: *Value share grew*
Sources: SMMT, NCBS

In addition to new car sales, sales of used cars and of spare parts for Volkswagens also increased (Figures 10 and 11).

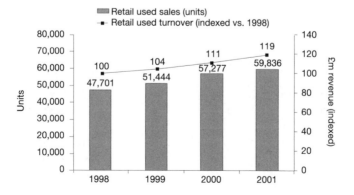

Figure 10: *Used car sales grew*[5]
Source: Volkswagen UK

---

5.   We do not have reliable data from before 1998.

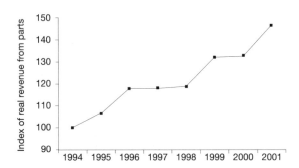

Figure 11: *Parts sales revenue grew*
Source: Volkswagen UK

Growth was profitable

The proportion of Volkswagen buyers who received an incentive decreased in absolute terms and relative to car buyers as a whole (Figure 12).

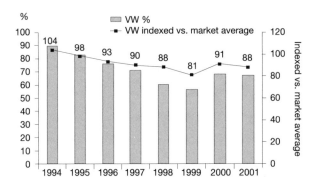

Figure 12: *The need to offer incentives was reduced: proportion of Volkswagen buyers who received an incentive*
Source: NCBS

The average amount paid for Volkswagen models increased relative to market sector averages.[6]

More cars were ordered and bought before they had actually been built. As a result, depths of stock were reduced by 30%. Hence, storage costs were reduced (Figure 13).

We cannot show any detailed profit figures, but we can say that as a result of all these favourable impacts on revenue and costs, Volkswagen's profitability was recovered.

---

6. This refers to 'transaction' price as recorded by NCBS: the amount people actually spent when buying a new car. The increase for Volkswagen reflected (1) people buying well-equipped and increasingly 'top end' variants within a model range (e.g. Golf *GTi*, Passat *V6*); (2) the reduced need for retailers to offer financial inducements to persuade them to buy.

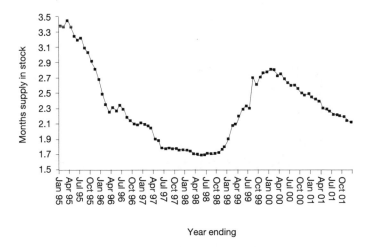

Figure 13: *Stock depths were reduced*[7]
Source: Volkswagen UK

Volkswagen's aspirational image wasn't eroded

In the period covered by this paper Volkswagen became a mass market player: a classy car make became a more common everyday car make. Yet its aspirational image was maintained. Owners' satisfaction with the reputation of their marque remained steady and strong. And there was no indication that new car buyers in general thought the brand was more common or run of the mill (Figures 14 and 15).

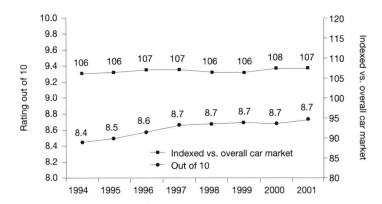

Figure 14: *Satisfaction with Volkswagen's reputation remained high*
Note: Figures have been rounded.
Source: NCBS

---

7. Stock depths increased in 1999 when Bora replaced Vento.

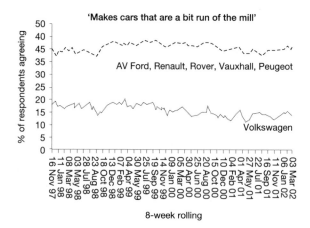

Figure 15: *Volkswagen did not become more 'run of the mill'*
Base: Marque non-owners[8]
Source: Millward Brown

ISOLATING THE EFFECT OF COMMUNICATIONS

It is something of a cliché when dealing with the car market to stress how hard it is to link communications with sales. This is because of the long interval between purchases and the range of non-communications-related factors which might influence people's eventual choice of car.[9] None the less, we believe we can show that:

- 'Passive stage' communications – principally national advertising – achieved its objectives of improving opinions of, and demand for, Volkswagens. In turn, this led to increased sales.
- 'Active stage' communications – direct marketing, the internet, PR and local advertising – achieved their objectives of providing information to active-stage buyers, and hence increased short-term sales.
- The influence of these channels was heightened by their effect on each other.
- No other factors can explain the magnitude of Volkswagen's growth between 1995 and 2001.

---

8. Thinking about the late Rosser Reeves, people are more likely to have a favourable impression of car brands that they have in their household. So, by factoring out people who own a car from the brand they are being asked about, we controlled for this potential bias. This concentration on 'marque non-owners' will be continued on all subsequent brand perception and advertising tracking charts.
9. This general problem is compounded by a more practical issue relating to data collection and management. Volkswagens are sold via franchised retailers, most of whom are themselves part of dealer groups selling a range of different cars from other brands too (on different sites). Each of these businesses has its own idiosyncratic way of recording sales, enquiries, and whether its customers have made use of or been exposed to marketing activity before walking through the door. Currently, this makes it extremely hard to link marketing activity to any *individual* new or used car sale.

'PASSIVE-STAGE' COMMUNICATIONS BUILT THE BRAND AND SALES

The channel best suited for passive-stage communications was broadcast national advertising. We will show that:

- it was famous, appealing, clear and stylish.
- it made people think better of Volkswagen.
- it increased demand for Volkswagen.
- it drove sales in both the long and the short term.

National advertising: famous, appealing, clear and stylish[10]

Volkswagen UK won more creative awards than any other advertiser during the period covered by this paper.[11] Much more importantly, its advertising has also claimed a place in the hearts and minds of new car buyers. On average it has generated 2% greater awareness per pound spent than the advertising of Volkswagen's main competitors.[12]

> 'I think they're the best car ads. Every other one has cars zooming down mountain roads. VW ads are always more interesting than that.'
>
> 'They're often better than the programme you're watching. There're not many adverts you can say that about.'
>
> 'You can always tell when it's going to be a Volkswagen ad. They are more clever. Quite often you don't seem to actually see the car until the end, but you always know it's going to be for Volkswagen because they look different.'
>
> 'They are an intelligent advertiser ... I find a lot of adverts quite patronising. With Volkswagen ads there's always a little bit to get, so I don't feel they're talking down to me.'
>
> 'They are the kind of ads you'll tell your friends about the next day.'
>
> Source: BMP qual 1995–2001

The advertising communicated as intended: on average, 77% of the audience 'took out' the intended primary message from each execution. And the ads were seen as clever, stylish and enjoyable (Figure 16).

National advertising made people think better of Volkswagen

In combination, the campaigns for the individual models were meant to position Volkswagen as well engineered, reliable, safe, and as cars you'd be proud to have on your drive. Judged against these measures, by the end of 2001 Volkswagen was ahead of the four other top five car brands (Table 4).

---

10. Since the growth strategy Volkswagen has run far too many individual campaigns for us to cover in detail in this paper. Hopefully, the following broad overview will suffice. (The successful 'Surprisingly Ordinary Prices' campaign was covered in detail in the 1998 Volkswagen case study.)
11. D&AD, Cannes Golden Lion, BTAA, Campaign Press & Poster, Creative Circle, and Eurobest.
12. This is over the time we have tracked ad awareness at an overall brand level; since March 1999. The main competitors are Ford, Vauxhall, Renault and Peugeot (as in the rest of paper).

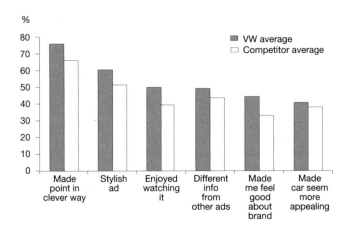

Figure 16: *Volkswagen ads were clever, stylish and enjoyable*
Base: Those who have seen ads
Source: Millward Brown

TABLE 4: VOLKSWAGEN BECAME IMAGE LEADER

% agreeing	Particularly well engineered (%)	Particularly reliable (%)	Proud to have on drive (%)	Feel safe driving (%)
Volkswagen	70	63	52	67
Ford	27	35	27	43
Peugeot	28	29	33	37
Renault	23	24	25	34
Vauxhall	20	25	23	35

Base: Non-owners of Volkswagens
Source: Millward Brown last 8 weeks of 2001

There was a highly significant correlation between adspend and each of these measures (Table 5).

TABLE 5: ADSPEND AND BRAND IMAGE

	Correlation with adspend (%)	Significance level[13] (%)
Well engineered	29.7	99
Particularly reliable	22.9	99
Safer to drive	40.9	99
Proud to have on drive	22.8	99

Base: Non-owners of Volkswagen
Sources: Millward Brown, Register-MEAL, MMS

In addition, those who were aware of the advertising were more likely to have a favourable impression of Volkswagen than those who were not (Figure 17).

---

13. That is to say, we can be 99% certain that there was a statistically significant relationship between these two variables: there was only a one in a 100 chance that the relationship was merely random.

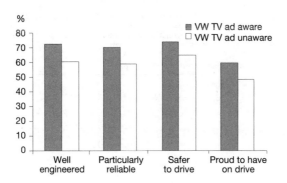

Figure 17: *Advertising drove brand image: Volkswagen image better among TV ad aware than TV ad unaware*
Base: Non-owners of Volkswagen
Source: Millward Brown

National advertising increased demand for Volkswagen

With advertising favourably affecting perceptions of the brand, demand for Volkswagen also increased. This was a key measure for the brand: while passive-stage car buyers were not currently thinking of buying a car, it was essential that, *when they did*, Volkswagen was among the two or three cars they would consider.

With the advent of the new strategy, Volkswagen went from being the least to the most considered of the five major car brands (Figure 18).

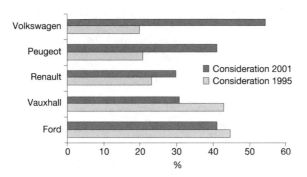

Figure 18: *After advertising, Volkswagen went from least to most considered marque*
Base: Non-owners of Volkswagen
Sources: Hall and Partners (9–10/1995), Millward Brown (Q4 2001)

More specifically, there was a highly significant correlation between advertising spend and consideration levels.[14]

---

14. Eight-week rolling TVRs vs. eight-week rolling consideration/shortlisting (same data for *change in* data below it).

TABLE 6: ADVERTISING AND DEMAND FOR VOLKSWAGEN

% agreeing ...	Correlation with adspend (%)	Significance level (%)
'I would consider buying...'	27.3	99
'I would definitely shortlist...'	15.6	99

Base: Non-owners of Volkswagen
Sources: Millward Brown, Register-MEAL, MMS

Finally, those who were aware of the advertising were more likely to consider Volkswagens than those who were not (Figure 19).

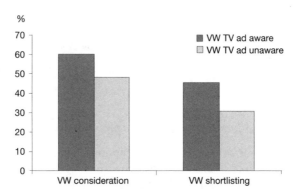

Figure 19: *Volkswagen consideration better among TV ad aware vs. TV ad unaware*
Base: Non-owners of Volkswagen
Source: Millward Brown

National advertising drove Volkswagen's sales

Improved opinions and increased consideration of Volkswagen translated into increased sales. There was a strong correspondence between Volkswagen adspend and market share (Figure 20).

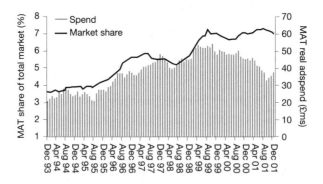

Figure 20: *Close correlation between Volkswagen spend and share*[15]
Sources: SMMT, Register-MEAL, MMS

---

15. To show this, we need to take a longer perspective: advertising might increase people's consideration of Volkswagen, but they might not actually be in the market for a new car until a long time after this. Hence the data are presented on an MAT basis.

There was a very strong and highly significant correlation between adspend and market share (Figure 21).[16]

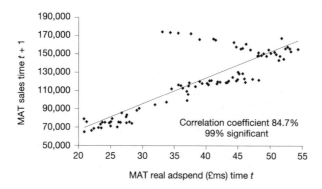

Figure 21: *Volkswagen spend correlated with sales*
Sources: MMS, SMMT

A comparison with Volkswagen's performance in other European markets puts this into perspective (Figure 22). In each, there has been a relationship between the change in adspend and change in share between 1994 and 2001. The UK's greater increase in adspend translated into higher share.[17]

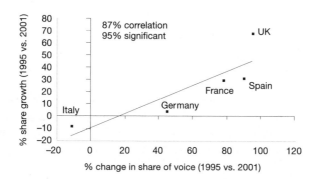

Figure 22: *UK's higher adspend leads to higher growth than Continent*
Sources: MMS, SMMT, and Continental equivalents

---

16. A one-month lag has been added to the data. On average, there is a five-week gap between a Volkswagen customer ordering a new car and that car being registered and delivered (source: NCBS 2001). It is at the point of registration that the car is officially recorded as 'sold' and picked up by SMMT sales data. Hence, when looking at the relationship between advertising and when the customer decides to buy a car, it is necessary to lag the sales data by one month. Ideally it would be five weeks, but the sales data are issued monthly.

17. This difference in growth rates cannot be attributed to fluctuations in Continental price levels between 1995 and 2001 (source: European Commission reports on car price differentials within the EU, 1995–2001). Nor can it be attributed to the competitive context being somehow weaker in the UK during that time period: Volkswagen's competitors sold – and sell – the same models all across Europe (with the honourable exception of the late and deeply lamented Renault Twingo).

In addition to a long-term sales effect, Volkswagen advertising also drove *short-term* sales (Figure 23): it worked against that 8% of new car buyers who happened to be in the market during the month when activity was run.

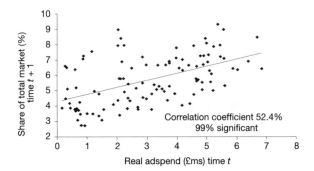

Figure 23: *Advertising drove short-term sales: Volkswagen* monthly *spend correlated with* monthly *share*
Sources: SMMT, MMS

The building blocks of this success were at a model level (Table 7). There was a highly significant correlation between each model's advertising spend and its share performance.

TABLE 7: MODEL ADVERTISING AND SHARE FOR THAT PARTICULAR MODEL

Model share/model spend	Correlation with adspend (%)	Significance level (%)
Polo share/Polo spend	82	99
Golf share/Golf spend	24	95
Passat share/Passat spend	67	99

Base: Non-owners of Volkswagen
Sources: SMMT, Register-MEAL, MMS

Furthermore, as we had intended (p. 506), advertising for one model had a 'halo' effect on the other Volkswagen models, thereby maximising the efficiency of the overall advertising investment (Table 8). In the context of mass market car brands, demonstrating such a halo effect is unprecedented.

TABLE 8: MODEL ADVERTISING AND SHARE FOR OTHER MODELS

Model share/model spend	Correlation with adspend (%)	Significance level (%)
Polo share/non-Polo VW spend	48	99
Passat share/non-Passat VW spend	61	99

Base: Non-owners of Volkswagen
Sources: SMMT, Register-MEAL, MMS

As one might expect, these correlations were not as strong as the correlation between a model's share performance and *its own* advertising. While advertising for one model *did* affect other models, the greater effect was on the model that it was advertising![18]

18. It is with regret that we were not able to show a link between advertising for non-Golf models and Golf share. Perhaps it will always be harder for Polo and Passat advertising to make the iconic Golf even more desirable.

Clearly, Volkswagen's passive-stage communication achieved its objectives. Admired, stylish and salient national advertising significantly affected people's perceptions of, and demand for, Volkswagen. This in turn drove sales in the long and short term at both a marque and model level. And this was achieved with the utmost efficiency, with advertising for one Volkswagen model influencing sales of other models.

ACTIVE-STAGE CHANNELS PROVIDED INFORMATION, STIMULATED RESPONSE AND GENERATED SALES

The primary roles of active-stage channels were to provide detailed information to people actively looking to buy a new car, facilitate further contact with Volkswagen and its retailers, and ultimately ensure that more of them went on to buy a Volkswagen. The channels employed for these tasks were direct marketing, the internet, PR and local advertising. All achieved their objectives.

Local advertising drove sales

Local advertising drove Volkswagen sales above and beyond the sales effect of national advertising. Controlling for the size of an individual retailer's catchment area and its relative affluence, there was a very strong correlation between the weight of an individual retailer's ad spend and that retailer's sales (Figure 24).

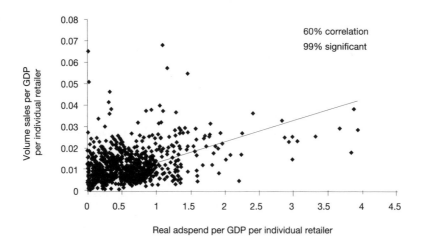

Figure 24: *Retailer local adspend and sales: local spend correlated with local sales*
Source: Volkswagen UK

There was also a strong relationship between *increases* in a retailer's adspend and that retailer's sales *growth* (Figure 25).

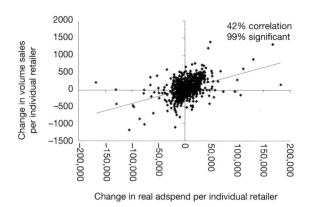

Figure 25: *Change in local spend correlated with change in local sales*
Source: Volkswagen UK

Direct marketing prompted excellent response and sales

Direct marketing generated a high response rate among its active-stage audience, and prompted a high proportion of these people to go on to buy a Volkswagen.

On average, Volkswagen's direct marketing response rate from March 1999 was an unusually high 6.5%.[19] We do not have access to car market norms, but response data from other markets suggest that 0.5% to 3% is a more common figure.

In turn, these responses translated cost-efficiently into thousands of sales – sales that paid for themselves. These figures only represent sales that could be tracked back to a centrally recorded response. They do not include those direct-marketing recipients who, having received the material, may have gone directly to their nearest Volkswagen retailer. Because many retailers currently have no mechanism in place to record what marketing activity may have driven customers through their doors, the figures therefore almost certainly underestimate direct marketing's overall contribution to sales.

Apart from the excellent standard of the creative work, the success of direct marketing may be put down to choosing the right channel for the job. It allowed us to talk to a focused and receptive audience – active new car buyers – in a relevant and cost-efficient way.[20]

The internet provided helpful information cost-efficiently

The website provided easy-to-understand and useful information to a large number of active-stage car buyers, and online advertising played an important role in channelling people to that site. Both achieved these ends cost-efficiently.

---

19. The results in this section are based on activity from March 1999. Prior to this, the accuracy of response and sales data for analysis purposes was poor. Nevertheless, even dealing with the period from March 1999 to December 2001 (as with the section dealing with national advertising), there were too many campaigns run in this period for us to look at individually within the constraints of the word-count.
20. Eight out of the ten direct-mail campaigns with the lowest cost-per-sale communicated a temporary offer that was available on a particular Volkswagen model (say, air-conditioning on a Polo). Such offers were relevant only to active-phase new car buyers. Arguably, the good response to these campaigns validates our decision to deploy direct marketing in a primarily active-phase capacity.

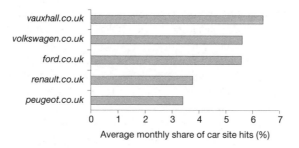

Figure 26: *Website traffic was high: Volkswagen had a higher share of car site hits than its market share would suggest*
Source: Hitwise

www.volkswagen.co.uk[21]

The website could be described as a convenient and highly interactive brochure. In 2001 it was visited 2.7 million times by 1 million 'discrete' visitors. This made it the second most popular car-maker's website – more popular than Renault and Peugeot, Volkswagen's nearest competitors in terms of market size (Figure 26).

Of these visitors, 71% were aiming to buy a new car in the next three months and 92% were seriously considering buying a new Volkswagen – our core active-phase target audience.[22] The site gave them the information they were looking for in a convenient, useful and enjoyable way. As one consumer described it: *'The site is a good ambassador for Volkswagen.'*[23]

The site was usable, useful and enjoyable

- Eighty per cent of visitors found it very/quite easy to find the information they needed.
- Eighty-four per cent of visitors described the usefulness of the site's content as good/very good.
- Sixty-six per cent of visitors described the site as very/quite enjoyable.

Source: Netpoll 2001

The average site user visited more pages than when on other car sites, suggesting a greater level of involvement – in internet parlance, the site was 'sticky'.[24]

Given the number of visitors and their positive experience of the site, we are confident that the objective of providing information to active stagers was achieved and at a cost of 56 pence per visitor, substantially cheaper than printing a brochure and sending it to someone!

Online advertising

We have reliable (2001) data for only two campaigns: one for Polo, one for the launch of the facelifted Passat.[25] The Polo advertising was for a limited edition

---

21. Unfortunately, we only have reliable data on this channel for 2001.
22. Source: Netpoll.
23. Source: Tribal DDB qualitative research, November 2001.
24. Source: Hitwise, 2001.
25. The Passat campaign is covered in more detail in the Passat case study also entered for these awards (p. 533).

model. It ran primarily on third-party websites that were likely to be visited by would-be car buyers. It was designed to be clicked on, sending people through to the relevant section of the website.

Some 50,500 people 'clicked through'. This represents a substantial proportion of the active small-car buyers who were in the market for a car when the activity ran. The cost-per-click-through was a mere £1.19 – again, substantially cheaper than sending someone a printed brochure.

We do not have a mechanism in place to make direct links between this web activity and people subsequently visiting a retailer and buying a Volkswagen. However, anecdotal feedback from Volkswagen retailers themselves suggests more and more customers are coming through their doors 'armed to the high teeth' with information gathered on the internet. The implication is that, when we establish appropriate measures, we will find online activity is a precursor to very many Volkswagen sales. Given the cost-efficiency of this new channel, the number of sales required for the channel to be shown to be paying for itself (and more so) won't have to be that high. Based on the figures shown above, we estimate only 1 in 400!

As with direct marketing, this demonstrates that Volkswagen UK has made the right decision about how a new and evolving channel can be best employed within the overall marketing mix.[26]

PR: *plentiful, good, and in the right places*

Volkswagen generated a great deal of PR, predominantly good in tone (Figure 27).[27]

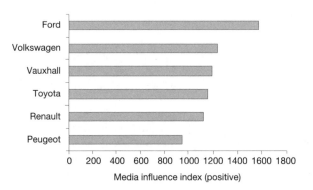

Figure 27: *Volkswagen second only to Ford in positive PR generated*
Source: Millward Brown Precis

Indeed, relative to its market share, Volkswagen received more good PR than any other manufacturer (Figure 28).

---

26. The importance of this should not be underestimated: arguably many marketers have wasted a lot of money trying to use the internet for jobs to which it was ill-suited.
27. These Millward Brown data are from the beginning of 1999. Data were not available prior to this date.

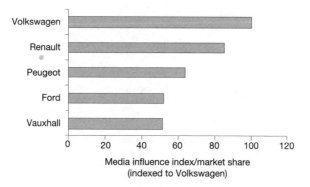

Figure 28: *For its market size Volkswagen receives most positive PR*
Source: Millward Brown Precis

Volkswagen sought to generate PR primarily around its quality (engineering, build, safety and reliability), to substantiate claims made by other channels at the brand level (Figure 29). In this it generated more PR than any other manufacturer.

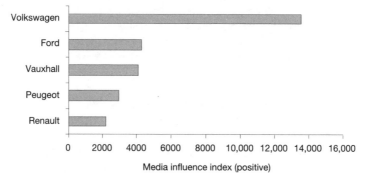

Figure 29: *Volkswagen receives most positive PR around 'quality'*
Source: Millward Brown Precis

As intended, a greater proportion appeared in titles likely to be read by people who were actively looking to buy a new car (Figure 30).

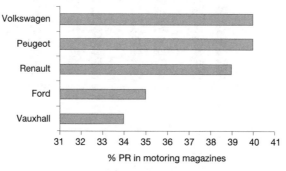

Figure 30: *A greater proportion of Volkswagen's PR is in 'active-stage' motoring magazines*
Source: Millward Brown Precis

There is significant evidence that the PR has been 'on message'. While journalists cannot be told what to say, they can certainly be pointed in the right direction. Here is one of the huge number of examples we could give you!

Excerpt from Volkswagen press release
Insurance groups for the new Polo have been confirmed by the ABI. Starting at Group 2 for the launch entry model, the 1.2-litre 65bhp, they represent a considerable improvement over those for the previous Polo.

Excerpt from article from *New Reg* magazine.
It's go low for Polo on the insurance front! A delighted Volkswagen say the all-new model will be from as low as Group 2. It's a major achievement for VW.

Further excerpt from Volkswagen press release
Lower repair costs are also key. For example, in a standard 10mph rear end impact, the new Polo's bumper will cost £153 to repair – that's almost £300 less than on the outgoing model.

Further extract from *New Reg* magazine
Low repair costs are also a key issue, say the German number-one sellers. In a standard 10mph rear-end impact, the new Polo's bumper will cost £153 to repair – almost £300 LESS than the outgoing model.

The excellence of Volkswagen's PR is reflected in The Guild of Motoring Writers' annual survey, in which journalists rank the manufacturers' performance in key areas of service to them.[28] In this, among every manufacturer, Volkswagen has come first in four of the past five years.

THE COMBINED EFFECTS OF
DIFFERENT COMMUNICATIONS CHANNELS

Each channel worked in isolation, but did they work together in a complementary way? Certainly, there is good evidence of an additive effect: the more communications people were exposed to, the better their opinions of Volkswagen (Figure 31).

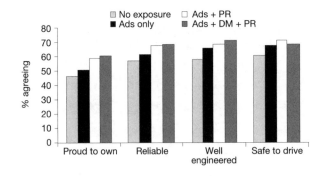

Figure 31: *The more channels seen, the better people's opinion of Volkswagen*
Base: Non-owners of Volkswagen
Source: Millward Brown, mean score 10/00–12/01[29]

---

28. For example, response to journalist's enquiries, providing press releases and pictures, loaning vehicles, professionalism.
29. We have tracked such channel exposure only since autumn 2000. 'Internet' is conspicuous by its absence.

Furthermore, multiple-channel exposure was linked to greater demand for Volkswagen (Figure 32).

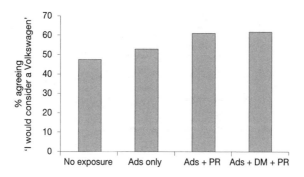

Figure 32: *The more channels seen, the greater the demand for Volkswagen*
Base: Non-owners of Volkswagen
Source: Millward Brown, mean score 10/00–12/01

OTHER FACTORS CANNOT EXPLAIN THE PATTERN OF VOLKSWAGEN'S GROWTH

Distribution

The number of Volkswagen retailers decreased (Figure 33).

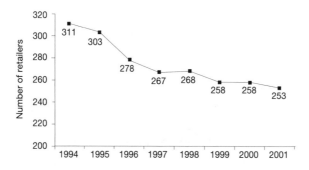

Figure 33: *Distribution decreased*
Source: Volkswagen UK

And there is nothing to suggest that the remaining retailers improved significantly: customer satisfaction levels remained steady, comparable to industry norms (Figure 34).

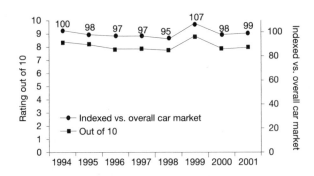

Figure 34: *Customer experience: the retailer 'experience' remained constant*
Source: NCBS

Pricing and discounts

Volkswagen's growth cannot be attributed to price decreases. Indeed, as we have noted, the average amount paid for Volkswagen models increased versus its competitors. Nor can it be attributed to discounts: as we saw in Figure 12 the proportion of Volkswagen buyers who received a financial discount decreased, both in absolute terms and relative to market averages.

Product range

Volkswagen entered three new market sectors between 1994 and 2001. However, most of the brand's growth came from sectors where it already had a model presence before 1994. And two of these new models, Lupo and New Beetle, were launched in 1999, four years after growth began (Figure 35).

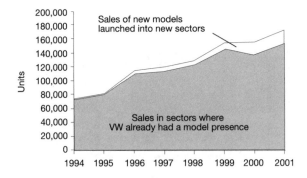

Figure 35: *Volkswagen sales in 'old' vs. 'new' market sectors*
Source: SMMT

Product quality

Volkswagen sells, launches and relaunches the same excellent cars all across Europe. But UK growth rates outstripped those in Continental markets (Figure 36).

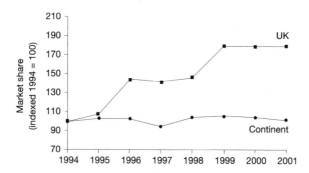

Figure 36: *UK vs. Europe share*
Source: SMMT and Continental equivalents

Fleet discounts

Some UK car-makers negotiate massive volume deals with organisations that need to buy large numbers of company cars. However, in line with its objective of achieving profitable growth, Volkswagen has refused to try and 'buy share' with such fleets.

OVERALL COMMUNICATIONS CONTRIBUTED SIGNIFICANTLY TO THE VOLKSWAGEN BUSINESS

Despite the difficulties associated with proving effectiveness in the car market, we have shown that 'passive-stage' communications made Volkswagens more desirable to a broad audience and, beyond that, drove sales – sales of the models being advertised, sales of other Volkswagen models, and ultimately sales of the overall brand.

'Active-stage' local marketing, direct marketing and the internet provided the narrower, more receptive, active car-buying audience with relevant information in a timely, cost-efficient and profitable way. These channels too drove sales, helped by a positive PR background in motoring magazines and motoring press. Their influence was heightened by their effect on each other: the more channels people were exposed to, the greater their influence.

And between 1995 and 2001, no other factors can explain the magnitude of Volkswagen's share growth. By way of summary, the communications programme in its entirety has been successful. During these years there was a strong and highly significant correlation between share and Volkswagen UK's overall communications investment (Figure 37).[30]

---

30. Annual total communications spend correlated to annual market share.

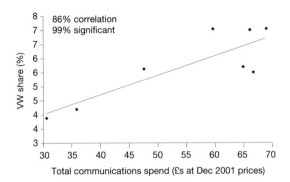

Figure 37: *VW share and total spend*
Sources: SMMT, MMS, Proximity, Tribal DDB

VOLKSWAGEN COMMUNICATIONS WERE EFFICIENT

Clearly, investment in communications has increased revenue for Volkswagen. Looking at the other side of the profit equation, it has also helped reduce costs by being efficient.

A comparison with Renault

Volkswagen and Renault have much in common:

- They are the only two true importers in the UK top five.[31]
- They offer a similar range of models competing in similar mass market sectors.[32]
- Renault too has significantly increased its communications budget (Figure 38).

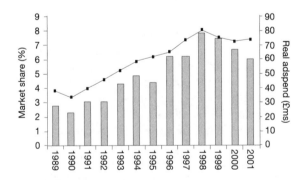

Figure 38: *Renault growth 1990–2001: Renault embarked on a growth strategy*
Sources: SMMT, Register-MEAL, MMS

---

31. The remaining three top five players, Ford, Vauxhall and Peugeot, have all (or, at least, had!) factories in the UK – and hence have different cost structures.
32. Each had four models in the three volume sectors of the market between 1995 and 2001. Renault had Clio, 19/Megane, Scenic and Laguna (accounting for 95% of its sales). Volkswagen had Polo, Golf, Vento/Bora and Passat (accounting for 91% of its sales). Source: SMMT.

- in the past 12 years both have increased their market share from just under 4% to just over 7% and have taken the same time to do so (Figure 39).

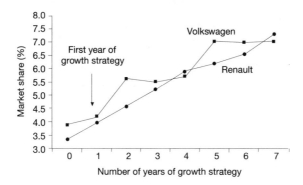

Figure 39: *Volkswagen and Renault had strikingly similar growth*[33]
Source: SMMT

However, Renault had to invest much more in communications than Volkswagen to achieve this position (Figure 40).[34]

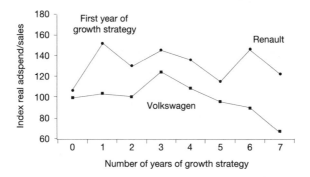

Figure 40: *Volkswagen's spend per car sold was lower than Renault's*
Sources: SMMT, MMS

Volkswagen communications were increasingly efficient

We have shown that Volkswagen invested in communications efficiently compared with a benchmark competitor. Beyond that, in an absolute sense, its investment was also increasingly efficient over time (Figure 41).

---

33. Year 0: Renault = 1990, Volkswagen = 1994.
34. We do not have access to reliable data on Renault's direct marketing, local advertising or internet spend over this period, so unfortunately this analysis can include only advertising. However, as with Volkswagen, it is almost certain that advertising would have accounted for the majority of communications investment over this period.

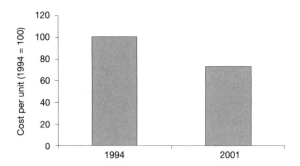

Figure 41: *Volkswagen's total communications cost per unit has improved*
Sources: MMS, Proximity, Tribal DDB

THE COMMUNICATIONS PAID FOR THEMSELVES

We have now seen that communications were effective in generating revenue for Volkswagen in a cost-efficient way. We now need to confirm that they did so profitably. We have already shown how direct marketing paid for itself, and suggested that internet activity is similarly 'profitable'; here we look at the remaining channels.[35]

Local advertising

We estimated return on investment by analysing the relationship between a retailer's yearly adspend and sales referred to earlier (Figures 24 and 25). We have calculated that for (say) every £10,000 spent by a retailer, it sells 96 more cars. Given the average price paid for a Volkswagen and the average retailer margin, this means the local advertising more than pays for itself.

National advertising

We have constructed an econometric model to quantify return on investment. Between 1995 and 2001 Volkswagen UK invested an extra £142 million in national advertising. The model indicates this extra investment has generated an additional 151,000 sales. In revenue terms this equates to £1.99 billion.[36] Given Volkswagen's profit margins, this means that the national advertising has already paid for itself.

There are further benefits. Tens of thousands of the buyers of those 151,000 cars were new customers for Volkswagen – as were many of the buyers brought into the brand by direct marketing. Motoring industry sources have put the average lifetime value of a customer at £156,000, including all the cars, parts and services

---

35. The only channel we have not been able to put figures to is PR. However, the costs associated with PR are relatively low and the PR push has been successful. Anecdotally, Volkswagen is in no doubt that its investment in PR has been amply returned.
36. 151,000 × average price paid for a Volkswagen. Source: SMMT.

they might buy from a manufacturer over this lifetime. So the longer-term return on investment is even more considerable.

More speculatively, it is possible that in strengthening the reputation of the Volkswagen brand, the communications programme has benefited, by association, other car marques in the Volkswagen Group, all of which have grown in the period covered by this paper.

AND FINALLY...

Different people in the marketing industry use the term 'integration' in different ways. For many, integration is when different channels work to the same creative idea – or at least the same strategy. Volkswagen's success, however, has been founded on integration of a different variety. It has been based on the recognition that different channels are effective in different ways, and may be used to target different audiences with different messages. Ultimately, the approach is based on a sound understanding of consumer buying behaviour and how consumers use different information sources on the 'road to purchase'.

The effectiveness demonstrated here is vindication of this approach. A mass media channel communicated fundamental product truths in compelling ways to a broad audience, and was hugely successful in building brand image and desirability. Simultaneously, more focused channels delivered product details to an information-hungry audience of 'primed' active new car buyers, generating responses and maximising the conversion of desire into sales. In combination, all glued together with a shared tone of voice, their effect on Volkswagen's business fortunes has been, as we have shown, quite considerable.

21

Volkswagen Passat

'Beautifully crafted': launching the facelifted Passat in 2001

Principal authors: Richard Butterworth, James Hillhouse
and Sara Donoghugh, BMP DDB
Collaborating authors: Claire Holland, Mediacom, Tom Goodwin, Tribal DDB,
and David Parslow, Proximity London

EDITOR'S SUMMARY

This case describes how an integrated multi-channel communications campaign was used to launch the facelifted Passat in 2001, leading to a 21% increase in volume share and a 30% increase in value share. With all the communications channels working together efficiently, spend per unit decreased by 9%. The case shows how launch communications directly led, profitably, to 8180 extra sales and £131 million extra revenue for Volkswagen UK in the short term, in addition to more long-term benefits.

This paper describes how in 2001 an integrated communications programme was used to help launch a facelifted version of the Volkswagen Passat in the face of more heavily supported and, ostensibly, more attractive new competition. It is quite a succinct paper insofar as it focuses on only one year's worth of activity and on only one marketing task.

THE PASSAT

The Passat is a model sold in the upper-medium sector of the car market (Figure 1). This sector accounts for around 17% of new car sales and includes models such as the Ford Mondeo, Renault Laguna, Peugeot 406 and Nissan Primera. Typically, models within the sector have a product life cycle of eight or nine years before they are replaced with a successor. Sometimes that successor carries the same name, sometimes a new name is introduced: Carina becomes Avensis, Cavalier becomes Vectra and so on.

Figure 1: *The Mark 5 Passat*

The most recent incarnation of the Passat – its fifth – was launched in spring 1997. This launch, supported by 'A Car Born Out of Obsession' advertising, was very successful. By the end of 1998 its sales were healthy and it had a reputation for engineering excellence which none of its competitors could match. Sales remained good in 1999 but as the model began to enter, in life cycle terms, its 'middle age', sales began to decline (Figure 2).

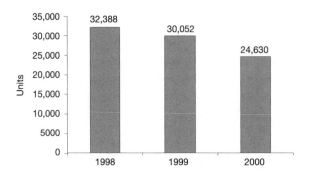

Figure 2: *Passat started to lose sales*
Source: SMMT

Cars as products are constantly evolving: advances in design, engineering, technology and manufacturing efficiency exert a constant influence on what is available to consumers. On a minor level, this might mean that a car-maker can afford to offer a piece of equipment such as ABS or air-conditioning as standard rather than as a paid-for extra. More fundamentally, this might mean that the introduction of a radically improved new model makes all its competitor models seem inferior and outdated – for a year or two at least.

This dynamic exerts a uniquely strong influence in the upper-medium sector of the car market. Buyers within the sector are predominantly middle-aged men; men with a typically blokish affinity for technical novelty. On top of this, a large proportion of these chaps get their cars through company car schemes. This involves choosing their car from a menu of available models or from within a set price band. As a result, novelty and technical progress become associated with status in the workplace car park. Among those drivers who haven't progressed to the heady upper management heights of being able to choose a BMW, Mercedes or Audi – that is to say, the vast majority of upper-medium drivers – driving 'the next new thing', the car with the latest advances, becomes a sign of where that driver is in the managerial pecking order.[1]

This means that cars in the sector cannot rest on their laurels for long. A model may have an eight or nine-year lifecycle. But during this time between launches of 'all-new' models, manufacturers need to give their wares a 'facelift'. These facelifts involve equipment upgrades and often significant changes to the car's interior and exterior, even though underneath the car is still largely the same.

FACELIFTING THE PASSAT

In 2000 Volkswagen decided to give the Passat a facelift so that it would remain competitive in the novelty-fixated world of the company car park. There were no fundamental product issues with the underlying car so the facelift was, on the scale of facelifts, more a nip, a tuck and a firming up at the health farm than a complete overhaul. Most obviously it was given a new expression around its lights, much more chrome and a spruce-up on the inside. Less obviously, the 'torsional rigidity' of the overall body was increased, some engine types/sizes were phased out and others were introduced to replace them. The launch date for this facelifted car was January 2001 (Figure 3).

Figure 3: *The facelifted Passat*

1. Source: BMP qualitative research, 1996–2000.

Motoring press comments on the facelifted Passat:

'The difference is not huge. Think of the contrast between tomato purée and tomato ketchup.'

Daily Telegraph, April 2001

'When restyling the Passat, Volkswagen took a cautious approach, preferring to build on the car's natural strengths rather than making dramatic changes.'

Auto Express, February 2001

'A new Passat goes on sale this month but you will have to give it a thorough inspection if you are to see what makes it stand apart from its illustrious predecessor.'

Scotsman, January 2001

'Open the door and VW's engineers have wisely left well alone. There was nothing really wrong with the old car's interior and the same is true here, where you'd be hard pressed to spot the changes.'

Sunday Express, January 2001

'The only visible difference I could discern is the boot, which is taller and longer than it used to be.'

Sunday Telegraph, March 2001

Such a facelift was a timely defensive step. Around the same time, two of the Passat's major competitors launched *all-new* and highly attractive models. The new Ford Mondeo was launched in December 2000. It had been deliberately designed to exceed the 1997 Passat's quality levels. When this New Mondeo was presented to the motoring press it received superlative reviews. And it went on to win *What Car?* and *Top Gear*'s Car of the Year awards.

The all-new Renault Laguna launched in February 2001. Its quality represented a step change for Renault in the upper-medium sector. The car was so well made that it became the first model ever to achieve five stars in the Euro-NCAP safety test. It too met with universal praise from motoring journalists and industry experts.

Motoring press comments on the new Mondeo and Laguna:

'Ford's new Mondeo goes on sale in the UK at the beginning of next month and will send its rivals scurrying back to their drawing boards faster than you can say "motorway service station". Make no mistake, the new Ford Mondeo will be the car in which any self-respecting sales rep should be seen hanging up his or her jacket next year.'

Sunday Express, November 2000

'The stylish new Laguna range goes on sale next February and from my brief experience I would say this car will cut short the honeymoon of Ford's new Mondeo.'

Mail On Sunday, November 2000

'The new Laguna was yesterday named the safest *ever* car. It scores a record five out of five stars in independent Euro-NCAP safety tests.'

The Sun, March 2001

This meant that the facelifted Passat was entering a challenging world, facing two extremely good, wholly new, competitors – competitors with much to shout about and, in all likelihood, with big launch communications budgets to match. None the less, Volkswagen's business objectives for the facelifted car were bullish:

- Increase sales from 25,000 in 2000 to 30,000 in 2001.
- Achieve this without resorting to the high levels of discounts and incentivisation which are prevalent in the UK car market.

LAUNCHING THE FACELIFTED CAR

Given the challenging context, Volkswagen's communication agencies were briefed to develop an integrated launch campaign where every penny spent worked as hard as possible. The overall communications objectives were as follows:

- Create awareness of launch.
- Communicate and reinforce what was most attractive about the facelifted Passat.
- Provide active 'in the market' new car-buyers with in-depth information about the car.
- Uncover potential buyers and encourage them to take test-drives.

A channel strategy was devised, taking account of the lengthy 'road to purchase' new car-buyers go through, the numbers of people at each stage in the process, their information needs at each stage, and the ability of particular channels to deliver that information and potentially influence behaviour.

PR, in the form of press relations, was the channel spearhead. It was used to maximise positive coverage of the car in the last quarter of 2000 when it received its UK debut at the October NEC Motorshow, and was scrutinised by motoring journalists for the first time. Its aim was to ensure that – inasmuch as such things can be influenced – specialist motoring correspondents alluded to those well-crafted attributes of the facelifted Passat which would subsequently be promoted in 'paid-for' communications channels.

Moving into 2001, as the Passat featured in more and more motoring press road-tests and reviews, PR was used to ensure that when active new car-buyers used that medium as a shortlist-narrowing information source, they would be more likely to have their perceptions of the Passat reinforced rather than contradicted.

National TV, poster, and print advertising was used to announce the car's arrival to a wide new car-buying audience, and to communicate what, broadly, made it attractive. People buy new cars about once every three years so it was recognised that the majority of this audience would not be in the market for a car until 2002 or 2003. Nevertheless, the hope was that this strand of activity – our most intrusive channel – would have a sales effect in 2001 by getting the Passat on to the shortlists of people looking to buy in that year.

National advertising was reinforced with *regional and local retailer advertising* aimed at people actively in the market for a new car. Recognising that people at this stage of the new car-buying process are looking for information to help choose between shortlisted cars (and that they use 'local' media to help do this), this local work went into more detail about Passat pricing and variants, and where people might buy one locally.

The *internet* was used in a similar way. As internet penetration has grown, this new channel has been used increasingly by new car-buyers in two ways: (1) as a means of investigating the details of their shortlisted models, both from the car-makers themselves and from objective third-party websites; and (2) as a convenient method of making comparisons between shortlisted models. Accordingly, the Passat pages on the Volkswagen website were used to provide rational product information about the car – information that was intended to support the claims being made by more broadcast communications channels. In a sense they served as a convenient, interactive, information-packed brochure.

More proactively, keyword placements in search engines and various forms of online ads were used to increase the likelihood in an online environment that new car-buyers would make their way to the Passat pages on the website.

Direct marketing was used to encourage people to test-drive the facelifted Passat. It was aimed at three key prospect audiences in decreasing order of 'hotness':

- Owners of three to five-year-old Passats: drivers who were likely to be nearing the time to think about replacing their current car (16,000).
- People who had expressed an interest in the Passat model when responding to past direct marketing activity (14,000).
- People on lifestyle-based mailing lists whose names fitted the general profile of past Passat buyers (100,000).

All three groups were sent information which supported and elaborated on the claims being made in national advertising.

Point-of-sale material for display in Volkswagen retailers at the time of launch was used to echo the national advertising claims. Its role, in the information-rich showroom environment, was to remind buyers teetering on the edge of purchase why they had come so close to buying a facelifted Passat in the first place – a last-minute emotional nudge for anyone who might be having any doubts.

THE 'BEAUTIFULLY CRAFTED' CREATIVE IDEA AND CREATIVE WORK

An idea was needed which had the scale appropriate to a launch – albeit a facelifted one – and the flexibility to unite all the complementary strands of activity which would be running in all the various communications channels. Lacking a single major 'flagship' product improvement as a focus, the communications brief emphasised the general emotional benefits of buying an extremely well-put-together and refined new car.

The resulting creative idea was based on a simple human insight: when you have just bought a brilliantly engineered new car you take great care of it. In fact, during this new car honeymoon period you sometimes go to quite absurd lengths to ensure the car stays as good as new, as clean as new, as smooth-running as new, for as long as possible. This creative idea was summed up by the line '*The beautifully crafted new Passat; you'll want to keep it that way.*' Such a driver-focused approach was relatively unusual for a car launch.

Powerful and flexible, this idea manifested itself in many forms. In national advertising it was dramatised in three TV executions: 'Dirty Dog', 'Driving Test' and 'Safari'. And exaggeratedly proud examples of owner behaviour were shown on poster and print executions. Tonally, all this work was in keeping with the style of all the other Volkswagen advertising which ran in 2001.

Local advertising used the idea to point potential buyers in the direction of the nearest retailer, and as a basis for showcasing product details.

Three online executions focused on particular 'beautifully crafted' product points and employed the creative endline (or a variant thereof).[2]

The award-winning direct marketing material developed the idea in a way which brilliantly exploited the strengths of the channel. The outer envelope of the mailers warned recipients that they might find the enclosed picture disturbing. Inside were shots of the Passat horrendously disfigured by muck and cobwebs. Recipients were directed to use the cloth enclosed in the pack to wipe the car clean: a feat which was possible because the dirt had been printed on special 'wipeable' paper. Such an imaginative approach was vital, given that many of our prospects were almost certainly being sent direct marketing activity by Ford and Renault at around the same time. This activity was supplemented with inserts in suitable publications.

The point-of-sale material simply reproduced some of the imagery from the national advertising.

All this material was implemented during 2001. Much of the activity began simultaneously in January. We would like to post-rationalise this as a concerted attempt to maximise overall marketing presence, launching as we were in a narrow window between the New Mondeo launch (in December 2000) and the New Laguna launch (in February 2001). But to do so would be somewhat disingenuous: the facelifted Passat came on to the market in January and it needed to hit the ground running for Volkswagen to hit its year-end targets. Hence nearly all the communications activity began at the same time!

That said, careful thought was given as to how impact could be maximised in the channels employed. In national advertising, which accounted for the lion's share of the launch communications budget, such impact was vital: the Passat launch was sandwiched between two major competitors and the core buying audience, ABC1 men aged 35 to 54, were relatively light viewers of TV. The response to this challenge was to strive for media quality rather than simply 'delivering the numbers'.

Maximising the impact of national advertising

- Heavyweight TV buying on 'launch day', Sunday, 7 January, buying spots in consecutive breaks in key programmes, and buying a roadblock at 1800 hours.[3] The aim was to ensure that as many of our target as possible saw all three TV executions, establishing the idea in their heads and boosting the resonance of every other piece of launch communications they were then exposed to.
- Weighting of spot-buying towards the weekends, this being when people are more likely to be thinking about buying a new car.

---

2. The Passat pages on the website didn't reference the campaign. This wasn't an omission. A decision was made that the pages should continue to conform with the overall tone and identity of the rest of the site. This was already well established, the design was demonstrably 'usable' (in an ergonomics sense), and set to stay long after the launch campaign was over. Put simply, long-term considerations of consistency outweighed the perceived benefit of greater short-term 'inter-channel resonance'. A recurrent question for a brand with many sub-brands: when you decide to integrate, how much should you integrate with longer-term, ongoing, elements of your overall communications programme?

3. A 'roadblock' involves airing the same ads simultaneously on different commercial channels. No escape!

- Careful cherry-picking of spots in TV programmes which indexed highly against the target audience.
- A year-long drip TV presence in the 17 Grand Prix televised by ITV – an appointment-to-view programme for our would-be kings of the company car park.
- The use of 'fireplace' formats in newspapers in order to stand out from the DPSs so beloved by other car advertisers.
- The use of an eclectic range of hobby lifestyle print titles which, again, indexed highly against the target audience.[4]
- Domination of outdoor landmark locations even if their cost, on paper, was high relative to potential audience delivery.[5]
- The use of the 'trade press' title *Fleet News* to ensure company car fleet managers were aware of the merits of the facelifted Passat.

And in an online environment where active avoidance of ads is common, different forms of online advertising were employed to maximise standout: banners, buttons and superstitials.[6]

THE FACELIFT LAUNCH WAS A TREMENDOUS SUCCESS

The sales objective of 30,000 was exceeded by over 3800 units. More significantly given the buoyant state of the overall new car market in 2001, volume share increased too (Figure 4).

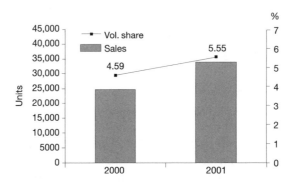

Figure 4: *Passat's sales and share 2001 vs. 2000*
Source: SMMT

Remarkably, even though the Passat had only been facelifted, the rate of this growth exceeded that of its two all-new competitors, the Mondeo and Laguna (Figure 5).

---

4. For example, *Yachting World, Golf World, Classic Cars*.
5. For example, Cromwell Road, Chiswick Roundabout, Vauxhall Cross.
6. A banner is an advertisement in the form of a graphic image that typically runs across a web page or is positioned in a margin or other space reserved for ads. A button is a small banner. And a superstitial is a large pop-up advertisement with full animation, sound, and graphics.

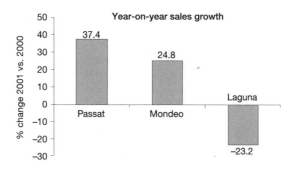

Figure 5: *The Passat's sales growth exceeded that of the New Mondeo and New Laguna – year-on-year sales growth*
Source: SMMT[7]

Although the upper-medium sector was buoyant in sales terms, discounting and incentivisation was fierce in 2001, reducing the overall value of the sector by 2%.[8] Against this background, a smaller proportion of Passat buyers received an incentive or a discount in 2001 than in the previous year (Figure 6).

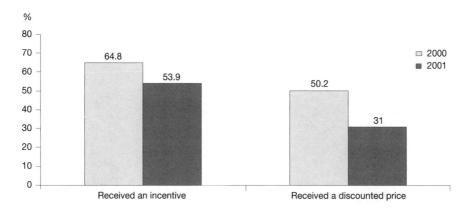

Figure 6: *Proportion of Passat buyers who received financial inducements 2001 vs. 2000*
Source: NCBS

To put this in context, the Mondeo and Laguna, brand new models though they were, had to offer more incentives and discounts to persuade people to buy them (Figure 7).

As a result of increased volume and reduced incentivisation, Passat was able to increase its value share by 30% from 4.7% in 2000 to 6.1% in 2001. In an absolute sense, its revenue contribution to Volkswagen UK that year was £543 million.[9]

From a budgetary point of view, all this was achieved efficiently. The Passat's spend per unit decreased by 9%. And, as far as we can tell from the information

---

7. The Laguna's performance was surprising and atypical for a new upper-medium–sized car in launch.
8. Sources: NCBS mean actual price paid for upper-medium cars multiplied by SMMT annual sector volume sales.
9. Sources: NCBS & SMMT.

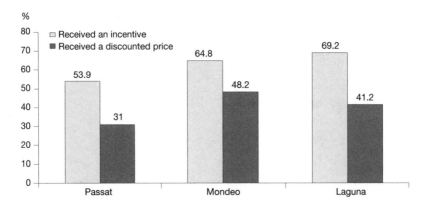

Figure 7: *Proportion of buyers who received a financial inducement in 2001*
Source: NCBS

available, the launch investment behind the Passat was much lower than that for the Mondeo and Laguna (Figure 8).[10]

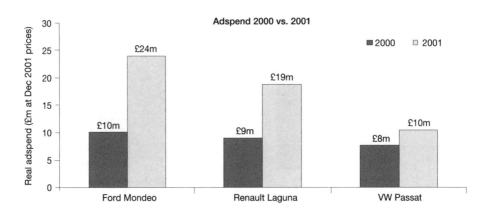

Figure 8: *The New Mondeo and Laguna launches were more heavily supported*
Source: MMS

ISOLATING THE EFFECT OF COMMUNICATIONS

Clearly, the launch of the facelifted Passat was a tremendous business success. The launch objectives were achieved, and they were achieved efficiently. But did communications contribute to that success? And if so, by how much? In trying to answer these questions we faced three challenges.

---

10. We don't have reliable data on the New Mondeo and New Laguna's direct marketing and internet spend levels so we have used national advertising figures as a proxy for overall marketing communications investment.

1. As is the case with all car market effectiveness case studies, the long inter-purchase interval can make it hard to show a clear link between communications activity and sales. This is a particular issue for communications channels whose primary role is to build long-term demand: activity which exerted an influence in one year may not translate into a sale until two or three years later. And that influence may itself be built upon by communications activity delivered via other channels as would-be new car buyers get ever closer to purchase.

2. Everything, apart from PR, happened everywhere at the same time. All the channels in the integrated armoury were brought to bear as the facelifted model came on to the market across the country. This is somewhat ironic: because the launch was so integrated, the success of that integration becomes more difficult to prove. Especially hard is separating the effect of the facelift from the effect of *communicating* that facelift.

3. At a more practical level, it is hard to collect truly integrated data. The retailers who sell Volkswagens are franchisees; separate partner businesses which are often part of other large dealer groups (e.g. Lex or Reg Vardy). Different businesses have different record-keeping procedures and capabilities. There isn't (yet) one single overall system allowing us to link all the various forms of marketing communications to individual sales. Car-selling as a business simply isn't as 'joined up' as some other categories.

Despite these challenges we believe we can show that communications played a vital part in the facelifted Passat's success. We can show that:

- The communications programme overall drove awareness of, and interest in, the launch.
- The individual channels were effective, in some cases having a direct impact on sales and share growth.
- Some of the channels had an additive effect on each other.
- It is hard to find an alternative explanation for the scale of the Passat's growth.

COMMUNICATIONS TOLD PEOPLE ABOUT THE LAUNCH AND MADE THEM INTERESTED IN IT

With products that are bought regularly, an improvement in quality can increase sales without buyers having to be told about that improvement: they buy the improved beans (say), enjoy eating them more than usual, and go on to buy them more often or in greater amounts.

This doesn't happen in the car market. Cars are an infrequent purchase so people have little opportunity to learn about improvements in product quality directly. Awareness of an improvement is a necessary precursor to subsequent sales success. This is why car makers spend so much money communicating new launches and facelifts!

In the case of the Passat, the launch communications activity clearly drove awareness of the facelift, starting with Motorshow-associated PR coverage (Figure 9).[11]

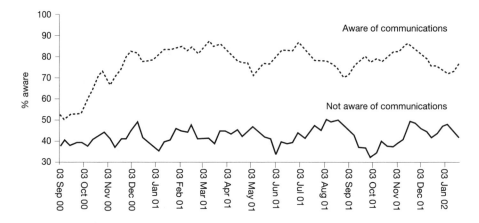

Figure 9: *Awareness of the Passat facelift*
Base: Upper-medium sector buyers excluding owners of any Volkswagen model
Source: Millward Brown

And beyond simply driving awareness, the launch communications also drove people's interest in the facelifted car (Figure 10).

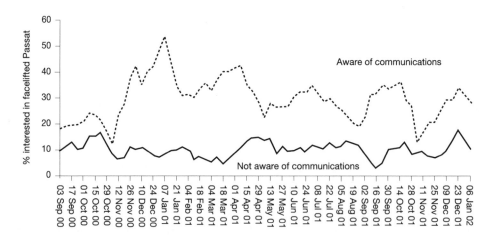

Figure. 10: *Interest in the facelifted Passat*
Base: Upper-medium sector buyers excluding owners of any Volkswagen model
Source: Millward Brown

11. 'Launch communications activity' includes only direct marketing, PR and (any form of) advertising. We sadly neglected to include the internet on the Volkswagen tracking study. The spectre of Rosser Reeves (and his infamous fallacy) suggests Volkswagen ownership might make people more inclined to notice and be interested in the facelift launch and its associated communications. Accordingly, this and all subsequent tracking charts control for ownership of a Volkswagen within the sample: owners were excluded.

THE INDIVIDUAL CHANNELS WERE EFFECTIVE

PR worked as intended

As mentioned in the previous section, our 'spearhead' channel achieved its objective: awareness of the facelifted Passat grew before the car's actual launch date as a result of press coverage linked to the Passat's first UK appearance at the NEC Motorshow (Figure 11).

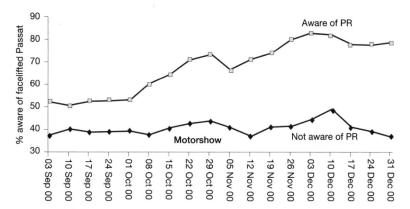

Figure 11: *PR drove pre–launch awareness*
Base: Upper-medium sector buyers excluding owners of any Volkswagen model
Source: Millward Brown

It is hard to prove whether this coverage would have been achieved if Volkswagen's PR department hadn't done such a good job. But we think the sheer scale of the coverage was remarkable given that it was picked up by Volkswagen's ongoing tracking study. Certainly, the fact that the coverage was overwhelmingly positive must have been to the Passat's benefit (Figure 12).

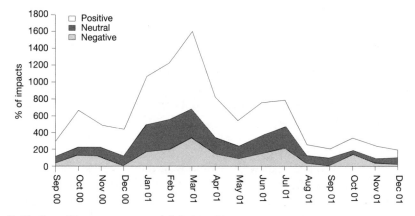

Figure 12: *The Passat PR coverage was overwhelmingly positive*
Source: Millward Brown Precis[12]

---

12. Millward Brown's Precis service is a sophisticated monitor of PR scale, placement and tone.

If industry praise can be used as evidence of the effectiveness of Volkswagen UK's Press Office, it is worth noting that in its 2001 annual survey The Guild of Motoring Writers – PR's most direct consumers – voted it ahead of all other mass-market car brands in its ability to liaise with and brief motoring journalists.[13]

National advertising worked as intended

The advertising was seen and it communicated what it was meant to communicate (Tables 1 and 2)

TABLE 1: ADVERTISING RECOGNITION

	%
Dog	69
Driving Test	63
Safari Park	62

Base: Upper-medium sector drivers excluding owners of any Volkswagen model
Source: Millward Brown 2001

TABLE 2: ADVERTISING COMMUNICATION: % AGREEING

	Dirty Dog	Driving Test	Safari Park
There is a new Passat	67	68	64
The Passat is a well-crafted car	69	72	72
The Passat is a car you'd be proud to own	75	69	68

Base: Upper-medium sector drivers who saw the ads, excluding owners of any Volkswagen model
Source: Millward Brown 2001

Advertising's visibility was achieved efficiently: the campaign achieved an Awareness Index score of 6–7, exceeding the car market average score of 4.[14]

As a result, the advertising successfully drove awareness that the Passat had been facelifted (Figure 13).

Looking at mean figures covering the whole of 2001, it is clear that advertising had a massive effect on driving awareness of, and promoting interest in, the facelifted car (Figures 14 and 15).

This interest, in turn, translated into business success: there was a highly significant correlation between Passat adspend and *orders* for the car (Figure 16).

There was a highly significant correlation between Passat adspend and *sales* for the car (Figure 17).

And, most importantly, there was a highly significant correlation between Passat adspend and *market share* (Figure 18).

And, remarkably, given that we are looking at only a year's worth of data in a market with an average inter-purchase interval of three years, there was a significant correlation between changes in adspend levels and the Passat's share *growth*. Advertising drove short-term market share (Figure 19).

---

13. Indeed, if it weren't for stable-mate Audi, it would have come top.
14. Source: Millward Brown.

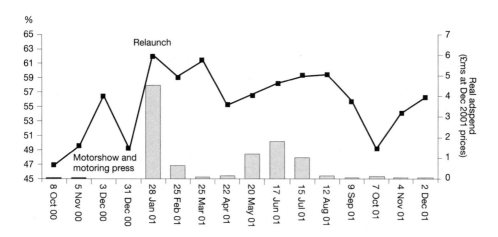

Figure 13: *Awareness of relaunch vs. adspend*
Base: Upper–medium sector drivers excluding owners of any Volkswagen model
Sources: Millward Brown, MMS

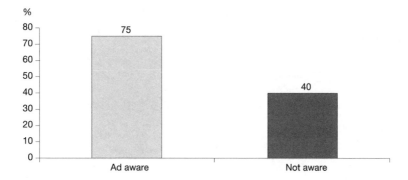

Figure 14: *Awareness of Passat relaunch*
Base: Upper-medium sector buyers excluding owners of any Volkswagen model
Source: Millward Brown

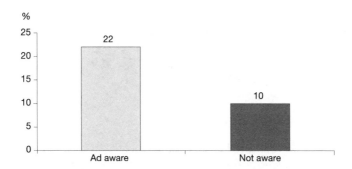

Figure 15: *Interest in relaunched Passat*
Base: Upper-medium sector buyers excluding owners of any Volkswagen model
Source: Millward Brown

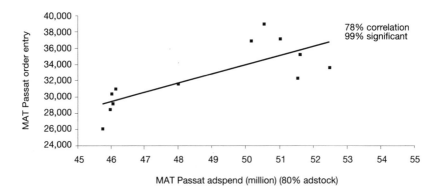

Figure 16: *Passat adspend vs. order entry*
Sources: MMS, Volkswagen UK

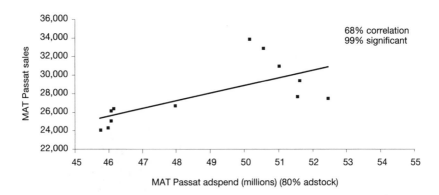

Figure 17: *Passat adspend vs. sales*
Sources: MMS, SMMT

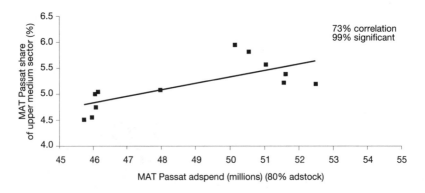

Figure 18: *Passat adspend vs. share*
Sources: MMS, SMMT

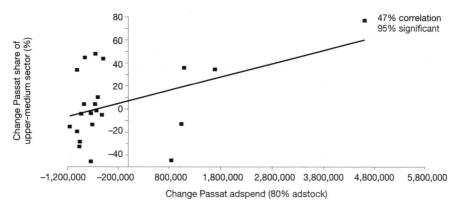

Figure 19: *Passat adspend vs. share*
Sources: MMS, SMMT

Direct-marketing worked as intended

The overall response rate to the direct marketing activity was 6.5%, exceeding all previous Volkswagen launch mailings, and very high when judged against direct marketing norms. Response targets among both prospects and cold names were exceeded (Table 3).

TABLE 3: DIRECT-MARKETING RESPONSE RATES

	Target (%)	Achieved (%)
Prospects	10	18.9
Cold names	5	5.4

Source: Proximity

So far, this activity has translated into 726 sales, boosted by a further 89 attributable to the insert activity.[15] These figures underestimate the overall sales effect. In a world of imperfect data-capture mechanisms, many sales attributable to direct marketing activity probably went unrecorded by retailers. In addition, some sales may be yet to happen – we know from past Volkswagen direct marketing activity that conversion figures can improve dramatically 18 months after that activity has run.

Online activity worked as intended

The online Passat ads were seen: they delivered an audience of 2.3 million, the online equivalent of 2.3 million OTS.[16] Beyond that, they provoked a response in the form of 10,900 'click-throughs' to the Passat pages of the Volkswagen website: an average click-through rate of 0.4%.[17]

---

15. Although we deal with total communications payback later in this paper it is worth noting that this represents a massive return on investment for Volkswagen.
16. To put this into context, delivering this same OTS level using posters would have cost substantially more. Source: Mediacom.
17. Source: Volkswagen UK. Although we cannot reveal precise details, some activity run in particular online locations achieved click-through rates of 2%, ten times greater than the norm.

Volkswagen has never launched a car using this channel to this kind of audience before, so we cannot put this result into context using past results. We know that the click-through rate outperformed generally accepted online industry standards of 0.2%.[18] But we decided to put this number into perspective by looking further afield:

- Looking at market sizes, the 10,900 'click-throughs' equate to a massive 20% of all online upper-medium car buyers in the months when the online activity ran.[19]
- Thinking about relative channel costs, the click-through rate was higher, and the cost-per-click lower, than we might have expected to achieve had we run a direct response piece of advertising designed to prompt a brochure request.[20]

Local advertising worked as intended

At least, we're pretty sure it did. We don't have a precise record of individual retailer adspend behind the Passat in 2001. This was because Volkswagen's 253 retailers had the flexibility to run copy for which ever of Volkswagen's seven models they felt needed most support given their local trading conditions on a week-by-week basis, choosing from an 'ad pack' of dozens of executions. Keeping track of who spent how much on what was a challenge we hadn't yet risen to.

That said, we do know that in 2001 local advertising drove overall Volkswagen sales above and beyond the effect of the other communications channels. It is likely that in launch year much of that local advertising copy related to the Passat. So, by inference, we are confident that Passat local advertising was effective.[21]

THE COMMUNICATIONS CHANNELS HAD AN ADDITIVE EFFECT

We don't have the measures, or sufficiently robust samples, to show how each and every channel might have influenced every other channel. And, even if we had, the near-simultaneous timing of activity in the different channels would have made such an analysis very hard. But we can show how some channels interacted.

Figure 20 shows how awareness of the facelifted Passat was significantly higher among people who were aware of both Passat-related PR and its advertising than among those who were aware of its advertising only. The picture is similar with people who had received direct marketing material: their awareness of the facelift was significantly higher too.[22]

---

18. Source: Admap/WARC.
19. A drab technical footnote. *A:* 155,620 upper-medium-sized cars were sold in the three months the online activity ran (source: SMMT). *B:* 35% of new car buyers used the internet when buying a new car (source: NOP). $A \times B$ = 54,467; 10,900/54,467 = 20%. This calculation ignores those car buyers who may have gone directly to the Passat web pages via their homepage. Unfortunately we didn't (at the time) have robust data on the number of people who visited by way of that most obvious route, the front door.
20. Source: Mediacom.
21. The effect of local advertising is dealt with in more detail in the Volkswagen brand paper.
22. Significant differences at the 99% confidence level.

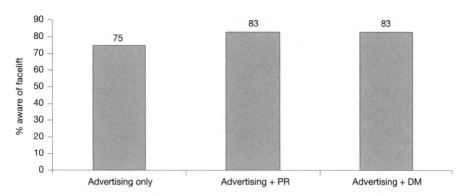

Figure 20: *The effect of different combinations of channel exposure on awareness of the facelifted Passat*
Base: Upper-medium sector buyers excluding owners of any Volkswagen model
Source: Millward Brown, 2001 average

Looking at interest in the facelifted Passat, there were similar significant differences (Figure 21). Interest in the car was much greater among people who had been exposed to two channels than among those who were aware only of the advertising. This shows the massive importance of PR and direct marketing in the overall channel mix.

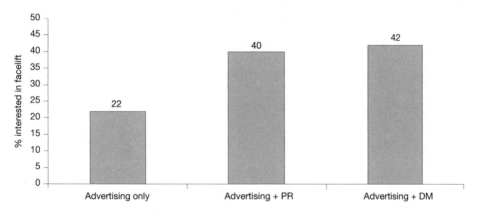

Figure 21: *The effect of different combinations of channel exposure on interest in the facelifted Passat*
Base: Upper-medium sector buyers excluding owners of any Volkswagen model
Source: Millward Brown, 2001 average

IT IS HARD TO ATTRIBUTE THE PASSAT'S SUCCESS IN 2001 TO OTHER FACTORS

A number of factors which might conceivably have driven the Passat's business success in 2001 may be ruled out quite quickly:

• Distribution didn't increase.
• The Passat's relative price wasn't cut.
• Incentivisation and discounting decreased (Figure 6).

Volkswagen's fleet department expended greater effort supporting the Passat in 2001 compared with the previous year; more focus, more man-hours. Although there are no publicly available data on competitive fleet man-hours activity, it is likely that (1) Volkswagen's competitors who weren't launching a new upper-medium model in 2001 defensively increased support of their current offering; (2) Ford and Renault increased support for their new upper-medium offerings. In other words, it is likely that Volkswagen had to run faster in order to keep up.

Much more fundamentally, what about an improvement in product quality? Can't the Passat's success in 2001 be attributed simply to facelifting the car? We believe it would be wrong to try to rule out the contribution made by quality enhancement. But we will argue that it was a necessary rather than a sufficient factor behind the Passat's growth. Our argument is based on the following two pieces of evidence.

Comparison with the New Ford Mondeo

If an improvement in product quality is a primary driver of subsequent growth, one would predict that the greater the improvement in product quality, the greater that growth would be: *launching a new car should drive growth more than merely facelifting a car*. But, as we have shown, sales of the facelifted Passat grew by more than sales of the all-new Mondeo, a car which was lauded with prizes and which consistently beat all-comers (including the Passat) in motoring magazine road-tests: 37% vs. 25% growth. This reversal of expectation suggests that the explanation for the scale of the Passat's growth must lie beyond an improvement in its product quality.

A facelift which wasn't communicated

We have benchmarked the Passat's performance against one of its competitors to see what might have happened had we *not* communicated news of its facelift. The Peugeot 406 and the Passat had much in common. Both came from manufacturers with similar overall market positions, offering a similar range of models. Both had a comparable position within the upper-medium sector.[23] Both had been supported by heavyweight communications in the first three years of their life cycles. And both received facelifts at similar points in those life cycles (Table 4).

TABLE 4: THE PASSAT AND PEUGEOT 406

	Passat	406
Model % market share of upper-medium sector, 2000–2001	6%	6%
Launch date	April 1997	December 1995
Facelift date	January 2001	April 1999
Time between launch and facelift	45 months	41 months

Source: SMMT

As with the Passat, the 406's facelift was a moderate one, primarily exterior.[24]

---

23. The most noteworthy difference between the two is that Peugeot offered a Coupé version of the 406 as well as the more standard saloon and estate body shapes. The Passat came only as a saloon or an estate. This explains the 406's overall sales advantage – until 2001 when it was overtaken by the facelifted Passat.
24. The styling update was overseen by the Italian company Pininfarina, whose brief was '*To give the car a greater presence through added value without losing the elegance of the original design*'.

But there was one illuminating difference between the two models: the Passat's facelift was announced with a major communications campaign, whereas *Peugeot chose not to communicate the news of the 406's facelift in mass communications.* Instead, it continued to support the 406 heavily with its extremely popular 'Heroes' advertising campaign.

Following its facelift the 406's share merely levelled out (Figure 22).

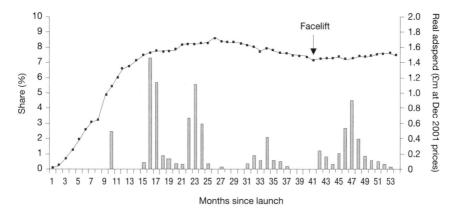

Figure 22: *The 406's share*
Sources: SMMT, MMS

In contrast, the Passat's share grew (Figure 23).

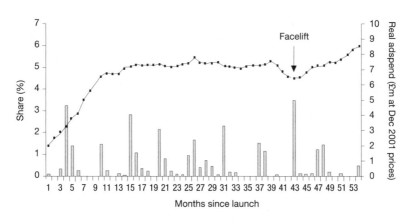

Figure 23: *The Passat's share*[25]
Sources: SMMT, MMS

The contrast between the fates of the two facelifted cars is shown more clearly in Figure 24.

We believe this difference in the two model's fates can only be explained by Volkswagen's decision to *communicate* that the Passat had been facelifted. Message, in this case, was everything: product improvements were the necessary

---

25. The Passat's sales dropped in months 39–41 as the last remaining stocks of the old, pre-facelift car were sold off.

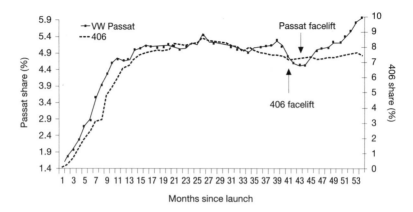

Figure 24: *The 406 vs. the Passat share*
Sources: SMMT, MMS

prerequisite for the Passat's growth, but highly effective communication of those improvements was the *catalyst* for achieving growth of such magnitude.

RETURN ON INVESTMENT

Although this is a slightly artificial exercise in a long-term market such as the car market, we have estimated the contribution of communications and calculated its immediate 'payback' in two ways (neither ideal).

Figure 25 shows the life cycle of a typical car in the sector. It is based on life cycle share data from 13 models. Most of these – as far as we could tell from published information – were facelifted at some point in their 'middle age' and most communicated news of that facelift.

The Passat, quite clearly, defied the trend in year 5. Had it followed the sector trend between years 4 and 5 (its facelift year), sales in 2001 would have been 8180 fewer than were actually sold.

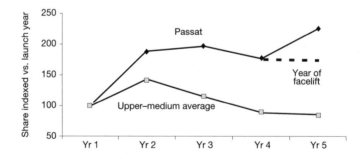

Figure 25: *The Passat share curve vs. upper-medium average*
Source: SMMT[26]

---

26. Mean score based on data from the following upper-medium sector models: Audi A4, BMW 3 Series, Citroën Xantia, (old) Ford Mondeo, Honda Accord, Mercedes C-Class, Nissan Primera, (old) Renault Laguna, Toyota Avensis, Vauxhall Vectra.

Returning to the Peugeot 406 comparison, if the Passat's share performance in 2001 had echoed 406's in its (uncommunicated) facelift year, the Passat would have sold 8398 fewer than were actually sold. Taking the more conservative of these two figures, we estimate that communicating news of the Passat's facelift resulted in 8180 extra sales in 2001. In revenue terms, this represents £131 million.[27]

The sum of £11.2 million was invested behind communicating the facelift launch. Volkswagen UK cannot disclose profit margins but we can state that the overall communications investment in 2001 paid for itself in the short term.

More sensibly, adopting a broader perspective, the return on investment is greater than these figures suggest. In a market with a three-year buying cycle, effective communication which ran in 2001 is likely to have a positive impact on sales, revenue and profit in 2002 and 2003.

Thinking about Volkswagen's overall range, all of its models are 'beautifully crafted'. We believe that the promotion of this message in a manner which was tonally in keeping with communications for the rest of the brand has benefited both the overall brand and, more specifically, sales of other Volkswagen models.[28]

Finally, six years ago car buyers were sceptical about Volkswagen's ability to operate in the upper-medium sector of the car market. The Passat's 2001 sales show how this scepticism has now been overcome. This step change in consumer opinion will help reduce the communications investment needed for Volkswagen to break into more premium sectors of the car market (as it plans to do in 2003).[29]

WHAT WE HAVE LEARNED

So many gaps to fill! Which channel generated the greatest return per pound spent? Was there any cross-channel duplication? Were direct marketing response rates or online advertising click-through rates influenced by concurrent national advertising? Was the Passat more successful among avid Grand Prix viewers? Did the point-of-sale material work? And was the most effective breed of dog used in the 'Dirty Dog' TV ad?

As you may have gathered by now, this paper has been written in a spirit of exploration and a lot of questions have gone unanswered. Accordingly, apart from the obvious message to ourselves of *'plug those darn gaps'*, we are reluctant to draw too many morals. None the less, three lessons we have learned are worth making. If you have news to communicate, communicate it. Play to the strengths of individual communications channels, basing their overall deployment upon a sound knowledge of consumer buying behaviour. Further, having an 'integrated communications idea' doesn't simply mean slapping an executional property from one of your TV ads on every other piece of communication you produce – it all takes a bit more crafting than that.

---

27. Units sold multiplied by average price paid for a Passat in 2001. Sources: SMMT and NCBS.
28. The ability of communications for one Volkswagen model to boost sales of other models is demonstrated in the Volkswagen brand paper entered for these awards.
29. Back in 1996, quotes such as these were typical: '*I just can't associate Volkswagen with this type of car, this type of market*', '*I'd want a better name if I was going to spend that kind of money*', '*I don't have to be sold on Volkswagen, but I just cannot make that transition from small cars to large cars*'. Source: BMP qualitative research, spring 1996.

APPENDIX: 'BEAUTIFULLY CRAFTED' CREATIVE WORK

Dog owner: 20 Dixon Road – will a tenner do it?
Taxi driver: Yes, sir

The dog shakes mud all over the inside of the taxi

 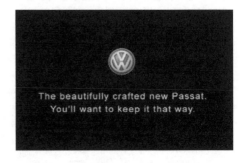

Facelifted Passat national TV advertising – 'Dirty Dog'

SILVER

Son: Dad, I passed!

Dad: Well done, son

Dad: How was his 3-point turn?
Examiner: Yeah, it was good
Dad: It's just his instructor says it's a bit dodgy

Examiner: No, it was definitely fine
Dad: Did he check his mirror correctly?
Examiner: Ye-es

Dad: You sure?

The beautifully crafted new Passat.
You'll want to keep it that way.

Dad: How long have you been an examiner?

Facelifted Passat national TV advertising – 'Driving Test'

Husband: Lovely here isn't it? Nice to get some fresh air
Wife: David, shouldn't we be getting back now?
Husband: No, no. Everything's fine. Much better than being cooped-up in the car!

Wife: Not too tired are you, mum?
Husband: Come on everyone, stick together!

[Loud monkey cries and lion roars]

Facelifted Passat national TV advertising – 'Safari Park'

22

Waitrose

David versus four Goliaths: how advertising quietly revolutionised a successful business

Principal author: Steve Hastings, Banks Hoggins O'Shea FCB

EDITOR'S SUMMARY

This case documents how Waitrose strengthened its position as the UK's pre-eminent food retailer despite tough competition from larger spending rivals. Increasing advertising budgets played a vital role in building loyalty and attracting new customers. Waitrose's share of the grocery market has increased from 3.17% to 3.70% since 1997, when it first started advertising seriously.

A UNIQUE CULTURE

Waitrose is part of the John Lewis Partnership and has a very strong culture based on co-ownership.

Figure 1: *Waitrose logo*

This culture is centred as much on the happiness of the partners as it is on profits. Any money spent on advertising is seen by the partners as coming from profit, which affects their annual bonus. So advertising has to be liked and effective to survive the unique democratic decision-making process at Waitrose.

In 1997 Waitrose had no significant advertising history or experience. Indeed many partners were advertising-suspicious, perhaps echoing the sentiment of the Partnership founder, who said:

'In business of our kind it is very difficult indeed to spend money largely on publicity without allowing yourself to be undersold.'

John Spedan Lewis (1968)

Waitrose, in 1997, was already a successful business. Yet its national market share was only just over 3%, and it faced the growing power of the 'big four' grocery retailers (i.e. Sainsbury's, Tesco, Safeway and Asda), who had rapidly grown their combined share of the British grocery market from 43.9% in 1985 to 65.5% by 1997.[1] Their growth continued, driven by large advertising spends and aggressive acquisition programmes. Their combined share had grown to almost 70% by 2001.[1]

Yet in the face of this onslaught Waitrose quietly managed to grow its share. They increased their advertising investment, grew sales per square foot and developed a more loyal customer base.

This paper shows how a larger advertising investment allowed Waitrose to compete more effectively against the grocery giants. Crucially, we will show how this advertising investment contributed incremental profit to the Waitrose business and in turn helped create an advertising-supportive environment where, previously, little support for advertising existed. We will also describe how the financial department took a lead role in evaluating the sales results of marketing, a move suggested by Tim Ambler (2001) but, until then, rarely seen.

Finally, we will show how the addition of television to the media mix gave Waitrose a fully integrated campaign with significant benefits.

---

1. TNS Till Roll Data.

SILVER

THE ROLE FOR ADVERTISING

With the growth in larger-format stores and the concentration of grocery turnover in just a few brands, Waitrose faced all the dangers of being a small player in the market. A vigorous store-opening programme increased the store count from 116 in 1997 to 136 branches by 2000. However, the lack of availability of new sites meant that Waitrose had to compete by being different rather than big.

The brief to the new agency was to take a fresh look at the role for advertising. How could Waitrose better employ advertising to protect and grow its position? We started by looking at the customer base.

The first insight was that too many people were going through Waitrose with a basket not a trolley. More people used Waitrose as a secondary ('basket') shop than a primary ('trolley') shop (Figure 2).

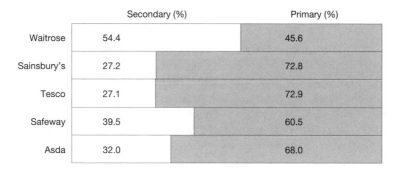

Figure 2: *Shopping behaviour at different grocery stores*
Base: All southern adults
Source: Target Group Index ©, BMRB, 1997

Why do Waitrose customers shop differently?

Our qualitative research showed basket shoppers had a very clear view of Waitrose as 'a different kind of supermarket'.

'There is a snob value.'

'A bit more of a classy shopper.'

'A bit more select.'

Source: BHO Qualitative Research 1997, Secondary Shoppers

Combined with this view came a strong sense that Waitrose was more expensive than its rivals.

'You always end up spending more there.'

'I go careful in Waitrose.'

Source: BHO Qualitative Research 1997, Secondary Shoppers

We found that a number of factors contributed to these price perceptions:

1. Although large by grocery standards, most Waitrose shops are smaller than Tesco and Sainsbury's. Since 'large equals cheap', small must be more expensive.
2. The Waitrose shops tend to be clean and uncluttered and fully stocked, giving the look and feel of an expensive shop.
3. The perception that Waitrose doesn't have special offers.

We learnt a valuable lesson by taking accompanied shopping trips with secondary shoppers. When they were shown the prices of everyday items, they were surprised by what they saw:

'We've been brainwashed into thinking Waitrose is expensive but it's not the case. Look at those prices.'

'The price of the dry pasta is the same.'

'Look at these special offers.'

Source: BHO Qualitative Research 1997, Secondary Shoppers

And while these shoppers knew Waitrose offered high-quality food they were unable to rationalise the difference in price, where one existed, with their 'regular' supermarket. For instance they didn't know that a Waitrose cod fillet is made from 100% cod fillet steak, not a mix of fish parts reconstructed into a 'steak' shape.

In short, many basket shoppers didn't feel they had permission to shop at Waitrose other than for top-up shopping (popping in for bread and milk because it's convenient) or for special occasion shopping (for a dinner party).

THE NEW CAMPAIGN

The broad role of communications was to reinforce and ring-fence Waitrose's position in the market. More specifically, we wanted to redefine 'value' as the balance between quality and price, not merely as 'low price'. We wanted secondary shoppers to reappraise Waitrose and to take larger baskets or even trolleys to the checkout.

This had to be achieved in a way that perpetuated the quality values of Waitrose for primary shoppers, staff and suppliers.

The core message

'Waitrose is committed to bringing their customers the finest quality fresh foods at prices which make them outstanding value.'

The Quality Food message chimes with the long-term consumer trend to eating better, healthier food and with the concerns caused by diseases such as foot and mouth and BSE.

The advertising dilemma

Retail advertising usually chooses one of two paths: tactically priced messages or more strategic brand messages. We noticed that they often veer from one extreme to the other; the price-led campaign can weaken the brand message, so is followed by a brand campaign which in turn weakens price perceptions, and so on. We decided that a focus on quality alone might just reinforce existing prejudices, and price messaging in national media was 'just not Waitrose'.

The creative solution was found by devising a story around individual products with a 'killer fact' about its provenance or the supplier relationship Waitrose has, and juxtaposing this with a subtle price tag which the target audience would recognise as good value.[2] The advertising was unusual because it never showed the product.

The Waitrose campaign has kept the same creative idea from its launch, with two distinct parts. The press-led integrated campaign established the advertising property (1997–2000), then TV was added in May 2001. Figures 3–8 show six press executions.

Figure 3: 'Fresh Icelandic Cod, £8.99/kg'
Waitrose cod has been supplied by the same Grimsby fish merchant for 17 years

Figure 4: 'Sunflower spread, 59p/500g'
Waitrose sunflower spread is made near Bruges, Belgium using locally pressed sunflower seeds

---

2. Our creative development research showed that secondary shoppers did understand these prices to be very competitive.

Figure 5: *'Fresh Brussel Sprouts, 99p/kg'*
Waitrose has all the ingredients for a Christmas dinner that everyone will relish. (Well, almost everyone.)

Figure 6: *'Organic Ice Cream, £1.99/500ml'*
Ice cream is just one of over 800 organic products available at Waitrose. Its superior flavour results from infusing the strawberries, chocolate or vanilla (all organic, of course) in the organic cream for at least 12 hours before freezing. Find out more at *www.waitrose.com/ice-cream*

Figure 7: *'Semi-skimmed Milk 89p/four pints'*
Just one of the hundreds of everyday items we price check every week

Figure 8: *'Vacherin Mont D'Or mountain cheese, £4.99/350g, £14.26 per kg'*
The summer mountain pastures of the Massif Mont D'Or are home to some very special cows. For it is their milk, and theirs alone, that gives this seasonal cheese its rich, creamy flavour. For more information, visit
www.waitrose.com/cheese

Harder-working media

The media budget gave Waitrose a 1.6% share of voice in the grocery sector (Figure 9).

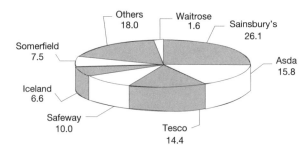

Figure 9: *Share of voice for supermarket and grocery chains, 1998*
Source: MMS

The Waitrose estate is based in the South, so the previous advertising that had been placed in national titles produced a large wastage. We improved the efficiency of spend by persuading the key titles to sell-on the Northern part of space we took to advertisers who were happy to have coverage in the North alone. This innovation produced an immediate cost-saving of 15–20% over the previous plan[3] (Figure 10).

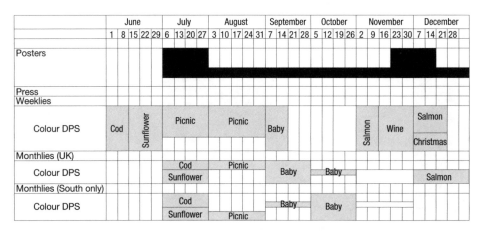

Figure 10: *Media plan, 1998*

Broadening the campaign

After an initial testing period with press advertising, positive results grew confidence and we were able to broaden the media to produce a multi-faceted campaign, taking each press subject into stores (shelf-barkers, tent cards, A-frames, advertisements in *Seasons*, the Waitrose free magazine), on to the internet (we directed readers of the advertisement to a micro-site, where they could find more detail about the product) as well as an article in *Waitrose Food Illustrated*, the Waitrose-backed food magazine (Figure 11).

---

3. Source: Billett.

Try our authentic Indian Meals

Shelf Barker

Microsite

Brand Double Page Spread

Try
*our authentic
Indian Meals*

A Frame

Tent Card

Seasons Advertising Feature

WFI Indian Supplement

Figure 11: *Integrated communications*

LEARNING FROM THE CAMPAIGN

The advertising worked in a number of ways. Advertising awareness proved responsive to advertising spend (Figure 12).

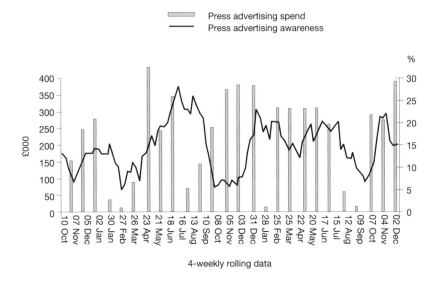

Figure 12: *Waitrose press advertising awareness (prompted from photos)*
Base: All respondents: 300 interviews per 4 weeks
Source: Consumer InSight Brand Tracking Study 1998–2000

The advertising also improved perceptions of Waitrose on a number of key dimensions (Figures 13–16).

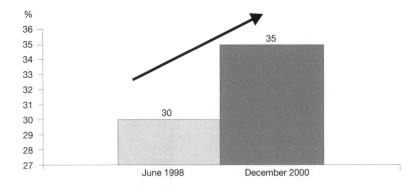

Figure 13: *'Waitrose offers a range of everyday family foods at competitive prices'*
Base: Waitrose Primary, secondary and non-shoppers
Source: Brand Tracking Study, Consumer InSight

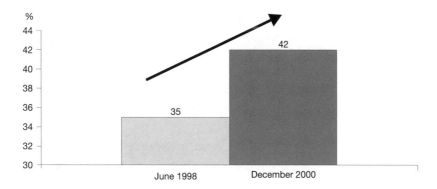

Figure 14: *'Waitrose works with its suppliers closely'*
Base: Waitrose primary, secondary and non-shoppers
Source: Brand Tracking Study, Consumer InSight

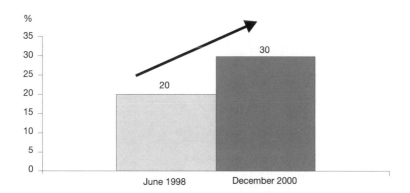

Figure 15: *'Waitrose is particularly careful in selecting food for its shops'*
Base: Waitrose primary, secondary and non-shoppers
Source: Brand Tracking Study, Consumer InSight

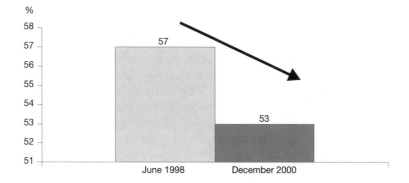

Figure 16: *'Waitrose is expensive'*
Base: Waitrose primary, secondary and non-shoppers
Source: Brand Tracking Study, Consumer InSight

At the same time the proportion of primary 'trolley' shoppers coming into the branches increased (Figure 17).

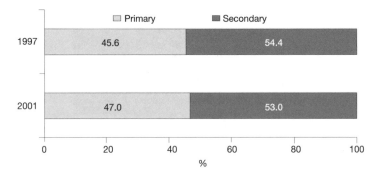

Figure 17: *Primary and secondary shopper proportions, 1997–2001*
Base: All Southern adults
Source: Target Group Index, BMRB, 1997, 2001

And as icing on the cake, sales per branch rose (Figure 18) and brand share improved from 3.17% in 1998 to 3.28% by February 2000.

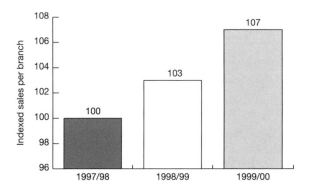

Figure 18: *Average sales per branch*[4]
Source: IGD, Waitrose

All the signs of a successful advertising campaign were in place. Our target customers were noticing the campaign, their views of Waitrose were changing as we wanted them to, more people were shopping with trolleys and we were seeing more sales per square foot. On top of that, we made a ripple in the market, with one major grocery retailer producing imitative advertising until complaints from Waitrose forced them to back down. Finally, the advertising received strong accolades from the advertising community; a useful endorsement because it helped

---

4.   The four new branches in 1999 were larger than the average Waitrose branch, yet sales per square foot across all branches increased year on year, indicating the business was becoming more efficient across the whole estate.

the agency attract the highest-quality people to work on the business:

> 'My favourite ad of the week also has a rural feel. The Waitrose advertising, particularly the sunflowers, are a joy.'
>
> Larry Barker, *Campaign*, 24 July 1998

With such positive results, we decided to look formally at the link between advertising and sales, using econometrics.

APPLYING ECONOMETRICS

Waitrose commissioned econometric analysis from Numbercraft, based on weekly data from 1997 to 1999. The following factors were available for inclusion in the econometric analysis:

- Waitrose revenue
- Total market revenue
- Waitrose share
- Advertising spend – total all supermarkets by media
  – Asda, M&S, Sainsbury's, Safeway, Tesco, and Waitrose by media
- Promotions
- Weather
- Holidays

No clear pattern

Isolating the effects of a relatively small advertising budget on a relatively small share brand will always be difficult, and so it proved here. Numbercraft based their findings on a share-based model. The key findings, quoting from their summary,[5] were:

- There is no significant link between relative ad spend and market share. This is probably a function of the small Waitrose market share compared with the big four (Tesco, Sainsbury's, Asda and Safeway).
- Seasonal effects, rather than advertising factors, account for much of the variation in Waitrose sales share.
- Waitrose benefits positively from advertising from some competitors (Sainsbury's and Tesco) and loses share with advertising from other competitors (Asda and Safeway).

As Peter Grindrod of Numbercraft summarised:

> 'Something is going on here as a result of the advertising but the Waitrose share is so small that other effects are drowning out the story.'

---

5. 'Impact of Advertising on Revenues', November 1999. Data from end of January 1997 to end September 1999.

We had fallen into the traditional conundrum facing smaller advertisers – just because the effects of advertising were not measurable didn't mean it wasn't working. However, we didn't yet have enough evidence to convince the sceptics that we should spend even more on advertising.

Nil desperandum! – entering the zone of efficiency

Although the Waitrose share of voice had grown from 1.6% in 1998 to 2.7% in 2000, further work by Numbercraft suggested that Waitrose was still spending advertising money at a rate that put the company below their advertising 'zone of efficiency' (Figure 19).

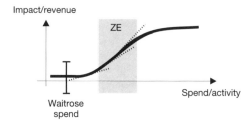

Figure 19: *Zone of efficiency*
Source: Numbercraft

Numbercraft calculated that to enter the zone of efficiency Waitrose would need to spend a minimum of £4.5–5.0m per annum on advertising, and for every £1m spent, extra revenue would be generated which would cover costs and make a contribution to profit. So, the Waitrose financial analysts saw that at the gross margins Waitrose achieve, raising advertising investment further would be a worthwhile proposition. At the same time, changes in the competitive situation meant Waitrose and the advertising agency took a fresh look at their media choices.

Market developments

In July 1999 Wal-Mart entered the UK grocery market, buying Asda. M&S were about to launch their first ever advertising TV campaign, Sainsbury's had launched the Jamie Oliver TV campaign promoting the Taste the Difference range, and Tesco showed it had distanced itself from its 'pile 'em high sell it cheap' days by introducing its Finest range.

It was decided to increase the budget to include TV, with the aim of:

1. Guarding the Waitrose position against 'the Goliaths' who wanted to migrate their own customers to higher-priced produce.
2. Giving secondary shoppers more reasons to shop at Waitrose, hence building their frequency and basket size.
3. Achieving a short-term revenue gain sufficient to suggest the advertising budget would produce a positive return over time.

THE TV CAMPAIGN

The campaign theme was deliberately maintained on television, with the aim of deepening and broadening the existing multi-media campaign. Three commercials were shown in May 2001 ('Cod', 'Wine' and 'Milk'), with five run between October and December 2001 ('Lamb', 'Stilton', 'Champagne Pudding', 'Wine', 'Indian Ready Meals') (Figures 20–22).

'COD'
Soundtrack: *Sitting on the Dock of the Bay* by Otis Redding

FVO: We will never, ever...

buy fish unless it achieves at least eight out of ten on the Torry institute scale ...

of freshness and quality.

Waitrose. Quality food, honestly priced.

Figure 20: *'Cod' – fresh Icelandic cod, £8.99/kg*

'WINE'
Soundtrack: *Red, Red Wine* by UB40

FVO: When the supermarket that's won more
wine awards than all the others put together ...

says a wine's worth drinking ...

 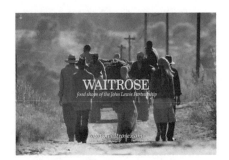

it's worth drinking

Waitrose. Quality food, honestly priced.

Figure 21: *'Wine' – Culemborg Pinotage, Western Cape, £4.59/75cl*

'MILK'
Soundtrack: *Good morning* from *Singing in the Rain*

FVO: Only one supermarket knows every farm
and farmer that supplies every pint …

of its fresh milk

Waitrose. Quality food, honestly priced.

Figure 22: 'Milk' – Select Farm Milk, 28p/pint

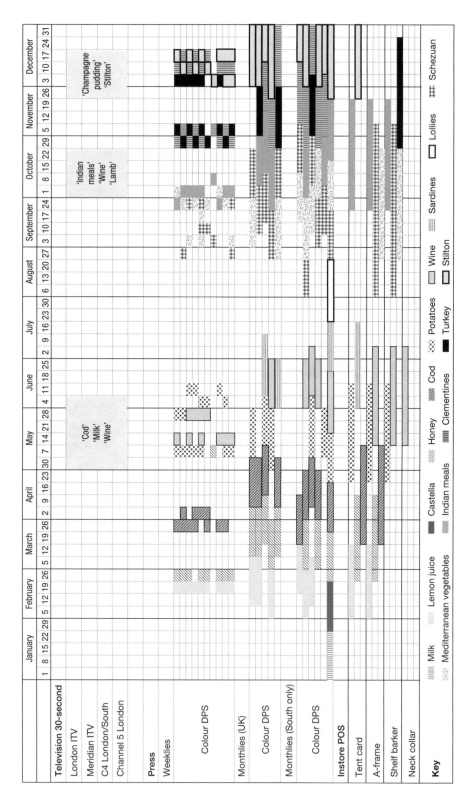

Figure 23: *Media plan, 2001*

Many of our audience are light television viewers: the schedule was bought to include the 'destination' programmes that these selective viewers choose, e.g. documentaries, natural history programmes. Also we placed advertisements for different products in the same programmes to ensure that a breadth of range and sense of scale was communicated.

Careful planning ensured that the TV commercials coincided with the press execution of the same subject, together with in-store activity to highlight the featured products (Figure 23). New press copy was introduced using weekly titles, then switched to monthlies to give the campaign longevity.

The campaign was fully integrated in two important ways. Running each product campaign successfully required the operational integration of the marketing, buying, selling and merchandise departments at Waitrose as well as the advertising and media agencies. Also, we integrated the different media channels around each product.

DID IT WORK?

Yes, and beyond expectations.

Given the size of Waitrose sales – £2.296bn in 2001–2002 – we needed only a small percentage increment in revenue to produce a profit on the marketing investment.[6] The factor we have to detect is the *difference* that advertising has made. The method we are going to use is to link the advertising effort to the sales success Waitrose has had, then, to look at qualitative research, the Brand Tracking Study and a MediaSpan assessor analysis from Taylor Nelson Sofres to assess the sales and profit contribution due to the advertising.

Waitrose sales and share growth

The advertising campaign has been associated with an unprecedented increase in Waitrose's fortunes. Waitrose sales growth has been well above that of the category despite the rise in selling space being at the same rate as the category also (Figure 24); brand share has therefore increased and sales per branch have also increased (Figures 25, 26).

Looking more closely at the TV advertising period, we can see the campaign 'bedding-in' and the later two bursts being associated with driving Waitrose revenue growth above the category growth (Figure 27).

---

6. At an industry average gross margin of 25%, we need a 1% increase in sales to cover the whole marketing budget.

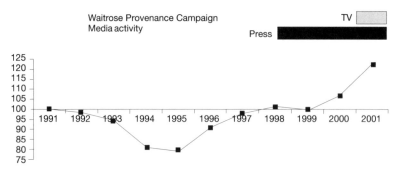

Figure 24: *Waitrose vs. category: difference in sales growth indices (1991 = 100)*[7]
Source: National Statistics © Crown Copyright 2001, SDM 28/Mintel

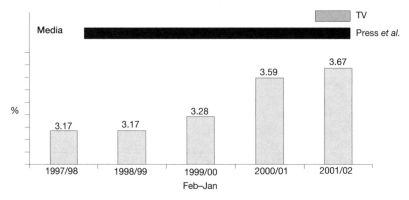

Figure 25: *Waitrose brand share*
Source: IGD, Waitrose

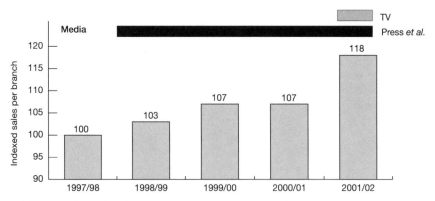

Figure 26: *Waitrose sales per branch*
Source: IGD, Waitrose

7. It is not possible to look at category like-for-like sales over this time period, as IGD calculate like-for-like as same stores operating within only the previous two years. However, during the period 1997–2001, Waitrose increased their sq. ft selling space by 27% which matched the category increase (Source: Mintel/ Annual Reports – Tesco, Sainsbury's, Asda, Safeway, Somerfield, Morrisons, Marks & Spencer, Waitrose and Co-op, included). Despite growth in sq. ft space for Waitrose being the same as the category, sales growth for Waitrose was greater than the category.

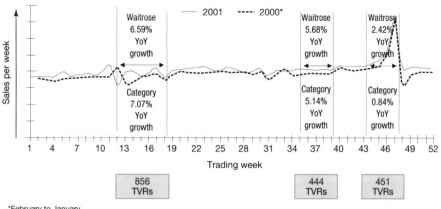

Figure 27: *Like-for-like total Waitrose revenue growth, 2000–2001*
Source: IGD, Waitrose

Evidence that advertising helped sales growth

We have used three related diagnostic methods to build the story of how the advertising worked to change opinion, build awareness and imagery and, vitally, encourage shopping at Waitrose. Firstly, the qualitative feedback from our key audiences was both rich and positive:

'They [the ads] look healthy don't they? Not processed. Back to nature in a healthy way. And that is what we are getting on our shelves, which is what I like.'

Waitrose primary shopper

'Very reliable. Very fresh. They know where the food is coming from.'

Asda primary shopper

'The ads are natural and full of goodness.'

Asda primary shopper

'I think it really fits. I think the whole advert fits with how I see Waitrose. The food they have. I think it's really, really good.'

Tesco primary shopper

'I like that. They're not saying "we're cheap". For me, that is value for money. I like those ads.'

Waitrose secondary shopper

Source: MBL/Banks Hoggins O'Shea.FCB Qualitative Research 2001/2002

The Brand Tracking Study, run by Consumer InSight, was able to indicate how the TV had been working by looking at TV regions against those Waitrose areas that had no TV.

Spontaneous awareness of Waitrose was boosted by both bursts of TV and showed a strong positive swing compared with non-TV areas (Figure 28).

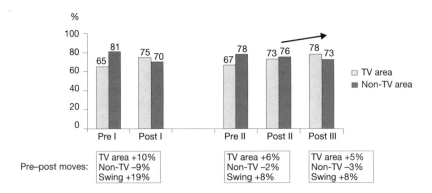

Figure 28: *Total spontaneous awareness of Waitrose*
Base: TV area: 1st Wave: Pre I (382) Post I (395), 2nd Wave: Pre II (372) Post II (399), 3rd Wave: Post III (396)
Non-TV area: 1st Wave: Pre I (112), Post I (218), 2nd Wave: Pre II (116) Post II (219), 3rd Wave: Post III (209)
Source: Brand Tracking Study, Consumer InSight

Also, TV worked well against all key audiences, including non-shoppers. This impact is important in attracting trialists (reported later) (Figure 29).

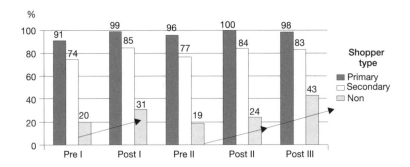

Figure 29: *Total spontaneous awareness of Waitrose by shopper type*
Base: TV area: Primary Shoppers: Pre I (95), Post I (100), Pre II (93); Post II (98); Post III (100): Secondary Shoppers: Pre I (191), Post I (196), Pre II (186); Post II (203); Post III (204): Non Shoppers: Pre I (96), Post I (99), Pre II (93); Post II (98); Post III (92)
Source: Brand Tracking Study, Consumer InSight

Waitrose gained a stronger uplift in spontaneous awareness than did its competitors (albeit from a lower base, but with a lower advertising spend) from the Pre Stage I to the Post III measure (Figure 30).

Furthermore, the campaign, led by TV, has quickly improved perceptions of Waitrose. Overall image endorsement has grown faster in the TV regions than elsewhere (Figure 31) and perception of value likewise (Figure 32).

But did sales improve as a result of the introduction of TV into the campaign?

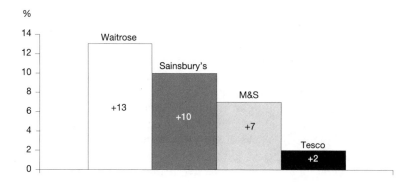

Figure 30: *Percentage uplift in total spontaneous awareness across the TV bursts in the region*
Source: Brand Tracking Study, Consumer InSight

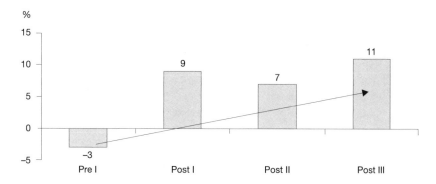

Figure 31: *Difference between average endorsement of Waitrose for all image statements in TV areas and non-TV areas*
Base: TV area: 1st Wave: Pre I (382), Post I (395), 2nd Wave: Pre II (372) Post II (399), 3rd Wave: Post III (396)
Non-TV area: 1st Wave: Pre I (112), Post I (218), 2nd Wave: Pre II (116) Post II (219), 3rd Wave: Post III (209)
Source: Brand Tracking Study, Consumer InSight

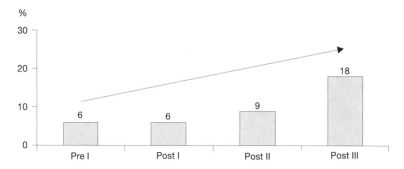

Figure 32: *Prompted image 'Are better value than they used to be': difference between TV areas and non-TV areas*
Base: TV area: 1st Wave: Pre I (382), Post I (395), 2nd Wave: Pre II (372), Post (399), 3rd Wave: Post III (396)
Non-TV area: 1st Wave: Pre I (112), Post I (218), 2nd Wave: Pre II (116), Post II (219), 3rd Wave: Post III (209)
Source: Brand Tracking Study, Consumer InSight

Tracking individual shoppers

We used Econometrics to argue the case for a larger advertising spend. With fewer than a year's data since TV was launched we had too few points with which to build an econometric model. Instead, we looked at individual purchasing data from the Taylor Nelson Sofres MediaSPAN Assessor to establish sales effects. This has the advantage of being based on the *real* behaviour of individuals, rather than the rolled-up aggregate data found in an econometric model.

MediaSPAN fused television viewing data from BARB with actual shopping behaviour from Superpanel, so we could look with confidence at the immediate sales effects among those exposed to the advertising, and contrast their behaviour with those who were not exposed to the advertising. The results were strong.[8]

The TV advertising increased the Waitrose share of shopping trips (Figure 33) and grocery expenditure (Figure 34), grew revenue (Figure 35) and generated a huge number of extra shopping trips – the latter campaign generating 932,000 extra trips, enough to fill the new Wembley stadium ten times over with reserves (Figure 36).

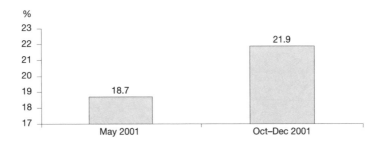

Figure 33: *Short-term incremental uplift in share of shopping trips*[9]
Date: May/October 2001
Source: TNS MediaSPAN

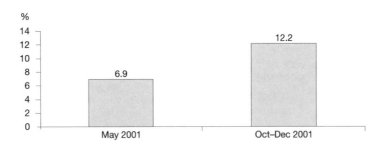

Figure 34: *Short-term incremental uplift in expenditure share*[10]
Date: May/Oct–Dec 2001
Source: TNS Superpanel

8. The analysis was completed over each of the two TV periods (May 2001 then Oct–Dec 2001). The analysis period was 10/16 weeks respectively following the start of the TV advertising. The advertising effect quoted is among people who saw the advertising within 28 days of purchase. The Superpanel sample is significant, at 5122 households in the Waitrose TV regions, of whom 1051 already shopped at Waitrose.
9. TNS confidence levels: at 90% ± 6.4 for both figures.
10. TNS confidence levels: at 90% ± 1.3 for both figures.

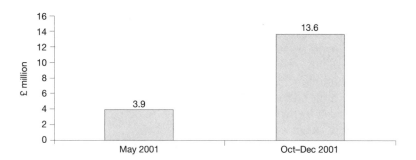

Figure 35: *Incremental sales revenue due to advertising*
Date: May/Oct–Dec 2001
Source: TNS MediaSPAN

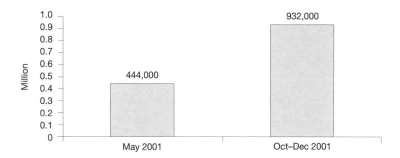

Figure 36: *Short-term incremental uplift n number of shopping trips*
Date: May/Oct–Dec 2001
Source: TNS MediaSPAN

To give these figures some perspective, each burst added hundreds of extra visitors to each shop, each week of the analysis period (Figure 37).

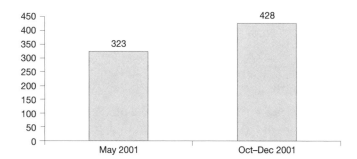

Figure 37: *Increase in number of shopping trips per store per week*
Date: May/Oct–Dec 2001
Source: TNS MediaSPAN

In total, the two bursts of TV-led activity have generated short-term increases of an extra 1,372,000 shopping trips to Waitrose and an extra £17.5 million revenue.

Taylor Nelson Sofres commented that it is extremely rare for a campaign to generate more top-line revenue in the short term than the cost of media. The TV media cost for Waitrose was £2.6 million, comfortably exceeded by the incremental revenue of £17.5 million.

The incremental uplifts in expenditure share generated *more* top-line revenue in the *short term* than the cost of media. In fact, the cost of TV media was more than comfortably exceeded by incremental revenue. TNS commented that it is extremely rare for a campaign to achieve this in the short term.

Indeed, the results we achieved are far higher than Taylor Nelson Sofres has recorded in previous studies, both for a leading competitive retailer, and for a basket of fmcg brands (Figure 38).

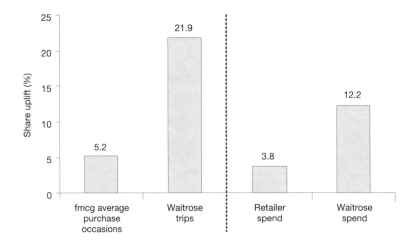

Figure 38: *Previous uplifts quantified for other advertisers*
Base: Superpanel 52-week continuous panel to 03/02/02
Respondents to the mediaSPAN Questionnaire
Note: The fmcg average and retailer results are from tvSPAN panel 1996; uplifts relate to Meridian region only
Source: TNS Superpanel

The campaign achieved these results by:

1. Raising the average basket value of existing shoppers by 11%.[11]
2. Increasing trial of Waitrose (during the May burst 5.8% of non-Waitrose shoppers tried Waitrose!).[11]

Clearly it was vital that trialists returned and didn't go back to their old habits. Happily, the proportion of trialists from the first TV burst returning in the second campaign period was 47%, with their basket size increasing by 38% from May to October–December (from £11.20 in May to £15.51 by October–December).[11] The campaign, then, is not only raising business from existing Waitrose users, but recruiting new users and building their 'Waitrose shopping habit'.

---

11. Source: TNS MediaSPAN.

The benefits of integration

What evidence did we have to support the value of running an integrated campaign?

Firstly, spontaneous brand awareness is enhanced among those who have seen both the TV and press campaigns (Figure 39).

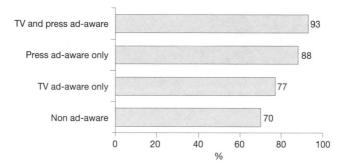

Figure 39: *Spontaneous brand awareness by advertising medium noticed Dec 2001*
Base: Just TV ad aware (branded awareness/recognition) (53); just press ad aware (branded awareness/recognition) (64); TV + press ad aware (branded awareness/recognition) (41); non-ad aware (238)
Source: Brand Tracking Study, Consumer InSight

Those who had seen both TV and press advertising were more likely to think better of Waitrose and claimed to be more likely to shop at Waitrose than those who had seen only one medium (Figure 40). As Consumer InSight summarised: 'The combination of press and TV advertising has a more positive effect on people's opinion of Waitrose than press or TV alone.'

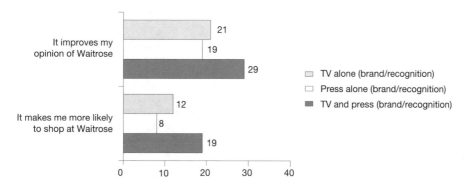

Figure 40: *How integrated advertising affects opinion of Waitrose (post III), by awareness of medium*
Base: TV area post stage: all who recall Waitrose advertising (brand recognition): just TV (52), just press (66), TV and press (42)
Source: Brand Tracking Study, Consumer InSight

The combination of all the media has given a small brand higher visibility and improved perceptions.

We also found that the best increments in spend levels were achieved by those exposed to *both* TV and press (Figure 41).

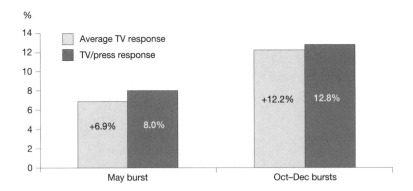

Figure 41: *Incremental share of expenditure*
Date: May/Oct–Dec 2001
Source: TNS MediaSPAN

These findings support the tracking study, suggesting it is the *combination* of media that works best to build awareness, image and, now, sales.

The longer-term value to Waitrose

These findings are based on the immediate period during and after advertising. At the gross margins which Waitrose enjoy, the £17.5 million short-term extra revenue from the TV regions alone is more than enough to cover the cost of television advertising in its entirety for the year 2001. We are not allowed to quote the Waitrose gross margin, so have used a lower approximation.

TABLE 1

Extra revenue generated	£17.50 million
Gross margin @ 25%	£4.38 million
TV media budget 2001	£3.00 million
Immediate contribution to profit	**£1.38 million**

Indeed, work by Andrew Roberts at TNS concludes that '72% of the full short-term effect of advertising will occur within the first 28 days' (Roberts, 1999). On this basis, with the two bursts summing to £17.5 million extra revenue, the full short-term returns to the advertising will be £24.3 million. This produces a healthy £3.08 million contribution to profit.

TABLE 2

Extra revenue generated	£24.30 million
Gross margin @ 25%	£6.08 million
TV media budget 2001	£3.00 million
Full short-term contribution to profit	**£3.08 million**

This rise of £24.3 million represents the lowest limit of return because it excludes any medium-term payback. However, the purpose of this paper (as it was of the Waitrose financial analysts), is to look at the long-term benefit to the business of spending money on advertising.

Advertising's benefits are likely to persist far beyond this immediate measurable short-term effect, because 47%[12] of those induced to try the shop when they consumed the advertising have returned, and because it has increased the loyalty (via larger basket values) of existing shoppers.

But what sort of carry-over effect can we assume?
A number of studies in the UK and the USA measure advertising's effects over 12 months as 2.5 times larger than the initial sales uplift (Broadbent, 2001). This multiple alone would suggest a benefit to Waitrose over 12 months of £17.5 million × 2.5, or £43.75 million. At this revenue, the profit benefit over 12 months to Waitrose would be £5.00 million:

TABLE 3

Extra revenue generated	£43.75 million
Gross margin @ 25%	£10.98 million
Total annual advertising budget 2001	£5.98 million
Medium-term contribution to profit	**£5.00 million**

We can have confidence in the figure because it is within the estimate Numbercraft derived from its econometric model. It suggested a £7.0 million budget would generate £49 million extra revenue, +/- £14 million.

Now we have two estimates of the annualised extra revenue for year one: Numbercraft +£49 million (+/- £14 million); and TNS-based estimate +£43.75 million.

But was this estimate realised in actual sales? Yes. Total sales increased by Waitrose's largest ever annual rise of £201 million between February 2001 and January 2002.

Revenue growth beyond our estimate for advertising is largely explained by the new branches maturing, retail price inflation and by general category growth. We estimate these three factors between them to have accounted for £155 million of the sales growth, leaving £46 million to be explained by marketing activities and other variables. With no other significant explanations available, advertising has contributed top-line sales of at least the £43.75 million estimated here.

Brand value

Although Waitrose do not need to value their brand – they are not quoted and are not for sale – a price/earnings ratio of 15 is average in the retail sector and easily achievable for Waitrose. At this ratio, the medium-term contribution to profits of £5.02 million would add over £75 million to the value of the Waitrose business.

The tough financial department at Waitrose

The financial department at Waitrose takes a hard view on all investments. The base question is 'If I put cash in now, when will I get cash out?'

---

12. TNS MediaSPAN.

Advertising spend is judged against two other key investment areas – capital expenditure on the estate, such as new stores, extensions and refurbishments, and systems investment. Waitrose have built a model of how they expect returns to flow into the business, and it is the financial department who have been responsible for judging the sales' effects of the marketing spend. They required 'an early demonstrable hit' from their advertising budget; they got it with the TNS MediaSPAN results.

Here is a summary of the report the financial department produced on the advertising investment:

> 'The advertising has clearly already paid for itself as well as achieving some soft targets (awareness, image-building) for the Partnership. It worked!'

Mark Turner, Head of Financial Analysis, Waitrose, October 2001

Advertising has quickly established itself at Waitrose as an important investment category, ranked alongside systems investment and branch expansion, where once it was frowned upon. The involvement of the financial department in measuring sales response has greatly helped this process.

Further benefits: Waitrose Partners' response

Given the need to gain the approval of the Partners, good feedback from them was crucial:

> 'I was really impressed. I thought it just summed up everything we do in the shops and I did wonder how on earth we were going to advertise on television – which is almost seen as quite tacky.'

> 'If you work for a company that has cracking adverts on TV it certainly makes you feel a bit more acknowledged.'

Lee Cutajar, Fruit and Veg Manager

> 'I felt very proud to work for Waitrose. When I saw the advertisements in a Special Managers' Meeting, at the end of it we all sat there smiling, thinking "Isn't it great? We work here!".'

Caroline Jackson, Branch Partner, Admin Office, Audit and Dining Rm.

The positive response extends all the way to board level:

> 'My first reaction was one of pride at my company doing this work.'

Geoff Salt, Distribution Director, Waitrose

Further benefits: supplier relationships

So enthusiastic is the head of meat, poultry, fish and dairy products (the largest buyership), he takes copies of the TV commercials to potential new suppliers to explain the Waitrose way.

> 'It shows the respect we have for our suppliers.'

Richard Sadler, Head Buyer, Waitrose

New or reaffirmed learning

1. Advertising is an engine for growth that can be ranked alongside other investment areas in the business. Judgement of returns should reflect the nature of this investment, which in this case will produce its major return over the medium to long term, yet indicated its potential and contributed to profits in the short term.
2. Involving the financial department in judging the sales effects of advertising can have a positive effect on advertising budgets and on the attitude to advertising as a primary source of business growth.
3. TV is a powerful medium on its own. However, the multiplier effect of other media working alongside TV in an integrated campaign make their consideration vital.

Summary

Since 1997 Waitrose has made a fundamental shift in its attitude towards advertising investment, and has produced a powerful supermarket advertising campaign that is the envy of many a 'Goliath'. At the same time its share of market has moved from 3.17% to nearly 3.7% despite the big four trying to win Waitrose customers with new product ranges. Some of this improvement has been due to a brave advertising campaign that now spans many channels to reach the same consumer with the same message. The arrival of television in 2001 proved beyond doubt that the advertising budget can be placed under the heading of 'investment' not 'cost'. Last but not least, the campaign has already contributed over £5 million extra to profits as well as growing Waitrose's position as the pre-eminent quality food retailer in the UK.

REFERENCES

Ambler, T. (2001) *Marketing and the Bottom Line*. FT/Prentice Hall: London.
Broadbent, T. (2001) How advertising pays back. *Admap*, November.
Lewis, J.S. (1968) *Retail Trading – the Philosophy and Practice of John Spedan Lewis*. Merritt Hatcher Ltd.
Roberts, A. (1999) Recency, frequency and the sales effects of advertising. *Admap*, February.

23

Walkers Crisps
Staying loyal to Lineker

Principal authors: John McDonald, Peter Knowland and Bridget Angear, Abbott Mead Vickers.BBDO
Collaborating authors: Marco Centonze, Andy Carrington

EDITOR'S SUMMARY

The Lineker campaign produced by Abbott Mead Vickers.BBDO continues to pay great dividends to Walkers Crisps. Between 1995 and 2000 it helped increase sales by 105% and share from 21% to 27% in grocery.

An increasingly effective campaign has doubled the awareness and enjoyment of Walkers' commercials. It's also bolstered consumers' loyalty to Walkers, helping it become Britain's biggest food brand. All achieved with a media spend that was only a fraction of their competitors' budget.

INTRODUCTION

'With an immediate ROI of £1.70, building to £5.10 in the long term, our loyalty to Gary Lineker has clearly paid off.'

This paper will prove that loyalty pays. We've remained loyal to the Gary Lineker campaign and enjoyed long-term success in both sales and advertising measures.

In 1995 Walkers Crisps introduced the 'No More Mr Nice Guy' campaign with a daunting set of objectives. It had to deliver well-branded news that could drive sales, in the short term, and brand health in the long term. It also had to appeal equally, across the board, to adults and kids.

The results so far

Between 1995 and 2002, Walkers sales grew from 1.34 billion to 2.75 billion packs per year – an uplift of 105%. Our market share rose 6% in grocery and 3% in impulse,[1] while our competitors' declined.

Econometric modelling reveals that, without this advertising over the past two years, Walkers Crisps would have foregone nearly 114 million pack sales. The same analysis shows that £1 invested in advertising generates a short-term revenue ROI of £1.70 (and three times that in the long-term). This compares to an average ROI of £0.24 for the bagged snacks market.

This has been achieved by establishing a 'loyalty chain' whereby everyone who participated has benefited.

We've remained loyal to Gary for seven years and 43 executions. There have been rocky patches, but by sticking with him, we found we could improve the campaign. Its effectiveness is now at an all-time high with record impact and branding, and more powerful communication of news.

This more effective campaign has helped protect brand loyalty, despite considerable competitive activity. Brand regard is at its highest level. So it's no surprise that, in a promiscuous market, Walkers' brand loyalty keeps strengthening while others' declines.

Consequently, the trade seriously values Walkers Crisps. When loyalty to individual supermarkets is declining, they place greater value on brands with high loyalty. And so they remain loyal to us, aiding our distribution.

Finally, Gary's career benefited by staying loyal to us. The fame gained from these adverts helped make him one of Britain's best-loved celebrities, with a varied media portfolio.

So loyalty – while laudable morally – also proves beneficial in practical terms.

---

1. 'Grocery' is defined by IRI as multiple grocers and co-ops. It includes major multiples (the big six supermarkets); Morrisons and Waitrose; minor multiples (e.g. Budgens and Cullens); and Co-ops. It excludes discounters (Netto, Lidl, Aldi), Boots, Superdrug and Marks and Spencer. 'Impulse' is defined as all other retail outlets not mentioned in grocery, including 'symbol independents'; multiple CTNs; unaffiliated grocers and CTNs; off-licences; forecourts; other (e.g. hospitals, schools and workplace). It excludes pubs. It is heavily dominated by local brands, so 60% was felt to be the maximum level for a national brand in impulse.

BACKGROUND

'Swedes 2, Turnips 1.'

Of all the dour performances in English football it was perhaps the most ignominious. The 1992 European Championships, England were playing Sweden and losing, 2-1.

They desperately needed a goal to avoid humiliating elimination in the first round. So, naturally, manager Graham Taylor takes off star England striker Gary Lineker. Gary trudges off, dejected. Unsurprisingly, his team lose and return home to unflattering comparisons with root vegetables.

The moral? Never substitute Gary Lineker.

Walkers Crisps have taken this to heart. At various times throughout the seven years and 43 executions it seemed the campaign might be wearing out; times when Walkers could have remonstrated: 'Do I not like that?!' and substituted him.

Fortunately, they didn't. And their steadfastness has paid off handsomely. This paper will demonstrate how.

Walkers Crisps history

Leicester during the Second World War. A pretty grim place. Rationing meant a lack of basic goods and a miserable populace. So local butcher Henry Walker's invention of 'Walker's Crisps' couldn't have come at a better time: deprived of treats, the town rapidly grew fond of this easily available source of solace.

By the late 1970s Walkers Snack Foods dominated the Midlands. In the 1980s they spread across the country at a speed that would put foot-and-mouth to shame.

By 1995 they covered all of Britain and were now the biggest salty snack company in Britain. Walkers Crisps – responsible for over 70% of their volume – was the key product (source: IRI). But, despite this, the business was facing many difficult challenges.

Business objectives

Walkers needed to find a new way to grow sales, grow in different retail channels and protect share against ever-tougher competition.

By 1995, distribution-fuelled growth was coming to an end. National distribution had reached 95% in grocery and 60% in impulse.

So the first business challenge was to find another way of generating growth. Second, Walkers was growing faster in grocery than in impulse. So it was essential to continue growing in grocery and also stimulating impulse (see Figure 1).

Finally, it was a competitive market, particularly against the predominant private label. And there were potentially huge brands looming on the horizon such as Pringles. Pringles is backed by the formidable marketing muscle of P&G and was felt to be a major threat at launch (see Figure 2).

The salty snacks market is highly promiscuous. People have a repertoire of about five brands and switch between them based on personal whim, deals and enticing news or promotions. For example, when Walkers 24-packs were on deal

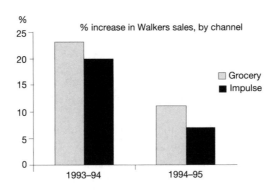

Figure 1: *Walkers' sales in grocery growing faster than their sales in impulse*
Source: IRI

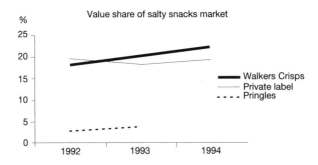

Figure 2: *Private label was key rival*
Source: IRI

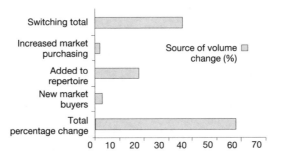

Figure 3: *Source of business for Walkers 24-pack when on deal*
Source: TNS Superpanel

recently, 36% of their additional sales came from switching. Clearly, a high proportion of consumers simply follow deals (see Figure 3).

So the final business challenge was to remain central in people's repertoire while defending against competitive threats.

MARKETING OBJECTIVES

Marketing had to:

1. Devise motivating news
2. Make news work in the short term and the long term
3. Appeal to a broad audience.

First, how to generate growth? Walkers knew that constant 'news' was the most effective way of stimulating short-term sales. Communicating news generates a significantly higher return on investment versus non-news communication (see Figure 4).

But what sort of news?

Recent 'news'
Flavours can be …

- New (Barbecue)
- Renamed (Salt 'n' Lineker)
- Upgraded (Cheese 'n' Onion '98)

Promotions can be …

- Collectable (Tazos)
- Altruistic (Books for Schools)
- Monetary (Moneybags)

Crisps can be …

- Fresher (Nitrogen-flush packaging)
- In bigger bags (several pack-size upgrades)

Sub-brands can deliver …

- More taste (MAX)
- Less fat (Lites)
- More interesting shapes (Squares)

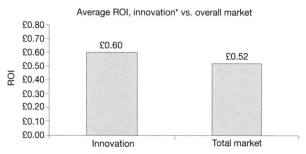

Figure 4: *Advertising 'news' has greater ROI than other types of advertising*
Source: IRI

Marketing had to devise compelling news, then ensure it was well-communicated and well-branded. While news did generate growth, the uplift is only partially sustained. We had to establish long-term growth by ... fortifying the long-term relationship consumers had with the brand (see Figure 5).

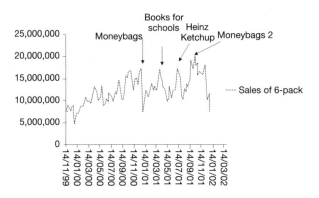

Figure 5: *Walkers' sales peak with 'news' then fall back*
Source: IRI

And finally, we had to exploit both impulse and grocery channels. What this effectively meant was that they had to target everyone (see Figure 6).

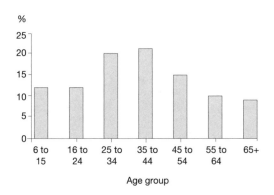

Figure 6: *Percentage of buyers of Walkers' Crisps, by age group*
Source: TNS

Children are significant consumers of snacks, and also purchasers (in impulse). Adults are main buyers (buying mostly in grocery) and heavy consumers themselves. So marketing had to appeal to a very broad cross-section of the population (see Figure 7).

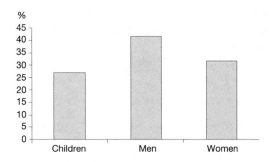

Figure 7: *Consumption of Walkers Crisps, by group (%)*
Source: TNS

ADVERTISING OBJECTIVES

Advertising needed to address a challenging set of objectives.

It had to communicate *impactfully* well-branded news that drove short-term sales and long-term brand health, while appealing to both kids and adults. Why? We've seen the importance of news to Walkers in driving sales. So advertising had to ensure that the news cut through and was clearly communicated.

Also, Walkers had discovered that more popular promotions were being aped by competitors. To preclude copying, it was important that people knew the promotions were 'owned' by Walkers. The campaign had to deliver well-branded news.

A crucial objective was to support brand regard. If we were going to keep consumers loyal in the long term, we had to protect brand measures against heavy-spending competition. Advertising had to strengthen brand loyalty.

Finally, we had this mass-market targeting issue. We needed a vehicle that two very different audiences – kids and adults – noticed and enjoyed.

How did the campaign address these objectives?

Campaign details

The nation had last seen Gary sloping off the football pitch in Malmö back in 1992. Suddenly, in 1995, he reappeared as the face of Walkers Crisps.

The 1996 IPA paper extensively describes the campaign development process. The primary aim of this paper is to show how the campaign remained fresh throughout the subsequent years. This section explains how Gary's resurrection took place.

Advertising strategy

Research identified the strategy of 'irresistibility'. A crisp so 'more-ish' that you can't resist it. A perfect crisp with the best flavours, freshness and the crispiest crunch.

Tonally, advertising couldn't be pompous as this didn't fit with the down-to-earth brand personality and simple nature of the product ('we take crisp-making seriously, but not ourselves').

Its humour had to appeal to both adults and kids – not too 'wacky snacky' as in much of the competitive activity.

Media choice

TV is the media battleground in salty snacks (75% share of spend, according to MMS 2001) and a brand's success is based on its ability to communicate within this medium. Walkers has invested 83% of its spend (source: MMS) in TV over the campaign. Initially, airtime was booked in both children's and adults' programmes to meet our dual target.

The creative idea

Gary Lineker was chosen as spokesman. He was popular with a broad cross-section: a renowned footballer and gentleman. The advertising poked fun at his 'nice guy' image: Gary's so overcome by the irresistibility of Walkers Crisps that he becomes nasty and steals them. The simplicity of this idea gives it scope to communicate a range of news. The logic: each piece of news makes Walkers even more irresistible, which is the reason Gary wants to steal them even more.

Keeping the campaign fresh

After a few years, we realised that the 'No More Mr Nice Guy' idea would not stretch for ever. So we took steps to refresh it, ensuring he would not always end up with the crisps. We decided to play with the storyline conventions. For example ...

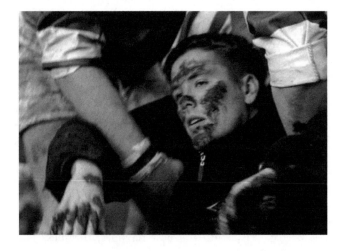

Figure 8: *Gary jealously guarding his 'arch crisp-thief' role, with young pretender Michael Owen duffed up by a rugby team*

Figure 9: *Gary foiled by wilier enemy, with Steve Redgrave even more determined to hang onto his Walkers*

Figure 10: *Gary foiled by bad luck, falling into a potato masher when he was just about to waltz off with the crisps*

Figure 11: *Gary cameo, generally used as the Walkers endorsement of a sub-brand (e.g. disguised as David Beckham to fool Victoria into handing over Sensations)*

We used celebrity 'foils'. Millward Brown evidence suggests a celebrity in your ads can improve effectiveness.

TABLE 1: CELEBRITY ADS ARE MORE EFFECTIVE

Mean scores	Celebrity ads	Non-celebrity
Brand cues	2.35	2.15
Branding	3.89	3.78
Understanding	3.45	3.40
Enjoyment	3.28	3.26
Passive/active (involvement)	4.93	4.61
Relevance	2.58	2.55
Similarity to other ads	2.07	2.03

Source: Millward Brown

So we inferred that having two celebrities (Gary plus one) might improve measures further. We also get huge amounts of PR from celebrity ads, which further aids overall awareness.[2]

Skewing the targeting

We monitor the appeal of the campaign and its spokesman across age groups. This shows us whether we should occasionally skew more to adults or kids to redress imbalances, for example:

Kids → Looney Toons Qubix
Adults → Lites or Sensations

Media

We gradually moved away from buying kids' airtime, realising that adults' airtime was more effective. Instead of splitting our buying, we could combine it in one strategy. That's because 75% of the top 20 adult programmes are also watched by kids (source: BARB/SPC) (see Figure 12).

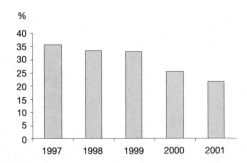

Figure 12: *Walkers' proportion of media spend on kids' airtime*
Source: BARB/DDS

---

2. The 2002 Ads That Make News study, carried out by media communications firm Propeller and monitoring company Media Report Editorial, revealed that Walkers and Pepsi (who also use celebrities) received more press coverage than any other brand during the first quarter of the year.

But what kind of adult programming?

We opted for premium, peak-time programmes that we knew had high attentiveness. Research carried out by Kate Lynch of Starcom *et al.* indicated that attentiveness (and factors which contribute to it such as loyalty and viewing duration) were more likely to generate high advertising recall. See Figures 13 and 14.

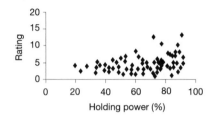

Figure 13: *Higher rating programmes in peak keep people 'tuned' through commercial breaks for longer*
Source: Starcom (Valuing Primetime, 1999)

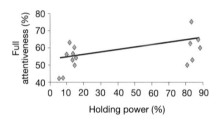

Figure 14: *There's a high correlation between 'holding power' and levels of viewing attentiveness*
Source: NBC/Starcom (MRI/Attention Scores)

Therefore, we abandoned a quest for pure GRP quantity, and instead went for quality programmes with loyal viewers (see Figure 15).

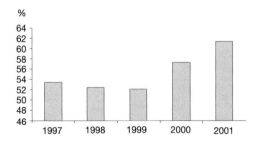

Figure 15: *Walkers' proportion of media spend on peak airtime*
Source: BARB/DDS

Summary

We've refreshed the campaign's advertising and media strategy to enable us to meet our objectives more effectively.

But the proof of the pudding, as they say, is in the eating. Pass the spoon.

What happened?

The campaign's ability to retain consumer loyalty helped Walkers gain share despite the arrival of new competitors (see Figure 16).

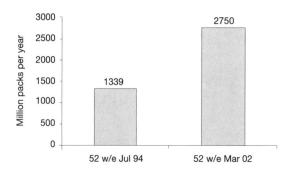

Figure 16: *Walkers Pack sales have increased 105% over the campaign*
Source: IRI

In fact, Walkers' share has grown in both grocery and impulse (see Figures 17 and 18).

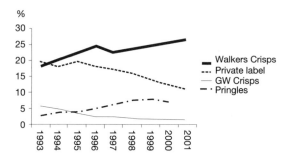

Figure 17: *Walkers' share of bagged snacks (grocery)*
Source: IRI

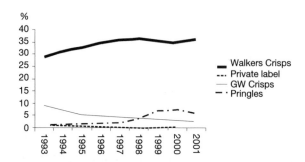

Figure 18: *Walkers' share of bagged snacks (impulse)*
Source: IRI

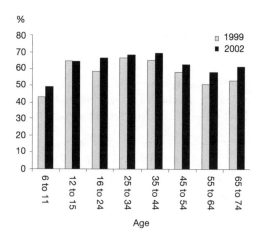

Figure 19: *Penetration has risen across ages: percentage of population buying Walkers Crisps*
Source: TNS

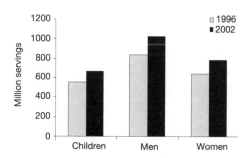

Figure 20: *Walkers Crisps servings consumed per year*
Source: TNS

This is due partly to increased penetration across all ages (Figure 19) and partly due to increased consumption, which rose 22.1%, while the market rose only 1.9%. Walkers consumption also increased among all age groups, see Figure 20.

It seems Walkers' growth occurred due to us stealing from private label (Figure 21).

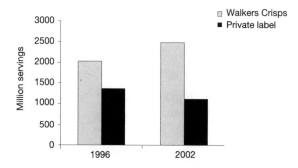

Figure 21: *Walkers Crisps servings consumed per year at expense of private label*
Source: TNS

It's a testament to the power of the brand that it could steal share from cheaper private label in such a cost-conscious market.

Summary
Walkers have grown total sales and share in both the grocery and impulse channels and, in addition, have staved off the threat of private label.

Now we'll show how advertising contributed substantially to this success.

PROOF OF EFFECTIVENESS

It's said that success breeds success. In a similar vein, loyalty breeds loyalty. We'll show how loyalty paid off for Walkers in four ways.

1. We've stayed loyal to the Gary campaign.
2. Consumers have remained loyal to Walkers Crisps.
3. The trade has remained loyal to Walkers Crisps.
4. Gary has remained loyal to us.

We've stayed loyal to the Gary campaign

The campaign was undoubtedly successful early on. In 1995 *Campaign* Magazine reported that Walkers Crisps commercials were the UK's best-recognised. In 1996 Walkers won an IPA Effectiveness award. The story of the next few years is one of vicissitudes (Figure 22).

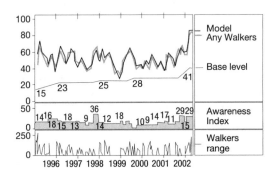

Figure 22: *Adult AIs 1995–2002 at very high levels*
Source: Millward Brown

Pre-campaign, the Awareness Index had been 8. Suddenly in the first few years of 'No More Mr Nice Guy', AIs among kids and adults shot up to around 18, even surpassing 30 at one point (the Spice Girls execution, at the height of their fame). This was against a category average of 8 (see Figure 23).

There were similarly impressive rises in advertising enjoyment scores (see Figures 24 and 25).

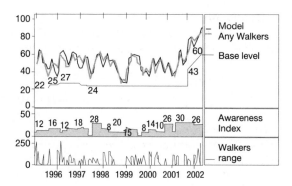

Figure 23: *Kids AIs 1995–2002 also reaching high scores*
Source: Millward Brown

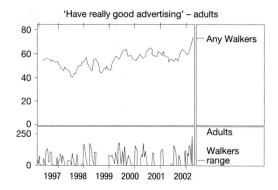

Figure 24: *Enjoyment consistently increased among adults*
Source: Millward Brown

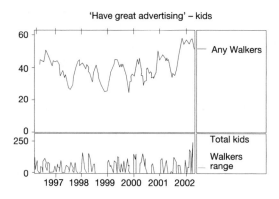

Figure 25: *Similarly increased pattern for kids*
Source: Millward Brown

But, after five years and 30 executions it seemed the campaign was wearing out. AIs weren't hitting earlier peaks. This was probably linked to waning enjoyment and overfamiliarity. We discovered that people were finding the idea predictable.

'Oh look – Lineker ends up with the crisps again. That's a surprise.'

Sarcastic male, 18–21 (AMV Qualitative Research)

Had the idea run its course? We could have jettisoned it then. Instead, we sought to refresh it. We evolved new storyline structures, used celebrities judiciously and bought more considered media (see Campaign details on p. 597).

The result? Dramatically improved advertising measures. It's more enjoyable than ever. 'Really good ads' rocketed recently. And our spokesman is still loved (see Figure 26).

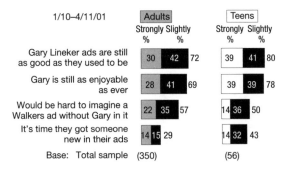

Figure 26: *Gary is still as popular as ever*
Source: Millward Brown

He's lost none of his charm for mums:

'Ooooooh, Gary Loinacher, I call him!'

Women 35–45 (AMV Qualitative Research)

Teenagers are as effusive as they ever are in focus groups:

'He's alright, I suppose'.

14-year-old boy (AMV Qualitative Research)

Today's kids are too young to know of Gary's past glories. To many he's just 'the crisps man'. Instead, the comic-book style of the advertising is most enjoyable.

'He gets hit on the head and it goes CLANG. He's funny.'

Child, Millward Brown Verbatims (Books for Schools, 2001)

Greater cut-through
Our impact is better than ever, with Walkers executions frequently charting at number one in *Marketing Magazine*'s Adwatch.

But we haven't just 'bought' this awareness. The AI factors-out spend, showing true impact and branding. Recent executions cut through even better than previous peaks. AIs have been enormous for recent executions – especially the Redgrave and Helena ones (30 and 29, versus a category average of 8).

Campaign AIs are in the top 4% of all campaigns Millward Brown track (and 2001's AIs are even higher) (see Figure 27).

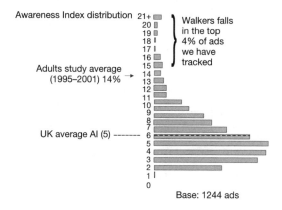

Figure 27: *The campaign has some of the highest ad efficiencies that Millward Brown track*
Source: Millward Brown

Furthermore, the campaign's base level awareness[3] has risen into the top 8% of all campaigns. This indicates the valuable advertising memories a campaign has established in customers' minds (Figure 28).

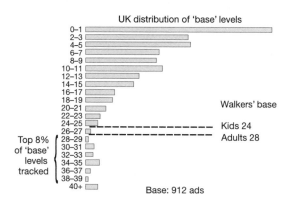

Figure 28: *The campaign has a substantial 'base' level of advertising memories*
Source: Millward Brown

Building on the existing campaign – rather than replacing it – has built up a huge 'adstock' that a new campaign couldn't match for years.

---

3. Base level is officially defined as 'the level of recall to which advertising falls after the brand has been off air for circa six months'. It is effectively the amount of 'recall' you would still get if you were not on air.

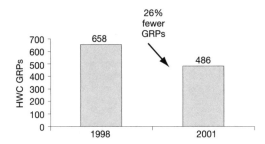

Figure 29: *Fewer ratings are required per burst of news than before*
Source: BARB/DDS

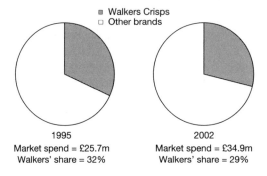

Figure 30: *Walkers' share of voice needn't be so high*
Source: MMS

And now people are so *au fait* with our campaign, we needn't spend so much on media, which means we can be less concerned with share of voice (see Figures 29 and 30).

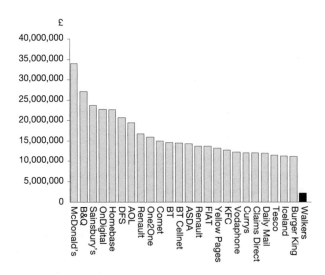

Figure 31: *Walkers' spending dwarfed by other big brands*
Source: MMS

In fact, Walkers need to spend very little, for a brand of their size. They are the second biggest brand in Britain but their spend is far from commensurate (see Figure 31). (The most recent *Marketing* report into brand size listed Walkers as the second biggest brand in Britain after Coca-Cola.)

So our loyalty has generated considerable media efficiencies.

Better news communication

Renewed concentration on communicating news has paid off (see Figure 32).

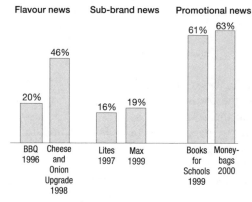

Figure 32: *'News' has been communicated better throughout the campaign*
Source: Millward Brown

In the Books for Schools promotion 92% of kids knew of the promotion and that it was by Walkers! Of those, 66% claimed their source of awareness was TV advertising. This close association of a promotion with Walkers is crucial. When competitors try to run similar school-themed giveaways their advertising gets misattributed to Walkers Crisps. So our promotions have been rendered more immune to copying.

So our faithfulness to the campaign was rewarded. We continue to meet our campaign objectives – indeed we meet them better than ever.

Consumers have remained loyal to Walkers Crisps

Walkers Crisps consumers are much more loyal than those of other snacks. And they are becoming more so. The proportion of spend that consumers give to Walkers Crisps (rather than salty snack competitors) has risen (see Figure 33).

We believe advertising plays a significant part in the strengthening of brand loyalty.

Learned articles[4] suggest the following way of getting consumers into the 'loyalty loop':

---

4. Light, L. *Brand Loyalty Management – the New Marketing Basic*, Admap, May 1998.

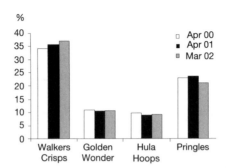

Figure 33: *Walkers' brand loyalty rising as others' falls: % of buyers' spend that is spent on that brand*
Source: TNS Impulse

- Advertising firstly makes a brand salient.
- It then conveys motivating news that gets people interested and creates expectations about the brand.
- If consumers then buy it, they'll form their own (hopefully positive) beliefs.
- Afterwards, advertising reinforces these beliefs among users and creates a stronger brand bond.
- Advertising attracts new customers, then keeps them more loyal afterwards (see Figure 34).

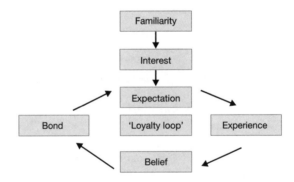

Figure 34: *How brand advertising works*

We believe that this has occurred for Walkers Crisps. Advertising has helped keep the brand salient. It communicates motivating news, while developing a brand personality that creates empathy with the mass of British consumers. This both attracts new customers and convinces existing ones they've made the right choice.

We've witnessed a direct relationship between advertising and brand measures. When we advertise, brand measures rise. When we cease, brand measures slide. (NB: sometimes there is a slight lag in this process.)

Brand measures have been sustained across the campaign, despite increased competition from Pringles who had a consistently high spend.

Obviously, advertising can't take full credit for improved brand regard. There have been new sub-brands (such as Lites in 1997 and Max in 1999),[5] flavour upgrades (such as improved Cheese and Onion in 1998), new flavours (Barbecue, Heinz Tomato Ketchup and Great British Flavours)[6] and new packaging[7] that have played a part. However, the last major innovation was in 1998.

Since then, we've used the same potatoes, same oil,[8] and same packaging. Something besides product innovation is sustaining brand image. So we can establish a connection between the communication[9] and the strengthening of brand loyalty.

The trade has remained loyal to Walkers Crisps

As we've established, loyalty to Walkers Crisps is higher than all other crisps. This is a good reason for the trade to remain loyal to Walkers. But there's another commercial imperative. Loyalty to big supermarkets is declining (Figure 35).[10]

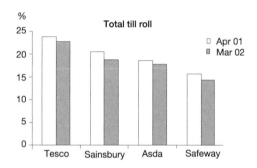

Figure 35: *Supermarket loyalty is declining*
Source: TNS Superpanel

So, by stocking a brand that retains high loyalty, supermarkets stand a better chance of arresting their declining loyalty (and if they don't stock it, customers may go elsewhere).

This is a useful asset for Walkers' sales teams and helps them gain distribution incredibly quickly. The trade know their allegiance will have sustained, lucrative results. For example, Sensations went from zero to 95% distribution in Asda, Tesco and Safeway in just two weeks!

---

5. As Lites and Max still represent less than a tenth of Walkers Crisps volume, they clearly have little effect on consumer regard.
6. Given that, throughout the campaign, approximately 75% of sales have always been the big three SKUs (Cheese 'n' Onion, Salt 'n' Vinegar and Ready Salted), new flavours/products can only have a minor effect on brand image.
7. In 1998 the revolutionary Nitrogen-flushed packaging slowed down oxidisation of the crisps and stopped crisps going rancid.
8. This year Lites started being cooked in sunflower oil for lower saturated fat but this is not the case for the main brand.
9. It could potentially be PR, website or point-of-sale activity. But, given that they all spring from the Gary campaign, this is more of a consequence of the campaign. Also promotions clearly play a large part in affecting brand regard. But they are always advertised so they act symbiotically.
10. People are spending more of their total spend within grocery – till roll in total multiples and Co-ops went up from 60.9 to 61.4 over the last year. But loyalty to each store has decreased. This is due to buyers shopping in more grocery outlets.

Gary has remained loyal to us

Gary's career has benefited from his fidelity to Walkers. Since 1995, he's moved from retired footballer to TV pundit, to panel game captain, to newspaper columnist. But he's remained spokesman for Walkers Crisps. He admits it's been important for his career: keeping him in the public eye, thus enabling him to move into new opportunities when others (like *Match of the Day*) end.

And the more jobs he undertakes, the more we benefit too.[11] Reciprocity is a wonderful thing. This is the final link in our loyalty chain. We've shown that loyalty pays dividends to all participants in that sequence.

Now we'll prove the payback of advertising in recent years.

Payback

It has not been possible to conduct an econometric analysis of the impulse channel.[12] However, a look at the trends supports the idea that the campaign generated considerable sales uplift. In Figure 36 the top line represents pack volume sales,[13] the bottom line, GRPs.[14]

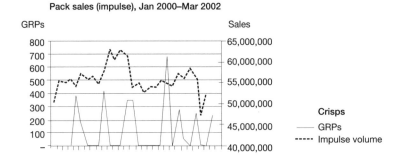

Figure 36: *Impulse sales show correlation with media spend*
Source: IRI, MMS

There's a correlation between the rise in sales and GRPs, albeit circumstantial. We have, however, constructed an econometric model for grocery sales. Over the last two years, every £1 spent on advertising generated £1.70 in retail revenue.[15] This equates to almost 114 million extra packs sold over the period as a direct result of advertising (see Figure 37).

11. On *They Think It's All Over* and *Match of the Day*, Walkers frequently receive overt or subtle referencing – generally from Gary's co-stars. Giles Smith in the *Telegraph* wrote recently: 'The BBC's coverage [of the FA Cup Final] was hosted with amiable aplomb by the face of a well-known brand of salted snack. Restrictions on advertising in this column mean we are unable to name him. We are, however, at liberty to use the name of the product he endorses – Walkers crisps – references to which were strewn over Saturday's programme like ... well, like so many discarded crisp packets on the terrace of life.'
12. Any source of fmcg sales data in the impulse channel, IRI included, will be largely based on audit rather than census scanning data, so store level econometric modelling is impossible. Aggregate level data are available, but the measurement of promotions and in-store display is extrapolated from a few observations and is not sufficiently granular to construct a regression model which will isolate the effect with any significant degree of confidence.
13. Four-weekly sales data, measured in packs or inner bags of a multipack.
14. 30-second equivalent, housewives and children.
15. This is not derived from the financial margin of each product but from the overall increase in revenue sales. Therefore it is not actual revenue to Walkers. Also, it does not include production spends – but neither do any of the brands featured in the averages charts.

WALKERS CRISPS `SILVER`

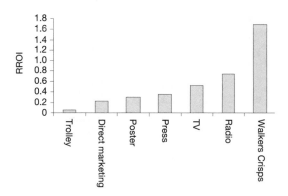

Figure 37: *We exceed the average RROI for all media*
Source: IRI

IRI believe £1.70 is an exceptionally high ROI. The average ROI for TV advertising is only £0.52. And it compares very favourably to a Bagged Snacks category ROI of 0.24 (see Figure 38).

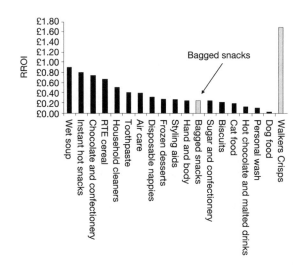

Figure 38: *Exceeding the category RROI by 7 times*
Source: IRI

Furthermore, some of our promotional executions generated especially large ROIs. The ROIs for two promotions – Moneybags 1 and Moneybags 2 – have been calculated as a massive £3.65 and £3.36 respectively (see Figure 39).[16]

It doesn't stop there. These are, of course, all short-term effects. But the advertising will continue to pay back into the long term, well beyond the two or

---

16. It has been impossible to separate out the effects of advertising and promotion in this case. To emulate it, we added the Moneybags total prize fund to the Spend section, i.e. £750,000 for Moneybags 1 and £1 million in the more generous Moneybags 2.

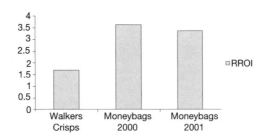

Figure 39: *Promotional advertising generates a particularly massive RROI*
Source: IRI

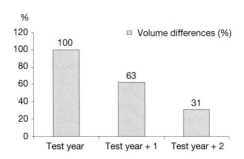

Figure 40: *Advertising continues to pay back: long-term effects on established products*
Source: IRI

three weeks the campaign is on air. It continues having an effect (albeit dwindling) throughout the first year, then beyond that (see Figure 40).[17]

Walkers' parent company, Frito Lay, works to the assumption that long-term effects will be three times those of short-term ones (this was the result of an internal Behaviour Scan study in Frito Lay markets).

So, in reality, £1.70 invested in advertising pays back approximately £5.10 in the long term.

CONCLUSION

If you're currently thinking your campaign is approaching retirement, it might be worth a rethink. We re-energised a campaign that appeared to be tiring and it's now got record advertising measures. Ones that would have taken a new campaign years to attain.

By remaining loyal to it, we've helped sustain brand regard, and by extension, brand loyalty. This has protected Walkers against the endemic promiscuity in the market. This, in turn, has protected their on-shelf presence by keeping stores loyal.

---

17. There seems to be consensus in the published press that there is a long-term effect of several times the short-term effect. Some further reading: Lodish, L. 'How TV advertising works', *Journal of Market Research* 32/2 1995.

Over the campaign period, Walkers Crisps sales have more than doubled in a market that was felt to be mature. Advertising itself was responsible in the last two years for 114 million packs being sold. Apropos of nothing, this is enough packets to cover the entirety of Holland – and who's to say we shouldn't?

£1 invested in advertising delivers an immediate benefit of £1.70 in revenue ROI, building to approximately £5.10 in the long term. It's an enormous ROI – seven times bigger than the category average.

The obvious success of the 'No More Mr Nice Guy' campaign has been recognised around the world. Ireland uses Gary in its own commercials. Frito Lay brands across the world, from Holland to Egypt to Turkey and now Australia, all have a local star.

Perhaps the best indication that we all believe in staying faithful is that Walkers and Gary have signed up together for another five years – another 25 commercials at least. So, for the foreseeable future, there will be plenty more Mr Nice Guy.

Section 3

Bronze Winners
(summaries)

Bakers Complete

From underdog to top dog: doubling market share with one-seventh of rivals' spend

SUMMARY

Context

As a Complete Dry Dog Food (CDDF) specialist, Edward Bakers Petfoods' (EBP) strategy was to facilitate sector growth, stealing share from canned dog foods. Its long-term mission was to be the number one CDDF brand, prioritising the grocery multiples for distribution. To this end, Bakers Complete was relaunched in 1995 with revised packaging, a revised formula and a new communications campaign.

The potential of Bakers Complete was characterised as a reservoir, being held back by a dam that advertising was to break. This was to be achieved in three ways:

1. **Convince sceptical consumers** of Bakers Complete's meatiness: research showed that can users felt that CDDF was not as good as real meat.
2. **Knock canned products** by stressing that Bakers Complete provides all the nutrition that cans do and more.
3. **To create an engaging personality for the brand**, becoming mainstream without the rather earnest imagery of other brands. The brand architecture, informed by qualitative research, defined this personality as more like Richard Branson than a 'top breeder' – down-to-earth, bright and lively, but most of all approachable.

The target was housewives aged 25–45, with children and from C1 C2 social grades. They were owners of everyday, family dogs, neither pampered pooches nor working dogs. They would come to appreciate the rational benefits of CDDF, (hygienic, healthy, cost-effective) and indeed some may have already tried it, but since we were trying to grow the CDDF market, they would mainly be users of cans.

Their prime motivation was that their dog should still *enjoy* its food.

Throughout, an important secondary target was trade, especially the multiple grocers, as without distribution and facings the brand would not grow quickly enough.

Strategy

The agency built on the emotional nature of the owner/dog relationship. This can vary from:

- Surrogate child: 'I love him, I adore him, I can't live without him'.
- My best friend: 'He's always there. He seems to know what I'm thinking'.

For full case history please contact the IPA Information Centre by emailing *info@ipa.co.uk*.

BRONZE

- Part of the family: 'A house isn't a home without a dog'.
- Employee: 'We got her because my husband is often away'.
- Part of the furniture: 'He's a nuisance really. He just gets in the way'.

The agency targeted 'best friend' with a campaign based on Pippin the brand 'spokesdog'. Pippin was a 'loveable rogue'.

The campaign launched in July 1995, beginning with 'shopping'. This aimed to educate that Bakers Complete is a stand-alone food, superior to canned food, and to create real emotional empathy.

Results

Sales

In the first year of the campaign, sales value had increased by 62.5%. After two years, sales had doubled and the brand has continued to show strong growth ever since.

The CDDF market, itself in danger of stalling in 1994, had been reinvigorated following the relaunch of Bakers Complete in 1995.

Shifts in imagery

Brand image has only been tracked since 1998. In spite of this data coming from the latest stages of brand development, advertising is still driving statistically significant image shifts.

By eliminating other factors the successful Bakers team have built a good case for the advertising, having developed both their market and their brand.

Benadryl
How the soft sell sold harder

SUMMARY

How does advertising work? Persuasion or involvement/saliency? A comparison of different campaigns for Benadryl explains why, in this case, it was all about involvement.

Context

At the launch, allergy remedy brand Benadryl had the product advantage of being faster-acting than its competitors. Advertising was developed along the rational persuasion model to explain this advantage and between 1998 and 2000 £3.5m was spent behind it. After a successful launch the brand plateaued. Competitors had come into the market with competitive speed claims and similar creative treatments.

Strategy

The decision was taken to launch a variant with a completely different creative treatment. The advertising idea was to 'criminalise' the causes of hayfever and to bring Benadryl to life as a police 'rapid reaction force', which responds immediately to stamp out the causes of hayfever.

Results

Both tracking data and qualitative data point to the level of consumer involvement in the tone of the advertising or driving the successful sales results.

The ROI at the sales level is estimated at £4.8 sales for every £1 spent in advertising.

For full case history please contact the IPA Information Centre by emailing *info@ipa.co.uk*.

BT Retail

Bringing people together: share defence with a big D

SUMMARY

'ROI's econometric modelling is an investment at the heart of BT's business strategy', states Simon Elwood, Head of Research and Planning, BT Retail. This case continues a strong BT tradition in the Awards, based on the clear importance they (and Abbott Mead Vickers.BBDO) attach to the management and analysis of data.

Context

This chapter of the BT story covers the decline of BT's share in the fixed line minutes market, which they once monopolised, and in which they now face competition from mobile phone operators, cable companies and resellers. The BT share of this market is now reduced to 63%, and had fallen by 20% in the five years to April 2001. The BT 'Together' campaign was designed to defend aggressively this share position by promoting a new flat monthly fee, unlimited calls plan and the 1571 answering service.

Strategy

The strategy was to celebrate BT's role, enabling people to make both emotional and physical connections. The new campaign idea was to dramatise an endless chain of connections in a flawed yet functioning society. All brought together under the new endline 'BT: Bringing People Together'.

Investment

BT spent £55.3m on the 'Bringing People Together' campaign since its launch in July 2001 across TV, press, radio, outdoor and online.

Return

The rate of decline has slowed from 9.2% p.a. in 2000/2001 to 4.5% in 2001/2002. Had the decline continued, BT's share would have fallen by another 1.9% or £227m. Intermediary measures show that the campaign has been successful in cutting through and establishing both the softer values BT wanted, as

---

For full case history please contact the IPA Information Centre by emailing *info@ipa.co.uk*.

well as the harder product messages. The 1571 service has proved to be BT's fastest-ever product launch.

Through modelling, this paper shows that the softer 'brand' elements of the campaign, and direct, harder product messages contributed to the protection of market share.

Dr Beckmann Rescue Oven Cleaner

A *new approach to oven cleaning that took the strength out of Mr Muscle*

SUMMARY

'Oven cleaning – yuck!' Yet this case proves how successfully taking on a Goliath (Mr Muscle) is still possible if there is a distinctive product advantage, an original creative approach and a single-minded media strategy.

Context

Mr Muscle dominates the oven-cleaning market. Part of the SC Johnson portfolio, it is supported by spend of £3m for the Mr Muscle range: 98% awareness and 43% household penetration is the result. However, in these environmentally sensitive times, it has a drawback. As the case writer puts it 'it's a thug!'. Mr Muscle is highly effective but also highly unpleasant to use.

It is this weakness that Dr Beckmann's Rescue sought to exploit. It is both eco- and user-friendly – and it works. However its first press launch campaign had been too low key and resulted in limited share gain and eventually a delisting from Tesco. The objective of the new campaign was to turn the previous one on its head.

Strategy

Focusing on the core product strengths, the proposition reads: 'The oven cleaner for the modern woman – effective, safe, pleasant, low stress and fast.' This was communicated via a £200,000 regional TV campaign in London and Central featuring a celebrity chef cleaning the oven and his hands with Dr Beckmann's.

Results

Two bursts of advertising contributed to a 20% growth in market share. Tesco agreed to relist Dr Beckmann and the team went on to advertise in Granada and Yorkshire. By the end of March 2002, a third burst had Dr Beckmann's share growing to 42%, not far behind Mr Muscle's 46%.

All this was achieved with an almost 30% price premium over Mr Muscle.

For full case history please contact the IPA Information Centre by emailing *info@ipa.co.uk*.

Lynx

'The penetration game': keeping up with the changing languages of youth

SUMMARY

The Lynx case is a lesson in how to use advertising over a long period of time to sustain a mass market youth brand. A combination of agile creativity in both content and media has resulted in a retail brand worth £65m p.a.

Context

Lynx's success is driven by penetration – particularly among 17–34-year-olds. More 15–24-year-olds use Lynx (75%) than surf the internet (63%), own a Playstation (46%) or even drink Coke (65%). The principal marketing challenge is to maintain the younger user base as each generation ages. Lynx has to recruit its entire 15–19-year-old user base every five years. The balance between penetration and retention was managed through a carefully judged relationship between advertising to drive penetration, and innovation to drive retention.

Strategy

The creative strategy was to link into 'every man's greatest desire' (17–19-year-old qualitative respondent) by promising manhood via the seduction of women. The imaginative leap was to move from the first stage of advertising for the launch and the early years (up to 1995), which featured fantasy men in real situations to the second stage (1995 onwards), which featured real men in fantasy situations. For example, 'House Party' 1996, 'Tribal Women' 1998.

Media

The channel mix kept pace with the audience by using 10-second time lengths, tactical advertising and private print in 'lads' mags'.

Results

Lynx generates £65m sales a year. The second-stage creative strategy, which this paper features, drove 10% of all sales in the 20-month period following its introduction. Penetration gains in the same period correlate with new executions, and while distribution and promotions can be excluded, the intermediate measures of awareness, re-engagement and positive shifts all point to an advertising success.

For full case history please contact the IPA Information Centre by emailing *info@ipa.co.uk*.

Manchester Evening News
Local paper bucks the trend with unexpected revenue boost

SUMMARY

Media owner papers are rare. This paper demonstrates how advertising can help drive recruitment advertising sales for the *Manchester Evening News*.

Context

For the *Manchester Evening News*, recruitment advertising revenue accounts for over 50% of total revenue. The recruitment advertising market moves with the economic cycle and the fourth quarter 2001 revenues were down 12% compared with the same period in 2000. The *Manchester Evening News* team decided to invest £210,000 to stimulate the market with three clear marketing objectives.

1. Increase advertising revenue by reassuring advertisers that the *Manchester Evening News* is the best place to place their recruitment ads.
2. Increase newspaper sales by encouraging people to turn to the pages of the *Manchester Evening News* to look for a new job.
3. Generate a feeling of goodwill towards the paper.

Solution

The advertising strategy focused on telling the consumer that the *Manchester Evening News* can provide its readers with a *better* job than the one they currently have.

Striking black and yellow type-only posters were created with yellow blanks marking where a word should be. People were encouraged to interact with the posters and fill in the blanks themselves. This had the desired effect but some consumers took the message literally and scrawled their own interpretation of the campaign on the posters.

A 30-second TV campaign was developed which depicted a day in the life of a less-than-satisfied office worker, who starts to think about how much he hates his job when he walks past one of the posters. The newspaper offers the frustrated character a new start as the last frame of the ad shows him happily sitting in his new place of employment, having got a new job from the *Manchester Evening News*.

The posters were up for one week before the TV campaign went on air to allow people time to familiarise themselves with the idea behind the campaign.

For full case history please contact the IPA Information Centre by emailing *info@ipa.co.uk*.

Equally important, a trade mailer mimicking the campaign went out to advertisers at the end of December to encourage them to place their ads in the *Manchester Evening News* in January.

Results

Recruitment advertising revenue increase

The measure of revenue success is gauged against forecast. The *Manchester Evening News* derives its forecast from three factors: actual revenue generated in the pervious year; financial targets set by the board; and a watchful eye on the economy.

The campaign started to have an effect at the end of the second week. This was expected as people are often on holiday for the first week of January. In addition, the TV did not air until w/c 7 January, and the air-time was weighted towards the Thursday of that week (the main job day).

The revenue increase over the advertising period more than covered the cost of the campaign.

Newspaper sales increase

During the campaign period, sales figures of the newspaper were significantly ahead of forecast. No other activity had taken place in the newspaper sales department, although it should be noted that the death of Princess Margaret on 9 February resulted in unusually high sales.

As readers of the paper are very familiar with the product, it is harder to shift their perceptions of the quality of the Jobs Section as they have first-hand experience of the paper. That said, upon seeing the advertising, more readers thought the newspaper had good-quality jobs. Those agreeing with this statement increased by 4% from 76% to 80%.

The advertising not only communicated that the *Manchester Evening News* was great for jobs but also it positioned the newspaper as a more desirable brand.

Goodwill towards the paper

Following the campaign, people were more positive about the newspaper and the perception of the paper was enhanced among both readers and non-readers.

Conclusion

The *Manchester Evening News* jobs campaign was an intrusive, engaging and effective piece of advertising that caught the imagination of the Manchester public.

Up against difficult economic conditions, the results exceeded expectations.

Advertising revenue increased during the campaign period and continued to be higher than expected in the subsequent months.

The newspaper sales department received a pleasant start to their new year with an increase of 5% on copy sales.

The tracking study showed that perception of the Jobs Section among both readers and non-readers improved upon seeing the advertising.

The *Manchester Evening News* as a brand benefited from the campaign as people felt more positive about the paper across a variety of indicators.

Mr Kipling
Reinventing a brand icon

SUMMARY

A traditional story in more ways then one. A tired but iconic brand personality, a brand suffering at the hands of own-label equivalents and a story of how a sensitively developed advertising idea can reverse a brand's fortunes in 12 months.

Context

By 1999, private label was dominating the ambient packaged cake market, overshadowing the branded leaders. Even the combined 21% of Manor Bakeries brands could not compete with the PL monolith.

Research commissioned by Manor Bakeries in 1999 made a stark discovery. Customers were buying products, rather than brands. If they were buying a brand it was by association with a product, 'Oh Mr Kipling, they do Cherry Bakewells'.

Products were acting as a filter for choice because brands were not seen to offer distinctive benefits or relevance to modern life.

It was clear that all was not well with the Mr Kipling brand.

By 1999, consumers no longer believed in the Mr Kipling brand. Continuous Millward Brown tracking showed that the brand had lost relevance for today.

In particular, Mr Kipling himself needed to be reassessed.

Strategy

The agency decided to reinvent Mr Kipling rather them replace him. The advertising featured a roguish Mr Kipling, a Mr Kipling who produced 'cakes that put you in such a good mood, you'd forgive him for anything'.

The advertising idea

The ads show Mr Kipling as an absent-minded professor-type who accidentally creates mayhem around him. Ordinarily such actions would put the recipients in a bad mood, but the happiness gained from eating his cakes defies this. 'Exceedingly good' is integrated as the resolution of each story.

Results

Brand share increased (see Figures 1 to 3).

For full case history please contact the IPA Information Centre by emailing *info@ipa.co.uk*.

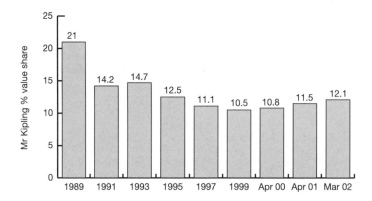

Figure 1: *Mr Kipling share back in growth*

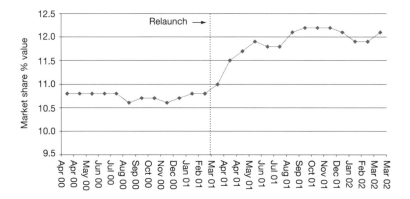

Figure 2: *52-week market share shows steady growth since relaunch*
Note: MAT 52 w/e (latest 31/03/02)

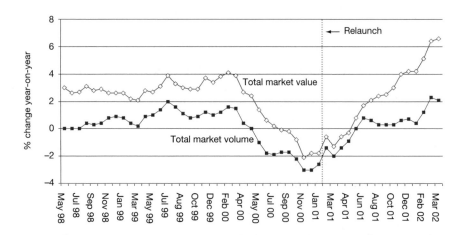

Figure 3: *Ambient packaged cake market in growth since time of Mr Kipling relaunch*

Post Office
The business of change

SUMMARY

Context

The Post Office is the retail arm of what was called Consignia and is now called the Royal Mail Group. It has 17,500 branches, more than all bank and building society branches in this country put together. They face the challenge of maintaining their network while losing their biggest customer-tied revenue from the payments of benefits over the counter. From 2003 all benefits will be paid directly into recipient bank accounts putting 36% of the Post Office revenue in terminal decline.

It was decided to manage the period of transition by promoting hero products within the travel sector, primarily Bureau de Change (BdC), and at a secondary level travel insurance and passport processing in order to:

1. Challenge current negative perceptions of the Post Office, forcing reappraisal and reconsideration.
2. Directly increase revenue from BdC and travel products.
3. Encourage consumers to use other Post Office channels, i.e. internet and telephone.

Strategy

£4m was spent behind a TV, press, poster and internet campaign around a 'what a good idea' creative route. This used the vehicle of entrepreneurs (Richard Branson, Stelios Haji-Ioannou), famous for being consumer champions, being surprised that the Post Office already provides such consumer-friendly services as 0% commission on foreign currency exchange.

Results

Image
Pre–post measures showed significant shifts (7% improvement) on brand values, e.g. setting the trends.

Responses
Significant increases in call centre and website activity.

For full case history please contact the IPA Information Centre by emailing *info@ipa.co.uk*.

Sales

BdC transactions reached an all-time high of £19 million in the first two weeks of August 2002 (a year-on-year increase of 125%).

ROI

ROI was measured in terms of:

1. Short-term value: £234m extra BdC business accounting for £9.4m revenue on £4.1m media.
2. Long-term value: Using the techniques of Brand Finance plc, this paper calculates the long-term payback of the campaign by forecasting cash flows over a four-year period from the campaign, and then calculates their net present value (NPV) to yield a £6m payback in the long term.

Interestingly Brand Finance also calculated the increase in the value of the Post Office brand as a trademark, which other brands pay a royalty to use (e.g. holiday car rentals). This concluded that an increase in royalty value of £3m could be attributed to the campaign.

Rimmel

Reclaiming the streets of London: from 'beauty on a budget' to 'beauty made in London'

SUMMARY

From beauty on a budget to beauty made in London, the Rimmel case is the first IPA case written in the new cosmetics category. It shows how a combination of a new positioning, a new face of Rimmel (Kate Moss) and a 360° media strategy resulted in a short-term ROI of 8%.

Context

Rimmel has established itself through the 1960s and 70s as the nation's favourite make-up. It was the first brand women bought and had been successfully positioned as 'beauty on a budget'. Its success was maintained through the 80s and 90s but by the end of the 90s it faced a crossroads. It was being crowded out by new entrants, it was being out-spent, it was being out-innovated, and it faced pressure from retailers' own brands.

The choice was made to change. To change and regain credibility among its core younger audience (16–24), while at the same time increasing prices to close the gap between Rimmel and the mass-market average. In short, to gain an added value positioning, rather than a cost-driven positioning in the market.

The new strategy

The new Rimmel strategy was to embody 'beauty inspired by the street' by claiming the street credibility of London for the brand.

London represented an edgy experimental interpretation of beauty and was neither pretentious nor perfect.

Rimmel = Beauty made in London became the brand positioning and Kate Moss, the iconic girl from Croydon, became its new face.

The channel strategy

A big brand experience was created by having a mixture of channels that worked around London, fashion and Kate Moss. Style, press and television sat alongside sponsorship of the vogue.com fashion week and the MTV European Music Awards, sampling through Sky Digital and sponsorship of the *Sugar* model competition.

For full case history please contact the IPA Information Centre by emailing *info@ipa.co.uk*.

Results

The paper describes short-term sales increases in Boots and Superdrug in both volume and value, despite an overall increase in price of 14%. Re-engagement with the young is shown through Millward Brown's link test data and through success among the younger profile Superdrug shopper and MTV viewer. As neither distribution nor promotional strategy changed, the case for a communications effect is clear. Quantification of the contribution made by the communication relies on a complex econometric model, which due to confidentiality is only partly revealed but does imply an 8% short-term ROI.

Sainsbury's
Attracting promotional customers without damaging the Sainsbury's brand

SUMMARY

'Two per cent of customers are lost when they first have children.' A case about how direct marketing helped to strengthen Sainsbury's hold on the value-sensitive family segment.

Context

In 2001 Tesco had 21% of the grocery retail market, a 5% lead on Sainsbury's. A key contributing factor was that as the market had focused on value, Sainsbury's had been left behind both in perception and in reality. This was particularly important because the price-sensitive family segment – the largest segment in the market – was, as a result, drifting away from Sainsbury's. Sainsbury's was overrepresented in the 'quality' segments but underrepresented in the family segments.

Programme

An evolving 12-month programme of mailings over three waves was devised. Each wave targeted households in three drive-time segments: 0–3 minutes from the store, 4–6 minutes, and up to 29 minutes drive-time.

The first wave tested both a 5% and a 10% discount offer.

As the programme developed, learning was passed from one phase to the next to improve ROI by being more precise about store selection, profile of respondents, and to perfect the mix between holders and non-holders of the Reward Card.

By the third wave, personalised discounts based on pre-spending at an individual customer level were being introduced.

Results

	Wave 1	Wave 2	Wave 3
Incremental sales	£21m	£21m	£18m
Incremental revenue per unit	£3.58	£4.21	£18.21
Net profit per unit	£–0.28	£–0.05	£2.31

For full case history please contact the IPA Information Centre by emailing *info@ipa.co.uk*.

Seatbelts

'Damage' campaign: no seatbelt, no excuse. Helping reduce road deaths by 13% in a year

SUMMARY

Public service advertising has a strong tradition in the Awards. This case adds to this tradition by describing how a particularly imaginative campaign had a very demonstrable effect in Northern Ireland.

Context

Road fatalities in Northern Ireland are substantially higher than in Great Britain. Some 9.5 per 100,000 population are killed on the roads in Northern Ireland compared to 5.9 in Great Britain. The overall seatbelt wearing ratio is also lower – 84% compared to 90% in Great Britain.

This campaign was designed to achieve awareness, shifts in attitude, and behavioural conversion among 16–34-year-olds. Therefore ultimately its objective was to save lives.

Strategy

The campaign was built on the insight that wearing a seatbelt currently felt as though one were being constrained within the social environment of the car. This social exclusion, which the target audience feared, had to be transferred so that it became associated with *not* wearing a seatbelt. It had to be cooler to wear one then not to wear one.

A show-and-shock strategy based on a 60-second TV narrative was chosen as the communication form to show the audience how not wearing a seatbelt can destroy everything you want (social success) and that it really could happen to anyone. Cinema and TV were backed up by 'point of danger' media including drive-time radio, car park barriers and petrol pumps.

Results

A 96% awareness among 16–34-year-olds and an 88% overall seatbelt-wearing rate (up 4%) show that there was an effect during the period of the advertising. The role of advertising is isolated by data that show that the key campaign elements, e.g. 'not wearing a seatbelt is selfish', had risen post-campaign, and that 93% of 16–34-year-olds claimed that the campaign had influenced them.

For full case history please contact the IPA Information Centre by emailing *info@ipa.co.uk*.

Stella Artois
The returning hero: reassuringly effective

SUMMARY

Stella Artois papers have delivered consistent new learning to the IPA dataBANK. This paper is no exception as it tackles the issue of the relationship between advertising and price promotions in the multiple retailers.

Context

Stella Artois is a dramatic success. The third largest grocery brand in the UK, it is worth £1.1bn, and 25 pints of it are drunk every second. It is still continuing to grow and this paper concentrates on the growth in the off trade (the 2000 paper had analysed the effect of advertising on trade distribution). Almost half of the off-trade business comes from multiple grocers. This paper shows how the competition between grocery retailers to deliver the most attractive promotions on leading brands, regardless of their own position (in Stella's case 'reassuringly expensive'), had the potential to undermine the brand's underlying dynamics, but did not.

The causes of Stella's multiple success

Two contributions stand out from the econometric analysis. The first is advertising, the second promotions. In 2001, two out of three cans were sold on promotion and Stella was on promotion in one or other of the major multiples for 46 weeks of the year.

The advertising contribution is well documented and is updated here. A consistent creative and media strategy around consistent positioning delivered exceptional long-term value.

The role of promotions

The paper isolates two effects of the promotions. The first is called 'by the book', by which is meant the short-term sales effect expected when an attractive brand is made better value. This effect is normally attributable to the extra buyers being infrequent Stella drinkers coming back to the brand rather than new buyers. The second is called the 'novel' effect – that because of the strength of the brand, the promotions are leading to increased penetration, i.e. new buyers being attracted into the Stella franchise.

Through the use of econometrics, the case is built on the fact that promotions have had a positive effect on both short-term and long-term penetration. That

---

For full case history please contact the IPA Information Centre by emailing *info@ipa.co.uk*.

promotions have worked so well is attributable in a large part to the role that advertising plays before consumers even step into the supermarket.

Conclusion

This paper breaks new ground in the analysis of the relationship between advertising and promotions.

Tommy's: The Baby Charity

Why the little things are infinitely the most important: how a little-known baby charity took its first steps

SUMMARY

No one could be unmoved by this cause. Tommy's funds research into the causes of miscarriage, premature birth and still birth. This paper succeeds in describing how communications can provide a route not only to the pockets of the general public, but also to the media owners who agreed to fund this campaign.

Context

Small charities like Tommy's are trapped in a vicious circle of low income – low marketing spend – low income, which is almost impossible to break out of. The large charities command big enough income figures to invest in communications and therefore reap the rewards. This paper shows that there is a clear correlation between voluntary income and share of voice, and in particular income and awareness. The task the Tommy's team set out for themselves was to break out of this vicious circle by embarking on an awareness-building campaign entirely funded through media-owner contributions aimed at mothers with children under five.

The creative solution

The creative idea centred on 'Tommy's: The Baby Charity – because every pregnancy should have a happy ending' and used the device of telling a story through children's literature about a birth which, shockingly, does not have a happy ending. Impact is achieved by using well-known children's characters thus raising expectations of a happy ending, which are then dashed.

The media solution

The creative work was powerful enough to persuade media owners to donate £1.1m in everything from cinema and TV to press, poster and radio. This in itself is used to justify the effectiveness of the campaign in its own right.

For full case history please contact the IPA Information Centre by emailing *info@ipa.co.uk*.

Results

In the financial year to April 2002, total income increased by £200,000. Some £35,000 was directly attributable to an advertising effect. The implication in this case is that there will also be a long-term effect of beginning to break out of the small charity vicious cycle.

How to Access the
IPA dataBANK

The IPA Effectiveness dataBANK represents the world's most rigorous and comprehensive examination of marketing communications working in the marketplace. Over the 22 years of the IPA Effectiveness Awards competition (1980 to 2002), the IPA has collected over 700 examples of best practice in advertising development and results across a wide spectrum of marketing sectors and expenditures. Each example contains 4000 words of text and is illustrated in full by market, research, sales and profit data.

ACCESS

The dataBANK is held in the IPA Information Centre for access by IPA members only. Simply contact the Centre by emailing *info@ipa.co.uk*. Simple or more sophisticated searches can be run, free of charge, by qualified, professional knowledge executives across a range of parameters including brand, advertiser, agency, target market (by age, sex, class, and so on), medium and length of activity, which can be specified by the user. The results are supplied by email or other means as required.

PURCHASING IPA CASE STUDIES

Member agencies will be allowed a minimum number of case studies for download per month, after which they will be charged at £20 each. Please note that these arrangements are currently under review. Alternatively, new members can sign up to WARC (see below) at a beneficial IPA rate and can then download case studies as part of that subscription.

FURTHER INFORMATION

For further information, please contact the Information Centre at the IPA, 44 Belgrave Square, London SWIX 8QS.
Telephone: +44 (0)20 7235 7020
Fax: 020 7245 9904
Website: *www.ipa.co.uk*
Email: *info@ipa.co.uk*.

WARC

The IPA case histories dataBANK can also be accessed through the World Advertising Research Center (WARC). Reached by logging on to *www.warc.com*, the world's most comprehensive advertising database enables readers to search all the IPA case histories, over 2000 case histories from similar award schemes around the world (including the Advertising Federation of Australia, the New York American Marketing Association and the Account Planning Group), plus thousands of 'how to' articles on all areas of communication activity. Sources include the Advertising Research Foundation, ESOMAR, *Admap*, the Association of National Advertisers, as well as the IPA.

IPA dataBANK Case Availability

* Denotes publication in the relevant *Advertising Works* volume

NEW ENTRIES 2002

2002	Aerogard Mosquito Repellent (Australia)
2002	Anti-Drink Driving*
2002	B&Q
2002	Bakers Complete*
2002	Barnardo's*
2002	Benadryl*
2002	Britannia Building Society*
2002	BT Cellnet*
2002	BT Retail*
2002	Budweiser*
2002	BUPA
2002	Chicago Town Pizza
2002	Crown Paint
2002	Dairy Council (Milk)*
2002	Debenhams
2002	DfES Higher Education
2002	Domino's Pizza*
2002	Dr Beckmann Rescue*
2002	Economist, The*
2002	Flowers & Plants Assoc
2002	Fruitopia
2002	Halifax Building Society*
2002	Hastings Hotels (Golfing Breaks)*
2002	Hovis*
2002	Imperial Leather
2002	Jeyes Bloo
2002	John Smith's
2002	Kellogg's Real Fruit Winders*
2002	Levi Strauss Engineered Jeans (Japan)
2002	Lynx*
2002	Manchester Evening News (Job Section)*
2002	Marmite*
2002	Mr Kipling*
2002	Norwich Union Pensions
2002	Ocean Spray*
2002	Olivio/Bertolli*
2002	Police Recruitment*
2002	Police Recruitment (Could You?)
2002	Police Recruitment Northern Ireland
2002	Post Office*
2002	Rimmel*
2002	Royal Mail
2002	Sainsbury's* (Jamie Oliver)
2002	Sainsbury's* (Promotion)
2002	Seafish Industry Authority

2002	Seatbelts*
2002	Senokot
2002	Shell Corporate
2002	Shell Optimax
2002	Skoda*
2002	Stella Artois*
2002	Strathclyde Police
2002	Tesco*
2002	Tommy's*
2002	Volkswagen (Brand)*
2002	Volkswagen Passat*
2002	Waitrose*
2002	Walkers Crisps*
2002	West End Quay
2002	Yorkshire Forward/Yorkshire Tourist Board
2000	1001 Mousse*

A

1982	Abbey Crunch
1990	Abbey National Building Society
1990	Abbey National Building Society (plc)
1980	Abbey National Building Society Open Bondshares
1990	Aberlour Malt Whisky*
1996	Adult Literacy *
1986	AGS Home Improvements*
1988	AIDS
1994	AIDS*
1986	Air Call
1990	Alex Lawrie Factors
1980	All Clear Shampoo*
1992	Alliance & Leicester Building Society*
1990	Alliance & Leicester Building Society*
1988	Alliance & Leicester Building Society*
1984	Alliance Building Society
1990	Allied Dunbar
1984	Allinson's Bread
1984	Alpen
1990	Alton Towers
1992	Amnesty International
1990	Amnesty International*
1990	Anchor Aerosol Cream
1994	Anchor Butter
1988	Anchor Butter
1992	Andrex
1994	Andrex Ultra
1986	Andrex*

1992	Central Television Licence Renewal	2000	Degree
2000	Channel 5	1980	Dettol*
1990	Charlton Athletic Supporters Club*	1984	DHL Worldwide Carrier
1980	Cheese Information Service	1998	Direct Debit
1996	Cheltenham & Gloucester Building	1992	Direct Line Insurance*
	Society	1990	Dog Registration
1988	Chessington World of Adventures	2000	Domestic Abuse*
1998	Chicago Town Pizza	1980	Dream Topping
1994	Chicken Tonight	1988	Drinking & Driving
2000	Chicken Tonight Sizzle and Stir*	1998	Drugs Education*
1994	Child Road Safety	1994	Dunfermline Building Society
1992	Childhood Diseases Immunisation	1980	Dunlop Floor Tiles
1990	Children's World	1990	Duracell Batteries
1984	Chip Pan Fires Prevention*	1980	Dynatron Music Suite
1990	Choosy Catfood*		
1998	Christian Aid*	E	
1992	Christian Aid	1988	E & P Loans*
1994	CICA*	2000	easyJet*
1992	Citroën Diesel Range	1992	Economist, The*
1988	Clairol Nice n' Easy	1994	Edinburgh Club*
1988	Clarks Desert Boots*	1990	Edinburgh Zoo
1996	Classic Combination Catalogue	1980	Eggs Authority
1994	Clerical Medical	1992	Electricity Privatisation
1992	Clorets	1980	Ellerman Travel & Leisure
1988	Clover	1996	Emergency Contraception
1984	Clover	1986	EMI Virgin (records)*
1980	Cointreau	1980	English Butter Marketing Company
1998	Colgate Toothpaste*	1986	English Country Cottages
1990	Colman's Wholegrain Mustard	1992	Enterprise Initiative
2000	Confetti.co.uk*	1992	Equity & Law
2000	Co-op*	1990	Eurax
1996	Cooperative Bank	1994	Evening Standard Classified
1994	Cooperative Bank*		Recruitment
1990	Copperhead Cider	1984	Exbury Gardens
1982	Country Manor (Alcoholic Drink)		
1986	Country Manor (Cakes)	F	
1984	Cow & Gate Babymeals*	1990	Family Credit
1982	Cracottes*	1998	Famous Grouse
2000	Crime Prevention	1982	Farmer's Table Chicken
1990	Croft Original*	2000	Felix*
1982	Croft Original	1996	Felix*
1980	Croft Original	1980	Ferranti CETEC
2000	Crown Paints*	1990	Fertilizer Manufacturers' Association
1990	Crown Solo*	1982	Fiat Auto UK
1984	Cuprinol*	1980	Findus Crispy Pancakes
1986	Cyclamon*	1988	Findus French Bread Pizza & Crispy
			Pancakes
D		1992	Findus Lasagne
1996	Daewoo*	1984	Fine Fare
1982	Daily Mail*	1982	Fine Fare*
2000	Dairylea*	1996	First Choice Holidays
1992	Danish Bacon & Meat Council	1992	First Direct
1980	Danum Taps	1998	First Direct*
1990	Data Protection Registrar	1992	Flowers & Plants Association
1980	Day Nurse	1994	Fona Dansk Elektrik
1994	Daz	1980	Ford Fiesta
1996	De Beers Diamonds*	1998	Ford Galaxy*
1980	Deep Clean*	1986	Ford Granada*

1984	Kraft Dairylea*	1998	Marmite*
1980	Krona Margarine*	1998	Marmoleum
1986	Kronenbourg 1664	1988	Marshall Cavendish Discovery
		1994	Marston Pedigree*
L		1986	Mazda*
1990	Lada	1986	Mazola*
1992	Ladybird	1998	McDonald's
1990	Lanson Champagne*	1996	McDonald's
1992	Le Creuset	1980	McDougall's Saucy Sponge
1982	Le Crunch	1990	Mcpherson's Paints
1990	Le Piat D'or	1988	Mcpherson's Paints
1986	Le Piat D'or	2000	McVitie's Jaffa Cakes
1996	Le Shuttle	1992	Mercury Communications
1990	Lea & Perrin's Worcestershire Sauce*	1988	Metropolitan Police Recruitment*
1980	Lea & Perrin's Worcestershire Sauce	1990	Midland Bank
1988	Leeds Permanent Building Society	1988	Midland Bank
1988	Lego	1992	Miele
1984	Leicester Building Society	1988	Miller Lite*
1996	Lenor	2000	Moneyextra*
1992	Levi Strauss UK*	1988	Mortgage Corporation*
1980	Levi Strauss UK	1984	Mr Muscle
1988	Levi's 501s*	1994	Multiple Sclerosis Society
1996	Lil-lets	1996	Murphy's Irish Stout*
1990	Lil-lets*	2000	Myk Menthol Norway*
1996	Lilt		
1992	Limelite*	**N**	
1980	Limmits	2000	National Code and Number Change
2000	Lincoln Insurance	1996	National Dairy Council – Milk*
2000	Lincoln USA	1992	National Dairy Council – Milk
1980	Lion Bar	1980	National Dairy Council – Milk
1992	Liquorice Allsorts	1992	National Dairy Council – Milkman*
1988	Liquorice Allsorts	1996	National Lottery (Camelot)
1988	Listerine*	1996	National Savings
1980	Listerine	1984	National Savings: Income Bonds
1998	Littlewoods Pools	1982	National Savings: Save by Post*
1992	Lloyds Bank	1986	National Westminster Bank Loans
1984	Lloyds Bank*	1982	Nationwide Building Society
1990	London Buses Driver Recruitment	1990	Nationwide Flex Account
1984	London Docklands*	1988	Nationwide Flex Account
1982	London Docklands	1990	Navy Recruitment
1990	London Philharmonic	1988	Nefax
1992	London Transport Fare Evasion	1982	Negas Cookers
1986	London Weekend Television	1982	Nescafé
1980	Lucas Aerospace*	2000	Network Q
1996	Lucky Lottery	1992	Neutrogena
1992	Lucozade	1982	New Man Clothes
1980	Lucozade*	1994	New Zealand Lamb
2000	Lurpak*	1980	New Zealand Meat Producers Board
1988	Lurpak	1996	Nike
1994	Lyon's Maid Fab	1994	Nike
1988	Lyon's Maid Favourite Centres	1994	Nissan Micra*
		2000	No More Nails*
M		1986	No.7
1988	Maclaren Prams	1988	Norsk Data
1990	Malibu	1998	North West Water
1982	Manger's Sugar Soap*	1998	North West Water – Drought
1988	Manpower Services Commission	1998	Norwich Union
1994	Marks & Spencer	1990	Nouvelle Toilet Paper

1990	Rowntree's Fruit Gums	1996	Stella Artois*
1992	Royal Bank of Scotland	1992	Stella Artois*
1986	Royal College of Nursing	1994	Strepsils*
1986	Royal Mail Business Economy	1990	Strongbow
1990	Royal National Institute for the Deaf	1982	Summers the Plumbers
1996	RSPCA	1980	Sunblest Sunbran
1988	Rumbelows	1990	Supasnaps
		2000	Surf*
S		1980	Swan Vestas*
1994	S4C	1984	SWEB Security Systems
1988	Saab*	1992	Swinton Insurance
1996	Safeway	1998	Switch
1996	Samaritans	1996	Switch
1986	Sanatogen		
1980	Sanatogen	**T**	
1988	Sandplate*	1992	Tandon Computers
1986	Sapur	1990	Tango
1992	Save the Children*	1986	TCP*
1988	Schering Greene Science	1986	Teletext
2000	Scoot.com*	1986	Territorial Army Recruitment
1980	Scotcade	2000	Terry's Chocolate Orange*
1984	Scotch Video Cassettes	2000	Tesco*
1998	Scotland on Sunday	1980	Tesco
1992	Scotrail	1990	Tetley Tea Bags
1992	Scottish Amicable*	1984	Thomas Cook
1998	Scottish Prison Service	1992	Tia Maria
1980	Seiko	1990	Tia Maria
1992	Sellafield Visitors Centre	1990	Times, The
1980	Shake 'n' Vac	1994	Tizer
1984	Shakers Cocktails*	1980	Tjaereborg Rejser*
1980	Shloer*	1980	Tolly's Original
1986	Shredded Wheat	1984	Torbay Tourist Board*
1990	Silent Night Beds*	1986	Toshiba*
1992	Skol	1986	Touche Remnant Unit Trusts
1982	Skol	1992	Tower of London
1980	Slumberdown Quilts	1996	Toyota RAV4
1990	Smarties	1982	Trans World Airlines
1980	Smirnoff Vodka	1984	Tri-ac
1980	Smith's Monster Munch	1980	Triumph Dolomite
1982	Smith's Square Crisps	1994	TSB
1992	Smith's Tudor Specials	1988	TSB*
1994	Smoke Alarms*	1986	TSB*
1992	Smoke Alarms	1982	Turkish Delight*
1996	So ...?	1986	TV Licence Evasion*
1986	Soft & Gentle	2000	Twix Denmark
1996	Soldier Recruitment		
1994	Solvent Abuse	**U**	
2000	Solvite*	1984	UK Canned Salmon
1996	Solvite	1986	Umbongo Tropical Juice Drink
1992	Sony	1998	UPS
1988	Sony	1990	Uvistat*
1992	Sony Camcorders		
1996	Springers by K	**V**	
1984	St Ivel Gold*	1988	Varilux lenses
2000	Standard Life	1994	Vauxhall Astra
2000	Star Alliance	1996	Vauxhall Cavalier
2000	Stella Artois*	1990	Vauxhall Cavalier
1998	Stella Artois	1996	Vegetarian Society

Index